973.2 R433   FV
RESISTANCE, POLITICS, AND THE
AMERICAN STRUGGLE FOR INDEPEN-
DENCE, 1765-1775
                              38.50

Resistance, Politics, and the American Struggle for Independence, 1765-1775

A book from the Program on Nonviolent Sanctions
in Conflict and Defense,
Center for International Affairs,
Harvard University
and the
Albert Einstein Institution

Resistance, Politics, and The American Struggle for Independence, 1765-1775

edited by
Walter H. Conser, Jr.
Ronald M. McCarthy
David J. Toscano
Gene Sharp

Lynne Rienner Publishers • Boulder, Colorado

To our families

Title page and part opening illustrations, pages 1 and 359,
courtesy of The John Carter Brown Library, Brown University

Published in the United States of America in 1986 by
Lynne Rienner Publishers, Inc.
948 North Street, Boulder, Colorado 80302

Library of Congress Cataloging-in-Publication Data

Resistance, politics and the American struggle for
    independence, 1765–1775

    Includes bibliographies and index.
    1. United States—Politics and government—Revolution,
1775–1783—Addresses, essays, lectures.   2. United
States—Politics and government—Colonial period, ca.
1600–1775—Addresses, essays, lectures.   I. Conser,
Walter H.
E210.R47 1986   973.2   85-31190
ISBN 0-931477-75-1

Distributed outside of North and South America and Japan by
Frances Pinter (Publishers) Ltd, 25 Floral Street,
London WC2E 9DS England.   UK ISBN 0-86187-671-7

Printed and bound in the United States of America

The paper used in this publication meets the minimum
requirements of the American National Standard for
Permanence of Paper for Printed Library Materials
Z39.48-1984

Instead of moping, and puling, and whining to excite compassion; in such a situation we ought with spirit, and vigour, and alacrity, to bid defiance to tyranny, by exposing its impotence, by making it as contemptible, as it would be detestable. By a vigorous application to manufactures, the consequence of oppression in the colonies to the inhabitants of Great Britain, *would strike home, and immediately. None would mistake it. Craft and subtilty would not be able to impose on the most ignorant and credulous; for if any should be so weak of sight as not to see, they would not be so callous as not to feel it.*

Daniel Dulany, 1765

I beseech you to implore every Friend in Boston by every thing dear and sacred to Men of Sense and Virtue to avoid Blood and Tumult. They will have time enough to dye. Let them give the other Provinces opportunity to think and resolve. Rash Spirits that would by their Impetuosity involve us in insurmountable Difficulties will be left to perish by themselves despised by their Enemies, and almost detested by their Friends. Nothing can ruin us but our Violence. Reason teaches this. I have indubitable Intelligence, dreadful, as to the Designs against us; consolotary, if we are but prudent.

Samuel Adams to James Warren, 21 May 1774

The Congress we hear have come into a conclusion that we import no *British goods . . . none I hope will be so inimical to his country, as to attempt to break the general union by refusing to comply therewith. But should there be any such; it becomes every one, that hath any regard to the liberties of his country, to treat with deserved neglect and abhorrence the wretch, that thus meanly seeks his own [enrichment] upon the ruins of his country's liberties—to break off all trade and dealings with such selfish miscreants and make them sensible, that without injuring their lives or property, their injured country can make them feel the weight of her vengeance, and rue the day they ever suffered a selfish spirit to banish all love to their country from their breasts.*

Rev. Ebenezer Baldwin, August 1774

Contents

Appendixes

Tables

Preface

The struggle for American independence has captured the attention of American historians since the beginning of our history as a nation. Since the time that writers first began examining the conflict, scholars have presented their interpretations of the events of the period, suggested reasons for their occurrence, and explored the significance of the events in America from the end of the Seven Years' War to the Treaty of Paris. Beginning with the resistance to the Stamp Act in 1765, these studies typically highlight the battles of Lexington and Concord and the exchange of shots between British soldiers and American colonists. In these interpretations, the events between 1765–1775 are not significant in themselves, but rather are only a prelude to the war. Our book questions this assumption and suggests that these forms of resistance—primarily nonviolent ones—pursued by the American colonists from 1765 to 1775 were of fundamental importance themselves for the outcome of the struggle for independence, shaping the growth of new political, economic, and social institutions which could sustain truly independent self-government.

The editors' interest in this decade began in the early 1970s, when we were involved in researching the use of nonviolent action as a pragmatic tool of civilian struggle. In our work, we discovered a large number of events in American colonial history—boycotts, nonimportation, noncooperation, and protest demonstrations of many kinds—all of which could be described as examples of nonviolent action. Indeed, the incidence and successes of nonviolent resistance seemed so significant that we were surprised that the subject had received so little attention. Although many scholars have described the decade in great detail, the richness and importance of the nonviolent activity was lost because of their emphasis on a seemingly inevitable rush toward war. This book demonstrates that the movement for independence was more complex than conventional analysis might have us believe.

Students of American colonial history are all too familiar with the many edited books in the field. Frequently in such studies, the articles are unconnected beyond a shared theme. This book is different. The chapters in this volume, most of which have never been published previously, relate integrally to one another and provide a complete narrative of the period. Our contributors are highly respected American and British historians whose writings are well known and whose scholarship is of the highest quality.

We recognize that no study is exhaustive or absolutely final. We realize that this book, if read carefully, is likely to spark scholarly controversy and argument. We welcome these discussions for we believe that such debate can clarify the issues explored in this volume and enhance the understanding of this critical decade in our history.

W. C.
R. M.
D. T.
G. S.

Acknowledgements

In a study of this kind the editors have many people to thank and many debts of gratitude to acknowledge. Foremost among these is the thanks owed our American and British contributors, whose intellectual conscientiousness was matched by their patience with our editorial requests. Some authors prepared their contributions several years before publication, including Paul Langford, C. C. Bonwick, and Ian R. Christie, who completed their chapters before 1980.

This project was originally conceived as a result of Gene Sharp's recognition that the American colonists had employed the techniques of nonviolent resistance in their struggle against Great Britain. He has been unfailingly helpful in the other editors' attempt to understand the significance of these actions and has been centrally responsible for placing this work within the context of contemporary Anglo-American scholarship. Editors Conser, McCarthy, and Toscano wish to take this opportunity to acknowledge their great debt to Gene Sharp and his effort to make the work as complete and rigorous as possible.

Several members of the American historical profession have aided us with their comments on various stages of the manuscript. We wish to thank Caroline Robbins, Edmund S. Morgan, and Alan Rogers for their insights and suggestions. They have often disagreed with the editors' viewpoint, but have always been helpful, and of course bear no responsibility for the conclusions this volume presents.

Many other persons have provided us with assistance and given us support in the research and preparation of this book. Nancy A. Tramontin completely and thoroughly edited the manuscript before it was accepted for publication. We wish to thank Marianne Morsilli McCarthy, Peter Dimmock, Marty Blatt, Agnes Brophy, Diana Murrell, Jennifer Bing, Philip Bogdonoff, Susan Abrams, and Connie Grice.

Special thanks go to the Program on Nonviolent Sanctions and to the Albert Einstein Institution for helping make the project a reality. Publication of this work was made possible by grants from the L. J. Skaggs and Mary C. Skaggs Foundation and the New York Friends Group, Inc.

PART 1
A Decade of Struggle, 1765–1775

The BOSTONIANS in DISTRESS.

London, Printed for R. Sayer, & J. Bennett, Map & Printsellers, N°53 Fleet Street, as the Act directs, 19 Nov. 1774.

·1·

The American Independence Movement, 1765–1775: A Decade of Nonviolent Struggles

WALTER H. CONSER, JR.
RONALD M. McCARTHY
DAVID J. TOSCANO

S ome years after his retirement from public office, John Adams paused to reflect on the nature of American colonial resistance to British rule. In a letter to Dr. Jedediah Morse in 1815, Adams described his feelings about the events of those earlier years:

> A history of military operations from April 19th, 1775 to the 3d of September, 1783, is not a history of the American Revolution. . . . The revolution was in the minds and hearts of the people, and in the union of the colonies; both of which were substantially effected before hostilities commenced.[1]

In Adams's view, the American revolution could not be explained merely as a series of military confrontations by which the colonials won independence from Great Britain. Resistance to British authority, as Adams well knew, had begun some years before 1775. It is this period and its events that brought about those changes that Adams found in the minds and hearts of the colonists. This first chapter of *Resistance, Politics, and the Struggle for American Independence* begins by reviewing the significance of this critical period before 1775, including the steps in the achievement of American independence accomplished in those years. After an overview of the three resistance campaigns of the era, the authors discuss the concept of nonviolent action and close with an introduction to the chapters that follow.

Historical scholarship also recognizes that colonial resistance did not begin with the skirmishes at Lexington and Concord. Nonmilitary opposition to British authority has its own history, beginning a full ten years before these famous battles. It is this decade of struggle to which Adams referred when he wrote of the alienation of American minds from Britain and the colonies' new allegiances. Historians and social scientists have described this period of colonial resistance, with its three major campaigns (against the Stamp Act of 1765, the Townshend Acts of 1767, and the Coercive Acts of 1774) in numerous articles and books. Some have gone so far as to suggest, as Adams did, that this decade was the most critical and creative period in the development of colonial grievances and movements in opposition to British colonial policy.

Many of these authors have been concerned with the development of the beliefs and ideas that supported independence. Others have studied military organization, the role of government institutions and ruling elites, and the periodic conflicts pitting class against class or the backcountry against the older settled regions. Scholars overlook, however, the degree to which the colonists used a kind of "weapons system" that operated without force of arms or violence in trying to compel the British government to change its policies.

As a technique of struggle, this weapons system is commonly known as *nonviolent action*. During their conflicts with Britain, the colonists developed and used nonviolent methods ranging from protest and noncooperation to the creation of parallel political, judicial, and executive institutions that challenged existing governments for ruling authority. Consequently, each of the major resistance campaigns contained not only a further development of the ideas of freedom and independence but also a lively debate about how these liberties should be sought and defended. In turn, the means by which the colonists chose to defend and support their liberty had an influence upon the eventual shape of American independence by providing the organizational basis on which it rested.

Each of the three campaigns was prompted by Britain's introduction of laws affecting the taxation and governing of the North American colonies. Believing that their liberty and prosperity was threatened by these laws, many colonists were convinced that they must resist. They were, however, often unsure about the most appropriate and effective form of opposition. Many viewed established constitutional avenues for redress as being incapable of achieving repeal of the offensive acts. Neither the statutes passed by colonial legislatures nor the decisions of colonial courts, for example, carried any weight in England. Moreover, the Crown often controlled the appointment of governors, officials, and judges, so that colonists in some places felt that the administrative personnel of their own governments were there to oppress them.

Even when the passions of the time led some colonists into crowd violence, the majority of the people found organized physical force unacceptable. Yet these same people often believed that giving in to the government in London meant, as they put it, trading the condition of free men for that of slaves. Clearly, another means of resistance was called for.

Believing some options to be ineffective and others unacceptable, the colonists explored and employed new techniques in their effort to effect changes in British policy. During the 1765–1775 decade, they used such nonviolent means as petitions, protest marches, demonstrations, boycotts, and refusal to work. When the Crown levied taxes on certain goods, Americans often refused to purchase them, or any other British export. In the words of leader John Dickinson, these boycotts meant "withholding from Great Britain all the advantages she has been used to receiving from us."[2]

Other methods were devised as well. If colonial merchants violated popular sentiments by continuing to import boycotted goods, people not only refused to buy from them but also to talk with them, to sit with them in church, or to sell them goods of any kind. At times, colonial activists conducted regular business in violation of British law by using documents without required tax stamps, by settling legal disputes without courts, and by sending protest petitions to England without the permission of royal governors. They organized and served on local, county, and province committees designed to extend, support, and enforce resistance. In 1774 and 1775, many of these bodies assumed governmental powers on their own initiative, acting as extralegal authorities with powers greater than the remnants of colonial government.

Nonviolent action in these many forms was the predominant, but not the only, method used by the colonists to resist British power in these years. Even when opposing the most oppressive acts, colonists never completely abandoned established constitutional forms of political action and redress. When possible, they worked through colonial agents in London, parliamentary contacts and appeals, and their governors to bring about a change of policy.

They also used extralegal methods that were neither nonviolent nor violent, in the sense that they involved destruction of property or material possessions without threatening injury to persons. The Boston Tea Party of 1773 is an example of such an act, as were crowd actions which, while tumultuous and even destructive, did not endanger the physical safety of their opponents.

Violent actions did occur as part of the American movement, however, but they have been greatly overemphasized and were of questionable value in countering parliamentary policy.[3] The famous Boston and New York "mobs," as well as those of other cities and towns, did indeed turn out for every resistance campaign. They were rarely as violent after 1765 as during the first phase of the Stamp Act crisis. Similarly, cases of tarring and feathering, supposedly the crowd's chief weapon, have been shown to number fewer than a dozen throughout the colonies from 1766 to April 1775.[4] All of these events, however, should be viewed within the context of a resistance movement that was overwhelmingly nonviolent.

Colonial nonviolent action was often improvised, particularly before the First Continental Congress of 1774 planned the final campaign of resistance in the Continental Association. The colonists frequently did not have a clear idea of what was involved in waging effective nonviolent struggle. They were at times confused about which steps to take when the impact of a particular method was lessening and often found it difficult to judge the relative effectiveness of a campaign. Despite these failings, colonial activists were acutely aware that some methods were more effective than others and acted pragmatically on that perception.

But, it can be asked, were the colonists actually aware that they were employing nonviolent means of struggle? Certainly such terminology did not exist in the eighteenth century, but, as subsequent chapters will show, there was an awareness on the colonists' part of the nature of the option they chose. At times, they knew they were choosing a method of active self-expression, as in the case of a 1770

New Hampshire petition intended to show Parliament "that we have Sensibility to feel the Oppression."[5]

In another case, a gathering in Massachusetts clearly demonstrated its support for means of action which neither accepted the injustice they perceived nor made a violent response. The Middlesex County Convention wrote: "There is a Mode of Conduct, which in our very critical Circumstances we wou'd wish to adopt, a Conduct, on the one Hand, never tamely submissive to Tyranny and Oppression, on the other, never degenerating into Rage, Passion, and Confusion."[6]

• STAGES IN THE STRUGGLE •

As the colonists resisted each challenge from the British government, the effects of this extensive use of nonviolent action exceeded their own intentions. Very few of the participants in the Stamp Act resistance of 1765–1766, for example, would have predicted the erosion of British authority through the ten succeeding years of essentially nonviolent struggle. The gradual transformation of British North American from colonies to an independent state involved five factors: (1) the collective expression of American political differences with Britain, (2) the growth of organizations and institutions that articulated colonial interests and argued against new British powers and controls, (3) open resistance to specific acts of the British government, (4) mass political and economic noncooperation with British authority, and (5) the development of parallel institutions, particularly institutions of government.[7]

Each of these factors was essential for effective opposition to the Crown and instrumental in the revolutionary breakaway of the colonies from Britain. All of the components existed simultaneously throughout the decade of resistance, though developed to varying degrees at different times. All five could be seen in the resistance to the Stamp Act, for example, yet they were not fully maintained once that campaign was over. The growth of organizations expressing American interests and the formation of new parallel institutions was not rapid until the latter part of the decade of resistance. Thus, the constituent parts of the process leading to independence were themselves developed and transformed in successive struggles, just as they contributed to the final achievement of independence.

The first stage in the struggle for independence might be termed the development of a *shared political consciousness*. Colonists of the most diverse personal interests and backgrounds slowly found themselves developing similar attitudes about the governance of the provinces. Over the course of the 1760s and 1770s, they began to view themselves as "Americans" with claims to rights of their own. This was essential to the independence movement, for no change would have been possible unless a large part of the American people realized their common grievances and goals. Their discontent had its source in the British domination of the provinces, which was in turn made possible by colonial cooperation. Until they became conscious of the need for change, the colonists showed no willingness or determination to act against Britain.

By the mideighteenth century, a cultural and political gap was growing between Great Britain and the colonies. British styles certainly set the trend in the social sphere, and Americans of means were eager to consume the new English fashions. Wealthy colonists, especially those in the South, aspired to live as genteely as Englishmen did. Many young men lived for a time in England, either to receive a formal education or to be introduced into the society of respectable families. A good number of Americans were true Anglophiles, even to the point of continuing to refer to England as home.

Nevertheless, Americans came more and more to resent the actions of British officials placed among them. British army and navy officers, for example, were often openly contemptuous of their American counterparts and were widely resented for it. In some areas, the navy actively impressed sailors despite the American belief that this practice was illegal. Customs officers, or at least the avaricious and contentious ones, also antagonized American merchants and seamen in the towns under their jurisdiction.

The Proclamation of 1763, intended to increase British control over colonial growth by restricting expansion to the west (into Indian lands), was widely resented in the southern and frontier colonies. Americans felt that the proclamation did little more than maintain an expensive and unnecessary army and block the colonists' aspirations to take land freely beyond the Appalachian Mountains. The belief became common that the army and Crown officials were only tools of royal oppression and that the people's own representatives were being made to appear as their willing accomplices. The various disputes of the period had, in a sense, translated individual discontents into public issues. Moreover, by acting, the colonists increased their awareness of the issues and confidence in their collective ability to resist Parliament's restrictions on their liberty. This confidence reaffirmed their growing identity as Americans.[8]

In the years after the end of the French and Indian War and the Proclamation of 1763, it became clear to many colonists that a fundamental transformation in their relationship with Great Britain was under way. Until the desire for actual independence overcame the wish to remain part of the British Empire, a common American demand during resistance campaigns was for a return to earlier conditions, especially those that prevailed before 1763. Such sentiments and arguments against British policy and in favor of colonial rights were frequently expressed by the emerging associations that were formed to support the colonial cause.

The *growth of institutions and organizations* that expressed colonial grievances and argued for changes in Crown policy was the second element critical to the development of independence. New organizations gave rise to a new colonial leadership capable of expressing public grievances while organizing protest actions. Leaders emerged from among occupational groups such as merchants and "mechanics" (artisans and small-scale manufacturers) who cooperated with, and sometimes pushed, more celebrated politicians and legislators to work for colonial rights. The leadership that developed over the years 1765–1775 often argued that the high importance of American goals made it all the more vital that demands be pursued in a peaceful manner. James Otis stated that the Townshend Acts of 1767 were a great "matter of grievance," but also held that "redress is to be sought in a legal and constitutional way." John Dickinson, in his *Letters from a Pennsylvania Farmer*, felt that the colonial cause was "of too much dignity to be sullied by turbulence and tumult." Finally, it was Joseph Warren who wrote, during the course of the final resistance campaign in 1774, that the colonists "choose to effect our salvation from bondage by policy, rather than arms."[9]

When British laws and policies appeared to threaten American liberties, colonial leadership, acting through the newly established organizations as well as existing ones, mobilized the populace for *open resistance,* the third element necessary for colonial independence. Mass meetings, petitions, and demonstrations encouraged resistance. Public statements by leaders such as Dickinson, Otis, and Patrick Henry galvanized the people and inspired many to confront British authority. The real work of the resistance was often carried on in villages and towns, in the country as well as the city, by forgotten patriots. These now nameless men and women were the people who spun, wove, and wore homespun cloth, who united in the boycott of British goods, and who encouraged their neighbors to join them and stand firm. Many came together in crowd actions and mass meetings to protest and served on, or supported, local resistance committees. They refused to obey the statutes and officers of the British Crown, which so short a time before had been the law of the land. It was these various acts of resistance and noncooperation that struck most openly at the authority of the Crown.

The resistance campaigns against the extension of Parliament's authority also created crises within the British government and its colonial branches. Officials were unwilling or unable to use military force against resisters. General Thomas Gage, commander in chief of British forces in North America, could do nothing to police all the colonies adequately. After refusing to order his troops to fire on a crowd threatening violence and protesting the Stamp Act in New York in November 1765, he wrote that "tho a fire from the fort might disperse the Mob, it would not quell them." He feared that a military confrontation would start "a Civil War, at a time when there is nothing prepared or timely can be so, to make opposition to it."[10]

Despite the general's fears, the Stamp Act resistance did not signal the beginning of civil war. On the contrary, colonial leaders reconsidered and largely abandoned violent crowd actions of the kind Gage encountered in favor of organized tactics of *noncooperation,* the fourth element in the independence process. This included refusal to use tax stamps, and later, refusal to quarter troops, petitioning Parliament without the consent of the colonial governor, deliberate continuation of bodies declared illegal or dissolved by Crown officials, and many other actions. Such events began early in the resistance movement, drawing for precedent upon more limited actions previously taken in the colonies and elsewhere. Economic and political noncooperation on a wide scale, however, increasingly threatened British authority. Thus, one result of widespread resistance was the beginning of a redistribution of power in the colonies. A new political base was created by the decisive shift away from dependence upon Britain. In many colonies, those political elites that strongly supported Britain sooner or later lost authority with the populace. Similarly, the desire to increase American autonomy contributed to the growth of economic structures based on homegrown agriculture and industry.

The ultimate transfer of power rested upon the establishment of various forms of *parallel government,* the fifth phase in the process leading to independence. It was the ability of the American colonists to do without British colonial administrative machinery, largely because they replaced it with governing mechanisms of their own, that signaled the beginning of American independence. Autonomous governing bodies arose in large numbers during the period of the Continental Association in late 1774 and nearly 1775.

In August and September 1774, for example, the courts and legislature of Massachusetts—and with them, all colonial government outside Boston—ceased to function. Juries refused to sit, sheriffs and justices of the peace refused to administer the law, and vast crowds blocked the court houses to prevent judges from acting under the Coercive Acts. Commanding General Gage, now the governor of Massachusetts, found to his surprise that disorder was not rampant. Although concerned about the crowds that shut down courts and demanded the resignation of officials serving under the Coercive Acts, Gage was confident that this indicated limited support for the movement and thus was certain that he could bring the resistance to an end.[11]

With the sanction of the First Continental Congress, extralegal committees and congresses that effectively adopted the functions of government appeared throughout the colonies in the last months of 1774. Their appearance some months before the beginning of the War of Independence indicates that self-government in the colonies was *not* gained by war, as it is usually assumed.

During the resistance campaigns preceding the Continental Association, the colonists had laid the basis in thought and action for their later attempt to achieve independence. In the earlier campaigns, tendencies toward independence and those leading toward whatever degree of social revolution the colonies finally experienced appeared together. Both were encouraged by the same events, although the trend toward independence and that toward revolution can be distinguished analytically. *Resistance, Politics, and the Struggle for American Independence* primarily lays stress upon those events that led people to desire political independence while also developing their capacity to achieve it.

It is clear that the political basis for independence existed in the Continental Association and the organizations aimed at bringing its goals to fruition. The evidence presented in Chapter Fourteen of this volume illustrates that, within the majority of colonies, the transfer of power from British officials to the provincial conventions and committees was strongly in evidence before 19 April 1775. Though complete separation from Great Britain was seldom considered seriously by the colonists before late 1775, the extralegal assemblies and committees rendered America independent in matters of government well before the first calls for a formal declaration were heard in Congress.

• THREE CAMPAIGNS OF RESISTANCE •

The movement toward colonial self-government began with the first open resistance campaign against the Stamp Act of 1765. Already concerned that they were losing the freedom of action they had enjoyed before 1763, the colonists were stunned by a comprehensive law placing taxes on numerous documents and paper goods. Before adoption of the Stamp Act, colonial complaints against British policies found their voice in petitions to Parliament from the colonial legislatures. With Parliament's enactment of the Stamp Act on 22 March 1765, the character of colonial dissent changed. Opposition now took many forms, including not only petitions for repeal of the law but also colonial refusal to pay the taxes, social boycotts against supporters of the act, and nonimportation and nonconsumption of British goods.

Within two months after the Stamp Act arrived in America, Massachusetts and Virginia legislatures passed resolutions protesting it. Several colonies laid plans to convene the Stamp Act Congress in October 1765. Several newspapers issued calls to oppose the parliamentary edicts, and demonstrations were organized in major cities to protest the British action.

Gatherings in several cities tried to secure the resignation of Crown-appointed stamp tax agents. Crowds hanged them in effigy and sometimes confronted them at their homes to persuade or coerce the agents into resigning their posts. During the month of August 1765, actions against tax officials took place in Massachusetts, Connecticut, New York, Rhode Island, and Maryland, with the result that most had resigned before the first stamped paper reached the colonies in September.

By the time the Stamp Act went into effect on 1 November 1765, colonial resistance was well underway. The Stamp Act Congress in October enacted a declaration of rights and drafted addresses against the act intended for the king and Parliament. Some newspapers announced that they were ceasing publication rather than use tax stamps. Others decided to defy Crown policy by continuing to publish without the stamps.

Actions such as these effectively nullified the Stamp Act in the colonies but did not bring about its desired repeal. That was the task of colonial nonimportation agreements entered into by merchants in the three major port cities of Boston, New York, and Philadelphia. On 31 October 1765, New York merchants pledged their refusal to import British goods until the repeal of the tax. Philadelphia merchants joined the agreements on 7 November, followed by Boston on 9 December. These accords had a significant affect on British trade and prompted a petition campaign by British merchants to repeal the Stamp Act.

By the date of its repeal in March 1766, the Stamp Act was a dead letter in the colonies. Numerous ports had reopened without the use of stamps, and various local courts throughout the provinces conducted business in violation of the British laws. Repeal brought a certain calm to North America, but the colonists did not forget their experience with the powerful methods of noncooperation and nonimportation.

When Parliament passed the Townshend Acts in 1767, colonial activists again turned to the weapon of nonimportation in an effort to overturn the revenue measures. At first, these duties encountered little resistance and, unlike the Stamp Act, went into effect (on 20 November 1767) without any attempt in the colonies to prevent their enforcement. A Boston town meeting of 28 October had voted to encourage domestic manufacturing and adopted a limited nonconsumption agreement to protest the acts, but colonial agitation remained slight until early 1768. Two events then brought colonial grievances into sharper focus and provided the impetus for further popular resistance. The first was the publication of John Dickinson's *Letters from a Pennsylvania Farmer.* Circulated weekly in newspapers throughout the colonies beginning in December 1767, the articles denied the right of Parliament to levy any kind of duties for revenue on the colonies. Dickinson spoke forcefully against British oppression and counseled colonial resistance through petition and nonimportation.

Following soon after Dickinson's first letters was the action taken by the Massachusetts House of Representatives. On 20 January 1768, it adopted a petition to the king and authorized Speaker of the House Thomas Cushing to send a letter describing its action to every other colonial assembly. Dispatched on 11 February 1768, the circular letter also expressed the hope that other assemblies would take proper constitutional action to secure repeal of the Townshend duties. The Virginia House of Burgesses was the first legislative body to vote its approval of the resolutions passed by the Massachusetts House. By the end of the year, every colonial assembly had adopted petitions to the king questioning or denying Parliament's right to levy taxes of any kind on the colonies.

While colonial assemblies acted on the Massachusetts letter, a movement for nonimportation began. Planning for such agreements commenced in Boston in March of 1768, but no accord was signed until 1 August. Later in August, New York merchants signed a pact similar to Boston's. In addition to nonimportation, they decreed that violators of the agreement, or merchants who refused to sign, should be boycotted and labeled "Enemies to their Country."[12] After some hesitation, Philadelphia merchants signed an agreement on 6 February 1769, and a number of smaller ports followed shortly thereafter.

Repeal of the Townshend Acts, except the duty on tea, came in April 1770, though it is not certain that the colonial commercial resistance was the most significant reason for Parliament's action. Nonimportation had not been as complete as during the Stamp Act resistance, and the British economy was not as susceptible to commercial pressure as it had been in 1765. Yet the nonimportation agreements succeeded in sharply reducing trade with Great Britain, and the lessons learned during this campaign were applied to the later nonintercourse agreements of 1774–75.

Shortly after news of partial repeal reached America, the New York merchants changed their nonimportation agreement to permit imports of all except duties articles. The virtual collapse of the nonimportation movement was later completed when the merchants of Philadelphia and Boston voted sweeping modifications as well. The second major campaign of resistance to British authority was over.

Collapse of the Townshend Acts resistance ushered in a three-year period of relative political calm. Despite the lack of resistance activity similar in scope to the Stamp Act and Townshend Acts campaigns, disputes arising between colonial assemblies and royal governors often provoked legal and extralegal actions by colonists in support of their self-proclaimed rights.

One of the more significant developments of the period involved the formation of the committees of correspondence in late 1772 and early 1773. Their organization was prompted by two developments in New England. One of these was the British response to the burning of the *Gaspée,* an armed schooner in the British Customs service, off of the coast of Rhode Island in June 1772; and the other was the controversy in the summer and fall of 1772 over whether Massachusetts Superior Court justices should be paid by the Crown from revenue raised by Customs.

By the end of December 1772, committees of correspondence had been formed throughout Massachusetts at the suggestion of the Boston town meeting. In March 1773, the Virginia House of Burgesses elected a standing committee of correspondence and requested that other assemblies appoint similar bodies. A network of intercolonial committees was firmly in place by early 1774.

At the time of the committees' formation, the colonials claimed that they would oppose British infringements of their "Rights, Liberties, and Privileges."[13] These claims were put to the test with Parliament's passage of the Tea Act in May 1773. By late fall, colonists organized a plan to nullify the act by securing the resignations of tea agents. Some resisters, however, took more direct action and proceeded to dump dutied tea into Boston harbor on 16 December 1773.

British reaction to the Boston Tea Party was swift and harsh. In an effort to punish the people of Massachusetts for their alleged flaunting of British authority over the last ten years, Parliament enacted a series of measures that came to be known as the Coercive Acts. News of the edicts reached the colonies in May 1774 and immediately prompted resistance. An extralegal meeting of the Virginia House of Burgesses, convened on 27 May in defiance of the governor's orders, called for an intercolonial congress. The Massachusetts House suggested a September meeting in Philadelphia and elected its own delegates to the proposed congress. By the end of August, all the colonies except Georgia had elected delegates to the congress, some in extralegal sessions prohibited by Crown-appointed governors.

As time for the intercolonial gathering approached, plans were readied in several colonies for the reinstitution of commercial sanctions. Support grew during the summer months for economic resistance, and a number of localities enacted their own nonimportation, nonconsumption, and nonexportation agreements. The extralegal Virginia Convention of 1 August 1774, for instance, adopted its own plan of nonintercourse, complete with the apparatus to enforce it.

The First Continental Congress met in Philadelphia on 5 September 1774. Before it disbanded on 22 October, it enacted a series of resolutions articulating the rights and grievances of the colonies and adopted the detailed program of economic noncooperation known as the Continental Association. This document, approved by Congress on 20 October, aimed at the redress of grievances through a "nonimportation, nonconsumption, and nonexportation agreement," which would prove to be the "most speedy, effectual, and peaceable" measure.[14] The association set 1 December 1774 as the date on which imports from Great Britain, Ireland, and the West Indies would stop. To increase compliance with the policy, the association called for colonial nonconsumption of restricted items. Finally, the agreement authorized nonexportation in the event that nonimportation should fail to secure redress of grievances. If needed, nonexportation, the commercial weapon that many colonists felt to be the most coercive measure available to them, would begin on 10 September 1775.

The Continental Association did not simply outline a program of economic resistance. Most significantly, it also designed means by which the nonintercourse agreement would be organized and enforced. The Association's enforcement provisions were quickly implemented throughout the provinces. As authorized by the Association, committees were organized in almost every town, city, and county to oversee the mandate of Congress. Violators of the association were ostracized and boycotted until they accepted the document's provisions.

Colonial noncooperation throughout the resistance to the Coercive Acts was not limited to a refusal to buy British goods, but was extended to all laws of royal government. Courts were closed, taxes refused, governors openly defied. The Suffolk Resolves, passed in September 1774 by Suffolk County, Massachusetts, counseled tax refusal, commercial nonintercourse, and noncooperation with the Crown-appointed governor and officials. Extralegal provincial congresses convened in 1774 and nearly 1775 throughout the colonies to oversee enforcement of the association and, in some cases, to debate the possibility of military confrontation with British forces. The "illegal" assemblies on the local, county, and provincial levels often assumed legislative and judicial functions in executing the wishes of the Continental Congress. As the conservative newspaper, *Rivington's New York Gazetteer,* wrote in February 1775, the association took "Government out of the hands of the Governor, Council, and General Assembly; and the execution of laws out of the hands of the Civil Magistrates and Juries."[15]

Naturally, the Crown did not look favorably upon these developments. On 18 November 1774, King George III sent a note to Lord North stating that "the New England Governments are in a State of Rebellion; blows must decide whether they are to be subject to this Country or independent."[16] The issue for Parliament and George III was no longer redress of grievances; the colonists had demonstrated that British authority was in jeopardy throughout North America and the Crown felt a need to put the colonies in their place. Consequently, Lord Dartmouth, in his letter of 27 January 1775, directed General Gage to quell the heretofore nonviolent rebellion by arresting and imprisoning "the principle actors & abettors in the [Massachusetts] Provincial Congress . . . if . . . they should presume to assemble . . . even though [this] be a Signal for Hostilities."[17] Gage took the offensive by attempting to seize military stores at Concord, where he clashed with colonial farmers on 19 April 1775.

Organizations throughout the colonies were immediately confronted with the decision over whether they should follow the Massachusetts farmers into armed struggle. Seven provinces, including Massachusetts, Connecticut, Rhode Island, Maryland, New Hampshire, South Carolina, and Virginia, had authorized the organization of local militias prior to Lexington and Concord, but these bodies were highly defensive in nature; they would be called upon only as a last resort.[18] With the initiation of hostilities, many of these militias were placed on a war footing.

When the Second Continental Congress convened on 10 May 1775, it assumed direction of the quickly developing military struggle. Washington was appointed commander in chief of the army of the United Colonies in June 1775, and military plans and regulations were constructed. In addition to creating a Continental Army, Congress authorized issuance of two million dollars in paper money to help finance its policies. Washington left Philadelphia to take command of troops in Massachusetts on 23 June, the day after news had arrived of the Battle of Bunker Hill, which left 366 British and Americans killed and 1,099 wounded.

On 15 July 1775, the Continental Congress modified the association to allow military goods to be imported. The policy of commercial coercion receded into the background. Arthur Schlesinger, Sr. suggested that the confrontation at Lexington and Concord "wrought a radical change" in the nature of the colonial struggle against the Crown. Schlesinger concluded: "Armed rebellion had superceded commercial coercion as the dependence of the radicals in their struggle for larger liberties. Thereafter, the Continental Association lost its distinctive character as a method of peaceable coercion; it became subordinated to the military necessities of the times."[19]

• THE NATURE OF NONVIOLENT ACTION •

The colonists who pursued the resistance against the British government which culminated in the achievement of de facto independence were faced, as discussed earlier in this chapter, with the dilemma of how to resist Crown authority most effectively. The most important technique of action chosen, both in terms of the frequency of its use and the results achieved, was nonviolent action. Colonial leaders did not adopt this technique in order to remain morally pure. Rather, their decision to use what we call nonviolent action was based on a strategic judgement of the most effective means of resistance. Similarly, colonial activists did not have a thorough understanding of the nature, dynamics, and scope of nonviolent action before they put it into use. As shall be described in later chapters, the colonists were not certain how effective a given method might be, and often made tactical and even strategic errors in applying the nonviolent technique. Of course, similar mistakes are frequently made by participants in both improvised and carefully planned military struggle, and sweeping judgements about the deficiencies or capacities of the nonviolent technique as a whole, based on this experience alone, are not appropriate. Colonial errors, as well as their successes, however, can provide students of resistance campaigns and social movements with critical insights into the nature of nonviolent or civilian struggle.

Many people are familiar with the term "nonviolent action," but few are sure of its precise meaning. The editors of this volume view nonviolent action as a technique used in social and political conflict which operates to bring about change through the use of methods which do not inflict, or threaten to inflict, physical injury upon an opponent, but instead serve to manipulate the shared social, cultural, economic, and political system in which the opposing parties engage in conflict. The methods of nonviolent action may attempt to convert an opponent by various appeals; they may inconvenience a rival, threaten profits, or weaken a tyrant's control over subordinates. If applied properly, nonviolent action can make it impossible for an opponent to continue onerous actions by removing the support of taxpayers, officials, and enforcement personnel. Activists employing the technique may also bring about the transfer of power from traditional authorities to extralegal institutions which are granted superior legitimacy and enjoy greater popular obedience.

The various methods of nonviolent action may be divided into three categories.[20] The first of these, *nonviolent protest and persuasion,* consists of methods which express the position of the activists in words and symbols. This class of methods includes the protest march and demonstration, the public speech or sermon of protest, the petition, and demonstrative fasts or funerals; all of which were used by the American colonists. Nonviolent actionists may also choose to employ techniques under the general category of *noncooperation.* Methods from this class used in the colonial struggle include nonimportation, nonexportation, refusal to obey "illegitimate" laws, and social boycott. Practitioners of this type of activity deliberately withhold or withdraw their usual cooperation in an effort to prevent or force change. These actions, which may be legal or illegal, can often paralyze an antagonist by slowing or halting normal activity.

The third category of methods, those of *nonviolent intervention,* pose a more direct and immediate challenge to an opponent than do the methods described above. Tactics associated with nonviolent intervention may disrupt or destroy normal patterns of behavior, or they may bring about the establishment of more desirable relationships and institutions. The most dramatic use of nonviolent intervention on the part of the colonists is found in their creation of new governmental bodies such as the provincial congresses and conventions. By receiving overwhelming support from the populace, these extralegal bodies and their local counterparts effectively replaced the Crown's established government in the colonies.

Both violent and nonviolent action can work against an opponent by reducing the sources of his or her power. Each technique, however, operates differently; while violence accomplishes its task by destroying both the antagonist's person and power, nonviolent action succeeds by rendering the opponent's sources of power unusable, unworkable, and uncontrollable. The nonviolent technique may be applied in a myriad of ways. When the needed conditions are met, it is capable of producing change in one of three basic ways.

The first mechanism by which nonviolent action may achieve success is called *conversion*. In conversion, the opponent is convinced that the protestors are correct in their position and agrees to make the requested changes. Change in the opponent may be brought about by appeals to reason, argumentation, or even through emotional pressure. In this process, nonviolent groups often attempt morally to uplift an oppressor by appealing to his or her inherent goodness. The conversion mechanism, of course, is most likely to operate when the opponent does not have a firm policy in the matter or when vital interests are not involved.

A much more common, and perhaps more typical, use of nonviolent action in social conflict is the mechanism of change known as *accommodation*. In accommodation, the opponent is neither convinced that the demands of the nonviolent actionists are just nor is the antagonist entirely coerced into making the proposed changes. The opponent is able to continue the struggle but decides to grant the nonviolent actionists' demands rather than risk a more unsatisfactory resolution of the conflict at a later date. Accommodation does not necessarily imply compromise. The opponent may agree to meet all of the demands of the resisters or may accede to only a few unimportant requests in order to end the open conflict by reducing the will of the nonviolent actors to continue their activity. In both the Stamp Act and Townshend Acts movements, for example, the accommodation of the ministry to the colonial position was sufficient to bring about a temporary halting of resistance activity.

The most dramatic of the three mechanisms, as well as the most difficult to achieve in mass action, is *nonviolent coercion*. Nonviolent coercion occurs when an opponent is forced against his or her will to grant the actionists' demands. In order for this mechanism to work, the opponent's sources of power must be nullified or reduced to a point where continuation of the struggle with the nonviolent actors is impossible. The opponent is often confronted by widespread defiance and disobedience and finds it impossible to act effectively to defend his or her objectionable policies. This may happen when a law is nullified by overwhelmingly popular noncooperation. It may also occur when political authority is transferred to alternative governing institutions, depriving the opponent of the ability to rule.

• OUTLINE OF THE BOOK •

Most American historians have largely ignored the colonists' use of nonviolent action or have mentioned it only in passing. Those who have recognized its existence have generally been unable to interpret either the dynamics or the consequences of actions such as nonimportation, court closings, refusal to obey Crown authority, and other nonviolent resistance methods. One problem in such an analysis occurs, in part, because the colonists did not use the modern terminology of nonviolent action; words such as "boycott" and "civil disobedience" simply had not yet been invented. Another difficulty results from the tendency of people to view nonviolent action as a pacifistic stance based on moral and ethical belief rather than as a pragmatic means of political struggle. Given this common but mistaken view of nonviolent action, it is not surprising that few historians would find examples of it in the colonial experience. Few activists of the time, however, justified their use of the technique on moral grounds; they were concerned primarily with winning redress of grievances. If the methods of nonimportation and nonexportation proved effective, they were employed. Despite the fact that colonists were not entirely conscious of the technique which they used, there was some recognition that violence was often an ineffective means of struggle. Even Samuel Adams, whom many contemporary historians associate with the tactics of violence, issued numerous statements prior to Lexington and Concord opposing the use of armed force by the colonists. In May 1774, for example, Adams cautioned colonial leader James Warren about the use of the tactic. Writing to Warren following his receipt of the Boston Port Bill, Adams warned: "Nothing can ruin us but our violence."[21] The Boston patriot was not the only colonial leader who counseled this way. The historical documents of the period prior to Lexington and Concord indicate a colonial concern that orderly struggle be maintained and engagements with British troops avoided.[22]

The contributions of nonviolent struggle to this critical period of American history are also neglected due to scholars' frequent propensity to ignore particular events in order to support certain viewpoints. Researchers often look throughout the length of a period for evidence of what they regard as its inevitable outcome. Students of colonial history, for example, may be looking for the roots of war and find them in mass violence or military preparations. In the process, they will fail to realize that a conflict may be fought in many ways and may ignore the contributions of alternative means to the outcome of that struggle.

Scholars inevitably face critical decisions of detail and scope in their presentation of material. The editors of this volume have tried to present a full description of events, both nonviolent and violent, so that readers might draw their own conclusions about this critical decade of history. Some of the facts published in this volume are new and extremely revealing; others have already been recounted in other works.

This book is divided into two parts. In the narrative section of the book (chapters Two–Eight), the editors have attempted to bring the important events of the period together in one place. These chapters are chronological treatments of the resistance campaigns and the British responses to them. They rarely make use of the term "nonviolent action"; instead, both our British and American contributors utilize the terminology of the day in their depictions of nonimportation agreements, provincial conventions, and the like. To complement the descriptive accounts contained in the narrative chapters, the editors have included an analytical section (chapters Nine–Fourteen), which provides various interpretations of the events of the decade. These contributions attempt to answer some of the questions raised by the previous chapters and suggest some areas for future research.

The narrative section begins with Walter H. Conser's review of colonial resistance to the Stamp Act (Chapter Two). Conser outlines the colonial nullification campaigns and details the formation and enforcement of nonimportation agreements in the major ports. As he notes, crowd activity of a violent nature did sometimes occur, but its impact upon the British decision to repeal the act was minor.

Conser's view that nonimportation was critically important to American success is supported by Paul Langford's chapter on the Rockingham Ministry (Chapter Three). Dr. Langford documents Rockingham's belief that Anglo-American commerce would be ruined if colonial resistance continued and details the campaign waged by British merchants and manufacturers in support of repeal. The pressure of British commercial interests, coupled with the ministry's brilliant orchestration of repeal testimony in Parliament, Langford claims, brought an end to the Stamp Act.

As Chapter Four and its Introduction indicate, a major reason for the passage of the Townshend Acts was political; Parliament wished to render civil government in the colonies more independent of popular rule. Leslie Thomas's work illustrates that colonial agitation again took the form of commercial resistance. Unlike resistance to the Stamp Act, however, nonimportation during this period was beset with difficulties, and debates persist as to its effectiveness. Ian Christie (Chapter Five), for example, argues that the British government was concerned more with the political implications of resistance, such as the breakdown of authority and perceived threats of violence, than with colonial economic sanctions. He claims further that nonimportation had little effect on British merchants and manufactures because of poor colonial enforcement and the opening of new British markets. Paul Langford (Chapter Seven) also points to the faulty implementation of nonimportation but believes the claim that British prosperity was maintained by the opening of new markets is overstated.

There is no doubt that the colonial activists made critical errors in the timing and execution of commercial sanctions during this period, but the evidence presented by Thomas suggests that certain colonial ports were nonetheless rigorous in their enforcement. In Chapter Nine, Ronald M. McCarthy and Walter H. Conser take a close look at the impact of commercial resistance and argue that the success of nonimportation is contingent on the following five critical factors: (1) the timing of economic resistance, (2) the effectiveness of enforcement, (3) the general economic situation in Great Britain, (4) the sectors of the British economy which were hurt and the impact of this injury, and (5) the ability of affected sectors to mobilize support in Parliament for colonial demands. Conser and McCarthy believe that the campaign against the Townshend Acts, while not a complete success, was nevertheless significant in its implications for future resistance activities. This chapter, as does the earlier piece by Dr. Langford, suggests that it is extremely difficult to assess the economic effects of nonimportation and calls for more research in this area.

Whatever the deficiencies of enforcement found during the commercial resistance to the Townshend Acts, they were effectively eliminated during the next nonviolent resistance activity of 1774–75. As David Ammerman (Chapter Six) illustrates, economic sanctions applied during this period were rigorously enforced throughout the colonies by extralegal local committees authorized by the Continental Congress. Great Britain, however, constantly underestimated the extent and character of the resistance. Both Paul Langford (Chapter Seven) and Ian Christie (Chapter Eight) explain that the Crown believed a small group of conspirators to be the core of resistance. This misunderstanding, claims Christie, provided a rationale for passage and attempted enforcement of the Coercive Acts.

Colonial resistance in 1774 and early 1775 was, of course, widespread, and nonimportation showed signs of significantly reducing trade between Britain and the North American provinces. Yet other powerful measures available to the colonists, such as nonexportation, were forgone until after the character of the struggle had changed fundamentally. Nonexportation, the method which many felt to be the most powerful weapon in the colonists' nonviolent arsenal, was never applied within the context of orderly resistance. Colonial failure to use this method earlier in the struggle against the Coercive Acts is cited by both American and British contributors in this volume as a crucial strategic error made by colonial activists.

The skill of the colonists in applying the methods of nonviolent struggle improved greatly over the decade. Similarly, the intellectual underpinnings of resistance in both colonial America and Great Britain were refined as well. Walter H. Conser (Chapter Ten) and C. C. Bonwick (Chapter Eleven) trace the evolution of religious and political thought in America and Great Britain and the role of the clergy in the movements of the day. Both chapters illustrate how proponents of change in both Britain and the colonies gave support to each other through correspondence and action. J. H. Plumb's contribution (Chapter Thirteen), like that of Dr. Bonwick, describes the support for American demands within Great Britain. Significantly, however, this encouragement was eroded by war, when support for America became "tainted with sedition."

If the nonviolent movement for change was so successful, one might ask why this strategy was abandoned in favor of military resistance. In Chapter Twelve, David J. Toscano, Ronald M. McCarthy, and Walter H. Conser, Jr. offer a number of alternative explanations for the shift to war. This piece traces the ideological justifications for military resistance and sketches the development of the militia and the committees of safety. Understanding the nature of American colonial struggles is seriously compromised by historians' failures to investigate these developments in detail. Many have viewed the war as inevitable, desirable, or both. Consequently, they have not considered research on the shift to war to be important. The editors believe that investigation of these questions should proceed and present this chapter as a tentative guide for future research.

In the concluding chapter, Ronald M. McCarthy summarizes the research of this volume and describes the political accomplishments of the independence movement. His chapter provides a detailed analysis of the extralegal colonial governments and their development prior to April 1775. McCarthy further documents the view expressed by the editors that independence in many of the colonies had essentially been achieved prior to the commencement of military hostilities at Lexington and Concord.

This book does not propose to answer all the questions surrounding this decade of struggle. Certain questions of interest to students of resistance struggle have not even been raised here. How did the use of nonviolent resistance, for example, affect social structure in the colonies? What were the effects of the adoption of military means? Did the move toward military resistance under the Second Continental Congress serve to strengthen that institution as a central governmental body in a way which altered the decentralizing tendencies of the local and provincial popular assemblies? Was previous British support for American positions eroded by the change to military struggle? To what extent were certain segments of the American public alienated by the use of violence? These questions, and others like them, require serious consideration and careful examination. The editors believe that they have contributed to the exploration of the critical issues surrounding the decade and hope that others will investigate the unanswered questions in further detail.

• NOTES •

1. John Adams to Dr. Jedediah Morse, 29 November 1815, *The Works of John Adams*, Charles Francis Adams ed., (Boston: Little, Brown, 1850–56),vol. 10, p. 182.

2. John Dickinson, *Letters from a Farmer in Pennsylvania to the Inhabitants of the British Colonies* (1767–68; reprint, New York: Outlook, 1903), pp. 29–30. See appendix B.

3. The case for the importance of violence in the movement is made by Richard Maxwell Brown, "Violence and the American Revolution," in Stephen G. Kurtz and James H. Hutson, eds., *Essays on the American Revolution* (Chapel Hill, N.C.: Univ. of North Carolina Press, 1973), pp. 81–120.

4. Bernhard Knollenberg, *The Growth of the American Revolution, 1765–1775* (New York: Free Press, 1975), p. 361, n. 64.

5. Nathaniel Bouton, ed., *Documents and Records Relating to the Province of New Hampshire from 1764–1776* (Nashua, N.H.: Orren C. Moore, State Printer, 1873), vol. 7, p. 250.

6. Middlesex County Convention resolution, 30–31 August 1774, L. Kinvin Wroth, et al., eds., *Province in Rebellion: A Documentary History of the Founding of the Commonwealth of Massachusetts, 1774–1775* (microform publication, Cambridge: Harvard Univ. Press, 1975),p. 886.

7. Crane Brinton, *The Anatomy of Revolution* (New York: Vintage, 1965); Charles Tilly, *From Mobilization to Revolution* (Reading, Mass.: Addison-Wesley, 1978).

8. The growth of an American identity, especially during periods of conflict with Britain, is discussed in Richard L. Merritt, "The Colonists Discover America: Attention Patterns in the Colonial Press, 1735–1775," *William and Mary Quarterly,* 3d ser., 21 (1964), pp. 271–85.

9. David Hawke, *The Colonial Experience* (Indianapolis: Bobbs-Merrill, 1966);

Dickinson, *Letters from a Farmer,* pp. 29–30; Richard Frothingham, *The Life and Times of Joseph Warren* (Boston: Little, Brown, 1865), p. 347.

10. Gage to Cadwallader Colden, 5 November 1765, *New-York Historical Society Collections* (1923), vol. 7, p. 70.

11. K. G. Davies, ed., *Documents of the American Revolution, 1770–1783 (Colonial Office Series)* (Shannon, Ireland: Irish Universities Press, 1975), vol. 8, pp. 117, 179–84; vol. 9, pp. 29–30, 51–52.

12. Quoted in Arthur M. Schlesinger, *The Colonial Merchants and the American Revolution, 1763–1775* (New York: Atheneum, 1968), p. 124.

13. Boston Committee of Correspondence, in *Boston Town Records 1770–1777,* pp. 95–108; quoted in Knollenberg, *Growth of the American Revolution,* p. 88.

14. Worthington C. Ford ed., *Journals of the Continental Congress, 1774–1798* (Washington, D.C.: Government Printing Office, 1904), vol. 1, pp. 75–81.

15. *Rivington's New York Gazetteer,* 18 February 1775.

16. Sir John Fortescue, ed., *The Correspondence of King George the Third . . .* (6 vols., London: Macmillan, 1927–28), vol. 3, p. 153.

17. Dartmouth to Gage, 27 January 1775, in Clarence Edwin Carter, ed., *The Correspondence of General Thomas Gage with the War Office and the Treasury, 1763–1775* (2 vols., New Haven: Yale Univ. Press, 1931–33), vol. 2, pp. 179–83.

18. A short description of the decisions made by Massachusetts, Connecticut, Maryland, Virginia, New Hampshire, and Rhode Island to authorize military preparations is provided in Knollenberg, *Growth of the American Revolution,* pp. 176–83. Prior to the Second Continental Congress, New Jersey, Pennsylvania, Delaware, and North Carolina took no measures, on a provincial level, to arm the populace. For a detailed treatment of military preparations taken by the colonists, see Chapter Twelve of this volume.

19. Schlesinger, *Colonial Merchants,* p. 541.

20. The discussion of the methods and mechanisms of nonviolent action is based upon Gene Sharp, *The Politics of Nonviolent Action* (Boston: Porter Sargent, 1973), Chapters Three–Eight, Thirteen.

21. Samuel Adams to James Warren, 21 May 1774, "Warren-Adams Letters," Massachusetts Historical Society, *Collections* 17 (1917).

22. See Pauline Maier, *From Resistance to Revolution* (New York, Knopf, 1972).

·2·

The Stamp Act Resistance

WALTER H. CONSER, JR.

The Stamp Act, passed in March 1765, was part of a larger colonial program that had begun a year earlier. In March 1764, George Grenville, chancellor of the exchequer, presented to Parliament the American Revenue Act. This American Revenue Act, or the Sugar Act, as it has become more commonly known, was designed for the specific purpose of raising money in the colonies for the Crown. This revenue was to be raised through increased duties on items as disparate as foreign refined sugar, coffee, textiles, indigo, and Madeira wine. The act also increased the list of American products such as iron, raw silk, and potash which could only be sold to Great Britain. The act banned the importation of foreign rum and French wines and doubled the duties on foreign goods reshipped from Britain to the colonies.

In presenting this Revenue Act, Grenville indicated his intention to carry out other reforms within the colonial system, most particularly of the Customs service. To do this, Grenville announced the establishment of a vice-admiralty court centered at Halifax, Nova Scotia, with jurisdiction over the American colonies. This enabled the British government to prosecute colonists there, far from their homes, rather than in local colonial courts. In addition, Grenville broadened the Customs officials' authority of investigation and seizure and established more rigid registration and bonding procedures for the shipping trades.

Measures to increase revenue from the colonies seemed quite justified to imperial administrators. A large national debt had accrued as a result of the Seven Years' War, a war fought in part for the protection of the American colonies. Also, a standing British army of approximately ten thousand troops was being garrisoned in America for protection from the Indians and a possible war of repossession by France. Although such revenue measures were potentially beneficial to the Crown treasury, they promised certain hardship to the colonists. By early 1764, the colonial economies had slumped badly. Prices were unstable, business slowed, and the economic outlook of the colonies was bleak. That gloomy outlook was exacerbated

22

by the increased duties and greater restrictions posed by the Sugar Act and the parliamentary prohibitions against colonial paper money. The new revenue duties fell hard on colonial trade and the shipping business.

Not surprisingly, the New England colonies, where mercantile interests predominated, were the first to respond to the Sugar Act. On 15 May 1764, a town meeting of Boston, Massachusetts chose a committee to draw up instructions to be given to Boston's four representatives in the General Assembly. The committee delivered its report on 24 May 1764. The Boston town meeting then voted to protest the Sugar Act. In their instructions, the Bostonians reminded their representatives of the need to remain vigilant against attacks on "the invaluable Rights and Privileges of the Province." The resolution also noted that the proposed duties would seriously depress trade. Appealing to economic motives, the Bostonians claimed that the mother country would receive more benefits from a flourishing colonial trade than she would from the duties which would arise from trade hampered and taxed. In their closing paragraph, the Bostonians highlighted their fears that these revenue duties were but a preparation for even grater taxes. "For if our Trade may be taxed why not our Lands?" the instructions queried.

> Why not the produce of our Lands and every Thing we possess or make use of? This we apprehend annihilates our Charter Right to Govern and Tax ourselves—It Strikes at our British Privileges which as we have never forfeited them we hold in common with our Fellow Subjects who are Natives of Britain: if Taxes are laid upon us in any shape without ever having a Legal Representation where they are laid, are we not reduced from the Character of Free Subjects to the miserable state of tributary Slaves?[1]

Clearly the brunt of these political instructions was directed to the economic hardships of the new duties. Political issues, however, were as crucial: in their coda, with its invocation of charter rights and its mention of the issue of representation, the Bostonians identified an issue of tremendous future significance.

Scarcely three weeks later, on 13 June 1764, the Massachusetts House of Representatives followed the lead of the Boston town meeting. In a letter to its agent in London, Jaspar Mauduit, the House lamented the passage of the Sugar Act and chastized him for not having put up greater resistance to the revenue bill. Calling upon Parliament to exercise greater moderation in the raising of revenue from the colonies, the Massachusetts House instructed Mauduit to work for the repeal of the Sugar Act and the prevention of any further duties and to join with the other colonial agents in such measures of prevention as were possible. In conjunction with this letter to Mauduit, the House formed a committee of correspondence consisting of James Otis, Oxenbridge Thacher, Thomas Cushing, Edward Sheafe, and Thomas Gray. The committee was to meet during the recess of the House and was authorized to write the other colonial governments calling on them to join in united opposition to the Sugar Act and in action to prevent any other duties or taxes.[2]

Massachusetts had taken an important step. This move was the more auspicious since rumors had been reaching the colonies of a new proposal by Grenville for a stamp tax of some sort. Agent Mauduit, in London, had sent word of the proposal to the Massachusetts representatives. This news had helped to provide the impetus for their circular letter of June. In late July 1764, the assembly of nearby Rhode Island met and formed a committee to assist in this proposed intercolonial drive for repeal of the Sugar Act. As with their northern neighbors, the Rhode Islanders were concerned in particular about preventing the levy of a stamp duty upon the North American colonies being considered at that time by Parliament; in general they were concerned about preventing "all such taxes, duties, or impositions, that . . . [were] inconsistent with their rights and privileges as British subjects."[3] The assembly then passed a resolution similar to the circular letter of Massachusetts in which it called for united action by the several American colonies to protest the recent parliamentary measures.[4] Finally, then, in November 1764, the Rhode Island Assembly drew up a petition to King George III in which it reiterated its opposition to the recent trade regulations and especially to the proposed internal tax on stamps.

The protests of the New Englanders were paralleled in the middle and southern colonies. In a strong statement, the New York Assembly on 18 October 1764 called for a total exemption from "involuntary taxes" or taxes not assessed by their own representatives.[5] In addition, the New Yorkers established their own committee of correspondence to channel protests in behalf of the repeal of the Sugar Act. In North Carolina, the assembly sounded the same message with its declaration on 31 October 1764 that the imposition of any taxes was regarded as the inherent right and exclusive privilege of that body alone.[6] Petitions of protest were also sent by the Pennsylvania Assembly and the Virginia House of Burgesses.[7] Together these protests provide a picture of growing political concern in the colonies over the infringement of rights and economic hardships portended by the new act.

In addition to these types of pressure set forth by the legislatures, a number of pamphlets were published which articulated the colonial grievances. During these months of developing opposition to the Sugar Act, three significant pamphlets appeared. Each was closely connected to the deliberations of the assemblies of the colonies in which their authors lived. For example, in May 1764, the Connecticut Assembly appointed a committee composed of the governor, Thomas Fitch, as well as George Wyllys, Ebenezer Silliman, and Jared Ingersoll. They were charged "to set in the most advantageous light all objections as may justly and reasonably [be] advanced against creating and collecting a revenue in America. . . . and especially against affecting the same by Stamp Duties, etc."[8] After some deliberation, the committee produced an essay entitled *Reasons Why the British Colonies in America, Should Not Be Charged with Internal Taxes, by Authority of Parliament*. The pamphlet asserted that "charging Stamp Duties, or other internal taxes on the colonies in America, by parliamentary Authority, will be an infringement of . . . Rights and Privileges and deprive the Colonists of their Freedom and Inheritance."[9] While not encouraging additional external taxes, the pamphlet acknowledged that: "reasons of State may render it expedient to prohibit some Branches of Trade and to burden other."[10] Such considerations, however, could never legitimately be countenanced at the cost of political liberty. Therefore, the colonists looked to the wisdom of the Crown to repeal the Sugar Act. Such action would restore the colonists' rights and enable Parliament to search out new sources of revenue. *Reasons* was a model of restraint and moderation, with its neat distinctions between internal and external taxation and its invocation of historical precedent and charter guarantees.

In June 1764, a slightly more polemical address appeared in Boston. Its author was James Otis, a popular leader in Boston, a member of the Massachusetts House, and a personal antagonist of Governor Francis Bernard and Lieutenant-Governor Thomas Hutchinson. Otis's pamphlet, *The Rights of the British Colonies Asserted and Proved,* squarely challenged the idea of internal as opposed to external taxation and did so on a much wider basis than mere charter rights. Not simply the guarantees of the Magna Carta but in addition "by the law of God and nature" were American colonists "entitled to all the natural, essential, inherent, and inseparable rights of our fellow subjects in Great Britain." Building from this premise, Otis included among such rights that "taxes are not to be laid on the people, but by their consent in person, or by deputation."[11] The upshot of this position was manifold. With rhetorical exuberance Otis acknowledged the authority of Parliament and reiterated his allegiance to the king. He insisted, however, that Parliament's authority was clearly restricted by these natural God-given rights. From this it followed that the king and his ministers must have been misinformed regarding this issue of colonial taxation. "There is no foundation for the distinction some make in England," Otis contended, "between an internal and an external tax on the colonies," and accordingly, Otis looked to Parliament to "afford us relief by repealing such acts, as through mistake, or other human infirmities, have been suffered to pass."[12] Combined with his dissolution of the internal and external issue was Otis's belief that Parliament had no right to levy any taxes in the American colonies since America had no representation in Parliament. Otis initially had been careful to set out a constitutional argument to correct ministerial ignorance. However, he now concluded that the real answer to these dilemmas would be the inclusion of American representatives in the British Parliament.

Otis ultimately retreated from some of the positions he had outlined. By November 1764, he had abandoned much of his "natural rights" position for one grounded again in charter rights. In so doing, he fell in line with the third significant resistance pamphlet of this period, *The Rights of the Colonies Examined.* The author of this pamphlet was Steven Hopkins, governor of Rhode Island. Published in November 1764, Hopkins's piece repeated the identity and equality of rights shared by British subjects both in Britain and America. Conceding that the regulation of trade might fall within parliamentary purview, Hopkins challenged the legitimacy of the proposed internal taxation through stamps. Ascribing the idea of such a tax to ministerial ignorance, just as Otis had done, Hopkins noted that the very proposal to collect taxes "in the colonies without their consent" had produced misgivings, consternation, and protest. Moreover, Hopkins concluded in a judicious understatement that, if such a project were carried out, "the colonies cannot help but consider [it] as a manifest violation of their just and long enjoyed rights."[13]

Each of these pamphlets was designed as a piece of polemic, information, and disputation. By concentrating their focus and distilling their arguments, the authors provided fuller treatment and greater clarification of the relevant issues than was provided by the legislative resolves alone. These essays were reprinted in newspapers and distributed as inexpensive pamphlets, thereby providing greater exposure to opposition ideas and helping to recruit a widespread and well-informed audience.

• POPULAR RESISTANCE TO THE SUGAR ACT •

Legislative resolves and philosophical debates were not the only forms of resistance activity. Nor were they the only means of encouraging and increasing involvement in the resistance to British authority. On 20 August 1764, a report appeared in the *Newport Mercury* of an agreement by some fifty Boston merchants to curtail their purchase of English imports. Lace, ruffles, and other "Superfluities in Dress" were to be entirely avoided; likewise no "English Cloth [was] to be purchased except at a fixed price." Furthermore, the "usual manner" of expressing bereavement for a deceased friend or relative "by covering themselves in Black, is also in the list of Superfluities, and no Part thereof, but the Crape in the Hat is retained."[14]

The motivation for such measures seemed self-evident to the newspaper, as "the causes of these prudent Measures, everyone will too easily suggest to himself to require any attention." Some skeptics claimed that the economics of full warehouses rather than the politics of protest were behind the merchants' agreements. Whatever their motivation, however, the newspaper heartily endorsed the proposed boycott. "As we have already manifested," the account concluded, "a great Attachment and Complaisance to Boston fashions, however ridiculous and extravagant, it is to be hoped that we shall not show an Aversion . . . but we shall cheerfully join in the above Resolutions."[15] The example was picked up, and the Boston papers reported similar ceremonies taking place in the following months. Here again, the ostentatious and expensive clothing formerly worn at funerals was now replaced by simple, frugal, American home manufactures. English lace and linen were now given up in an attempt to curtail the purchase of British goods.[16]

Other kinds of activities were developed at this time. On 6 September 1764, the Boston papers reported a boycott agreement reached in Philadelphia. According to the report, "a great Number of Gentlemen in the City have actually engaged Suits of Cloth to be spun and wove in this Province . . . and are determined henceforward to have no part of their Dress, but of the Manufactures of their own Country." Citing the tremendous financial savings that avoidance of British goods would entail, the article closed with the charge to tell all Pennsylvanians:

> [There is] no Benefit in Wearing English Wollens but dishonor, while they can wear their own Manufactures! Tell them of the great Discredit they draw on themselves, by eating English Cheese, and drinking English Beer and Cyder, while they have better made at Home! Tell the fair Ladies also, how much more amiable

they will appear in decent, plain Dresses made in their own Country, than in the gaudy, butterfly, vain, fantastick, and expensive Dresses brought from Europe.[17]

Another newspaper article of 5 July 1764 recounted similar actions occurring in New York City. The story closed stating that, since "many of the most considerable Gentlemen in this City are determined to wear the Manufactures of this Country, and to encourage the Use of whatever is our own Produce, it is earnestly hoped, that every Lover of their Country will follow their laudable example."[18] In the same spirit, students at Yale College in Connecticut agreed unanimously to abstain from foreign liquors.[19] Such attention to American products which grew out of the concern over the parliamentary duties sometimes resulted in energetic competitions to produce bigger and better domestic items. In December 1764, for example, the New York Society for the Promotion of Arts, Agriculture, and Oeconomy awarded a number of prizes for the domestic production of such products as cloth, wine, and animal skins. Significantly, the Society also took notice that "no member of the Society after Six Months on the Death of any Relative put himself in Mourning," as well as disapproving of any "extravagant funerals."[20]

Attempts to reduce the economic dependence of the colonies and simultaneously to search for profitable and useful home manufacture had a long history in the American colonies. Moreover, this economic resistance to the Sugar Act was confined largely to urban areas such as Boston, Philadelphia, and New York. Few contemporaries, therefore, assigned much significance to these fledgling boycott attempts. These efforts were rather part of a larger tradition of popular resistance.

Popular resistance took a variety of forms. One of the most extreme cases was an attack in Rhode Island on a group of British naval officers as they attempted to apply the new Customs regulations. Lieutenant Thomas Hill of H. M. S. *St. John* later recounted that on 30 June 1764, while he was patrolling off the coast of Newport, Rhode Island, he encountered a ship which he suspected of smuggling. He seized the cargo and prepared to take the ship and its master to the vice-admiralty court at Halifax, Nova Scotia. Then, Lieutenant Hill, much to his surprise, found *himself* under arrest for detaining civilians without proper credentials. The lieutenant was soon released and returned to Boston to rectify the credentials dispute. Shortly thereafter, on 9 July, the officers of the *St. John,* now docked at Newport, arrested a man believed to be a deserter. Quickly, however, a large group of people assembled, rescued the arrested individual, and drove the naval officers off the dock under a rain of stones and rocks. The crowd traded jibes and jeers with the naval officers and their crew. Near six o'clock that evening as the *St. John* sailed past an island in the middle of the harbor, the crowd commandeered the guns of the island's battery and fired eight rounds at the ship. The shots caused little damage, though the mainsail was split in half. When the captain of the *St. John* reported this affair to the governor and council of Rhode Island, he found them unsympathetic to the plight of Customs officers. The officials were willing to investigate the matter only "when they thought it necessary."[21]

Popular resistance, combined with legislative and judicial action and political argumentation, failed to achieve repeal of the Sugar Act. Not only did Prime Minister Grenville refuse to repeal the Sugar Act, but in August 1764, he sent a circular letter to all colonial governors in America requesting a list of all items used in public transactions, law proceedings, grants, conveyances, and land or financial securities.[22] In such an action, Grenville clearly was anticipating the passage of a stamp tax and was assembling a list of potentially taxable official documents used in America.

Colonial protests against the Sugar Act and the rumored new stamp tax still continued to arrive in London. In January 1765, the legislatures of Massachusetts, Rhode Island, Connecticut, New York, Virginia, and Georgia had each petitioned against Grenville's proposed stamp tax. Nonetheless, in March 1765, Parliament reconvened and passed the Stamp Act.

The proposed act, to become effective on 1 November 1765, placed a tax on a variety of paper materials—documents, diplomas, bonds, licenses, deeds, clearing papers for ships in harbor, newspapers and their advertisements, playing cards, dice, calendars, almanacs, and the like. The actual stamps, then, were pieces of vellum, parchment, or paper upon which a stamp of the prescribed denomination had been previously imprinted. Thus, "stamps" were not individual adhesive pieces which would later be affixed to the dutiable documents, but rather embossed sheets available for purchase by the Americans from the official stamp distributors. In the case of dice and playing cards, these items were to be packaged in stamped paper, and one card in each pack was marked with an appropriate embossment.

Several other enactments were included in the bill. All monies which accrued from this act as duties, forfeitures, or penalties were to be paid in sterling. Any violations of the Stamp Act provisions were liable to prosecution in the vice-admiralty courts, where cases (except felonies) were decided by a single judge without a jury, according to the rules of civil law. In those cases in which fines and forfeitures were inflicted, the penalties were to be divided as follows: one third to His Majesty's government, one third to the governor of the colony in which the offense took place, and one third to the person who informed or brought suit on behalf of the government in the case. Finally, it was specified that all colonial governors, by the first of November, 1765, take an oath in support of the Stamp Act and pledge to do their utmost to see that it was enforced.

The cost of the stamped paper varied with the item and ranged from a halfpenny for newspaper copy to ten pounds for an attorney's license. To George Grenville, the stamp tax possessed the beauty of efficiency and simplicity. The entire enterprise would require but a few tax officers, he thought, and promised a ready source of new income once set into motion. Moreover, to allay possible American misgivings, Grenville agreed to appoint Americans as stamp distributors and officials in order that their greater familiarity with the colonial situation might temper any bureaucratic excesses.

Jared Ingersoll, who attended the parliamentary session as the agent for Connecticut, recounted the passage of the bill in a letter to Governor Fitch.[23] Upon the presentation of the bill by George Grenville, debate ensued. Supporters of the bill argued that the additional revenue was needed and that, despite colonial protests, the Americans were indeed represented in Parliament. If not actually represented, asserted Thomas Whately, secretary to Grenville and principal architect of the Stamp Act, the colonists were virtually represented because Parliament represented the whole of the empire, not simply the boroughs that elected its members. Not surprisingly, the Grenville bloc refused to receive any colonial petitions which challenged the right and authority of Parliament to assess such taxes. In a concluding flourish, Charles Townshend spoke on behalf of the bill, and after observing the care, protection, and nurture which the Americans had received so extensively from Parliament, he chastised the colonists for their niggardly refusal to contribute in Britain's time of need.

In what was to be the only high point for the bill's opposition forces, Colonel Isaac Barré rose to answer Townshend's charges. "They planted by your Care?" Barré demanded.

> No! Your Oppressions planted em in America. They fled from your Tyranny to a then uncultivated and unhospitable Country—where they exposed themselves to almost all the hardships to which human Nature is liable, and among others to the Cruelities of a Savage foe, the most subtle and I take upon me to say the most formidable of any People upon the face of God's Earth. And yet, actuated by Principles of true english Lyberty, they met all these hardships with pleasure, compared with those they suffered in their own Country, from the hands of those who should have been their friends. They nourished by your indulgence? They grew by your neglect of Em:—as soon as you began to care about Em, that Care was exercised in sending persons to rule over Em, in one Department and another, who were perhaps the Deputies of Deputies to some Member of this house—sent to Spy out their Lyberty, to misrepresent their Actions and to prey upon Em; men whose behaviour on many Occasions has caused the Blood of those Sons of Liberty to recoil within them. . . . The People I believe are as truly Loyal as any Subjects the King has, but a people Jealous of their Lyberties and who will vindicate them, if ever they should be violated.[24]

The speech, Ingersoll reported, was stirring. Yet Barré's eloquent rhetoric was no match for Grenville's forces. The bill passed its first reading in the Commons by a vote of two hundred fifty to fifty. The second reading of the bill occurred on 15 February, and it breezed through without even a division. Thereafter, the bill was sent to the House of Lords, where it was approved without debate or division, and finally, by reason of the illness of the king, was given the royal assent by special commission on 22 March 1765.

News of the passage of the Stamp Act reached America in April 1765. Certainly the Virginian agent, Edward Montague, was not the only witness to write of the act's passage, but when his letter was printed in the *Pennsylvania Gazette* on 18 April, it received the dubious distinction of being the first harbinger of the fateful news. Nevertheless, no action was taken in the colonies until the following month. On 30 May 1765, during the last days of its May session, the Virginia House of Burgesses considered a series of resolutions against the Stamp Act. Introduced by Patrick Henry, then a young lawyer and newly elected member from Louisa

County, the series of five resolutions asserted that, as confirmed by royal charter and past precedent, only the people themselves or their duly chosen representatives possessed the power to tax. Thus, only the Burgesses could legitimately tax Virginians, and any taxes proposed or enacted by any other body would be unconstitutional. Accordingly, in their fifth and final resolution, the Burgesses built upon these arguments to conclude that "every Attempt to vest such Power [to tax] in any other Person or Persons whatsoever other than the General Assembly aforesaid has a manifest tendency to destroy British as well as American Freedom."[25] The resolution, in so many words, accused the Parliament of tyranny. In his famous concluding speech, Henry moved in the direction of implicating the king himself. As the speech was recreated by an anonymous eyewitness: "one of the members stood and said he had read that in former times tarquin and Julius had their Brutus, Charles had his Cromwell, and he Did not Doubt but some good american would stand up, in favour of his Country."[26] Challenged as treasonous by the Speaker of the House, Henry retreated and reaffirmed his allegiance to the king.

Further developments followed the Burgesses' vote on 30 May. On the next day, the five resolutions came up for review. In Governor Fauquier's opinion, the passage of the resolutions in the first place was attributable to Henry's influence among the "young and giddy members" of the assembly. Now, on 31 May 1765, Henry had left for home and the Burgesses rescinded the fifth resolution which they had previously passed. No other resolutions were revoked. On 1 June 1765, the governor dissolved the Virginia Burgesses.[27]

Neither Fauquier's action nor the Burgesses' revocation prevented the other colonies from hearing about the Virginia Resolves. On 24 June 1765, the *Newport Mercury* printed what purported to be the resolutions of the Virginians. Interestingly, this account retained the excised fifth resolution, in addition to a sixth resolve which read: "Resolved that his Majesty's liege People, the Inhabitants of this Colony, are not bound to yield Obedience to any Law or Ordinance whatever, designed to impose any Taxation whatsoever upon them, other than the Laws or Ordinances of the General Assembly aforesaid." Here was not only an affirmation of charter rights but also a call to disobedience. Consequently, while this account contained one resolve which they had repudiated and another upon which they had never voted, the Virginians were hailed as leaders of the opposition to the Stamp Act from New Hampshire to Georgia and wherever else the *Newport Mercury* account circulated.[28]

To the north in Boston, colonial officials were unsure in their forecasts and expectations of the act's import. They were also uneasy as to whether the people would accept or resist the act, even though it was not to become effective until 1 November. Upon hearing of the act's passage, Lieutenant-Governor Thomas Hutchinson of Massachusetts had predicted that "the discouragements, discontents, and disaffection to the Mother Country which will be caused in many of the Colonies will eventually more than balance all the profit that will ever be received from Taxes."[29] In early June, Hutchinson, not yet aware of the actions of the Virginia Burgesses, guardedly suggested that the "Stamp Act is received with us as decently as could be expected." While anticipating that the "Act will execute itself," Hutchinson still foresaw considerable hardships, particularly as "it would lessen the number of law suits among us" and would be especially "hard upon the college."[30] The governor of Massachusetts, Francis Bernard, however, was not sanguine. He found the people of Boston "extremely out of Humour with the Stamp Act." Moreover, the recent appearance of the Virginia Resolves in the *Newport Mercury* was especially disturbing. "The Spirit of Rebellion, which these Resolutions, whether Authentic or Factitious, breathe," Bernard insisted, "is such as must make them abhorred by all loyal subjects: yet it is inconceivable how they have roused up the Boston Politicians, and been the Occasion of a fresh inundation of factious and insolent pieces in the popular Newspaper."[31]

Resistance organization went deeper in Boston than legislative politics and newspaper articles. Sometime in the early summer of 1765, a group was founded, calling itself the Loyal Nine and dedicating its energies to the repeal of the Stamp Act. The forerunner in conception and often in personnel of the Boston Sons of Liberty, the nine were John Avery Jr., Thomas Crafts, John Smith, Henry Welles, Thomas Chase, Stephen Cleverly, Henry Bass, Benjamin Edes, and George Trott. Most of the nine were shopkeepers and artisans, while Edes was the copublisher of the *Boston Gazette*. This small cadre kept in communication with legislative leaders, such as Samuel Adams and James Otis, but remained largely out of the public's eye. Of equal importance with their legislative connection was the Loyal Nine's alliance with the leaders of the Boston populace, especially Ebenezer MacIntosh. For a number of years, by then long enough to have dimmed the memory of the reasons why, two sections of Boston had annually engaged in raucous celebrations and occasional brawls. The two sections of the city, the North End and the South End, usually took the occasion of 5 November, or the Pope's Day (in which Guy Fawke's gunpowder plot of 1605 was commemorated), to square off and contend for supremacy over one another. MacIntosh was a shoemaker by trade and the leader of the South End side. Thus, if and when it became necessary to enlist the support and participation of the people, the Loyal Nine hoped that the spirited energies of the North and South End groups could be applied under MacIntosh's leadership to the defeat of the Stamp Act.[32]

• POPULAR DISCONTENT WITH THE STAMP ACT •

The month of August quickly demonstrated to all observers the popular discontent with the Stamp Act and the determination and energy available for its defeat. On the morning of 14 August 1765, an effigy representing Andrew Oliver was prominently displayed hanging from a tree in the center of Boston.[33] Oliver, it was reported, had been named as the stamp distributor for Massachusetts. Accordingly, the effigy was initialed with the letters A.[ndrew] O.[liver] on the right hand, and a label on the breast signified that the effigy was intended for the stamp officer. Near the effigy was a large boot (a pun on the Earl of Bute, a friend and political mentor of George III) with a Greenvile sole and a devil rising out of it. Due to its strategic position, the scene attracted a large crowd. Lieutenant-Governor Hutchinson, upon hearing of this episode, sent the sheriff to cut down the effigy. Unfortunately, the sheriff reported, the crowd was quite large and so determined to keep the effigy in place that his men had been unable even to approach the tree from which poor Oliver's likeness was suspended. Governor Bernard, meanwhile, had called his council, but they too thought it best to let things cool down.

Near dusk of that same day, according to a Boston newspaper, "a number of respectable people assembled" and cut the effigy down from the tree—henceforth known as the Liberty Tree. They placed the effigy "on a bier, and covering it with a sheet, they proceeded in a regular and solemn manner" through the streets. The crowd, cheering and applauding, soon passed under the windows of the council, still in session, and made their way to a small warehouse owned by Mr. Oliver. Inasmuch as Oliver had only recently built the warehouse, it was assumed that he intended to distribute the stamps from it, so the crowd tore the structure down. From there, they took the boards up to Fort Hill and kindled a bonfire into which they placed a "burnt-offering of the effigies for those sins of the people which had caused such heavy judgments as the Stamp Act, etc." Unfortunately for Oliver, his troubles were not over yet. According to Hutchinson, at this point, "the heads of the mob then gave direction to carry the image to fort hill being near Mr. O. and then burn it but to do no damage to his dwelling house." Nonetheless, as the crowd was approaching the hill, Hutchinson, the sheriff, and a neighbor named Paxton rushed to Oliver's house and convinced him and his family to evacuate, while Hutchinson and the others remained. Whether intended by Hutchinson or not, the situation now pitted the intransigent Hutchinson against the spirited crowd. For, as reported in the same newspaper accounts, as Oliver's house

> stood near the aforesaid hill, and by that means it received from the populace some small insults, such as breaking a few panes of glass in the windows of his kitchen as they passed his house, which would have ended there, had not some indiscretions, to say the least, been committed by his friends within, which so enraged the people that they were not to be restrained, tho' hitherto no violence had been offered to any person, and the utmost decorum had been preserved.[34]

As the crowd battered their way into the house, Hutchinson left for reinforcements, but upon his return to Oliver's house, he was again greeted with a fresh volley of rocks and garbage, and he beat a hasty retreat to his own home. By the end of the evening, Oliver's grounds and property were quite the worse for wear as several fences had been torn up, gardens and fruit trees demolished, and silver plates scattered in the street.[35]

Not surprisingly, there was concern among official circles to apprehend those responsible for the destruction. The *Boston Gazette* noted: "it is supposed by some people, that the effigies exhibited in this town on Wednesday last (ACTUALLY or VIRTUALLY) originated in Cambridge." Others, however, suspected Ebenezer MacIntosh of the South End to be the instigator of the action. Governor Bernard believed that "respectable people" were behind the demonstration, and he and his council offered a reward of £100.[36] The original object of attention, Oliver himself, was less concerned with the apprehension of the rioters than with the immediate resignation of his stamp distributorship. In reply to a delegation of gentlemen who visited him in the morning and requested his resignation, Oliver said that he would gladly comply. As he had not yet received official word of his appointment as stamp distributor, he could only agree to do nothing to carry out the act. This was sufficient for most people, and that evening, as the crowd reconvened, there were praises and toasts to Oliver, where the night before there had been jeers.

Boston was to see more turbulence before the month of August was out. On the evening of the fifteenth, the same night Oliver's resignation was read to the crowd, a group gathered in front of Lieutenant-Governor Hutchinson's house and called for him to come out. Several of Hutchinson's neighbors and one old man, in particular, persuaded the crowd to disband without incident or altercation. Tranquility prevailed for the ensuing week, but on the night of 26 August, renewed disorders erupted. As recounted by a Boston newspaper, "a number of rude fellows" gathered that evening in downtown Boston, their numbers steadily increasing once they had kindled a bonfire—the traditional gathering signal for a mob.[37] At this point, the crowd proceeded to the house of William Story, register of the Court of Vice-Admiralty, entering his offices, and proceeded to destroy the files and records of the court. From Story's house, the crowd next marched to the house of Benjamin Hallowell, comptroller of Customs, where they ruined much of his private and public papers, assaulted his house and property, and drank all his liquor. Whether following a predetermined plan or merely emboldened at the ease and success of their efforts so far, the assemblage then wound their way to Hutchinson's house. Forewarned of their approach, Hutchinson was determined to remain alone and defy the mob. At the last moment, however, he consented to his daughter's pleas and removed with the rest of his family to a neighbor's house nearby. Almost at the exact moment that Hutchinson escaped out the back, the crowd made their way in through the front. By daylight the next day when they stopped, the crowd had destroyed most of Hutchinson's house and gardens, as well as scattering and looting his clothing, silverware, manuscripts and papers, and a sum of cash. Understandably unnerved, Hutchinson, who presided over court on 27 August in a borrowed suit of clothes, cut short the session and retired into seclusion for rest.

Though the level of destruction on the night of 26 August far surpassed that previously seen in Boston, neither Story, Hallowell, Hutchinson, nor any of their families had been physically injured. There are several possible interpretations of the motivations of the rioters. To be sure, all three, Story, Hallowell, and Hutchinson, had some connection to the Customs service, which was itself the object of great resentment in Boston. This Customs connection might help to explain the somewhat greater restraint and specificity—the destruction of the vice-admiralty court records at Story's and the public papers at Hallowell's—of the crowds in the earlier part of the evening. As for the more extreme demolition of Hutchinson's possessions, perhaps this reflected the crowd's anger at his defense of Oliver the previous week, his support for the Customs service in the years past, or possibly just his haughty manner and obvious wealth. Of course, one could also mark up such riotous proceedings to simple lawlessness, and undoubtedly, there were those who did so.

In any case, the ferocity of the rioters' activities alarmed many in Boston. On 27 August 1765, the Boston town meeting met and denounced the attacks of the previous day. Proclaiming the town's "utter detestation of the extraordinary and violent proceedings," the meeting unanimously voted that the town officials "suppress the like disorders for the future."[38] The *Boston Gazette* editorialized that "most people seem disposed to differentiate between the Assembly on the 14th of the Month and their transactions, and the unbridled Licentiousness of this Mob, judging them to proceed from very different Motives as their Conduct was most evidently different."[39] On his part, Hutchinson believed he had been unfairly targeted as a supporter of the Stamp Act. He was firm in the belief that "this violence is by no means to be charged upon the whole country, nine tenths or more of the people in it I am sure would detest these barbarous proceedings against me." And in conclusion, he noted, "we are in the most deplorable state and all who are in authority stand in need of more than human wisdom and fortitude upon this occasion."[40]

Governor Bernard, at this point residing in Castle William in Boston harbor, echoed Hutchinson's plea for strength, but his conception was of a rather more military sort. On 18 August 1765, Bernard ruminated about the recent Oliver disturbance and concluded: "I am entirely at the Mercy of the Mob . . . I have no Place of Safety to resort to but this fort with a weak Garrison." It was true, Bernard admitted, that "nothing has been urged against me yet but as no lies are spared to incense the people . . . I know not how long I shall be spared."[41] No attack on Bernard came, and days later, he conceded: "I consider myself only as a prisoner at large, being wholly in the Power of the People. They let me remain as a nominal governor, that what is done may not appear to be an actual Revolt, and I am desireous to keep my part as long as I can for the same reason: but I am wholly without Authority."[42] In another letter written during the same period, the governor reiterated this assessment and concluded that even

in case of a Popular Tumult I cannot command ten men that can be depended upon; the Militia are worse than no Soldiers at all and there is not, as I know of, a Corps of Regulars within 200 miles of me . . . [the people] see that at present they have it in their power to choose whether they will submit to this act or not . . . they see their own Government unable to resist them and therefore they conclude they shall be able to oppose the Power of Great Britain. A single Regiment would have prevented this Insurrection; possibly it may require many to reduce it. The People depend much upon their example being followed in other governments and expect they shall be supported in the generality of their own.[43]

Bernard's remarks were surprisingly prescient, for in many ways the activities of the Bostonians—petitions and boycotts as well as effigies and visitations—were indeed to be followed. To the south in Rhode Island, the town meeting of Providence on 13 August had instructed their representatives in the assembly to petition for the postponement of the introduction of the Stamp Act into the colonies. Mindful of the recently passed Virginia Resolves, the town meeting called on the assembly to adopt similar measures, as well as to send capable men to the convocation recently proposed by a Massachusetts circular letter.[44] In this letter, James Otis, at the order of the Massachusetts House, had called on all the other colonies to send representatives to New York in October of that year in order to consider possible united action against the Stamp Act. This assembly, since known as the Stamp Act Congress, represented a significant early step in the development of intercolonial collaboration.[45] Providence's exertions were duplicated by the small, rural town of Little Compton, Rhode Island, where the town meeting likewise called for strong support for the Stamp Act Congress, invoking the same litany of threatened colonial rights and the need for intercolonial cooperation.[46]

These legislative maneuvers were temporarily eclipsed, however, by further developments that month in Newport, Rhode Island. On the night of 26 August, effigies were constructed of Augustus Johnston, the stamp distributor for Rhode Island, as well as Martin Howard and Thomas Moffatt, two prominent individuals who had vocally supported the imposition of a stamp tax. According to newspaper accounts, the effigies hung from the gallows from mid-morning until late in the afternoon, at which point, "some combustibles being placed under the Gallows, a fire was made, and the Effigies consumed, amidst the Acclamations of the People—the whole was conducted with Moderation, and no Violence offered to the Persons or Property of any Man."[47] On the following day, a heated exchange of words and blows between a local Newporter and Howard resulted in a mob forming and invading Howard's house. After breaking windows and furniture, the crowd proceeded to Moffatt's residence and did the same again. Johnson, the stamp distributor, was the next target. After he promised to resign his commission, however, no harm was done to him or to his property.[48]

Public animosity toward stamp distributors continued to grow, and many of those so appointed found themselves the object of strident disapproval. Jared Ingersoll's case in Connecticut was one such example. Previously, Ingersoll had acted as the colonial agent for Connecticut. In that capacity, he had collaborated with the other agents in opposing the passage of the Stamp Act in 1764. Failing to prevent its passage, Ingersoll had been instrumental in a number of modifications which reduced the scope of the final bill and thereby ameliorated its effects. Pleased to have accomplished that much, Ingersoll accepted the post of stamp distributor for Connecticut in the hopes of advancing himself through the position and continuing his service to his fellow colonists. Upon his return to America, Ingersoll found that either he had misjudged the temper of his countrymen or his position on the Stamp Act had been badly misrepresented. In New London and Norwich, Connecticut, Ingersoll was satirized in public ceremonies. Festooned with the Devil on its shoulder and a copy of the Stamp Act pinned to its breast, an effigy of Ingersoll was paraded through the streets on a stick, then hanged on the gallows and burned.[49]

In New York, the stamp distributor, James McEvers, informed Lieutenant-Governor Cadwallader Colden that it was impossible for him to perform his office.

Fearful of receiving the treatment meted out to Andrew Oliver in Boston and cog-
nizant that stamp distributors were not better loved in New York, McEvers resigned
rather than risk the public's wrath.[50] Further to the south in Maryland, the stamp
distributor was Zachariah Hood. Hood was a native of Maryland and, as such,
again exemplified the belief of British officials in London that the Americans
would take more kindly to a native-born distribution and collection service than to
placemen from Britain. However, Hood was roundly criticized and condemned as
the worst of "sycophants" in the contemporary *Maryland Gazette*. The paper in-
toned: "May the man forever be accursed, who owes his greatness to his country's
ruin." Not surprisingly, effigies of Hood sprang up throughout Maryland. On 29
August 1765, the *Maryland Gazette* published an account of an effigy and parade
at Annapolis. "On Monday morning last," reported the paper:

> A considerable number of people, asserters of British American privileges, met
> here to show their detestation of, and abhorrence to, some late attacks on liberty;
> and their dislike to a certain late arrived officer, a native of this province. They
> curiously dressed up the figure of a man, which they placed on a one-horse cart,
> malefactor-like. . . . In this manner, they paraded through the streets of the town
> till noon, the bells at the same time tolling a solemn knell, when they proceeded
> to the hill.

Thereafter, the crowd took the effigy and "placed it in the pillory, from whence
they took it, and hung it to a gibbet erected for that purpose, and then set fire to a
tar barrel underneath, till it fell into the barrel." Similar episodes occurred in Baltimore on 28 August and at Elk Ridge and Frederick on 29 August.[51]

With the Stamp Act not to go into effect until 1 November and with popular
feelings so agitated, the months of September and October promised continued
resistance. As before, the agitation utilized the methods of legislative protest and
remonstrance, popular visitations and demonstrations, and discussions of political
principles and grievance in pamphlets and essays. There was also a renewal of
earlier attempts at economic coercion through boycotts and nonimportation campaigns. Early in its September session, for example, the assembly of Rhode Island
passed a series of resolutions similar in tone and content to those of Virginia. In
two important aspects, however, the Rhode Island resolves surpassed those of the
southern colony. In its fifth resolution, the assembly explicitly indicted the Stamp
Act: "the inhabitants of this colony are not bound to yield obedience to any law or
ordinance designed to impose any internal taxation whatsoever upon them, other
than the laws or ordinances of the General Assembly, aforesaid." This, of course,
was the famous resolution which the Burgesses had revoked but which had been
credited to them in the newspaper account. The Rhode Islanders went further than
this injunction, however, when they indicated in their final measure: "that all the
officers in this colony, appointed by the authority thereof, be, and they are hereby,
directed to proceed in the execution of their respective offices in the same manner
as usual; and that this Assembly will indemnify and save harmless all the said officers, on account of their conduct agreeably to this resolution."[52] In such action, the
Rhode Island Assembly had not declared support for the Stamp Act to be treason-

ous; nonetheless, their declaration of no internal taxation without proper represen-tation and, especially, their willingness to indemnify all government officials who proceeded in their offices without stamps transformed the Rhode Island govern-ment into a resistance organization for noncooperation with the Stamp Act.

On 9 September, George Meserve, the stamp distributor for New Hampshire, arrived at Boston harbor and immediately knew something was amiss. The pilot who was to guide his ship into the harbor delivered a letter to Meserve from a group from Portsmouth, New Hampshire, informing him that it would be unwise for him to come ashore until he had resigned his office. Meserve, unable to disembark be-cause of the crowd on shore, remained aboard ship for two more days. Finally, he announced his resignation. He was then greeted on the docks with cheers and applause. Merserve's troubles were not quite over yet, as he was made to reiterate his resignation publicly after he arrived in Portsmouth.[53]

On 18 September 1765, the Boston town meeting instructed its representatives to the General Assembly to pledge their support to the upcoming Stamp Act Con-gress and to refuse forthrightly to comply with the provisions of the Stamp Act. On 23 September, one of the first shipments of stamps arrived in Boston harbor. It was immediately stored in Castle William by Governor Bernard. The next day, the Bos-ton town meeting again renewed its call for the representatives in the House "to comply with no measures or proposals for countenancing the same or assisting in the Execution of it by all lawful Means, consistent with our Allegiance to the King, and relation to Great Britain to oppose the Execution of it." Similar remonstrances were delivered by the townspeople of Marblehead and Weymouth in Mas-sachusetts.[54]

The Massachusetts representatives followed the wishes of their constituents quite well. On 26 September 1765, Governor Bernard officially informed the Mas-sachusetts House and Council of the arrival of the stamps in Boston. Bernard took this opportunity to point out that because Andrew Oliver had already resigned his commission as stamp distributor, responsibility for the stamps, in Bernard's opin-ion, devolved upon the House and council. He further noted, however, that the council had referred the matter to the legislature as a whole, and so he now asked the legislature for their advice and assistance in this matter. The House responded to Governor Bernard later that same day. Their reply was short and direct. "As the stamped papers, mentioned in your message, are brought here without any direc-tions to this government," the message explained, "it is the sense of the House that it may prove of ill consequence for them any ways to interest themselves in this matter. We hope, therefore, your Excellency will excuse us if we cannot see our way clear to give you any advice or assistance herein."[55]

Such obstinacy had its effect on colonial officials. Governor Bernard, survey-ing this scene from his self-imposed exile in Castle William, was disconsolate. Reflecting upon the destruction of Hutchinson's property and the concern, as evi-denced by the town meeting resolutions and newspaper editorials, of many Boston-ians, Bernard informed the Earl of Halifax that: "the Horror of this last affair has not at all abated the Spirit of the People against the Stamp Act. I am again assured that this Town and Country about it . . . are as resolute as ever to oppose the Execution of the Stamp Act and to suffer the utmost Extremities rather than to submit to it." Bernard expected little change in this intransigent popular opinion until there was "a fuller prospect of the Anarchy and confusion which must take place when the Courts of Justice and public offices are shut up; as they must be on the first of November, unless stamps are allowed to be used."[56] With no judicial decisions or public documents legally valid unless they were on stamped paper, the nonuse of such material and the closing of public courts which would follow could only produce disruption and confusion, or so it seemed to Bernard.

In Connecticut, renewed pressure was being exerted during the month of September on Jared Ingersoll to resign his office. At first, Ingersoll agreed not to exercise the office, as he claimed he had received no official notification of his appointment as stamp distributor and thus had no position officially to resign. Later in the month, Ingersoll agreed to attend a meeting at Hartford called by the governor to discuss the Stamp Act. On his way there, he was met by a band of horsemen and agreed to resign the office completely. Escorted by the horsemen, he continued to Hartford and publicly repeated his resignation before the Connecticut Assembly.[57]

Demonstrations and protests against the Stamp Act occurred in virtually all the provinces of the middle colonies during the month of September. In Philadelphia, there was a demonstration on 16 September celebrating the fall of George Grenville's ministry. "The Day was spent," as one observer put it, "in Congratulation upon a Revolution . . . at night, the Bells rang, Bonfires were made, and every Demonstration of Joy, given."[58] Part of the revelling crowd assembled in front of the house of John Hughes, stamp distributor for Pennsylvania, and called out for his resignation, but soon retired. During the previous week, the Pennsylvania Assembly had acted upon the circular letter from Massachusetts by appointing Joseph Fox, John Dickinson, John Morton, and George Bryan as their delegates to the Stamp Act Congress. On 21 September, the assembly, following the lead of Rhode Island and Virginia, passed a series of resolves protesting the Stamp Act.[59]

In neighboring New Jersey, it was rumored that William Coxe, the stamp distributor, had been unable to rent a house "unless he would insure the House from being pulled down or damaged." To this the anonymous epilogue was added: "Query, whether it would not be prudent for all Stamp Officers to insure their Houses?"[60] Coxe's house was never pulled down, but the suggestion that it might was evidently enough to intimidate him. On 3 September, Coxe resigned his office, notifying the governor that he had returned the papers commissioning him as a stamp distributor to London and promising to forward any relevant stamp materials to the governor. Later, on 28 December 1765, Coxe was visited by a deputation of two of the Woodbridge Sons of Liberty. The delegation delivered a letter which read:

> Whereas you have been appointed to the most odious and detestable office of the Distributor of Stamps for the government of New Jersey; and whereas the former resignation (said to be yours) is no way satisfactory to the inhabitants of the same:

> We the Sons of Liberty in said Government, hereby desire your resignation, in as ample form and manner as possible; expressing and solemnly declaring, upon the veracity of a gentleman and man of honour, that you will never, directly or indirectly, yourself or by deputation under you, ever distribute said stamps, or be any ways accessary in putting said Act in Force, in the government aforesaid.

Upon reading the letter and conversing with the delegation, Coxe repeated his resignation to them. He further assured them that he had taken no steps toward finding a replacement for himself nor had he in any way encouraged or executed the distribution of the stamps in New Jersey or elsewhere. The delegation was entirely satisfied with Coxe's acquittal of himself. After thanking him in the hopes that "your example may influence those to do the like, who yet hold that detestable office," they drank toasts of long life and prosperity to King George III and William Coxe and of "Confusion to every American Stamp-Master, unless he resigns his abhorred and detestable office." The delegation thereafter departed for Woodbridge and reported their experiences to the Sons of Liberty of that town.[61]

This call for the resignation of all stamp distributors was echoed in a newspaper piece by an inhabitant of New Jersey who took the *nom de plume*, Caesariensis. This writer heartily applauded the resignation of Coxe and foresaw the day when:

> The conduct of the stamp officer will give the true political complexion of every colony; if the stamp officer cannot execute his office with any degree of comfort and reputation, and thereupon resigns, then it will be evident that the inhabitants of that colony are sensible of the imposition [of the tax], and spurn at it; if on the other hand, they supinely submit to the unconstitutional exaction, and suffer the unrighteous taskmasters to live at ease, it may be certainly concluded, that the inhabitants of such colony are insensible, and see not, or at least regard not the difference between freedom and slavery.[62]

Various additional actions occurred in New Jersey. On 14 September, a prominent citizen of Elizabethtown died and was buried in the "new mode," with both mourners and the deceased clad without the traditional English lace or ruffles.[63] At the commencement at Princeton that year, a series of orations on "Patriotism, Frugality and Liberty" were given while the bachelor of arts candidates appeared on their own accord dressed in plain homespun and homewoven clothes.[64]

Perhaps most significantly, the New Jersey bar, at a meeting held 19 September 1765 at Perth Amboy, unanimously decided not to use the stamps for any purpose. The result of such an action would obviously be to stop all legal business in the colony. The following day, the lawyers met with the chief justice of the New Jersey Court, Frederick Smyth, and again reaffirmed their decision. They would "rather suffer their private interest to give way to the public interest," declared the lawyers, "protesting at the same time against all indecent and riotous behaviour, which they will discountenance by every means in their power to preserve order, and by an absolute refusal to make use of the Stamps and other quiet methods, endeavour to obtain a repeal of the law."[65] The lawyers concluded by advising the chief justice, in answer to a question raised by him, that the governor had no power to appoint the chief justice as a temporary stamp distributor and that the chief justice, if so appointed, need not accept the job.

The governor of New Jersey, William Franklin (son of Benjamin Franklin of Philadelphia), had reported all these proceedings to the colonial officials in London. Back in June, the New Jersey Assembly had received the Massachusetts invitation to the Stamp Act Congress on the last day of its session and had closed without taking action. On the following day, 21 June 1765, the Speaker of the New Jersey House had reconvened the majority of the members in an extralegal session in Perth Amboy, and this body had elected three men to represent them in New York in October. In the opinion of the governor, this extralegal meeting was clearly "an irregular and unconstitutional Meeting" and just as clearly at odds with the royal provincial government.[66] On his part, Governor Franklin felt that the conduct of the people had been lawful and that, "although many of them have objections to the Act, yet none of them would have endeavoured to prevent its Execution by Violence or otherwise."[67]

Sometime in September, reputedly out of New Jersey, a one-issue newspaper, the *Constitutional Courant,* was published. Across its masthead, the *Courant* featured the subsequently well-known illustration of a snake divided into several parts and juxtaposed to the motto "Join or Die." The snake was divided into eight sections which were labeled with abbreviations for New England, New York, New Jersey, Pennsylvania, Maryland, Virginia, North Carolina, and South Carolina. Georgia was omitted. In the depiction used on the *Constitutional Courant,* the snake figure was printed below the motto "Join or Die," which was itself centered on the masthead between the words "Constitutional" and "Courant." The image proved to be quite popular and was reprinted in various forms.

The *Courant* itself belonged to that on-going series of pamphlet literature with its part-expository, part-hortatory purposes. The present situation was a tragic one, declared the writer, *"Philo Patriae"*: "Our liberty, in being subjected to laws that we had no share in making; our property in being taxed without our own consent . . . and in our trials by juries, because any informer or prosecutor has it in his choice, whether to try the matter in a court of common law or a court of admiralty. . . . This is a real representation of the slavish state we are reduced to by the Stamp Act." The writer believed that the recent destruction of property reflected the level of popular animosity against the Stamp Act and those who would enforce it. However, he concluded that he:

> would wish my countrymen to avoid such violent proceedings, if possible; but at the same time to oppose the execution of the Stamp Act, with a steady and perpetual exertion of their whole power,—and by all means, to endeavour, jointly and severally, to throw all possible obstructions in the way of its taking effect, and to treat with the utmost ignomiy and detestation, all those enemies and betrayers of their country's most sacred rights, who officiously endeavour to inforce it: I would wish them never to pay one farthing of this tax, but leave the infamous officers, if they will have it, to take it by force, by way of robbery and plunder.

From such strident phrases, the author went on to reaffirm his allegiance to the Crown and to recommend that all the colonies "lay before his majesty a united representation of their grievances, and pray a redress."

Consistent with many other American writers of the time, the author of the *Constitutional Courant* consciously placed the blame for such problems as the colonies faced on the ministry at Whitehall. Consequently, the conclusion of the piece looked forward to the demise of Grenville's ministry and its replacement by one better informed and more favorable to American sentiments.

In nearby Maryland, pressure for the resignation of Zachariah Hood, the stamp distributor, was growing. In the opinion of Charles Carroll of Carrolton, "our stamp-master, Zachariah Hood, is hated and despised by everyone." Furthermore, Carroll continued, Hood had been the object of public ridicule as a likeness of him was made which was then "whipped, pilloried, and hanged in effigy." Added to hate and ridicule, Carroll noted that "the people seem determined not to buy his goods."[68] Those with any possible connections to Hood were quick to disclaim any relation. For example, on 26 September 1765, one Thomas Hyde informed the public that:

> Whereas it hath been reported, that the Subscriber is in Partnership with Mr. Zachariah Hood, and that my Son was sent for from Philadelphia to keep his store and assist him in his Office: This is to inform the Public That this Report is without Foundation, and that I never had any such thought, nor have I any connection in Business with Mr. Hood of any kind, and that the Whole Reason of my Son's coming to Maryland was to see me, there being a Vacation in the College, where he lives, to give the Youth an Opportunity to visit their Friends.[69]

It was just as well that Mr. Hyde's son had no intention of working at Hood's shop, for on 2 September, a crowd of three or four hundred had gathered and demolished Hood's warehouse, much as had happened to Andrew Oliver in Boston the month before. The incident so unnerved Hood that he requested Governor Horatio Sharpe to advise him on the feasibility of resigning his post. Governor Sharpe refused to offer Hood any advice, so Hood went to New York in the hopes of avoiding further confrontation.[70] Hood's arrival in that city was discovered by the New York Sons of Liberty, and on 28 November 1765, a number of them visited Hood and received his resignation. The action by the New Yorkers was cordially applauded by the Baltimore Sons of Liberty in a note late in November.

Back in Annapolis, the assembly met on 24 September 1765 to consider the Massachusetts circular letter. Despite Governor Sharpe's hope that the members would forgo the New Englanders' invitation, the assembly that same day chose three of its members to represent Maryland at the Stamp Act Congress. The three individuals, Colonel Edward Tilghman, William Murdock, and Thomas Ringgold, were also voted £500 toward expenses by the legislature. In further actions, the House composed its own resolution protesting the Stamp Act and declined to advise the governor on the care of the stamps should they arrive from England. Though such actions by the Maryland House were clearly a rebuff of his hopes and suggestions, Governor Sharpe chose to ignore them. In a letter to Lord Calvert of

10 September 1765, Sharpe recounted the activities surrounding Hood's resignation and the opposition to the Stamp Act, noting: "The People here being in general actuated by the same kind of Spirit that possess't the Inhabitants of the other Colonies." Sharpe also informed Lord Calvert of a recent altercation at Annapolis between Customs officials and townspeople. Blows were traded by the two sides, but Sharpe thought it more important to warn against simplistic comparisons least the Customs episode "be blended with the behaviour of the Populace towards Mr. Hood."[71] In another letter two weeks later to General Thomas Gage, Governor Sharpe again differentiated between the Hood episode and that of the Customs officers, but he happily concluded that there has not "been any Mob raised or the least Violence committed here since that Night [of the Customs incident]."[72]

Virginia had been relatively quiet since the passage of Patrick Henry's resolutions in May. On 23 September 1765, the day of the meeting of Westmoreland County Court, effigies of George Grenville and George Mercer, the stamp distributor for Virginia, were put up. In full view of the crowds attending court day, the effigies were tried, condemned, and loaded on a cart. From there the two effigies, the one of Grenville, wearing a placard which identified him as "the infamous projector of American Slavery," and Mercer's, which was decorated with the adage "Money is my God," were paraded through the streets to the gibbet.[73] Of equal drama and perhaps more consequence was the resignation notice on the following day by the magistrates of the Westmoreland Court. They informed the governor and his council that:

> After the First Day of November next, We the under written Magistrates of Westmoreland, find Ourselves compelled, by the strongest Motives of Honour and Virtue, to decline Acting in that Capacity; because from that Period, the Act for establishing Stamps in America commences; which Act will impose on us a Necessity, in consequence of the Judicial Oath we take, of Acting in Conformity to its Directions, and, by doing so, to become Instrumental in the Destruction of our Country's most essential Rights and Liberties.[74]

The month of October was remarkable for its wide variety of resistance activities. The Stamp Act Congress met in New York City for the majority of the month, and popular demonstrations continued throughout the length of the colonies, as provincial legislatures simultaneously continued to pour out resolutions protesting the Stamp Act. News of reactions from London to the activities in America—both supportive and otherwise—began to reach the colonies. On the supportive side, there appeared in the *Newport Mercury,* on 14 October 1765, a report from London indicating that the Stamp Act was to be repealed. Such reports, however, reflected more hopes than facts. More typical of the ministry's perception was the circular letter sent to all the colonial governors by Henry Conway on 24 October. In this letter, Conway, the secretary of state for the southern department, lamented the recent disturbances and "the ill-advised intemperance" which had occurred in North America. Confiding that he expected that the unlawfulness originated with the "lower and more ignorant of the people," Conway suggested that such open resistance could only alienate support in Britain and wreck all chances for repeal. In conclusion, he called on the governors to restore tranquility and good order and instructed them to request reinforcements from the army if more pacific means failed. The issue at hand was more than a simple protest and redress. In Conway's estimation, the very sovereignty of the Crown was under attack and, "however unwillingly His Majesty may consent to the exertion of such powers as may endanger the safety of a single subject, yet can he not permit his own dignity and the authority of the British Legislature to be trampled on by force and violence, and in avowed contempt of all order, duty, and decorum."[75]

If Conway misjudged the social composition of American resistance, his instincts were at least correct regarding the erosion of decorum. In Wilmington, North Carolina, a rambunctious and spontaneous demonstration occurred on the evening of 19 October. There reportedly had been public gatherings during the course of the summer at Cross-Creek, New Bern, and Edenton, North Carolina. On the night of the nineteenth, however, some five hundred people gathered and tarred and torched the effigy of a stamp supporter. Continuing their protest, "they went to every House in Town, and brought all the Gentlemen to the Bonfire, and insisted upon their drinking, 'Liberty, Property, and no Stamp Duty,' and 'Confusion to Lord B-te and all his Adherents,' giving three Huzzas at the Conclusion of each Toast." The revelry continued, according to the newspaper account, "until 12 of the Clock, and then dispersed, without doing any Mischief."[76]

Later that month, on the eve of All Saints Day, the townspeople of Wilmington were again out in force. This time an effigy of Liberty was produced, "which they put into a Coffin, and marched in solemn procession with it to the Church-yard, a Drum in Mourning beating before them, and the Town Bells, muffled ringing a doleful Knell at the same time." But, in the midst of the procession and before they had interred the coffin, "they thought it advisable to feel its Pulse, and when finding some Remains of Life, they returned Back to the Bonfire ready prepared, placed the Effigy before it in a large Two-armed chair, and concluded the Evening with great Rejoicings, on finding that Liberty had still an Existence in the Colonies—Not the least Injury was offered to any Person."[77]

The activities in Wilmington were more than matched in neighboring South Carolina. Again on 19 October, an effigy of a stamp distributor was erected in the central square of Charleston. On the gallows from which the figure hung were the words "Liberty and no Stamp Act," and pinned to the clothes of the effigy was a warning against meddling with the figure. Later that evening, the figure was paraded through the streets by a crowd of some two thousand persons. The procession stopped at the house of the soon to arrive stamp distributor, George Saxby, but left upon finding no stamps within his house. The crowd moved on to the town common, where the effigies were burned and a coffin was buried with the inscription, "American Liberty."[78]

Five days later on 23 October 1765, it was rumored that the stamps had been landed. In the course of the day, a crowd formed and called on Colonel Henry Laurens to demand if he had the stamps. Surprised at the visit, Laurens assured those present that he had no idea of the stamps' location. A thorough search of his house ensued, but Laurens' report was correct, so the crowd thanked him and continued their search. They next visited the chief justice of the court, Charles Shinner. The justice outdid his investigators, however, by providing punch and leading them in toasts of "Damnation to the Stamp Act!" Lieutenant-Governor William Bull had meanwhile placed the stamps in Fort Johnson, and on the following day, he had a notice put up to that effect. Calm was still not in the offing, however, for on 26 October, George Saxby and his assistant Caleb Lloyd arrived from England. Uneasy about coming ashore, the two disembarked at Fort Johnson. Within hours they had both agreed not to exercise their offices but to await answers to the colonists' petitions for repeal. The declarations were publicly read the following day, and on 28 October, Saxby and Lloyd came across to the docks. They were met by a large concourse of people and, after reiterating their pledge, were escorted to a tavern and then home. The scene was a festive one, with bells ringing and cannons firing. By mid-afternoon most had retired, and at night the streets were patrolled by civilians to preserve order.[79]

Lieutenant-Governor William Bull had believed that New Englanders were the cause of the troubles in South Carolina. If not in person, then by the "artifices of some busy spirits" by which the Carolinians were "poisoned with the principles which were imbibed and propagated from Boston and Rhode Island." As for the crowds, they were simply not Conway's "ignorant populace" but prominent citizens of Charleston who had been involved in the various demonstrations. It was of no surprise to Bull, then, when the South Carolina Assembly, on 26 July 1765, appointed delegates to represent the colony at the upcoming intercolonial Congress in New York.[80]

While Lieutenant-Governor Bull blamed the New Englanders for his troubles, Governor Wright of neighboring Georgia held the South Carolinians responsible for the instigation of resistance activities in Georgia.[81] Wright perhaps overestimated his situation, for the only major complaint that he mentioned was the burning of an effigy after a general muster. The Georgia legislature even acceded to his wishes and sent no formal delegation to the Stamp Act Congress. The Speaker of the Georgia Assembly, Alexander Wylly, had convened an extralegal meeting of the House to respond to the Massachusetts invitation, but when the deliberations were finished, Wylly could only inform the northerners of Georgia's pledge to cooperate.

The month of October saw two important debates and series of resolutions come out of the assemblies of New England. In Massachusetts, the assembly had been adjourned for most of the month of October. On 26 September, Governor Bernard had requested advice and assistance on the matter of handling the newly arrived stamps. He found the assembly unwilling to assist in any way, so he prorogued the session. Prior to taking this action, the governor lectured the legislature on the inappropriateness of resisting parliamentary authority. If the Stamp Act had been passed as an expedient measure, Bernard maintained, then its repeal would occur upon demonstration of its inexpediency, not upon a futile disputation of Parliament's right to tax the colonies. If, when 1 November came, no stamps were used, then the courts and ports would close. Bernard posed the question:

> When the courts of justice are shut up, no one will be able to sue for a debt due to
> him, or an injury done him. Must not then all credit and mutual faith cease of
> course, and fraud and rapine take their place? Will any one's person or property be
> safe, when their sole protector of the law is disabled to act. . . . If trade and navi-
> gation shall cease by shutting up the ports of this province for want of legal clear-
> ances, are you sure that all other ports which can rival these, will be shut up also?
> Can you depend upon recovering your trade again entire and undiminished, when
> you shall be pleased to resume it? Can the people of this province subsist without
> navigation for any time? What will become of the seamen who will be put out of
> employment? What will become of the tradesmen who immediately depend upon
> navigation for their daily bread. . . . These are serious and alarming questions,
> which deserve a cool and dispassionate consideration.

On 23 October, when the Massachusetts House was finally reconvened, it took the
first opportunity to respond to Governor Bernard's address of the previous month.
The assembly assured the governor of their utmost attention to the troubled times
in which the province was passing through. However, they respectfully suggested
that the governor exaggerated the peril and especially the violence, as in the attack
on Hutchinson's house which Bernard alleged to be so threatening. As for the consequences of nonuse of the stamps, the House declared: "If any individuals of the
people have declared an unwillingness to subject themselves to the payment of the
stamp duties, and choose rather to lay aside all business than make use of the
stamped papers, as we are not accountable for such declarations, so neither can we
see anything criminal in them." As for the matter of the right and power of Parliament to tax Americans, the assembly wished Governor Bernard to note that: "there
are certain inherent rights belonging to the people, which the Parliament itself cannot divest them of, consistent with their own constitution: among these is the right
of representation in the same body which exercises the power of taxation." Continuing their rebuttal, the representatives declared: "There is a necessity that the
subjects of America should exercise this power within themselves, otherwise they
can have no share in that most essential right, for they are not represented in Parliament, and indeed we think it impracticable." Accordingly, it was the obligation of
the representatives to protest such parliamentary actions as the Stamp Act out of a
sense of duty to the king and Parliament.

> The very supposition that the Parliament though the supreme power over the sub-
> jects of Britain universally, should yet conceive of a despotic power within them-
> selves, would be most disrespectful; and we leave it to your Excellency's consider-
> ation, whether to suppose an undisputable right in any government, to tax the sub-
> jects without their consent, does not include the idea of such a power.[82]

After the Massachusetts Assembly had answered Governor Bernard in the
form of a general address, it drew up a series of fourteen resolutions. The content
of the resolutions reiterated the general points which the body had made to Bernard: the existence of essential rights, as in the power of taxation being based in
representation; that the inhabitants of Massachusetts were not, never have been,

and cannot be represented in the Parliament of Great Britain; from which it followed that "all acts, made by any power whatever, other than then General Assembly of this province, imposing taxes on the inhabitants, are infringements of our inherent and unalienable rights, as men and British subjects, and render void the most valuable declarations of our charter." The resolutions then closed with a testimony of allegiance to King George and the instruction that "all the foregoing resolves be kept in the records of this House; that a just sense of liberty, and the firm sentiments of loyalty may be transmitted to posterity."[83]

On 25 October 1765, the assembly of Connecticut passed a series of resolutions similar to those of Massachusetts. Underscoring the duty to themselves, Parliament, and posterity to protest the injustices which they considered were occurring, the assembly drew up a list of eleven resolves. They too drew attention to the issue of representation, noting that "the Consent of the Inhabitants of this Colony was not given to the said Act of Parliament personally or by Representation, actual or virtual, in any Sense or Degree, that at all comports with the True intendment, Spirit, or equitable Construction of the British Constitution." Consequently, as "the only legal Representatives of the Inhabitants of this Colony are the Persons they elect to serve as Members of the General Assembly . . . it is the Opinion of this House that the said Act for granting and applying certain Stamp Duties, etc., as aforesaid, is unprecedented and unconstitutional."[84]

Neither Massachusetts nor Connecticut had done more than go on record in opposition to the Stamp Act; neither had moved beyond registering protest to support extralegal measures of pressure for repeal. Yet in their energetic protests and their utilization of lawful avenues of protest and petition, they joined the other colonial assemblies in maintaining a constant voice of dissatisfaction with Parliament's actions and, thus, an important pressure on Parliament itself for repeal.

Not all protest activity in New England during October was confined to the solemn chambers of the legislatures, however. In a more lighthearted vein, there was a report in the *Newport Mercury* of twenty-three couples who decided to marry early in order to avoid paying the stamp duty on their marriage licenses. The motivation may have been purely economic, but the newspaper account applauded the action in glowingly patriotic terms.[85]

Not so lighthearted were the month's activities in the middle colonies. On 3 October, stamps arrived for New Jersey but were left on board H. M. S. *Royal Charlotte* for safekeeping. The governor of New Jersey, William Franklin, was not at all sanguine about the custody of the stamps. He told Captain Hawker of H. M. S. *Sardoine* that "the stamps might as well be given directly to the Populace, as to send them into New Jersey."[86] Popular demonstrations continued in New Jersey. The freemen of Essex, New Jersey, for example, met on 25 October, and in a spirited statement declared the Stamp Act unconstitutional and vowed to oppose its execution. They also asserted that they would:

> detest, abhor, and hold in utmost contempt, all and every person or persons who shall meanly accept of any employment or office relating to the said Stamp Act, or shall take any shelter or advantage from the same: and all and every Stamp

> Pimp, informer, favourer, and encourager of the said act, and they will have no communication with any such person, nor speak to them on any occasion, unless it be to inform them of their vileness.[87]

A similar declaration of the act's unconstitutionality and the threat of complete social ostracism was also agreed upon in neighboring Elizabethtown.

At this time, the citizens of Philadelphia also gave evidence of their opposition to the Stamp Act. On 5 October, the date stamps arrived, there was a popular demonstration with several thousand in attendance. As recounted in the newspaper, the colonists "met at the Statehouse to consider the proper Ways and Means for preventing the unconstitutional Act of Parliament being carried into Execution."[88] A delegation then visited John Hughes, the stamp distributor for Pennsylvania, and requested his resignation. Hughes agreed not to execute the act "until it was generally complied with in the other Colonies, but refused to sign any resignation at that Time."[89] Despite the rebuff, the crowd remained peaceful and soon retired with the assurance that the stamps would remain aboard the ship. The assembly had already chosen its delegates to the Stamp Act Congress, so they closed their current session by sending yet another protest to London.

In New York City, resistance activities were hectic. On 10 September, a large crowd had paraded the effigies of George Grenville, General Murray, and Lord Colville for their support of the Stamp Act.[90] On 22 October, stamps arrived at New York harbor, but the presence of a large and vocal crowd prevented their landing. Accordingly, since James McEvers had already resigned his commission as stamp distributor and would have nothing to do with them, the stamps were transferred from the ship to Fort George. The next day there appeared handbills throughout the city which warned:

> Pro Patria
> The first Man that either
> distributes or makes use of Stampt
> Paper, let him take care of
> his house, person, and effects
> Vox Populi

The warning did not daunt the lieutenant-governor, Cadwallader Colden, or his son, David, for on the night of 31 October, the lieutenant-governor took an oath to uphold the act, while his son applied for McEvers' old job as stamp distributor.[91]

If the Coldens thought they would see an end to the resistance, they were sorely deceived. For on the very night on which they were writing London, popular demonstrations were being carried on in the streets and would continue through the week. Less noticed but just as important was a meeting held by the merchant community. On 31 October, a group of two hundred prominent New York merchants agreed to boycott English goods. In addition, they established a committee of correspondence composed of Isaac Sears, John Lamb, Gershom Mott, William Wiley, and Thomas Robinson. All of these men belonged to the New York Sons of Liberty and were instructed by the New York merchants to secure the cooperation of the merchants in the other colonies. The resolutions of the New York merchants were surprisingly broad. All orders regularly sent from Britain were counter-manded, as were all commissioned goods until the Stamp Act was repealed. In a separate action that same night, the retailers of New York City agreed to a similar boycott of British goods, which in this case was to begin on 1 January.[92]

Two other important events occurred at this time—the publication of Daniel Dulany's pamphlet *Considerations on the Propriety of Imposing Taxes in the British Colonies, for the Purpose of Raising a Revenue, by Act of Parliament* and the convening of the Stamp Act Congress in New York. Dulany was a successful lawyer in Maryland, and the pamphlet reflects his concern over the legal and constitutional issues posed by parliamentary taxation. As much of the pamphlet was concerned with the impropriety of Parliament imposing taxes on the colonies, Dulany took great pains to attack the current idea of "virtual representation," which had been presented to counter the colonists' charge that they should not be taxed by a legislature in which they were not represented. In Dulany's view, the Americans and the British simply held no common ground, no similar interests. Thus, America was categorically not represented, virtually nor in any other way by the British Parliament. Dulany's critique of virtual representation was consonant with much colonial sentiment. In Dulany's own Maryland, the freeholders of Anne Arundel County had met and, in a resolution not inspired by Dulany, had informed their representatives in the Maryland Assembly that "the minister's virtual representation adduced argumentatively in support of the tax on us is fantastical and frivolous."[93]

Dulany had helped lay to rest the delusion of virtual representation. He was also concerned with resolving further the question of taxation in the colonies. If the Americans were not virtually represented in Parliament, then where were they represented, if they were at all? For Dulany, the answer was only in their own colonial assemblies, and as a bedrock of English constitutional experience claimed that there could be no taxation without the taxpayers' consent or that of their representatives, the logic of Dulany's argument clearly placed the power to tax in the several colonial assemblies. Dulany's concern, as was the case with many of the pamphleteers of the Stamp Act resistance, was to describe the legitimate limits of parliamentary power, all the while conceding Parliament's authority within the empire.

It was only at the close of the pamphlet that Dulany left the arena of political theory for more practical suggestions. If Parliament violated or trespassed on colonial rights, wrote Dulany, then the colonists "*instead of moping, and puling, and whining to excite compassion . . . ought with Spirit, Vigour, and Alacrity, to bid Defiance to Tyranny, by exposing its Impotence, by making it as contemptible as it would be detestable.*"[94] The presumption was that, by united action, the colonists could make tyranny impotent—a significant political doctrine. Dulany also suggested that the development of American home manufactures, with the pressure that it would produce on the British merchant community and subsequently on Parliament, was a sure avenue for redress. In advocating the boycott of British merchandise and their replacement by indigenous American industries, Dulany drew back from any endorsement of extralegal or illegal activities. Neither destruction of property nor assault on persons were countenanced. Resistance activity, in Dulany's view, while it could expand to other forms than legislative protests, must, nevertheless, remain within the bounds of law.

The meeting of the Stamp Act Congress, which assembled in New York in early October, represented a significant and innovative step in intercolonial cooperation. Previous meetings of the colonies, such as the Albany Congress in June 1754, had been held to confer primarily on problems of internal defense. Now in October, Parliament, not Indians, was the focus of colonial concern. Attention was drawn away from primarily local and particularist concerns so that the delegates, as the invitation suggested, might consult together on the difficulties occasioned by the Stamp Act as well as to petition the king and Parliament for relief. Not all colonies were formally represented. Of the British colonies in North America, only the thirteen continental American colonies were invited. Nova Scotia, Quebec, East and West Florida, and the islands of the West Indies had no part in the assembly.

In New England, official delegations were sent from the legislatures in Massachusetts and Rhode Island, and both of these delegations were empowered to enter into any reasonable common agreements. Connecticut sent a delegation specifically instructed not to enter into any binding agreement without prior authorization of the assembly. New Hampshire sent no delegation because its assembly was prorogued. However, its Speaker did send word of their willingness to join in a united address to the king. Ironically, the assembly of the host colony of New York was also prorogued. Lieutenant-Governor Colden viewed the proposed meeting with great suspicion, calling it "an illegal convention. . . . whatever plausible pretences may be made for their meeting, their real intention may be dangerous."[95] Consequently, when Colden refused to reconvene the New York Assembly, an extralegal committee was formed to appear at the Congress on behalf of New York. Similarly in New Jersey, an extralegal assembly was convened by the Speaker, Robert Ogden, and they sent an informal delegation to the Congress. The assemblies of Pennsylvania, Delaware, and Maryland were in session when they received the Massachusetts invitation, and each sent official delegations to the convention. The situation was somewhat different in the South. Of the four southern colonies, only South Carolina was officially represented. In Virginia, the Burgesses were not in session, nor was the North Carolina Assembly. Georgia, for its part, decided not to send a delegation, but the Georgians did pledge their moral support.

The Congress finally gathered on Monday 7 October 1765.[96] In its first order of business, the group chose Timothy Ruggles and John Cotton, both of Massachusetts, as their chairman and clerk. Thereafter, the Congress spent the next two weeks in debate, working to hammer out a statement of colonial rights as well as a definition of the proper sphere of parliamentary authority. By the time they had drawn up the final draft of the resolutions, the delegates had a comprehensive and well formed statement of the colonial position. Much of the content of this draft, entitled a *Declaration of Rights,* was familiar. It began with a reaffirmation of the colonists' allegiance to the Crown and of their "due subordination" to Parliament. It declared that American colonists had the same rights as native-born Englishmen, among which was no taxation except by the taxpayers' consent or that of their representatives. Moreover, Americans were not virtually represented in Parliament, but rather only in colonial assemblies. Accordingly, as governments, on Locke's account, were established to protect life, liberty, and possessions, taxes were a free gift of the people and thus doubly outside parliamentary purview. In a further resolution, the colonists objected that the establishment of vice-admiralty courts violated the traditions of trial by a jury of one's peers. Having raised these constitutional issues, the *Declaration* now turned to two economic considerations. In the colonists' view, the demand that duties be paid in specie worked an unfair hardship on an already depleted colonial economy. This was but an illustration of the larger point that open and prosperous trade was more beneficial and profitable to Great Britain than a trade curtailed and opposed. For clearly, the full development of the colonies was dependent upon the enjoyment of proper rights and liberties within the context of a mutually advantageous relationship with the mother country.

With the completion of the *Declaration of Rights,* Congress's attention quickly turned to the writing of an *Address to the King,* a *Memorial to the House of Lords,* and a *Petition to the House of Commons.* These three documents varied little in substance from the positions taken in the *Declaration of Rights.* All the documents were presented by the subcommittee chosen to draft them to the Congress as a whole. The delegations from Massachusetts, Rhode Island, Pennsylvania, New Jersey, Delaware, and Maryland all signed. The delegations from Connecticut, New York, and South Carolina were not empowered to sign but first had to report back to their respective assemblies. Two men, Timothy Ruggles of Massachusetts and Robert Ogden of New Jersey, refused to sign any of the statements. The convention met for the last time on 25 October 1765, having decided to send a set of the *Proceedings* to each of the thirteen colonies and one set to Great Britain as the united appeal of the American colonies.

The delegates now returned to their colonies with the news of the Congress's activities. In Massachusetts, the assembly thanked two of its delegates, James Otis and Oliver Partridge. However, it severely censured Timothy Ruggles for refusing to sign the petition and thereby, it said, bringing ignominy to the Bay Colony. In Connecticut and New Hampshire, the respective assemblies quickly gave their approval to the petitions and sent them off to London. Such action by the Connecticut legislature did not deter the governor, Thomas Fitch, from pledging an oath of support for the Stamp Act before several members of his council. (In the elections the following spring, neither the governor nor the council members who administered the oath were reelected.) At its first meeting, the several assemblies of New York, Delaware, Pennsylvania, and Maryland received reports of the gathering and immediately voted their approval of the documents and their thanks to the delegates. In New Jersey, Robert Ogden, the only other individual who refused to sign the petition, was given a hostile reception upon his return. An effigy was hung in New Brunswick, New Jersey, accusing Ogden of betraying the colony's trust and calling him an "abandoned miscreant."[97] Ogden soon resigned from the assembly and re-tired to private life. In the southern colonies, the South Carolina Assembly warmly received news of the deliberations in New York as did the assembly of Georgia. Virginia and North Carolina, however, were still prorogued, and consequently, they were the only two colonies which did not send petitions to England.

The month of October had been marked with demonstrations, resignations, and an important intercolonial association. However, many felt as if they were marking time. As the first of November approached, all wondered what would hap-pen when the Stamp Act officially went into effect. Much, of course, had hap-pened already. On 4 November 1765, the *Newport Mercury* noted in summary: "At present, as we are informed, there is not one of the persons appointed from New Hampshire to Georgia that will execute the odious office—so that the Stamps are now a commodity no body knows what to do with. It is more dangerous to buy or sell or meddle with a stamp, than it is to encounter all the dangers and penalties attending the want of them."[98] Thus by 1 November, severe pressure had been placed on all the appointees for the stamp distributorships. Most had been the ob-jects of popular demonstrations. Many had been abused, ridiculed, and even hanged in effigy. Some had even had their property destroyed, as in the cases of Andrew Oliver and Zachariah Hood. None of the appointees was physically in-jured or killed. However, this is probably accountable to their willingness to resign in the face of such popular intimidation rather than to the good will of the demon-strators whom they faced. In short, as Charles Thomson, a Philadelphia merchant, informed his London friends on 7 November, "the stamp officers have everywhere (except Nova Scotia and Canada, which are under the power of a military force) been obliged to resign their offices; the several assemblies have passed and pub-lished resolves declarative of their rights."[99] Neither colonial governors nor colo-nial legislatures seemed to want to step into the breach. There was no one to take charge of the sale of the stamps. As for the stamps which had arrived in America, they were so closely guarded that they were unavailable even for those who wished to use them.

• RESISTANCE CONTINUES •

It came as little surprise, then, that the patterns of demonstration throughout the colonies continued on 1 November. In Portsmouth, New Hampshire, the morning began with the tolling of the church bells and lowering of all flags to half-mast. Notices were posted throughout the city for "the friends of Liberty" to attend her funeral that afternoon. The procession met and carried the casket through the streets. Upon entering the cemetery, however, the remains of Liberty were per-ceived to be still alive, and accordingly, a copy of the Stamp Act was immediately thrown into the grave and buried. The assemblage then retired to a tavern and toasted "Liberty revived." As for the stamped papers, they were still stored in the fort at Newcastle, where, said the newspaper account, "they are to remain as a dead inactive lump of matter, till they are sent back to their native country."[100]

In Boston, Governor Bernard expected dire events to happen on 1 November. Nonetheless, in writing to his friend John Pownall, Bernard described the day with some degree of relief. Anticipating that there would be disturbances throughout the city on 1 November, Bernard, with the support of the council, had called out the militia. To his consternation, Bernard was informed by the commanding officer of the regiment that he "could not execute my order, for he could not get a Drummer to beat a drum, one who had attempted it had his Drum broke; the others were bought off; the People would not muster." Unable to raise the militia, Bernard revoked the order. At this point, he indicated that from some unnamed source:

> We were assured that if the Guard was dismissed the Town would be quiet, otherwise not; that there would be a procession the next day 1 November, but there should be nothing in it to affront this Government; that if any images were made for that purpose, they should not be exhibited; that nothing would more tend to disturb the Peace of the Town than opposing this procession, nor to preserve it than permitting it.

Effectively unable to prevent the proposed parades, Bernard acquiesced and the stage was set. On the next day, "about two o'clock the procession began with carrying the Images thro' the publick streets accompanied with an innumerable people from the Country as well as the Town walking in exact order. At last they [the effigies] were carried to the Gallows out of Town, and there tore to pieces and hanged. After which the Mob dispersed, and the Town was perfectly quiet." If the orderliness of the crowd surprised Bernard, he found their leaders even more astonishing: "It is remarkable on this occasion that the ringleaders of the Mob which demolished Mr. Oliver's house was employed with his Corps to keep the Peace and prevent mischief; and I was told that he was engaged so to do, as an assurance that no mischief would be done. This man whose name is MacIntosh is a noted Captain of a mob and has under him 100 or 150 men trained as regular as a Military Corps." Relieved at the orderliness of the day's proceedings and surprised by the self-control of the crowd and its leaders, Bernard could still only deplore the situation he found himself in. Ruefully, he thought again of MacIntosh and concluded: "to this man it was thought proper to commend the Care of the Town on this occasion: So totally is the Town and consequently the Government in the hands of the Mob."[101]

The Boston papers drew an explicit contrast between the activities of 1 November and those of 26 August. The self-discipline shown by the crowd was applauded, and one paper hoped that the order and calm would show that the destruction of Hutchinson's property "was not agreeable to the Sentiments of the Town but was only the lawless Ravages of some foreign Villians who took advantage of the overheated tempers of a very few People of this Place."[102] Even if the crowds remained quiet on 1 November, as Bostonians well knew, 5 November, or Pope's Day, was a traditional occasion for rowdy contests between North and South Enders. However, this year there were no brawls or disorders. Ebenezer MacIntosh, now known in Boston as the "First Captain General of the Liberty Tree" for his part in various resistance campaigns, was joined by Samuel Swift, leader of the North End contingent. Together with their followers, MacIntosh and Swift paraded through the town, first to the Liberty Tree and then up to a nearby hill. There the crowd torched effigies, which they had been displaying during the parade, and then retired without further commotion.[103]

In New York City, the people had been out in the streets on the night of 31 October. There had been, however, no damage to property nor injury to persons.[104] Lieutenant-Governor Colden had informed Secretary Conway on 23 September that the garrison at Fort George had been strengthened. Colden promised to "do everything in my power to have the stamped paper distributed at the time appointed by Act of Parliament, and if I can have this done, I believe the present bustle will soon subside." Colden, however, was soon to see events move completely beyond his control. On the morning of 1 November, an anonymous letter addressed to the lieutenant-governor was posted at a prominent coffeehouse, there to remain until it was delivered to Colden himself. The letter called Colden the "Chief Murderer" of the colonists' rights and privileges for having taken the oath in support of the Stamp Act the previous night, and it pledged spirited resistance against any measures of enforcement he should try. That evening a large crowd gathered in front of Fort George and hung two effigies—one of Colden and the other of the Devil—from a gibbet in plain sight of the fort. The whole ensemble was then lifted up and paraded through the streets. Just before returning to the area of the fort, some persons broke into Colden's coach house and brought out his coach and two other pieces of livery. The scene grew more hectic by the minute. One observer declared:

> It is impossible sufficiently to admire and commend the patience and temper of the officers and soldiers. The Populace knocked at the gate, placed their hands on top of the Ramparts, called out to the guards to fire, threw bricks and stones against the Fort and not withstanding the highest provocation was given, not a word was returned to the most opprobrious language. From this description, you will perhaps conclude that it was the design of the people to provoke a fire. I must leave you to judge from appearances. I can do no more.[105]

The assemblage moved from the fort, with effigies, gibbet, and coach, to a nearby hill, where the entire ensemble was consigned to the flames. At this point, a smaller party splintered off from the main body and proceeded to the home of Major Thomas James. James had had the temerity, in referring to the opposition by the colonists, to announce publicly that he would "cram the stamps down their throats," a comment which in no way endeared him to the local populace. Growing in size as it neared James's house, the crowd demolished the structure and scattered and destroyed his possessions.

Lieutenant-Governor Colden stayed in Fort George throughout the length of these proceedings. On the following day, 2 November, he agreed to wait until the arrival of Sir Henry Moore, the governor-elect of New York, before taking any actions regarding the stamps. Such assurances were not sufficient for all New Yorkers, however. Although on 4 November Colden pledged not to issue the stamps at all, rumors circulated throughout the city that there would be a full-scale attack on the fort on the evening of 5 November. That afternoon, a compromise was reached in which the Corporation of the City of New York would take custody of the stamps.

At first, Colden had approached Captain Kennedy and others of His Majesty's Navy, but none of them would accept custody of the stamps. It was at this point that the New York City officials entered into the situation. As recorded in the minutes of the Common Council of the City of New York for 5 November 1765:

> It is therefore resolved that it appears to this Board Absolutely Requisite to Remove the present Dissatisfaction and save the City from the most Distressing Confusion; That a Committee Immediately wait upon his honour and in the most Respectfull manner acquaint him of the present dangerous State of Things and Request that for the Peace of the City and the Preventing of an Effusion of Blood, he would please to Direct that the Stamped Paper, be delivered into the Care of the Corporation, to be deposited in the City hall and Guarded by the City watch; and this Board Do Further Resolve and Engage to make Good all such sums of money as might be Raised by the Distribution of such of the Stamps as Shall be Lost, Destroyed, or Carried out of the province.

The delegation from the City Corporation met with Colden, and he readily agreed to give them custody.[106]

Anxious to defend his actions, Colden explained his rationale to Henry Conway in a letter of 9 November. "What I have at last yielded to," Colden declared, "I should gladly have done at the time the Stamp Papers were imported as I have no Kind of direction relating to them but I should have been thought mad at that time to have proposed it to them. Has not the Mayor and Corporation by taking the stamp'd paper voluntarily into their custody assumed the office of Distributor of Stamps?" As for the ringleaders of "the present sedition" afflicting New York, Colden said, "I have the strongest presumption from numerous circumstances to believe that the Lawyers of this Place are the Authors, Promotors, and Leaders of it. People in general believe it and many must with certainty know it." Finally in closing, the lieutenant-governor suggested: "If Judges be sent from England, and with an able Attorney General and Soliciter General to make examples of some very few, this Colony will remain for many years quiet. One complete Regiment with the Ships of War now in their Port, and the garrison at this time in the Fort, to assist the Civil Officers I believe may be sufficient for this purpose."[107] No troops were forthcoming from Conway, but as Colden had suggested, New York once again quieted down.

The preceding week's events were the subject of much discussion. On 6 November, an anonymous handbill addressed to the "Freeholders and Inhabitants of the City of New York" congratulated the citizenry upon their acquisition of the stamps from the royal authorities. "We have entirely accomplished all we wanted in rescuing the Stamps from the Hands of our inveterate Enemy," declared the authors of the piece. Accordingly, now was the time to consolidate the gains made, and to join "Hand in Hand in effecting the Peace that now subsists," for to "proceed any further would only hurt the good Cause in which we are engaged."[108] Not everyone was as conscious of a victory having been won. James Otis, for one, could only remark that he was "much surprised at the violent proceedings at New York, as there has been so much time for people to cool, and the outrages on private property are so generally detested."[109]

While Lieutenant-Governor Colden was privately of the opinion that a show and perhaps application of military might would be sufficient to beat down colonial resistance, General Gage was much less certain of that solution. "When I consider the present moment," Gage declared,

> that though a fire from the Fort might disperse the Mob, it would not quell them, and the consequence would in all appearances be an Insurrection, not only of the Inhabitants, Sailors, etc., in this city but of the Country people who are flocking in, and those from the Neighboring Provinces who would likewise assist . . . it seems to me that a Fire from the Fort would in this situation of things be the Commencement of a Civil War. . . . The Fort, though it can defend itself, can only protect the Spot it stands on.[110]

While the citizens of New York were actively protesting Parliament's actions, other colonies were actively boycotting British goods. To the north, forty-eight merchants in Albany agreed to follow the lead of the New York mercantile community and join in a boycott of British goods.[111] In November, Maryland merchants informally agreed not to use British goods, while the Philadelphia merchant community likewise pledged themselves to a nonimportation pact on 7 November. According to Charles Thomson, the Philadelphia merchant, the impetus for the agreement came from popular pressure. The people were exasperated, said Thomson, and "it would be unsafe for any man to import while the Stamp Act continues unrepealed, the people are determined not to use the manufactures of Great Britain."[112]

Thomas Wharton, another prominent Philadelphian, described the significance of the activities to his friend Benjamin Franklin. In Wharton's opinion, demonstrations would not bring about repeal. Instead, the economic boycott promised to be much more powerful and effective. "I cannot doubt but before this," Wharton wrote to Franklin, "thou are apprized of the Imprudent and Unwarantable Steps, which the several Colonies have taken in Order to render the late Act of Parliament Void . . . and which steps I fear When fully known at Home, will rather tend to Injure then relieve Us." Wharton agreed that the Stamp Act was wrong. Moreover, it was obviously inexpedient, and he suggested to Franklin "that if they would not hear our Cries, I could not doubt, but the Parliament would pay a Regard to the Prayers of the Merchants and Manufacturers of Britain." With this hope in mind, Wharton continued:

> In Order to obtain the desirable End of the repeal of the Stamp Act, an Association was formed this day, and Articles signed by a very great Number of Merchants, and will be subscribed by All, enjoining, that They will not Import from Britain any Goods or Merchandize, until that Act be repealed. . . . by this Means We shall be able to plead thro' themselves more effectual, than all We could Otherwise do: and I see this Method far more Eligible then the Conduct of all the Governments Around Us.[113]

Resistance in the southern colonies continued to grow throughout November. Virginia, for example, had lost its stamp distributor, George Mercer, on 31 October 1765. The North Carolina distributor, William Houston, arrived in Wilmington on 16 November. He was immediately visited by a crowd numbering between three and four hundred, which insisted upon knowing whether he intended to execute the Stamp Act. In reply: "he told them, he should be very sorry to execute any Office disagreeable to the People of the Province. But they, not content with such a Declaration, carried him into the Court-house, where he signed a Resignation satisfactory to the whole." At this point, the crowd lifted him into an armchair and, with loud acclamations, escorted him to his lodgings, where the whole group toasted his health and an end to the Stamp Act. The entire episode was conducted, the newspaper noted, "with great Decorum, and not the least Insult offered to any Person."[114]

Though he had just been deprived of his stamp distributor, the North Carolina governor, William Tyron, still hoped to be able to obtain cooperation in the execution of the Stamp Act. On 18 November, he invited fifty of the leading gentlemen of the colony to dine with him and, in the course of the evening, expressed his hopes that North Carolina would obey the royal authorities and the acts of Parliament. He implored these men to take the lead in such obedience and even promised to help defray such incidental expenses as would accrue from the taxes. The fifty gentlemen thanked the governor for his comments. On the morning of the next day, the gentlemen informed the governor that the Stamp Act was destructive of their rights as Englishmen and that any submission to it would be "a direct inlet for slavery." Moreover, while they too cherished peace and good order, they noted that as "the office of Distributor of the Stamps is so detested by the People in general," they did not think any applicant for the job safe from the resentment of the people.[115] Governor Tyron's attempts at cajoling compliance were dashed by a series of demonstrations in the end of November. On the night of 20 November, a massive crowd gathered and performed the familiar ritual of hoisting up an effigy of the governor, then lighting it afire as they toasted confusion to Lord Bute and "Liberty, Property, and no Stamp Duty!" Days later, an equally large crowd gathered to witness the burial of "Liberty," only to discover that her pulse still beat, and appearances to the contrary, she was still alive.[116]

In Georgia, the press had carried reports in October that "to the northward they have begun to show their Attention to Stamp Officers in such a manner that 'tis said the gentlemen appointed for that Office in Massachusetts, New Hampshire, Rhode Island, Connecticut, New York, New Jersey, Virginia, and North Carolina have declared they will resign." Accordingly, at a November meeting of the Sons of Liberty in Georgia, it was thought only proper that when the Stamp distributor for the colony arrived, "he should be waited upon, and as he is a stranger, to be acquainted with sentiments of the people."[117] As it was to turn out, the Georgia stamp distributor was not to arrive from England until early January 1766. Nonetheless, a large crowd turned out on 5 November to protest the Stamp Act and to demonstrate their opposition to anyone who would try to enforce it.

As the end of the year approached and royal officials assessed their situation, they could only be despondent. "All of the distributors of Stamps between Halifax and St. Augustine have been compelled to resign their commissions," advised Charles Steuart, the surveyor-general in America. Moreover, according to the chief Customs agent of Philadelphia,

> What has lately happened in New York (and the same spirits prevail as strongly here) is sufficient to convince us that it is vain for us to contend against the general voice of a united people. We have not the least hope of enforcing the act by anything we can do at present. . . . As there is not the least possibility of getting them [the stamps], we must submit to necessity and do without them, or else in a little time people will learn to do without them or us.[118]

Colonial officials were equally gloomy about their predicament. In a letter written on 26 December 1765, Samuel Ward, governor of Rhode Island, told the treasury officials in London that: "People of every Rank and Condition are so unanimous in their Opinion that the Operation of the Act for levying Stamp Duties in America would be inconsistent with their natural and just Rights and Privileges, injurious to His Majesty's Service and the Interest of Great Britain, and incompatible with the very Being of this Colony, that no Person I imagine will undertake to execute that Office."[119] In describing the situation in Massachusetts, Governor Bernard likewise noted the determined opposition to the Stamp Act and concluded: "At this time I have no real Authority in this place, and am much in the hands of the People, that is, if it was to be known here that I received a power to distribute the Stamps, I should have my house surrounded and be obliged, at least, to give public assurances that I would not undertake the Business."[120]

As if to validate these officials' opinions, resistance activity continued. In New England, town meetings continued to issue statements protesting the Stamp Act and countenancing noncooperation. For example, on 25 December 1765, "at a large meeting of the respectable Populace" in Pomfret, Connecticut, the town drew up a series of eleven resolves. Pledging allegiance to the king, they noted "that God and Nature brought us into the World Freemen," a condition since recognized "by Solemn Charter, Compact, and Agreement." From here, the town's declarations turned to Jared Ingersoll, the former stamp distributor.

> Whereas our Stamp-Master was appointed Agent for this Colony at the Court of Great Britain, with Confidence that he would exert his utmost endeavours to prevent said Act; nevertheless, he returned the executioner of those Evils he was sent to defend us from: And notwithstanding his Solemn Resignation, and Engagements to the contrary, has and still obstinately persists to plot the ruin and total overthrow of his native Country, by all the ways and means his Malice and Craft suggests, or his unbridled Audacity can attempt.

Following these strong words, the town challenged Ingersoll to appear in a public meeting and clear himself. Furthermore, they concluded, "that we do earnestly recommend to the Civil Authority of this Colony to proceed in Business as usual; as our Cessation and Delay of Business will be construed an implicit acknowledgment of the validity of the Stamp Act."[121]

In Boston on 9 December 1765, two hundred fifty merchants subscribed to a nonimportation agreement. The agreement countermanded existing orders to Great Britain, though it did exempt from restriction articles necessary to fishing and manufacturing. In addition, they resolved "not to purchase any Goods that may be imported into this province by any Persons whatsoever, for Sale, contrary to the Spirit of the above Agreement; but that we will take every prudent Measure in our Power to discourage the Sale of such goods." These colonial nonimportation and nonconsumption resolutions were to be in effect until 1 May 1766, by which time it was hoped that repeal of the Stamp Act would be underway. The merchants of Salem and Marblehead, Massachusetts, signed similar nonimportation agreements, thereby uniting the merchants of the major New England ports with their brethren in New York and Philadelphia.[122]

To most observers of the colonial situation, it was clear that the Stamp Act had aroused widespread and determined opposition throughout the length and breadth of Britain's American colonies. In hindsight, it is now apparent that new social dimensions and configurations were growing out of the dynamics of this popular resistance to the Stamp Act. These new dimensions concerned not so much the fact that the colonists were protesting nor even the forms, such as the boycotts and legislative remonstrances, which this opposition was taking. Americans had registered their dissatisfaction with other aspects of Britain's mercantile system before, as in the protests against the Navigation Acts of 1696 and the Currency Act and Sugar Act of 1764. Likewise, the colonists had experimented with legislative protest, and even economic noncooperation, as in the case of the Sugar Act, had been tried.

But unlike previous imperial legislation, the Stamp Act touched on many more aspects of everyday colonial life. Dice, marriage licenses, newspapers, shipping permits, legal decisions, and land securities were all within the orbit of the stamp tax. For common people, powerful merchants, and lawyers alike, the tax would be a daily confrontation, its very comprehensiveness preventing it from being shunted off to the periphery of colonial experience. The conflict which ensued over the tax was not only focused on the menace of higher taxes—taxes felt to be unconstitutional—but there was in addition the direct economic threat to those two powerful colonial interests, the lawyers and merchants. For merchants, such as Charles Thomson of Philadelphia or John Rowe of Boston, the Stamp Act resistance meant joining a nonimportation agreement and perhaps even participating in a demonstration. It came as no surprise to colonial observers to find that these same lawyers and merchants, the so-called better sort of colonial society, participated along with (indeed often disguised as) their artisan neighbors in such activities. Involvement by the merchants could come in response to popular pressure or in hopes of influencing policy or both. The result of this wide social spectrum of involvement was not only the increased politicization of individual groups but, rather unexpectedly, the increased politicization of the whole of colonial life. Politicization, on one level, meant the increased recognition by such merchants of their need to participate to a larger extent in the political sphere of their society. It also meant the growing awareness that this political sphere extended to London as much as it included America.

Thus, the Stamp Act's ability to galvanize and solidify popular opinion caused it to become quickly embroiled in the labyrinth of local colonial politics. Whether it was religious liberals ("New Lights") and religious conservatives ("Old Lights") in Connecticut, or proprieters and antiproprieters in Pennsylvania, or First Families and nouveau riche in Virginia, each side tried to tar its opponents with the brush of complicity in the Stamp Act. Each side also simultaneously vied for continued or increased support from allies in London. Moreover, the continued attention to political questions through demonstrations, pamphlets, newspapers, and legislative discussion and resolves not only kept the Stamp Act in the limelight, but it often elevated these local disputes and power plays to the level of principled confrontations over political authority and power. In short, in the midst of all this political discussion and activity, there occurred within colonial society an easy going transference of attention from local politics to imperial politics and vice versa. This entanglement between local prerogative and imperial policy, if not entirely unprecedented in colonial life, was of a scale large enough to introduce a new complexity to colonial life. In ways not seen before, the avenues of political participation were broadened, and the experience of political participation was deepened. This process of greater political participation would go much further by the end of the decade with the development of parallel government in America. But even in 1765, the changes were apparent, and Governor Francis Bernard, as he surveyed the results of popular demonstrations and the increasing pressure being brought to bear on colonial officials such as himself, could only characterize the results with that word so opprobrious to him: democracy.[123]

Bernard also knew well that yet another result of the dynamics of this process of politicization was the isolation of imperial authority from the popular sources of support within the colony. To be sure, this was a gradual process, yet one inexorably added to by the political activities surrounding the Stamp Act. Time and again, one finds the royal governor and often his council pitted against the lower house in a struggle for power and allegiance. The final result of this contest would be the identification of the governor with the so-called imperial interests, while the colonial assemblies, in their own quest for power, would correspondingly take up the American interest.[124]

The interplay, then, of local political conditions and imperial dictate was significant in the resistance to the Stamp Act, as it had been throughout the course of America's colonial experience.

The colonists had been discussing which strategy for resistance would be most effective ever since Andrew Oliver had been induced to resign in mid-August 1765. Some commentators hypothesized on the several alternatives open to the colonists in the face of the Stamp Act and on their likely consequences; others— usually royal officials—surveyed the multitude of colonial demonstrations which had taken place searching for their plan and meaning. An article which appeared in the *Newport Mercury* on 2 September 1765 set forth some of the available options within the context of Andrew Oliver's recent resignation.

> Since the resignation of the Stamp-Officer, a question has been thrown out—How shall we carry on trade without the stamp'd paper?—Carry on no trade at all, say some, for who would desire to increase his property, at the expense of liberty— Others say, that in case there shall be no officer to distribute the Stampt papers after the first of November, a regular protest will justify any of his Majesty's subjects, in any court of justice, who shall carry on business without them.

Repercussions from the imposition of the act were clear, for: "should the colonies cease to take the manufactures of Great Britain, as they will be under a necessity of doing very soon, unless she alters her measures, thousands of her useful labors and their families must starve—so great a dependence has the mother upon her children."[125]

In the same month of September, General Thomas Gage traced the developments as he saw them for Henry Conway. Writing on 23 September, Gage noted:

> The general Scheme, concerted throughout, seems to have been, first by Menace or Force to oblige the Stamp Officers to resign their Employment, in which they have generally succeeded, and next to destroy the Stampt Papers upon their Arrival; that having no Stamps, Necessity might be an Escape for the Dispatch of Business without them; and that before they could be replaced, the Clamor and outcry of the People, with Addresses and Remonstrances from the Assemblys might procure a Repeal of the Act.[126]

Gage was a keen observer and accurately portrayed the interconnection of popular and legislative activities. Yet to Francis Bernard, perhaps a bit skittish by the end of 1765, not repeal in London, but the overthrow of his government seemed to be the logical end of all the agitation in Massachusetts. Writing to Lord Colville on 11 December 1765, Bernard declared that "the present Subject of Clamour is the Custom House refusing to give unstamped Clearances: Merchants, Traders, and Mob all join in this. I have nothing to do in this business: but when the Mob is up, I am not sure they will observe distinctions of departments." If the Custom House could be pressured into opening, Bernard predicted, "they will set about obliging the Judges to administer Justice without stamps, and in that business or the next step after, it will arrive at the Governor and Council. So that I think my turn must come some time or other."[127]

Stamped papers were needed for all shipping permits and all legal documents. Accordingly, there were several possibilities which the colonist might face. Perhaps by 1 November, or shortly thereafter, there would be stamps and distributors to make them available. In this case, any permits or documents without the stamps would be illegal. A second possibility might be that stamps would be available but that all concerned persons—merchants, lawyers, litigants, and the like—would boycott the use of these ports and courts. Next, there was the chance that stamps would be available but that justices and court officials would choose to operate in defiance of the law by not insisting upon their use. Finally, there was the strong likelihood that neither stamps nor distributors would be available; in which case, the ports and courts would either have to close down completely or open and operate in defiance of the law.

In the months between November 1765 and the repeal of the Stamp Act in March 1766, a variety of resistance activities focused on this issue of the opening and closing of courts and ports. As early as September 1765, the New Jersey bar had decided not to use stamps for any purpose. During the same month, the magistrates of Westmoreland County in Virginia had unanimously decided to resign their offices rather than to remain open and use the stamps.[128]

Such closures, occasioned by boycotts and resignations, had several implications. Another Virginian, George Washington, commented on one of them as follows: "Our Courts of Judicature must be inevitably shut up, [Washington wrote], for it is impossible . . . under our present Circumstances that the Act of Parliament can be complied with . . . and if a stop be put to our judicial proceedings I fancy the Merchants of G. Britain trading to Colonies will not be among the last to wish for a Repeal of it."[129] As Washington correctly saw, the closure of courts in America could have ramifications for merchants in London. Trade could be paralyzed, as bills might go uncollected, and debtors remained untouched. In short, the regular course of life would come to a standstill. Hardships for creditors would occur on the domestic scene as well. For example, as the merchant Charles Thomson reported in early November: "The Confusion in our City and Province, and indeed thro the whole Colonies, are unspeakable by reason of the late Stamp Act. The Courts of Justice and the office of Government are all shut up; numbers of people who are indebted take advantage of the times to refuse Payment and are moving off with all their effects out of reach of their Creditors." Thomson also foresaw a possible effect on British merchants. He gloomily concluded: "Where this will end God Knows—but if relief does not come, and that speedily we who have imported Goods from Great Britain are ruined, and how far our Ruin may affect the Trade and Manufactures of Great Britain they best can tell."[130]

While Thomson spoke of "numbers of people" taking advantage of the court situation to avoid debts, it is difficult to substantiate the actual scope of this practice. Interestingly, some months later, there was a report of a case in which the tables were turned. In this instance,

> a certain person being duned for a debt, he gave his creditor to understand, that as there was no law, he would not pay him, whereupon the creditor seized him by the shoulder, and called out 'here is a man that wants stamps!' he was in a little time surrounded by a number of people, who would make a sacrifice of him, who dared to take the advantage of the distressing situation of his country, had he not immediately paid the money, and made an acknowledgement of his fault.[131]

Stamps were not required in the criminal courts but were required in the admiralty courts and the civil courts. With the local admiralty courts closed, the mechanism for enforcing the Stamp Act was removed, unless prosecutors were willing to take their cases to the admiralty court in Halifax, Nova Scotia. Thus, the implementation of imperial policy, as well as many local matters, was interrupted whenever courts were inoperative. Several other courts shut down during

November. On 1 November, the courts in New Hampshire were closed because there were no stamps to be had. Soon after, the citizens of Portsmouth formed an independent association to protect property, anticipating quite possibly the very debtor situation of which Charles Thomson complained. In South Carolina, Chief Justice Shinner indicated that as no stamps were available, no business of the court would be transacted. Accordingly, he adjourned his court until 3 December, at which time it was continued until 4 March 1766. The same circumstances occurred in Georgia, though this time the governor adjourned the court. Somewhat differently, in North Carolina, Governor Tryon noted: "No business is transacted in the Courts of Judicature, tho' the Courts here have been regularly opened." There the courts were in effect closed as a result of the boycott of the facilities by both lawyers and litigants.[132]

Noncooperation in the form of official resignation or the popular boycott of institutions was joined by scrupulous attention to legal and bureaucratic detail as a reason for refusing to use the stamps. Governor William Franklin mused, "we might legally go on with Business in the Usual Way, much as if the Stamps had never been sent, or had been lost at sea, seeing that no Commissioner or instructions have been sent to any Body to execute the Act in this Province."[133] At other points, legislatures refused to advise royal governors on stamp matters, claiming that such issues did not fall properly within their legislative purview. For example, as mentioned previously, on 25 September 1765, Governor Bernard of Massachusetts requested the advice and assistance of the Massachusetts Assembly in the care of the stamps. The assembly responded to the governor that, "as the Stamped Papers, mentioned in your Message are brought here without any Direction to this Government, it is the Sense of the House that it may prove of ill Consequence for them in any ways to interest themselves in this matter." In a similar vein, the assembly of South Carolina interrogated Lieutenant-Governor Bull as to whether a copy of the Stamp Act, "said to have been passed in Parliament," had been received, and if so, from whom? Had he received the copy from an authentic and reliable source such as the secretary of state or the Lords of Trade? Bull responded that his copy came from the governor, though he did not indicate from whom the governor received his copy.[134]

Other options remained besides those forms of noncooperation which resulted in court closings. One was to remain open continuously in defiance of the law. Another was to reopen without the use of stamps. In December 1765, Charles Carroll of Carrollton recommended this former choice "since a suspension from business implies a tacit acquaintance of the Law, or at least ye right of ye power of imposing such Laws upon us: the right we deny upon ye soundest of reasoning, and the power we should oppose by all lawful means."[135] Significantly, in Carroll's own Maryland, the courts of Frederick County had already decided by November 1765 to remain open.[136]

In the months between December 1765 and March 1766, the scope of these court-related resistance activities grew throughout the colonies. In December, the lawyers in Philadelphia and New York voted to continue their practices, but under no conditions to use the stamps.[137] Also in December, the Boston town meeting called for the local courts to reopen. A memorial of 18 December 1765 from the town to the governor noted, "the Courts of Law within the Province in which alone Justice can be distributed among the people, so far as respects Civil Matters are to all intents and purposes shut up, for which your Memorialists apprehend no Just and Legal Reason can be assigned." The town meeting therefore called upon the governor and his council to direct the officers of the courts to reopen. In response, the council refused to act, claiming "the Subject Matter of this Memorial is not proper for the determination of this Board" and was best left to the justices of the court themselves to determine appropriate action. Pressure to reopen the Massachusetts courts continued as the new year began. By 16 January 1766, it was reported to the Boston town meeting that the Inferior Court of Common Pleas for Suffolk County along with the Court of Probate were now open. The town meeting voted on the same day to instruct their representatives in the Massachusetts House to see that "Justice be also duly administered in all the Countys throughout the Province." In short, now that the Suffolk County courts were open, the Bostonians saw no reason for any other Massachusetts courts to be closed.[138]

On 24 January 1766, the Massachusetts House addressed the Bostonians' concerns. The House resolved "that the Shutting up the Courts of Justice in general in this Province, particularly the Superior Court, has a manifest tendency to dissolve the Bonds of Civil Society, is unjustifiable on the Principles of Law and Reason," and thus was a pressing matter which deserved immediate attention. Once such attention was given, it was clear which course of action should be taken: "the Judges and Justices, and all other publick Officers in this province ought to proceed in the discharge of their several functions as usual."[139] Despite the forthrightness of the House's resolution, the Superior Court of Massachusetts remained closed until March 1766. At that point, it ruled on a single case which had begun prior to 1 November 1765, after which the court suspended operation again until June 1766.

Other courts throughout the colonies wrestled with the question of how to proceed. On 6 January 1766, a notice in the *Boston Gazette* indicated that the courts in Providence, Rhode Island, had remained open since November and were continuing to do so.[140] Within the month, the inferior courts of New Hampshire had resumed their operations without stamps, and by early February, the superior courts were open again as well.[141] In Virginia, Judge Edmund Pendleton of Caroline County urged that "we must resolve either to admit the stamps or to proceed without them, for to stop all business must be a greater evil then either." For his own part, Pendleton said, "I thought it my duty to sit, and we have constantly opened Court." In nearby Northampton County, the court not only remained open, but on 11 February 1766, the judges unanimously declared the Stamp Act unconstitutional. The Stamp Act "did not bind, affect, or concern the inhabitants of this colony," the judges ruled, "inasmuch as they conceive the same to be unconstitutional, and the said several officers [of the court] may proceed to the execution of their respective offices without incurring any penalties by means thereof."[142]

In New Jersey, a meeting of the bar was held on 13 February 1766. The courts of New Jersey had been closed since November for lack of stamp distributors and of judges willing to sit illegally. Now in February, many lawyers wanted to find a way to resume some sort of practice. So too did the New Jersey Sons of Liberty. They attended the February meeting and called on the bar to resume practice without the use of stamps. After a long meeting, however, the bar decided to continue "to desist from this practice till the first day of April next," after which if the Stamp Act was still in effect, to resume their practice in defiance of the law. Repeal occurred before April came, thereby relieving the New Jersey lawyers of the opportunity. However, before repeal took place, the county courts of Sussex and Cumberland in New Jersey had both reopened.[143]

Judicial developments in South Carolina and Maryland demonstrated popular concern over the courts in the southern colonies. In South Carolina, the courts had been closed since November. On 4 March 1766, three new judges were appointed to assist Chief Justice Shinner. A case was presented at this time, but the court decided to postpone consideration until its meeting of 1 April 1766. On that day, the three new judges overrode Shinner's negative vote and agreed to hear the postponed case. At this point, Dougal Campbell, clerk of the court, refused to enter the case on the docket or to empanel a jury. The court, Shinner excluded, appealed to Lieutenant-Governor Bull to suspend Campbell, but Bull refused to do it. The three judges next turned to the assembly, hoping to pressure Bull into cooperation. The assembly drew up a series of resolutions indicating that the court had jurisdiction over its own affairs and should not be obstructed by the clerk's intransigence; that Dougal Campbell, by his refusal to obey the orders of the court, was guilty of contempt of court and ought to be suspended from his post; and finally, that Campbell and all who supported him in his position were acting in contradiction to the behavior of good British subjects. The resolutions accurately mirrored the feelings of the assembly, but they did not produce the desired results. Bull remained firm, Campbell remained clerk, and the South Carolina courts remained closed.[144]

In Maryland, the Sons of Liberty of Baltimore and Anne Arundel counties, together with a deputation from Kent County, assembled on 1 March 1766 at Annapolis. Their purpose was to try to persuade the chief justice of the provincial court to reopen. The group requested the chief justice and the judges of the land office to open their offices by 31 March, or earlier, if a majority of the superior courts of the northern colonies should reopen prior to that date. When the end of the month arrived, the situation seemed at a stalemate, for the chief justice refused to reopen court. Finally, after promises to the judges of financial assistance in the event they were fined for their actions, the provincial court of Maryland passed the following order: "It is by the court here ordered that the clerk of this court, from henceforth . . . transact all business whatsoever, in his office, for which application shall be made to him, by any inhabitant of this province, as usual without stamped paper."[145]

While the lawyers of the colonies were engaged in their battle over the courts, two other groups—newspaper editors and merchants—were undertaking a parallel fight. The movement to reopen the courts had obtained mixed results. The majority of noncriminal legal proceedings appeared to have been suspended in the colonies from November through the repeal. To be sure, no courts operated regularly with the stamps. However, few courts continued proceedings or resumed operations.

The resistance activities surrounding newspapers and ports had results as diverse as those concerned with courts. For example, on 10 October 1765, the *Maryland Gazette* informed its readers that it was ceasing publication because of the financial burdens soon to be imposed by the Stamp Act. Newspapers were especially hard hit by the act. Its regulations assessed duties on the sheets of paper upon which the news was printed: a halfpenny on each copy of a newspaper printed on what was called "half a sheet" and a full penny on the next larger size of paper. Moreover, for each advertisement which the paper carried, an additional two shillings was charged. As the publisher usually received only three to five shillings for each advertisement, such a rate of tax was felt to be excessive. Thus, when the Philadelphia publisher Benjamin Franklin gloomily predicted that the tax "will affect the Printers more than anybody," he echoed the fears of many of his fellow printers.[146]

When the 10 October issue of the *Maryland Gazette* appeared, it wore a different masthead. Within a black band was printed "The Maryland Gazette Expiring: In uncertain Hopes of a Resurrection to Life again." In the corner of the front page, instead of a stamp, appeared a death's-head.[147] The funeral bands and editorial farewells gained wider usage by the end of the month. On 31 October, the *New Hampshire Gazette,* the *New York Gazette or Weekly Post Boy,* the *Pennsylvania Journal,* the *Pennsylvania Gazette,* and the *South Carolina Gazette* all informed their readers of their cessation. The *Pennsylvania Journal* outdid the *Maryland Gazette* in funeral display. Its front page resembled a tombstone with mortuary urns and skulls and crossbones. Under the title appeared the legend, "Expiring: In Hopes of a Resurrection to Life Again," while the marginal captions read, "Adieu, Adieu to the Liberty of the Press." On the last page was a coffin, indicating the paper's demise "Of a Stamp in her Vitals."[148] For its part, the *South Carolina Gazette* kept its regular masthead, but its editor, Peter Timothy, indicated that the *Gazette* would suspend its publication because numerous subscribers had indicated they would not buy any newspapers that appeared with stamps.[149] It seemed to many publishers that the newspapers were to be bankrupted if they attempted to operate with the stamps either because of the increased cost from the stamp duties or due to the boycott of their entire paper if they used the stamps.

Other options remained for the newspapers, though, and some papers chose or were pressured to remain open and not suspend their publication. The *New London Gazette* and the *Connecticut Gazette* continued to publish on 1 November without using stamps. The *Georgia Gazette* did likewise, explaining that "No Stamp-Officer having yet arrived . . . this paper will be carried on as usual till he arrives and begins to issue his stamps." As events turned out, pressure from the royal governor put an end to the *Georgia Gazette* by the end of November. More fortunate was the *Boston Gazette,* which resumed publication on 4 November and continued thereafter.

The continuation of papers such as the *Boston Gazette* and the support which they gave to the resistance campaign were often tied to the efforts and presence of the Sons of Liberty in the colonies. Benjamin Edes, copublisher of the *Boston Gazette,* was a member of the local chapter, as were William Goddard, publisher of the *Providence Gazette,* and William Bradford, printer of the *Pennsylvania Journal.* The opposition to the Stamp Act by the Sons of Liberty was well known, and they were generally thought to be responsible for those cases in which newspapers were forced to continue publication. For example, John Holt, publisher of the *New York Gazette or Weekly Post Boy,* was informed that "should you at this critical time, shut up the Press, and basely desert us, your House, Person, and Effects, will be in imminent Danger." Holt's paper appeared on 7 November with the banner: "The United Voice of all His Majesty's free and loyal subjects in America— Liberty, Property, and No Stamps." In another case, Andrew Steuart, printer of the *North Carolina Gazette,* tried to suspend his paper's operation by 1 November. On 16 November, the local Sons of Liberty requested that he keep his paper open or face "the Hazard of Life, being maimed, or have his Printing Office destroyed." Not surprisingly, Steuart acceded and continued his paper, but it was later closed down by the North Carolina governor.[150]

Other stratagems were used by the newspapers. Some papers retained their regular titles but appeared anonymously without the editor or printer specified. The *Newport Mercury* appeared this way for two issues before resuming undisguised. Likewise, the *Boston Post Boy,* the *New Hampshire Gazette,* the *Boston Evening Post,* the *Massachusetts Gazette,* and *Boston News-Letter* continued under this guise. Finally, further to the south, the *Pennsylvania Journal,* the *Pennsylvania Gazette,* and the *New York Mercury,* after using captions such as "No Stamped Papers to be had," published in this way, though after a few weeks they restored their regular titles.

Several papers which had suspended publication later reappeared. As early as 25 November, the *New York Gazette* of William Weyman resumed publication without stamps. To the surprise of Maryland's inhabitants, the *Maryland Gazette* reappeared on 10 December. This time the *Gazette*'s readers were informed that the piece was "an apparition of the late *Maryland Gazette* which is not dead, but only sleepth." The issue lasted only for a day; but on 30 January 1766, there appeared the *Maryland Gazette, Reviving;* and finally on 20 February, the *Maryland Gazette Revived.* In Providence, Rhode Island, William Goddard's paper could only muster the wherewithal to reappear once on 12 March 1766, as the *Providence Gazette Extraordinary.*

Finally, two brand new papers started publication. In South Carolina, Peter Timothy had closed his *Gazette* on 31 October. On 17 December 1765, a former apprentice, Charles Crouch, began the *South Carolina Gazette and County Journal.* The new paper was successful enough that as late as three years later, long after the Stamp Act struggle had ended and the *Gazette* had resumed publication,

Timothy complained that he was being discriminated against for the closure of his paper. In Williamsburg, Virginia, Alexander Purdie started his *Virginia Gazette* on 7 March 1766 on unstamped paper. Purdie was suspected of being under the influence of Governor Francis Fauquier. Consequently, another paper, under the editorship of William Rind, lately of the *Maryland Gazette,* began on 16 May 1766.[151]

As the Sons of Liberty and many other colonials evidently realized, the newspaper provided important services to the opposition to the Stamp Act. To the extent that the newspapers remained open, they provided a *prima facie* example of defiance to the Stamp Act. Such action provided clear examples of the possibility of resisting British authority and thus served to encourage resistance in general. Moreover, the newspapers were significant for the communication of resistance activities and news. Such intercolonial communication provided information and facts but also served as a means of reinforcement and support for those opposed to the Stamp Act throughout the colonies. In short, while a few newspapers suspended publication after 1 November in order to avoid the use of stamps, in the opinion of one historian, "most printers ignored the requirement that news sheets be stamped and continued business as usual."[152]

Perhaps because of their organization and political clout or perhaps just by their larger numbers, the colonial mercantile establishment had much success in reopening ports and resuming normal trade relations. Just as all legal documents were supposed to be on stamped paper, so too were all shipping permits. Yet what should one do if stamps were unavailable or if there was no stamp distributor to parcel them out? One answer became quickly apparent. For as early as the first week of November, ships were clearing out of ports in Virginia with unstamped permits. The practice had begun on 2 November, and by the seventh, Governor Fauquier gave his explicit approval, since the tobacco crops were ready for market and there were no stamps to be had. Similar circumstances occurred in Georgia and Rhode Island in the month of November. In Rhode Island, ships cleared out on unstamped paper from the end of the month on, while this practice lasted only into the end of November in Georgia.[153] In these cases where there were neither stamps nor distributors, Customs officials would issue "let passes" to ship captains. A typical certificate would indicate that "no Stampt Papers being distributed in this Province, We are therefore obliged to grant the clearances and Cocquetts on unstampt Paper as formerly." As the surveyor-general in Virginia characterized the situation, ships needed to be cleared, but there were no stamps and "impossibilities will not be expected of us, and from the Nature of the Case our Conduct will stand justified."[154]

More ports opened during December. Portsmouth, New Hampshire, opened early in the month after a temporary closure, while the Connecticut ports of New London and New Haven soon followed suit. The harbor of New York City and the ports of New Jersey resumed trade in the first week of December on unstamped clearances. Before the week was out, the surveyor general of the colonies of New Jersey, Delaware, Pennsylvania, and New York declared that vessels could be cleared on unstamped paper if conditions warranted it. The surveyor general's statement was merely an admission of the conditions his Customs agents faced, for in each of these colonies there were no stamp distributors to hand out the stamps. In Philadelphia, merchants had tried to clear out as many full ships as possible before 1 November. Thereafter, in an interesting variation on usual policy, clearance papers were given to any ships partially loaded by 31 October, and undated additions were allowed for several weeks.[155]

In Boston, there had been pressure to keep the port open all along. As Andrew Oliver had already resigned in August 1765, there was no one officially to distribute the stamps. Nonetheless, merchants and Customs officials both continued to request that Oliver (despite his resignation) adjudicate the situation. Mindful of his 14 August experience, Oliver sent them to the attorney general, Edmund Trowbridge, and to the advocate general of the admiralty court, Robert Auchmuty. This administrative merry-go-round continued into December. By that time, the Boston Sons of Liberty had begun to doubt the sincerity of Oliver's August resignation and asked him to perform another public recantation under the Liberty Tree on 17 December 1765. Oliver appeared on the appointed day and repeated his resignation for the large crowd of Bostonians which had assembled for the occasion. With popular agitation at such a high-pitch and lacking strong administrative support, the Customs officials capitulated, and by 17 December, the Boston port was open.[156]

Several significant developments related to the ports occurred during January and February 1766. In Maryland, the ports of Oxford and Annapolis opened, while in North Carolina, the important port of Wilmington reopened. However, in January there were a few cases of ships clearing from port on stamped papers. Though Governor James Wright of Georgia had originally permitted ships to clear from Savannah on unstamped paper, he stopped this practice at the end of November. In January 1766, George Angus, the Georgia stamp distributor, finally arrived from England, and some sixty ships officially cleared the Georgia port between 17 January and 30 January with the required stamps. The captains of the ships were not subjected to any local pressure. The same evidently was not true for George Angus, for by the end of January, he had left for the Georgian countryside "to avoid the resentment of the people." As for the stamps themselves, they were moved for safe-keeping when the governor learned that six hundred Georgians were proposing to march to Savannah from the outlying districts to prevent any further use of the stamps.[157] By mid-February, the Georgia ports were opening again, this time without stamps.

Actions such as these, however, could not make up for stamps having been used in Georgia. The use of stamped papers to clear ships particularly incensed merchants in North Carolina. As of January 1766, the North Carolina merchants had been faced with a major problem. Royal frigates continued to patrol the waters off Cape Fear, stopping and seizing all ships which lacked properly stamped papers. Any ships which were thus seized, either on the high seas or even in other ports under British jurisdiction (such as in the Caribbean), were liable to prosecution in the admiralty courts. Thus, the North Carolinians were especially angered at Georgia's use of the stamps and at her seeming traitorous defection from the ranks of the resistance campaign. The citizens of Charleston, South Carolina, did more than complain. They inaugurated a boycott of all Georgian goods and trade and refused to send any rice to the southern colony.[158] The South Carolina boycott was backed with the threat of death to any who attempted to break the boycott and supply the Georgians. In March 1766, a schooner laden with rice for Georgia attempted to leave under the cover of darkness, but the master and the owner were stopped by a warning that the penalty for such action would be carried out, and they then discharged their cargo.[159] The South Carolina secondary boycott was not unparalleled. Other such boycotts occurred elsewhere. In January 1766, a ship arrived in Portsmouth, New Hampshire, from the Barbados cleared with stamped paper. The stamped clearances were taken by the local Sons of Liberty, and other ships were advised to stay clear of the West Indian island. Similar incidents occurred in which ships left Caribbean ports with stamped clearances bound for North American harbors. In some cases, as in Boston and Philadelphia, members of the local Sons of Liberty confiscated the stamps and warned against trading with the ship's captain.[160]

Pressure to reopen ports in North and South Carolina reached a peak in February 1766. By 12 February, all North Carolina ports except Wilmington were open. On 18 February, after three more ships had been seized coming out of that harbor, a large group of North Carolinians met and marched to New Brunswick. This group was later to form the Wilmington Association and was responsible for obtaining promises by the governor and Customs officials to give clearances on unstamped paper. Shortly thereafter, Governor Tryon admitted to royal officials in London that: "These Southern Provinces will regulate their Future Obedience and Conduct agreeable to the measures that are adopted by the more Formidable Colonies to the Northward."[161] In South Carolina, shipping had been paralyzed in Charleston, with some two hundred fifty vessels idle in the harbor. Lieutenant-Governor Bull resisted efforts by the merchants to obtain unstamped clearances. Finally in late January, as William Saxby, the resigned stamp distributor, categorically refused to deal with the stamps at all, Bull relented and agreed to furnish unstamped shipping clearances on 4 February 1766.

Thus by the end of February 1766, all ports south of Quebec and Nova Scotia were opened in defiance of the Stamp Act by the officers simply giving unstamped clearances to vessels when the law said that all such clearances must be stamped. Most of the ports had been reopened within two months of the date on which the Stamp Act went into effect. The movement to reopen ports, as that to reopen courts and to resume publication of newspapers, formed an important part of the resistance to the Stamp Act. In conjunction with other aspects of the resistance campaign (the legislative resolves and the intimidation of appointed stamp distributors by destruction of property and even threats of personal injury, which led to their subsequent resignation), the actions of the ports, newspapers and courts as forms of popular noncooperation with British authority achieved what one historian has aptly called the "nullification" of the Stamp Act.[162] "Nullification" was an appropriate word, for while the act was legally binding, the level and extent of colonial noncooperation was so great as to make it seem as if it had never passed.

As if to bear out this observation, various forms of resistance activity continued, even as the lawyers and merchants were working to open the courts and ports. In the first week of January 1766, a shipment of stamps for New York and Connecticut arrived in New York harbor. The ships were boarded in the night and the stamps taken off and burned. In other cases, stamps were landed safely, but once they were delivered, the local citizenry captured and destroyed them. According to the *Boston Gazette,* such destruction of stamps occurred in Milford, Connecticut, and Marblehead, Massachusetts, during January.[163]

Further reports of widely diversified resistance activity continued to appear in the colonial newspapers throughout February and March. For example, the town of Wallingford, Connecticut, assessed a fine of twenty shillings on any inhabitant who "shall introduce, use, or improve any stampt vellums, parchment, or paper for which tax or tribute is or may be demanded." Representatives from the Sons of Liberty from New York, Connecticut, Boston, and Portsmouth, New Hampshire gathered at Portsmouth on 10 February 1766. The meeting, attended by over one thousand persons, expressed "in the strongest Manner, their Affection to and Loyalty for their rightful sovereign George the III" and further called for united action in defense of their liberties and in defiance of the Stamp Act as a proper testimony of that respect for the sovereign.[164]

On 20 February 1766, the Sons of Liberty of Woodbridge, New Jersey, following the suggestion of the New York Sons of Liberty, met to take action against the Stamp Act. The Woodbridge group resolved that, "as we are of the unanimous Opinion of our countrymen, that the Stamp Act is unconstitutional, we will pay no Sort of Regard to it; but are resolved to oppose it to the utmost, with our Lives and Fortunes, if the glorious Cause of Liberty requires it." To that end, a committee of five persons was delegated "to act in conjunction with the several Committees of our neighboring Township . . . that we may be in actual Readiness on any Emergency." The point of such resolutions was "only to communicate our Sentiments for them to improve upon; and [we] shall be ever ready to hear other Proposals that they shall think more conductive to the Public End aimed at, namely, the Union of the Provinces throughout the Continent." Similar meetings of the Sons of Liberty occurred throughout New Jersey. On 11 March 1766, the Sons of Liberty of Piscataway met and resolved "at all events [to] oppose the Operation of that detestible Thing called the Stamp Act in this Colony." Moreover, they agreed "always [to] hold ourselves in Readiness and with the utmost Cheerfulness assist any of the neighboring provinces, in Opposing every Attempt" to infringe upon their rights as Englishmen. On 18 March, the Sons of Liberty of Hunterdon County, West Jersey, and on 3 April 1766, the Sons of Liberty of Freehold, East Jersey, each met and drew up resolutions protesting the Stamp Act and pledging support to any intercolonial efforts to defeat it.[165] Even the animal kingdom conspired to resist the Stamp Act, or at least they were sometimes given the credit. One report from Philadelphia indicated that "a Quantity of the Stamp Paper, on board the Sardoine

Man of War, has been gnawed to pieces by the Rats!"[166]

Resistance activity of still another sort continued as three independent popular associations were formed in Maryland, North Carolina, and Virginia. While each of these three cases was associated with the issue of the use of stamps (opening ports and courts, and the like), their example as autonomous political organizations within each of their colonies was highly significant. On 24 February, several of the "principal gentlemen" of Baltimore gathered at the market-house and organized an association to compel the officers at Annapolis to resume legal business without stamped paper. They notified the officials that the assembly would adjourn until 1 March, at which time they and at least twelve representatives from each of the other counties of Maryland would be present to urge a complete reopening of all official business. On the appointed day, the various representatives and their supporters reconvened at Annapolis, and at their insistence, many offices, particularly the courts, were reopened as usual without stamps.[167]

On 18 February, a mass meeting was held in Wilmington, North Carolina, at which the so-called Wilmington Association was drawn up. After reiterating their allegiance to King George, the subscribers to the Association claimed they were "fully convinced of the oppressive and arbitrary tendency" of the Stamp Act. Accordingly, "preferring death to slavery . . . and with a proper and necessary regard to ourselves and Posterity, [we] hereby mutually and solemnly plight our faith and honor, that we will at any risque whatever, and whenever called upon, unite and truly and faithfully assist each other, to the best of our Power, in preventing entirely the operation of the Stamp Act."

On the following day, the assemblage set out to see the governor. By the time it had reached the home of Governor Tryon, its numbers had increased measurably. Immediately, they informed the governor "that we are fully determined to protect from insult your person and property," and offered a bodyguard as an example of good faith. On 20 February, the Association's representatives obtained a promise from the port authorities that no further inspection and seizures for lack of stamps would occur, at least until the arrival of the surveyor general of the Customs. The next day, however, the Custom officials were pressured by the governor, and the people feared a recantation of the previous agreement. Accordingly, the Customs officials were escorted to town, "where they all made oath, that they would not, directly or indirectly, by themselves, or any other person employed under them, sign or execute in their several respective Offices, any stamped Papers, until the Stamp Act should be accepted by the Province. All the Clerks of the Courts, Lawyers, etc. who were present were sworn to the same effect." As had the newspaper accounts of the Maryland experience, the report of the Wilmington affair noted and applauded the goals and behavior of the resisters, suggesting that there was no "injury offered to any person, but the whole affair conducted with decency & Spirit, worthy of the imitation of all the Sons of Liberty throughout the Continent."[168]

The third episode took place in late February in Westmoreland, Virginia. Archibald Ritchie, a wealthy merchant who had a cargo bound for the West Indies, claimed that he knew where he could obtain stamps and was going to use them. It was in this same Westmoreland in September 1765 that the magistrates of the county court had resigned to wide popular acclamation rather than execute the Stamp Act. Ritchie's declaration was bound to be unpopular. On the evening of 27 February, 115 men, led by Richard Henry Lee, gathered and drew up the Westmoreland Association. Similar to the Wilmington Association, the subscribers to the Westmoreland agreement pledged their faith to King George and their lives to the protection of their rights and the defeat of the Stamp Act. As for "every abandoned wretch who shall be so lost to Virtue and publick good" as to use any stamps, the Association promised to work to convince "all such Profligates, that immediate danger and disgrace shall attend their prostitute Purpose." In the concluding resolutions, the subscribers agreed to inform each other if such a stamp user was discovered, and should any subscriber suffer repercussions for his resistance activity, the Association vowed "at the utmost risk of our lives and Fortunes to restore such Associate to his Liberty, and to protect him in the enjoyment of his Property." The significance of all this activity for Archibald Ritchie was clear. On the following day, the whole Association plus several hundred supporters gathered at Ritchie's house. A delegation visited Ritchie and demanded that he publicly recant his previous statement. Ritchie hesitated, whereupon he was informed that if he refused, he would be stripped to the waist, dragged at the end of a cart to the pillory, and left there for an hour. Ritchie acquiesced and read the statement prepared for him, which in part said: "Sensible now of the high Insult I offered this Country. . . . I do hereby solemnly Promise and Swear on the Holy Evangels, that no Vessel of mine shall Sail Cleared on Stampt Paper, and that I never will on any Pretence make Use of, or cause to be made use Stampt Paper, unless the Use of such Paper shall be authorized by the General Assembly of this Colony." With the retraction secured, the assembly adjourned peacefully, and Ritchie returned home.[169]

In addition to political and legal noncooperation, various forms of economic resistance persisted. As has been noted, sporadic attempts at organized nonconsumption and nonimportation of British goods had occurred against the Sugar Act. These efforts were renewed in the resistance to the Stamp Act with much wider scope and success. Consequently, between 31 October and 8 December 1765, the majority of the mercantile community along the eastern seaboard cities joined in an economic boycott of British goods. The solidarity of the boycott agreements was surprisingly tight. In one instance of an attempted breach of the boycott agreement, merchants in Philadelphia confiscated the proscribed articles and ordered that they be locked up until the repeal of the Stamp Act. In a similar case, the Sons of Liberty of New York took charge of goods shipped from England and returned them at the first opportunity.[170] Boycotts could also be directed at Americans and, as seen in the secondary boycott of Georgia by South Carolina merchants, could be quite effective.

Once an economic boycott was undertaken, its consequences could be double-edged. It could aid and promote the manufacture and use of American products in preference to English goods. Moreover, the boycott of British goods would inevitably hurt the pocketbooks of British merchants as these goods were either given up by Americans or substituted by American products. Both of these consequences occurred, although in different degrees. Several kinds of products began to be produced and purchased in America—scythes, spades, shovels, wallpaper, liquors, cordials, cloth, and clothing. It was in this area of clothing that the most visible activity took place. Homespun American linen, made of native-grown and spun flax, became a symbol of patriotic devotion for American liberty and corresponding opposition to the Stamp Act. According to Arthur M. Schlesinger, more than three hundred persons in New York City were engaged in the manufacture of linen, and the volume of home produced goods was sufficient in that city to warrant a fortnightly market for the sale of New York manufacturers. Likewise, in Philadelphia, a market met three times a week to sell homemade linens, shallons, flannels, ink-powder, and other wares.[171]

Writing under the name "Homespun," Benjamin Franklin applauded the resiliency of American boycott efforts. To the charge that American diets, lacking boycotted English delicacies, were bland, Franklin recounted to his opponent, "Vindex Patriae," a long list of native grown products. Moreover, Franklin continued, Indian corn, no matter how bland, could never be "as disagreeable and indigestible as the Stamp Act." In this vein, Franklin summarized the state of the boycott:

> They resolved to wear no mourning; and it is now totally out of fashion with near two millions of people; and yet nobody sighs for Norwich crapes, or any other of the expensive, flimsey, rotten, black stuffs and cloths you used to send us for that purpose. . . . They resolved last spring to eat no more lamb; and not a joint of lamb has since been seen on any of their tables, throughout a country 1500 miles extent, but the sweet little creatures are all alive to this day with the prettiest fleeces on their backs imaginable.[172]

Whether Franklin realized it or not, his summary aptly captured the dual nature of the American's boycott effort. In one sense, it was an effort directed at economics, hence the eating of lamb was abandoned in order not to interfere with the production of American wool. In another way though, the American effort drew on the sentiments and social habits of the Americans and developed an opposition consciousness or at least a willingness on the part of the people to identify with the resistance to the Stamp Act. Here, as Franklin saw, it was now "out of fashion" to wear the articles that heretofore had been habitual.

Bearing out Franklin's assessment were other examples of American productions and, especially, changes in American habits. For example, on 3 February 1766, a group in New York City promised: "we will not buy or suffer to be bought for our use, any Lamb before the first day of August next; and that we will not buy any Meat from any Butcher that shall expose any Lamb to Sale before the Day aforesaid, and will give all manner of Discountenance to such Butchers for the future." So too on 17 March 1766, the Boston town meeting chose a committee "to procure Subscriptions for not purchasing Lamb the ensuing season."[173] American herbs—sage, sassafras, and balm—were now promoted as more healthy than

British tea. Finally of some significance, if only of restricted scope, young women at Providence and Bristol, Rhode Island, agreed not to admit the addresses of any man who favored the Stamp Act.[174]

Courting and mourning, working and drinking, in short, much of everyday life became an arena for small acts of resistance. Awareness of such actions could hardly go unnoticed. Even Thomas Hutchinson admitted:

> When I first saw the proposals for lessening the consumption of English manufactures, I took them to be mere puffs. The scheme for laying aside mourning succeeded to my surprise, and scarce any body would now dare to wear black for the nearest relative. In this town there is yet no very sensible alteration in other articles, but in the Country in general, there is a visible difference, and the humour for being clothed in homespun spreads every day not so much for economy as to convince the people of England how beneficial the Colonies have been to them.[175]

As Hutchinson recognized though, a clear intention of the boycott agreement was to put pressure on British merchants who in turn would demand the repeal of the Stamp Act. Many colonists had voiced such a hope, none more clearly than Daniel Dulany in his pamphlet, *Considerations on the Propriety of Imposing Taxes in the British Colonies.* Said Dulany: "Let the Manufactures of America be the Symbol of Dignity, the Badge of Virtue, and it will soon break the Fetters of Distress. . . . By a vigorous Application to Manufactures, the Consequence of Oppression in the Colonies to the Inhabitants of Great Britain would strike Home and immediately."[176]

Yet the boycott campaign was a complicated venture and built on several strategic calculations. The consequences for Britain, suggested by Dulany, could be foreseen. Conceivably, the development by Americans of their own manufactured goods might progress to the point where the American economy, or at least its manufacturing sector, would become not only independent from the British economy but eventually even in competition with it. If such direct competition, especially in the fledgling manufacturing sectors, were to occur, then widespread unemployment of British workers could be expected.[177] At the very least, even if American manufacturing remained undeveloped, the longer the boycotts continued, the greater would become the stockpile of unsold British inventories. With no business, British workers would have to be laid off, unemployment would rise, and the nation, as well as the mercantile community, would be severely hurt. In either case, the specter of unemployment and the increased potential for social unrest loomed large. Consequently, in order to relieve this situation and mend the economic ties between Britain and America, the British government would have to repeal the Stamp Act.

These were the hopes and expectations of the Americans for their boycott efforts, and in some quarters, at least, they seemed to come true. For example, as early as August 1765, a merchant in Bristol, England, noted: "The Avenues of Trade are all shut up. . . . We have no remittances, and are at our Witts End for Want of Money to fulfill our Engagements with our tradesmen." Further news reached Parliament that the once flourishing export trade from Great Britain to

America was in a crisis. Merchants and manufacturers from London, Bristol, Liverpool, Halifax, Leeds, Lancaster, and several other towns petitioned Parliament for help, citing economic stagnation and precipitous drops in trade.[178]

The testimony of a handful of British merchants, however, can hardly prove the success of the American effort or demonstrate damage to the British economy. Unfortunately, comprehensive statistical information on the impact of the Americans' boycotts on the British economy has never been assembled. Nonetheless, as is more fully discussed in Chapter Nine, a decline in the size of exports from Britain to the American colonies in 1765–66 is apparent. The situation might indeed have seemed harsh to the British mercantile community, for in February 1766, the American debt to merchants in the trading centers of London, Bristol, Glasgow, Liverpool, and Manchester exceeded £4,450,000. A debt of this size would hardly go unnoticed, and in the opinion of Horace Walpole at least, "the weapon with which the Colonies armed themselves to most advantage, was the refusal of paying debts they owed to our merchants at home, for goods and wares exported to the American provinces."[179]

These forms of economic resistance played an important part in the more general resistance campaign against the Stamp Act. However, the significance of the economic resistance in this particular conflict does not lie primarily in its impact on the development of an independent American economy. Instead, it was important for the political bonds it built between Americans and as a pressure mechanism on British politicians. Participation in the rituals of spinning homegrown flax, subscription with others to a nonimportation agreement, even the ready acknowledgment of those who wore homespun American clothes—and those who did not— were all ways in which political allies were identified, political organizations were developed, and political power was experienced. All of these aspects grew increasingly important as the decade continued and resistance to British authority grew. Of course, the immediate test for this political power came in the contest for repeal in Parliament. This contest was in reality much more complex than merely the subscription by Americans to economic noncooperation. Still, to the Americans their involvement in such activities had been very important.

The colonists were well aware that one possible response to their various forms of resistance might be the implementation of a draconian military action by the British. Such an alternative had been proposed to and often suggested by colonial governors in America. Several objections were raised against the implementation of such a military policy. In October 1765, for example, the *Georgia Gazette,* in the course of arguing against the Stamp Act, had forecast that "to attempt the enforcement of an act on the colonies by military strength would tend to destroy their usefulness to the mother country—Commercial interests must in great measure, if not totally cease—And besides a colony of soldiers is, in effect, no colony at all."[180] Benjamin Franklin, writing under the pseudonym "Pacificus," satirized this same military solution. Citing the need for "an absolute Submission to the Tax" imposed by Parliament, "Pacificus" proposed:

That all the Capitals of the several Provinces should be burnt to the Ground, and that they cut the throats of all the Inhabitants, Men, Women, and Children, and scalp them, to serve as an Example; that all the Shipping should be destroyed, which will effectually prevent Smuggling . . . No Man in his Wits, after such a terrible Military Execution, will refuse to purchase stamped Paper. If any one should hesitate, five or six hundred Lashes in a cold frosty Morning would soon bring him to Reason. If the Massacre should be objected to, as it would too much depopulate the Country, it may be replied, that the Interruption this Method would occasion to Commerce, would cause so many Bankruptcies, such Numbers of Manufacturers and Labourers would be unemployed, that, together with the Felons from our Gaols [jails], we should soon be enabled to transport such Numbers to repeople the Colonies, as to make up for any Deficiency which Example made it Necessary to sacrifice for the Public Good. Great Britain might then reign over a loyal and submissive People, and be morally certain, that no Act of Parliament would ever after be disputed.[181]

The Americans were also well aware of British support for their position. Sometimes the support was dramatic, as in the case of the ship captain from London who had left ten boxes of stamped paper on the English wharves rather than risk the displeasure of the Americans. Other times support took the form of lobbying for repeal by the British mercantile community. The colonists had many diverse connections and avenues of influence, such as colonial agents, personal friends, and transatlantic organizations by which they frequently tried to influence the course of those politics. Thus, it was not surprising to find letters and notices of support from English sympathizers with the American cause reprinted in American newspapers.[182] One such letter, printed in Boston, testified to this support but also recounted, in the author's view, the counterproductiveness of violence, or at least the difficulty such violence posed for those British who wished to support the colonials and to work for repeal.

In general [the writer related], our opposition to the Stamp Act has been highly approved in England—except the acts of violence—the destruction and plunder of private property, which though generally disapproved among us, and executed by men not all concerned in our Cause, who taking occasion from the tumults which oppression naturally produces, to perpetuate their evil designs without discovery, furnish the enemies of the colonies with arguments which they are glad to improve against them.[183]

Similar sentiments regarding the disadvantages of violence were expressed by the townspeople of Plymouth, Massachusetts. In a letter read before the Boston town meeting of 10 March 1766, the town of Plymouth complimented Boston "for the invariable attachment you have on all Occasions and particularly the present shown to the Principles of Liberty." The Bostonians were to be applauded for their "Loyal and Legal Endeavours to secure to our Country the uninterrupted Enjoyment" of that liberty. This example, the letter concluded, "we think sufficient to destroy all those injurious reflections the work of some Peoples Imaginations; and from which they affect to draw Consequences not only disadvantageous to you, but to the whole Country."[184]

Interestingly though, not all destruction of property nor intimidation of persons was committed by those opposed to the Stamp Act. In at least one case in Georgia, several of the Sons of Liberty were collared one evening in January 1766 by a member of a pro-stamp faction and were beaten for their resistance views. According to the newspaper, the Stamp Act supporters did not intend for there to be any assaults. Apparently, it was sometimes as easy for the activities of pro-stamp persons to get out of hand as had occurred in anti-Stamp Act protests and demonstrations.[185]

• REPEAL OF THE STAMP ACT •

On New Year's Day, 1766, John Adams had mused that "we are now upon the beginning of a year of greater expectation than any that has passed before it. . . . The eyes of all America are fixed on the British Parliament."[186] Throughout the first three months of 1766, Parliament, as if to return the gaze, did indeed focus its attention on the state of affairs of the colonies. In July 1765, George Grenville's ministry had been replaced by that of the Marquis of Rockingham, who was thought to be more sympathetic to colonial complaints. On 14 January 1766, Parliament reconvened after a long summer recess. George Grenville and William Pitt, neither of whom were officially attached to the Rockingham ministry, yet both of whom were intimately interested in the American question, squared off. Grenville characterized the American situation as being an open rebellion on the brink of revolution. "They are now grown to disturbances, to tumults and riots," said Grenville of the situation in America; "they border on open rebellion; and . . . I fear they will lose that name to take that of revolution." Some days later, in reply to criticism of his position, Grenville called for "firm and temperate measures to prevent this scene of blood which indecision and uncertainty will produce. . . . Let those who encourage America [in its resistance] and have raised and increased this condition by such encouragement extricate us out of it and God grant they may meet with success."

Grenville's great protaganist in these debates was William Pitt. Pitt applauded the resistance of the Americans and thoroughly chastised the ministry for its imposition of the Stamp Act in the first place. "I have been charged with giving birth to sedition in America," Pitt noted: "They have spoken their sentiments with freedom, against this unhappy act, and that freedom has become their crime. . . . The gentleman tells us, America . . . is almost in open rebellion. I rejoice that America has resisted. Three millions of people, so dead to all the feelings of liberty, as voluntarily to submit to be slaves, would have been fit instruments to make slaves of the rest." In his famous peroration, Pitt asked

to tell the House what is really my opinion. It is, that the Stamp Act be repealed absolutely, totally, and immediately. That the reason for the repeal be assigned, because it was founded on an erroneous principle. At the same time, let the sovereign authority of the country over the colonies, be asserted in as strong terms as can be devised, and be made to extend to every point of legislation whatsoever, that we may bind their trade, contain their manufactures, and exercise every power whatsoever, except that of taking their money out of their pockets without their consent.[187]

Other information was presented to Parliament. Benjamin Franklin appeared before the House of Commons on 12–13 February, and testified on behalf of the American's cause (see Appendix A). Reiterating the arguments of internal versus external taxation and the nonrepresentation of the colonies in Parliament, Franklin effectively parried many of the points which Grenville and the other critics of America's resistance had raised. To the question of whether anything less than military force could carry out the Stamp Act, Franklin replied in the negative. "I do not see how military force can be applied to that purpose," Franklin stated. "Suppose a military force sent into America, they will find nobody in arms; what are they then to do? They cannot force a man to take stamps who chuses to do without them. They will not find a rebellion, they may indeed make one." In his concluding statement, Franklin took note of the support for mercantile boycotts in America and predicted increased economic hardship for Britain as a result. Respect and esteem too had been lost, that "affection" which America held for Great Britain. Both economic equilibrium and political difference could be regained, Franklin suggested, but not before repeal and not if it ever cost the Americans their political liberty.[188]

George Mercer, former stamp distributor of Virginia, also appeared and spoke tellingly of the Americans' resistance and the difficulties of enforcement. These very difficulties pointed up to Parliament the financial catastrophe which the Stamp Act represented. The total receipts from the sale of stamps, even including the areas of greatest cooperation such as Grenada, the West Indies, Nova Scotia, and Quebec, was £3,292. This stunted amount gives effective testimony to the success of the various efforts at nullification and resistance which the colonists had carried on. Parliament, however, was more aware that it had already spent £6,837 just for the initial expenses of the act, such as printing the stamps. As for those printed stamps, if the stamp distributors had been obliged to pay for the amount of stamps consigned to them, their debt would have been £64,115. Whether Parliament checked their expected revenues of £60,000 or their initial outlay of £6,837 against the revenues in hand, they had lost badly. More bad news was coming though. According to the British merchant community, which by this time was actively working for repeal, the previous trade with the colonies amounted to £2,000,000. Now in 1766, the Americans owed British merchants approximately £4,450,000. Bankruptcy and economic distress were already a reality and growing every day.[189]

All this testimony produced its desired effect, and on 4 March 1766, a repeal bill passed the House of Commons. Little noticed at the time, the bill out of the Commons also included a Declaratory Act, which asserted that Parliament had full authority to make laws binding the American colonists "in all cases whatsoever." The House of Lords was quick to follow suit, and on 18 March 1766, the repeal bill received the royal assent and became law.

The news of repeal produced joyful celebrations in Britain. The manufacturing and trading towns that had seen their trade to America dry up so completely now rejoiced at the prospect of renewed trade. Cartoons appeared in the British papers satirizing the Grenville ministry and applauding the repeal, while Rockingham, Pitt, and others instrumental in the repeal received accolades and praise for their actions. In London itself, fifty coaches of merchants who traded with North America went in solemn procession to the Houses of Parliament at Westminster to pay their respects to His Majesty and express their pleasure at the repeal. Throughout much of the city church bells rang, and at night houses were illuminated to commemorate the repeal.[190]

Word of the repeal reached America soon thereafter. On 31 March 1766, Henry Conway dispatched a circular letter to the colonial governors in America informing them of Parliament's action.[191] News of the repeal actually reached Boston on 16 May and Philadelphia three days later. Popular celebrations took place up and down the coast as the news spread. In Boston, the Liberty Tree was bedecked with 108 lanterns under the direction of the still powerful Ebenezer MacIntosh. In Philadelphia, a large crowd gathered and saluted King George with toasts. The citizens of Annapolis, Maryland, celebrated twice: when they first learned of the repeal, they gathered for the drinking of "all patriotic toasts," and in June, when official notification had been received, they had a city commemoration, directed by the mayor. In Virginia, news of the repeal first reached Williamsburg on 2 May. A ball and general illumination to celebrate the repeal was held here on 13 June. News of the repeal reached Charleston, South Carolina, on 6 May. That night bonfires, ringing bells, and orderly parades heralded the event. During the next week, the South Carolina Assembly commissioned the portraits of its delegates to the Stamp Act Congress and voted to have a statue of William Pitt made and sent to Charleston from England. Interestingly, one member moved to have the statue constructed of King George, rather than of Pitt; however, the motion died for lack of a second.[192]

Not all Americans were so overjoyed with the repeal as to keep from offering a few critical remarks. Christopher Gadsden, for example, appreciated the significance of the Declaratory Act and warned against too complete a trust in Parliament's beneficence. A writer in the *Virginia Gazette* likewise suggested that the British merchants' part in the repeal campaign indicated only self-interest on their part and neither support for, nor real understanding of, the American position. "The Relief they have given," he said, "is professedly for their own Sakes, not ours." Another writer in the same issue of the paper gave the honor of victory to the Americans and their resistance, for "had we tamely submitted, would the Justice of our Cause have procured us Relief?"[193]

Many colonists had evidently agreed that tame submission was not the answer to the Stamp Act. A remarkable degree of solidarity and intercolonial cooperation, surprising all the more for the very tenuousness of previous intercolonial ventures and the improvised nature of efforts such as the Stamp Act Congress, had been achieved. So too, a willingness to undergo the rigors of participation in various forms of resistance activity—demonstrations, boycotts, nonconsumption agreements—had been seen. As they viewed the months before March 1765 and March 1766, colonial governors gave widely different pictures of their experiences. Governor Bernard in Boston informed the Lords of Trade: "Popular violences indeed have ceased together with the apprehension of them, but the Spirit of weakening the Power of Government, already reduced to a great impotence by all legal methods and bringing it still nearer and nearer to the level of the common people continues in as much force as ever." James Wright, governor of Georgia, on the other hand, congratulated the members of the legislature for: "having no Injuries or Damages either of a publick or private Nature (with respect to property) to compensate . . . no Votes or Resolutions injurious to the Honor of his Majesty's Government or tendency to destroy the Legal and Constitutional Dependency of the Colonies on the Imperial Crown and Parliament of Great Britain to reconsider."[194]

Whatever the differences in resistance activity between Massachusetts and Georgia, they had seen in common, as had all the other colonies, an unprecedented display of popular political power. The meaning of such an experience was not lost on at least one observer. Thomas Hutchinson concluded of the resistance to the Stamp Act: "An experiment had been made, which persuaded them, that, by union and firmness, the colonies would be able to carry every point they wished for. Power, once acquired, is seldom voluntarily parted with."[195] Resistance to the Stamp Act had indeed been an experiment. To the colonists' delight, with the repeal secured, the experiment had been successful. Yet with the inclusion of the Declaratory Act by Parliament, grounds for future conflict and, thereby, further experimentation in what Hutchinson had called "union and firmness" seemed apparent.

· NOTES ·

1. Instructions to Royal Tylor, James Otis, Thomas Cushing, and Oxenbridge Thacher, *A Report of the Record Commissioners of the City of Boston containing The Boston Town Records, 1758 to 1769* (Boston: Rockwell & Churchill, 1886), pp. 119–22.

2. *Journals of the House of Representatives of Massachusetts, 1764–1765* (reprinted., Boston: Massachusetts Historical Society, 1971), vol. 41, pp. 72–77 (hereafter cited as *Mass. House Journals*).

3. "Proceedings of the General Assembly," 30 July 1764, in John Russell Bartlett, ed., *Records of the Colony of Rhode Island and Providence Plantations in New England,* (Providence: A. C. Greene, 1856), vol. 6, p. 403.

4. See the account of the receipt of this resolution on 18 October 1764, by the Pennsylvania Assembly in Charles H. Lincoln, "The Revolutionary Movement in Pennsylvania," in *Publications of the University of Pennsylvania,* Series in History 1 (Philadelphia: Univ. of Pennsylvania Press, 1901), p. 128.

5. *Journals of the Votes and Proceedings of the General Assembly of the Colony of New York* (New York: J. Buel, 1851), vol. 2, pp. 776–79.

6. William L. Saunders, ed., *Colonial and State Records of North Carolina* (10 vols.,

Raleigh: Trustees of the Public Libraries, 1886), vol. 6, p. 1261.

7. See the 18 September instructions of the Pennsylvania Assembly to agent Richard Jackson to protest the Sugar Act and the further identical instructions the following month, in Lincoln, "The Revolutionary Movement in Pennsylvania," pp. 127–28. For the 14 November 1764 resolution of the House of Burgesses, see John P. Kennedy, ed., *Journals of the House of Burgesses of Virginia, 1761–1765* (Richmond: The Colonial Press, 1907), pp. liv, 254–56.

8. Charles J. Hoadly, ed., *The Public Records of the Colony of Connecticut* (Hartford: Lockwood & Brainard, 1850), vol. 12, p. 256.

9. Thomas Fitch, *Reasons Why the British Colonies in America, Should Not Be Charged with Internal Taxes, by Authority of Parliament* (New Haven: Meacom, 1764), p. 14.

10. *Ibid.*, p. 19.

11. James Otis, *The Rights of the British Colonies Asserted and Proved* (Boston: Edes & Gill, 1764), pp. 35, 37.

12. *Ibid.*, p. 42.

13. Stephen Hopkins, *The Rights of the Colonies Examined* (Providence: W. Goddard, 1764), pp. 15, 16.

14. *Newport Mercury,* 20 August 1764.

15. *Ibid.*

16. *Boston Post Boy and Advertiser,* 1 October; 8 October 1764.

17. *Boston Newsletter,* 6 September 1764.

18. *Ibid.*, 5 July 1764.

19. *New York Gazette and Post Boy,* 22 November 1764.

20. *Boston Gazette,* 31 December 1764.

21. Bartlett, *Records of Rhode Island,* vol. 6, pp. 428–30.

22. See, for example, William Nelson ed., *Archives of New Jersey* (Paterson: Call Publishing Co., 1903), vol. 9, p. 448.

23. Jared Ingersoll to Governor Thomas Fitch, "Fitch Papers," Connecticut Historical Society, *Collections* 18 (1920), pp. 317–26.

24. *Ibid.*, pp. 322–24.

25. See the text of the resolutions in Kennedy, *Journals of the House of Burgesses, 1761–1765,* pp. lxiv–lxv.

26. See the firsthand account of Henry's speech by an anonymous traveler in, "Journal of a French Traveller in the Colonies, 1765," *American Historical Review* 26 (1921), pp. 726–47.

27. Henry Fauquier to the Board of Trade, 5 June 1765, Kennedy, *Journals of the House of Burgesses, 1761–1765,* pp. lxvii–lxviii.

28. *Newport Mercury,* 24 June 1765.

29. Thomas Hutchinson to ———, 9 April 1765, "Hutchinson Correspondence," Massachusetts Historical Society, vol. 26, p. 135.

30. Hutchinson to Richard Jackson, 5 June 1765, *ibid.,* p. 140.

31. Francis Bernard to Thomas Pownall, 5 June 1765, "Bernard Papers," The Houghton Library, Harvard Univ., vol. 4, p. 5. For Bernard's assessment of the Virginia Resolves, see Bernard to Thomas Pownall, 20 July 1765, *ibid.,* pp. 7–9.

32. See the discussion of the Loyal Nine in Edmund and Helen Morgan, *The Stamp Act Crisis* (Chapel Hill: Univ. of North Carolina Press, 1953), pp. 121–22.

33. This account is drawn from Thomas Hutchinson to ———, 16 August 1765,

"Hutchinson Correspondence," vol. 26, pp. 145a–145b; *Boston Gazette,* 19 August 1765; *Boston Evening Post,* 19 August 1765. Both of these Boston newspaper accounts were reprinted in the *Newport Mercury,* 26 August 1765.

34. *Boston Evening Post,* 19 August 1765.

35. Thomas Hutchinson to ———, 16 August 1765, "Hutchinson Correspondence," vol. 26, pp. 145a–145b.

36. *Boston Gazette,* 19 August 1765; Bernard to John Pownall, 18 August 1765, "Bernard Papers," vol. 4, p. 12; Hutchinson to ———, 16 August 1765, "Hutchinson Correspondence," vol. 26, pp. 145a–145b.

37. *Boston Gazette,* 2 September 1765.

38. *Boston Town Records, 1758 to 1769,* p. 152.

39. *Boston Gazette,* 9 September 1765.

40. Hutchinson to Thomas Pownall, 31 August 1765, "Hutchinson Correspondence," vol. 26, p. 149; Hutchinson to Richard Jackson, 30 August 1765, *ibid.,* pp. 146–47.

41. Bernard to John Pownall, 18 August 1765, "Bernard Papers," vol. 4, p. 13.

42. Bernard to Earl of Halifax, 22 August 1765, *ibid.,* pp. 144–48.

43. Bernard to Richard Jackson, 23 August 1765, *ibid.,* p. 19.

44. *Newport Mercury,* 19 August 1765.

45. *Mass. House Journals,* vol. 42, pp. 108–11.

46. *Newport Mercury,* 2 September 1765.

47. *Ibid.*

48. *Ibid.*

49. On Ingersoll, see Morgan and Morgan, *The Stamp Act Crisis,* pp. 231–35; on the demonstrations, *Newport Mercury,* 2 September 1765.

50. E. B. O'Callaghan, ed., *Documents Relative to the Colonial History of the State of New York* (Albany: Weed, Parsons, & Co., 1855), vol. 7, p. 761.

51. For an account of these episodes, see Thomas Scharf, *History of Maryland* (reprint ed., Hatboro, Penn.: Tradition Press, 1969), vol. 1, pp. 525–26.

52. Bartlett, *Records of Rhode Island,* vol. 6, pp. 451–52.

53. *Newport Mercury,* 11 November 1765.

54. *Boston Gazette,* 14 October 1765; 21 October 1765.

55. Alan Bradford, ed., *Speeches of the Governor of Massachusetts, 1765–1775; and the Answers of the House of Representatives to the Same* (Boston: Russell & Gardiner, 1818), p. 49.

56. Bernard to Earl of Halifax, 21 August 1765, "Bernard Papers," vol. 4, p. 155.

57. *Boston Gazette,* 9 September 1765; 30 September 1765.

58. Samuel Wharton to Benjamin Franklin, 13 October 1765, Leonard W. Labaree, ed., *The Papers of Benjamin Franklin* (New Haven: Yale Univ. Press, 1968), vol. 12, pp. 315–16.

59. Charles Hoban, ed., *Pennsylvania Archives* 8th ser. (Philadelphia: T. Fenn, 1935), vol. 7, pp. 5767–68, 5779–80.

60. Nelson, *Archives of New Jersey,* vol. 24, p. 600.

61. *Ibid.,* vol. 25, pp. 6–10.

62. *Ibid.,* vol. 24, pp. 616–18.

63. *Ibid.,* pp. 619–20.

64. *Ibid.,* pp. 632–38.

65. *Ibid.,* pp. 639–40.

66. William Franklin to Lords of Trade, 18 December 1765, *ibid.,* vol. 9, pp. 524–

25.

67. William Franklin to Secretary Henry Conway, 23 September 1765, *ibid.*, pp. 492–93.

68. Charles Carroll to Edmund Jennings, September 1765, quoted in Paul Giddens, "Maryland and the Stamp Act Controversy," *Maryland Historical Magazine* 27 (1932), p. 84.

69. *Maryland Gazette,* 26 September 1765.

70. Governor Horatio Sharpe to Lord Halifax, 5 September 1765; Sharpe to Lord Baltimore, 10 September 1765, in William H. Browne, ed., *Correspondence of Governor Horatio Sharpe, in Archives of Maryland* (Baltimore: Maryland Historical Society, 1883), vol. 3, pp. 221–24.

71. Sharpe to Lord Calvert, 10 September 1765, *ibid.*, pp. 224–27.

72. Sharpe to General Gage, *ibid.*, pp. 228–29.

73. John C. Matthews, "Two Men on the Tax," in Darrett Rutman, ed., *The Old Dominion: Essays for Thomas Abernathy* (Charlottesville: Univ. Press of Virginia, 1964), pp. 100–101.

74. The notice appeared in the *Pennsylvania Gazette,* 31 October 1765, and is reprinted in Robert Scribner, ed., *Revolutionary Virginia: A Documentary History* (Charlottesville: Univ. Press of Virginia, 1973), vol. 1, p. 19.

75. H. S. Conway to Sharpe, Browne, *Correspondence of Sharpe,* vol. 3, pp. 234–35.

76. Saunders, *Records of North Carolina,* vol. 3, p. 123.

77. *Ibid.,* vol. 7, p. 124.

78. Edward McCrady, *The History of South Carolina under the Royal Government, 1719–1776* (London: MacMillian, 1899), pp. 565–66.

79. *Ibid.,* pp. 568–72.

80. William Bull to Lords of Trade, 3 November 1765, Merrill Jensen, ed., *English Historical Documents* (London: Eyre & Spottiswarde, 1953), pp. 680–82; A. S. Salley, ed., *Journal of the Commons House of Assembly of South Carolina, January 8, 1765–August 9, 1765* (Columbia: Historical Commission of South Carolina, 1949), p. 151.

81. James Wright to Henry Conway, 31 January 1766, quoted in Charles Jones, *The History of Georgia* (Boston: Houghton, Mifflin, 1883), vol. 2, p. 61.

82. Bradford, *Speeches of the Governor . . . Answers of the House of Representatives,* pp. 43–48.

83. *Ibid.,* pp. 50–51.

84. Hoadly, *Records of Connecticut,* vol. 12, 421–25.

85. *Newport Mercury,* 14 October 1765.

86. William Franklin to James Hawker, 9 November 1765, Nelson, *Archives of New Jersey,* vol. 9, p. 519.

87. *Newport Mercury,* 4 November 1765.

88. Supplement to *Boston Gazette,* 21 October 1765.

89. *Pennsylvania Gazette,* 10 October 1765.

90. *Boston Gazette,* 30 December 1765.

91. For the governor's oath, see "The Letters and Papers of Cadwallader Colden," New York Historical Society, *Collections* 7 (1923), p. 64; for David Colden's request, see David Colden to commissioners of the Stamp Office, "The Colden Letter Books," New York Historical Society, *Collections,* 2 (1877), pp. 50–52.

92. *Newport Mercury,* 18 November 1765.

93. 24 October Supplement to *Maryland Gazette,* 10 October 1765.

94. Daniel Dulany, *Considerations of the Propriety of Imposing Taxes in the British Colonies, for the Purpose of Raising a Revenue, by Act of Parliament* (North America [Boston]: n. p., 1766), p. 40. Italics added.

95. Colden to H. S. Conway, 23 September 1765, O'Callaghan, *Documents Relative to New York,* vol. 7, pp. 759–60.

96. This account of the Stamp Act Congress draws on LeRoy Joseph Bennish, "The Stamp Act Congress" (Ph.D. diss., Duke Univ., 1967).

97. Nelson, *Archives of New Jersey,* vol. 24, pp. 669–70.

98. *Newport Mercury,* 4 November 1765.

99. Charles Thomson to Messers. Welsh, Wilkinson, & Co., "Charles Thomson Papers," New York Historical Society, *Collections* 11 (1878), p. 12.

100. *Newport Mercury,* 18 November 1765.

101. Bernard to John Pownall, 1 November 1765, "Bernard Papers," vol. 5, pp. 16–21.

102. *Boston Gazette,* 4 November 1765.

103. See Bernard's account of the 5 November activities, Bernard to John Pownall, 26 November 1765, "Bernard Papers," vol. 5, pp. 43–46.

104. This account of the activities in New York draws on Colden to H. S. Conway, 23 September 1765, O'Callaghan, *Documents Relative to New York,* vol. 7, p. 260; Colden to H. S. Conway, 5 November 1765, *ibid.,* pp. 771–72; and the manuscript account quoted by Henry Dawson, *The Sons of Liberty in New York* (Poughkeepsie: Platt & Schram, 1859), pp. 93–97.

105. Robert Livingston to General Monckton, 8 November 1765, Massachusetts Historical Society, *Collections,* 4th ser., 10 (1872), p. 560.

106. The minutes of the corporation and the responses by Colden are quoted in Dawson, *Sons of Liberty in New York,* pp. 102–3.

107. Colden to Conway, 9 November 1765, O'Callaghan, *Documents Relative to New York,* vol. 7, pp. 773–74.

108. "To the Freeholders and Inhabitants of the City of New York," in "C. Colden Papers," New York Historical Society, *Collections* 7 (1923), p. 91.

109. James Otis to W. S. Johnson, 12 November 1765, quoted in E. Edward Beardsley, *Life and Times of William Samuel Johnson* (New York: Hurd and Houghton, 1876), p. 33.

110. Gage to Colden, 5 November 1765, "C. Colden Papers," New York Historical Society, *Collections* 7 (1923), p. 70.

111. *New York Gazette and Post Boy,* 31 October 1765; 7 November 1765.

112. For descriptions of the agreement by Maryland merchants, see Ronald Hoffman, *The Spirit of Dissension* (Baltimore: Johns Hopkins Univ., 1973), p. 37. Charles Thomson is quoted in Thomson to Messers. Welsh, Wilkins, & Co., 7 November 1765, "Thomson Papers," New York Historical Society, *Collections* 11 (1878), pp. 5–6.

113. Thomas Wharton to Franklin, 7 November 1765, Labaree, *Papers of Benjamin Franklin,* vol. 12, pp. 357–58.

114. Saunders; *Records of North Carolina,* vol. 7, p. 124.

115. *Ibid.,* pp. 127–29.

116. *Newport Mercury,* 20 January 1766.

117. *Georgia Gazette,* 3 October 1765; 7 November 1765.

118. Charles Steuart to commissioners of Customs, 8 December 1765, quoted in

Mary Alice Hanna, "Trade of the Delaware District Before the Revolution," *Smith College Studies in History,* vol. 2, no. 4 (July 1917), pp. 296–97; collector and comptroller of Customs to commissioners of Customs, 1 December 1765, quoted in *ibid.,* pp. 295–96.

119. Samuel Ward to commissioners of the treasury, Bartlett, *Records of Rhode Island,* vol. 6, pp. 478–79.

120. Bernard to G. Cooper, 22 December 1765, "Bernard Papers," vol. 5, pp. 63–64.

121. *Boston Gazette,* 13 January 1766.

122. See the text of the resolutions and mention of similar adoptions in Salem and Marblehead, *Boston Gazette,* 16 December 1765.

123. Speaking of the effects of crowd action, Bernard wrote John Pownall: "I shall now proceed to show what effect these Assemblies have had to establish a formal Democracy in this town" (Bernard to John Pownall, 26 November 1765, "Bernard Papers," vol. 5, p. 43).

124. See the analysis of the growth of assembly power in the southern colonies in Jack P. Greene, *The Quest for Power: The Lower Houses of Assembly in the Southern Royal Colonies, 1689–1776* (Chapel Hill: Univ. of North Carolina Press, 1963).

125. *Newport Mercury,* 2 September 1765.

126. Gage to Conway, 23 September 1765, Clarence Edwin Carter, ed., *The Correspondence of General Thomas Gage with the War Office and the Treasury, 1763–1775* (2 vols., New Haven: Yale Univ. Press, 1931–33), vol. 1, p. 67.

127. Bernard to Lord Colville, 11 December 1765, "Bernard Papers," vol. 4, pp. 85–86.

128. For the New Jersey activities, see Nelson, *Archives of New Jersey,* vol. 24, pp. 639–40; for Virginia, see Scribner, *Revolutionary Virginia,* vol. 1, p. 19.

129. Washington to Francis Dandridge, 20 September 1765, John C. Fitzpatrick, ed., *The Writings of George Washington* (Washington D. C.: U. S. Government Printing Office, 1932), vol. 2, pp. 425–27.

130. Thomson to Messers. Cook, Lawrence, & Co., 9 November 1765, "Thomson Papers," New York Historical Society, *Collections* 11 (1878), pp. 7–8.

131. Nelson, *Archives of New Jersey,* vol. 25, p. 31.

132. Jeremy Belknap, *The History of New Hampshire* (Dover: Mann & Remick Inc., 1812), p. 253; McCrady, *History of South Carolina,* pp. 573–75; Allen Candler, ed., *Colonial Records of Georgia* (Atlanta: Franklin-Turner Co., 1908), vol. 9, p. 443; Governor Tryon to Henry Conway, 26 December 1765, Saunders, *Records of North Carolina,* vol. 7, p. 144.

133. William Franklin to Benjamin Franklin, 13 November 1765, Labaree, *Papers of Benjamin Franklin,* vol. 12, p. 369.

134. *Mass. House Journals,* vol. 42, pp. 124–26; John Drayton, ed., *Memoirs of the American Revolution Relating to the State of South Carolina* (Charleston: A. E. Miller, 1821), vol. 1, p. 38.

135. Charles Carroll to Daniel Barrington, 22 December 1765, Thomas M. Fields, ed., *Unpublished Letters of Charles Carroll of Carrollton* (New York: United States Catholic Historical Society, 1902), p. 104.

136. Browne, *Correspondence of Sharpe,* vol. 3, p. 253–54.

137. Theodore Thayer, *Pennsylvania Politics and the Growth of Democracy* (Harrisburg: Pennsylvania Historical and Museum Commission, 1953), p. 124; *Boston Gazette,* 30 December 1765.

138. *Boston Town Records,* 1758–1769, vol. 16, pp. 159–61.

139. *Mass. House Journals,* vol. 42, p. 124.

140. *Boston Gazette,* 6 January 1766.

141. *Pennsylvania Gazette,* 13 February 1766; "Superior Court Records of New Hampshire," New Hampshire Historical Society, quoted in Morgan and Morgan, *The Stamp Act Crisis,* p. 178.

142. David J. Mays, *Edmund Pendleton* (Cambridge, Mass.: Harvard Univ. Press, 1952), vol. 1, p. 170; "Records of the Northampton County Court," in Scribner, *Revolutionary Virginia* vol. 1, pp. 20–21.

143. Nelson, *Archives of New Jersey,* vol. 9, pp. 506–8, n. 1; *ibid.,* vol. 25, p. 40.

144. Christopher Gadsden to William S. Johnson, 16 April 1766, Richard Walsh, ed., *The Writings of Christopher Gadsden* (Colombia: Univ. of South Carolina Press, 1966), pp. 69–71; McCrady, *History of South Carolina,* pp. 574–76.

145. *New York Gazette,* 24 March 1766; Scharf, *History of Maryland,* vol. 1, p. 550.

146. Franklin to David Hall, 14 February 1765, Labaree, *Papers of Benjamin Franklin,* vol. 12, pp. 65–67.

147. *Maryland Gazette,* 10 October 1765.

148. See the account in Arthur M. Schlesinger, *Prelude to Independence: The Newspaper War on Britain, 1764–1776,* (reprinted., New York: Vintage, 1965), pp. 69–79.

149. *South Carolina Gazette,* 31 October 1765.

150. Schlesinger, *Prelude to Independence,* pp. 77–79.

151. *Ibid.*

152. Morgan and Morgan, *The Stamp Act Crisis,* p. 188.

153. Lawrence Henry Gipson, *The British Empire Before the American Revolution,* vol. 10, *The Triumphant Empire: Thunder Clouds Gather in the West, 1763–1766* (New York: Knopf, 1961), pp. 340–41.

154. The certificate is quoted from Alfred Martin, "The King's Customs: Philadelphia 1765–1774," *William and Mary Quarterly* 3d ser., 5 (1948), p. 305; Peter Randolph, surveyor general, to collector of Customs at Norfolk, 2 November 1765, *Pennsylvania Magazine of History* 2 (1878), pp. 298–99.

155. *Boston Gazette,* 16 December 1765; *Connecticut Courant,* 10 February 1766.

156. Bernard to H. S. Conway, 19 December 1765, "Bernard Papers," vol. 4, pp. 180–82; *Boston Gazette,* 23 December 1765; Morgan and Morgan, *The Stamp Act Crisis,* pp. 135–36.

157. Governor Wright to Henry Conway, 31 January 1766, quoted in Jones, *History of Georgia,* vol. 2, pp. 62–63.

158. Saunders, *Records of North Carolina,* vol. 7, p. 159; *Virginia Gazette,* 4 April 1766.

159. Arthur M. Schlesinger, *The Colonial Merchants and the American Revolution, 1763–1775* (New York: Atheneum, 1968), p. 82.

160. *Boston Gazette,* 6 January 1766, 30 December 1765, 3 March 1766.

161. William Tryon to Lords Commissioners of the Treasury, 5 April 1766, Saunders, *Records of North Carolina,* vol. 7, pp. 195–96.

162. Gipson, *British Empire,* vol. 10, *The Triumphant Empire: Thunder Clouds Gather in the West, 1763–1766,* Chapter Fifteen.

163. Governor Henry Moore to Henry Conway, 16 January 1766, O'Callaghan, *Documents Relative to New York,* vol. 7, pp. 805–6; General Gage to H. S. Conway, 16 January 1766, Carter, *Correspondence of Gage,* vol. 1, p. 81; *Boston Gazette,* 10 February 1766.

164. The account of the Wallingford fine is in the *Newport Mercury,* 10 February 1766; the Portsmouth meeting is in *Boston Gazette,* 17 February 1766.

165. Nelson, *Archives of New Jersey,* vol. 25; pp. 42–43, 63–65, 71–73.

166. *Boston Gazette,* 17 February 1766.

167. Scharf, *History of Maryland,* vol. 1, p. 550; Charles Barker, *The Background of the Revolution in Maryland* (New Haven: Yale Univ. Press, 1940), pp. 310–11.

168. Saunders, *Records of North Carolina,* vol. 7, pp. 168c–168e.

169. Kennedy, *Journals of the House of Burgesses, 1761–1765,* pp. lxxii–lxxiv; *Maryland Gazette,* 27 March 1766.

170. Schlesinger, *Colonial Merchants,* p. 81.

171. *Ibid.,* p. 77.

172. Labaree, *Papers of Benjamin Franklin,* vol. 13, pp. 7–8.

173. *Boston Gazette,* 17 February 1766; 17 March 1766.

174. Schlesinger, *Colonial Merchants,* p. 77.

175. Thomas Hutchinson to Thomas Pownall, 8 March 1766, "Hutchinson Correspondence," vol. 26, pp. 200–206.

176. Dulany, *Considerations,* pp. 39–40.

177. See the full discussion of this point in Chapter Three of this volume.

178. Quoted from Lawrence Henry Gipson, *The Coming of the Revolution, 1763–1775* (New York: Harper, 1962), p. 106.

179. The quote by Walpole and the figure of American indebtedness is quoted from Gipson, *ibid.,* pp. 106–7.

180. *Georgia Gazette,* 10 October 1765.

181. Labaree, *Papers of Benjamin Franklin,* vol. 13, pp. 54–58.

182. *Boston Gazette,* 6 January 1766; 12–19 May 1766. Also see Chapters Three and Eleven of this volume.

183. *Boston Gazette,* 3 March 1766.

184. *Boston Town Records,* 1758–1769, vol. 16, p. 168–70.

185. *Boston Gazette,* 10 February 1766.

186. John Adams, "Diary," Charles Francis Adams, ed., *The Works of John Adams* (10 vols., Boston: Little, Brown, 1850–56), vol. 2, p. 170.

187. Quoted from Gipson, *British Empire,* vol. 10, *The Triumphant Empire: Thunder Clouds Gather in the West, 1763–1766,* pp. 378–79, 392. For an analysis of these debates, see Chapter Three of this volume.

188. See the full text of Franklin's testimony in Appendix A.

189. The figures on stamp costs and revenues are quoted from Gipson, *British Empire,* vol. 10, *The Triumphant Empire: Thunder Clouds Gather in the West, 1763–1766,* pp. 328, 381.

190. See, for example, the cartoons contained in Appendix I. The account of the celebration of repeal in London is taken from Gipson, *British Empire,* vol. 11, *The Triumphant Empire: The Rumbling of the Coming Storm, 1766–1770,* p. 3.

191. Conway to governors in America, 31 March 1766, O'Callaghan, *Documents Relative to New York,* vol. 7, pp. 823–24.

192. See the following accounts for these several incidents, Colonial Society of Massachusetts, *Publications,* vol. 26, pp. 30–31; *Pennsylvania Gazette,* 22 May 1766; Barker, *Background of the Revolution in Maryland,* p. 331; Charles Campbell, *The History of the Colony and Ancient Dominion of Virginia* (Philadelphia: J. B. Lippincott, 1860), p. 544; McCrady, *History of South Carolina,* p. 586–87.

193. *Ibid.*, p. 589; *Virginia Gazette,* 30 May 1766.

194. Bernard to Lords of Trade, 7 July 1766, "Bernard Papers," vol. 4, p. 229; James Wright to assembly and council, 16 July 1766, Candler, *Colonial Records of Georgia,* vol. 14, pp. 370–71.

195. Thomas Hutchinson and Lawrence S. Mayo, eds., *The History of the Colony and Province of Massachusetts Bay* (Cambridge, Mass.: Harvard Univ. Press, 1936), vol. 3, p. 107.

·3·

The First Rockingham Ministry and the Repeal of the Stamp Act: The Role of the Commercial Lobby and Economic Pressures

PAUL LANGFORD

It was an abiding belief of Americans in the years between 1766 and 1776 that in economic sanctions they had a weapon of overwhelming power in their disputes with the mother country. The nonimportation campaigns of 1768–70 and of 1774–75 were based not merely on pious hopes of success but on what seemed positive evidence of their effectiveness. In the repeal of the Stamp Act, the colonists had won a major victory against the imperial government and had apparently done so by the leverage exerted through their commercial hold on the British economy. Nonimportation agreements had followed fast on the heels of the Stamp Act itself, and it was not difficult to argue that they had been the decisive consideration in the final determination of the government and of Parliament to remove the offending legislation. Yet the proposition was not necessarily as convincing as it seemed at first sight. There were, after all, alternative explanations of the *volte face* which took place in imperial policy in 1766, not all of them closely related to either the political or economic activities of the colonies.

An English Whig, for example, would have argued that it was the change of ministry in the summer of 1765 which worked the transformation. This is a claim worth considering in detail, for if the ministers in power during the Stamp Act crisis were committed to repeal, it would hardly be possible to attribute much significance to the economic pressures exerted in America. The administration of the Rockingham Whigs replaced that of George Grenville for purely domestic, indeed palace, reasons, but great hopes were from the beginning entertained that the new ministers would quickly remove the American taxation laid by their predecessor. Joseph Sherwood, for example, the Rhode Island agent in London, wrote home to Governor Samuel Ward: "I give you Joy on the Revolution in the Ministry. . . . It is confidently Asserted these Changes will produce great Ease to the Inhabitants of America," while the American newspapers were quick to "declare their expectations."[1] In part, these hopes rested on the simple assumption that "the new State Physicians will naturally find fault with the Prescriptions of the Old Doctors," and certainly Rockingham and his colleagues were determined to discredit and undo much of Grenville's work.[2] But there appeared more solid grounds for expecting relief because some of those newly in office had opposed the Stamp Act at Westminster in the previous spring. Henry Conway had been one of only two members of Parliament prepared to deny the legality of taxing the Americans, and several of his colleagues and associates had at least objected to the expediency of the tax. But the significance of this opposition was limited. As Jared Ingersoll pointed out, it was the opposition of a "few of the heads of the minority who are sure to athwart and oppose the Ministry in every measure of what Nature or kind soever."[3] Moreover, it had been far from unanimous. "We had a sad division on adjourning," George Onslow had reported to Newcastle on 6 February 1765; "49 to 245. Many of our People with them."[4] Perhaps Benjamin Franklin's assessment of the significance of the change of ministry was the fairest. "Some we had reason to Doubt of are removed," he wrote, "and some particular Friends are put in place."[5] There was, from the colonial point of view, reason for hope, but not necessarily for confidence.

Nonetheless, this hope seemed at first capable of realization. Though the Board of Trade flatly declared that the Virginia Resolves against the Stamp Act amounted to an "absolute Disavowl of the Right of the Parliament of Great Britain to impose Taxes upon her Colonies, and a daring Attack upon the Constitution of this Country," and strongly advised vigorous measures, the ministers showed no anxiety to act precipitately.[6] The cabinet did not discuss the Virginia Resolves until 30 August 1765,[7] and the resulting dispatch from the secretary of state's office was not transmitted until 14 September. The tenor of the discussion and dispatch was firm but far from harsh. Lieutenant-Governor Francis Fauquier's report that the Resolves were the work of "Young, hot, and Giddy Members" permitted Conway to express the hope that they would quickly be revoked in the next session.[8] Conway's directions to Fauquier were confined to a general exhortation: "by every prudent Measure in your Power, at once to maintain the just Rights of the British Government, and to preserve the Peace and Tranquillity of the Province committed to your Care."[9] It would seem that at this juncture the ministry was not particularly dismayed by developments in America which would provide them with an opportunity simultaneously to discredit Grenville and to demonstrate their own preference for a liberal and popular policy. That this was so is also suggested by a letter written by Joseph Harrison. A Customs officer at New Haven, Harrison had come to England to further his career and had established contact with Rockingham and William Dowdeswell, later becoming an assistant to Edmund Burke in his secretarial work for Rockingham.[10] By 11 October, he was writing to his colleague John Temple in Boston:

> Wee have lately had strange accounts from Boston of the riots and disorders there and at Rhode Island. Surely the people are distracted and infatuated. The ministry would certainly have relieved them from those grievances they have so much complained of had they behaved with tollerable decency. But now they must expect no favour. What measures will be taken is not determined. I shall know when any

resolutions are formed; and shall give you the earliest advice.[11]

Harrison's belief that the Boston riots, in which the property of royal officials was destroyed and all possibility of operating the Stamp Act without military backing nullified, dramatically affected imperial policy was undoubtedly correct. "All America is in confusion," Conway told Rockingham on 10 October 1765.[12] Almost overnight, a relatively minor colonial problem was transformed into virtual rebellion. The ministry recognized this by referring a long-term solution to the consideration of Parliament. By way of the formal machinery of the Privy Council, the reports of the American governors and representations of the Board of Trade were henceforth directed to await the attention of the legislature.[13] However, an immediate policy was required and this time there was little delay. The critical information from Governor Francis Bernard of Massachusetts was received on 5, 13, and 14 October.[14] The treasury dispatched orders as early as 8 October; the secretary of state, who had to await the results of a cabinet meeting on 13 October, dispatched his on the twenty-fourth. These instructions were quite explicit. Grey Cooper, as the secretary to the Treasury Board, ordered Bernard to appoint a new stamp distributor (Andrew Oliver, the old one, had been compelled to resign) and to "inforce a due Obedience to the Laws, and to take care that His Majesty's Revenue suffers no Detriment, or Diminution."[15] Conway expressed surprise that troops had not already been used, and while advising "lenient and persuasive Methods" where possible, he specifically ordered "such a timely Exertion of Force as the Occasion may require."[16] Later, there was to be much dispute as to the precise implications of these orders. Once the ministry had come to a decision to repeal the Stamp Act, it was naturally anxious to insist that it had never wavered in its attachment to this policy. The Opposition's interpretation varied. Charles Lloyd's pamphlet *The Conduct of the Late Administration Examined,* published in 1767, characterized "the whole tenor" of Conway's dispatches as "languor and debility."[17] On the other hand, in February 1766, when Grenville sought to demonstrate the inconsistency of his opponents, he constantly reiterated that the ministry's policy of October 1765 had been one of enforcement. In the debates of 3 and 7 February, after Conway had rashly asserted that "he would sooner cut off his hand" than employ force, Grenville waxed sarcastic at his expense: "The present administration [is] eager and desirous to carry orders into execution. They will not sleep till orders are sent to the Admiralty and the misery that will follow it was of no consequence, as all the Governors have already orders by Conway's circular letter to carry the laws into execution."[18]

It is difficult not to sympathize with Grenville's interpretation. When Newcastle later reexamined the orders of October 1765, he was compelled to note that they strongly recommended "The Execution of The Stamp Act" and, if necessary, the "Use of Force."[19] Meanwhile, something like an impartial assessment is provided by John Campbell, M. P. for Corfe Castle and a correspondent of Lord Holland's. Campbell did not attend the repeal debates of 1766 and wrote to Holland on 6 April of that year: "I have seen some letters [in the printed Papers] from the submissive secretary, to Gov[erno]r Bernard and another, which seem to me quite inconsistent with the repeal of the Stamp Act. Surely both cannot be right."[20]

In fact, it is perfectly clear that, at the time, Conway and his colleagues really did intend the use of force in America. General Thomas Gage, the commander-in-chief in North America, received explicit orders to supply troops to governors who required them, and Lord Colville, the naval commander, was directed by the Admiralty to provide transport where necessary.[21] Sir Roger Newdigate, a Tory with intensely authoritarian views on the American crisis, noted, "Total Languor and want of Energy in Government," on hearing the dispatches of 24 October read in the Commons three months later. However, even felt compelled to add, "P. S. orders sent to L[or]d Colville etc. to send forces from Nova Scotia."[22] As Grenville maintained in the Commons, bloodshed was averted not because the ministers refused to endorse it but because the machinery of enforcement in America proved incapable of effective action. The critical drawback was that the military could only be employed at the specific request of the civil power, in this case the governors and their councils. But colonial councils proved understandably reluctant to call in troops against countrymen who were unanimous in their opposition to the Stamp Act and with whom in many cases they were in complete agreement. At Boston, for example, the council flatly refused to ask for military aid, and although Bernard had the courage to write privately for troops to Gage, who devised an elaborate procedure for them to act independently if the council attempted to restrain their use, he preferred to back down in the event.[23] In New Jersey, Governor William Franklin, who strongly advised the use of force, found his hands tied by his councillors,[24] and at New York, where Gage actually had his headquarters, the same difficulty prevented action, even though the commander in chief had asked Cadwallader Colden, the lieutenant-governor, to make a requisition.[25]

> Notwithstanding what has passed [Gage wrote home], No Requisition has been made of Me for assistance, which I must acknowledge I have been sorry for, as the disturbances, which have happened, have been so much beyond riots, and so like the forerunners of open Rebellion, that I have wanted a pretence to draw the troops together from every post they cou'd be taken from, that the Servants of the Crown might be enabled to make a stand in some spot, if matters should be brought to the Extremitys, that may not without reason be apprehended; And I have been the more anxious in this Affair, as from the distance of the Troops, and the Season of the Year it wou'd require a very Considerable time before a respectable force could be assembled, and if the Requisition from the Civil Power is postponed 'till sudden emergency's do happen, it will not be in my power to give the assistance that will be wanted.[26]

By the time the Ministry's orders reached America, it was perfectly clear that the cumbersome procedure required for the employment of the military, the unhelpful deployment of troops in North America, and the total paralysis of colonial administration in the face of a united opposition to the Stamp Act all made impossible the execution of those orders. As reply after reply to the dispatches of Cooper and Conway explained the impossibility of carrying out the instructions from home, it must have been with considerable relief that the ministers, by then committed to a policy of repeal, found that their initial measures had miscarried.[27]

While there is no positive evidence, there are strong indications that the Duke of Cumberland was the prime mover of the ministry's policy of enforcement and repression. The critical cabinet meeting of 13 October which resulted in Conway's dispatch of 24 October was held at Cumberland's house. A policy of enforcement, if necessary with troops, would certainly coincide with Cumberland's conservative and military cast of mind, and there were those who did not hesitate to lay the policy at his door. "Mr. [Richard] Jackson," Thomas Hutchinson's son wrote of the agent for Connecticut and Pennsylvania, "in Conversation gave it as his Opinion that if the Duke of Cumberland had not died, instead of a repeal of the Act, there wou'd have been a number of Regiments in America before this."[28] A correspondent of Charles Jenkinson's postulated a similar outcome, "if a certain great Duke had lived. Entrenous God has been most kind to this Kingdom, if we were but sensible of it."[29] Certainly Cumberland's death came at a fortunate moment for the Americans. It is difficult to believe that the conciliatory policy adopted by Rockingham and his friends at the close of 1765 could have been pursued under Cumberland's regime.

Indeed, that conciliatory policy owed nothing to the attitudes of the Rockingham ministry in its early months but rather was the rest of a substantial change which took place after the Duke of Cumberland's death on 31 October 1765. In part, this was simply because Rockingham, on whose shoulders Cumberland's mantle naturally fell, did not hold all his master's views on the American question. Some hint of his attitude, even in October, is clear from his remark to a Yorkshire friend that "the notable confusion which he [Grenville] has raised in America, Tho' it lays difficulties upon the present administration, yet so far it serves them, as it shows that he had neither prudence or foresight."[30] In November, this obvious desire to discredit his predecessor at the treasury was augmented by the discovery of a completely new angle to the Stamp Act crisis. In the week after Cumberland's death, Rockingham received two letters of critical importance, which convinced him that the arguments involved in the problem were as much economic as constitutional. One was from his old friend Sir George Savile, whose influence as M. P. for Yorkshire on Rockingham was great. Savile enclosed a letter from a Boston man complaining bitterly that "The Government at home has taken the most effectual Methods to destroy all Trade."[31] Though this complaint was a vague one, Savile pointed the moral: "They speak as ignorant men. Our trade is hurt, what the devil have you been a doing? For our part, we don't pretend to understand your politics and American matters, but our trade is hurt; pray remedy it, and a plague if you wont."[32]

The second letter, received a few days later, on 6 November, was from Barlow Trecothick. Trecothick was a prosperous and prominent figure in the American trade, who had led the London North America Merchants in their opposition to the Stamp and American Mutiny acts in the previous spring.[33] Clearly, he was very much a coming man when he wrote to Rockingham. His letter forecast disaster not merely in the colonies but in Britain if speedy action was not taken. Since the Americans were evidently determined not to accept the Stamp Act, he argued, all commercial business requiring stamps would grind to a halt. The British export market in America would then collapse, the manufacturing industries would experience a severe slump, and chronic unemployment would ensue—with large numbers of laborers "without Employ and of course without Bread!" Trecothick wrote:

> Here I must stop, not daring to pursue any further the dreadful Chain of Consequences. . . . My great fear is, that too great Delay and Caution in administering the Remedy, may render the Deseases of this embarrassed Nation incurable and even a virtuous Administration may therefore be deemed accountable for Effects proceeding from the Error of their Predecessors.[34]

The effect of these two letters on their recipient can scarcely be exaggerated, for they established a line of argument, a causal chain between Grenville's legislation, economic distress in America, and a fatal slump in Britain, all of which was to lead first Rockingham, then the administration, and finally Parliament itself to a liberal and conciliatory colonial policy. Rockingham himself was an almost immediate convert to the cause of relief. While expressing anxiety about the constitutional issues raised, he arranged a meeting with Trecothick and began to search for corroborating evidence. By 15 November 1765, Jackson, the Connecticut agent, was aware that the Cumberland policy was to be reversed: "I have within the Compass of a week conceived hopes [hc wrote to Governor Fitch], that Measures may be taken here, that will perfectly conciliate the minds of the Americans, but have reason to believe that such Measures are by no means, what were to have been expected a Month ago and yet depend upon the Moderation of what we hear from New York."[35]

At the end of the month, Rockingham's rough notes of a "Plan of Business" for the parliamentary session were already in the strain which was in fact to be adopted three months later.

> Que. Consideration of N[orth] A[merica] in the Commercial—to be first brought on—
> Que. to avoid the discussion on the Stamp Act—till Good Principles are laid down for Easing and Assisting N[orth] America and being well informed of the high Importance of the Commerce to N[orth] A[merica] respectively to the Mother Country.[36]

On 28 November, the day on which these notes were written, Grenville was writing to the Duke of Bedford of reports that the ministers were "resolved (if possible) to repeal the American tax."[37] In fact, at that time, a precise policy was far from formulated. Trecothick himself had only asked for "repeal or suspension," and certainly Rockingham had not yet decided on the former. What is certain is that he already viewed the problem in economic rather than legalistic terms and that he was already disposed to advise a policy of relief for the colonies on the basis of British commercial interests.

This need not be surprising, for Rockingham was always ready to listen to the merchants. In part, this was doubtless connected with the general anxiety of the

"Old Whigs" to attract the support of extraparliamentary and popular elements, among which the merchants were important if not preeminent, but it was also a very personal interest closely related to Rockingham's Yorkshire heritage. Since his father's death, he had played a major part in the politics of his home county, and Yorkshire politics had not a little to do with the commercial and industrial concerns of the West Riding and Humber regions. Throughout the 1750s, he had taken great care, with his ally Sir George Savile, to concern himself with the economic problems of the North. Of course this was partly self-interest. Referring to the threat to bullion imports in October 1765, he told Charles Yorke, "I don't know what will become of Yorkshire Rents—If Portugal Coin—was not brought there—in return for Cloth etc."[38] Nonetheless, his background had inevitably given him, impressionable as he was, a quite genuine and sincere belief in the importance of trade. In notes made in the early months of 1766 for a speech on American business, which was never given, he stated proudly: "Bred in a Manufacturing County—Fond of giving every Encouragement—The Existence of the Country."[39] Yorkshiremen were certainly aware of his uncharacteristic energy when it came to commercial matters. One of them informed Rockingham in early December that the country gentlemen and manufacturers of Yorkshire intended, though only if he approved their doing so, to petition for a prohibition on grain exports, and added: "They who have so often experienced your Lordships readiness to serve them on all Occasions wherein either their Trade or their Interest were concerned, can think of no Person to whom they can so properly apply as to your Lordship to Present their Petition if you will Please to permit them so to do so."[40]

Rockingham himself placed great emphasis on this aspect of his work. "It is with no small Satisfaction," he was to inform the Bristol merchants on leaving office, "that I can look back upon the Measures of the last Session of Parl[iamen]t because I think that at no Time the Commercial Interest of this Country was more the Object of Government."[41]

This is not to claim that the Rockingham ministry moved at once openly towards the repeal of the Stamp Act under the stimulus of the economic pressures revealed in November 1765. On the contrary, Rockingham and his colleagues formally decided in favor of repeal only in the middle of January 1766 when Parliament itself was about to consider the problem of America. For this there were many reasons. Perhaps the most important was the great strength and influence of those, particularly in the political establishment, who opposed the abolition of the colonial stamp tax. The Stamp Act had been overwhelmingly supported by heavy majorities in almost all quarters when passed in the session of 1765. It was not to be expected that this support would be abandoned overnight simply because the Americans had displayed their displeasure. On the contrary, the violence of the American response to the Stamp Act was more likely to provoke retribution than conciliation. In Parliament, opinion was largely hostile, not merely among the friends of Grenville and Bedford but more importantly among the independent M. P.s who ultimately decided the fate of controversial legislation. The king himself was deeply perturbed by the Stamp Act riots and not inclined to favor a liberal policy. Even the cabinet was deeply divided, with Lord Chancellor Northington bitterly opposed to concession. Not until at least significant sections of this generally anti-American block were won over, would Rockingham be able to carry through repeal, however convinced he was of its merits.

In the event, Rockingham and his colleagues proved surprisingly successful in creating a climate of opinion which favored the elimination of the stamp tax. Contemporaries considered the Elder William Pitt's declaration of support for repeal, which was made in the House of Commons on 14 January 1766, a crucial development. But more important was the expedient of the Declaratory Act, the statutory declaration of Britain's right to tax the colonies, which was actually strongly disapproved by Pitt and which made repeal of the Stamp Act possible. It is inconceivable that king, cabinet, and Parliament would have agreed to submit to colonial demands without the face-saving permitted by the Declaratory Act. Whatever the logical absurdity of asserting a right while repealing its only practical application, the state of politics clearly required such a maneuver.

If the Declaratory Act made repeal possible, more was needed to convince all parties that repeal would be positively beneficial. Rockingham himself had been primarily influenced by the economic consideration, though the practical difficulties of enforcing the Stamp Act in the colonies no doubt played their part in his thinking. But the economic arguments were to be the crucial factor determining the ultimate fate of the Stamp tax. Fortunately for the ministry, and indeed with its connivance and collaboration, a great campaign out of, as well as in, Parliament forcibly demonstrated the dangers for British prosperity and economic stability in continuing an unpopular colonial policy. In this campaign, the pressures brought to bear from America were of critical importance. Ever since the autumn of 1764, it had been obvious that something was seriously amiss with the North American economy. In the spring of 1765, London merchants were testifying that returns from the American colonies "are fallen very short," while colonial merchants like John Hancock of Boston, William Davidson of New York, and William Allen of Philadelphia all complained bitterly of severe business difficulties.[42]

At first, the Sugar Act and Grenville's Customs regulations were blamed for this recession, but the Stamp Act put previous legislation into the background. "I hear the stamp act is like to take place," wrote Hancock earlier in 1765: "it is very cruel, we were before bothered, we shall not be able much longer to support trade, and in the end Great Britain must feel the ill effects of it. I wonder the merchants and friends of America don't make a stir for us."[43] Gradually, as it became clear that colonial society as a whole was heavily opposed to the Stamp Act, it turned into the principal grievance of the merchants, and ultimately its repeal came to appear synonymous with the return of economic prosperity. By the autumn of 1765, American merchants were warning their British counterparts that unless relief were speedily granted, trade would grind to a complete halt. The logical conclusion of their argument was reached with the nonimportation agreements, which were passed in the three great centers of New York, Philadelphia, and Boston respectively on 31 October, 7 November, and 9 December 1765, and which were to take effect from 1 January 1766.[44] The agreements were carried out with some vigor. Thus, Richard Neave and Son of London soon learned from Samuel Mifflin of Philadelphia that all orders for shipment were countermanded.[45] Barnards and Harrison were similarly informed by Hancock that unless the act were repealed, they would lose a customer who refused to be a "Slave to enrich Placement."[46] In the face of such action, it is scarcely surprising that the merchants in Britain acted quickly. Whether they agreed with the American attitude—whether even, they accepted the logic of the colonial merchants—was irrelevant. With business bad for the past year and faced now by the prospect of complete disaster, they had little choice but to obey their clients' demands. Thus Hancock bluntly informed Barnards and Harrison: "You may bid Adieu to Remittances for the past Goods, and Trade in future. . . . We are a people worth a saveing and our trade [is] so much to your advantage worth keeping that it merits the notice of those on y[ou]r side who have the Conduct of it but to find nothing urg'd by the merch[an]ts on your side in our favour Really is extraordinary."[47] English merchants were by no means slow to take the hint.

There was nothing new about an attempt by the mercantile interest to influence imperial policy. Only the previous winter, Trecothick, a "steady, cool but firm friend to America," as Jared Ingersoll called him, had led the London North America Merchants in an organized effort to modify Grenville's colonial legislation.[48] Though their opposition to the Stamp Act was unsuccessful, they succeeded, in cooperation with the American agents, in having a clause deleted from the American Mutiny Act allowing the billeting of troops in private houses.[49] "The Colonys," the Rhode Island agent, Joseph Sherwood, wrote home in May 1765, "are under great Obligations to the Merchants of London for their Assistance and Influence in this most Important Attack, had it not been for their Aid, I do believe the Measure would have been carried."[50] However, influencing a minister to alter minor legislative provisions was scarcely comparable to the task of completely converting opinion both inside and outside Westminster from an attitude of total hostility to the colonies to one of readiness to repeal the Stamp Act. If the Americans were right in thinking that the most effectual way to get the Stamp tax revoked was through the British merchants, success was not to be achieved without considerable skill and labor on the part of the latter.

Their campaign began in the metropolis on 4 December when a new London North America Merchants Committee, which included well-known names like Barclay, Mildred, Hanbury, Neave, and Dennys DeBerdt, was elected under the chairmanship of Trecothick to work for the repeal of the Stamp Act.[51] Two days later, on 6 December, the committee agreed on a circular which was to be dispatched "to the outports and to the manufacturing Towns."[52] This circular revealed the two essential points in the merchants' campaign: first, the object was a concerted movement to petition Parliament and to pressure local M. P.s in favor of repeal, and second, there was to be no discussion of the constitutional issues or, indeed, of the colonists' resistance to imperial authority at all. "We mean to take for our sole Object," it stated, "the Interest of these Kingdoms it being our Opinion, that conclusive Arguments for granting every Ease or Advantage the North Americans can with propriety desire, may be fairly deduced from that Principle only."[53] According to Trecothick, this circular was sent to some thirty towns throughout the provinces.[54] The response was enthusiastic. At Bristol, for example, where a good deal of press coverage was given to American problems in general and to the nonimportation agreements in particular, both the Society of Merchant Venturers and traders outside the society petitioned Parliament and sent three representatives—William Reeve, the Quaker leader of the Bristol merchants, Joseph Farrel, and Thomas Farr—to bear the petitions to London.[55] At Birmingham, where there was great anxiety about unemployment, the local manufacturers met on 23 December to elect a committee, and by 4 January, they had produced not merely a petition to the legislature but letters to all the M. P.s and peers in the district.[56] Altogether some twenty-five towns, from all the key trading and industrial areas, petitioned Parliament.[57]

Not every appeal was successful, and when the Mayor of Norwich replied in distinctly cool vein to the circular, Trecothick assured him:

> [The Committee] desire me to acquaint you that they confine their object in the intended Application to Parliament to the Honour and Real Interest of Great Britain, which in their Apprehension are both inseparably connected with the Welfare of the Trade to North America, they propose to petition Parliament on the Subject of the present Declension and the Prospect of a total Failure of that Trade. And hope for the Concurrence of a City so greatly concerned as yours is in the Event. [T]he present State of the Demand for the Manufactures will doubtless afford Matter whereon to found such Petition from you. And they wish to have it supported by the Countenance of the worthy Members for the City and County.[58]

Yet despite this pressure, despite the fact that there was undoubted and publicized economic distress in Norwich, and despite the existence of sufficient organization and vigor for a petition about grain prices there, the Stamp Act campaign was ignored.[59] Doubtless this was because the chief political interest in the city was that of Grenville's friend, the Earl of Buckinghamshire, who received copies of the correspondence with Trecothick from the mayor together with congratulations on sentiments "founded on such principles as can alone Support the Honour and true Interest of Great Brittain."[60] At Liverpool, too, the corporation had political interests which differed from those of the merchants. There Trecothick's circular was suppressed and produced only after Sir William Meredith, M. P. for Liverpool, had informed the local traders of its existence.[61]

These cases were atypical, however. For the most part, the circular was astonishingly productive. Indeed, the response was so widespread that the Opposition was forced to doubt not its extent but its authenticity. Faced by a flood of petitions and evidence from the provincial towns, Grenville and his friends could only argue that a gigantic fraud had been practiced; that the manufacturers had "been deceived by false representations,"[62] and that the ministry, in this deception, "took the lead, and employed for this purpose every engine in their power,"[63] "encouraging petitions to P[arliamen]t, and instructions to Members from the trading and manufacturing towns, against the act."[64] Certainly, there was a good deal of suspicion of the merchant classes. One of Charles Jenkinson's Scottish friends refused to believe "the sad Tales—which the Glasgow Sugar-mongers and Tobacconists sour their Punch and light their Pipes with," while from the embassy at The Hague, Sir Joseph Yorke opined: "as to the Clamour of the Merchants and Manufacturers that is all an artifice, (I don't mean there is not a Stagnation or Embarrassment) to force Government to give up its powers."[65]

How much truth there was in these charges is not easy to determine. Trecothick was certainly anxious to avoid the imputation, which was made to his face in the Commons' Committee on 11 February 1766, that the London merchants had dictated the pattern of the protests.[66] In this respect, the activities of the Bristol merchants were somewhat embarrassing. They had obtained a copy of the Liverpool petition, in order, they wrote, "that we may be as uniform as possible in our application."[67] They also offered to send Birmingham a copy, though fortunately the manufacturers in that town declined the offer.[68] When Reeve and his colleagues asked Trecothick for instructions as to the petition, he insisted that "the particular distresses of Commerce in each port and in each manufacturing Town will best be expressed from their own feelings" and that "such only as either are or soon expect to be aggrieved should complain."[69] Nonetheless, he did go on to outline the London petition, and in drawing up their own, the Bristol merchants proved remarkably slavish in following its pattern. Grenville asked scornfully in the Commons: "Is it difficult for Ministers to get Pet[itio]ns ag[ain]st Taxes. I opposed the Tax upon Beer, could not I first Com[missione]r of Treas[ur]y have got Pet[itio]ns from all the Mughouses in London."[70] Despite this, the sheer volume of protest throughout the country belied the notion that it was largely an invention on the part of the ministry and the London merchants. As Trecothick remarked in the Commons: "In General I believe the petitions would have come though Letters had not been sent."[71]

More serious was the charge that deliberate deception of another sort was involved. One of the reasons for the great success of the campaign was the relative importance of the manufacturing as against the mercantile element among the petitioners. Though Trecothick and his friends provided the basic organization, it was the great outburst of opinion from manufacturing towns in Yorkshire, Lancashire, and the Black Country which, with its serious implications for local society, made a deep impression on opinion inside and outside Westminster. Their contribution stemmed, in the first instance, from the cessation of orders from the merchants who marketed their wares in North America, and in one case, at least, it is certain that a degree of disingenuity was practiced. Henry Cruger, a Bristol merchant of American birth, informed one of his Rhode Island customers that although he had received no instruction to cancel orders from him, he had taken upon himself the responsibility of doing so. "I cou'd not think of giving out any of your orders untill I saw which way this Momentous Affair wou'd turn, and terminate."[72] However, this case was doubtless exceptional. There can be little question that demand had indeed severely decreased and that, for the most part, the pressure on the manufacturers was both spontaneous and genuine.

The precise relationship between the ministry and the merchants' campaign is somewhat obscure, though there is no doubt that some of the ministers cooperated closely with the merchants. Rockingham was in constant touch with Trecothick— indeed according to the endorsement on the copy of the merchants' circular preserved among the Rockingham Papers, it was "concerted between the Marquess of R[ockingham] and Mr. Trecothick."[73] Rockingham was regularly informed of the progress of the movement, writing, for example, to Newcastle on 2 January, "Tregothick and the Merchants and Trading and Manufacturing Towns, etc. go on well."[74] Similarly, Dartmouth at the Board of Trade advised Samuel Garbett, the leader of the Birmingham industrialists, and received regular reports on the headway made in the Midlands.[75] It is interesting that in each of these cases, the wheels of cooperation were oiled by personal interests. Trecothick was, incidentally, the leader of the Grenada proprietors who were petitioning the Privy Council for an island assembly,[76] while Garbett was corresponding with William Burke, as well as his superiors in the administration, about problems involving the iron industry.[77] It is evident from the interest which Rockingham and his more liberal friends took at this time in the concerns of the merchants in general, and in their petitioning campaign in particular, that they were as much the directors as the victims of the mercantile and manufacturing lobby which was so rapidly gaining strength.

This was probably equally true of the other interests and groups with which the ministry was in contact. Inevitably, Rockingham and his colleagues were subject to immense pressure from interested parties on the American issue. A mass of material and information from American agents, merchants, manufacturers, speculators, administrators, writers, experts, and mere busybodies is still to be found among Rockingham's papers at Sheffield.[78] Dartmouth, as well as receiving the usual flood of advice and information, was also much influenced by quite close friends and acquaintances. Dennys DeBerdt, a London merchant who plied him with a stream of propaganda on the Stamp Act controversy, had been specifically selected as special agent for Massachusetts because of his known connection with Dartmouth,[79] while Dr. John Fothergill, a noted Quaker with extensive American connections and a friend of Dartmouth's, was constantly in touch with him.[80] However, ministers were as anxious to consult the experts as the latter were to influence them. Quite apart from the better-known Americans such as Franklin and Ingersoll, who were constantly being consulted by Rockingham, Conway, and Dartmouth, far less distinguished figures were involved. A West Riding manufacturer like Joseph Milnes could be asked to supply information about the American trade when calling at Wentworth Woodhouse, Rockingham's country seat, and a friendship as nonpolitical as that between Dartmouth and George Whitefield could be used to obtain evidence from the other side of the Atlantic.[81] Whatever the amateurism and naïveté of the young ministers, there is no denying their industry or enthusiasm in the autumn of 1765. As in the case of the campaign organized by Trecothick and the London merchants, so in relation to the activities of the innumerable groups and individuals around the ministry in 1765–66, it is clear that what began as an attempt to pressure the ministers soon became a great movement in cooperation with them to influence public and parliamentary opinion.

The organization of a great campaign in favor of repealing the Stamp Act was merely a preliminary to convincing Parliament. Yet in the Commons, where the great battle took place, the extraparliamentary campaign too was a reasonable success. The critical divisions of 7 and 22 February showed a massive majority, 274 to 134 and 275 to 167 respectively, not merely against Grenville's proposal to enforce the Stamp Act but in favor of a total repeal. For virtually six weeks, the Commons was preoccupied with the American issue, and by the end of that time, it had overwhelmingly determined on the removal of a tax which it had laid with equally overwhelming support a year previously. Yet the crucial consideration in this determination was scarcely the elaborate constitutional argument conducted in the great set-piece debates. For the most part, the arguments expressed were exceedingly stereotyped and repetitive. They had already been rehearsed in countless pamphlets and papers and were not noticeably improved by their airing at Westminster. "Every point now turns immediately into something American," wrote one M. P. after a debate on army estimates had been used to discuss the Stamp Act.[82] It was scarcely surprising that many began to find the arguments tedious. "Mr. Burke," the young William Baker remarked after the debate of 24 February, "was the only man who could keep up the attention of the House on a subject already threadbare," while Burke himself recorded of the debate on the third reading of the repeal bill that "The house was teezed to Death and heard nobody willingly."[83] The debating strategy of both administration and opposition was simple enough. The essence of the ministry's approach throughout had been to concede everything demanded in terms of constitutional rights, in order to clear the way for a repeal based on expediency. The king's Speech and Address of 14 January, the rejection of the Stamp Act Congress's petitions on 27 January, the elaborate series of resolutions condemning the colonists' activities, and above all the resolution which was to become the Declaratory Act all were intended to pave the way for what the Duke of Newcastle called "the immediate Repeal of The Stamp Act; not as an illegal Act; But, as the most Imprudent, and pernicious One, That ever was made."[84]

Against this, the Opposition was concerned to treat the repeal of the Stamp Act as a purely constitutional question—to describe it as a "glaring absurdity"[85] to declare a right while repealing its only legislative application, to point out that "the disgrace of departing from the inforcing the laws by constraint, and by open rebellion of the Colonists, can't be wiped off by the power of any words whatsoever,"[86] to insist that the Americans were seeking not the redress of specific grievances but ultimate independence, and to prophesy that repeal would merely encourage them to make new demands. The sole object urged by the Opposition was the submission of the Americans—"the Palladium," Bedford called it, "which if suffered to be removed, puts a final period to the British Empire in America."[87] The sole solution suggested was the enforcement of the Stamp Act, based, Henry Cruger wrote, upon "this Argument, that since you snarle and begin to shew your Teeth, they ought to be knocked out before you are able to bite."[88] This was the essence of the arguments employed in the debates on the imperial problem, the framework on which the seventy-nine speakers in those debates, all but a handful of them committed party politicians, hung their remarks.[89] It was obviously important to state the different viewpoints clearly, but it can hardly be maintained that they were decisive as such. It was evidence, not argument, that was responsible for what Bamber Gascoyne, M. P. for Midhurst, described as "such an alteration in men's minds."[90] The administration had hit on a formula acceptable to the House, provided it could demonstrate that the Stamp Act was as damaging from the purely British point of view as it was for the colonies. In consequence, the decisive battle was fought not in the drama of debate but during the examination of evidence and witnesses to the effects of the act. It was this battle, notable for what Charles Garth, one of the American agents, described as "the very great Attention and minute Enquiry which has been had and given upon this Occasion in the House of Commons," which it was the administration's concern to win.[91]

To a great extent, the ministry's task had been eased in advance by the change wrought in the climate of opinion in which the legislature found itself considering a course of action. If it is true that the initial reaction in England to news of the disturbances in America had been one of intense hostility, it is also the case that by February 1766 public opinion appeared to be overwhelmingly in favor of repeal. The immense flood of propaganda poured out with the active connivance of the ministry had had an undoubted impact. Pamphlets, newspapers, petitions, even cartoons had been employed by the merchants, on the one hand, and by the ministry, on the other, to influence opinion.[92] Pitt's declaration in support of repeal and the administration's readiness to satisfy all scruples on the score of rights had assisted this development. "The Vox Populi," wrote Henry Cruger on 14 February, "now begins to gain ground, and I think since the Legality of Taxation is allowed, the Act will be repeal'd upon the Grounds of Expediency," while Richard Champion, another Bristol merchant, thought that "Out of Doors the whole Kingdom seem to be united upon the same Sentiment."[93] This extraordinary turnabout was bound to have its effect at Westminster.

However, the main emphasis must be on the efforts made to put pressure on M. P.s and peers directly. For ministers who had a reputation (which they posthumously retain) for being ineffectual, Rockingham and his friends showed unexpected efficiency in organizing this campaign. From the beginning, they had worked in harness with the merchants' petitioning movement; in the critical period of January–February 1766, ministers, merchants, and American agents and experts all joined in the attempt to ensure the maximum impact for their case in Parliament. For example, Samuel Garbett, the Birmingham industrialist, circularized Staffordshire and Warwickshire peers and M. P.s with long and detailed accounts of the plight of the local economy as a result of the Stamp Act crisis.[94] Henry Cruger was also very busy. "I was three Weeks in London," he later wrote to his father, "and every Day with some one Member of Parliament, talking as it were for my own Life. [I]t is surprising how ignorant some of them are of Trade and

America."[95] Similarly, William Strahan's account of Benjamin Franklin's activities commented that:

> The assiduity of our friend Dr. Franklin is really astonishing. He is forever with one Member of Parliament or other (most of whom by the bye seem to have been deplorably ignorant with regard to the Nature and Consequence of the Colonies). . . . This is the most necessary and essential Service he could possibly perform on this Occasion; and so effectually hath he done this, and I will venture to say, he hath thrown so much Light upon the Subject, that if the Legislature doth not now give you ample redress, it is not for want of the fullest and most distinct Information in respect of the real Merits of the Case.[96]

Of course, the main effort took place in the Commons' Committee of the Whole House on the American Papers. Twenty-two witnesses gave evidence in favor of repeal. On 31 January, four victims of the American riots had testified to the violence of the disturbances in the colonies. The remainder were heard, once the constitutional questions had been resolved, on the consequences of the Stamp Act: three London merchants prominent in the American trade, on 11 February, and on the following day, three Americans with some knowledge of commerce, as well as six manufacturers from the English provinces. On 13 February, three merchants from the outports, two manufacturers, a goldsmith, and quite unclassifiably, the celebrated Franklin testified.

The ministers obviously chose these witnesses with great care, though they occasionally met with difficulties. For example, Garbett, who had throughout played a major part in the campaign in the Midlands, told Dartmouth that he "should with great reluctance attend the House of Commons upon the Plan your Lordship mentions or be Instrumental in Occasioning any of my Neighbours to Attend."[97] However, there was no shortage of witnesses. Fifty-three were ordered to attend the Commons' Committee, though of course some were summoned by the Opposition, and in any case, less than half were actually examined at the bar. The basis of this selection was obviously to demonstrate the unanimity, not merely of the Americans but, far more important, of the British merchants and manufacturers in their opposition to the Stamp Act. Already the Commons had been subjected to a carefully marshaled onslaught of twenty-seven petitions from the trading and manufacturing towns, and now the impression of an economy under siege was to be driven home by viva voce evidence from all quarters.[98] Various friends of the ministry in the Commons were apparently allotted specific tasks to ensure that when the witnesses were questioned in Committee, the maximum effect would be achieved. For example, Sir George Savile was active in coordinating the evidence of the Yorkshire West Riding textile manufacturers, with whom he was well acquainted, and the copious lists of prearranged questions which he drew up with them still survive.[99] Burke directed the activities of the merchants of Lancaster and Glasgow and manufacturers of Birmingham,[100] while Sir William Meredith dealt among others with the Liverpool representatives.[101] Richard Jackson methodically rehearsed with William Kelly, a New York merchant, the questions he was to ask him in the House, and Barlow Trecothick, whose role was probably more important than that of any other witness, was equally well-prepared.[102] The questions he was asked were based on his own paper "Proofs and Observations on Allegations in the London Merchants' Petition,"[103] and when he was examined in the Commons, it was reported to Newcastle that he "stated every thing as he did to your Grace this morning."[104] Naturally the Opposition did all in its power to reduce the impact and credibility of the witnesses—apparently the procedure was for alternate questions from each side, with Conway and Grenville taking the lead, but as little as possible was left to chance, and the result was impressive.

Thanks to the preservation of the written record of the viva voce evidence, it is possible to be certain of the principal considerations which interested the Committee of the Whole House in its examination of witnesses.[105] There can be little question that the emphasis was on the damage done to the British economy by the Stamp Act and its repercussions. Recently some weight has been attributed to the military and diplomatic factors—the expense and difficulty of reducing the Americans to submission by force, and the threat of Bourbon intervention in any Anglo-American conflict—a view which apparently rests primarily on some remarks made by Conway in his speeches of 7 and 21 February.[106] But Conway's allusions to the problems of imperial strategy must be seen in the context of long perorations largely concerned with the economic aspects. Indeed, in his great speech of 21 February, problems of imperial strategy apparently seemed so insignificant that some of those who reported the debate and speech made no note of them.[107] Beyond this there is, in any case, little to suggest that the military and diplomatic considerations had any influence. One or two questions were asked of the American witnesses as to the military potential of the colonists, though very little attention or emphasis was bestowed upon the subject. It would be surprising if the contrary were the case. A few years after Bourbon power had been shattered by English arms, and over a decade before it was demonstrated how formidable American antagonists could be, Englishmen were not likely to be impressed by such an argument and tended to agree with Pitt's assertion that if necessary, "the force of this country can crush America to atoms."[108] That it was a minor consideration which needed stating may be conceded. That it was the critical one is suggested neither by the evidence of the debates nor by the observations of contemporaries.

The primary concern of the administration was to demonstrate, in Newcastle's words, "That the Interest, and The very being of This Country, as a Trading Nation, depends upon The immediate Repeal of The Stamp Act."[109] Of course, much of the evidence was concerned necessarily with the situation in America, though the ministry vainly attempted to limit the scope of the inquiry to safer topics.[110] The inability of the colonists to pay the sums required by the Stamp tax; the total unacceptability of modifying, as opposed to repealing, the Stamp Act; and the certainty of a grateful submission to British authority on the part of the Americans once repeal had been obtained—these points were driven home time and time again by the American witnesses, despite strenuous efforts by the Opposition to demolish them. Franklin was particularly useful in this respect. His knowledge of American conditions and his skill in evading the attempts of the Opposition's questioners to trap him into expressing constitutionally subversive doctrines made a considerable impact. Rockingham himself apparently attributed great weight to Franklin's testimony.

> To this very Examination [Strahan wrote to his partner in Philadelphia], more than to anything else, you are indebted to the speedy and total Repeal of this odious Law. The Marquis of Rockingham told a Friend of mine a few Days after, That he never knew Truth make so great a Progress in so very short a Time. From that very Day, the Repeal was generally and absolutely determined, all that passed afterwards being only mere Form.[111]

This was probably something of an exaggeration, and indeed, it is possible that the publication of Franklin's evidence and the predominance of the constitutional issue in the later stages of the American Revolution have bestowed on his role rather more significance than it strictly merited.[112] The essential task was to prove that, quite apart from other considerations, purely British interests were at stake, and this was achieved not by Franklin, but by Trecothick and his friends.

Most of the witnesses were British merchants and manufacturers, who had first to paint a dire picture of home industry and commerce and secondly to establish that it was Grenville's American legislation and, in particular, the Stamp Act that was to blame. Six merchants—Trecothick, Hanbury, Mildred from London, Glassford from Glasgow, Reeve from Bristol, and Halliday from Liverpool—all testified to the drastic decline of the American trade in 1765, to the refusal of their colonial colleagues to place orders until the Stamp Act had been repealed, to the huge British debts tied up in the colonies at the mercy of the insurgents, and in general, to the prospects of a total collapse of Anglo-American commerce unless the colonists' grievances were redressed.[113] Equally significant were the testimonies of the manufacturers, no less than eight of them, representing the key industrial centers of Manchester, Leeds, Bradford, Nottingham, and Leicester, as well as London. Again their reports of a major slump and chronic unemployment in the manufacturing trades were carefully linked to the cessation of orders from America, so that the clear impression was gained of an almost catastrophic economic crisis directly caused by the colonial disturbances. What must finally have decided the issue was Grenville's total failure to reverse this impression when he called his own witnesses on 17 and 18 February. The only authority he was able to summon on the colonial trade was Richard Oswald, who, it transpired, had abandoned his American business some twelve years previously in favor of government contracting in Germany. In the course of the interrogation, his complete ignorance of current American affairs was exposed, and his testimony utterly demolished by the administration's questioners. He was dismissed with the withering question: "When you were a Contractor in Germany and wanted Flour in a distant Country did you enquire of the Price of it from a Person who had not been in that Country for twelve years?"[114] For the rest, Grenville seems to have been concerned partly to exculpate himself from the charge that his Customs reforms had been responsible for wrecking the Spanish bullion trade in the West Indies and partly to play for time.[115] His patent inability to produce any expert evidence on his side greatly enhanced the impact of the testimonies procured by the administration.

That the commercial consideration was the decisive one in the ultimate triumph of the campaign for repeal can scarcely be doubted. According to Horace Walpole, "it was the clamour of trade, of the merchants, and of the manufacturing towns, that had borne down all opposition," and his verdict must be confirmed by the historian.[116] But it must not be assumed that the Commons were motivated in their decision simply by a concern for the merchants, in particular, or the economic plight of the country, in general. One of the topics raised in the Committee had a significance which went beyond the purely economic. This was the unemployment which was said to be a product of the Stamp Act crisis, a matter on which many witnesses were most emphatic. For example, Robert Hamilton, a Manchester manufacturer, claimed to have laid off some 2,400 workmen; William Reeve, the leader of the Bristol merchants, spoke of heavy unemployment in the West Riding and testified to the dismissal of 30 percent of the labor force of his district.[117] A Cheapside shoemaker connected with Trecothick, one John Hose, was trapped by an Opposition questioner into the unfortunate admission that he thought boots and shoes bore a Stamp duty.[118] But this transparent ignorance merely added point to the patent honesty and therefore effect of his testimony—that he had laid off all but forty-five of his three hundred workmen and that he had done so because Trecothick's American orders had suddenly dried up.

The corollary of this anxiety about unemployment was concern about the American industrial potential and the determination of the colonists to manufacture for themselves the goods, which they declined to order from Britain, and this seemed scarcely less important than the nonimportation agreements themselves. The possibility of industrial expansion in the colonies was repeatedly raised during the Committee's examination of witnesses with some knowledge of America, though this fear was in reality a superfluous one.[119] The labor shortage and bias in favor of agricultural and commercial enterprise in the colonies militated strongly against serious industrial development during the foreseeable future, and Thomas Whately's belief that "all Attempts to establish Manufactures in America, to an Extent that may be alarming to Great Britain must prove abortive in the End," was quite justified.[120] Nonetheless, much was made of this danger, and the claims of Franklin and his friends that the Americans were indeed capable of dispensing with British manufactures were most influential, endorsing the view that what was at issue was not merely a temporary depression, but a long-term threat to English industry.[121]

The Commons' evident anxiety about unemployment reflected their concern with the social as well as economic consequences of the Stamp Act crisis in England. An industrial slump was potentially as dangerous to law and order as to commercial prosperity. As the Duke of Grafton later pointed out in the Lords, at the very least, there was the prospect of a heavy addition to the burden of maintaining the poor, at most, the danger of severe disturbances,[122] even, according to DeBerdt, the possibility that the unemployed might "fall on the Lands of the Nobility and Gentry."[123] This consideration had been heavily emphasized to the ministry by the merchants and agents in the previous autumn, and great use was made of it in the Commons. According to Henry Cruger, it was the most influential factor there. Referring to the evidence of a Leeds manufacturer that he had laid off half his employees, he remarked:

> This fact will have great weight when added to many more evidences of the like kind. The Country Members are somewhat alarmed at so many People losing Employ, if anything repeals the Act, it must be this. [T]he present Ministry see and have declared the Expediency of repealing on this ground. [I]f the late Ministers come in again, and enforce the Act, they will have 20,000 unemployed Poor in a suppliant manner petitioning a Repeal of the S[tamp] Act.[124]

How seriously these prophecies should be taken is uncertain. It is difficult to believe that the fears expressed were never a little extravagant and fanciful. On the other hand, many were quite obviously very alarmed.

> Every member of the Community [Garbett assured Dartmouth], from his Majesty to the Peasant must soon feel the Effects in numberless Instances—here I must Stop—as Dangers arise which I must not point out—for I would most unwillingly be thought Seditious—but I will venture to say that Gentlemen are not aware of the numerous ill consequences that will be produced by Violence by Indecision or by suspence in their determination respecting America.[125]

Another Birmingham man, John Twiggs, was equally apprehensive, writing to William Reeve in December that "We are very fearful the Country will rise before [that] Time [the meeting of Parliament] comes; but sho[ul]d not the Act be repeal'd 'tis impossible to prevent it, dreadful and alarming indeed is our Situation.[126]

Whatever the truth of the matter, it was an effective ploy. That it was a critical consideration is confirmed by the attitude of the Opposition, which treated the grievances of the merchants as the deceptions of "Interested Men,"[127] but which did not attempt to deny the "distress of our manufactures at home."[128] Bedford considered that "they ought in such an emergency to be employed by Government," and the very concern to find a solution to the problem amounted to a tacit recognition of its importance.[129] Its impact was heightened by what DeBerdt called "a recent instance thereof"—the Spitalfields riots of May 1765.[130] These riots have been obscured in historical perspective by the Gordon Riots, but heavy concentrations of troops had to be employed before they subsided, and they made a deep impression at the time. Fundamentally, the riots had been the product of a slump in the silk industry in the year or two after the Seven Years' War, and there was some excuse for expecting a repetition of such disturbances in 1766. It was scarcely surprising that Newcastle, alarmed by the rapid growth of unemployment, could write, "I dread The Consequence of what may happen even in This Capital," or that the Commons recognized the domestic implications of the Stamp Act crisis.[131] It was not only the prospect of a decline from commercial greatness that ensured the success of the repeal agitation; it was also the threat of popular disturbances and the specter of severe social dislocation.

Fundamentally, the Commons approved the policy of repeal because it accepted the existence of a causal link between Grenville's American legislation and the commercial and industrial crisis in Britain. Whether the historian should be equally trusting is more than doubtful. In this connection, a paper possibly drawn up by Charles Jenkinson early in 1767 merits extensive quotation.

> It was represented to Administration, and afterwards given in Evidence in Parliament, in March 1766, by those who solicited the Repeal of the Stamp Act, that a very considerable Part of the Orders for Goods, which had been transmitted from America in the Year 1765, had been afterwards suspended; but that, in Case the Stamp Act was repealed, those Orders were to be executed in the present Year 1766, in Addition to the Orders for the Supply of that Year; that in Consequence, the Exports to the Colonies had, in the Year 1765 been greatly diminished, and the Trade of Great-Britain thither entirely at a Stand. Whereas, should the Stamp-Act be repealed, Trade would again flourish, and the Exports to the Colonies, in the present Year 1766, would be at least double the Value of the Exports in the past Year. The Stamp-Act was repealed, and every other American Proposition adopted; and from the Custom-House Entries, it now appears, that the Exports to the North American Colonies in the Year 1766, instead of being double the Value, as was promised, actually fell short of the Exports in 1765, no less than 176,884£ so greatly was the Administration and Parliament abused by those they confided in, and so dangerous it is to allow interested Traders to direct the Measures of Government.[132]

Though Jenkinson was admittedly an opponent of repeal, his comments were substantially correct. Lavish promises of great improvement had been made in order to ensure the passage of repeal, and these promises were indeed belied by events. Exports from the American colonies, far from reviving after repeal, continued to decline. For example, the value of goods exported to New York, which had fallen some £130,000 from their 1764 figure of £500,000, fell a further £50,000 in 1766.[133] Shipments to Pennsylvania, which stood at £435,000 in 1764, fell by a sixth in 1765 and a further ninth in 1766. These figures were typical of the general pattern. Apart from Georgia, a tiny plantation which for no clear reason did not conform, exports to the colonies suffered a general decline. It was not surprising that by the end of 1766, the New York merchants were again complaining of their commercial troubles, and, in their mystification at the origin of these troubles, were blaming both Rockingham and Grenville. Nor was it surprising that John Hancock, the most celebrated of the Boston merchants, was writing in 1766, "Our trade is very dull, money very scarce and but an indifferent prospect of carrying on Business to any advantage."[134] Not until two years later, long after the remedies applied by the Rockingham administration had been carried out, were there any signs of improvement.

The failure of the colonial economy to respond to the measures of 1766 must largely be explained by reference to the fact that the depression in American markets was by no means local. Trecothick pointed out in the Commons that "[The] Trade of Gr[eat] Britain to every Q[uarte]r of the World is upon the decline," and certainly, all the key markets for British manufactures suffered heavily in the mid-1760s.[135] Export values to Germany, which had reached a record £2.3 million in

1764, sank steadily to £1.2 million by 1770. Those to Holland, over £2 million in 1764, fell by a quarter in 1765 and 1766, while the Portuguese trade, which could normally absorb up to £1 million a year, accounted for less than half that figure in the middle sixties. The Spanish trade displayed a similar trend, and even exports handled by the East India Company were reduced by over a third between 1764 and 1766. Only Ireland and Russia of the important markets sustained their level of demand in what T. S. Ashton has described as a "reaction—common to all overseas markets—from the post-war boom."[136] Indeed, the recession was not limited to commerce. A major financial crash originating at Amsterdam in 1763, a succession of bad harvests and exceptionally high food prices, together with the stresses and strains consequent upon a return to peacetime conditions all aggravated the basic problem of the depression which followed the inflated prosperity of 1763 and 1764.

The precise connection of the Stamp Act crisis with this depression is not easily assessed. However, it is clear that there were two major fallacies in the argument which the House of Commons heard and endorsed in 1766. One lay in the undue significance attributed to colonial trade. It is true that great emphasis was placed on the American market in the overall picture of British trade by some merchants and manufacturers and that historians have also stressed its strategic importance; "the principal dynamic element in English export trade," it has been called.[137] Nonetheless, it is possible to overestimate its significance. In the great year of 1764, British exports to America amounted to some £2.8 million. Yet Germany and Holland each took over £2 million in the year, while Ireland, Spain, Portugal, and the East Indies all commanded well over £1 million each. It was natural for merchants who derived their livelihood from the American trade to stress the national importance of their business, but it must be remembered that the continental colonies accounted for only an eighth of all exports, a very large, but by no means a dominating proportion.

The second misapprehension was scarcely less serious. The basic assumption on which both administration and the House of Commons acted, namely, that the severe decline in colonial commerce was directly attributable to the legislation of the Grenville ministry, was far from sound. There was and is no reliable evidence that the Sugar Act and Stamp Act were responsible for the slump in the colonial economy. In particular, the impression was deliberately given that the heart of the problem lay in the nonimportation agreements, which so dismayed British merchants. Yet these agreements were not made until November 1765 (the earliest, that of New York, was reached on 31 October) and were not to come into operation until 1 January 1766, long after the symptoms of a commercial malaise had begun to appear in Britain and America in the autumn of 1764.[138] Doubtless, the Sugar and Stamp acts and the accompanying measures had an adverse effect on the colonial economy, both in the restrictions they imposed on trade and in the demands they made on specie. But the fundamental cause of the economic problem lay elsewhere. Wartime conditions, especially the artificial stimulus injected by the presence of large military concentrations across the Atlantic and the temporary British possession of the great Spanish and French islands in the West Indies, had raised commercial activity to quite unprecedented heights. The consequent glut in continental and Caribbean markets and the drastic shrinkage produced by the coming of peace led inevitably to a severe recession. One Opposition M. P. properly inquired of Trecothick "whether [the] encrease in 1764 did not occasion the market being glutted and decrease the y[ea]r 1765."[139] Both the American and Spanish trades were victims first and foremost of this development. In consequence, it is scarcely surprising that the nullification of Grenville's colonial measures by the Rockingham administration and Parliament in 1766 failed to produce any significant improvement. What was at issue was not a regional decline in American trade but a widespread depression—aggravated by, but fundamentally independent of, political discontents and government measures—which had afflicted Britain, its empire, and indeed, the whole Western world. The Americans, the merchants and manufacturers in Britain, Rockingham and his colleagues, and in the last resort, the House of Commons all came to an essentially erroneous conclusion—that the critical factor in the crisis at home and in the colonies was the Stamp Act and Grenville's other imperial policies.

Had Grenville been able to prove to the House of Commons that the premises on which the administration based its case for repeal were false and had he been able to show that repeal would not improve the economic situation, it is unlikely that Rockingham's policy would have found the favor it did. However, the fact that the economic basis of the ministry's policy was faulty rather adds to its significance. It is no coincidence that the British Parliament came nearer than ever after to a genuinely conciliatory attitude at a time of severe economic unrest. Ten years later, the situation was very different. Apart from the financial crash of 1772–73, the early 1770s were a prosperous period for English trade and industry. The political inactivity of the merchants in 1774–75 as opposed to 1765 is well known.[140] But in 1765, the commercial scene was almost universally bleak. In 1775, it was surprisingly bright—even the American trade on the eve of the War of Independence prospered, while employment was full and industrial growth rapid.[141] Not until the American war was well under way and Bourbon intervention inevitable did the severe economic recession of the late 1770s develop. It would be unwise to underrate the differences between the administrations of North and Rockingham or to attribute changes in imperial policy to crude economic factors. Yet the fact remains that in 1766, in the midst of an alarming if largely fortuitous depression, both government and Parliament opted for a conciliatory policy, while in 1774–75, when commercial prospects were so good that not even those "interested men," the merchants, were inclined to protest, there was overwhelming support for a rigidly authoritarian policy.

From a purely domestic point of view, the economic basis of repeal was equally significant. The agitation for repeal is usually treated as an affair of the merchants. Certainly, it was so in America, but in Great Britain, while the role of Trecothick and his friends in supervising the campaign was of the first importance, a critical part was also played by the manufacturers, so that the Opposition could even talk of "The Manufacturing Interest against The Interest of The Nation."[142] Nearly twenty years before the period of industrial takeoff and the political activities of Wedgwood and his fellow manufacturers, Parliament was displaying intense interest in the economic problems and social repercussions of British industry and its development. Their preoccupation, not merely with trade and navigation but with manufactured exports and industrial employment, is a pointer to the rapidly changing balance of power in the community. The prominence of the disparate financial and mercantile interests—North America, East India, and West India—in the early years of George III's reign must not be allowed to obscure the role of the manufacturing interest, as yet unorganized and incoherent, but nonetheless, a growing power in the land. Not the least remarkable feature of the Stamp Act crisis is its powerful testimony to the burgeoning importance of the new cities and new men of the industrial North and Midlands, as against the traditional influence of the mercantile elites of the metropolis and outports.

In retrospect, indeed, it is the general effectiveness of the various external pressures operating on administration and Parliament in the Stamp Act crisis which is particularly impressive. The Rockingham Whigs, apart from rather vague good intentions, had shown little enthusiasm for the colonial cause in their early months of power. Indeed, despite the record for liberalism which the repeal of the Stamp Act was to earn them, they were always to remain deeply conservative in their attitude toward America.[143] In 1765–66, it was primarily their fear of the economic consequences for the empire of a continuing crisis in Anglo-American relations which put them on the road to the repeal of the Stamp Act. This was still more true of Parliament, where the general attitude was profoundly hostile to the colonial viewpoint. Only under the great pressures brought to bear by an intensively organized campaign in and out of Westminster was parliamentary opinion convinced of the need to repeal the Stamp Act, not least in the purely domestic interest. The fact that much of the argument advanced and information purveyed was completely misleading is scarcely relevant in this context. Ultimately, what mattered was that the combined pressures of American political discontent and economic sanctions together with the great weight of the commercial and industrial lobby in Britain were sufficient to transform a basically unpromising political situation. Colonial opinion was ultimately to misinterpret the significance of these developments and to find that nonimportation campaigns were not automatically effective in every circumstance. Yet it is difficult in retrospect not to sympathize with those who saw the events of 1765–66 as conclusive evidence of the vulnerability of the British establishment to organized pressure.

• NOTES •

1. Gertrude S. Kimball, ed., *The Correspondence of the Colonial Governors of Rhode Island: 1723–1775* (Boston and New York: Houghton-Mifflin, 1902–1903), vol. 2, p. 367: 16 July 1765.

2. Sheffield City Library, Wentworth Woodhouse Muniments (hereafter cited as WWM), R1-522: copy of a letter from America, 8 November 1765.

3. Ingersoll to Fitch, 6 March 1765, "The Fitch Papers," Connecticut Historical Society, *Collections* 17 and 18, vol. 2 (1918, 1920), p. 334.

4. British Library (formerly British Museum), Additional Manuscripts (Add. MS.) 32965, f. 346, 6 February 1765.

5. Franklin to Thomson, 11 July 1765, Leonard W. Labaree, ed., *The Papers of Benjamin Franklin* (New Haven: Yale Univ. Press, 1959–66), v. 12, p. 207.

6. Board of Trade's Representation, 27 August 1765, British Public Record Office, Colonial Office (C. O.) 5/1368, f. 133.

7. Minutes of "a meeting of his M[agesty]'s Ser[van]ts at his R[oyal] H[ighness] the Duke of Cumberland's," See Add. MS. 32969, f. 257. Conway's dispatch of 14 September adhered very closely to the directions of the Minute.

8. Fauquier to Board of Trade, 5 June 1765, C. O. 5/1331, f. 29.

9. Conway to Fauquier, 14 September 1765, C. O. 5/1345, f. 84.

10. On Harrison, see D. H. Watson, "Barlow Trecothick and other Associates of Lord Rockingham during the Stamp Act Crisis" (M. A. thesis, Sheffield Univ., 1958), pp. 100–128.

11. "The Bowdoin and Temple Papers," Massachusetts Historical Society, *Collections* 6th ser., 10 (1897), p. 70.

12. WWM, R1-502.

13. James Munroe, ed., *Acts of the Privy Council of England: Colonial Series* (6 vols., London: His Majesty's Stationery Office, 1911), vol. 4, p. 732. The clearest summary of the proceedings of the treasury, council, and secretary of state is at the British Public Record Office, Treasury Papers (hereafter referred to as T.), 1st ser., vol. 447, ff. 135–36.

14. Bernard's letters of 15, 22, and 31 August (the last was received first) to secretary of state and Board of Trade, C. O. 5/755, ff. 261–300; 891, ff. 541–78, T. 1/439, ff. 67–68.

15. *Ibid.*

16. WWM, R29: Three different dispatches were signed by Conway on 24 October, that to Bernard, a circular to all American governors, and instructions to Gage. All used similar expressions.

17. C. Lloyd, *Conduct of the Late Administration Examined, Relative to the American Stamp Act,* 2nd ed. (London, 1767), p. 74.

18. P. D. G. Thomas, ed., "Parliamentary Diaries of Nathaniel Ryder, 1764–67," Royal Historical Society, *Camden Miscellany* 23 (1969), p. 258.

19. "Mem[orandum]s upon The American Abstracts," 24 January 1766, Add. MS. 33001, f. 54.

20. 6 April 1766, Add. MS. 51406, f. 138.

21. Conway to Gage, 24 October 1765, C. O. 5/83, f. 449, Conway to Admiralty Lords, 15 October 1765, British Public Record Office, Admiralty Papers 1st ser., vol. 4126; Munroe, *Acts of the Privy Council: Colonial Series,* vol. 4, p. 733.

22. Notes, 31 January 1766, Warwickshire Record Office, Newdigate Manuscripts, B2545—17.

23. Edward Channing and Archibald Cary Coolidge, eds., *The Barrington-Bernard Correspondence and Illustrative Matter, 1760–1770* (Cambridge, Mass.: Harvard Univ. Press, 1912), pp. 227–38.

24. W. Franklin to Conway, 23 September 1765, C. O. 5/987, ff. 135–38; Donald L. Kemmerer, "New Material on the Stamp Act in New Jersey," *Proceedings of the New Jersey Historical Society* 56 (July 1938), pp. 220–25.

25. "The Letters and Papers of Cadwallader Colden," New York Historical Society, 1775, *Collections* 56 (1923), pp. 57–71.

26. Gage to Barrington, 10 January 1766, Clarence Edwin Carter, ed., *The Correspondence of General Thomas Gage with the War Office and the Treasury, 1763–1775* (2 vols., New Haven: Yale Univ. Press, 1931–33), vol. 2, p. 334: Gage to Barrington, 16 January 1766. See also John R. Alden, *General Gage in America* (Baton Rouge, La.: Louisiana State Univ. Press, 1948), pp. 113–14ff.

27. The replies, almost all of which insisted on the impossibility of enforcing the Stamp Act without large reinforcements, are to be found at C. O. 5/310, ff. 84–85; 390, ff. 70–71; 658, ff. 112–17; 755, ff. 455–58; 934, ff. 54–56; 1098, ff. 36–39; 1280, ff. 37, 123–24, 176–77.

28. 1 July 1766, quoted in Michael G. Kammen, *A Rope of Sand: The Colonial Agents, British Politics, and the American Revolution* (Ithaca: Cornell Univ. Press, 1968), p. 123.

29. T. Ramsden to Jenkinson, 15 January 1766, Add. MS. 38205, f. 32.

30. Rockingham to [Viscount Irwin], 25 October 1765, *Historical Manuscripts Commission Various Collections*, vol. 8, p. 133.

31. "Extract of a Letter from Boston," 16 August 1765, WWM, R1-482. It is a reasonable assumption that this was the enclosure in Savile's letter.

32. George Thomas, Earl of Albermarle, *Memoirs of the Marquis of Rockingham and his Contemporaries* (London: R. Bentley, 1852), vol. 1, p. 253. The original, which is not quite accurately reproduced by Albermarle, is at Savile to Rockingham, 1 November 1765, WWM, R1-519.

33. For details of Trecothick, see Theodore D. Jervey, "Barlow Trecothick," *South Carolina Historical and Genealogical Magazine* 32 (July 1931), pp. 157–69; and Watson, "Barlow Trecothick," pp. 20ff.

34. Trecothick to Rockingham, 7 November 1765, WWM, R24-43a.

35. Richard Jackson to Fitch, 15 November 1765, "Fitch Papers," vol. 2, p. 376.

36. Rockingham's notes, dated 27 November 1765, but from the day of the week given, in fact (28) November, WWM, R49-6.

37. Bedford Manuscripts, Bedford Estate Office, London, 1ii, ff. 228–29; the version at Lord J. Russell, ed., *Correspondence of John, Fourth Duke of Bedford* (London, 1846), vol. 3, p. 323, is not wholly accurate.

38. 24 October 1765, Add. MS. 35911, f. 64.

39. Notes in Rockingham's hand, undated, WWM, R49-31.

40. Samuel Lister to Rockingham, 7 December 1765, WWM, R1-538.

41. Rockingham to [William Reeve?], August 1766, unfinished draft, WWM, R1-670.

42. Jackson to Fitch, 9 February 1765, "Fitch Papers," vol. 2, pp. 316–17; A. E. Brown, *John Hancock His Book* (Boston: Lee & Shepard, 1898), pp. 63–64; Albert Matthews, ed., "Letters of Dennys DeBerdt, 1757–1770," Colonial Society of Massachusetts, *Publications*, vol. 13, *Transactions, 1910–11* (1912), p. 441; Lewis Burd Walker, ed., *The Burd Papers: Extracts from Chief Justice William Allen's Letterbook* (3 vols., Pottsville, Pa.: Standard Pub. Co., 1897–99), vol. 1, p. 67.

43. Hancock to Barnards and Harrison, 22 March 1765, Brown, *John Hancock,* p. 69.

44. On these, see Arthur M. Schlesinger, *The Colonial Merchants and the American Revolution, 1763–1775* (New York: Columbia Univ. Press, 1917), pp. 79–80.

45. Historical Manuscripts Commission, *Dartmouth Manuscripts,* William Salt Library, Stafford, vol. 2, p. 23.

46. December 1765, Brown, *John Hancock,* p. 104.

47. 14 October 1765, *Ibid.,* pp. 86–87.

48. "Communication to Connecticut Gazette," 10 September 1765, Franklin B. Dexter, ed., "A Selection from the Correspondence and Miscellaneous Papers of Jared Ingersoll," *Papers of the New Haven Colony Historical Society* 9 (1918), p. 332.

49. See Jack M. Sosin, *Agents and Merchants: British Colonial Policy and the Origins of the American Revolution, 1763–1775* (Lincoln, Neb.: Univ. of Nebraska Press, 1965), pp. 33–36.

50. Sherwood to Governor Hopkins, 2 May 1765, Kimball, *Correspondence of the Colonial Governors of Rhode Island,* vol. 2, pp. 363–64.

51. Trecothick to Principal Magistrate of Leeds, enclosing Minute of Proceedings of 4 and 6 December 1765, WWM, R1-537.

52. "General Letter from Com[mitt]ee of North American Merchants," 6 December 1765, WWM, R1-535.

53. *Ibid.*

54. Trecothick's evidence in Committee on American Papers, 11 February 1766, Add. MS. 33030, f. 105.

55. W. R. Savadge, "The West Country and the American Mainland Colonies," (B. Litt. Thesis, Oxford, 1951), pp. 212–13ff.

56. Garbett to Dartmouth, 21 December 1765, Garbett to Dartmouth, 4 January 1766, *Dartmouth MSS.*

57. The petitions, with dates of presentation to the House of Commons, were as follows: from the Lancashire region: Liverpool, Lancaster, Manchester, (17 January); Macclesfeld (20 January); from Yorkshire: Halifax, Leeds (17 January); Birmingham, Coventry, Wolverhampton, Stourbridge, Dudley (20 January); Nottingham (28 January); Worcester (24 February); from the West Country and Cotswolds: Bristol, two petitions, Bradford (17 January); Frome (20 January); Minehead (21 January); Taunton (22 January); Witney (23 January); Chippenham (27 January); Melksham (30 January); also London (17 January) and Glasgow (27 January).

58. Trecothick to J. Poole, 27 December 1765, Add. MS. 22358, f. 33. For Poole's original reply, see 14 December 1765, f. 33, and for the circular sent, f. 32.

59. F. J. Hinkhouse, *The Preliminaries of the American Revolution as seen in the English Press: 1763–1775* (New York: Columbia Univ. Press, 1926), p. 63.

60. J. Poole to Buckinghamshire, 10 February 1766, Add. MS. 22358, f. 34.

61. Meredith to Burke, 1 January 1766, WWM, Bk. 1-44.

62. Bedford's notes, Bedford MSS. liii, f. 18.

63. Lloyd, *Conduct of the Administration Examined,* p. 117.

64. Nugent in the Commons, on 14 January 1766, as reported in the *Universal Magazine,* vol. 38, p. 244.

65. G. Middleton to Jenkinson, 1 December 1765, Add. MS. 38205, f. 12; Sir J. Yorke to Hardwicke, 14 January 1766, *ibid.,* 35368, ff. 3–4.

66. Trecothick's evidence on 11 February 1766, Add. MS. 33030, ff. 105–6; and

Newdigate's notes of the evidence, mistakenly dated 10 February 1766, Newdigate MSS., B2545-20.

67. Quoted in Walter E. Minchinton, "The Stamp Act Crisis: Bristol and Virginia," *Virginia Magazine of History and Biography* 73 (April 1965), p. 153.

68. Savadge, "The West Country," p. 216.

69. Trecothick to Reeve, 2 January 1766, quoted in *ibid.*, p. 221.

70. Grey Cooper's report of the debate of 3 February 1766 in Commons in C. H. Hull and H. V. Temperley, eds., "Debates on the Declaratory Act and the Repeal of the Stamp Act, 1766," *American Historical Review* 17 (April 1912), p. 572.

71. Trecothick's evidence of 11 February 1766, Add. MS. 33030, f. 106.

72. Henry Cruger, Jr., to Aaron Lopez, 1 March 1766, "Commerce of Rhode Island, 1726–1800," Massachusetts Historical Society, *Collections,* vols. 9 and 10 (1914–15); vol. 1, p. 145.

73. WWM, R1-535. According to Watson ("Barlow Trecothick," p. 36), Lady Rockingham was the author of this endorsement.

74. Add. MS. 32973, f. 13.

75. Garbett to Dartmouth, 21 December 1765, 4 January 1766, *Dartmouth MSS.,* 130, 147; [Garbett] to Dartmouth, 9 February 1766, Northants Record Office, Fitzwilliam Manuscripts, A. xxvi. 18.

76. Trecothick to Rockingham, 30 November 1765, WWM, R43-8, 9, 10, 11; *Journal of the Commissioners for Trade and Plantations, from January 1764 to December 1767* (London, 1936), pp. 226–27.

77. Joseph Redington and R. A. Roberts, eds., *Calendar of Home Office Papers . . . 1760–1775* (4 vols., London: Longmans, 1878–79), 1760–65, pp. 605–6, 620, 637–38; 1766–69, pp. 24–25, 27, 37, 38, 41–42; *Dartmouth MSS.,* vol. 3, p. 180.

78. For a detailed analysis of much of this material, see Watson, "Barlow Trecothick."

79. Thomas Cushing and Samuel Adams to ———, 11 November 1765, *Dartmouth MSS.*

80. For Fothergill's letters to Dartmouth, see 7/8 August and 29/31 August 1765, *ibid.,* 75, 81; and 6 December 1765, WWM, R65-5.

81. Milnes to Rockingham, 21 and 24 November 1765, WWM, R24-37, 38, 39; *Dartmouth MSS.,* 331–32.

82. J. Yorke to Hardwicke, 14 February 1766, Add. MS. 35374, f. 286.

83. D. H. Watson, ed., "William Baker's Account of the Repeal of the Stamp Act," *William and Mary Quarterly,* 3d. ser., 26 (April 1969), p. 262; Burke to O'Hara, 4 March 1766, T. W. Copeland, ed., *Burke Correspondence,* (Cambridge Univ. Press, 1958–79), vol. 1, p. 241.

84. Newcastle to Seeker, 2 February 1766, Add. MS. 32973, f. 342.

85. A paper of about February 1766 in Bedford's hand, *Bedford MSS., l iii. f. 18. The Opposition held meetings to marshal its arguments at Halifax's house on 24 January and at the Star and Garter on the twenty-ninth (ibid.,* ff. 14–15, 22–23).

86. Bedford, "Thoughts in the Proper Manner," 24 January 1766, *ibid.,* f. 14.

87. *Ibid.*

88. Henry Cruger, Jr., to Henry Cruger, Sr., 14 February 1766, "Commerce of Rhode Island," vol. 1, p. 141.

89. The breakdown of the 79 speakers is as follows: 9 Grenvilles, 8 Bedfords, 7 Pittites, 10 Independents (including 3 Tories), 16 King's Friends, and 29 Administration.

90. Gascoyne to Strutt, 8 February 1766, Strutt Manuscripts.

91. Garth to Tilghman, etc., "Stamp Act Papers," *Maryland Historical Magazine* 6 (1911), p. 304.

92. See Douglas Adair, "The Stamp Act in Contemporary English Cartoons," *William and Mary Quarterly,* 3d ser., 10 (October 1953), pp. 538–42; M. D. George, "America in English Satirical Prints," *William and Mary Quarterly,* 3d ser., 10 (October 1953), p. 517–18.

93. Cruger to H. Cruger, Sr., 14 February 1766, "Commerce of Rhode Island," vol. 1, p. 142; Champion to C. Lloyd, 15 February 1766, G. H. Guttridge, ed., *The American Correspondence of a Bristol Merchant, 1766–1776* (Berkeley: Univ. of California Press, 1934), p. 11.

94. Copies of letters to Newdigate, Barre, J. Mordaunt, Denbeigh, Shelburne, Sir C. Mordaunt, and Dartmouth, 15 February 1766, Fitzwilliam MSS., A. xxvi. 18.

95. Henry Cruger, Jr. to Henry Cruger, Sr., 14 February 1766, "Commerce of Rhode Island," vol. 1, p. 139.

96. "Correspondence between William Strahan and David Hall, 1763–1777," *Pennsylvania Magazine of History and Biography* 10 (1886), p. 92; see also Edwin Wolf 2nd, "Benjamin Franklin's Stamp Act Cartoon," *Proceedings of the American Philosophical Society* 99 (December 1955), pp. 388–96.

97. [Garbett] to Dartmouth, 9 February 1766, Fitzwilliam MSS., A. xxvi. 18. Garbett seems the most likely author of this letter which exists only in the form of a copy in the hand of Joseph Harrison.

98. See Watson, "Barlow Trecothick," pp. 41–42, for the organized presentation of the petitions.

99. WWM, R42-5 to R42-12. Savile's friend David Hartley also helped to organize the Yorkshire campaign (Hartley to ———, 7 February 1766, Berkshire Record Office, Hartley Manuscripts, 0.19).

100. Copeland, *Burke Correspondence,* vol. 1, p. 235; Burke, notes "Names to the Birmingham Petition," Fitzwilliam MSS., A. xxv. 79.

101. "Minutes of Evidence from Sir William Meredith," Bk. 1-44, Meredith to Burke, 1 January 1766, WWM, R42-2, 3, 4.

102. "Papers relating to the Questions that Mr. Jackson asked Mr. Kelly." WWM, R96-11, 12. A number of draft questions with answers.

103. WWM, R57-2. The petition itself is at WWM, R57-1.

104. West to Newcastle, 11 February 1766, Add. MS. 32973, f. 411, Franklin was similarly prepared, see Labaree, *Papers of Benjamin Franklin,* vol. 12, p. 129.

105. The official record, which bears witness to the inability of the clerks to keep pace with the speakers, is to be found at Add. MS. 33030, f. 78–203 and WWM, R-27. Other sources for the evidence are Thomas, "Parliamentary Diaries of Nathaniel Ryder," pp. 291–302; "Commerce of Rhode Island," vol. 1, pp. 139–40; West to Newcastle, 11 February 1766, Add. MS. 32973, f. 411; Newdigate's notes, Newdigate MSS. B2545-15, 16, 17, 18, 19, 20, 21, 22. A useful analysis of the evidence is in B. R. Smith, "The Committee of the Whole House to consider the American Papers (January and February 1766)" (M. A. Thesis, Sheffield Univ., 1957).

106. Lawrence Henry Gipson, "The Great Debate in the Committee of the Whole House of Commons on the Stamp Act 1766, as Reported by Nathaniel Ryder," *Pennsylvania Magazine of History and Biography* 36 (January 1962), pp. 40–41; see also *idem., The British Empire Before the American Revolution,* vol. 10, *The Triumphant Empire:*

Thunder Clouds Gather in the West, 1763–1766 (New York: Knopf, 1961), pp. 480–9.

107. West to Newcastle, 21 February 1766, Add. MS. 32974, f. 45; Lionel Cust, ed., *Records of the Cust Family, Series 3* (London: Mitchell, Hughes and Clark, 1927), p. 96.

108. Pitt's speech of 14 January as reported in *Universal Magazine*, vol. 38, p. 248.

109. Newcastle to Archbishop of Canterbury, 2 February 1766, Add. MS. 32973, f. 342.

110. Meredith's motion to this effect on 11 February was negatived (West to Newcastle, [11 February 1766] *ibid.*, f. 411).

111. "Correspondence between William Strahan and David Hall," pp. 220–21: 10 May 1766.

112. For the examination, which was later printed, see Labaree, *Papers of Benjamin Franklin*, vol. 13, pp. 124–62 and Appendix A. Though the most quoted point made by Franklin is the celebrated distinction between internal and external taxes, the most influential was probably his insistence that modification of the Stamp Act, the only alternative by this stage to repeal, would be totally repugnant to the colonists. For the impression made by his testimony on this matter, see *Selection from the Family Papers Preserved at Caldwell* (Glasgow, 1854), Part II, vol. 2, pp. 71–75, and for the problem of Franklin's role in general, see Smith, "The Committee of the Whole House," p. 275.

113. Much was and is made on the importance of these debts, (see, for example, Emory G. Evans, "Planter Indebtedness and the Coming of the American Revolution," *William and Mary Quarterly,* 3d ser., 19 [October 1962], pp. 511–33). It must be stressed however that their influence lay less in affecting the Commons than in moving the merchants to press for the repeal campaign in the first place.

114. Add. MS. 33030, f. 200.

115. William S. Taylor and John H. Pringle, eds., *Correspondence of William Pitt, Earl of Chatham* (4 vols., London: John Murray, 1839), vol. 2, p. 387. Grenville called seven witnesses on 17 and 18 February. The evidence for 18 February is not in the official record, but some of it was noted by Newdigate (Newdigate MSS., B.2545-15).

116. Horace Walpole, *Memoirs of the Reign of King George III* (London: Lawrence and Bullen, 1894), vol. 2, pp. 211–12.

117. Add. MS. 33030, f. 154, 151, 145.

118. *Ibid.,* f. 180.

119. *Ibid.,* f. 99, 100, 111, 119, 131, 144, 150, 168, 170.

120. Thomas Whately, *The Regulations lately made concerning the Colonies, and the Taxes Imposed upon Them, considered* (London, 1765), p. 67.

121. For Franklin's testimony on this point, see Labaree, *Papers of Benjamin Franklin*, vol. 13, pp. 143, 160–61; and for its incompatability with other remarks made by him, see Victor S. Clark, *History of Manufactures in the United States, 1607–1860* (reprint ed., New York: P. Smith, 1949), vol. 1, p. 218.

122. Hull and Temperley, "Debates on the Declaratory Act," p. 581; see also John Fothergill, *Considerations Relative to the North American Colonies* (London, 1765), p. 14.

123. DeBerdt to Halifax, n.d., Matthews, "Letters of Dennys DeBerdt," p. 429.

124. Henry Cruger, Jr., to Henry Cruger, Sr., 14 February 1766, "Commerce of Rhode Island," vol. 1, p. 140.

125. Garbett to Dartmouth, 9 February 1766, Fitzwilliam MSS., A. xxvi. 18.

126. J. Twiggs to W. Reeve, 26 December 1765, quoted in Savadge, "The West Country," p. 217.

127. Newcastle's Notes "from the Book," 11 March 1766, Add. MS. 33001, f. 155.

A remark apparently made by Lord Coventry in the Lords.

128. Jenkinson's speech on 21 February 1766, Thomas, "Parliamentary Diaries of Nathaniel Ryder," p. 305.

129. A paper of about February 1766 in Bedford's hand, Bedford MSS., liii. f. 18.

130. DeBerdt to Dartmouth, July 1765, Matthews, ed., "Letters of Dennys DeBerdt," p. 432.

131. Newcastle to Archbishop of Canterbury, 15 February 1766, Add. MS. 32974, f. 5.

132. "Exports to North America in 1765 and 66," Add. MS. 38339, f. 303. This document was subsequently published in William Knox's pamphlet, *The Present State of the Nation* (London, 1768).

133. The statistics are taken from Sir C. Whitworth, *State of the Trade of Great Britain in its Imports and Exports* (London, 1776), which was based on the Inspector-General of Customs' ledgers. While the general value of this work is limited, it is adequate for the purpose of year-by-year comparisons of exports in this period.

134. Hancock to Barnards and Harrison, 15 October 1766, Brown, *John Hancock,* p. 134.

135. Newdigate's notes of 11 (wrongly dated 10) February 1766, Newdigate MSS., B. 2545-20.

136. T. S. Ashton, *Economic Fluctuations in England, 1700–1800* (Oxford: Clarendon Press, 1959), p. 154.

137. Ralph Davies, "English Foreign Trade, 1700–1774," *Economic History Review,* 2d ser., 15 (December 1962), pp. 285–303.

138. The standard authorities, (Ashton, *Economic Fluctuations,* p. 154; and Walter E. Minchinton, ed., *The Growth of English Overseas Trade in the Seventeenth and Eighteenth Centuries* [London: Methuen, 1969], p. 17), recognize the existence of a deepseated depression after the Seven Years' War, yet persist in attributing a key role to the agreements, though the timing does not correspond.

139. Newdigate's Notes of 11 (wrongly dated 10) February 1766, Newdigate MSS., B. 2545-20.

140. Bernard Donoughue, *British Politics and the American Revolution: The Path to War, 1773–1775* (London: Macmillan, 1964), pp. 152–56.

141. Little attention has been bestowed on this problem from the British angle in any detail, but for one useful, if limited, investigation, see M. L. Robertson, "Scottish Commerce and the American War of Independence," *Economic History Review,* 2d ser., 9 (August 1956), pp. 123–31.

142. Newcastle's Notes "from the Book," 11 March 1766. Add. MS. 33001, f. 155. A remark apparently made by Lord Coventry in the Lords on that day.

143. See Paul Langford, "The Rockingham Whigs and America 1767–1773," in Anne Whiteman, J. S. Bromley, and P. G. M. Dickson, eds., *Statesmen, Scholars, and Merchants: Essays in Eighteenth-Century History Presented to Dame Lucy Sutherland* (Oxford: Clarendon, 1973).

Reprinted from Paul Langford, *The First Rockingham Administration, 1765–1766* (Oxford: Clarendon Press, 1973) with the permission of the publisher. A fuller and more detailed account of the politics of the Stamp Act crisis in Britain appears in this earlier book.

Circular Letters, Customs Officers and the Issue of Violence: The Background to the Townshend Acts Resistance
Introduction to Chapter 4

WALTER H. CONSER, JR.
RONALD M. McCARTHY

News from Britain which came into American ports during the winter of 1765–66 gave the American colonists reason to hope that the Stamp Act would be repealed, and the spring ships in 1766 confirmed that their protests had been successful. Once free of the restrictions imposed by the Stamp Act and nonimportation, trade between England and America increased so much that 1766 became a record trading year. Most colonists hoped that life would now quickly return to normal.

There still existed some American grievances, however. The merchants of New York, for example, hoped to follow their success in the Stamp Act struggle with pressure for changes in the Currency Act of 1764. With the aid of their allies among the British merchants, they felt that American trade could be placed permanently on a more favorable footing. The British merchants assured their American trading partners that they would help where possible but cautioned the Americans not to gloat over their success, lest important allies in England be offended.[1] Neither these merchants nor most Americans saw any grievances which could not be handled within the existing framework of Anglo-American politics.

Important events occurred during 1767 to alter this perception and to lead Americans again to seek to force Britain to change its political and commercial policies toward the American colonies. Chapter Four will describe the course of the resistance campaign against the Townshend Acts of 1767. This Introduction will demonstrate the inception and intent of the Townshend Acts, the origins of American resistance to them, and discuss some aspects surrounding the problem of the use of violence in the renewed resistance against the government of Great Britain.

The British government in 1766 and 1767 clearly did not share the views of the American colonists about the future of the empire. The new ministry of Lord Chatham (William Pitt) took the position that, in the words of the Declaratory Act, Parliament could legislate for the colonies "in all cases whatsoever." A major figure in this ministry dealing with American policy was Charles Townshend, chancellor of the exchequer. Prior to 1766, Townshend had been concerned with American questions while a member of the Treasury Board. He had long favored Parliament's asserting and using its right to tax America.[2]

During 1767, Townshend was central to the ministry's development of plans to change Anglo-American relationships by statute in order to increase imperial control over the colonies and to tax their imports. His office researched and produced not only the revenue acts of that year but also the administrative changes made. The government's plans to change the structure of colonial administration were partly aimed at convenience and efficiency of administration. Thus, both the structure of admiralty courts and of the Customs service were altered, and the Sugar Act of 1764 was simplified, affording Britain increased economic and governmental control over the American colonies.[3]

The revenue acts, proposed by Charles Townshend in 1767 and enacted by Parliament with the ministry's support, taxed a variety of items that the American colonists imported directly from Great Britain. Among them were several grades of British-made paper and glass, painters' colors, and tea. Most were of little economic significance except for the tea. These taxes were laid in the form of import duties to be paid by the American merchants directly to the Customs officers at the port of entry into the colonies. Tea, for example, was taxed at the rate of 3d. per pound. The plan also strengthened the Customs service in America by appointing an American Board of Customs Commissioners and by broadening the conditions under which writs of assistance were to be granted. Admiralty court jurisdictions were refined by setting up courts in major port cities, and an office of secretary of state for the colonies was established.

In addition, a bill was introduced in Parliament designed to punish the colony of New York for refusing to provide funds for the army. Under the Quartering Act, troops billeted in or passing through a colony were to be partially supported by that colony's government. The assembly of New York declined to appropriate money to provide for the British troops. The ministry was angered by this and pushed the New York Restraining Act through Parliament. Under its provisions, no bill passed by the New York Assembly would be allowed to become law until the assembly bowed to the Quartering Act's requirements.[4] Townshend had a hand in the planning and passage of all these acts. With their passage between January and June 1767, the foundation of his system was complete.

That administrative reform was the intent even of the revenue portions of the Townshend program was quite clear. Although the British politicians often expressed both their concern over the high land tax and their hope that American revenues might reduce domestic taxes, Townshend's scheme was primarily aimed at expenses of the administration in America itself, especially for the military establishment. The preamble to the Revenue Act explicitly stated that the revenues were to be used to provide salaries for the governors and other civil officers, who were ordinarily paid by the assemblies alone. If the ministry saw fit, money could be taken from the Townshend Act revenues and paid directly to the officials. This was not done for several years, but the provision remained in force, even after the repeal of the majority of the duties, and was later used, notably in Massachusetts.[5]

Faced with threatened punishment as a result of their defiance of the Quartering Act, the New York Assembly appropriated money in June 1767 which the governor could use for the troops. This accommodation was accepted by the ministry as being in substantial compliance with the Quartering Act, and the New York Restraining Act was suspended before it went into effect.[6] Resistance against the other portions of the Townshend scheme—the taxes especially—did not develop immediately. It was only with the publication of *Letters from a Farmer in Pennsylvania to the Inhabitants of the British Colonies* by John Dickinson, which appeared in newspapers throughout the colonies in early 1768, that awareness of the Townshend Acts as a grievance began to increase.

Reminded by Dickinson of their grievances and encouraged by members who opposed the Townshend Acts, as discussed in Chapter Four, the Massachusetts legislature issued a circular letter on 11 February 1768 calling upon all the colonies to protest the acts. This circular letter, sent by the Massachusetts legislature to the Speakers of each of the other colonial assemblies, adopted a respectful tone toward the Crown but also asserted that the colonies must protect their rights. "Parliament is the supreme legislative Power over the whole Empire," the letter admitted, yet it held that Parliament's powers were limited and could not be exercised arbitrarily. The circular letter argued strongly against the right of Parliament to tax American colonists. It was, the Massachusetts legislature claimed, "held sacred and irrevocable by the Subjects within the Realm" that no political power could take any portion of people's possessions except through their direct consent or by the decision of the duly authorized representatives of the people. But since distance and other factors precluded any representation of the Americans in Parliament, only their own colonial assemblies, and no other body, might legitimately tax the American people. The circular letter closed with an assurance to the other colonial assemblies that Massachusetts had no interest in taking over the leadership of the colonies and renewed the colony's allegiance to the king and his ministers. Far from demanding resistance, the circular letter's suggestion for action was that the colonial assemblies should all petition Parliament to repeal the Townshend Acts.[7]

Petitioning Parliament for redress of grievances was a time-honored practice, but the British government could not accept the suggestion of collective action contained in the circular letter nor the denial of a right of Parliament confirmed by the Declaratory Act of March 1766. The British government's reaction was swift and unmistakable. Lord Hillsborough, recently appointed secretary of state for the colonies, quickly sent two letters to colonial officials. The first of these was a circular letter to the governors of all the American colonies, dated 21 April 1768. In this letter, Hillsborough cited the opinion of the king and his government that the Massachusetts circular letter was of "a most dangerous and factious tendency." He instructed the governors to "exert your utmost influence to defeat this flagitious attempt to disturb the public peace by prevailing upon the Assembly of your province to take no notice of it, which will be treating it with the contempt it deserves."

Hillsborough directed the governors that if these efforts failed and the assembly insisted upon taking up the Massachusetts circular letter, the assembly must be immediately dissolved.

Lord Hillsborough's second letter, dated 22 April, was to Governor Francis Bernard of Massachusetts, instructing him to demand of the Massachusetts House of Representatives that it immediately rescind the circular letter or face the consequence of being dissolved on the spot. Governor Bernard presented Hillsborough's demand to the Massachusetts House, which overwhelmingly rejected it, by a vote of ninety-two to seventeen, on 30 June 1768. Following his instructions, Bernard immediately dissolved the House. The "Glorious Ninety-two," as the legislators who refused to rescind were soon called, were acclaimed all over the colonies, while the seventeen "Rescinders" were portrayed in a widely circulated cartoon, drawn by Paul Revere, as being consigned to hell for their sins.[8]

Lord Hillsborough's instruction that other assemblies be dealt with as the Massachusetts House had been if they persisted in taking up the circular letter did not prevent a rapid and favorable response to the Massachusetts circular letter from several colonial assemblies. The New Jersey Assembly petitioned the king on 6 May 1768, declaring that the colony could not be taxed except by taxes "imposed on them by themselves or their Representatives." The same kind of expressions of support for the ideas contained in the circular letter came from the assemblies of South Carolina, Maryland, Delaware, Pennsylvania, New York, Connecticut, and New Hampshire.[9] In Rhode Island, the assembly voted on 16 September to petition the king in protest of the Townshend Acts. The next day, the assembly declared the action of Massachusetts to be: "a just representation of our grievances. . . . Therefore the Assembly, instead of treating that letter with any degree of contempt, think themselves obliged, in duty to themselves and to their country to approve the sentiments contained in it."[10]

The Georgia Assembly also met and passed a resolution of agreement with the Massachusetts letter. Governor James Wright, who had warned the assembly of the consequences of considering the circular letter, thereupon dissolved it. The North Carolina General Assembly, led by Speaker John Harvey, adopted an address to the king protesting the Townshend Acts on 11 November 1768. In the address, the assembly argued that this tax was just the sort of thing that "the acknowledged principles of the British Constitution ought to protect us from." Another southern legislature, the Virginia House of Burgesses, was one of the first to act on the circular letter. It voted on 14 April 1768 to adopt a petition to the king opposing taxation of the colonies by Parliament. Moreover, the House of Burgesses composed its own circular letter in which the Burgesses called upon the colonies to "unite in a firm but decent Opposition to every Measure which may effect the Rights and Liberties of the British Colonies in America."[11]

At the same time that the British North American colonies were working toward a resistance movement in which they would begin to treat the problems of acting collectively and responsibly while maintaining their traditional independence, the imperial government was revealing its inability to deal effectively with the colonies. Convinced that the conflict over Parliament's right to tax Americans was settled by the Declaratory Act, Lord Hillsborough thought only to suppress dissent or to prevent it from spreading by muzzling the assemblies. His attempt to suppress conflict without meeting it head on had, rather, the effect of increasing colonial awareness of the conflict and determination to act. The refusal of Parliament and the administration to be questioned or opposed and their ineffective responses to American demands would continue, and both would become a major part of the context of struggle between the colonies and the imperial government for many years.

Taxation was by no means the only issue raised by the Townshend Acts. While the grievance which prompted John Dickinson to write his *Letters from a Pennsylvania Farmer,* the suspension of the New York Assembly, was soon settled, the precedent appeared to Dickinson to be very threatening. In Massachusetts, other parts of the Townshend system also had important consequences. The American Board of Customs Commissioners, which arrived in Boston in November 1767, had its headquarters in that city. From its inception, there was conflict between the Board and its officers, on one side, and the people of the town of Boston, on the other. The Board's actions in enforcing the Customs laws, the highhandedness with which they were performed, and the personal ostentation of the commissioners made them detested by those who made their living in trade and from the sea. The members of the Board concluded soon after reaching Boston that they could not enforce the acts of navigation (the Customs statutes) without the aid of British troops, and they took this conflict with the people of the town as an occasion to ask for military support in early 1768. On 18 March 1768, a crowd celebrating the second anniversary of the Stamp Act repeal shouted in the streets of the town and broke some windows. The commissioners, feeling threatened, desperately requested troops. After the seizure by Customs men of the sloop *Liberty* in June 1768, the Board sent an officer, who had been hurt by the crowd which had gathered to oppose the seizure, home to England to plead for aid. By this time, however, Lord Hillsborough had already decided to send troops to Boston.[12]

Four regiments of troops came almost in secret to Boston. Governor Bernard knew that the troops were being sent, but did nothing to inform the town or province officially. On 3 September 1768, Bernard informally mentioned their expected arrival to a member of the council. When the town discovered that the troops were on the way, many feared it to be an army of occupation coming to enforce the Townshend Acts. They considered desperate measures, possibly military opposition to the army. James Otis declared that there was "nothing to do, but to gird the Sword to the Thigh and Shoulder the Musquet."[13]

The Boston town meeting of 12 September 1768 sent a delegation to Governor Bernard asking him to reconvene the House of Representatives. They told Bernard that there was a danger of invasion by the French—a pretext used by those who wanted to arm the populace. The House, though, had been dissolved because it refused to rescind the circular letter, and Bernard refused to recall it earlier than the next spring. Blocked, the town meeting considered other measures by which the representatives of the people could consider the danger and perhaps lend support to Boston in its opposition to the troops. On 13 September, the town meeting sent a letter to the selectmen of each town in the province, calling for a convention of delegates to meet in Boston to consider the crisis.

Approximately ninety-six towns responded to Boston's request by sending delegates. This meeting, the Massachusetts Convention of Towns, was condemned by Thomas Cushing, as its chairman and chose several committees to report to the Convention on the problems raised by the imminent arrival of the soldiers. While half in Boston, the Convention elected the Speaker of the House of Representatives, Thomas Cushing, as it chairman and chose several committees to report to the Convention on the problems raised by the imminent arrival of the soldiers. While half of the membership of the Convention were former legislators, many members were new to colony-wide politics. Several towns which ordinarily did not choose a representative to the House took the situation seriously enough to send delegates, while many towns—notably those represented in the last House by the "Rescinders"—refused to join.

The Convention met for a week, until 29 September 1768. One of its first acts was to send a delegation to Governor Bernard, assuring him that the Convention was not trying to usurp the legislative power. Bernard was again asked to convene the legislature and again refused, condemning the Convention as an illegal meeting and refusing to have anything to do with it. The Convention refused to support those who had wanted military opposition to the troops, an option not given serious consideration after the first days of fear about what the army might do. Citing fear of the French, the Convention supported the proposal that the citizens arm themselves, but it also cautioned the people against "any undue expression of resentment" against the troops. After adopting a petition to the king, to be sent to the colony's London agent for delivery, as well as a series of resolutions asserting the colony's rights and condemning the dispatch of the troops, the Convention adjourned. The troopships were already in the harbor.[14]

In Hutchinson's opinion, this meeting and its outcome "had a greater tendency towards a revolution in government than any preceding measures in any of the colonies."[15] This Convention did not assume legislative power in the sense that it enacted laws or tried to enforce its decisions. Nor did it go beyond its original mandate of considering what, if any, steps would be taken to oppose the landing of the troops or whether some other form of resistance would prevail. Nevertheless, the Convention marked the first instance when the forces opposed to policies of the British government in Massachusetts had independently come together from across the province to consider resistance measures. During the later Continental Association (1774–75), this meeting and the independent meetings of legislatures that several other colonies, Virginia and North Carolina among them, had undertaken would stand as precedents for the development of the provincial congresses and conventions which seized the legislative power away from British imperial institutions.

· THE ISSUE OF VIOLENCE ·

When the soldiers, who were sent from Halifax, Nova Scotia, to garrison the town of Boston, came ashore on 9 October 1768, they were met with silence and disdain, the people refusing whenever possible to aid the army in its occupation of their town. Nonimportation continued against the Townshend act regulations despite the presence of the British troops. The troops were never used in any way to aid Customs officers in enforcing the law, nor did they ever protect the commissioners or other officers from the townsfolk, except on occasions when the commissioners fled to Castle William, a royal fortress built on an island in the harbor. Nevertheless, with their arrival, Boston entered a new period. The historians of the late nineteenth and early twentieth centuries and, following them, some more recent writers have often seen this as a period filled with violence against the troops, Customs officers, and importing merchants.

On the evening of 28 October 1769, John Mein, publisher of the *Boston Chronicle* and a strong opponent of nonimportation, was walking along King Street on his way home. The latest issue of the *Chronicle* had just appeared, containing Mein's latest and most effective attacks against the Boston nonimportation agreement. Mein had attempted to prove that the agreement was not being adhered to in Boston by showing that plenty of goods were still moving through the Custom House. Mein was recognized and soon surrounded by a crowd of angry men, a crowd which Mein later claimed was encouraged by "the Principle People." Prominent in the crowd was William Molineux, Boston's "first Leader of Dirty Matters."[16] The crowd shouted at Mein and threatened him. When Edward Davis swung at him with a club, Mein cocked his pistol and pointed it at the threatening crowd. Mein backed up King Street toward the safety of the main guard, vowing to fire if he was touched. Mein reached the guard at the Town House and had turned to go inside when Thomas Marshall struck him on the back with a spade, cutting his shoulder. As Mein fled inside, he fired his pistol, wounding a soldier on guard duty. While Mein took refuge in the Town House, a warrant for his arrest (for waving the pistol and assault on the soldier) was obtained from magistrate Richard Dana. While sheriff Stephen Greenleaf, Samuel Adams, and Molineux searched for him, Mein disguised himself as a soldier and fled, later taking refuge on a warship in the harbor. Soon afterward, he sailed to England.

Meanwhile, another crowd, soon augmented by the original one, seized George Greyer, "a sailor."[17] They stripped Greyer, "painted him all over with Tar & then covered him with Feathers & then put him in a Cart & carried him thro' all the main Streets of the Town."[18] As the crowd carted Greyer through the streets, members shouted to people in the houses to put candles in their windows as a sign of support for the crowd's actions. The crowd paraded Greyer most of the evening, not freeing him until late that evening when it dispersed.[19]

This scene has been interpreted by many historians as being typical of the violence against persons which so characterized the "violent period" that preceded the

War of Independence. Violence is viewed as having been a major tool of the American Whigs against their political opponents in the nonimportation movement. In this view, violence and its threatened use were commonly employed to enforce the agreements, to silence by means of intimidation those who opposed the agreements, and to cow those who too actively supported British policies. By attacking Mein, Greyer, and others like them, these historians argue, the colonial radicals (especially in Boston) created a climate of intimidation and fear, without which their campaigns to boycott British goods and to maintain their powerful position in the colonial legislatures could not have been successful.[20]

Not all historians agree with this interpretation, and there is a growing body of opinion that holds that violent action by crowds was not central to the conduct of the independence movement. Bernhard Knollenberg, for example, believed the use of violence in the movement to have been limited and noted how restrained it appears to have been. On the specific issue of tarring and feathering, which the historian R. S. Longley believed to be "fairly common by 1768," Knollenberg pointed out that "fewer than a dozen" actual cases for the period 1766 to April 1775 had come to his attention.[21]

Historians who gaze with horror on the cruelties of the American crowds, such as those which carried on the tarring and feathering of Greyer, seldom mention violence by British officials and their supporters. The paramount example of this violence was naval impressment, the practice of seizing American sailors from their ships and forcing them to man naval vessels whose crews had been reduced by desertion or death. This practice had actually been forbidden in American waters by the British law known popularly as "the Sixth of Anne." Despite this law, impressment was carried on throughout these years.[22]

There was also violence by individual supporters of the Crown against their political opponents, notably in Boston. Two of these incidents occurred well before the mobbing of John Mein. In September 1769, John Robinson, a Customs commissioner, and James Otis argued in the British Coffee House. On this pretext, Robinson beat Otis severely with the help of some other men. Otis was cut on the forehead and badly bruised before he was rescued.[23] Otis may have suffered permanent injury as a result, and he soon lost his central place in the politics of the town. In an earlier, and even less well-known case, John Mein himself attacked a rival printer. After a letter criticizing him appeared in the *Boston Gazette* on 7 January 1768, Mein demanded that the publishers, Benjamin Edes and John Gill, tell him the identity of the pseudonymous author. When they refused, Mein promised them the punishment he had reserved for the writer of the letter. On 26 January 1768, Mein met Gill on the street and caned him. At his trial for assault, Mein's defense cited the "insults" he had met as an excuse for his brutality, but he was found guilty and fined.[24]

More important than the examples of the occurrence of interpersonal violence were patterns of violent conflict between Americans and British officials. These took two important forms: those directed against the Customs officers and those directed against the soldiers. Again, these were most noticeable in Boston, although not restricted to that city. But violence was not the only response, or even the major one, to either of those groups. The Customs commissioners arrived in Boston on 5 November 1767. This day was the anniversary of the Gunpowder Plot, celebrated in England as Guy Fawkes Day and in Boston as Pope's Day. Before 1765, rival gangs of men and boys from different quarters of the town had waged fierce fights to decide which group would have the honor of holding a bonfire at the end of the celebration. Despite this tradition of fighting with one's foes on this day, the large crowd assembled on the day the commissioners landed did them no harm at all. The townspeople expressed their opposition by placing the motto "Liberty, Property, and no Commissioners" on their Pope's Day effigies.[25]

On 18 March of the next year, 1768, the second anniversary of the repeal of the Stamp Act, effigies of one of the Customs commissioners and of the inspector-general of Customs were hanged from the Liberty Tree. In the evening, a crowd shouted in the streets for a few hours and broke some windows. Shortly after that, there was trouble aboard John Hancock's sloop *Lydia* when he refused to allow two Customs officers to search the vessel without a warrant. On 10 June, officers seized Hancock's ship, *Liberty,* for breach of the Customs laws and, with the help of a boatload of sailors and marines, removed it from the dock to the harbor to be anchored under the guns of the British warship, *Romney.* This situation exacerbated fears of what more the officers might do and also of further impressment like that previously carried out by the officers of the *Romney.* These circumstances combined to provoke the crowd, which had collected during the seizure, to attack both of the officers and the son of one.[26] The commissioners became frightened and fled to the protection of Castle William in the harbor, where they remained until after the arrival of the troops in October 1768.

From that time, whenever the commissioners became frightened by activities in the town, they fled to Castle William for safety. Yet little serious threat was ever offered by the crowds.[27] Nor were there any crowd actions against the commissioners' property in their absence. Nonetheless, it was the commissioners' reports, among others, that convinced the ministry of the terrible violence of the Boston mob.

One result of reports of violence to the ministry was the occupation of Boston by British troops in October 1768. Of the four regiments sent to carry out the occupation, two were removed in July 1769. None of the troops were ever called upon to strengthen the hand of government in any way, beyond guarding people who came to Castle William for protection. The troops were, however, often involved in fights as individuals, not as military units, with the townspeople.

The Boston Massacre of 5 March 1770, in which five Bostonians were killed and a number wounded by gunfire from a small detachment of British troops, has been interpreted in widely differing ways over the years. In particular, historians have disagreed as to its role in the independence movement. The Massacre took place during the Townshend Acts resistance, and the Bostonians successfully argued that the troops must be removed from the town in the aftermath of the Massacre. Moreover, the occurrence of the Boston Massacre was not entirely a surprise to many in the town; Samuel Adams for one. Because of this, some historians have concluded that it was planned by the Whigs or at least was a natural outgrowth of a deliberate policy of harassing the soldiers.

Two recent interpretations of the Massacre which take this point of view are those of Hiller B. Zobel[28] and Dirk Hoerder.[29] Zobel viewed the Massacre as a direct outcome not only of Samuel Adam's policy of "putting the enemy in the wrong" but also of all the other violence which had occurred since 1765.[30] Hoerder did not contend that the Massacre was a plot but did see a deliberate policy of harassment against the troops during 1769, a policy which created the conditions for the Massacre.

Important questions must be asked about any such interpretation, however. Zobel, in particular, viewed any cases of violent conflict between persons in which the person attacked was a Crown supporter to be directly connected (he does not specify the mechanism) to all other such acts of violence. Thus, in setting the stage for the Massacre, Zobel described, among other events, the death of a young naval officer who was killed by Irish sailors as he attempted to impress them into the Navy.[31] This event happened at sea many miles from Boston. It is certainly true that there were a number of conflicts, many of them petty, between the soldiers and the Boston townspeople in the year before the Massacre. It is also true, though, that soldiers regularly took part in town life without incident.

Another historian of the Massacre, Jesse Lemisch, argued that the Massacre was part of a generally antagonistic relationship between Customs officers and townspeople, which often had specific economic conflicts at its basis.[32] As Lemisch pointed out, British soldiers in a garrison town competed with unskilled workers for jobs. When the troops were stationed in a peacetime garrison in a town, their pay was cut by the amount that it was felt they could earn on the outside—a few shillings a week. Although their pay was reduced, it was still steady, and they could therefore afford to work at quite low wages to make up the amount lost.

In March 1770, colonial Boston was jammed with British soldiers and sailors, as well as commercial seamen laid off from mercantile ships which had entered port in late 1769 in order to wait out the winter storm season. In such a situation, unskilled dockyard jobs were at a premium. No unemployed person wanted to compete with other workers who were willing to work for less than a living wage. The discontent caused by British soldiers and American civilians vying for the same jobs was worsened by an incident on the Boston dockyards on 3 March 1770. On that day, Samuel Gray, employed as a ropemaker and later to die in the Massacre, insulted a British soldier. The soldier was looking for work, and Gray sneeringly offered him a job cleaning the outhouse. The soldier answered by getting together his friends and trying to assault Gray and his coworkers.[33] This incident led to other fights around the town two nights later. It is clear that the incident which precipitated the Massacre—a crowd abusing the lone guard at the Town House—was not the only occurrence that night. Groups of soldiers and groups of townsmen were ready to settle their differences with their fists. In fact, some accounts make it appear that the streets in the sections of town near the docks were alive with groups of would-be street fighters.[34]

The historian may not, without further evidence, assume that because two events occur in a single city during the same period of time, they are causally related. Clearly, animosities and street fights between the Bostonians and the troops or the Customs agents influenced and were influenced by the context within which the resistance to the Townshend Acts took place. These brawls did *not*, however, constitute one of the major techniques of resistance. Even though Customs officers collected the hated tax, they were rarely mobbed. In fact, they continued to collect the taxes, and in the cases of the sugar and tea revenues, in rather large amounts. Never were the Customs as an institution or the army as an institution primarily opposed by violent means.

The single most abhorred crowd action—to later historians—was tarring and feathering. This was indeed a terrible punishment. It was not, however, a punishment used by the resistance movement. Instead, it had private motives. Tarring and feathering was a punishment inflicted upon people not because they were Customs officers—which might make it political—but because they were Customs *informers*. These were people, such as George Greyer mentioned previously, who turned in information about a merchant importing illegally in hopes of receiving a third share of any resulting seizure. None of the sufferers in these cases were major figures in the imperial conflict. There were no commissioners and no inspectors involved. Those subjected to the treatment were, like John Malcom, George Greyer, and Owen Richard, accused of being petty informers who threatened the livelihood of smugglers and those whose income came from the sea. The tarring and feathering of John Malcom in Boston in 1774 was, in fact, condemned in the newspapers by the "Committee on Tarring and Feathering," a mythical body whose "proclamation" was intended to control and restrain tarring and feathering, not to promote it.[35]

Many did not approve of the tarring and feathering of these men, as Governor Hutchinson reported to Hillsborough, the secretary of state for the colonies, in 1770.[36] Popular leaders obviously did not have the degree of control over crowds sometimes attributed to them, though, and were not able to restrain the rage of the people once it had reached the boiling point. Likewise, as Lemisch pointed out, the goals of the resisters did not necessarily include the goals of the poor, for example, the sailors, who made up some of the crowds.[37] The Whigs and those known to be among their supporters often tried to restrain the crowds if they could. During the *Liberty* riot, a speaker invoked the biblical phrase, "To thy tents, O Israel," in an attempt to get the crowd to disperse. When an importer killed a child in a crowd with a musket shot from his window, a Liberty Tree placard asked the people to leave revenge to the courts.[38]

Perhaps most damaging to the contention that the crowd was a vicious and terrible weapon in the hands of the Whigs is the observation that some individuals were willing to defy crowds which made demands on them and did not in return suffer either violence or destruction of their property. This occurred within the context of the resistance campaigns. Examples of this are offered in other chapters.

Only two need be given here.

A Philadelphia Stamp Act mass meeting in October 1765 demanded the resignation of stamp distributor John Hughes. Hughes refused to resign but pledged that he would not execute the act unless it was implemented in other colonies. A later mass meeting accepted the compromise.[39] In Boston, as well as the other port cities, there were merchants who never joined the nonimportation agreements and who continued to import goods, even tea, upon which the duty was paid. While they were boycotted, criticized, and even harassed, violence was seldom done to them. In January 1770, some Boston merchants tried to circumvent the nonimportation agreement, as is described in the following chapter. These importers were "visited" at their homes and shops by crowds numbering in the thousands trying to convince them to return to the fold. While these importers did all soon comply with this request, they often refused to meet the demands of the crowd at that time. Yet none suffered physically for doing so.

Even when tempers were at their highest, as was the case just before the Tea Party in 1773, some men safely refused to assent to the crowd's desires. At the mass meetings which preceded the Tea Party, a variety of demands were placed upon Frances Rotch, the captain of a tea ship. While standing in the middle of the crowd, he simply refused to comply with all the crowd's demands. The people may have resented him, but they did not harm him.[40]

Boston was not the only city which experienced violence between the townspeople and the soldiers or Customs officers. New York, long a garrison town, saw bitter street fighting between soldiers and civilians, often prompted by the soldiers' attempts to cut down the Liberty Pole. One New Yorker was killed in the fighting just before the Boston Massacre. Tarring and feathering of informers also occurred elsewhere in Massachusetts, one at Salem and another at Gloucester. Similarly, Philadelphia experienced acrimonious disturbances which included Customs officers as their targets.[41]

While violence was rarely used against the socially prominent supporters of imperial policy, threats and intimidations sometimes were. Anne Hulton recorded a crowd attack on the house of her brother, Customs Commissioner Henry Hulton, in June 1770. Frightened by the attack, in which the windows on the first floor of the house were broken and the crowd shouted curses at Hulton in the dark of the night, the family soon sought the protection of Castle William.[42]

Another attack upon a house occurred in the fall of 1773, when importer Richard Clarke's house was surrounded and damaged by a crowd, and he and his sons were threatened. The firm of Clarke and Sons was a tea consignee of the East India Company and one of the firms which initially refused to pledge to reject the arriving tea.[43] Threatening crowds also confronted Massachusetts men chosen to the council by the Crown in the summer of 1774, frightening them and causing several to flee Boston to seek the protection afforded by the troops.[44]

A variety of forces caused the individual cases of known violence between persons or by crowds against individuals. Some were scarcely connected with politics at all. (Both Massachusetts and Virginia experienced violent crowd action connected with smallpox scares.[45]) Likewise, some cases of violence, or perceived threats of violence, occurred when previously nonviolent crowds became frightened or enraged—perhaps by rumors or the sight of a hated opponent. In addition, many cases of violence or threatened violence appear to have occurred at times of the greatest stress in a movement. This was particularly true when movements were just beginning, and no firm policy on the use of violence could be enforced. This happened in 1765 at the outset of the Stamp Act resistance. It was also the case in 1773 at the time of the tea agitation and again in 1774 in the weeks preceding the meeting of the First Continental Congress and the establishment of a firm plan of resistance. Another period of violent conflict in New York, Philadelphia, and Boston occurred in the months during which nonimportation was breaking up in 1770. This was surely a very stressful period for the movement against British taxation (although the violence was only indirectly connected with nonimportation).

Taking the period from the summer of 1765 to April 1775 as a whole, it becomes clear that far from being a mainstay of the independence movement, violence was irregular and sporadic, especially as compared with the organization and unity of action of the merchant and legislative bodies, the committee structure, and the local communities.

• NOTES •

1. The New Yorkers' continuing concern over the Currency Act of 1764 and British government resentment over the timing of their petition for repeal is discussed in Joseph A. Ernst, "The Currency Act Repeal Movement: A Study in Imperial Politics and the Revolutionary Crisis, 1764–1767," *William and Mary Quarterly,* 3d ser., 25 (April 1968), pp. 195–96. The committee of London merchants trading to North America, so instrumental in the repeal of the Stamp Act, feared that American response to the repeal would only antagonize British politicians, and told their major correspondents so in a series of three circular letters in the spring of 1766 (see, for example, John Hancock of Boston's responses to his correspondents in London, the firm of Barnards and Harrison, 30 April and 30 June 1766, A. E. Brown, *John Hancock His Book* [Boston: Lee and Shepard, 1898], pp. 124, 131–32).

2. Robert Chaffin, *Prologue to War: The Townshend Acts and the American Revolution, 1767–1770* (Ph.D. diss., Indiana Univ., 1967), pp. 39–50, 57; Bernhard Knollenberg, *The Growth of the American Revolution, 1766–1775* (New York: Free Press, 1975), p. 38.

3. The significance of these alterations in the imperial structure for the colonies is discussed in Chapter Fourteen of this volume.

4. Nicholas Varga, "The New York Restraining Act: Its Passage and Some Effects, 1766–1768," *New York History* 37 (July 1956), pp. 237–50.

5. The development by Townshend and the ministry and the passage by Parliament of the Townshend plan is discussed in the following works: Chaffin, *Prologue to War,* pp. 137–38, 145, 149, 151, 152, 156, 165, 166–67, 173–79; Thomas C. Barrow, *Trade and Empire: The British Customs Service in Colonial America, 1760–1775* (Cambridge, Mass.: Harvard Univ. Press, 1967), pp. 216–34.

6. Varga, "New York Restraining Act," pp. 250–52.

7. Henry Steele Commager, ed., *Documents of American History* (New York: Crofts, 1934), pp. 66–67.

8. Both of Hillsborough's letters to the governors are quoted appropriately in Knollenberg, *Growth of the American Revolution,* pp. 55–56. See also Chapter Five of this volume. On the refusal to rescind and its effect upon intercolonial resistance, see Pauline Maier, *From Resistance to Revolution* (New York: Knopf, 1973), pp. 169–70. Besides the rather crude cartoon, Revere also executed one of his most famed works for the "Glorious Ninety-Two," the "Liberty Bowl" of 1768, commemorating the legislators' decision "not to rescind," which he made on commission from a group of Boston Sons of Liberty (Elbridge H. Goss, *The Life of Colonel Paul Revere* [Boston: Joseph George Cupples, Bookseller, 1891], vol. 1, pp. 62–65).

9. Knollenberg, *Growth of the American Revolution,* pp. 55, 57.

10. Edward Field, *The State of Rhode Island and Providence Plantations at the End of the Century: A History* (Boston: Mason, 1902), vol. 1, pp. 219–20.

11. E. Merton Coulton, *Georgia: A Short History* (Chapel Hill: Univ. of North Carolina Press, 1947), p. 114; Hugh T. Lefler and Albert Newsome, *North Carolina: The History of a Southern State* (Chapel Hill: Univ. of North Carolina Press, 1954), p. 199; Knollenberg, *Growth of the American Revolution,* pp. 54–55.

12. Chaffin, *Prologue to War,* pp. 187–207; Oliver M. Dickerson, *The Navigation Acts and the American Revolution* (Philadelphia: Univ. of Pennsylvania Press, 1951), pp. 198–99.

13. James Otis is quoted by John C. Miller, "The Massachusetts Convention: 1768," *New England Quarterly* 7 (September 1934), p. 450.

14. *Ibid.,* pp. 445–74; Richard D. Brown, "The Massachusetts Convention of Towns, 1768," *William and Mary Quarterly,* 3d ser., 26 (January 1969), pp. 95–104.

15. Thomas Hutchinson, *The History of the Province of Massachusetts-Bay* (London: John Murray, 1828), vol. 3, pp. 205.

16. John Rowe thus characterized Molineux at his death in 1774, Anne Rowe Cunningham, ed., *Letters and Diary of John Rowe: Boston Merchant 1759–1762, 1764–1779* (Boston: W. B. Clarke, 1903), p. 286.

17. As he is called by Hutchinson, *History of Massachusetts-Bay,* vol. 3, p. 259. He was also called an informer.

18. Cunningham, *Letters and Diary of John Rowe,* p. 94.

19. This account is taken from those in John E. Alden, "John Mein, Scourge of Patriots," Colonial Society of Massachusetts, *Publications (Transactions,* 1937–42), pp. 586–89; Cunningham, *Letters and Diary of John Rowe,* p. 194; Hutchinson, *History of Massachusetts-Bay,* vol. 3, pp. 258–60; and R. S. Longley, "Mob Activities in Revolutionary Massachusetts," *New England Quarterly* 6 (March 1933), p. 116.

20. This view is summarized by Richard Maxwell Brown, "Violence and the American Revolution," in Stephen G. Kurtz and James H. Hutson, eds., *Essays on the American Revolution* (Chapel Hill: Univ. of North Carolina Press, 1973). Quotation from p. 84.

21. Longley, "Mob Activities," p. 115; Knollenberg, *Growth of the American Revolution,* pp. 100, 361, n. 4.

22. Maier, *From Resistance to Revolution,* pp. 6–7, 20; Neil R. Stout, "Manning the Royal Navy in America," *American Neptune* 23 (July 1963); G. G. Wolkins, "The Seizure of John Hancock's Sloop 'Liberty'," Massachusetts Historical Society, *Proceedings* 55 (1921–22), pp. 249–50; Jesse Lemisch, "Jack Tar in the Streets: Merchant Seamen in the

Politics of Revolutionary America," *William and Mary Quarterly,* 3d ser., 25 (July 1968), pp. 383–89.

23. Henry H. Edes, "Memoir of Dr. Thomas Young, 1731–1777," Colonial Society of Massachusetts, *Publications* (Transactions, 1906–1907), pp. 5–6. John Mein stood surety for Robinson.

24. Alden, "John Mein," pp. 582–86.

25. Knollenberg, *Growth of the American Revolution,* p. 61.

26. *Ibid.,* pp. 64–65; Dickerson, *Navigation Acts,* pp. 237–42; D. H. Watson, "Joseph Harrison and the *Liberty* Incident," *William and Mary Quarterly,* 3d ser., 20 (October 1963), pp. 585–95.

27. Ann Hulton, who accompanied her brother, Commissioner Henry Hulton, to Boston, records that the wife of Customs officer Burch feared threats from crowds before the *Liberty* riot in June 1768. Hulton's Brookline home was attacked by a crowd in 1770, as described below, an attack later blamed on the jealousy of Customs Commissioner John Temple, who had lost his previous post when the Board was formed (*Letters of a Loyalist Lady: Being the Letters of Ann Hulton, Sister of Henry Hulton, Commissioner of Customs at Boston, 1767–1776* [Cambridge, Mass.: Harvard Univ. Press, 1927], pp. 11, 22–24, 39–40).

28. Hiller B. Zobel, *The Boston Massacre* (New York: Norton, 1970), see also pp. 70, 150, 177, 214.

29. Dirk Hoerder, *People and Mobs: Crowd Action in Massachusetts During the American Revolution* (Inaugural-Dissertation, Freie Universität Berlin, 1971), pp. 320–33.

30. Adams is quoted by John C. Miller, *Sam Adams: Pioneer in Propaganda* (Stanford: Stanford Univ. Press, 1960), p. 24.

31. Zobel, *Boston Massacre,* pp. 113–31.

32. Lemisch, "Jack Tar in the Streets," pp. 393–400.

33. *Ibid.,* p. 400.

34. Zobel, *Boston Massacre,* pp. 185–88; John Shy, *Toward Lexington: The Role of the British Army in the Coming of the American Revolution* (Princeton, N.J.: Princeton Univ. Press, 1965), p. 316; Jesse Lemisch, "Radical Plot in Boston (1770): A Study in the Use of Evidence," *Harvard Law Review* 84 (December 1970) notes, in a hostile review of the position of Zobel, that a number of the key figures on both sides in the Massacre had been involved in the fighting of the last few days before the Massacre.

35. Frank W. C. Hersey, "Tar and Feathers: The Adventures of Captain John Malcom," Colonial Society of Massachusetts, *Publications (Transactions, 1937–42* [1943]) pp. 439–44; Walter Kendall Collins, "Tarring and Feathering in Boston in 1770," *Old-Time New England* 20 (July 1929), pp. 30–45, records several cases connected with informing, most not in Boston, but on Cape Ann. See also the account in Zobel, *Boston Massacre,* p. 230.

36. K. G. Davis, ed., *Documents of the American Revolution, 1770–1783* (Colonial Office Series), (Shannon: Irish Univ. Press, 1975) vol. 1, p. 107.

37. Lemisch, "Jack Tar in the Streets," pp. 389–91, 396. The actions of unemployed sailors were feared by Whig leaders in Charleston during the Stamp Act resistance, when the closing of the port threw many out of work (Robert A. Woody, "Christopher Gadsden and the Stamp Act," *Proceedings of the South Carolina Historical Association,* 1939 [no vol.], pp. 7–8).

38. Oliver M. Dickerson, "The Commissioners of Customs and the Boston Massacre," *New England Quarterly* 27 (September 1954), p. 311; Hoerder, *People and Mobs,*

p. 269. After the Robinson-Otis fight, a crowd threatened a justice of the peace who refused to arrest anyone for the attack. An unnamed Whig leader told them, "No violence or you'll hurt the cause," and the crowd released the justice (Zobel, *Boston Massacre,* p. 151).

39. John J. Zimmerman, "Charles Thomson: 'The Sam Adams of Philadelphia,'" *Mississippi Valley Historical Review* 45 (December 1958), pp. 469–70.

40. L. F. S. Upton, "Proceedings of Ye Body Respecting Tea," *William and Mary Quarterly,* 3d ser., 22 (April 1965), pp. 287–300. Several tea consignees did move to Castle William for safety, and public indignation was very high against them for refusing to pledge that they would not accept the tea consignments in time to have the tea kept out of the town.

41. Lemisch, "Jack Tar in the Streets," p. 400; In Salem, Robert Wood and Thomas Rowe were tarred and feathered as informers. Rowe was a tidesman, James Duncan Phillips, *Salem in the Eighteenth Century* (Boston: Houghton-Mifflin, 1937), p. 296; Hutchinson, *History of Massachusetts-Bay,* vol. 3, p. 283; Arthur L. Jensen, *The Maritime Commerce of Colonial Philadelphia* (Madison: State Historical Society of Wisconsin, 1963), pp. 149–52.

42. Hulton, *Letters of a Loyalist Lady,* pp. 22–25.

43. Draft of petition, 17 November 1773, Colonial Society of Massachusetts, *Publications (Transactions, 1902–1904* [1906]), p. 84; Hulton, *Letters of a Loyalist Lady,* pp. 64–65.

44. This period is described in Ronald M. McCarthy, "Popular Power and Institutional Reconstruction: Massachusetts, 1774–1775," presented at Spring Meeting of the New England Historical Association, April 1977.

45. Patrick Henderson, "Smallpox and Patriotism: The Norfolk Riots, 1768–1769," *Virginia Magazine of History and Biography* 73 (October 1965), pp. 413–24; George A. Billias, "Pox and Politics in Marblehead, 1773–1774," *Essex Institute Historical Collections* 92 (January 1956), pp. 43–58. In the Virginia case, the Whigs were on the anti-innoculation side and the Tories on the other; in Marblehead, the roles were reversed. In both cases, public fear of this terrible disease—which spread so easily in the crowded port towns—overcame whatever political connections existed.

·4·

The Nonconsumption and Nonimportation Movement Against the Townshend Acts, 1767–1770

LESLIE J. THOMAS

• THE RISE OF THE NONIMPORTATION MOVEMENT IN THE NORTHERN COLONIES •

The Nonconsumption Movement in New England

T he Townshend Acts furnished abundant material for a new series of attacks on parliamentary authority, and the attempt to enforce them provoked measures of resistance from the very beginning. Already during the summer and fall of 1767, before the Townshend Acts went into effect, the radicals began to formulate plans for resistance, and rumors of a nonconsumption agreement circulated in Boston. Massachusetts political leader Thomas Cushing wrote agent Dennys DeBerdt concerning reports received from England that the government was going to send troops to America to enforce the collection of the Townshend revenue duties. In Cushing's opinion, nothing would serve to alienate the people and drive them into a nonconsumption agreement sooner than the policy of the British government outlined in these rumors from England. In his own words:

> No one measure I could think of, would so effectually drive them [the colonists] into resolutions, which in the end would prove detrimental to Great Britain. I mean, living as much as possible within ourselves, and using as few as possible of your manufactures.[1]

Cushing attributed the popular opposition to the fact that the Townshend duties were to be levied for the purpose of raising a revenue which was to be applied toward the creation of a civil list and not to the amount of the duties themselves or their effect upon trade:

> As to imposing duties, so long as they are confined to the regulation of trade, and so conducted as to be of equal advantage to all parts of the empire, no great exception could be taken to it; but duties are laid with a view of raising a revenue out of the Colonies, and this revenue also to be applied to establish a civil list in America, . . . it apprehended [this] cannot be done without vacating our charter, and in effect overthrowing our present constitution.[2]

The suggestion of a plan for using nonconsumption as a means of resisting the Townshend program by economic coercion of Great Britain came from one of the radical leaders of the popular party in Boston.[3] The first protest against this proposal appeared in the *Boston Evening Post* on 7 September 1767. One writer argued that any attempt to force such an agreement upon the merchants against their will would be as obnoxious as the Townshend Acts themselves.[4]

A division of opinion between the popular party and the mercantile aristocracy in the province is further revealed in an article by an anonymous writer in the press about a week later. He was concerned about the increasing consumption of British manufactured goods by the colonies and the resulting balance of trade against the colonies. "To be in debt to our Mother Country, I confess is not so formadable, as to a foreign state, but to be long under a growing debt to our best friends, is to put it in their power to become our masters, if the adage of the wisest of men be right, that 'the borrower is servant to the lender.'"[5] He noted the current inclination to economize, which was gaining ground among the people, but expressed the fear that their resolutions would be overcome by the temptation to buy on easy credit terms and the fallacious argument that European goods were not only cheaper but better in quality than goods manufactured in the colonies. This situation was not only dangerous for the people as debtors but also to the long-run interests of the merchants as their creditors. "It is not to be supposed," he commented, "that those who would not take pains to save their own estate and liberty, will labour any more to save from a different kind of destruction, the interest of their master."[6]

The solution, as another writer, "Philo Patrie," saw it, was for those people with capital to turn their talents and funds in the direction of establishing manufacturing in the colony. This would serve two purposes; it would establish an economy to replace that based on the impoverished shipping industry, and it would provide employment for the unemployed mechanics and tradesmen who were sorely in need of relief. A linen manufactory, in particular, was proposed.[7]

Despite merchant opposition, plans formulated by the popular party were pushed through the Boston town meeting on 28 October 1767. After the reading of the address by "Philo Patrie," the town took into consideration a petition asking "that some effectual Measures might be agreed upon to promote Industry, Oeconomy and Manufactures, thereby to prevent the unnecessary Importation of European Commodities which threaten the Country with Poverty and Ruin." It was then resolved that "the excessive use of foreign superfluities is the chief Cause of the present distressed state of this Town, as it is thereby drained of its Money, which Misfortune is like to be increased by means of the late additional burthens and impositions on the Trade of this Province." The town should thus take measures to encourage the produce and manufactures of the province to lessen the use of superfluities and especially the items enumerated. A committee was appointed to prepare a form for subscription to such an agreement and to solicit subscriptions to it.[8] This was a nonconsumption, but not yet a nonimportation, agreement. The subscribers agreed to encourage the consumption of all articles manufactured in any of the British American colonies, especially in Massachusetts, and not to purchase any of a list of enumerated articles after 31 December of that year. It was also a-greed to observe frugality with regard to the purchase of gloves and new garments for funerals. The meeting passed a resolution to publish the nonconsumption agreement and to distribute it among the inhabitants of the town, and copies were sent to the selectmen of the other towns in the province.[9]

The action taken by the Boston town meeting on 28 October did not have the unanimous approval of the inhabitants. The popular party had successfully engineered its program of nonconsumption through the town assembled in its corporate character. Some degree of authority was essential for the success of the nonconsumption policy since it ran contrary to the economic self-interest of a socially prominent and financially powerful minority of the community. That minority was composed of the merchant aristocracy and the officials of the British government acting in the colony. The nonconsumption agreement was opposed by individuals in these two groups as the work of a discontented, radical minority. Two weeks after the event, Massachusetts' governor, Francis Bernard, reported that the nonconsumption agreement "has been so generally rejected & discountenanced by the Principal Gentlemen of the Towns, that it can have no Effect."[10] A writer in the press, styling himself "A True Patriot," declared that the nonconsumption agreement was "no more than the result of a very few and impotent Junto."[11]

The selectmen of Boston replied to the accusations that the nonconsumption agreement adopted by the town meeting was nothing but the political scheme of a faction. They recommended the agreement and denied the charge that it was "merely a Party-Business, and the Proposal only of a Junto." Declaring that they were opposed to mob action and riotous assemblies, they stressed their support for the subscription as a peaceful means of obtaining redress of their grievances.[12]

The nonconsumption movement spread to the other towns in Massachusetts and to the other colonies in New England.[13] At a Providence, Rhode Island, town meeting held on 2 December 1767, an agreement was adopted which provided not only for the nonconsumption of a comprehensive list of articles after 1 January 1768 but also stated that these items were not to be imported after that date for either sale or family use. Any person who refused to sign this agreement or who violated its provisions was to be "discountenanced, in the most effectual, but decent and lawful Manner." The meeting also agreed to discourage the excessive use of tea, chinaware, spices and black pepper, and all other British superfluities.[14]

Newport also adopted a nonconsumption agreement on 4 December, which was patterned closely after that of Boston. On 22 February 1768, it was reported that the economizing program had been enthusiastically received throughout Rhode Island. The tailors of Newport agreed to charge fourpence less per day when working on cloth of colonial manufacture than on cloth manufactured in Europe and to charge twenty-five percent more than the customary rates for making any garment of velvet, silk, or broadcloth which cost more than ten shillings sterling per yard.[15]

In Connecticut, Norwich led the way in adopting a nonconsumption agreement, followed by other town meetings at New London, Windham, Mansfield, and

New Haven.[16] The town meeting at New Haven adopted an agreement on 22 February 1768 not to purchase any of a list of articles after 31 March 1768 and to encourage the consumption of articles manufactured in the province.[17] On 29 December 1767, a public meeting at New York appointed a committee to report on a plan for cutting expenses and giving employment to the local tradesmen and the poor. The report was adopted at a meeting on 2 February 1768, but it did not include a nonconsumption agreement.[18] A meeting was also called at Philadelphia to consider what action to take with regard to Boston's example, but the result was disappointing to those in favor of adopting some form of nonconsumption because the assemblage voted only an expression of sympathy.[19]

The Boston Merchants' Nonimportation Agreement of 4 March 1768

The effort of the radical group in Boston to arouse public opinion in support of their measures for resisting the Townshend Acts was invaluably aided by the appearance of John Dickinson's "Farmer's Letters." They appeared weekly in the *Pennsylvania Chronicle* from 2 December 1767 to 15 February 1768. Each was reprinted in all but four of the newspapers printed in the thirteen colonies. In these letters, Dickinson provided a new basis for the constitutional arguments advanced by the colonial agitators in opposition to the threat to civil and political liberties contained in the Townshend Acts. In his third letter, which appeared on 14 December, Dickinson recalled the effectiveness of legislative petitions and nonimportation agreements in securing the repeal of the Stamp Act and urged the people in the various colonies to revive these agencies of protest.[20]

The essence of Dickinson's refinement of the colonial constitutional argument in this second stage of the taxation controversy (the first having been the Stamp Act resistance) was denial of the right of Parliament to levy any tax whatever on the colonies, whether internal or external, while conceding the legal authority of Parliament to regulate the trade of the empire. This distinction between the right of Parliament to regulate trade and the authority of Parliament to tax the colonies necessarily raised the question of revenue resulting from the regulation of trade. Dickinson's answer to this was that the intent of the act would determine the question.[21]

In this series of essays, Dickinson reviewed the history of the Navigation Acts and pointed out that they were concerned solely with the regulation of trade until innovation of raising a revenue in the colonies was introduced by the Grenville ministry in the Sugar Act of 1764. The Stamp Act and the Townshend duties were merely continuations of this policy initiated by Grenville. In answer to the argument that Britain had the right to levy a duty upon her exports, Dickinson argued that the Townshend duties were just as much a tax for revenue as was the stamp tax, because the colonies were prohibited from importing the taxed commodities from any place but Britain. He also pointed out that it would be impossible for the colonists to evade the duties by establishing manufactures in the colonies because the manufacture of one article made the manufacture of another necessary, thus forming a complicated interrelationship. In addition, he noted that the colonists had conceded the indisputable right of Britain to prohibit the manufacture of certain articles in the colonies and that therefore such newly established manufactures could be placed on the prohibited list.[22]

Dickinson's argument was an attempt to compromise by adopting the middle-of-the-road view of the jurisdiction of Parliament outside of the realm, with the avowed aim of keeping the empire intact. He tried to persuade his countrymen to adopt a policy of conciliation and to seek redress of their grievances by legal and peaceful methods.[23]

Governor Bernard of Massachusetts had delayed calling the fall session of the General Court until late in December, probably to avoid any preliminary disputes over the Townshend Acts, which went into effect on 20 November 1767. If this was his motive, he had diagnosed the situation correctly because the popular party in Boston shifted their efforts from the Boston town meeting to the provincial assembly as soon as it met. A committee was appointed at the town meeting on 20 November to formulate instructions to the representatives from Boston in the General Court.

The committee submitted its report on 22 December.[24] It emphasized the need for economizing in the consumption of imports and the establishment of industry and manufacturing in the colony. The report contended that "our Trade by which alone we are enabled to balance our Accounts with Great Britain is in almost every branch of it burthened with Duties and Restrictions, whereby it is rendered unprofitable to us."[25]

The Massachusetts General Court met on 30 December 1767 and appointed a committee to consider the Townshend Acts.[26] Four of the members were from Boston—Samuel Adams, James Otis, John Hancock, and Thomas Cushing. The committee proceeded to carry out the instructions given to the Boston representatives by the town meeting. They drafted letters to Dennys DeBerdt—the agent of the House of Representatives—Lord Shelburne, the Marquis of Rockingham, the Earl of Chatham, and Henry Conway, and sent a petition to the king.[27]

These letters raised both constitutional and practical objections, claiming the rights of all Englishmen for the colonies while pointing out that the colonists were already subject to economic subordination to the British Isles. In addition, the House stressed its fear of the arbitrary action of designing officials paid in Britain and unchecked in America.

The Boston representatives and their allies then turned to their next objective, that of securing the united action of the American colonies in resisting the Townshend Acts. The committee on the state of the province drafted a circular letter to the other colonial assemblies which was an implicit invitation to join the lower house of the Massachusetts assembly in resisting the enforcement of Townshend's program by taking such constitutional steps as were open to them.[28] The motion to send the circular letter was voted down in the House on 21 January 1768. By working diligently behind the scenes, however, the radicals succeeded in securing a reconsideration of the subject and the motion to send a circular letter was later adopted. It was also decided to expunge all reference to the previous defeat from the House *Journals*.[29] The circular letter of 11 February 1768, the authorship of which is credited to Samuel Adams, informed the other American colonial assemblies of the steps which the Massachusetts assembly had taken to oppose the enforcement of the Townshend program. Since it was assumed that this matter was one of common concern to all the colonies, the Massachusetts assembly took the opportunity to submit its opinions to the other colonial assemblies for their consideration and invited them to suggest any further action thought necessary.

If nonconsumption was to be effective, it was essential to obtain support in the countryside. Only by cutting off the extensive rural market could the merchants be compelled to curtail imports from Britain in their own economic self-interest. The task of organizing a nonconsumption movement among the backcountry towns and rural population and of enforcing it would have been extremely difficult, as compared to the task in the seaport towns where the population was more concentrated. A simple way of handling the situation was to obtain a resolution in support of the nonconsumption policy from the lower house of the assembly. In this way, the popular party could claim the support of the entire province for its policy. Such a pledge from the representatives of the people might convince the merchants that they would be unable to sell their goods in the face of such popular resistance and that therefore prudence required the curtailment of their imports.

On 25 February 1768, the House voted to refer the subject of nonconsumption to a special committee of five members—four of whom were definitely members of the radical group in the assembly.[30] On 26 February, the committee submitted its report in the form of resolutions, which were adopted by the vote of eighty-one to one.[31]

The resolutions read as follows:

> Whereas the Happiness and well-being of civil Communities depend upon Industry, Oeconomy & good Morals; and this House taking into serious Consideration the great Decay of the Trade of the Province; the Scarcity of Money; the heavy Debt contracted in the late War which still remains on the People, and the great Difficulties to which they are by these Means reduced:
>
> Resolved, That this House will use their utmost Endeavours, and enforce their Endeavours by Example, in suppressing Extravagances, Idleness, and Vice, and promoting Industry, Oeconomy and good Morals in their respective Towns.
>
> And in order to prevent the unnecessary Exportation of Money, of which this Province has of late been so much drain'd, it is further Resolved, That this House will by all prudent Means endeavor to discountenance the Use of foreign Superfluities and to encourage the Manufactures of this Province.[32]

The fact that the argument of economic expediency was used to justify the resolution in support of the nonconsumption policy does not necessarily detract from the force and validity of the political aspects of the popular party's protest. The two aspects, political and economic, were so interrelated in the Townshend Acts themselves that it is impossible to consider one apart from the other.

The first step toward nonimportation in Boston was taken on 29 February

1768. A notice was inserted in the newspapers calling a meeting of the merchants and traders on 1 March, "to consult on proper Measures relating to our Trade, under its present Embarrassments."[33] On the evening of 1 March, ninety-eight merchants met and William Phillips was chosen moderator. The meeting voted to adopt measures for stopping the importation of goods from Great Britain. A committee of nine was appointed to draw up an agreement. This committee met on 3 and 4 March and formulated the articles of the agreement, and on that evening, it reported back to the meeting of the merchants. The indebtedness of the merchants resulting from excessive importation in the face of restrictions on trade was declared to be endangering their own welfare as well as the welfare of their creditors in England. Reference was also made to the threat of the Townshend Acts to the liberties enjoyed by the colonies under the British Constitution.[34]

The merchants voted not to send for any European commodities for one year, certain necessary items excepted.[35] Other trading towns within the province and other provinces in New England, together with the commercial towns in New York, New Jersey, and Pennsylvania, were to be invited to join in the agreement. The terms of the agreement were to be effective only when those or similar resolutions were adopted by the main trading towns in Massachusetts and by the neighboring colonies. Manufacturing in the colonies was to be encouraged by using colonial goods. Necessary articles were to be purchased from those persons who subscribed to this agreement in preference to others. It was also voted to inform their various correspondents in Britain of the reasons which made it necessary for the merchants to withhold their usual orders for British manufactures. A committee was to be appointed to correspond with the merchants in the various towns and provinces and inform them of the agreement.[36]

On 9 March, the merchants' meeting agreed that subscribers would not order any additional goods until the first Tuesday in May while awaiting the decision of the merchants and traders in the neighboring towns and colonies. A committee was appointed to correspond with them, and letters were sent out on 16 March urging the merchants to cooperate in the nonimportation movement as a more effective means than mere remonstrances of obtaining a redress of grievances from Parliament.[37]

The Boston nonimportation scheme probably received its initial impetus from the same group of radical politicians who had previously maneuvered the nonconsumption agreement through the Boston town meeting and secured a resolution in support of the principle of nonconsumption from the Massachusetts House of Representatives. The success of the nonconsumption scheme could be assured only if the merchants could be induced or compelled to stop importing.

There is some indication that the nonconsumption policy coerced the merchants into adopting a nonimportation agreement. Thomas Cushing wrote in a letter to agent DeBerdt:

> The traders here in the English way, begin to feel the effects of the measures entered into last fall, by the people here, to promote frugality and economy. As the consumption of British goods lessens, their sale diminishes, and I guess it will

not be long before the merchants on your side [of] the water will have reason to complain. . . . I believe the gentlemen in trade are one and all convinced that it will be to no good purpose for them to import English goods as usual, under the present distressed and embarrassed state of the trade. They despair of ever selling them, and consequently of ever being able to pay for them.[38]

The Reaction of New York and Philadelphia to the Boston Nonimportation Movement

During the latter part of March 1768, the New York merchants received a letter from the committee of merchants in Boston urging them to follow Boston in adopting a nonimportation agreement.[39] Meetings were held by the merchants of New York. Governor Henry Moore brought the matter before the council and declared that the merchants' meetings for the purpose of drawing up a plan of nonimportation were illegal and dangerous to the tranquility of the province. The council disagreed with him, maintaining that the people had a right to assemble and adopt rules of economy in accordance with their right to dispose of their money as they saw fit. Moore then announced that he would support anyone who refused to join.[40]

Soon after the middle of April, the New York merchants adopted a nonimportation agreement, acting on the report of a committee appointed to obtain the opinions of the merchants, importers, and retailers. The merchants and importers agreed not to sell on their own accounts, or on commission, nor buy or sell for any person, any goods (except a few enumerated articles), shipped from Great Britain after 1 October 1768 until the Townshend Acts were repealed. The agreement was to go into effect if Boston and Philadelphia adopted similar measures by 1 June.[41] The agreement was signed within two days by every merchant and trader in New York except for two or three of minor importance.[42]

On 2 May 1768, the merchants of Boston accepted the nonimportation resolutions of the merchants and traders of New York.[43] The attempt of the Boston merchants to unite the leading commercial provinces in a coordinated plan of nonimportation now depended on similar action by Philadelphia.

The response of the merchants in Philadelphia was slow and hesitating. In March 1768, the General Assembly had instructed its agents in Britain to join with the agents of the other colonies to solicit the repeal of the Townshend duties.[44] When the nonconsumption resolutions of the Boston town meeting of 28 October 1767 arrived in Philadelphia, a meeting of the people was called to consider similar action. However, the results were disappointing; all that could be gotten was a vote of sympathy for the action taken by the people of Boston.[45]

When the Boston merchants adopted their conditional nonimportation agreement on 4 March, they wrote to the merchants of Philadelphia and New York, informing them of the decision to stop importation if the other commercial towns and provinces did likewise. The Philadelphia merchants held a meeting on 26 March 1768 to consider the letter from Boston.[46] The Boston proposal was not acceptable to the Philadelphia merchants, and the meeting adjourned without taking definite action. They were willing to extend nonimportation only to the articles actually taxed under the Townshend Act. They objected that the late date at which the Boston agreement was to go into effect would allow the merchants to build up large stocks of goods. The Philadelphia merchants were inclined to be suspicious of their New England brothers anyway, in view of the notorious reputation of the New England ports for smuggling. They believed that under such conditions, a nonimportation agreement would have little effect on the Boston merchants while practically destroying the trade of Philadelphia.[47]

Since there seemed to be no hope of any compulsory action on the initiative of the merchants themselves, the popular party in Philadelphia attempted to organize a voluntary association of merchants to stop importing goods after 1 October 1768. A meeting was held on 25 April and they persuaded John Dickinson to address the merchants in order to induce them to sign the voluntary association.[48] Dickinson recommended the adoption of nonimportation as a peaceful and constitutional means of supporting the petitions of their representatives for the repeal of the Townshend Acts.[49]

In spite of Dickinson's influence and prestige with the leading merchants, the attempt to obtain a voluntary nonimportation association was a failure. The controversy was transferred to the newspapers, and Charles Thomson led off with an attack on the merchants of Philadelphia for considering their own private interests over those of the public and for failing to join New York and Boston in adopting a nonimportation agreement.[50] This sentiment was echoed by Arthur Lee when he declared: "It is with unspeakable concern, that I have perceived the Spirit of Liberty so luke-warm in this powerful and important city."[51]

These condemnations of the Philadelphia merchants were answered by Joseph Galloway, writing under the signature of "A Chester County Farmer." He defended the conduct of the merchants by asserting that the article by "A Freeborn American" censuring the merchants for not adopting nonimportation in conjunction with Boston and New York was written by a Bostonian in Philadelphia. "Chester County Farmer" recalled that the inhabitants of Philadelphia had adopted similar nonconsumption resolutions at the time of the Stamp Act. They had agreed to wear only clothing made in the colonies and not to purchase lamb so that the number of sheep would be increased and thus the supply of wool. Weavers and spinners had been encouraged to resume their work, and cloth was produced in sufficient quantity for sale in the city, where it found a ready and profitable market prior to the repeal of the Stamp Act. Upon the repeal of the Stamp Act, the townspeople abandoned their resolutions, and the cloth manufactured in the colonies was left without a market. The "Chester County Farmer" wanted to know, in the event that such resolutions should be entered into again, what guarantee could be given to the farmers and weavers that the townspeople would adhere to their resolutions to purchase and wear only clothing manufactured in the colonies.[52]

The merchants of New York had notified the merchants of Philadelphia of the nonimportation agreement which they had adopted. The first letter was sent 16 April, but since they had not received an answer from Philadelphia, the New York merchants sent another letter on 6 June reminding their colleagues that their failure to act within the time limit stated would absolve the merchants of New York and Boston from their agreements.[53] The Philadelphia merchants were not moved by this last plea for united action.

• THE INDEPENDENT NONIMPORTATION AGREEMENTS IN THE NORTHERN COLONIES •

The Independent Nonimportation Movement in Boston

With the refusal of the Philadelphia merchants to join Boston and New York in adopting the policy of nonimportation, the movement for the cooperation of the three leading ports collapsed. The merchants in Boston were now faced with the choice of giving up their agitation for the redress of commercial grievances or entering into an agreement independently of the other commercial centers. Meanwhile, a combination of events affecting the internal political and economic situation contributed to the support of the radical popular party's program of resistance to the enforcement of the Townshend Acts.

The American Board of Customs Commissioners had arrived at Boston on 5 November 1767 and had begun holding sessions on 18 November. On 9 May 1768, John Hancock's sloop *Liberty* entered Boston harbor with a cargo of Madeira wine. The cargo was landed, whale oil and tar were loaded, and the ship was ready to depart on 9 June. At this time customs officer Thomas Kirk informed the collector that he had earlier refused to allow several casks of wine to be unloaded illegally from the *Liberty*, and had been held prisoner in the hold for three hours while the goods were unloaded. On 10 June, the collector seized the *Liberty*, and it was towed out into the harbor and anchored under the protection of the warship *Romney*. This action caused a riot to break out in the city, which resulted in the commissioners taking refuge at Castle William. A boat belonging to the collector was dragged up on Boston Common and burned.[54] The *Liberty* was later condemned in the Admiralty Court.

The popular excitement over the seizure of the *Liberty* had not yet subsided when the news reached Boston of the ministry's decision to send troops. There was no direct connection between the *Liberty* episode and this decision; Lord Hillsborough had made the decision before the event. General Thomas Gage had received orders by the July packet from England to alert troops at Halifax but not to send them to Boston unless Governor Bernard requested them. This Bernard refused to do without the support of the council.[55] On 27 July, he put the question before the council, and on the twenty-ninth the council rejected any idea of asking Gage to send troops to Boston. The council blamed the illegal seizure of the *Liberty* for the disorders of 10 June and asserted that the commissioners had left voluntarily, denying that any attack had been made on their persons or property. The use of troops was denounced as unfriendly to peace and order.[56]

The proposal to send troops to Boston in the summer of 1768 drew support to the radical party from many who were not in sympathy with their program of opposition to the Townshend Acts, but were willing to support them in opposition to the use of troops to enforce the authority of the customs commissioners. It undoubtedly strengthened the support of the nonimportation policy and was a factor in prompting the merchants to take steps toward drawing up a nonimportation agreement late in July.[57]

At this point, Hillsborough ordered the Massachusetts House to rescind the circular letter sent to the Speakers of the other assemblies during the previous session. The opposition of the ministry was incurred mainly because the letter suggested intercolonial opposition to the acts of Parliament. In letters to the governors of the colonies, Hillsborough declared the circular to be "a most dangerous and factious Tendency, calculated . . . to promote an unwarrantable Combination, and to excite and encourage an open Opposition to and Denial of the Authority of Parliament."[58] The governors were urged to exert their influence to get the assemblies of their respective provinces to "take no Notice of it, which will be treating it with the Contempt it deserves." In the event of refusal on the part of the assembly to comply with this request, the governor was instructed to prorogue or dissolve the house immediately.[59] On 30 June the Massachusetts House of Representatives refused to rescind the circular letter by a vote of ninety-two to seventeen.[60] Bernard then carried out his instructions and dissolved the body.

Hillsborough's attempt to force the Massachusetts House to rescind the circular letter and the threat that the British government might resort to the use of troops to enforce the Navigation Acts in the colony was closely followed by action on the part of the merchants' committee at Boston. On 18 July, the merchants' standing committee issued a call for a general meeting at Faneuil Hall "to consult measures for the better regulation of the trade." The general meeting was postponed until 1 August, however, and on 28 July, the committee drew up resolutions.[61] On 1 August 1768, sixty-two merchants met at Faneuil Hall, where the resolutions were presented, adopted, and signed.[62]

In order to relieve trade, the merchants agreed not to order any more goods from Britain during the fall season other than what had already been ordered. No goods were to be imported from Great Britain, either on their own account or on commission, from 1 January 1769 to 1 January 1770, except for certain articles absolutely essential for the fishery. No goods usually imported from Great Britain were to be purchased from any factors between these dates. It was also agreed not to purchase any British goods from persons who imported them from another American colony. After 1 January 1769, no tea, paper, glass, or painters' colors were to be imported into the colony until the acts imposing duties on these articles had been repealed.[63] Sixty of the sixty-two merchants who attended the meeting on 1 August signed the agreement, and the next day additional subscribers were obtained.[64] At a meeting on 8 August, only one hundred merchants attended, and it is likely that this was all that had subscribed to the agreement up to this time.[65]

In contrast to the agreement adopted on 4 March of the same year, the agreement of 1 August 1768 was entirely independent of any action which other colonies might take. Nor was the nonconsumption movement in Boston relaxed after the adoption of the merchants' nonimportation agreements of March and August. In May 1768, Samuel Adams wrote to Dennys DeBerdt warning that the nonconsumption movement should not be taken too lightly in England and that the disposition of the people to abstain from the purchase of foreign goods was bound to have a telling effect upon the consumption of British manufactured goods in the long run.[66]

The Independent Nonimportation Movement in New York

The independent action of the Boston merchants on 1 August 1768 was closely followed in point of time by the New York merchants. At a meeting at Bolton and Sigell's tavern on the evening of 25 August, the merchants of New York met to consider further action, and on the twenty-seventh, they signed an agreement.[67] No orders, other than what had been sent, were to be given for goods imported from Great Britain, either on their individual accounts or on commissions. No goods shipped after 1 November 1768 were to be imported from Britain on individual accounts or commissions nor purchased from any factor until the Townshend duties were repealed. Certain essential articles were exempt from this restriction if imported after 1 November. No other goods, excepting those which had already been ordered, were to be imported from Hamburg and Holland, except tiles and bricks. All orders sent to Britain after 16 August were to be countermanded at once. All persons who subscribed to the agreement and imported any of the prohibited articles, either directly or indirectly, contrary to the true intent and meaning of the agreement, were to be treated as enemies of their country. Any goods sent contrary to this agreement were to be stored in a public warehouse until such time as the Townshend duties were repealed.[68]

On 1 September, the New York merchants sent a copy of their nonimportation agreement to the Philadelphia merchants, calling attention to the respects in which it differed from the Boston agreement and urging Philadelphia to adopt a similar one.[69] On 5 September, the retailers and tradesmen of New York entered into a nonconsumption agreement designed to support the merchants' nonimportation agreement of 27 August. An element of compulsion was involved in the clause stating that they would resort to every lawful means in their power to prevent anyone from dealing with violators of the agreement and to halt the sale of goods imported contrary to it. They pledged to publicize the names of those who refused to subscribe to the agreement or violated its terms and to treat them as enemies.[70] The importers of Albany also concurred in the New York merchants' agreement.[71] The assembly met in late October, and on 17 December, it addressed a petition to the House of Lords complaining that the trade of the colony was languishing, that the system of jury trial was being threatened, and that, above all else, the colony was in danger of losing its legislative independence as a result of the restraint placed upon it by the special act of Parliament.[72] On 31 December, the assembly heard a reading of the Massachusetts circular and ordered an appropriate answer to be drawn up. The House then resolved itself into a committee of the whole and passed a series of resolutions. The legislators declared that no tax of any kind or for any purpose could be levied upon the persons, estates, or property of the subjects of that colony except by their own representatives convened in General Assembly. The restraining act of Parliament was declared to be a violation of the constitutional rights of the colonial legislature. Finally, it was resolved that the assembly had an indisputable right "to correspond and consult with any of the neighbouring colonies . . . in any Matter, Subject or Thing whatsoever, whereby they shall conceive the Rights, Liberties, Interests or Privileges of this House, or of its Constituents, are or may be affected."[73]

The protest in the assembly against economic and financial conditions was followed by a tightening up of the enforcement of the nonimportation agreement when the merchants appointed a committee of inspection on 13 March 1769.[74] The artisans also tightened up their agreement by adding resolutions of nonconsumption. On 13 April 1769, the Cordwainer's Society resolved not to eat any more lamb until 1 August. On the same day, the Sons of Liberty, meeting at the Province Arms tavern, subscribed to a similar agreement with the object of increasing the supply of wool to encourage home manufacturing of cloth.[75]

The unity of all groups in support of the nonimportation policy was given further expression after the newly elected assembly met on 4 April 1769. On 10 April, the assembly passed a motion introduced by Philip Livingston stating:

> That the thanks of that house be given to the merchants of that city and colony for their repeated disinterested Public Spirit & patriotic conduct in declining the importation, or receiving of goods from Great Britain until such Acts of Parliament as the Assembly had declared unconstitutional and subversive of the rights and liberties of the people of this Colony, should be repealed.[76]

Accordingly, on 2 May, John Cruger, who was Speaker of the assembly and also president of the chamber of commerce, delivered the vote of thanks to the merchants.[77]

The Independent Nonimportation Movement in Philadelphia

The Philadelphia merchants seemed determined not to resort to the policy of nonimportation until all other means of obtaining redress had been exhausted. These took the forms of legislative petitions to Parliament and memorials of the merchants themselves to the merchants and manufacturers of Great Britain, designed to prod British business interests into exerting pressure upon Parliament, as they had done at the time of the repeal of the Stamp Act.

On 30 July 1768, a meeting of the inhabitants of Philadelphia voted instructions to their representatives in the assembly which called for sending a petition to the king, a memorial to the House of Lords, and a remonstrance to the House of Commons. The instructions were presented to Joseph Galloway and James Pemberton to be communicated by them to the assembly.

In accordance with the instructions to the representatives of Philadelphia, petitions to the king, Lords, and Commons were drawn up and adopted on 22 September and transmitted to the agent of the colony, along with a letter from the committee of correspondence in the assembly.[78]

After the Boston merchants adopted the nonimportation agreement of 4 August, their standing committee wrote to the merchants of Philadelphia urging them to adopt a similar agreement. The merchants of Philadelphia appointed a committee to consider the proposal, but after meeting several times and consulting with various merchants of the city, the committee failed to obtain a general concurrence. The next step taken by the committee was to consult eight or ten of the leading mercantile firms in an attempt to get their support. The hope was that with such backing the nonimportation measure could be carried. This attempt also failed because none of these firms would consent to a general nonimportation agreement. They offered to subscribe to an agreement only if it applied to nonimportation of articles on which duties had been or should be levied and to certain luxury items. This proposal of limited nonimportation was rejected by the committee.[79] A meeting called by the committee for 23 September was attended by fewer than one-fourth of the dry goods merchants. This was taken as conclusive evidence that the majority of the merchants were opposed to general nonimportation.[80]

Philadelphia was severely criticized in the New York press for its inaction, but was defended by "Philadelphus" in the *Pennsylvania Gazette* of 20 October 1768. "Philadelphus" began his defense by stating that the merchants of Philadelphia were not unaware of the grievances of the colonies resulting from the recent impositions on their trade and the political implications of the ministerial policy of raising a revenue in America. At the same time, he noted:

> Had the people of the northern colonies been more prudent in their measures, and less violent in their publications, the misrepresentation of the enemies of North-America would have had less weight; they would, in all probability, never have experienced the hardships they at present labour under,—and our burthens would have been relieved, perhaps, with more ease then we can at present expect.

"Philadelphus" informed the public that the merchants' committee had prepared a memorial to the merchants in England, with the aim of convincing them that the colonies could not pay their debts or import goods under the present impositions on their commerce. The memorial urged English merchants to join the colonies in obtaining redress in their mutual interest, as they had done at the time of the repeal of the Stamp Act. The merchants of Philadelphia were inclined to place their faith in the influence which the English merchants could exert with the ministry, if they could only be persuaded to join with the colonies in working for repeal of the acts. There was a general disposition to await the results of the petitions and memorials before taking any further action.[81]

The memorial mentioned by "Philadelphus" was sent to the merchants and manufacturers of Great Britain on 1 November 1768. Its emphasis was not on the unconstitutionality of the acts, but on the anticommercial character of the Townshend duties and the restrictions on colonial trade in general.

The course of events soon forced Philadelphia merchants to take further action. Some were planning to send orders by a vessel scheduled to leave in the middle of February 1769. There was no indication from England that Parliament was disposed to grant any relief. Since the sending of these orders promised to complicate any agreement which might be adopted in the event that Parliament failed to act, a meeting of the merchants was held on 6 February. At that time it was agreed that all orders for goods should be cancelled unless they were shipped before 1 April and that no further orders were to be sent before 10 March. By that time they expected to receive more definite news as to the result of their memorials.[82]

Another memorial was drafted at the meeting of 6 February 1769 and sent to their individual correspondents in the English cities. In this petition, the Philadelphia merchants raised the constitutional issue, which had hitherto been confined to the petitions of the legislative bodies. When the Philadelphia merchants resorted to these arguments, they alienated many of the English merchants who had sympathized with the colonial merchants' protests as long as they were concerned strictly with commercial grievances.[83] It soon became evident that no relief was to be expected either from Parliament or from the efforts of the merchants in England on behalf of the colonies. The advice of the London merchants to the merchants of Philadelphia was to continue their measures of nonconsumption, the promotion of manufacturing, and nonimportation in hopes that Parliament would be more favorable to a repeal of the Townshend duties in its next session. They cautioned their friends in Philadelphia, however, to avoid any kind of violence: "We wish you may stand your Ground, at the same Time flatter ourselves, the Conduct of our Friends in Pennsylvania will be pacific, and not run into any tumultuous Proceedings."[84]

The vacillating policy of the merchants of Philadelphia was drawing to a close, due chiefly to popular pressure in the form of a nonconsumption movement. Agitation for such measures appeared in a newspaper letter from "A Tradesman" as early as October 1768. He encouraged the merchants to follow the example of New York in adopting general nonimportation.[85]

Early in February 1769, the nonconsumption movement was taken up by the various fire companies in the city of Philadelphia. Three of them adopted resolutions to abstain from purchasing mutton during the year in order to increase the supply of wool for use in the manufacture of woolen cloth. A number of citizens also agreed to avoid all unnecessary consumption of wool and to wear leather jackets thereafter.[86]

As a result of this popular pressure and the despair of obtaining any redress of grievances, either from the petitions of the assemblies to Parliament or from the memorials to the merchants in England, the Philadelphia merchants took the final step in the adoption of a nonimportation agreement on 10 March 1769. At that time, it was agreed that no goods shipped from Britain after 1 April 1769 would be imported, except for a list of twenty-two articles used for local manufacturing, ship-ballast, and medicinal and educational purposes. In order to deny special advantages to smugglers, these conditions were extended to include goods imported from continental Europe. The subscribers pledged not to buy goods imported contrary to the agreement and to discountenance by all lawful measures any person who refused to abide by the resolutions. The agreement was to remain in effect until such time as the Townshend duties were repealed or until a general meeting of the subscribers should determine otherwise. The resolutions were circulated among the merchants and traders of the city, and a large majority signed during the next few weeks. At a later date, the merchants decided that goods arriving in Philadelphia contrary to the agreement should not be stored, but should be returned to England. The principle of the boycott was also extended to provide that any person who violated the agreement, in letter or spirit, should be stigmatized as an enemy of his country, and his name published in the newspapers.[87]

The Adoption of Nonimportation in the Smaller New England and Middle Colonies

Within a few months after the Boston merchants adopted their nonimportation agreement of 4 August 1768, similar agreements were adopted by neighboring Massachusetts towns. Salem adopted an agreement on 6 September 1768, followed soon after by Newburyport. Both were essentially the same as Boston's.[88] The merchants and traders of Marblehead held meetings from 20 to 26 October 1769 and framed their agreement.[89]

The New York merchants compelled the merchants in Albany to enter into an agreement before July 1769. The Albany merchants and traders wanted to include certain Indian goods in the list of exempted articles, but the New York merchants refused to give their consent. The result was that the Albany merchants were dissatisfied with their agreement from the very beginning. The increasing scarcity of goods for the Indian trade not only worked economic hardship, but the Indians were also suspicious of a conspiracy against them and were unable to understand why the traffic in furs suddenly stopped. Under the threat of an outbreak of Indian hostility, the Albany merchants soon clandestinely broke their agreement and imported goods for the Indian fur trade through Quebec and Montreal.[90]

New Haven adopted an agreement on 10 July 1769. On 9 October 1769, the Connecticut Assembly passed resolutions expressing its approval of the conduct of the merchants who had entered into nonimportation agreements, sacrificing their private interests in the cause of liberty.[91]

At the August session of the grand jury of Newcastle County on the Delaware, a nonimportation agreement closely patterned after Philadelphia's was drafted. On 28 August 1769, a meeting of the freeholders and freemen of the county met and signed the compact.[92] The New Jersey Assembly passed a vote of thanks to the merchants of New Jersey, New York, and Philadelphia for their nonimportation policy.[93]

Only two provinces remained outside of the nonimportation movement among the northern group. New Hampshire was predominantly agricultural and expressed little opposition to the acts until after the Boston Massacre in 1770. Rhode Island's failure to follow the other northern colonies into the policy of nonimportation caused much concern because of the importance of Newport as a commercial center. The notorious reputation the Newport merchants had as smugglers carried over into the extralegal nonimportation movement. The other colonies threatened to take commercial action against Rhode Island, particularly after Newport received a shipload of goods which had been turned away elsewhere.[94] Under this pressure, the merchants of Providence were the first to take action. On 10 October 1769, they met and agreed not to import any goods from Britain until the Townshend duties were repealed. Fourteen items were enumerated in this agreement as being exceptions to the prohibition against importation.[95]

At another meeting on 24 October, the merchants, traders, and other inhabitants resolved not to import, either for sale or family use, or purchase any of a list of articles enumerated in the town's nonconsumption agreement of 2 December 1767.[96]

Pressure was also exerted to compel the Newport merchants to adopt nonimportation. The Philadelphia merchants' committee sent a letter to Newport notifying the merchants there that plans were being made to halt all commerce with that port unless they entered into an agreement. Boston had already severed commercial relations with Rhode Island, and similar steps were being taken at Charleston, South Carolina. The Newport merchants met on 30 October 1769 and adopted an agreement patterned after those of the other colonies.[97]

· THE ADOPTION OF NONIMPORTATION AGREEMENTS IN THE PLANTATION PROVINCES ·

The Virginia Association of 18 May 1769

The first organized protest against the Townshend Acts in Virginia took the form of petitions from various counties presented in the House of Burgesses in April 1768. Petitions from several counties protesting the acts as unconstitutional were favorably received by the House of Burgesses, and a committee was appointed to draft memorials to the king, Lords, and Commons.[98] By 14 April, memorials embodying the principles of taxation and representation expressed in the county petitions received the approval of the House.[99] On 16 April, the body adjourned and did not meet again until 8 May 1769. In the interval, Governor Francis Fauquier died and Lord Botetourt was appointed by the Crown to succeed him.

When the House of Burgesses met again on 8 May 1769, the Massachusetts circular letter had been received. It was known that Hillsborough had ordered the Massachusetts Assembly to rescind their resolution to send the letter and that his order had been rejected. The news was also received from England that Parliament had revived an obsolete statute which allowed the government to transport persons accused of committing treason to England for trial. These factors gave rise to a series of resolutions which were passed by the House of Burgesses on 16 May 1769. These resolutions stated the rights of Virginians to tax themselves and to be tried by a local jury. They were embodied in a petition to the king, and copies were sent to the other colonial assemblies.[100] On 17 May, Governor Botetourt dissolved the Burgesses, in accordance with his instructions from the Crown. The members retired at once to a house in Williamsburg and proceeded to adopt resolutions of nonimportation.

The idea of economic coercion of Great Britain had persisted in the minds of the planters ever since their experience at the time of the Stamp Act. As early as January 1769, an anonymous writer in the *Virginia Gazette* reviewed the constitutional issue involved in Britain's attempt to tax the colonies for the purpose of raising a revenue and hinted at the advisability of reviving the policy of economic coercion. He asked: "Can we reflect one moment on the commercial interest of Britain, and not know that they may be brought to reason, by being made to feel the effect of their folly? . . . Our success is already warranted by experience."[101]

George Washington expressed his approval of the idea of a nonimportation plan for Virginia in a letter to George Mason, dated 5 April 1769.

> We have already . . . proved the inefficacy of the addresses to the throne, and remonstrances to parliament. How far, then, their attention to our rights and privileges is to be awakened or alarmed, by starving their trade and manufactures, remains to be tried.

Washington emphasized that nonimportation could be successful in Virginia only by appealing directly to the people. If they could be persuaded not to purchase imported articles, the factors who represented English merchants would be forced to be cautious about importation, even though they would not enter into the association.[102] Mason agreed, and added:

> It may not be amiss to let the ministry understand that, until we obtain a redress of grievances, we will withhold from them our commodities, and particularly refrain from making tobacco, by which the revenue would lose fifty times more than all their oppressions could raise here.[103]

The plan for a Virginia nonimportation association was submitted by Washington at the meeting in Williamsburg on 17 May, and the Association was signed the next day. The draft corresponds exactly to the plan drawn up by George Mason, except for the addition of two articles and the omission of one of Mason's, advocating the nonexportation of certain enumerated articles.[104]

The Burgesses unanimously accepted several provisions in the text of their agreement. First, they agreed to promote industry and frugality while discouraging any sort of luxury or extravagance. They agreed not to import any goods taxed by

Parliament for the purpose of raising a revenue in America and not to purchase such goods from anyone after the first of September. A third clause enumerated certain articles not to be imported from Great Britain or Europe until repeal of the Townshend duties should take place. If any of these goods were shipped anyway, contrary to the spirit of the agreement, the recipients were pledged to refuse to receive them or to allow themselves to be charged for the goods. Lastly, there were also provisions for the nonimportation of slaves and wine and the nonconsumption of lamb.

The agreement was signed by eighty-eight members of the House of Burgesses, and the document bears the signatures of nineteen additional subscribers.[105] George Wythe, clerk of the House of Burgesses, later submitted the names of eleven more members of the House who were not present at the time the Association was adopted but had later subscribed.[106]

Nonimportation seems to have been generally accepted among the planters in the various counties. George Wythe reported that in Dinwiddie County alone over a thousand persons subscribed to the agreement.[107] Robert Carter Nicholas, writing to John Norton in London, said:

> I suppose Mr. Cheap & Co. have drawn upon you for my annual Pipe of Wine; but I shall give them directions to ship me no more 'till farther Orders. You may expect very few Orders for Goods next Year; for my own Part, I am resolved to import Nothing that I can possibly do without, & believe this is the Resolution of most.[108]

The Adoption of Nonimportation in South Carolina

Charleston, the largest port in the plantation provinces, was not affected economically to the same extent as the commercial centers of the northern and middle provinces by the passage of the Townshend Acts. Most of the marketing of the staple products of the colony was handled by English and Scottish merchants and factors.[109] As a result, they were reluctant to join the merchants in the other provinces in adopting the policy of nonimportation. In September 1768, the Boston Committee of Merchants sent a letter to the Charleston merchants urging them to adopt an agreement, but the Charleston merchants did not even assemble to discuss the matter.[110] Although the initiative for resistance to the British government's revenue policy was lacking among the mercantile group, the provision that the revenue raised by the Townshend duties was to be used, in part, to pay the salaries of the judges and civil officials aroused legislative resistance to the constitutional implications.

When the assembly met on 16 November 1768, the governor, Lord Charles Montagu, informed the Commons of Hillsborough's instructions to the governors regarding the Massachusetts circular. The letters from the legislatures of Massachusetts and Virginia were both referred to a committee, which returned a report endorsing them. It also recommended that an address be sent to the king for a redress of grievances and that the Speaker inform the Massachusetts and Virginia assemblies that their letters had met with the approval of the Commons of South

Carolina. In response, Governor Montagu dissolved the assembly and kept them from meeting again until 27 June 1769.[111]

On 17 August 1769, the Virginia Resolves of 1769 were laid before the assembly. The Commons unanimously concurred with them and passed similar resolutions. On 23 August, the lieutenant-governor prorogued the assembly.

The planters in South Carolina, and in the plantation provinces generally, constituted the largest and most influential discontented group. In addition to their opposition to the policies of the British government, the South Carolina planters had certain other economic grievances in common with the other colonies, such as their opposition to the Currency Act of 1764. Since the merchants and factors in the plantation provinces refused to adopt the policy of nonimportation of their own accord, the nonconsumption of British goods by the planters and working people was designed to coerce them into stopping their importation.[112] On 2 February 1769, an agreement for the nonconsumption of imports was published, but was not adopted by any group at that time.[113]

During June and July 1769, nonimportation agreements were proposed to both the mechanics and the planters. At first, these groups were unable to arrange the details of an agreement which would protect the interests of both sides. The merchants proposed their own agreement after meetings on 30 June and 7 July 1769. The mechanics objected to the terms of this agreement on two points. It failed to include a clause pledging support for local manufacturing, and it failed to mention the restriction on the buying and use of mourning wear and gifts.[114] On 22 June, Christopher Gadsden, writing in the press under the pseudonym "Pro Grege et Rege," urged the planters and mechanics to adopt a policy of nonconsumption, which would force the merchants to stop importing. He denounced the importing merchants as "strangers" in the province whose private interest was opposed to the welfare of the people.[115]

The merchants, on the other hand, objected to the nonrepresentative character of the meetings which had formulated the mechanics' and planters' agreements. They accused the other groups of permitting the importation of articles which they regarded as indispensable while the mercantile group was not granted any concessions. The merchants were especially opposed to prohibiting the purchase or use of mourning goods with which their stores were heavily stocked.[116] In response, a committee of merchants was appointed to develop an alternative to the agreement promulgated by the mechanics and planters. The joint committee completed its work on 19 July, and the next day the merchants formally adopted the plan and appointed a committee of thirteen to enforce the new agreement. On 22 July, a meeting of the mechanics and planters adopted the compromise plan and appointed a committee of thirteen planters and thirteen mechanics to serve with the merchants' committee as a joint committee of thirty-nine. At the meeting of the planters and mechanics on 22 July, 286 people signed the agreement, and by 27 July, 142 merchants had also signed.[117]

The resolutions adopted on 22 July encouraged the use of American, especially local, manufactures, economy in funeral practices, and nonimportation. No goods of British, European, or Indian manufacture were to be imported from Britain, Holland, or any other port, and orders already sent were to be countermanded. Nor were slaves or wine to be imported, and transient traders and nonsubscribers were to be boycotted.[118] In October 1769, the general committee met and amended the agreement to prohibit the exportation of tanned leather because no saddlery or shoes were to be imported until the revenue acts were repealed.[119]

There still remained a core of loyal supporters of the Crown among the merchant-planters who opposed nonimportation. The most eloquent of these was William Henry Drayton, who especially resented the tyrannical methods employed by the Liberty Tree party in enforcing the agreement and its intimidation of all who opposed the policy of nonimportation by stigmatizing them as enemies of their country. He attacked them in the press under the signature of "Free-Man," arguing that the only authority which could legally stigmatize a man as an enemy to his country was the legislature of the province.[120]

On 14 September, it was announced that there were only thirty-one nonsubscribers in the whole town, exclusive of the Crown officials. Their names were published in handbills and circulated.[121] William Henry Drayton was among those thus publicized. On 5 December, Drayton petitioned the assembly for redress of injuries received in consequence of the nonimportation resolutions. He asked that his rights as a freeman be guaranteed against what he regarded a conspiracy contrary to the constitutional law of the land.[122] The lower house refused to receive Drayton's petition, and all but one of the town's printers refused to publish it in their paper.[123]

The Adoption of Nonimportation in Maryland and Georgia

In Maryland, the first action against the Townshend Acts was taken by the assembly. The lower house of the assembly was informed by Governor Horatio Sharpe of Hillsborough's instruction to ignore the Massachusetts circular letter of June 1768.[124] The assembly refused to recognize this order and petitioned through agent Charles Garth, asking the king to repeal the acts.[125] They also informed Massachusetts Speaker Thomas Cushing that Maryland supported the principles expressed in the circular letter.[126]

The first action in the direction of organizing a nonimportation movement in Maryland was not taken until 20 March 1769, when the Baltimore merchants signed an agreement. Acting under pressure from the Philadelphia merchants, who had adopted a nonimportation agreement only ten days previously, the Baltimore merchants agreed not to purchase British manufactures until after the repeal of the Townshend duties.[127] On 23 May, the meeting at Annapolis entered into an agreement not to send any orders for goods to Great Britain until 30 June 1769 and not to import British goods.[128] This agreement at Annapolis was the action of a county, Anne Arundel, rather than merely of one town, and this procedure set the pattern for the province of Maryland.[129]

The controversy over the adoption of nonimportation in Georgia revealed the same split between the merchants and the mechanics and planters that existed in South Carolina. On 2 September 1769, a meeting of a group known as the "Amicable Society" in Savannah issued a public notice to the planters, merchants, tradesmen, and all other inhabitants that a meeting would be held on 12 September to consider means of obtaining relief from the Townshend Acts. On the appointed date a committee was selected to draft a nonimportation agreement and instructed to report at the next meeting, to be held on 19 September.[130]

The merchants of Savannah, in an attempt to divert the popular movement for nonimportation, held a meeting at the house of Alexander Creighton on 16 September 1769. They drew up a statement of their grievances, in which they denounced the Townshend Acts as unconstitutional. The merchants adopted a resolution not to import any articles on which such duties were levied.[131] On 19 September, a mass meeting at Savannah, with Jonathan Bryan as chairman,[132] adopted a comprehensive nonimportation agreement patterned on that adopted in South Carolina.[133]

The Adoption of Nonimportation in North Carolina

North Carolina was the last of the plantation provinces to adopt the policy of nonimportation. On 30 September 1769, the Sons of Liberty of Wilmington and Brunswick adopted nonimportation resolutions. Their next effort was to obtain a nonimportation agreement which would apply to the entire province.[134]

On 23 October 1769, the General Assembly met at New Bern and on 26 October adopted the Virginia resolutions. North Carolina's governor, William Tryon, thereupon dissolved the assembly on 6 November. Consequently, sixty-four of the seventy-seven members immediately met at the courthouse in New Bern, organized as a convention, and appointed a committee to draw up a nonimportation association. The next day, the committee's report was presented and the nonimportation agreement formally signed by the sixty-four members of the assembly who were present.[135] The agreement was made effective 1 January 1770, and in all other respects it was closely modeled after the Virginia Association of 18 May.[136]

• THE ENFORCEMENT OF THE BOSTON NONIMPORTATION AGREEMENT, 1769–70 •

The Shift from Voluntary Compliance to Coerced Conformity

During the year in which the other major trading towns and colonies were adopting nonimportation, Boston was occupied by a force of British troops. After discovering in August 1768 that the troops were soon to arrive in Boston, the popular party attempted to influence Governor Bernard to recall the assembly, dissolved since its refusal to rescind the circular letter in June 1768. On 12 September, the Boston town meeting petitioned the governor to convene the assembly so that it might deliberate on the coming of the troops. Bernard refused on the grounds that he had not received official notice that troops were being sent. He also pointed out that in this case, the calling of the assembly depended upon orders from the Crown. The town then resolved to call a "committee of convention" and invited the other towns of the province to send delegates to meet with those of the town of Boston on 22 September.[137] The letter, sent out by the selectmen of Boston to the other towns on 14 September, reviewed the grievances of the colony and protested the sending of troops. The purpose of the troops, the letter declared, was "nothing short of enforcing by military power the execution of acts of parliament, in the forming of which the colonies have not, and cannot have, any constitutional influence."[138]

On 22 September, seventy delegates representing sixty-six towns in the province met in Boston. The convention held sessions until 29 September. Several petitions were drawn up and presented to Governor Bernard, a letter was drafted to the colonial agent of the House of Representatives, and a set of resolutions was framed. The papers were not concerned with opposition to the expected troops but emphasized, instead, the grievances of the colony and the need for holding new elections and calling the general court.[139] These resolutions represented a victory for the moderate elements in the colony. The radicals in Boston had called a convention, but the conservative delegates from the rural areas of Massachusetts refused to follow the leadership of the radical faction in Boston.[140]

Despite the inability of the popular party to put across their program in the convention, their power increased greatly at the next election. Their electoral success was so great that Bernard soon wrote to John Pownall that the "faction" was unopposed in the council, and barely opposed in the House.[141]

The increase in the political power and prestige of the popular party was followed by changes in the method of enforcing the nonimportation policy. Initially, subscription to the agreement in Boston was voluntary and the task of supervising it was left with the merchants' organization. In the spring of 1769 an element of coercion in enforcement was introduced. Committees of inspection were appointed to check the manifests of all cargoes and the names of those violating the terms of the agreement were published. Boycotts were instituted against those who refused to subscribe to the nonimportation agreement, and popular demonstrations were organized against the few who persisted in their refusal to abide by the agreement.

The nonimportation agreement went into effect 1 January 1769. On 21 April, a meeting of the merchants in Boston appointed a committee to inspect the manifests of vessels arriving from Britain and to report the names of those merchants who had imported goods and broken the agreement. On 27 April, the committee reported that six subscribers had imported in violation of the agreement and six more had imported who were not signers. The subscribers agreed to store their goods with the committee, and the committee was instructed to confer with the nonsigners.[142] On 9 May, the Boston town meeting recommended that the inhabitants of the town boycott those merchants who had imported goods contrary to the merchants' resolutions.[143] Shortly afterwards, handbills were circulated advising the people to boycott the various firms which had imported.[144]

This thrust by the popular party was met by John Mein, the publisher of the *Boston Chronicle,* who launched a campaign designed to destroy the public's confidence in the good faith of the Boston subscribers to the nonimportation agreement. With the cooperation of government officials, he printed the cargo lists of all the ships that had entered the port of Boston since the nonimportation agreement had gone into effect, together with the names of the consignees. He emphasized that individuals who had signed the agreement had hypocritically imported anyway.[145] He asserted that an accurate account revealed that 190 different persons, many of whom were signers of the agreement, had imported in violation of the agreement, and he substantiated his point by listing the number of trunks, bales, cases, boxes, casks, etc., although without classifying their contents. The defense of the merchants' committee in the *Boston Gazette* of 12 June 1769 emphasized that Mein had stated the quantity of goods without differentiating between those permitted under the agreement and those which were prohibited.[146] Nevertheless, Mein's challenge prompted the merchants to take steps to tighten enforcement of the agreement.

On 26 July, the merchants met and worked out a system of boycott that more effectively dealt with those who continued to import. It was agreed to withhold their business from the master of any vessel who loaded any prohibited merchandise at any English port. In the event that any of the prohibited goods should be consigned to them or sent contrary to orders, the merchants resolved not to accept them or to pay the freight charges. Another committee was appointed to inspect the cargo manifests of all vessels arriving at Boston before 1 January 1770 and to publish the names of those violating the agreement unless the importer agreed to turn over the goods for storage.[147]

In the face of this increase in enforcement, merchants William Jackson, Jonathan Simpson, the Selkridge brothers, John Taylor, and Samuel Fletcher, all of whom had continued to advertise goods in the newspapers, accepted the agreement. They promised to store their fall imports with the committee of merchants.[148] On 11 August, another meeting of the merchants was held. It resolved to publish the names of those who refused to subscribe and who continued to import goods of the kind banned by the agreement.[149] A man named John Greenlaw appeared before the meeting and admitted that he had purchased from importers. He agreed to store the goods until the resumption of importation.[150] A committee was also appointed to draw up an agreement restricting the town's vendue masters (auctioneers) from selling goods imported in breach of the merchants' agreement. Those who refused to sign would have their names published in the newspapers.[151] The firm of Richard Clarke & Son, once accused of violating the agreement, was exonerated by the merchants' committee in an item placed in the press on 21 August.[152]

The next month and a half were chiefly occupied by a renewal of John Mein's attack on the subscribers for receiving imports which appeared to conflict with the terms of the agreement. The dispute between Mein and the committee of merchants was basically a question of interpretation. Mein interpreted the agreement literally, and his case rested on a refusal to differentiate between those articles which were prohibited under the agreement and those which were allowed. He also tested the efficacy of the agreement by including on his list the importations of nonsubscribers as well as subscribers, of persons living outside of Boston, and of nonmerchants as well as merchants. The merchants' case rested upon a reasonable interpretation of the agreement, which stressed the strict adherence of the subscribers and brought pressure to bear upon the nonsubscribers who continued to import. [153]

Temporary Change in the Aim of the Nonimportation Movement in Boston: The Agreement of 17 October 1769

The coercive element in the method of enforcement was accompanied by a change in the objective of the nonimportation movement in Boston. [154] Lord Hillsborough, in a circular letter of 13 May 1769, assured the colonies that the ministry had no intention of proposing further taxes for revenue and that it intended to propose repeal of the duties on glass, paper, and painters' colors at the next session of Parliament. This pledge was regarded with alarm by the popular party. They feared that many merchants, particularly those who had earlier refused to subscribe, would abandon the agreement. In order to prevent this, the popular party determined to strengthen enforcement of nonimportation.

The adoption of coercive methods of enforcement was accompanied by the popular party's campaign to convince the people that the ministry's promise of partial repeal was merely a ruse to defeat nonimportation. They pointed out that the tax on tea was retained to vindicate Parliament's right to tax the colonies and argued that if the colonies acquiesced in the partial repeal, it would constitute an acknowledgement of this right. [155]

The first step in this direction was taken at the meeting on 26 July 1769. [156] It was unanimously voted that the removal of the duties on glass, paper, and painters' colors alone would not relieve the commercial difficulties of the colonies and that it was intended by the ministry merely to quiet British manufacturers and to prevent the establishment of manufacturing in the colonies. The meeting resolved to adhere strictly to the nonimportation agreement and to order no more goods from Great Britain until the revenue acts were repealed. At the same time, the list of exceptions which might nevertheless be imported under the terms of the agreement was extended. [157]

The radicals were also faced with the terms of the agreement of August 1768, which stated that nonimportation was to end on 1 January 1770. New York and Philadelphia had made their agreements conditional upon the repeal of the Townshend duties. In the early part of October 1769, there were reports that Boston had proposed extending its agreement until repeal. [158] The merchants themselves undoubtedly realized that the repeal of the Townshend duties alone would not relieve the distress which the commerce of New England, especially, was suffering. Although the earlier wine and molasses duties had not specifically been mentioned in the agreement of August 1768, on 17 October 1769, the merchants of Boston altered their agreement to make it effective until the revenue acts were "totally repealed."[159] The revised agreement was circulated among the importers, and by 13 November, it reportedly had been signed by all the merchants in town except ten or twelve.[160]

On 2 September and 25 October, letters were sent to the Philadelphia merchants informing them of the steps that Boston had taken and urging them to take similar measures.[161] The Philadelphia merchants admitted that the wine and molasses duties were as unconstitutional as the Townshend duties but declined to concur in the proposed changes.[162] The New York merchants also rejected the Boston proposal.[163] On 4 December, the merchants in Boston gave up the attempt to lead the other ports into including the wine and molasses duties as grievances of the nonimportation movement. At the same time, they extended their agreement to run until the total repeal of the Townshend Acts, instead of ending on 1 January 1770.[164]

The Enforcement by the "Body of the People" as the "Tyrants of the Times"

By the spring of 1770, the conservative elements in the nonimportation movement had lost whatever degree of control they had previously exercised over the methods of enforcement. Enforcement had formerly been in the hands of the standing committee of merchants and the committee appointed to inspect cargoes arriving at Boston. Now the handling of enforcement tended increasingly to be assumed by a mass meeting called the "Body of the People," which on some occasions numbered about a thousand persons. More drastic measures were adopted to compel the minority who still refused to subscribe to the agreement or to store their prohibited goods. The Boston town meeting also took steps to enforce the policy of nonimportation. Some merchants who had accepted the former agreement refused to subscribe to the modified agreement of October 1769. It was then expected that after the first of the year some who had stored their goods would demand that they be returned and that they would offer the goods for sale.[165]

Late in December, the standing committee of inspection conducted a survey of the goods which had been stored in the merchants' own shops, in rooms for which the committee held the keys. In the cases of John Taylor and Theophilus Lillie, they found quantities missing, and on 28 December, a meeting of the merchants voted a boycott against Taylor and Lillie and all who traded with them.[166] In spite of these measures, some of the merchants who had not subscribed to the agreement, but who had stored their goods under the original agreement, resumed sale of their merchandise after 1 January 1770.[167]

In mid-January 1770, a series of meetings of the merchants and inhabitants (the Body of the People) was called in an attempt to break down the opposition to continuing nonimportation. The committee of inspection informed the first of these meetings, on 17 January, that some merchants who had previously accepted the agreement were now selling or planning to sell their stored goods.[168] These importers refused to meet with committees sent to negotiate with them. The entire Body assembled that day then marched to the house of Richard Jackson, who also refused to meet with them.

On 18 January, the Body met again and voted to censure each of the eight firms that had violated their agreement to keep goods in storage. They resolved to visit each as a body and to demand, through spokesman William Molineux, that all goods previously stored should be returned to the custody of the committee of inspection until general importation was resumed.[169] Molineux informed the Body on 19 January that only Nathaniel Cary had agreed to their demands. Moderator William Phillips also told the meeting that acting Governor Thomas Hutchinson's sons had agreed to return their unsold tea to storage, which the Body voted to be acceptable.[170] Reconvening on 23 January, the Body voted to cease all commercial dealings with the four who continued to refuse to store their goods and with the traders who dealt with them. On the same day, Hutchinson challenged the authority of these assemblies by sending the sheriff to order the meeting to disperse and to avoid all unlawful disturbances of the peace in the future. The assembly ignored the order.[171]

On 13 March 1770, the Boston town meeting took up the question of strengthening the merchants' nonimportation agreement. It appointed a committee to obtain subscriptions to an agreement among the shopkeepers not to sell any more tea until the Townshend duty on that article should be repealed. Similar steps were taken at another town meeting on 16 March, and the names of those persons who had been publicly advertised by the merchants' committee as violators of the nonimportation agreement were entered on the town records.[172]

The strongly-worded censure of the "Infamous Importers" was viewed with repugnance by government party supporters. Robert Auchmuty deplored the fact that

> Persons of the most abandon'd characters, warmly espousing what is erroneously called the interest of the people, are almost the objects of their adoration. Such, however before despised, as selfish & base, now have an arbitrary sway in the town of Boston. They, back'd by a wrong headed deluded populace, are the tyrants of the times.[173]

The Enforcement of Nonimportation Outside of Boston

The Salem agreement, adopted in September 1768, seems to have been conscientiously enforced. However, the merchants and traders of Salem encountered a certain amount of difficulty, because some of the violators of the Boston merchants' agreement sent goods into Salem and attempted to dispose of them there. On 30 June 1769, a meeting of the merchants and traders of Salem publicly denounced this practice and resolved to discourage the sale of such goods by not purchasing any of them. Those traders in Salem who had violated the agreement of the town were warned that their names would be publicized if they continued to purchase goods of persons who refused to subscribe to the various nonimportation agreements.[174]

The merchants of Marblehead did not adopt an agreement until 26 October 1769. It was reported that between fifty and sixty merchants and traders had already signed the agreement by 27 October and that two more promised to store all the nonexcepted goods when they arrived, even though they had not signed the agreement.[175] Between March and May 1770, various other town meetings in Massachusetts joined in adding their support to the nonimportation agreement of the Boston merchants and in denouncing the conduct of those merchants who continued to import despite the agreement.[176]

In response to a letter from the committee at New York, in April 1769, the merchants and traders of New Haven, Connecticut, met on 10 July and entered into an agreement. In August of the same year, the merchants and traders of New London and Groton adopted similar resolutions. The support of the province's farmers was expressed in a resolution, passed by the assembly on 12 October 1769, which declared its approval of the action of the merchants of Connecticut and other provinces.[177]

The merchants of Portsmouth, New Hampshire, remained unsympathetic toward the nonimportation movement and continued to import from Great Britain. On 11 April 1770, however, action was taken by the town meeting of Portsmouth to enforce nonimportation, even though the merchants refused to adopt a formal agreement. The occasion was the arrival from Boston of importer Patrick McMasters. Having been boycotted in Boston for importing contrary to the general agreement of the merchants there, he intended to dispose of his goods in Portsmouth. The town meeting resolved not to purchase any goods from McMasters or to encourage him by providing him with warehouses or places to vend his wares.[178]

On 18 June 1770, the Boston merchants' committee instituted a boycott against the merchants of New Hampshire. The committee of inspection was instructed to see that no goods were imported from New Hampshire and that none from Boston were exported to that province.[179]

News of the partial repeal of the Townshend Acts prompted both Providence and Newport, Rhode Island to break their agreements in early 1770. Providence soon reinstated its agreement after being censured by the other towns; the merchants returning to their resolves on 6 June 1770.[180] The artisans, tradesmen, and mechanics of Philadelphia, on hearing of Newport's defection, met and adopted a resolution not to have any dealings with that town until the merchants there renewed their agreement. After this, the condemnation of Rhode Island spread throughout the colonies.[181] The Newport merchants renewed their agreement on 20 August, and Boston promised to intercede with the southern colonies to get them to resume commercial intercourse with Rhode Island.

• THE ENFORCEMENT OF NONIMPORTATION IN PHILADELPHIA AND NEW YORK, 1769–70 •

The first case of enforcement in Philadelphia occurred in connection with the arrival of a cargo of malt on the ship *Charming Polly,* which arrived in Philadelphia on 17 June 1769. The committee immediately investigated the circumstances of the shipment, and it was revealed that the consignee had not ordered the cargo and that the arrival of the vessel was his first notice of the matter. Since these were the first imports that breached the agreements, the committee of merchants called a general meeting for the next day.[182]

The brewers attended the meeting as a body and read an agreement which they had signed. The brewers regarded the shipment as contrary to the spirit of the agreements of the merchants and traders. They declared that they would not purchase or use any part of the cargo despite their need for the product.[183] The meeting resolved that no person ought to purchase any part of the cargo and that anyone who did so, or in any way aided in unloading, storing, or selling it, should be deemed an enemy of his country.[184] The result of this episode was the alienation of the Quakers and their formal decision to withdraw their support from the nonimportation policy. Fearing the use of coercive measures of enforcement, the monthly meeting of the Friends advised their members to withdraw from the nonimportation association and to refrain from giving such measures their support in the future.[185]

On 29 July, the brig *Speedwell* arrived at Philadelphia with goods from Liverpool, some of which were contrary to the merchants' agreements. The committee's investigation learned that the goods were mainly the result of orders which had been sent to the inland parts of Great Britain and had been filled and sent to Liverpool before the countermanding orders were received. The merchants to whom the goods were consigned agreed to store them until the Townshend duties were repealed.[186]

On 2 August, the merchants and traders of the city of Philadelphia resolved that thereafter the committee should not be authorized to receive any more goods to be stored if sent on consignment from Great Britain or if ordered after 6 February 1769.[187] This resolve was tested when the brig *Friends Good Will* arrived with a cargo of merchandise shipped by British merchants and consigned to various merchants in Philadelphia. The brig was sent back to England with her entire cargo intact.[188]

As soon as the effects of nonimportation began to cut into the profits of the dry goods importers of Philadelphia, without any apparent adverse effects upon the manufacturers and merchants in England, their enthusiasm for the nonimportation policy began to wane.[189] As early as December 1769, Henry Drinker expressed doubt that the merchants would hold to their resolutions not to import. "Interest, all powerful interest will bear down on Patriotism. This I think will be verified in the Colonies ere long, should the Parliament be obstinate."[190]

Importers who wished to alter the agreements or bring them to an end requested the merchants' committee to call a general meeting of subscribers, which was then scheduled for 3 May 1770. This meeting was subsequently postponed until 15 May 1770, a date undoubtedly chosen with a view toward sending orders to England on a ship owned by Abel James and Henry Drinker should importation be resumed.[191] Prior to this general meeting, the dry goods merchants held several meetings of their own to consolidate the forces attempting to end the agreement. Each agreed to be prompt in his attendance and to make a point to bring a friend along. This scheme was discovered at the last minute and exposed in a broadside addressed to the artisans, manufacturers, and mechanics. When the meeting was held, it was decided to postpone any definite action until 5 June in order that the merchants of New York and Boston could be consulted concerning a joint alteration of their agreements.[192]

The issue involved a difference of opinion between the importing merchants and the nonmercantile portion of the population. The merchants were inclined to accept Parliament's offer of a partial repeal of the Townshend duties as a sufficient concession to warrant the resumption of trade relations. The artisans, mechanics, and tradesmen, on the other hand, tended to regard the issue of taxation as unresolved until the Townshend duties had been totally repealed.

Between the meeting of 14 May and the meeting scheduled for 5 June, the question of continuing the nonimportation agreement was taken up by various writers in the newspapers. One suggested that the people indemnify those importing merchants who had been particularly hard hit by the nonimportation agreement.[193] Another denied that only the importers should have the determining voice in deciding whether to break or continue the nonimportation agreement. The writer pointed out that the consumers had willingly paid the higher prices for goods caused by the shortage. Now, if the dry goods merchants should import once again despite the continued existence of those reasons by which the merchants had justified adoption of nonimportation, they might be accused of entering into the agreement for reasons of gain.[194]

The merchants of Boston and New York had declined to make any changes in their agreements. At a general meeting of the subscribers in Philadelphia on 5 June, it was finally decided that no changes should be made in the nonimportation agreement at that time.[195] This decision was not the result of a unanimous approval of the nonimportation policy among the dry goods importers. In the following issue of the *Pennsylvania Gazette,* an article signed "A Spectator" criticized the manner in which the Boston merchants were observing their agreement, accused them of smuggling, and pointed out that many merchants feared the dictatorial methods of the 5 June meeting.[196]

In general, New York enforced nonimportation more strictly than Philadelphia or Boston, as revealed in individual cases during the period. In April 1769, a mercantile house in Philadelphia offered to supply a New York merchant with all the goods he could dispose of on commission. The merchant accepted the offer. Soon after, he learned that the people would regard his receiving the goods as contrary to the spirit and intent of the agreement, although he probably had not violated its letter. The merchant wrote to Philadelphia countermanding his previous orders, but the goods had already been shipped. They arrived at New York with a document revealing that they had been sent from Great Britain before 1 November of the previous year. The importing merchant publicly announced his intention to ship the goods back to Philadelphia.[197]

About the first of May 1769, a ship arrived at New York from London with goods sent contrary to orders. The merchants' committee met the next day and decided to store the goods in a public warehouse, but this did not satisfy the people. The city was flooded with handbills calling a meeting at the coffeehouse at ten o'clock in the morning. The meeting demanded that the merchants who had imported goods should ship them back to England, and the merchants who were consulted readily agreed to this condition.[198]

In the early part of July 1769, Alexander Robertson tried to import goods from Philadelphia. Under pressure from the committee of inspection, Robertson published an apology to the public and certified that he had reshipped the goods. It was later discovered that Robertson had returned only the empty casks and intended to sell their contents. In the face of this condemning evidence, he was publicly declared an enemy of his country.[199]

Upon partial repeal of the Townshend duties, the merchants of Albany rescinded their agreement, except as it applied to the importation of tea. However, opposition from the New York merchants forced them to resume their old agreement soon afterwards.[200]

• THE ENFORCEMENT OF NONIMPORTATION IN THE PLANTATION PROVINCES •

Although the Virginia Association of 18 May did prohibit the importation of wine and slaves, it was sumptuary in character in that it permitted the importation of all goods and merchandise other than those items which were specifically mentioned in the agreement. One purpose which the framers had in mind, judging by the goods enumerated in addition to taxed items and slaves, was to curtail the expenditures for luxuries. Naturally this type of an agreement left the subscribers in Virginia much more latitude than did the agreements of the northern provinces.

Another outstanding defect in the Virginia Association was its lack of support and cooperation among the merchants and factors of Williamsburg and Norfolk. The effectiveness of the agreement relied wholly upon the strictness with which the planters themselves observed their resolutions not to import and the nonconsumption by the rest of the population of goods imported by the factors. There was no mechanism of enforcement provided for in the Association of 18 May 1769. Moreover, no committees of inspection were provided for until the Association was revised on 22 June 1770.

The nonimportation agreement in Virginia was not strictly adhered to. An extract of a letter from London, dated 14 October 1769, stated, "there has been, and still are, large Supplies of all Sorts of Goods going to Virginia; a Ship of 300 Tons, full loaded for that Colony, sails this Day."[201]

In an attempt to render the Association more effective, a general meeting of the Williamsburg associators resolved on 1 June 1770 to extend an invitation to all gentlemen, merchants, traders, and others to meet with the associators in Williamsburg on 15 June to take appropriate action.[202] The movement to strengthen the nonimportation agreement had the organized support of the leading merchants of Norfolk and Williamsburg. Articles of association adopted on 22 June 1770 were essentially the same in principle as those of 18 May 1769. There were, however, three important alterations, made along lines suggested by George Mason in his letter to Richard Henry Lee.[203]

Committees of five persons were to be chosen in every county to inspect the invoices of incoming shipments. If any goods contrary to the Association were found, the committee was to request that such goods be reshipped immediately. In the event that violators refused, popular pressure was to be brought to bear by the newspaper's publication of their names together with an account of their violations. Goods imported contrary to the Association were not to be opened or stored but were to be reshipped to their point of origin. It was also agreed not to make any advance in the prices of goods already on hand or imported as a result of orders placed before 15 June 1770 and imported before 25 December, the deadline for receiving bona fide orders.[204]

Despite these changes, agreed to by 166 planters and merchants, the renewed Virginia Association was not successfully enforced. George Mason offered some reasons for it. In his opinion, the nonimportation agreements had been too hastily drawn up and were based on erroneous principles. Also, Mason pointed out, fortuitous circumstances had frustrated the scheme: namely, the unusual demand for British goods in northern Europe at this time and the unfortunate lack of uniformity among the provinces.[205]

A meeting of subscribers was scheduled for 11 December 1770, but so few of the associators attended that no action was taken, and the meeting adjourned until the following summer.[206] Despite this discouragement, some county committees attempted to enforce the Association into the spring of 1771. Formal records of modification or repeal of the nonimportation agreement in Virginia could not be located, but it is apparent that by July 1771 nonimportation had been abandoned except for dutied articles. George Washington, writing to Robert Cary & Co. in England, issued the following instructions:

> Our Association in Virginia for the Non-importation of Goods is now at an end except against Tea, paper, glass, and painters' Colors of Foreign Manufacture: You will please, therefore, to be careful that none of the glass, Paper, &c. contained in my Invoices, are of those kinds which are subject to the duty Imposed by Parliament for the purpose of raising a Revenue in America.[207]

The leading case in Maryland's enforcement of nonimportation was that of the *Good Intent*. The brigantine *Good Intent* was chartered in England to carry a cargo to Baltimore, arriving on 17 February 1770. The shipper evidently tried to use a loophole in the agreement to send goods which had been ordered before the agreement—orders considered dead by the consignees because of the passage of time. The major consignees, the firm of Dick and Stewart, invited a committee to review the case after the arrival of the ship.[208] After reviewing the evidence, the committee, which was specially called for the investigation, decided not to allow the cargo to be landed and the *Good Intent* sailed back to England on 25 February 1770.[209]

Committees of enforcement were appointed in a number of counties and districts of Maryland, and their investigations resulted in other shipments being stored under their watch.[210] During July and August 1770, the committee of Annapolis itself became embroiled in accusations of violating the Association. After charging Williams & Co. with exorbitantly raising the price of tea forbidden by the agreement, committee members Thomas Harwood, J. Brice, and Joshua Johnson were in turn accused of improper importation and profiteering.[211] Williams & Co. feared being made a scapegoat in the committee's attempt to squelch the rising discontent among merchants with the policy of nonimportation, a fear which probably contained an element of truth.

After the British government had shown a willingness to make concessions by repealing all of the Townshend duties except those on tea, the argument that the colonies adopt a conciliatory policy in return gained adherents.

The enforcement of the nonimportation agreement in South Carolina was complicated by the fact that nonimportation was laxly enforced in the two neighboring provinces of North Carolina and Georgia. Nonetheless, the committees attempted to make enforcement effective. Alexander Gillon, of Charleston, was compelled to sign an agreement to store wine which he had imported in January 1770.[212] Later, committees of inspection were appointed to examine the contents of shiploads of goods entering the province. Two firms were found to have sold goods which they had agreed to store. Both admitted that they had done wrong and agreed to return the goods to storage.[213]

In Georgia and North Carolina, the popular parties did not have the cooperation of the importing merchants. Also, they were not able to mobilize public opinion behind the nonimportation movement to the extent necessary to coerce the merchants.

Enforcement of the nonimportation agreement in Georgia was ineffective from the very beginning. The division between merchants and the popular party had been clearly revealed when the merchants attempted to avert a comprehensive nonimportation agreement by adopting a watered-down agreement on their own initiative. On 27 June 1770, a general meeting of subscribers and inhabitants at Charleston voted unanimously that Georgia ought "to be amputated from the rest of their brethren, as a rotten part that might spread a dangerous infection."[214]

The nonimportation agreement seems to have been generally ignored by the merchants of North Carolina as well. Indeed, Governor Tryon could write, on 1 February 1771, that "notwithstanding the boasted associations of people who never were in trade, and the sham patriotism of a few merchants to the southward of the province, the several ports of this province have been open ever since the repeal of the Stamp Act for every kind of British manufactures to the full extent of the credit of the country."[215]

• THE BREAKDOWN OF NONIMPORTATION IN NEW YORK, PHILADELPHIA, AND BOSTON •

The Conservative Reaction Against Nonimportation and the Abandonment of the Agreement in New York

The increasing tendency in New York to resort to coercive methods to enforce the nonimportation agreement caused alarm among the more conservative merchant group. The employment of violence was not part of their program for obtaining commercial reforms. Also, propertied interests in New York remembered similar experiences in connection with the Stamp Act. They feared the increasing tendency of the popular party leaders to organize demonstrations at which violators proscribed by the merchants' committee of inspection were hauled up before the crowd and forced to confess their guilt publicly and agree to store their goods with the committee. In addition, the economic crisis in the city in the winter of 1769–70 was accompanied by a new outbreak of crowd violence and rioting.

Another factor in the merchants' dissatisfaction with the nonimportation policy was the laxness with which it was enforced in Boston. News had also filtered back from London of large shipments of goods to the colonies, especially to the plantation provinces. All this convinced the New York merchants that they were being made the victims of a scheme which enabled smugglers to take advantage of them under the guise of patriotism.[216] The more conservative of the merchants were also opposed to the utilization of their economic protest in a struggle for constitutional rights as interpreted by the Sons of Liberty. By the spring of 1770, the fair traders and the more wealthy importers were convinced of the futility of continuing nonimportation and were willing to side with the conservative propertied interests in opposition to those who favored continued nonimportation.

A group called The Friends of Liberty and Trade appeared in early 1770 to oppose continuing nonimportation. They sought a solution that would achieve their objectives without sacrificing their principles.[217] They formed the solid core of the membership of the chamber of commerce, incorporated on 13 March 1770. The passage, in April, of partial repeal of the Townshend Acts together with a special act permitting New York to issue £120,000 in bills of credit were factors which gave further weight to the arguments for making a concession in return for one made by Parliament. Convinced that the policy of nonimportation was no longer serving their interests, the conservatives increasingly felt that the agreement should be revised. Their goal was to relieve the commercial situation and, by refusing to import tea only, still retain a semblance of protest against the principle of taxation. In May 1770, the New York merchants had received notice that the merchants of Philadelphia were considering altering their agreement.[218] When partial repeal of the Townshend duties became known in New York, the merchants notified Philadelphia that they would unite in agreeing to a general importation of everything except tea. A favorable reply was received from merchants (although not necessarily the committee) in Philadelphia.

The committee of merchants decided to take steps toward modifying the agreement to continue nonimportation only with respect to dutied articles. A circular letter dated 2 June was sent to commercial towns in the other colonies inviting the merchants there to send a delegation of six deputies to meet at Norwalk, Connecticut, on 18 June to formulate an intercolonial nonimportation agreement which would apply only to duties articles. In this way, it was hoped to avoid any one colony from being censured for modifying its agreement in accordance with the proposed changes.[219] The proposal met with a definite refusal from most of the merchants in the neighboring colonies of Massachusetts, Pennsylvania, and New Jersey.

On 11 June 1770, a group of merchants requested the committee of inspection to conduct a poll of the city on the question of whether to continue the nonimportation agreement as it stood or to confine nonimportation to tea and other duties articles provided that Boston and Philadelphia should concur in the alterations.[220] The poll was conducted on 12 June. It was not confined to the legally qualified voters, but since the conservatives had a majority, it did not matter anyway. On 16 June, letters were sent to Boston and Philadelphia with the news of New York's vote of 1180 to 300 in favor of resuming a general importation in cooperation with the two cities.[221]

On 18 June, the proposed terms of the modified agreement were made public. After the act partially repealing the Townshend duties became effective on 1 December, no goods were to be imported until the duty on that article was repealed. Any goods imported contrary to this agreement were to be reshipped.[222]

By 2 July, the answers of Boston, Philadelphia, and the counties in New Jersey were known in New York. All had rejected New York's proposal for modifying the agreements. On 5 July, the merchants met and publicly resolved to send orders for all commodities except tea on the next packet sailing for England. On 7 July, the merchants met again with members of the committee of inspection and decided to take another poll of the city. They also requested that the packet for England be delayed until the poll could be completed in order that orders might be sent on this vessel.[223] Upon order of the committee of merchants, two persons were appointed to canvass each ward and ask whether, in light of the opposition of Boston and Philadelphia, nonimportation should be continued.[224]

The radicals, led by Isaac Sears and Alexander McDougall, met and unanimously declared against modifying the agreement and resolved to use all lawful means to prevent it.[225] In spite of this protest, the poll was taken and completed on the evening of 9 July. The results proved an overwhelming victory for the merchants, and the committee of merchants immediately resolved to send orders for goods on the packet which sailed 11 July for England.[226] Messengers were sent to Boston and Philadelphia at once to inform the merchants of those cities of the decision. On 24 July, a circular letter justifying New York's action was sent by the committee to the other colonies.[227]

The Controversy in Philadelphia over Abandoning Nonimportation

The merchants' committee of New York informed Philadelphia's merchants' committee of their decision to resume importation and that they were sending orders for goods on the packet ship which was due to sail. They suggested that the Philadelphia merchants would be able to send orders on a ship sailing from Philadelphia within the next few days if they decided to follow New York's example. The merchants' committee of Philadelphia replied immediately and expressed their regret that the inhabitants of New York had sacrificed the cause of liberty and weakened the unity of the colonies by deciding to break their nonimportation agreement.[228]

The popular attitude was expressed at a meeting of the inhabitants of Philadelphia on 14 July, which adopted a series of resolutions condemning New York. The resolutions declared that the nonimportation agreements entered into by the merchants and traders of the various colonies were a constitutional method of asserting their rights, which, if maintained, would produce the desired results.[229]

The inhabitants of the various counties and towns of New Jersey entered into similar resolutions against New York. At Princeton, on 13 July, the students solemnly assembled to watch a hangman burn the letter from the merchants in New York to the merchants in Philadelphia, accompanied by the tolling of the college bell.[230]

The action of the New York merchants stimulated the Philadelphia dry goods importers to resume their agitation for modifying their nonimportation agreement to permit the general importation of everything except tea. During a two month newspaper controversy, the merchants in favor of modifying nonimportation and the popular forces opposed to any change hotly debated the question.

The dry goods merchants were not to be thwarted in doing away with the nonimportation agreement. Six of the former members of the committee of inspection joined with eleven other merchants in proposing to the merchants' committee of Philadelphia that a poll be conducted among the subscribers. They maintained that:

> Many of the Inhabitants of this city, who some Time since entertained Hopes of Advantage from a Continuation of our Nonimportation Agreement, being now fully convinced it cannot answer the End proposed, and that the Trade of this City must severely feel the Effects of adhering to that Measure, while the Colonies around us are enjoying the Advantages of our Inactivity, are of Opinion, it is a proper Time to make an Alteration in said Agreement. . . . the Sentiments of the Subscribers to the Non-importation Agreement should be taken, whether said Agreement should continue, or be dissolved, so far as to open the Importation of Goods from Great-Britain as usual, Tea, and such other Articles as are, or may be subject to Duties, for the Purpose of raising a Revenue in America, excepted.[231]

The group proposed that two of the subscribers, two members of the merchants' committee, and two or three other reputable citizens not engaged in the importing trade be appointed to take a poll of the subscribers.

The committee replied that according to the terms of the nonimportation agreement, alteration of the agreement could be made only by a general meeting of the subscribers called after three days' public notice. They were willing to call a general meeting of the subscribers if requested, but declined to participate in the proposed poll because they said it was beyond their authority under the terms of the agreement itself.[232]

The group of dissentients then took the initiative and called a meeting at Davenport's tavern on 20 September 1770, without consulting the merchants' committee. The merchants' committee attended and submitted a set of questions stressing the necessity of preserving the unity of the colonies in their opposition to the Townshend duties. The first resolution proposed that the other colonies be consulted before any changes were made in the nonimportation agreement. Second, the committee asked whether an agreement similar to those of Maryland and Virginia might not be adopted in the interest of preserving the unity of the colonies, providing New York and Boston would consent to adopting similar agreements.

There were 135 subscribers present at the meeting on 20 September 1770. The group in favor of altering the agreement was in the majority, and an alternative set of proposals was submitted by them. In a preliminary test of strength, a vote was carried to consider the proposals of those who were in favor of importing before taking up the questions posed by the merchants' committee.[233] Resolutions altering and, in fact, ending the nonimportation agreement were soon voted by the subscribers before the merchants' committee's questions were taken up. The first question of the committee was finally put to a vote and rejected by a majority of eighty-nine to forty-five. The committee then proposed that the inhabitants of the city should be allowed to vote on altering the agreement or, at the very least, that the subscribers who had not attended the meeting should be consulted. Once again, the committee was voted down.[234] At this point in the meeting, Charles Thomson, speaking for the members of the merchants' committee, announced that they considered the nonimportation agreement to be abolished by the resolutions passed at the meeting, and they therefore resigned as a committee. The meeting then voted to call together all subscribers on the next Saturday in order to elect eleven persons to replace the members of the committee who had resigned.[235]

Many of the nonmercantile groups of Philadelphia were opposed to ending the movement. On 24 September 1770, the grand jury for the city and county of Philadelphia met and passed a series of resolutions directed against the action taken by those who wanted to resume trade with England.[236] The resolutions of the grand jury, in effect, were a recommendation for the inhabitants of the province of Pennsylvania in conjunction with the other colonies. These resolutions undoubtedly represented the attitude of that portion of the population not engaged in the business of importing British dry goods and tea.

The popular reaction against the attempt to abandon nonimportation was further shown by the calling of a meeting of the freeholders and inhabitants of Philadelphia for the afternoon of 27 September 1770. An advertisement calling the meeting was published in the press and handbills were circulated in the city and suburbs. The meeting assembled at the appointed time and place, Joseph Fox was unanimously elected chairman, and the meeting proceeded to pass a series of resolutions directed against the action taken by the dry goods importers at the meeting of 20 September.[237]

In the event that the merchants and traders should adopt an agreement similar to that of Maryland, the meeting of inhabitants pledged their support to enforce it and to take every lawful step to prevent any person from importing goods from any other colony until the spring shipments arrived.[238]

This popular protest did not prevent the Philadelphia merchants from reopening trade with Britain. The merchants appointed a new committee to supervise the enforcement of the altered agreement. On 29 September 1770, the *London Packet* sailed with their orders for spring shipments.[239]

The Collapse of Nonimportation in Boston

By April 1770, the popular party in Boston was faced with a crucial struggle to save nonimportation from collapse due to laxity on the part of merchants who had hitherto been supporters of the agreement. Between 17 April and 25 April, six ships arrived at Boston with prohibited merchandise which was not consigned solely to the proscribed "Infamous Importers." At a merchants' meeting on 20 April, Samuel Adams and other popular leaders stressed the necessity of strictly enforcing the agreement at this critical moment, and a committee, headed by William Molineux, was appointed to visit each of the merchants who had imported goods on those ships and to demand that they ship them back to England. When the committee reported to the merchants' meeting on 21 April that all the importers had refused to reship their goods, the committee was instructed to propose a compromise whereby each of the importers would agree to store his goods instead of reshipping them, under the threat of having his name advertised in the newspapers for two years afterward if he refused this demand.[240]

On 26 April 1770, the "Body of the People" met jointly with the Boston merchants in Faneuil Hall where, one observer noted, "the heads of the faction being opposed by a number of principal Merchants found it necessary to make use of more decisive arguments than they had adopted before." As a result, the meeting voted that nothing less than shipping all the prohibited goods back to England would satisfy the Body of the People, and a committee was again sent to each of the importers to demand that they reship their goods.[241] When the Body met again on 28 April, the committee reported that after "a due reflection on their own mistaken conduct," and "as they were convinced their re-shipping them would be more satisfactory to the Body of the People," all the importers had "voluntarily" consented to ship their goods back to England.[242]

Hutchinson and others of the government party viewed this reference to the "voluntary" nature of the importers' decision to reship their goods as farcical. It was generally understood that if any merchant refused these demands, he would be visited in the evening by a crowd of several thousand men, and it was the fear of mob violence that compelled the importers to comply with the Body's demands. Hutchinson cryptically summed up the situation when he remarked that "the lower sort of people who were called in as servants in order to intimidate such as refused to join in the Combin[ation] are now become Masters."[243]

Another government party observer also noted indications of a growing uneasiness among the genuine merchants in response to popular coercive methods. The meetings of the Body continued through 3 May, although they had won their demands on 26 April, and this observer saw no purpose to these subsequent meetings other than "to keep up the spirit of rioting among the lower class of people" since "the only business they did was calling people before them who they said had spoke disrespectfully of that body, and obliging them to make proper concessions, nobody daring to resist their almighty power." On 1 May, about fifty "real merchants" met at the British Coffee House, "in order to consult what measures were to be taken with the trade, which they said was now got intirely under the direction of the Mob." It was proposed that the importation of goods for the fall trade should be allowed because the town could no longer stand the economic distress which nonimportation had brought upon it. But their "Faneuil Hall friends" sent a message to the "real merchants" at the British Coffee House, ordering them to disperse immediately because they had no right to make any decision without the advice and consent of the whole Body. "By this you will see that the Merchants have raised a power which is now got above their controul," the writer commented, and he predicted that "the real Merchants would be very glad to shake off their Faneuil Hall friends, but this they will find no easy matter to accomplish."[244]

The split between the "real merchants" and their "Faneuil Hall friends" broke out into the open on 22 May 1770, when the Boston merchants' committee received a letter from a group of Philadelphia merchants, dated 14 May, proposing to abandon nonimportation except for tea. In the forenoon, about forty or fifty "real merchants" met and resolved in favor of joining with the Philadelphia merchants. This shocked the popular party leaders into hasty action, Hutchinson noted. William Molineux condemned the merchants' meeting as "rebels" and "usurpers," and the church bells were rung calling an emergency meeting of the Body at Faneuil Hall that same afternoon, where some "warm debates" took place.[245] It was quite evident, Hutchinson commented, that at this meeting of the Body on 22 May, "the real Merchants who in the heighth of their zeal called in the populace to their aid are now restrained by the populace from acting according to their Sentiments."[246]

One of the Green family, a "real merchant" who had been among those who met in the forenoon and voted to abandon nonimportation, declared that "it was unreasonable that the Merch[an]ts should be restrained from dissolving an agreement they had made among themselves by the people who were then assembled, most of whom had no concern in Trade nor any property." This verbal bombshell turned the Body into a furor. John Ruddock, one of the popular party's trustworthy justices of the peace and a Boston selectman, was "so angry that he burst into crying & said his Indignation was raised to hear a young man utter such an affront to that body who had been called in by the Merch[an]ts to their aid & having made use of them would willingly throw them off, but they were mistaken." And others justified the right of the Body to decide the question of adhering to or abandoning nonimportation on the grounds that "if they had no property they had Liberty & their posterity might have property." William Molineux "harangued the populace & frightned some of the young Merch[an]ts to such a degree that they deemed better to withdraw their names from a paper wch they had signed declaring they desired a general Importation," Hutchinson reported.[247]

As a result of this tumultuous session, the Body voted to adhere strictly to the nonimportation agreement until all the Townshend revenue duties, including the tax on tea, were repealed. The popular party's newspaper account of these proceedings attempted to cover up the fact that a substantial number of the "real merchants" in Boston favored abandoning nonimportation and were held to it only by their "Faneuil Hall friends." The *Boston Gazette,* 28 May 1770, said that "the Spirit and Resolution manifested by 99 out of a hundred, to support their Rights and Priviledges at all Events, would do honor to any People." It also said that the Body voted "almost unanimously" to adhere strictly to the nonimportation agreement.

Thomas Hutchinson anticipated that the popular leaders would try to conceal the serious split in their ranks when he wrote to Governor Penn, of Pennsylvania, and Governor Colden, of New York, warning that the merchants should not be misled by the popular party's false account of the situation at Boston. He told Governor Colden: "I am well informed that the major part of the Merchants wish to see the Trade free from restraint but having in the heighth of their zeal called in the populace as their servants are forced now to submit to them as Masters."[248]

During the month of June 1770, the populace engaged with fanatical zeal in a renewed campaign of crowd intimidation against the "Old Importers." Their attention was directed at two of the "Old Importers" in particular—Hutchinson's nephew, Nathaniel Rogers, and the McMasters brothers—although boycott demonstrations against William Jackson and Theophilus Lillie were continued weekly with relentless regularity.[249] After fleeing to New York City to escape an anticipated crowd attack in Boston, Nathaniel Rogers was hounded out of New York by the local Sons of Liberty for being one of the "infamous Boston importers."[250] Upon returning to Boston, Rogers petitioned the Body for reinstatement in the community upon any terms it prescribed, but the Body rejected his request because of his long record of "political iniquity," for which he was about to be rewarded by being appointed provincial secretary. It was also noted that forgiving him now would not only be politically convenient for him, but economically expedient as well since it would give him an excuse to ship goods back to England which he could not sell because of the consumers' boycott against him. The relentless intimidation was thought to have contributed to Rogers's premature death, on 9 August 1770. He suffered an apoplectic fit and died upon returning from a justice of the peace where he had sworn out a complaint against one of his assailants.[251]

Simultaneously with the Nathaniel Rogers incident, the campaign of intimidation against the McMasters brothers reached a climax. After a meeting of the Body on the night of 1 June, a crowd led by Dr. Thomas Young marched to the McMasters' store and warned them to close their shop and leave town within three days. The *Boston Gazette* on 4 June 1770 hailed this ultimatum as evidence that "the bold and generous spirit of freedom encreases every day among us." The McMasters brothers asked to appear before the Body to make concessions, but they failed to keep the appointment when it met on 7 June.

On 19 June, a crowd seized Patrick McMasters, carted him through the streets, and prepared to tar and feather him, but fright caused him to collapse and he was spared that ordeal. Instead, McMasters was hauled to the gallows and forced to swear that he would leave town immediately and never return, with the warning that it would mean instant death if he ever came back. The Sons of Liberty hauled him to the city limits and forced him to walk a gauntlet. The Sons of Liberty of Roxbury were planning a similar reception for him when he crossed the town line, but he managed to escape into the woods and gain refuge at Castle William, where he joined another of his brothers. The third brother's location was unknown after he fled Boston for Marblehead and was forced to leave there.[252]

The crowd put in a long day. About midnight, it attacked the house of Henry Hulton, Customs Commissioner, at Brookline. After smashing all the downstairs windows and pounding on the walls with clubs, yelling threats to get Hulton dead or alive, the crowd marched off "huzzaing," leaving Hulton and his family huddled in an upstairs bedroom, terror-stricken. The next day, Customs Commissioners Hulton and William Burch abandoned their houses and moved their families to Castle William.[253]

Thomas Hutchinson accurately described the situation in Boston when he wrote to a friend, William Parker, on 26 August 1770:

> You certainly think right when you think Boston people are run mad. The frenzy was not higher when they banished my great grandmother, when they hanged the Quakers, when they afterwards hanged the poor innocent Witches, when they were carried away with a Land Bank, nor when they all turned new Lights, than the political frenzy has been for a Twelve month past.[254]

While the Boston Sons of Liberty were resorting to terroristic tactics to hold the merchants in their nonimportation agreement in mid-1770, they seem oblivious to the indisputable fact that nonimportation was on the verge of collapse in New York and Philadelphia. On 8 June 1770, the Body unanimously and indignantly voted to reject a proposal from the New York merchants' committee to hold an interprovincial "Congress of the Trade" at Norwalk, Connecticut, to relax their nonimportation agreements.[255] On 25 June 1770, in response to a message from the New York merchants proposing that there should be a general relaxation of their nonimportation agreements, the Body at Boston passed another resolution to maintain nonimportation "without the least Deviation" until the tax on tea was totally repealed.[256] After the New York merchants abandoned nonimportation, except for tea, on 9 July, their letter was read to a large meeting in Boston on 24 July. The Body pretended that the letter was torn into pieces and thrown to the winds as being "unworthy of the least Notice." Afterward, the Body voted to adhere "steadfastly and religiously" to nonimportation and sent a letter to the New York merchants urging them to countermand their orders for goods and to resume their agreement.[257]

The popular leaders in Boston were furious with the New York merchants for defecting from nonimportation and seemed determined, Hutchinson noted, in their "political frenzy" to keep nonimportation, even if they destroyed Boston economically. In a letter of 26 July to Lord Hillsborough, the secretary of state for the colonies, Hutchinson asserted that "altho 9 in 10 of the Merch[an]ts wish to import they dare not appear altho scarce any Merch[an]ts except Hancock & Phillips appear with the populace." However, Hutchinson doubted that the merchants had courage enough to oppose the populace because "the lowest class of the people still have the Rule in Boston, a few Merchants countenancing and encouraging them." A poll of public opinion, such as was conducted by the New York merchants, was impossible in Boston, Hutchinson declared, because "the Selectmen of Boston are the creatures of the Populace and would be deterred from any measure contrary to the minds of the Populace if they were of different sentiments themselves."[258]

Writers in the popular-party press denounced the manner in which the New York merchants had abandoned nonimportation and expressed the hope that political salvation did not depend upon these "lovers of filthy lucre" and a "few mercenary traders," but upon the virtue of the Body in every colony who had it in their power, by a consumers' boycott, to prevent British manufactures being imported, in spite of the merchants' betrayal. Another writer charged that the origin of the defection at New York was in Boston itself when those forty or fifty "real merchants" met at the British Coffee House on 22 May and signed a declaration in favor of abandoning the nonimportation agreement. Immediately after this, "the tares began to sprout at New York," he asserted.[259]

At a meeting of the Body of the People on 31 July 1770, William Molineux, William Phillips, William Cooper, Ebenezer Storer, and William Greenleaf were appointed to visit Salem, Marblehead, and Newbury to investigate rumors that the towns had abandoned their nonimportation agreements. And a larger committee was appointed to consider measures that ought to be adopted for "strengthening the Union of the Colonies and effecting the salutary Design this Body had in view in coming into the Agreement for a Non-Importation." The membership of this committee, composed of the popular party leadership, clearly shows that the Body was not dominated by the "real merchants." The committee members were: John Hancock, William Phillips, Samuel Adams, William Molineux, William Greenleaf, John Adams, Josiah Quincy, Richard Dana, Henderson Inches, Thomas Cushing, Jonathan Mason, and Doctors Joseph Warren and Thomas Young.[260]

At another meeting of the Body on 7 August, the Molineux committee reported that Salem, Marblehead, and Newbury were adhering to nonimportation. The Body also appointed another committee, composed of William Molineux, William Cooper, Thomas Boylston, William Whitwell, and Jonathan Mason, to visit Providence and Newport to confer about the urgency of these towns maintaining their nonimportation agreements. The Body also ordered the newspaper publication of all persons' names who refused to ship goods imported contrary to the nonimportation agreement back to England.[261]

The popular party leaders in Boston were grasping at straws, trying to create the public impression that they were finding strict adherence to nonimportation everywhere in the colony. As Hutchinson commented late in August:

> The distresses of the Town of Boston have not yet opened its Eyes. . . . The infamous Molineux & Young with Cooper, Adams and two or three more still influence the Mob who threaten all who import, but it seems impossible that it should hold much longer. Many who at first were zealous among the Merchants, against importing are now as zealous for it.[262]

Hutchinson was correct in predicting that the popular leaders could not hold the "real merchants" in nonimportation much longer, not even by the threats of crowd intimidation. On 10 September, the Boston newspapers printed an advertisement of a meeting of the merchants the next day, at the British Coffee House. The declared purpose of this meeting was to consider "conciliating Measures with Respect to the present critical State of the Trade," in preparation for a meeting of the Body of the People on 13 September. The *Boston Gazette* predicted in the same issue that the meeting of the Body at Faneuil Hall would be "the greatest Meeting of the Trade and Inhabitants of this Town . . . that ever was known." All business would be suspended on that day, the shops and warehouses remaining closed, and

> the whole Attention of the Town will be employ'd to settle upon the surest Basis, the Non-Importation Agreement, that it may be permanent against the least infraction, and that a Number of Warehouses will be taken up for the housing and re-shipping of all Goods that may arrive at any Time after that Day contrary to the Agreement, untill the Act imposing a Duty on the remaining Article TEA is totally repealed.[263]

The juxtaposition of these two notices in the same newspaper on 10 September clearly indicates the struggle for power that was taking place between the "real merchants" and their "Faneuil Hall friends." The declared objective of the merchants' meeting to consider "*conciliating Measures*" was in direct contradiction to the popular party's prediction that the nonimportation agreement would be strictly enforced as long as the tax on tea remained in effect. As subsequent events demonstrated, what the "real merchants" had in mind, following the example of their defecting colleagues in New York, was a drastic relaxation of nonimportation or perhaps even outright abandonment of the policy except as it applied to tea.

The closing of all stores and warehouses and cessation of all business on 13 September, when the Body was to meet, was not primarily to free the merchants but to enable the popular party leaders to muster all their nonmercantile, tradesmen, and small shopkeeper supporters to that crucial meeting. They realized only too well that they were fighting to save nonimportation. However, the popular party leaders were frustrated for they dared not resort to their usual tactics and turn the crowd loose against these British Coffee House merchant defectors because they were not the infamous "Old Importers," but former adherents to the nonimportation agreement, and many of them were hitherto respectable "Sons of Liberty."

According to the published report of the proceedings of the Body on 13 September, there were at least one thousand persons present. The dual nature of the personnel in attendance was tacitly admitted in the newspaper account, which said that there were "a very great Number of the principal and mostly wealthy Merchants, as well as the most respectable Tradesmen of the Town."[264]

The meeting of the Body continued for three days, and there was obviously a concerted effort made by the "real merchants" who met at the British Coffee House in the forenoons and then attended the meetings of the Body at Faneuil Hall in the afternoons.[265] The merchants did not openly propose abandonment of nonimportation. Instead, they sought to accomplish this objective in the guise of a proposal to invite the Philadelphia merchants to join with the Boston merchants in organizing an intercolonial congress of merchants' committees to consider a plan for a uniform "relaxation" of their nonimportation agreements if they should decide that it was necessary. But until then, the present nonimportation agreements should remain in force. In accepting this proposal of the "real merchants," the popular leaders of the Body specified that if the proposal for such a congress were accepted by the other colonies, the merchants' committee would then have to call a meeting of "the whole Body of Merchants, Tradesmen, and all others connected with trade" to choose the delegates to the intercolonial congress "by ballot." Thus, once again a distinction was indicated between the "merchants" and "tradesmen and all others connected with trade," by which the popular party leaders meant all other inhabitants. Also, the Body specified a loophole by which they could reject the final decision of the merchants' congress when it voted that it was the "declar'd sense both of the Merchants & Tradesmen" that "in Case the Report of the Committee should not be judg'd likely to answer the grand Purpose for which the [nonimportation] Agreement was originally enter'd into, namely the Preservation of our sacred and invaluable Rights, the People should then take such Measures as they should judge to be adequate."[266]

However, the proposed intercolonial congress of merchants' committees never took place, because on 20 September 1770 the Philadelphia merchants voted to alter their nonimportation agreement and allow the importation of all goods except tea. Faced with the defection of the Philadelphia merchants following those of New York, the Boston merchants could not be held to nonimportation much longer. As soon as news arrived from Philadelphia of the merchants' abandonment of nonimportation, the Boston merchants moved swiftly. On 8 October 1770, a meeting of merchants at the British Coffee House unanimously voted to alter their nonimportation agreement to allow the importation of all goods except tea. The following week, the goods stored by the merchants' inspection committee were delivered to their respective owners for open sale.[267]

Thus, the popular party was unable to hold the merchants in nonimportation because, as the Reverend Andrew Eliot accurately assessed the situation:

> Some who have been leaders, would have been glad to have held out longer, but persons in trade were weary, and, as interest is generally their god, began to be furious. The zeal of the populace, by which they had been restrained a great while, gradually abated, and it was impossible to prevent a general importation.[268]

Samuel Adams admitted that although the merchants had defected from their nonimportation agreement, "they held it much longer than I ever thought they would or could."[269] It was satisfying for him that "the Body of the people remained firm till the Merch[an]ts receded," but he was "very sorry that the [nonimportation] Agreem[en]t was ever enterd into as it had turned out ineffectual." However, Adams, the indefatigable militant, urged that they should "forget that there has been such a futile Combination" and convince their enemies that the colonists were "united in Constitutional Principles, and are resolved they *will not* be Slaves; that their Dependance is not upon Merch[an]ts or any particular Class of men, nor is their dernier resort, a resolution barely to withhold Commerce, with a nation that w[oul]d subject them to despotic Power."[270]

The popular party leaders were disgusted with the merchants and disillusioned because the people no longer responded to the usual appeals to patriotism. William Palfrey observed:

> Everything here seems to be tending fast towards that stupid senseless state of Slavery which commonly follows a long but unsuccessful struggle for Liberty. Even the most animating examples have lost their usual effect, and the people seem to be quite borne down by the powerful opposition of their enemies.[271]

Palfrey thus referred to one of the chief problems faced by politicians, then as well as now. It is impossible to keep the public emotionally keyed up indefinitely. After a period of time, people seem to reach a state of psychological exhaustion, and in the following period of emotional relaxation, public opinion tends to become apathetic. Palfrey found that the usual rhetoric of "Liberty and Property" no longer stimulated people to demonstrate their zeal in defense of these sacred principles by going out and tarring and feathering people, applying a coat of "odoriferous paint" to the houses and stores of obnoxious persons, or chasing them out of town.

In a last desperate effort to keep the flickering flame of the economic boycott alive, Samuel Adams and other leaders of the popular party in Boston pushed a "Plan for encouraging Arts, Agriculture, Manufactures and Commerce within this Province" through the meeting of The Body on 13 September, and the Boston selectmen were requested to insert it in the warrant calling the next town meeting on 20 September. And at the town meeting, a committee was appointed to consider this proposal to form a society to promote agriculture and manufacturing, and the committee filed a report with the town clerk on 29 September.[272]

As usual, the Boston town meeting was merely a platform for launching their program in the House of Representatives, and on 16 October, the House appointed a committee to consider the state of the province, which included the four Boston representatives (Speaker Thomas Cushing, Samuel Adams, John Hancock, and John Adams). On 16 November, the House passed resolutions reported by this committee in which the members pledged they would set an example to discourage "prodigality and extravagance" and the use of "foreign superfluities" by promoting "industry and frugality" and manufacturing in the towns. The four representatives from Boston were appointed along with five others as a committee to prepare a plan for "the Encouragement of Arts, Agriculture, Manufactures and Commerce," and instructed to report at the next session.[273]

Thus, the popular party leaders were reduced to passing an innocuous nonconsumption resolution conspicuously lacking in any punitive provisions. After three years of effort the situation remained as it was when they launched their political-economic program on 28 October 1767: the Declaratory Act asserting the unqualified legislative supremacy of Parliament and its right to tax the colonies in all cases whatsoever remained on the statute book, and the tax on tea remained as a symbol of that principle.

The Collapse of Nonimportation in Maryland and South Carolina

In Maryland, the growing attitude among the merchants that the nonimportation policy had failed to achieve its purpose was counteracted by the planters' determination to hold the line of resistance. The decisive blow to the nonimportation movement in Maryland came when the Philadelphia dry goods importers abandoned their nonimportation agreement on 20 September 1770.

When the New York merchants broke their agreement in July 1770, the general feeling in Charleston was very antagonistic to this betrayal. On 22 August, a general meeting of the inhabitants denounced New York's defection.[274] In the latter part of October, the general committee sent a circular letter to Philadelphia, New Jersey, and Connecticut urging these provinces to withdraw their trade from New York.[275]

This suggestion of the committee ignored the strong sentiment in favor of discontinuing nonimportation which existed within South Carolina. A meeting was called for 13 December 1770 at which a series of proposals to break through the agreements were proposed.[276] These resolutions were quickly adopted and, although protested by some members, soon spelled the end of nonimportation in America.[277]

• SUMMARY AND CONCLUSIONS •

The nonimportation movement of 1767–70 has been the subject of concentrated research by two eminent historians: Arthur M. Schlesinger and Charles M. Andrews.[278] Both scholars concluded that it was primarily a movement initiated by the merchants to bring about a redress of commercial grievances. Their goal was commercial reform and ultimately a return to the commercial system as it existed prior to 1764. But the organized agitation of this economic group within the colonial community, in these historians' analyses, had an unexpected effect upon the nonmercantile community and released social forces which alarmed conservatives more than did the parliamentary restrictions on commerce. Control of the nonimportation movement passed out of the hands of the merchants and into the hands of political radicals who were concerned with the natural rights of man and constitutional freedom, rather than with commercial grievances. The raising of the constitutional issue, which was nothing less than a claim to the right of self-government, spelled defeat for the merchants' objective of simple commercial reform.

This point of view, however, overemphasizes the fact of the merchants' agitation for commercial reform to the neglect of another more properly political aspect. Townshend's program was a conscious attempt to halt encroachment on the royal prerogative by the colonial assemblies, and to this extent it was a direct challenge to colonial aspirations in the direction of self-government. Thus, by 1767 the question was not whether the merchants were or were not in favor of colonial self-government, but rather a question of the methods to be employed in resisting the imperial policy and, specifically, the program promulgated under the names of the Townshend Acts.

At the time of the Stamp Act, the merchants and others of the ruling aristocracy had willingly enlisted the aid of the lower classes in the towns in their organized opposition to the enforcement of that obnoxious piece of legislation. However, the political propaganda in defense of natural and constitutional rights directed against the British government by the popular party leaders revealed to the conservatives the danger inherent in the situation. If these same arguments for natural and constitutional rights should be turned against the ruling aristocracy at home, social forces might be set in motion which would be more obnoxious and even more dangerous than Parliament's assertion of its supreme authority over the American colonies. With this thought foremost in their minds in 1767, the conservatives were reluctant to cooperate in another popular movement in resistance to an act of Parliament.

As has been seen, agitation for nonconsumption of British goods did not come from the merchants' organizations in Boston. The nonconsumption scheme was denounced by most merchants as a political plot of a discontented, militant minority group. The specific objective of the nonconsumption movement was to compel the merchants to curtail their imports from Britain, and consequently the merchants opposed the nonconsumption agreements.

Both Schlesinger and Andrews acknowledged the fact of nonconsumption movements in the various colonies but treated them as a part of the nonimportation movement which, they asserted, was initiated by the merchants for their own economic reasons. In failing to differentiate between nonconsumption and nonimportation, both authors overlooked a vital point.

It is even doubtful if the Boston merchants would have resorted to nonimportation to obtain a redress of their commercial grievances if it had not been for the popular pressure exerted through the nonconsumption agreement. Under the coercion of the nonconsumption movement, the Boston merchants attempted to meliorate their situation by promoting a coordinated nonimportation movement among the leading commercial towns in Massachusetts as well as New York and Philadelphia. In this way they undoubtedly hoped to avoid the commercial disadvantage which Boston merchants would suffer if they adopted a nonimportation agreement and the merchants of neighboring towns and colonies did not. The attempt to unite the northern commercial centers in a nonimportation policy failed, but the popular pressure in Boston was so great that the merchants were forced to adopt a nonimportation agreement independent of the other towns and colonies. It is only in this limited sense that it may be said that the merchants initiated the nonimportation movement.

The split, then, between the conservatives and the militants over the adoption, enforcement, and retention of the nonimportation policy reveals a division in colonial society which was both economic and political in nature. The popular parties seized upon the political issues involved in the Townshend Acts to launch a political and economic program which was not only a defense of colonial self-government, but was implicitly a challenge to the aristocratic control of government within the colonies. The nonconsumption and nonimportation movements were an attempt on the part of the popular party leaders to formulate governmental policy. They used economic coercion at home to compel the conservatives to adopt a policy of economic coercion of Parliament. They utilized their positions in the colonial assemblies to promote legislative cooperation among the colonies in opposition to the Townshend Acts. In this sense, the nonimportation movement of 1767–70, was a period during which the militants not only defended colonial self-government but made a bid for more control over local governmental decision-making.

· NOTES ·

1. Thomas Cushing to Dennys DeBerdt, 9 May 1767, Massachusetts Historical Society, *Collections,* 4th ser., vol. 4, pp. 348–49.

2. *Ibid.,* p. 349.

3. "The plan called for a combination 'to eat drink & wear nothing of any sort imported from Great Britain'; the leader said an agreement 'would be universal and include all ranks of people'" (*Massachusetts Archives,* vol. 26, p. 281; "Hutchinson Correspondence," 18 July 1767, quoted in Ralph V. Harlow, *Samuel Adams: Promoter of the American Revolution* [New York: H. Holt, 1923], p. 102, n. 12).

4. *Ibid.*

5. Articles dated 20 October 1767 in *Massachusetts Gazette* and *Boston News-Letter,* 29 October 1767.

6. *Ibid.*

7. *Boston Post Boy & Advertiser,* 9 November 1767.

8. Boston Record Commissioners, *Report,* vol. 16, pp. 221–22.

9. *Ibid.,* pp. 223–24.

10. Quoted from "Bernard Papers," The Houghton Library, Harvard Univ., 14 November 1767, vol. 6, pp. 252–53, in Harlow, *Samuel Adams,* p. 104.

11. Quoted from *Boston Evening Post,* 23 November 1767, in *ibid.,* pp. 104–5.

12. "The Subscription-Rolls, for encouraging Oeconomy, Industry, our own Manufactures, and the Disuse of foreign Superfluities, are in the Town-Clerk's Hands, open to all Persons who have not yet subscribed. The Selectmen strongly recommend this Measure to Persons of all Ranks. . . ." (letter dated 26 November 1767, in *Boston Post Boy & Advertiser,* 30 November 1767).

13. Arthur M. Schlesinger says that by the middle of January 1768, twenty-four towns in Massachusetts had adopted the Boston plan of nonconsumption. See Arthur M. Schlesinger, *The Colonial Merchants and the American Revolution, 1763–1776* (New York: Columbia Univ. Press, 1918), p. 110, n. 5. In the *Pennsylvania Gazette,* 11 February 1768, the towns of Chelmsford, Westford, Groton, Harvard, Ashby, Easton, Wareham, and Medway are also listed as having adopted nonconsumption agreements.

14. *Pennsylvania Gazette,* 24 December 1767.

15. *Ibid.,* 24 March 1768.

16. Schlesinger, *Colonial Merchants,* p. 112.

17. Hezekiah Niles, ed., *Principles and Acts of the Revolution in America* (New York: Barnes, 1876), p. 141.

18. Schlesinger, *Colonial Merchants,* p. 113.

19. P. L. Ford, ed., *The Writings of John Dickinson, 1764–1774* (Philadelphia: J. B. Lippencott, 1895), pp. 409–10.

20. See Appendix B.

21. Ford, *Dickinson Writings,* vol. 1, pp. 345–46, 349.

22. *Ibid.,* pp. 313–20.

23. *Ibid.,* pp. 323–24.

24. Boston Record Commissioners, *Report,* vol. 16, pp. 225–26.

25. *Ibid.,* p. 228.

26. Richard Frothingham, *The Rise of the Republic of the United States* (Boston: Little, Brown, 1910), p. 210.

27. See Harry A. Cushing, ed., *The Writings of Samuel Adams* (New York: G. P. Putnam's Sons, 1904), vol. 1, pp. 152–93; also a letter of transmittal from Thomas Cushing to Dennys DeBerdt, 30 January 1768, in Massachusetts Historical Society, *Collections,* 4th ser., vol. 4, p. 350.

28. "The House of Representatives of the Province, have taken into their serious Consideration, the great difficulties that must accrue to themselves and their Constituents, by the operation of several acts of Parliament, imposing Duties & Taxes on the American colonys. As it is a subject in which every Colony is deeply interested, they have no reason to doubt but your Assembly is deeply impressed with its importance, & that such constitutional measures will be come into, as are proper. . . . " (Cushing, *Writings of Samuel Adams,* vol. 1, p. 184).

29. Bernard to Barrington, 20 February 1768, in Edward Channing and A. C. Coolidge, eds., *The Barrington-Bernard Correspondence, 1760–1770* (Cambridge, Mass.: Harvard Univ. Press, 1912), pp. 145–46.

30. See William V. Wells, *The Life and Public Services of Samuel Adams* (Boston: Little, Brown, 1865), vol. 1, p. 176.

31. Harlow, *Samuel Adams*, p. 111. The single dissenting vote was cast by Timothy Ruggles, an arch-conservative representing the town of Hardwick.

32. See *Massachusetts Gazette*, 17 March 1768.

33. *Boston Evening Post*, 29 February 1768, quoted in Harlow, *Samuel Adams*, p. 113.

34. Anne Rowe Cunningham, ed., *Letters and Diary of John Rowe: Boston Merchant 1759–1762, 1764–1779* (Boston: W. B. Clarke, 1903), entries of 1, 3, and 4 March 1768, pp. 152–53.

35. Salt, coals, fishing lines, fish hooks, hemp, duck, bar lead, shot, wool cards, and card wire.

36. Cunningham, *Letters and Diary of John Rowe*, entry of 4 March, p. 153.

37. The committee was composed of John Hancock, chairman, John Rowe, Edward Payne, Wm. Phillips, Melatiah Bourne, Henderson Inches, and John Erving, Jr. (Charles M. Andrews, "The Boston Merchants and the Nonimportation Movement," Colonial Society of Massachusetts, *Publications*, vol. 19 [*Transactions* 1916–1917], p. 202).

38. Letter from Thomas Cushing to Dennys DeBerdt dated 18 April 1768, Massachusetts Historical Society, *Collections*, 4th ser., vol. 4, pp. 350–51.

39. Letter from Governor Moore to Hillsborough, 12 May 1768, E. B. O'Callaghan, ed., *Documents Relative to the Colonial History of the State of New York* (Albany: Weed, Parsons, & Co., 1853–57), vol. 8, pp. 68–69.

40. *Ibid.*

41. *Pennsylvania Gazette*, 21 April 1768.

42. Schlesinger, *Colonial Merchants*, p. 116; *Pennsylvania Gazette*, 28 June 1770.

43. Cunningham, *Letters and Diary of John Rowe*, entry of 2 May 1768, p. 161.

44. *Pennsylvania Gazette*, 31 March 1768.

45. Ford, *Dickinson Writings*, vol. 1, pp. 409–10.

46. *Pennsylvania Gazette*, 31 March 1768.

47. Ford, *Dickinson Writings*, vol. 1, p. 410.

48. *Ibid.*

49. *Ibid.*, p. 411–17.

50. Article signed "A Freeborn American," in *Pennsylvania Gazette*, 12 May 1768, in Ford, *Dickinson Writings*, vol. 1, p. 435; Schlesinger, *Colonial Merchants*, p. 119.

51. Letter signed 'A. L.' in *Pennsylvania Chronicle*, 30 May 1768.

52. *Pennsylvania Gazette*, 16 June 1768.

53. Letters from the merchants of New York to the merchants and traders of Philadelphia dated 6 June 1768, *Pennsylvania Gazette*, 28 June 1770.

54. Edward Channing, *History of the United States* (6 vols., New York: Macmillan, 1912), vol. 3, p. 94.

55. Bernard to Barrington, 30 July 1768, Channing and Coolidge, *Barrington-Bernard Correspondence*, p. 169.

56. Bernard to Barrington, 20 July 1768, *ibid.*

57. Harlow, *Samuel Adams*, pp. 115–16, 125–26.

58. *Colonial Records of Pennsylvania*, vol. 9, pp. 546–47. Andrew Eliot wrote, concerning the contribution of Hillsborough's letter to colonial unity: "The Ministry could not possibly have contrived a more effectual method to unite the Colonies, than the writing of that Circular Letter" (see Massachusetts Historical Society, *Collections*, 4th ser., vol. 4, p. 439).

59. *Colonial Records of Pennsylvania*, vol. 9, pp. 546–47.

60. Cunningham, *Letters and Diary of John Rowe,* entry of 30 June 1768, p. 167.

61. Andrews, "Boston Merchants and Nonimportation," p. 204.

62. Cunningham, *Letters and Diary of John Rowe,* entry of 1 August 1768, p. 171.

63. Andrews, "Boston Merchants and Nonimportation," p. 205.

64. Cunningham, *Letters and Diary of John Rowe,* entry of 2 August 1768, p. 172.

65. *Ibid.,* entry of 8 August; Andrews, "Boston Merchants and Nonimportation," p. 206.

66. Cushing, *Writings of Samuel Adams,* vol. 1, pp. 217–18.

67. J. G. Wilson, ed., *Memorial History of the City of New York* (4 vols., New York: New York Historical Company, 1892), vol. 2, p. 392.

68. *Pennsylvania Gazette,* 15 September 1768.

69. *Ibid.* On 13 September 1768, the Boston town meeting voted their approval of the terms of the New York merchants' agreement (Boston Record Commissioners, *Report,* vol. 16, p. 264).

70. Schlesinger, *Colonial Merchants,* p. 125.

71. Historical Manuscripts Commission, *Dartmouth Manuscripts,* vol. 2, "American Papers," William Salt Library, p. 64.

72. *Massachusetts Gazette,* 5 January 1769.

73. Wilson, *Memorial History of New York,* vol. 2, p. 397. Becker has pointed out that the composition of the merchants' committee of inspection reveals that the mercantile interest had not yet split into radical and conservative factions. The controversy over the continuation of the nonimportation policy in June and July 1770 resulted in the final division into radical and conservative parties.

74. Wilson, *Memorial History of New York,* vol. 2, p. 400.

75. O'Callaghan, *Documents Relative to New York,* vol. 8, pp. 194–95.

76. Wilson, *Memorial History of New York,* vol. 2, p. 399.

77. Samuel Hazard, ed., *The Register of Pennsylvania* (1828–1836), vol. 8, pp. 121, 131–34.

78. Letter signed "Philadelphus," *Pennsylvania Gazette,* 20 October 1768.

79. *Ibid.*

80. Hazard, *Pennsylvania Register,* vol. 2, p. 222.

81. Schlesinger, *Colonial Merchants,* p. 128.

82. Andrews, "Boston Merchants and Nonimportation," pp. 209–10.

83. Letter from London, 13 May 1769, *Pennsylvania Gazette,* 20 July 1769. Charles M. Andrews believes that the advice "to stick to the nonconsumption and nonimportation agreements and avoid riots, mobs, and such illegal measures, and lay less stress upon constitutional rights, came from men who were certain to lose by the process and so were based on honest conviction. That there was less sympathy for the American cause among the British merchants in 1769 than had been in 1765 is unmistakable, and there is nothing to account for it except the advance in the American claims" (Andrews, "Boston Merchants and Nonimportation," pp. 210–11, n. 3).

84. *Pennsylvania Chronicle,* 10 October 1768, Postscript.

85. *Pennsylvania Chronicle,* 20 February, 13 March 1769.

86. Schlesinger, *Colonial Merchants,* pp. 129–30.

87. Georgia Gazette, 26 October 1768.

88. Pennsylvania Gazette, 16 November 1769; Benjamin W. Labaree, *Patriots and Partisans: The Merchants of Newburyport, 1764–1815* (Cambridge: Harvard University Press, 1962), p. 24.

89. Andrews, "Boston Merchants and Nonimportation," pp. 212–13.

90. Andrews, "Boston Merchants and Nonimportation," pp. 212, 212–13n, 240.

91. Charles J. Hoadly, *The Public Records of the Colony of Connecticut* (Hartford: Lockwood & Brainard, 1855), p. 235.

92. *Pennsylvania Gazette,* 31 August 1769. No action was taken, apparently, by the other counties on the Delaware at this time. The Newcastle agreement was the only one which appeared in the press.

93. William Nelson, ed., *Archives of New Jersey* (Paterson: Call Publishing Co.), vol. 26, p. 546. The merchants and traders of New Jersey apparently adopted nonimportation agreements because when New York abandoned nonimportation in 1770, the inhabitants of Essex, Sussex, and Burlington counties in New Jersey met and passed resolutions to adhere to their agreements and sever all commercial relations with New York.

94. *Pennsylvania Gazette,* 31 August 1769.

95. *Boston Evening Post,* 16 October 1769.

96. *Ibid.,* 6 November 1769.

97. *Pennsylvania Gazette,* 16 November 1769.

98. John P. Kennedy, ed., *Journal of the House of Burgesses of Virginia, 1766–1769* (Richmond: Virginia State Library, 1906), pp. 145–46, 148.

99. *Ibid.,* pp. 165–71.

100. *Ibid.,* pp. 214, 215–16.

101. *Virginia Gazette,* 12 January 1769.

102. Washington to George Mason, 5 April 1769, Kate Mason Rowland, *Life of George Mason, 1725–1792* (2 vols., New York: G. P. Putnam's Sons, 1892), vol. 1, p. 139.

103. Mason to Washington, 5 April 1769, *ibid.,* pp. 141–42.

104. *Ibid.,* p. 143.

105. Kennedy, *Journals of the House of Burgesses, 1766–1769,* pp. xlii–xliii.

106. *Virginia Gazette,* 27 July 1769.

107. *Ibid.*

108. Letter dated 31 May 1769, in Frances Norton Mason, ed., *John Norton & Sons: Merchants of London and Virginia, 1750–1795* (Richmond: Dietz Press, 1937), p. 96.

109. Schlesinger, *Colonial Merchants,* p. 135.

110. *Ibid.,* p. 141.

111. William Roy Smith, *South Carolina as a Royal Province, 1719–1776* (New York: Macmillan, 1903), pp. 362–64.

112. Schlesinger, citing the *South Carolina Gazette,* 1 June 1769, refers to an article by a planter urging the promotion of local manufacturing and the patronage of nonimporters only. "'You cannot expect the merchants will begin this matter themselves', he wrote. ' . . . Oblige them to it, by declaring you will deal with none that do import extra articles,' and, by this method, you will bring about 'a happy Coalition of our Interest and that of Merchants into one immediate self-interest'" (Schlesinger, *Colonial Merchants,* pp. 141–42).

113. *Pennsylvania Chronicle,* 20 February 1769; *Maryland Gazette,* 12 March 1769.

114. Leila Sellers, *Charleston Business Before the Revolution* (Chapel Hill: Univ. of North Carolina Press, 1934), p. 208.

115. Schlesinger, *Colonial Merchants,* p. 142, citing the *South Carolina Gazette,* 22 June 1769.

116. *Ibid.,* p. 144.

117. *Ibid.*

118. Andrews, "Boston Merchants and Nonimportation," pp. 218–19.

119. News from Charleston, dated 26 October, in *Pennsylvania Gazette*, 16 November 1769.

120. Marion Dargan, Jr., *William Henry Drayton and the Revolution in South Carolina* (Ph.D. diss:, Univ. of Chicago, 1927), p. 41, citing *South Carolina Gazette*, 3 August 1769.

121. *Pennsylvania Gazette*, 19 October 1769.

122. Edward McCrady, *History of South Carolina Under the Royal Government, 1719–1776* (New York: Russell and Russell, 1969), p. 660.

123. Dargan, *William Henry Drayton*, p. 46.

124. *Maryland Gazette*, 30 June 1768.

125. *Maryland History Magazine*, vol. 12, p. 377.

126. *Maryland Gazette*, 28 July 1768.

127. Charles M. Barker, *The Background of the Revolution in Maryland* (London: H. Milford, Oxford Univ. Press, 1940), pp. 320–21.

128. *Maryland Historical Magazine*, vol. 3, pp. 143–44. I have not been able to locate copies of the exact terms of either the Baltimore or Anne Arundel county agreements.

129. Barker, *Background of the Revolution in Maryland*, pp. 320–21.

130. *Georgia Gazette*, 6 September 1769; 13 September 1769.

131. *Ibid.*, 20 September 1769.

132. Bryan was a member of the council at the time. In a letter to Governor Wright, dated 9 December 1769, Hillsborough ordered that Bryan be suspended from the council and removed from any office which he might hold in Georgia. His removal was reported by Wright in a letter to Hillsborough on 1 March 1770 (see Charles C. Jones, Jr., *The History of Georgia* [2 vols., Boston: Houghton Mifflin, 1883], vol. 2, p. 115).

133. *Georgia Gazette*, 20 September 1769.

134. Schlesinger, *Colonial Merchants*, p. 148.

135. *Georgia Gazette*, 27 December 1769.

136. Schlesinger, *Colonial Merchants*, p. 149.

137. Harlow, *Samuel Adams*, p. 129.

138. *Pennsylvania Gazette*, 29 September 1768.

139. Harlow, *Samuel Adams*, p. 130.

140. Andrew Eliot to Thomas Hollis, Massachusetts Historical Society, *Collections*, 4th ser., vol. 4, p. 428.

141. Quoted by Frothingham, *Atlantic Monthly* 10 (August 1862), pp. 199–200.

142. Schlesinger, *Colonial Merchants*, p. 157.

143. Boston Record Commissioners, *Report*, vol. 16, p. 289.

144. Schlesinger, *Colonial Merchants*, pp. 158–59. The names of the firms as given by Schlesinger were as follows: William Jackson, Jonathan Simpson, J. and R. Selkridge, John Taylor, Samuel Fletcher, Theophilus Lillie, James McMasters & Co., Thomas and Elisha Hutchinson, and Nathaniel Rogers.

145. Andrews, "Boston Merchants and Nonimportation," pp. 413–16.

146. Schlesinger, *Colonial Merchants*, p. 161.

147. *Boston Evening Post*, 31 July 1769.

148. Schlesinger, *Colonial Merchants*, p. 163.

149. The names published were: Richard Clarke & Son, John Bernard, Nathaniel Rogers, Theophilus Lillie, James McMasters & Co., John Mein, and Thomas and Elisha Hutchinson (*Boston Evening Post*, 14 August 1769).

150. *Ibid.*

151. *Ibid.*

152. *Ibid.*, 21 August 1769.

153. Schlesinger, *Colonial Merchants*, p. 170.

154. See Harlow, *Samuel Adams*, pp. 144–45.

155. Thomas Hutchinson, *History of Massachusetts-Bay* (London: M. Richardson, 1828), p. 252.

156. Hutchinson observed that "men who had no concern in trade had the greatest influence at this meeting" (see *ibid.*, p. 253).

157. *Boston Evening Post*, 31 July 1769.

158. *Ibid.*, 9 October 1769.

159. *Ibid.*, 20 November 1769.

160. *Ibid.*, 13 November 1769.

161. Schlesinger, *Colonial Merchants*, pp. 131–32.

162. *Ibid.*, p. 132, citing *Papers of the Committee of Merchants of Philadelphia, February 6, 1769–December 16, 1769*, Papers Relating to New England, 4 vols., Sparks Manuscripts 10, Houghton Library, Harvard Univ. (hereafter cited as Sparks MSS. 10). In a letter to the committee of Philadelphia, merchants wrote: "We think ourselves obliged to inform you, that though the Merchants have confined their agreement to the Repeal of the Act laying a duty on Tea, Paper, Glass, &c. yet nothing less than a Repeal of all the Revenue Acts, and putting Things on the same Footing they were before the late Innovations can or will satisfy the Minds of the People . . ." (*Pennsylvania Gazette*, 10 May 1770).

163. Colden to Hillsborough, 4 December 1769, in O'Callaghan, *Documents Relative to New York*, vol. 8, p. 191.

164. *Boston Gazette*, 22 January 1770.

165. Andrew Eliot to Thomas Hollis, 25 December 1769, in Massachusetts Historical Society, *Collections*, 4th ser., vol. 4, p. 446.

166. Schlesinger, *Colonial Merchants*, p. 175. Others who were advertised as violators from time to time were: John Bernard, Patrick and James McMasters, John Mein, Anne and Elizabeth Cummings, and Henry Barnes, a trader in the town of Marlborough (see *Boston Evening Post*, 25 December 1769; *ibid.*, 8 January 1770).

167. For example, Benjamin Greene & Son, who defended their action on the ground that they had not specified any definite time for storing their goods.

168. *Boston Gazette*, 22 January 1770.

169. *Ibid.*

170. Schlesinger, *Colonial Merchants*, p. 175; Andrews, "Boston Merchants and Nonimportation," p. 232.

171. Cunningham, *Letters and Diary of John Rowe*, pp. 196–97.

172. Boston Record Commissioners, *Report*, vol. 28, pp. 12, 16; *Boston Evening Post*, 26 February 1770.

173. Robert Auchmuty to Joseph Harrison, 15 March 1770, Sparks MSS. 10, "New England Papers," vol. 3, p. 72.

174. *Boston Gazette*, 10 July 1769.

175. *Boston Evening Post*, 6 November 1769.

176. See *Boston Gazette*, 12 March 1770; *Boston Evening Post*, 19 March, 9 April, 16 April, 11 June, and 25 June 1770.

177. *Ibid.*, 7 August 1769; Schlesinger, *Colonial Merchants*, pp. 150–51.

178. *Boston Evening Post*, 16 April 1770.

179. *Ibid.*, 25 June 1770.

180. Andrews, "Boston Merchants and Nonimportation," p. 238.

181. *Ibid.*, pp. 236–37.

182. *Pennsylvania Gazette,* 20 July 1769.

183. *Pennsylvania Chronicle,* 4 December 1769.

184. *Pennsylvania Gazette,* 20 July 1769.

185. See Isaac Sharpless, *The Quakers in the Revolution* (Philadelphia: J. B. Lippincott, 1899), p. 79.

186. *Pennsylvania Gazette,* 3 August 1769.

187. *Ibid.*

188. *Ibid.*

189. Charles H. Lincoln, "The Revolutionary Movement in Pennsylvania," *Publications of the University of Pennsylvania,* Series in History 1 (Philadelphia: Univ. of Pennsylvania, 1901), pp. 151–52.

190. Henry Drinker to Abel James, 9 December 1769, in *Pennsylvania Magazine of History and Biography* 14 (1890), p. 41.

191. Drinker to James, 29 April 1770, *ibid.*, pp. 43–44.

192. Schlesinger, *Colonial Merchants,* p. 219.

193. *Pennsylvania Gazette,* 24 May 1770.

194. *Ibid.*, 31 May 1770, Supplement.

195. *Ibid.*, 7 June 1770.

196. *Ibid.*, 14 June 1770.

197. Postscript to *Boston Weekly News-Letter,* 27 April 1769.

198. Letter from New York in *Massachusetts Gazette,* 11 May 1769.

199. *Maryland Gazette,* 6 July 1769; *Boston Evening Post,* 10 July 1769. Occasional other cases arose through the summer of 1769.

200. Andrews, "Boston Merchants and Nonimportation," pp. 212–13, 240.

201. *Maryland Gazette,* 15 February 1770.

202. *Virginia Gazette,* 31 May 1770.

203. Rowland, *George Mason,* vol. 1, pp. 144–46.

204. *Journals of the House of Burgesses, 1770–1772,* pp. xxix–xxxi.

205. Rowland, *George Mason,* vol. 1, 148–49.

206. Letter dated 19 December 1770, in *Journals of the House of Burgesses, 1770–1772,* p. xxxi.

207. John C. Fitzpatrick, *The Writings of George Washington* (Washington, D.C.: U.S. Government Printing Office, 1931), vol. 3, p. 60.

208. *Maryland Gazette,* 25 January 1770.

209. *Ibid.*, 15 February 1770.

210. *Ibid.*, 12 April, 19 April 1770.

211. *Ibid.*, 26 July, 2 August, 16 August 1770.

212. McCrady, *History of South Carolina,* pp. 664–65.

213. *Pennsylvania Gazette,* 28 June; McCrady, *History of South Carolina,* pp. 671–72.

214. Andrews, "Boston Merchants and Nonimportation," p. 237.

215. Letter to Hillsborough in William L. Saunders, ed., *Colonial and State Records of North Carolina* (10 vols., Raleigh: P. M. Hale, 1886–90), vol. 8, p. 496.

216. Letter from London, dated 26 March 1770, *Maryland Gazette,* 31 May 1770.

217. Carl L. Becker, *The History of Political Parties in the Province of New York,*

1760–1776 (Ph.D. diss.: Univ. of Wisconsin, 1909), p. 87.

218. Colden to Hillsborough, 16 May 1770, O'Callaghan, *Documents Relative to New York,* vol. 8, p. 214.

219. *Ibid.,* vol. 27, pp. 169–70, 193–94.

220. Wilson, *Memorial History of New York,* vol. 2, p. 406.

221. Schlesinger, *Colonial Merchants,* p. 223.

222. *Maryland Gazette,* 28 June 1770.

223. Colden to Hillsborough, 10 July 1770, in O'Callaghan, *Documents Relative to New York,* vol. 8, p. 218.

224. *Boston Gazette,* 23 July 1770.

225. Letter of Alexander Colden to Anthony Todd, 11 July 1770, O'Callaghan, *Documents Relative to New York,* vol. 8, pp. 218–20.

226. Becker, *Political Parties in New York,* pp. 92–93.

227. Wilson, *Memorial History of New York,* vol. 2, p. 407.

228. *Pennsylvania Gazette,* 12 July 1770.

229. Letter dated 11 July 1770, *ibid.,* 19 July 1770.

230. Nelson, *Archives of New Jersey,* vol. 27, p. 203.

231. Letter of 12 September 1770, *Pennsylvania Gazette,* 20 September 1770.

232. Letter of 14 September 1770, in *ibid.*

233. Circular letter from the committee in Philadelphia to the committee of merchants at Boston dated 25 September 1770, in *ibid.,* 4 October 1770.

234. *Ibid.*

235. *Ibid.,* 27 September 1770.

236. *Ibid.*

237. *Ibid.,* 4 October 1770.

238. *Ibid.*

239. Schlesinger, *Colonial Merchants,* p. 232.

240. "Narrative of Occurences at Boston from March 26 to April 21, 1770," Sparks MSS. 10, "New England Papers," vol. 3, p. 76 (hereafter cited as "Ocurrences at Boston"). See also the letter from the merchants' committee at Boston to the merchants' committee at New York, 5 May 1770, *Pennsylvania Gazette,* 24 May 1770, Supplement; and the *Boston Gazette,* 23 April 1770.

241. "Occurences at Boston from April 25 to May 4, 1770," Sparks MSS. 10, "New England Papers," vol. 3, p. 77; *Boston Gazette,* 30 April 1770.

242. *Ibid.* See also the letter of the Boston merchants' committee to the New York merchants' committee, 5 May 1770, in the *Pennsylvania Gazette,* 24 May 1770, Supplement.

243. Hutchinson to Hillsborough, 18 May 1770, "Hutchinson Correspondence," vol. 26, p. 485.

244. "Occurences at Boston, April 24 to May 4, 1770," Sparks MSS. 10, "New England Papers," vol. 3, p. 77. The British Coffee House had been the customary meeting place of the Boston "Merchants' Club" for twenty years, which is another indication that the people who met there at this time were the "real merchants" (see Charles Francis Adams, *The Works of John Adams* [10 vols., Boston: Little, Brown, 1850–56], vol. 2, p. 290).

245. Hutchinson to ———, [22] May 1770, "Hutchinson Correspondence," vol. 26, p. 492.

246. Hutchinson to Governor Penn, 28 May 1770, *ibid.,* p. 494. See also Hutchinson to ———, 27 May 1770, *ibid.,* p. 495.

247. Hutchinson to ———, [22] May 1770, *ibid.*, p. 492.

248. Hutchinson to Cadwallader Colden, 2 June 1770, *ibid.*, p. 498. For Hutchinson's letter to Governor Penn, 28 May 1770, see *ibid.*, pp. 494–95.

249. Hutchinson to ———, 24 May 1770, *ibid.*, p. 491.

250. See the account under a New York dateline, 14 May 1770, including a copy of the letter to Rogers from the New York Sons of Liberty, dated 10:00 P.M., 10 May, in the *Boston Gazette,* 21 May 1770. For a similar treatment of Rogers at Shelter Island, 28 May, see the account under a New London dateline of 1 June, in *ibid.,* 11 June 1770.

251. *Ibid.;* Hutchinson to [Bernard?], 12 August, and to [Hillsborough], 14 August, and to ———, 19 August 1770, "Hutchinson Correspondence," vol. 26, pp. 534, 536, 537–38.

252. See the petition of James, Patrick, and John McMasters to Lieutenant-Governor Hutchinson for protection, 5 June 1770, in the British Public Record Office, Colonial Office (C.O.), 5/759, p. 543. See also the proceedings of the "Body of the People," 7 June, in the *Boston Gazette,* 11 June 1770. For the newspaper account of the mob intimidation of Patrick McMasters, see the *Boston Evening Post,* 25 June 1770. For McMasters's personal account, see his petition to the Earl of Hillsborough, 27 June 1770, C.O. 5/759, pp. 547–48. See also Ann Hulton's description of McMasters's ordeal in a letter of 25 June 1770 in Ann Hulton, *Letters of a Loyalist Lady: Being the Letters of Ann Hulton, Sister of Henry Hulton, Commissioner of Customs at Boston, 1767–1776* (Cambridge, Mass.: Harvard Univ. Press, 1927), pp. 26–27; and the account of John Fleeming written to John Mein from Castle William, where he was also a fugitive from the mob, 1 July 1770, in Sparks MSS. 10, "New England Papers," vol. 4, p. 5.

253. See Ann Hulton's letter, 25 July 1770, *Letters of a Loyalist Lady,* p. 22–23. See also John Fleeming to John Mein, 1 July 1770, Sparks MSS. 10, "New England Papers," vol. 4, p. 5.

254. "Hutchinson Correspondence," vol. 26, p. 540.

255. Proceedings of The Body in the *Boston Gazette,* 11 June 1770.

256. Resolutions of The Body, 25 June 1770, *Boston Evening Post,* 2 July 1770.

257. Proceedings of The Body, 24 July 1770, in the *Boston Gazette,* 30 July 1770.

258. Hutchinson to [Hillsborough?], 26 July 1770, "Hutchinson Correspondence," vol. 26, pp. 522–23. Robert E. Brown, in *Middle Class Democracy and the Revolution in Massachusetts, 1691–1780* (Ithaca, 1955), p. 273, misquotes Hutchinson's statement in this letter when he cites Hutchinson as his authority for saying that "actually only some nine or ten merchants wanted to follow New York's lead, for popular spirit in Boston was still very strong, but pressure to import was beginning to build up." It makes a great deal of difference in interpreting the situation at this crucial moment in the nonimportation movement whether only "*nine or ten*" merchants wanted to abandon the nonimportation agreement, or whether "*nine in ten*" of the Boston merchants wanted to do so. Brown's misquotation of Hutchinson's statement supports his consensus thesis, whereas what Hutchinson actually said contradicts it. For statements corroborating Hutchinson's assessment of the situation at this time, see also a letter of Ann Hulton, 25 July 1770, in Hulton, *Letters of a Loyalist Lady,* p. 26, and Samuel Prince to Dr. Isaac ———, 28 July 1770, "Miscellaneous MSS.," vol. 13, in the Massachusetts Historical Society.

259. *Boston Gazette,* 6 August 1770, Supplement.

260. Proceedings of the Body, 31 July, *ibid.,* 13 August 1770.

261. Proceedings of the Body, 7 August, *ibid.,* 13 August 1770. The names of the merchants who were advertised by the inspection committee for refusing to ship goods back

to England were: William Bowes, Rufus Greene, Edward Church, Nathaniel Cary, and William Coffin, Jr. These men were *not* the infamous "Old Importers" who were regularly advertised as "Enemies to their Country." See *ibid.*, 20 August 1770, for both lists. The advertisement of merchants who were not among the "Old Importers" at this time indicates a growing opposition among the "real merchants" in Boston to the nonimportation policy.

262. Hutchinson to [Bernard?], 28 August 1770, "Hutchinson Correspondence," vol. 26, pp. 540–41.

263. *Boston Gazette,* 10 September 1770.

264. *Ibid.,* 17 September 1770.

265. Cunningham, *Letters and Diary of John Rowe,* entries for 10–15 September 1770, pp. 205–7, for the number of merchants who attended the merchants' meetings.

266. Proceedings of the Body, 13 September, in the *Boston Gazette,* 17 September 1770.

267. *Ibid.,* 15 and 22 October 1770.

268. Andrew Eliot to Thomas Hollis, 26 January 1771, Massachusetts Historical Society, *Collections,* 4th ser., vol. 4, pp. 457–58.

269. Samuel Adams to Stephen Sayre, 16 November 1770, Cushing, *Writings of Samuel Adams,* vol. 2, p. 58.

270. Samuel Adams to Peter Timothy, 21 November 1770, *ibid.,* p. 65.

271. William Palfrey to John Wilkes, 23 October 1770, Colonial Society of Massachusetts, *Publications,* vol. 34, p. 419.

272. The committee members were John Hancock, Thomas Cushing, Samuel Adams, Thomas Boylston, John Adams, Dr. Joseph Warren, and William Dennie. See the *Boston Gazette,* 17 September 1770; also, Thomas Young to Hugh Hughes, 15 September 1770, "Miscellaneous MSS.", vol. 13, Massachusetts Historical Society.

273. *Journals of the House of Representatives,* 16 October 1770 and 16 November 1770, pp. 97, 164, in Records of the States of the United States of America: A Microfilm Compilation Prepared by the Library of Congress in Association with the University of North Carolina, ed. William Sumner Jenkins; microfilmed by the Library of Congress Photo-duplication Service, 1949.

274. Andrews, "Boston Merchants and Nonimportation," p. 248.

275. Nelson, *Archives of New Jersey,* vol. 27, p. 293.

276. McCrady, *History of South Carolina,* p. 679.

277. *Ibid.,* pp. 680–81.

278. Schlesinger, *Colonial Merchants;* Andrews, "Boston Merchants and Nonimportation."

·5·

British Response to American Reactions to the Townshend Acts, 1768–1770

IAN R. CHRISTIE

Decisions for which the British government was largely responsible provide a complex but fairly clear chain of causation from the passage of the Townshend Acts to the Boston "Massacre." The reasoning behind various British reactions is not always explicit in the evidence available, but one circumstance is perfectly apparent. Moves made in London were not solely or even mainly in response to the colonial nonconsumption and nonimportation agreements themselves but to events which accompanied them. The government assumed that the agreements would eventually come to an end, owing to the economic depression they would generate in the colonial commercial community; indeed, until well into 1769 they were sceptical, from the information at their disposal, about the agreements taking effect at all. Even after that, British policy was not shaped by any feeling that an effective display of colonial nonviolent resistance made retreat essential. British ministers were much more concerned about the breakdown of the king's peace in the enforcement of the agreements by violence or threats of violence. They were also worried by the extension of violent action against the agents of the imperial authority engaged in enforcing the laws of trade and navigation. Because Boston seemed to be the focus of the trouble, they were gradually led to conclude that steps were necessary to overhaul the whole institutional machinery responsible for law and order in Massachusetts.

During February and early March 1768, the ministers pushed through Parliament an act establishing four district vice-admiralty courts in leading American commercial centers in place of the single court which had been set up at Halifax, Nova Scotia, in 1764. This measure was in itself an attempt to improve and strengthen imperial institutions. One object was to meet a legitimate complaint that a single such court at Halifax lay so far away that its jurisdiction would be a serious inconvenience and imposition. News from Boston of intentions to boycott British goods may have had a marginal effect in inclining the government to bring it forward, but the decision was plainly due much more to other considerations. The additional courts had been planned before the fall of Grenville's ministry, and Grenville blamed his successors for neglecting to implement the scheme. Information was coming in from various sources that smuggling was on the increase in America and that the collection of revenue was running far below expectation, while debates in Parliament on military supply served once more to draw attention to the fiscal burden of defense to which the colonies appeared not to be making any appreciable contribution. There was also an impression in London that, to some extent, the colonial criticism of the provincial vice-admiralty courts was justified by the poor professional quality of the judges and their vulnerability to corrupt pressures. It was believed that professionally staffed courts manned by fully trained lawyers from Britain not financially dependent on the colonial legislatures would do their duty to the general satisfaction. A major purpose of the measure was to secure a more effective enforcement of the laws of trade, navigation, and revenue. Only insofar as colonists might seek to obtain from illicit sources the goods they refused to buy from Britain had the act any possible connection with the threatened nonimportation agreement, and no evidence has been found that its enactment was based on any such consideration.[1]

The passage of this act might be taken as a sign of determination to enforce the Townshend Revenue Act, but in fact such a conclusion would be well away from the mark. Doubts about the Revenue Act were being voiced from the beginning of 1768, and these doubts had nothing to do with any colonial reaction against it. The greater part of the Revenue Act was to be repealed in February 1770 on commercial principles, and the government of that day, in thus resting its case, was by no means simply having recourse to pretense.

Lord Hillsborough, secretary of state for the colonies from the beginning of 1768, seems to have disapproved of the Townshend Act from an early stage. By his own account to the Connecticut agent, William Samuel Johnson, in October 1768, "one of the first things he had proposed to Lord North at his coming into administration was the repeal of this Act as being extremely anti-commercial."[2] While there is no other evidence for his views in January and February, it is not necessary to assume that he was simply striking a pose for the agent's benefit, and it is good ground for accepting the truth of what he had said. For it was the case that in this act, as in other (abortive) proposals, Charles Townshend had flown in the face of current mercantilist thinking. In a recent and most authoritative statement regarding British colonial and commercial policy, published at the beginning of 1765, George Grenville's then secretary to the treasury, Thomas Whately, had pointed out that in the nature of things, "the manufactures . . . of Great Britain must on all . . . accounts be superior in quality and lower in price than those of America." He was also of the opinion that by avoiding taxes on exports, so keeping the prices low, and by paying bounties on such raw materials as flax and hemp, the home country could always discourage the colonists from manufactures.[3]

During 1768, another member of Grenville's able little brain trust was to be found voicing the same doctrine. William Knox wrote to Grenville in July: "I am inclined to think it will be impracticable to raise anything from [the colonies] by parliamentary taxes of any kind, duties indeed I think highly impolitic to be laid for that purpose as they must operate as premiums on their own manufactures."[4] Governor Thomas Pownall was to make the same point a few months later in his speech of 19 April 1769 calling for the repeal of Townshend's act. The act, he declared, contradicted "every maxim and principle of the policy of commerce," tended "to obstruct the vent of British manufactures," operated "as a bounty to American manufactures," and encouraged "the contraband trade and supply from foreign markets." He laid stress on the existing potential for the manufacture of paper in the colonies and the actual development of glass production in Pennsylvania.[5] George Grenville himself, in the debate on repeal in March 1770, described the act as "diametrically repugnant to the principles of commerce."[6] No doubt, these arguments were elicited as part of opposition parliamentary tactics, but it is unlikely that they would have been so often reiterated, and apparently not seriously controverted in the Commons, if there had not been a considerable measure of truth in them.[7]

Hillsborough had long been a friend of Grenville and had moved in his circle. Moreover, he had had a professional connection with the group in his role as first commissioner of the Board of Trade in Grenville's ministry, a position where commercial considerations were a primary concern. It is therefore reasonable to believe that he accepted the view that Townshend's duties on paper, glass, red and white lead, and painters' colors were economically unsound because they would create an incentive for the production of these goods by local American industry. Tea did not fall into this category because it could not be produced in the colonies, but the tea duty could nevertheless be criticized on the ground that it would impose an undesirable check upon the consumption of a commodity, on the sale of which the prosperity of the East India Company was thought to depend.

Accepting that Hillsborough held these views in January and February 1768, it also follows that his approach to Lord North was in no way dictated by alarm at colonial threats of a nonconsumption agreement. At the beginning of the year, the reports coming in suggested there was little support for this idea. Governor Francis Bernard of Massachusetts, in a dispatch of 14 November, received in London on 16 January, stated that "the subscription . . . to engage people not to buy certain enumerated goods . . . [had] been so generally rejected and discountenanced by the principal gentlemen of [Boston] that it [could] have no effect."[8] His three subsequent letters, reaching London in January and March, gave no grounds for believing otherwise.[9] Not until 15 April did Hillsborough learn from him that James Otis's party had carried through the assembly the resolution to inform the legislatures of other colonies of the protests it was making.[10] Dispatches arriving from New York over the same period make no mention of a nonconsumption agreement.[11] In a more general way, this impression was underlined in a letter from the commander in chief in America, General Thomas Gage, which reached the office on 29 February, but Gage's observations could also have confirmed Hillsborough in his views of the inexpediency of Townshend's measure. During a recent visit to Philadelphia, Gage had been much struck by the development of trade and industry, and he wrote:

> They talk and threaten much in other provinces of their resolution to lessen the
> importation of British manufactures and to manufacture for themselves; but they
> are by no means able to do it. The people of Pennsylvania lay their plans with
> more temper and judgment, and [pursue] them with patience and steadiness. They
> don't attempt impossibilitys, or talk of what they will do, but are silently stealing
> Mechanics and Manufacturers; and if they go on as they have hitherto done, they
> will probably in a few years supply themselves with many necessary articles,
> which they now import from Great Britain.[12]

In January and February 1768, Hillsborough may therefore be understood to
have been favorably disposed to the repeal of the whole of Townshend's revenue
duties and to have begun the process of convincing his colleagues. It is thus one of
the many ironies in the history of British-American relations during these years of
crisis that the direct colonial repudiation of parliamentary authority in matters of
taxation, renewed by the Massachusetts Assembly in February and learned of by
Hillsborough on 15 April, cut the ground for such a policy from beneath his feet by
destroying its political acceptability in London. Where would such attrition end?
On 16 April Hillsborough had on his desk a private letter to Viscount Barrington,
the secretary-at-war, in which Gage expressed the disturbing opinion:

> From the denying the right of internal taxation, they next deny the right of duties
> on imports, and thus they mean to go on step by step, 'till they throw off all subjec-
> tion to your laws. They will acknowledge the King of Great Britain to be their
> King, but soon deny the prerogatives of the Crown, and acknowledge their King
> no longer than it shall be convenient for them to do so.[13]

A policy which was commercially right was now seen in the circumstances to
threaten political disaster. The following October, William Samuel Johnson set
down a verbatim record of what Hillsborough had told him when he urged a repeal
of the act:

> The colonies have rendered it impossible, by imprudently uniting to dispute the
> right of Parliament, which, since the late declarative act especially, we cannot
> permit to be called in question. I am sorry that your colony, which you have so
> often represented to me in so favorable a light, have listened to the factious sug-
> gestions of the Massachusetts Bay. Had they petitioned on the grounds of expe-
> diency only, they would have succeeded; but while you call in question the right,
> we cannot hear you.[14]

Johnson parted from Hillsborough apprized of the fact that the ministers, for their
own reasons, were dissatisfied with the act. "There is room for hope," he wrote,
"that some expedient may be hit upon to save the honor of Parliament, about which
they are so exceedingly concerned, and at the same time to get rid of the Act, which
is agreeable to none on either side of the question." The following January Benjamin Franklin gave a similar and rather more elaborate appraisal not only of Hillsborough's view but that of the government in general:

> The majority really wish the Duty Acts had never been made; they say they are

evidently inconsistent with all sound commercial and political principles, equally prejudicial to this country as to America; but they think the national honour concerned in supporting them, considering the manner in which the execution of them has been opposed. They cannot bear the denial of the right of Parliament to make them, tho' they acknowledge they ought not to have been made.[15]

The sine qua non of the ministers for a repeal was the abandonment of the colonial challenge to parliamentary supremacy. They earnestly sought this during the winter of 1768–69. In late November 1768, Hillsborough summoned the agents together to a meeting, and told them that, "if they would waive the point of right, and petition for a repeal of the [Townshend] duties as burdensome and grievous, Administration were disposed to come into it."[16] At once, he came up against the blank wall of the instructions which various colonial committees of correspondence had relayed to their agents, telling them to insist upon the question of right. Under these circumstances, he could see no way to repeal the act and said so not only privately but also publicly in the course of debate in the House of Lords. Even in the debate, however, he avowed his willingness to see it repealed, if the question of right was laid aside.[17] His next step was to frame a plan which might hold out an inducement to colonies to offer an effective alternative. We know of this scheme only from the form it took in a memorandum submitted by Hillsborough to George III on 15 February 1769. It was on the cabinet's agenda both before and after this date. Hillsborough proposed:

> To move the repeal of Mr. Townshend's last Revenue Act, which is expressly said in the preamble to be intended to raise a revenue for the support of the civil establishment of the colonies, with respect to Virginia and the West India Islands where provision has already been amply made for that service, and to declare that it shall remain in force with regard to the other colonies no longer than untill each shall have made such permanent provision for its own establishment as his Majesty shall approve in council.[18]

George III commented:

> The conduct of the Virginians was so offensive the last spring that the altering the Revenue Act in their favour and in that of the West Indies this session would not be proper; tho' any hint that could [might] be given that those colonies which submit to that law and make proper establishments for the governors and other services expressed in the aforesaid Act, may another year be exempted from every article of it except the tea duty.[19]

It is not unlikely that the king's comments reflected the views of other cabinet ministers, and this particular suggestion went no further. But ministers continued to discuss ways of getting rid of the duties if only it could be done in a manner not harmful to the authority of Parliament. Early in March, Henry Wilmot, agent for New Jersey, who also happened to be secretary to the Lord Chancellor, reported to his fellow agents that they "might depend on the Act's being repealed next session by the Ministry themselves, but that no consideration would induce them to do it this year."[20] William Samuel Johnson reported with a slightly different emphasis, on 23 March, that the colonies were left "with only a kind of *ministerial encourage-*

ment that, if they are *very quiet* and *quite silent upon the right, and* will *humbly ask it as a favor, perhaps* the offensive Acts shall be repealed next winter."[21] Among the considerations which may have shaped ministerial views during the late winter and early spring were the constitutional defiance apparent in the petitions from Pennsylvania and New York, the only provinces to submit petitions to Parliament against the revenue duties this session, and the final refusal of the colonial agents, after some hesitant consideration, to enter into a petition on their own account praying for the repeal on commercial grounds only. Furthermore, the many loopholes in the colonial nonimportation agreements up to the spring of 1769 left the London merchants trading to America in no mind to raise a petition themselves unless they could get strong political backing for it from either the ministry or the parliamentary Opposition—and neither would give it.[22]

Ministers made their final decision on the matter at a cabinet meeting on 1 May 1769, immediately after the end of the parliamentary session.[23] In face of continued colonial obduracy on the constitutional issue, they felt it impossible to take any action earlier than the following session of Parliament, and now that obduracy further determined their course of action. Four members of the cabinet—Grafton and his associates—were prepared to repeal the act in full. The other five present, including Hillsborough and Lord North, felt that Parliament's authority to raise a civil list revenue in the colonies must be maintained by the retention of the tea duty.[24] A year later North told the House of Commons:

> Indeed, I heartily wished to repeal the whole of the law, from this conciliating principle, if there had been a possibility of repealing it without giving up that just right which I shall ever wish the mother country to possess, the right of taxing the Americans. But I am sorry, heartily sorry to say, that the colonies, so far from deserving additional instances of tenderness, did not deserve the instance then shewn, for their resolutions became more violent than ever; their associations instead of supplicating proceeded to dictate, and grew at last to such a meridian of temerity, that administration could not, for its own credit, go as far as it might incline to gratify their expectations.[25]

No doubt, he spoke for those members of the cabinet who, on 1 May 1769, voted to retain the tea duty. By publishing this decision through a circular letter to the colonial governors, the ministry virtually bound itself to act in this sense at the beginning of the following parliamentary session.[26]

The repeal of all the Townshend duties except that on tea was duly effected early in 1770. It follows from the preceding account that North's emphasis in the House of Commons on the fact that the duties did not make commercial sense and that "it must astonish any reasonable man to think how so preposterous a law could originally obtain existence from a British legislature" was not mere flummery, but reflected a perfectly genuine point of view.[27] The circumstances preclude the conclusion that the repeal took place because of the colonial nonconsumption and nonimportation agreements, and indeed the whole trend of the argument from the evidence adduced here appears to controvert such a view. The ministry undoubtedly hoped that the partial repeal would reduce the tension between the government and the colonies, but this was not the main, or perhaps even the major reason, for the action. They did not act under economic pressure. On this point, the report by the Connecticut agent is categorical. Johnson wrote on 5 December 1769 that the failure of the nonimportation agreement to make any serious impression on merchants and manufacturers had greatly strengthened the ministry's hand, and he attributed this fact to a number of circumstances: in part, to breaches of the agreements, but much more to a vast Russian demand for goods stimulated by the Russo-Turkish war, to a growth of German trade, to some openings for export trade to France, and to the canal boom in Britain itself, which had created an enormous demand for labor.[28] Although North drew attention to a considerable reduction in colonial imports of British goods at the beginning of 1770, he measured this against an excess demand the previous year, when colonial merchants had been stocking up in anticipation of nonimportation, and he expected a breakdown of the nonimportation agreements of 1769, as stocks of manufactures became exhausted.[29]

In sum, in 1769 the ministers agreed upon, and in 1770 they put into effect, a measure which they regarded as second best. On economic grounds, they would have preferred complete repeal of the Townshend Act. Because the vital question of constitutional principal obtruded itself, they could not go so far as this. They jettisoned those duties most likely to encourage colonial industrial competition with British manufactures but left in force the tea duty as a symbol of Parliament's right to provide a civil list revenue, because in this case, whatever the economic drawbacks might be, at least no potential competition with British products was involved.

The nature of American protest also created problems for British ministers of a kind quite distinct from the question of the expediency or nonexpediency of retaining the Townshend Act. Hillsborough's concern over events in Massachusetts, in particular, arose from the nature of the reports received by his office from the governor during the previous two years (with the formation of the colonial office, dispatches received by the Earl of Shelburne on colonial business were transferred from the southern department, and those which continued to arrive from officials in America addressed to Shelburne were passed to Hillsborough as a matter of course).

Material in the letters of Governor Bernard, supported to some extent by evidence from elsewhere, gave rise in London to a belief that trouble in the province was being fomented by a minority which had successfully exploited the passions of the Boston mob in order to intimidate its opponents. In one of these letters Bernard declared: "The troubles of this country take their rise from and owe their continuance to one man [James Otis], so much that his history alone would contain a full account of them." Bernard attributed the opposition to royal government led by Otis and his friends, whom Bernard came to style "the faction," to malice arising from thwarted ambition. Seen in this light, the recent disturbances and other difficulties in Boston over the Stamp Act appeared to be not a genuine protest over a constitutional issue but an artificially-inspired agitation fostered by a group of local politicians on the make, who were out to exploit any circumstance to their advantage. The Stamp Act, Bernard wrote:

> Let loose all the ill humours of the common people and put them into the hands of designing men, to be employed not so much for the defence of their real and constitutional rights, as to humble the government and bring it to the level of the very people. . . . The opposing the Stamp Act has been made a mask for a battery, a stalking horse to take a better aim at the royalty of the government, [a fact] apparent while the repeal was in suspence but since it has passed . . . put out of all doubt.

As evidence in support of this assertion, Bernard pointed to the concerted attack on the councillors and assemblymen who had given him support during the session of 1766, resulting in the rejection at the ensuing elections that spring of nineteen representatives "noted for their attachment to government" and the new assembly's refusal to elect the lieutenant-governor, Thomas Hutchinson, and other officerholders to membership of the council.[30]

A year later, in November 1767, Bernard noted that his relations with the provincial legislature had been smoother, but he does not seem to have made the obvious connection between this fact and the general satisfaction with the repeal of the Stamp Act. It is of a piece with his insensitivity to colonial susceptibilities on constitutional issues that he appears to have implicitly attributed his growing troubles in 1768 simply to a recrudescence of the ambitions and malice of the Otis faction. In his dispatches, the words "the Party" and "the Faction" were used with increasing frequency to describe the opposition both in and outside the assembly and council, and his emphasis on its attempts at intimidation of officialdom became more marked.[31] On 5 March 1768, Bernard described proceedings in the legislature concerning his complaint against a paragraph planted by Otis and Samuel Adams in the *Boston Gazette:*

> Otis upon this occasion behaved like a madman; he abused everyone in authority and especially the council in the grossest terms. The next morning he came into the council chamber before the board met, and having read the council's address, he with oaths and imprecations vowed vengeance upon the whole council at the next election.[32]

The annual election of the council, Bernard added, was "the canker-worm of the constitution of this government." His next letter, giving a detailed narrative of the first outburst, during March 1768, of riots and demonstrations intended to intimidate the Customs commissioners and the Customs officials in Boston, made clear the uselessness of appealing to the council for support in restraining such activity. In particular, they would refuse consent to any proposal to bring in troops in support of the civil arm. "It is vain," he wrote, "to put such a question to the council; for, considering the influence they are under from their being creatures of the people, and the personal danger they would be subject to in assisting in the restraining them, it is not probable that the utmost extremity of mischief and danger would induce them to advise such a measure." It would be "dangerous," he argued, to call on troops on his own account—a clear hint to Hillsborough that, if any regulars were to be detached to Boston to help maintain law and order, this must be on Hillsborough's own initiative. "The peace of the town," he added, "is to depend upon those who have the command of the mob."[33]

The decision of the assembly not merely to petition George III for the repeal of the Townshend Act but to notify the other colonial legislatures of its course of action appeared to Hillsborough an attempt to extend throughout America a conspiracy directed against royal and parliamentary authority. He regarded the move as "seditious." In this matter, Hillsborough's own response was limited to an instruction to Bernard to dissolve the Massachusetts Assembly if it refused to rescind its motion and to the issue of Hillsborough's circular letter to governors of 21 April 1768 directing them to try to prevent discussion of the Massachusetts circular and to dissolve any assembly which failed to conform with these instructions.[34] This was a maladroit and abortive move, likely to cause resentment for the interruptions to business and the necessity for new elections which it imposed. The issue of the circular was thus blown up into something of greater importance.

The March riots in Boston seemed to present a more serious problem: a breakdown of law and order in face of a factious conspiracy, whose leaders were exploiting the forms of the provincial constitution and were using the weapon of mob terror, which the governor had declared himself unable to remedy. Both immediate and more long-term measures seemed necessary.

In Hillsborough's view, the short-term solution was to reinforce a presumably well-meaning but impotent provincial magistracy by putting troops at their disposal, a move which would relieve them from the threats to their own safety, which were discouraging them from action, and would put in their hands the power to maintain law and order. Since the council was too cowed to support the governor in calling on the commander in chief in America for troops, London must take the initiative in sending them. Once the troops were there, Bernard presumably would get more support from his council, and other magistrates also would take a firmer line, calling on the troops to put down riots when necessary.

Hillsborough's view is nowhere fully documented, but this deduction with regard to it follows from the contemporary British understanding about the use of troops in such circumstance.[35] In Britain, either militia or regular troops might be used to enforce law and order against rioters. No body of civil police was available for this purpose. There were occasions when recourse was had to regular troops rather than the militia because of well-grounded suspicions that men called up for militia service might tend to sympathize with the rioters. Some confusion existed regarding the circumstances in which troops could be used and the extent of the activity they might undertake. Under English Common Law, any public assembly which became involved in some infringement of the law would become "unlawful," and under the appropriate circumstances it might be classed as a "riot" or a "rebellion." If a felony was committed, all the people involved in a riot could be treated as felons, subject to criminal conviction for the penalties appropriate to that class of offense. Also, under the Common Law, magistrates, and indeed all citizens, had a right and also a duty to use reasonable force to suppress any form of unlawful assembly. But the law contained a sting, since it was interpreted to mean that neither too much nor too little force should be used, and the suppressor of a riot might find himself in trouble in the courts on either count. Soldiers, as individual subjects, had the same Common Law right and duty as everyone else.[36]

Under the terms of the Riot Act of 1715, the reading by a magistrate of the proclamation contained in the act, which commanded those assembled to disperse within the space of an hour, gave an added statutory definition of the offense being committed and provided some protection for agents of law enforcement. The act laid down that if twelve or more persons so assembled refused to disperse as required, they would be guilty of felony, and that if a proclaimed riot had to be dispersed by force, then those who took action to disperse it had an absolute indemnity against any penalty for the injuring or killing of a rioter.

The object of the statute had been to clarify and supplement the Common Law. But very soon after its passage, it seems to have been very generally regarded as having supplanted it. The Common Law duty laid upon everybody, including soldiers, to suppress riots, faded from view. An assumption gained ground that it was illegal to call in the military to aid the civil power and suppress a riot unless the proclamation was read and an hour given thereafter for rioters to disperse. To some extent, the degree of the confusion is indicated by the fact that until 1735 the secretary-at-war, the official responsible for arranging troop movements, usually directed army officers to refrain from the use of force in dealing with riots unless directed by a civil magistrate. After 1735, the army officer was usually left discretion in his orders, but there was a common belief in the army that it was illegal to take action against civilians until a magistrate had given orders to do so. Even if officers received this authority, they were somewhat loath to act unless the Riot Act had been read, since they might find themselves in trouble over the Common Law rule that the use of excessive force might bring retribution in the courts.[37]

The forms of direction given by the secretaries-at-war in the mid-eighteenth century regularly reflected this diffidence. In the 1750s and 1760s, acting on the basis of the somewhat equivocal advice given from time to time by the law officers of the Crown, these officials usually briefed military officers sent on riot duty with some such phrase as, "not to repel force with force, unless it shall be found absolutely necessary, or being thereunto required by the civil magistrate." In 1753, Henry Fox, the current secretary-at-war, included in his orders to officers involved with riots at Leeds the injunction which he was to repeat on other occasions: "I must recommend it to you to take care a civil officer be always present, when the repelling force with force may be necessary, that the proceedings may be legal." In 1765, Viscount Barrington, who was secretary-at-war throughout most of the revolutionary crisis, used the even more restrictive formula, "unless in case of absolute necessity and being thereunto required by the civil magistrate."[38]

Because of these inhibitions, strongly felt by all those involved in military action against riot, the Gordon Riots in London, a few years later, were to rage unrestrained for several days. That situation was very analogous in principle to what might have come about at Boston after October 1768 and again after May 1774, when the unwillingness of army officers to expose themselves by proceeding against disorder without the instructions of magistrates was paralleled by the unwillingness of magistrates to involve themselves in any way.

The basic common assumption, then, on which mid-eighteenth century authorities acted, was that troops supported law and order when called into action by magistrates and under their authority and in accordance with their instructions and that it was dubious if they could act in any circumstances without magisterial sanction. There is no reason to doubt, and at least some indirect evidence for believing, that it was in the light of this assumption that Hillsborough made his decision to send troops to Boston.[39] Once they were there, the men on the spot would presumably use them, but indeed, the very knowledge that this was so would probably contribute to the maintenance of the peace by the mere threat alone.

Bernard's report of the March 1768 riots seems to have been delayed by the need to find a "safe" conveyance, and it was June before the Government in London began to react. These events raised much wider issues than merely the Townshend Act. The British Customs service in North America operated not merely to collect the taxes which Townshend had caused to be laid but also others decreed by other statutes, particularly the Plantation Acts of 1764 and 1766. Furthermore, tax collection was only one of its functions, for it was also responsible for the general enforcement of the trade and navigation acts. The American customs commissioners, apprehensive for the safety of themselves and their families as well as for their freedom to perform their duties, had made application without success to Bernard for support and protection by the civil power. Bernard's letter of 18 March seemed to make it clear that the civil power must be reinforced. Accordingly, on 8 June, Hillsborough sent instructions to General Gage at New York to send one regiment, or such force as he might think necessary, "to give every legal assistance to the civil magistrate in the preservation of the public peace; and to the officers of the revenue in the execution of the laws of trade and revenue."[40] This particular step was, for the time being, abortive, for the dispatch was delayed in transit and did not reach Gage until early September, by which time other action was in train. The following month, Hillsborough also ordered the naval rendezvous on the North American station to be moved from Halifax to Boston, in order "to check further violences, prevent illicit trade," and support the local magistrates and Customs officials.[41]

Bernard's reports of the much more serious riots arising out of the case of the *Liberty* at Boston reached Hillsborough on 16 and 19 July 1768. They threw him into a near panic, made worse three days later when he received the uncompromising Virginia protests against the Townshend Act. On 19 July, he wrote to George III: "I have this moment received the inclosed papers by express from Governor Bernard, and think them of so much consequence that not a moment's time is to be lost in laying them before your Majesty."[42] With the king's agreement, he sought to call the cabinet together for 21 July.[43] Writing again to the king on 22 July, he described the dispatches from Virginia as "still more alarming than those from Massachusetts Bay" and asked for leave to make provisional arrangements for troop transports.[44] A letter from the secretary to the treasury, Thomas Bradshaw, to the premier, the Duke of Grafton, gives the fullest impression of the colonial secretary's state of mind:

> He has received dispatches from Virginia of the most alarming nature, and thinks that colony in a much worse state, than even the colony of Massachusets' Bay, he earnestly wishes for your Grace's return to Town, to take these very serious matters into immediate consideration, as he is of opinion, that parliament should meet, as soon as its forms will allow of it. His Lordship seems really alarmed . . . General Gage cannot send a great force to any part of America, and if that force should meet with a check, it is but too likely that the whole Continent would join in actual opposition to government—the *Council* as well as the Assembly of Virginia, have joined in the most indecent remonstrances against the late Act of Parliament, and they have called on the other colonies to make it a common cause.[45]

Hillsborough's efforts to convene the cabinet at once appear to have been frustrated by Grafton's reluctance to leave the rural pleasures of Euston and Newmarket. Not until 27 and 28 July did the members assemble and endorse his proposals.[46] It seems evident that, in their view, the focus of the whole trouble was Massachusetts, and it was to this province that they bent their chief attention. The Virginia dispatches simply showed the dire consequences that might follow from a failure to take firm measures with regard to Boston. The ministers persisted in believing that the Massachusetts circular letter and manifestations of defiance were merely the actions of a small faction, arguing to this effect from the circumstance that these measures had been "rejected in full house the beginning of the session, and taken up again at the end of it when the house was thin."[47] Moreover, only at Boston had there been a violent challenge to British authority. Ministers evidently thought that, if this form of challenge was not checked, it would spread to an uncontrollable extent. Accordingly, their decision was to provide strong military support for the civil power in Massachusetts, and they went far beyond the steps already taken in this direction by Hillsborough in June, by ordering the immediate dispatch of two regiments from Ireland to Boston.[48] Gage learned of this action only early in September, by which time, in accordance with Hillsborough's letter of 8 June, he had ordered two regiments to move down to Boston from Halifax.[49] It was as a result of these different initiatives that four regiments came to be concentrated there in the autumn of 1768. By that time, both the ministry and Gage saw them as available to deal with either of two situations. The troops could answer a call to back up the civil power in maintaining law and order. Alternatively, they might respond to a rebellion, as both Gage at New York and the ministers in London briefly apprehended when they learned of the Boston town meeting's resolutions of 12 and 13 September. On those days, the town issued a call for an extralegal convention and called on householders to prepare for possible war, as they said, with the French. "Whilst laws are in force," Gage wrote to Hillsborough on 26 September, "I shall pay the obedience that is due to them, and in my military capacity confine myself solely to the granting such aids to the civil power, as shall be required of me; but if open and declared rebellion makes its appearance, I mean to use all the powers lodged in my hands, to make head against it."[50] Early in the following year, the House of Commons recorded its conclusion, that the presence of troops was necessary for the former of these purposes. In the words of its resolution, the situation had become such that "the preservation of the public peace and the due execution of the laws became impracticable without the aid of a military force to support and protect the civil magistrates and the officers of his Majesty's revenue."[51]

As armed rebellion did not rear its head in Massachusetts, the use of the troops depended on a summons from the civil power. None was forthcoming. Bernard and then Hutchinson were powerless to ask for them owing to the refusal of the council to agree to any such move. Without such a sanction, other magistrates would make no appeal for military assistance. Perhaps they would not have done so in any case, for their hearts were with the resistance to Parliament's laws, a fact apparently not yet understood in Whitehall. The British soldiers in Boston remained, kicking their heels inactive and bored and a provocation to the inhabitants, until the last of them were withdrawn after the "Massacre."

The long-term measure for strengthening civil government in Massachusetts which commended itself to Lord Hillsborough was an alteration in the composition of the provincial council. The annual election of the council by the assembly appeared to be the factor which caused it to be overawed and dominated by the popular party in the province, a feature which Bernard had stigmatized as the "cankerworm" of the constitution.[52] Although this project did not mature during the period dealt with in this chapter, a good deal of thought was given to it, colonial agents were aware that it was under consideration, several of the ministers came round to the view that it was desirable. Thus, a brief outline of its history at this stage helps to explain later events.

The prolegomenon was provided by parliamentary debates on the recent events in Massachusetts, based on a comprehensive dossier of papers laid before the two Houses during the weeks before and after Christmas 1768.[53] This material included reports of what were seen as failures of duty by the provincial council, of the riot at Boston on 18 March, and a copy of the evidence given viva voce before the Treasury Board on 21 July by the then newly returned Comptroller of the Customs at Boston, Benjamin Hallowell, detailing injuries he had sustained at the hands of the mob.[54]

On 15 December, Hillsborough moved in the Lords a series of resolutions condemning various votes and proceedings of the Massachusetts Assembly and of the Boston town meeting as illegal, unconstitutional, and subversive, and he put on record the fact that the council and the magistrates of the colony had failed in their duty to preserve law and order and suppress disturbances. Then, in a proposal which pointed particularly at the town meeting resolutions of 12 and 13 September, the Duke of Bedford, probably acting by arrangement with the ministers, moved and secured agreement of the House of Lords to an address to the king requesting that all possible steps should be taken to secure information about the acts of treason or misprision of treason in the colony, with a view to bringing those guilty to Great Britain for trial before a special commission.[55] After Christmas, the Commons gave their concurrence, after still more papers had been laid before them disclosing the attitude of the council and other proceedings following the arrival of the troops at Boston the preceding October. Commons resolutions of 8 February 1769 included one pointing directly at the shortcomings of the council, declaring that "it appears that neither the Council of Massachusetts Bay, nor the ordinary civil magistrates, did exert their authority for suppressing the said riots and tumults."[56]

In raising the question of treason trials, it appears as if the ministers were more concerned with drawing attention to the possibilities, in order to bring Boston radicals to a sense of their wrongdoing, rather than with actually pursuing the course of action foreshadowed in the Commons debates. The agent for Connecticut drew the conclusion that ministers thought it a mere "*brutum fulmen* . . . they hope it will make the people of Boston tremble, and wish it may even strike terror through the continent." And during debate on 8 February, Grey Cooper, the secretary to the treasury, let the cat out of the bag with the observation: "This is no more than a solemn notice and warning to America."[57] However, ministerial opinion was by no means unanimous. Hillsborough and some, at least, of his cabinet colleagues were anxious to do something more positive than merely pass resolutions. His friend Viscount Barrington, the secretary-at-war, commented bitterly after the Lords' approval of the address:

> I wish there were a better prospect of such measures at home as will tend to preserve the obedience of the colonies and such have been proposed: I can moreover assure you that they have been relished by the majority of the cabinet; but by some fatal catastrophe two or three men there, with less ability, less credit, less authority, and less responsibility than the rest, have carry'd their point and produced that flimsy unavailing Address.[58]

After the Commons had accepted the address, he delivered himself more fully of views which, by his account, were not singular to himself:

> [The address] . . . tho' voted by the two Houses, I believe is not approved by five men in either: some thinking it too much and others too little in the present crisis. I am one of those who think the measure futile and in no respect adequate. I am convinced the Town Meeting at Boston which assembled the States of the Province against the King's authority, and armed the People to resist his force, was guilty of high crimes and misdemeanors, if not of Treason; and that Mr. Otis the *Moderator* (as he is improperly called) of that Meeting together with the Selectmen of Boston who signed the Letters convoking the Convention should be impeach'd. This would convey terror to the wicked and factious spirits all over the Continent and would shew that the subjects of Great Britain must not rebel with impunity anywhere. Five or six examples are sufficient; and it is right they should be made in Boston, the only place where there has been actual crime; for as to the opinions almost universally held throughout America, concerning the claim of taxation, I think every man has a right to judge and to speak his judgment concerning laws, tho' he has no right to disobey them.[59]

It was this body of opinion that Hillsborough represented when, on 13 February, immediately after the passage of the address, he brought forward for cabinet discussion, among other less important suggestions, the proposals that the appointment of the Massachusetts Council be vested in the Crown, according to the pattern in other "royal" governments, and that any future denial by the assembly of the principle laid down in the Declaratory Act of 1766 should involve automatic forfeiture of the colony's charter. Broadly speaking, the Bedfordite section of the ministry approved these suggestions, but the Chathamite group demurred. Hillsborough noted especially in a letter to the king two days later: "The Duke of Grafton still entertains doubts with regard to the alteration of the council of Massachusetts Bay, which I am very sorry for as I think it's absolutely necessary to the restoration and establishment of civil government in that province." In a further comment which reflects a general and long-held ministerial misconception of the colonial situation, he continued: "However those disposed to clamour may endeavour to represent that measure, I am almost convinced it will be generally approved at home, and be popular in the colony."[60]

George III took a more cautious view of the situation than his colonial secretary. Almost certainly, conversations with Grafton and Lord Chancellor Camden had given him cause to think hard about the other aspects of the matter before he minuted his comment that "the vesting in the Crown the appointment of the Council of Massachusetts Bay may from a continuance of their conduct become necessary; but till then ought to be avoided as the altering Charters is at all times an odious measure."[61] No minister could carry a proposal against half the cabinet without the strong support of the king, and perhaps not even then, and for the time being Hillsborough had to drop the idea.

But he returned to it in 1770. By this time the composition of the ministry had changed, both Grafton and Camden, the chief opponents of the measure, having resigned, and there had been the further provocation of the Boston "Massacre." The colonial secretary saw this incident as a direct outcome of the weakness in the provincial administration. On 12 June 1770, he wrote to Gage:

> Had the magistrates of Boston, and the principal persons of interest and credit in that place shewn that zeal and good disposition to prevent and appease quarrels between the soldiers and inhabitants, and to discountenance riot and tumult, of which they had so good an example in the case of New York, the unfortunate event of the 5th of March might have been prevented; but what has happened serves to expose the timidity of, and total neglect of duty (not to say worse) in the magistracy, and plainly points out that all measures for the support of the constitutional authority of this kingdom in Massachusetts Bay will be ineffectual and delusive, untill the government of that province, upon just principles of dependency on the Mother Country, can be restored to its proper vigour and activity.[62]

A new and even wider-ranging investigation of affairs in Massachusetts was set on foot in the plantation committee of the Privy Council, as soon as the end of the parliamentary session released the time of ministers for other activities. Documents were assembled and oral evidence taken. The retired governor, Bernard, himself gave verbal testimony, as did various merchants and ships' captains and officers of the Customs service recently returned from Boston. Much of the information clearly pointed to defiance of law and order and to the use of actual violence or threats of violence in the Bay capital against those who tried to maintain the king's peace and uphold the laws.

Benjamin Hallowell, the Comptroller of Customs, gave evidence that when he seized the *Liberty* for smuggling on 10 June 1768, he and his colleagues were subjected to mob violence—"the people abused, beat and wounded him and the collector [Joseph Harrison] very much." Harrison confirmed that he and his son, who was one of his clerks, had been "much abused and wounded," that his pleasure boat had been smashed and burned, and that his home only saved from destruction by the interposition of the landlord. Hallowell deposed also that, after the condemnation of the *Liberty,* the Boston mob had determined at a town meeting that the Customs commissioners, who had taken refuge aboard the warship *Romney,* "should not come on shore again," and afterwards handbills threatening them were posted up in various parts of the town. The magistrates "were acquainted with the riot, but did not exert themselves to quell it," nor did the General Court take any steps to do so. John Robinson, one of the commissioners, gave evidence of a "great tumult" in April 1768 and of a "very great riot" on 10 June and reported that the commissioners moved to Castle William because "they considered their persons in danger of insult and violence, and that their commission might be dishonoured by staying in town." He added, also, that in March 1770, during the days between the "Massacre" on 5 March and his taking ship for England on the sixteenth, "there were a number of men under arms every night . . . under pretence of defending the town from the military." Moreover, Privy Councillors heard that it was not only Customs officials who bore the brunt of popular hostility. Mr. Bridgeham, a merchant, deposed that violence had been committed against people not observing the nonimportation agreement—"such violences have always been perpetrated in the night"—and he knew of no action taken by the magistrates, who "must have known of these disorders." Bernard told the committee that the nonimportation agreements were "intirely done by force, and to this hour intirely effected by having a trained mob—that the mob was disciplined and that the people were obliged to send their goods home," and that the leaders "had created a sort of state inquisition and summon people there for speaking against them."

On 4 July, the investigating committee drew up a sweeping indictment of "lawless" elements in the province, condemning the "seditious and libellous" publications that had appeared at Boston, the violence used against Customs officers, the "illegal" proceedings of the town meeting and the provincial convention, the nonimportation agreements, the declarations and the doctrines promulgated by the assembly, and—once again—the conduct of the council. It noted that "goods lyable to dutys have been forceably landed without payment of those duties; and lawful seizures have been rescued by force of arms, and the officers of the revenue insulted, abused and violently treated, in the execution of their duty." It concluded that "the instructions from the town of Boston to their representatives on the 15th of May 1770, shew an evident disposition to support by force the unconstitutional doctrines, which have been inculcated." In view of the violence that had occurred, the committee proposed that Boston be once again made the headquarters of the North Atlantic squadron instead of Halifax and that armed force should be made available "to defend and support the officers of the revenue in the execution of their duty and the magistrates in the enforcement of the law." Castle William should be made a place of strength as a refuge for royal officials in case of need. Finally, Parliament should be asked to attend to the problem of the "weakness of magistracy and the inefficacy of the law"—a suggestion pointing towards legislation which might involve establishing a nominated council or giving fuller powers of appointment of magistrates to the governor.[63]

In these proceedings can be traced the genesis of the Massachusetts Charter Bill, which was to pass into law some four years later. Such evidence as is available concerning ministerial discussions during the rest of the year—and it rests mainly on the information reported by colonial agents—makes it clear that during the second half of 1770 ministers were busy preparing legislation to strengthen the administration of Massachusetts Bay, and all the reports point towards an intention to remodel the council. William Samuel Johnson, agent for Connecticut, gained a shrewd idea that this was in the wind before the plantation committee had even made its report, merely by inquiring what questions had been asked of some of the witnesses.[64] Lord George Germain, though not then in the secrets of administration, wrote truly when he observed to a friend that the investigations would end "in something more decisive than a spirited letter" and that Hillsborough would "not chuse to be the author of more letters to the colonies to hear them commented upon by Wedderburn and such troublesome critics."[65] Thomas Pownall, at that time a vigorous critic of government policy, gave a much clearer impression of developments in a letter of 14 July 1770 to an American correspondent, James Bowdoin, and as his brother John was one of Hillsborough's undersecretaries, his information perhaps deserves the more credence. He believed that an alteration of the province's charter was intended "to make the Council derive from the nomination of the Crown instead of arising from election." He also reported other plans: "The dividing the legislative from the privy council hath been talked of. The first to be *quamdiu se bene gesserint;* the other to be *durante bene placito.* The giving your governors, etc., independent salaries is, I believe, certainly intended." He also feared that the governor might be deprived of the control of the military in favor of the commander in chief in America—a step, which it can be said with reasonable certainty, the government never had in contemplation, for they took pains to avoid it in the much more tense circumstances of 1774.[66]

On 4 August 1770, Hillsborough wrote to Gage:

> I think I can now confidently assure you, that right principles and purposes with regard to America are adopted by all the king's confidential servants; and I make no doubt that the measures which will be pursued at the opening of the next session of parliament will warrant me in this information.

There can be little doubt that the "right" measures both he and Gage had in mind included the reshaping of the council, and the reference to Parliament is meaningless unless legislation was being planned.[67] The confident spirit of the letter seems to indicate that, in a cabinet in which Grafton and Camden were no longer present to raise objections, Hillsborough felt sure he commanded adequate support to see his proposals carried to completion. By 15 November, the Connecticut agent had news that a bill was in preparation.[68] On 2 January 1771, he explicitly confirmed this information. At the same time, he explained the delay in bringing it forward:

> The Bill . . . has been settled and approved by many principal officers of state; yet so strong have been the applications against it, and such the representations of the injustice and the ill-consequences which would attend it, such is the situation of things, and let me add, to do justice, such is the moderation of *some* of his Majesty's ministers, that I believe that it will go no further at present.[69]

It is difficult to know what weight to attach to Johnson's attribution of "moderation" to some of the ministers, for no direct evidence of it has been found. Four of Hillsborough's six colleagues in the cabinet at this time—Lord North, Lord Rochford, Lord Weymouth, Earl Gower—were to be associated with a firm policy towards the colonies in the years ahead. A fifth, Lord Halifax, seems likely, from his past record at the Board of Trade in the 1750s, to have sympathized with this point of view. The sixth, Sir Edward Hawke at the admiralty, was unlikely to have much weight in questions of this kind.[70] Some elements in the American situation may have led some of the ministers to feel that legislation was now a matter of less urgency. Both the withdrawal of New York from the nonimportation agreement, presaging its ultimate collapse, and the relatively satisfactory outcome of the trials at Boston of the soldiers involved in the "Massacre" may have helped to create a less tense attitude in London. But there can be little doubt that the international diplomatic crisis which broke out over the Falkland Islands in the autumn of 1770 was in itself a sufficient "situation of things" to drive out of ministers' heads any sense of urgency about the affairs of Massachusetts. The secretary-at-war, receiving late in November a plea from Gage for the establishment of a nominated council and royal control over magisterial appointments, replied to him on 3 December: "I cannot tell you whether anything has yet been determined in our cabinet concerning America. Everybody's attention is fixed on our negotiation with Spain; nobody here can tell how it will end."[71]

Although the Falklands' crisis was over by the end of January 1771, the cabinet did not again take up Hillsborough's plans for Massachusetts. Evidence to account for this inaction is lacking, but no doubt it can largely be attributed to the aftermath of distraction about the international situation among the ministers. The agreement between Britain and Spain still had to be implemented, and this was perhaps no time to get embroiled with one of the colonies. The momentum Hillsborough had built up in the previous summer and autumn had been lost. For the time being, he contented himself with one minor measure in support of gubernatorial power. Thomas Hutchinson, Bernard's successor as governor was allotted a salary of

£1,500, and Andrew Oliver, the new lieutenant-governor, one of £300, both chargeable against the proceeds of the American tea duty.

• NOTES •

1. Stat. 8 Geo. III c.22, passed on 8 March 1768 (*Journals of the House of Commons* [London, 1803], vol. 31, p. 661 [hereafter cited as *Commons Journals*]). See also P. D. G. Thomas, "Parliamentary Diaries of Nathaniel Ryder, 1764–67," Royal Historical Society, *Camden Miscellany* 23 (1969), p. 309 (at foot); Carl Ubbelohde, *The Vice Admiralty Courts and the American Revolution* (Chapel Hill: Univ. of North Carolina Press, 1960), esp. pp. 92, 113, 130.

2. W. S. Johnson to W. Pitkin, 20 October 1768, Massachusetts Historical Society, *Collections,* 5th Ser., vol. 9, p. 296.

3. Thomas Whately, *The Regulations lately made concerning the Colonies and the Taxes imposed upon them considered* (London, 1765, n.p.), pp. 65, 69.

4. British Library (formerly British Museum), Additional Manuscripts (Add. MS.) 42086, f. 52.

5. William Cobbett and Thomas C. Hansard, eds., *The Parliamentary History of England . . . to 1803* (36 vols., London: T. C. Hansard, 1806–20), vol. 16, cols. 619–20.

6. *Ibid.,* col. 871.

7. Both houses of Parliament were quick to show their displeasure at attempts to pull the wool over their eyes with nonarguments, as was shown by William Pitt's experience in early 1766 (Ian R. Christie, "William Pitt and American Taxation, 1766: A Problem of Parliamentary Reporting," *Studies in Burke and his Time,* vol. 17, [1976], pp. 167–79, csp. p. 175).

8. British Public Record Office, Colonial Office (C.O.) 5/757.

9. Bernard to Shelburne, 21 November 1767, 21, 30 January 1768, *ibid.*

10. Bernard to Shelburne, 18 February 1768, *ibid.*

11. Cadwallader Colden to Shelburne, 27 November 1767, 21 January 1768, Sir Henry Moore to Shelburne, 20, 26 January, 5 March 1768, C.O. 5/1099.

12. Gage to Shelburne, 23 January 1768, Clarence Edwin Carter, ed., *The Correspondence of General Thomas Gage with the War Office and the Treasury, 1763–1775* (2 vols., New Haven: Yale Univ. Press, 1931–33), vol. 1, p. 161.

13. *Ibid.,* vol. 2, p. 450; acknowledged in Barrington to Gage, 16 April 1768, Gage Manuscripts, W. L. Clements Library.

14. W. S. Johnson to W. Pitkin, 20 October 1768, Massachusetts Historical Society, *Collections,* 5th series, vol. 9, p. 296.

15. Leonard W. Labaree, ed., *The Papers of Benjamin Franklin* (New Haven: Yale Univ. Press, 1959), vol. 16, p. 11. See also Massachusetts Historical Society, *Collections,* 5th Series, vol. 9, p. 318.

16. W. Knox to Grenville, William J. Smith, ed., *The Grenville Papers* (4 vols., London: J. Murray, 1852–53), vol. 4, pp. 400–401. See also Charles Garth to the South Carolina Committee of Correspondence, 10 December 1768, *South Carolina Historical and Genealogical Magazine* 30 (1929), p. 234; W. S. Johnson to W. Pitkin, 3 January 1769, Massachusetts Historical Society, *Collections,* 5th Series, vol. 9, pp. 304–5.

17. *Ibid.;* Cobbett and Hansard, *Parliamentary History,* vol. 16, col. 477 (n.).

18. Sir John Fortescue, ed., *The Correspondence of King George III* . . . (6 vols., London: Macmillan, 1927–28), vol. 2, pp. 83–84.

19. *Ibid.,* p. 85.

20. Albert Matthews, ed., "Letters of Dennys DeBerdt, 1757–1770," Colonial Society of Massachusetts, *Publications,* vol. 13, *Transactions,* 1910–11, p. 367.

21. Massachusetts Historical Society, *Collections,* 5th series, vol. 9, p. 324. See also B. Franklin to N. W. Jones, 3 April 1769, Labaree, *Papers of Benjamin Franklin,* vol. 16, p. 79.

22. B. Franklin to J. Galloway, 29 January 1769, *ibid.,* p. 30; Dennys DeBerdt to Thomas Cushing, 1 February 1769, to Richard Cary, 2 February 1769, to the Delaware Committee, 2 February 1769, Matthews, "Letters of Dennys DeBerdt," pp. 355–56, 357–58, 359.

23. Cabinet minute, 1 May 1769, Grafton Manuscripts, printed in Sir William R. Anson, ed., *Autobiography and political correspondence of Augustus Henry, third Duke of Grafton* (London: J. Murray, 1898), p. 232.

24. *Ibid.,* pp. 229–30.

25. Cobbett and Hansard, *Parliamentary History,* vol. 16, col. 854.

26. For a copy of the circular letter, see Anson, *Autobiography of Grafton,* p. 233.

27. Cobbett and Hansard, *Parliamentary History,* vol. 16, col. 853.

28. Massachusetts Historical Society, *Collections,* 5th series, vol. 9, pp. 383–84.

29. Cobbett and Hansard, *Parliamentary History,* vol. 16, col. 855.

30. Bernard to Shelburne, 22 December 1766, C.O. 5/892, printed in Merrill Jensen, ed., *English Historical Documents,* volume 9, *American Colonial Documents to 1776* (London: Eyre & Spottiswarde, 1969), pp. 732–36.

31. Bernard to Shelburne, 14, 21 November 1767, 21, 30 January 1768, 18, 20 February 1768, C.O. 5/757.

32. Bernard to Shelburne, 5 March 1768, *ibid.*

33. Bernard to Hillsborough, 19 March 1768, *ibid.,* printed in Jensen, *American Colonial Documents,* pp. 736–39.

34. Circular letter to colonial governors, 21 April 1768, *ibid.,* pp. 716–17.

35. For background to the following discussion see M. A. Thomson, *A Constitutional History of England, 1642–1801* (London: Methuen & Co., 1938), pp. 425–27; E. N. Williams, *The Eighteenth Century Constitution, 1688–1815* (Cambridge: Cambridge Univ. Press, 1960), pp. 408–10.

36. This legal position of the soldier was not clearly and authoritatively restated until 1780, well after the American crisis, and on the occasion of the Gordon Riots, when it was spelled out by Lord Chief Justice Mansfield in debate in the House of Lords (see *ibid.,* pp. 417–20).

37. A. J. Hayter, "The Army and the Mob in England in the generation before the Gordon Riots" (Ph.D. diss., Univ. of London, 1973), pp. 13–18, 45–47; and *The Army and the Crowd in mid-Georgian England* (London: Macmillan, 1978), pp. 9–15.

38. Compare Hayter, *The Army and the Crowd,* pp. 28–34; "The Army and the Mob," pp. 16–17. I am grateful to Dr. Hayter for leave to quote these passages. The whole tenor of his thesis suggests that the inhibitions on the use of violence by troops against civilians anywhere in the king's dominions were stronger than is indicated in John Shy, *Toward Lexington: The Role of the British Army in the Coming of the American Revolution* (Princeton, N.J.: Princeton Univ. Press, 1965), p. 394.

39. See the reference at notes 40 and 50 below. The most striking evidence is the secre-

tary-at-war's description of the similar situation in the autumn of 1774 (Barrington to Dartmouth, 12 November 1774, in Shute Barrington, *The Political Life of William Wildman, Viscount Barrington* [London: W. Bulmer & Co., 1814], p. 140).

40. Carter, *Correspondence of Gage*, vol. 2, pp. 68–69.

41. Hillsborough to the Admiralty, 7 July 1768, British Public Record Office, Admiralty Papers, 1/4128.

42. Fortesque, *Correspondence of George III*, vol. 2, no. 637.

43. To Lord Gower, 19 July 1968, Granville Manuscripts, British Public Record Office, 30/29/7/2, fols. 104–5.

44. Fortesque, *Correspondence of George III*, vol. 2, no. 638.

45. 22 July 1768, Grafton MSS.

46. Smith, *The Grenville Papers*, vol. 4, pp. 320, 321–22; Add. MS. 35374, fols. 352–53.

47. Dennys DeBerdt to Thomas Cushing, London, 29 July 1768, Matthews, "Letters of Dennys DeBerdt," p. 336.

48. Carter, *Correspondence of Gage*, vol. 2, pp. 72–73.

49. *Ibid.*, vol. 1, pp. 191, 195.

50. *Ibid.*, p. 196.

51. *Commons Journals*, vol. 32, p. 186.

52. See note 32.

53. For the papers laid before Christmas see *Commons Journals*, vol. 32, pp. 74–76, and for the later submission, pp. 123–24.

54. *Ibid.*, 74–76. The nature of Hallowell's evidence can be inferred from his later testimony before the plantation committee of the privy council (*Acts of the Privy Council, Colonial Series*, vol. 5, pp. 249–50).

55. Cobbett and Hansard, *Parliamentary History*, vol. 16, cols. 476–80.

56. *Ibid.*, cols. 484–511; J. Wright, ed., *Sir Henry Cavendish's Debates of the House of Commons During the Thirteenth Parliament of Great Britain* (2 vols., London: Longmans, 1841–43), vol. 1, pp. 185–225; *Commons Journals*, vol. 32, p. 186.

57. Massachusetts Historical Society, *Collections*, 5th series, vol. 9, p. 317; Wright, *Sir Henry Cavendish's Debates*, vol. 1, p. 209.

58. Edward Channing and Archibald Cary Coolidge, eds., *The Barrington-Bernard Correspondence and Illustrative Matter, 1760–1770* (Cambridge, Mass.: Harvard Univ. Press, 1912), p. 182.

59. *Ibid.*, p. 184.

60. Fortesque, *Correspondence of George III*, vol. 2, no. 701 and enclosure.

61. *Ibid.*, no. 701A.

62. Carter, *Correspondence of Gage*, vol. 2, p. 103.

63. On this inquiry see K. G. Davies, ed., *Documents of the American Revolution, 1770–1783 (Colonial Office Series)*, (Shannon: Irish Univ. Press, 1971), vol. 2, pp. 110–28; *Acts of the Privy Council (Colonial Series)*, vol. 5, pp. 246–64; Massachusetts Historical Society, *Collections*, 5th series, vol. 9, pp. 442–43.

64. *Ibid.*

65. Germain to General Irwin, 30 June 1770, Historical Manuscripts Commission, *Report on the Manuscripts of Mrs. Stopford Sackville, of Drayton House, Northamptonshire*, (2 vols., London: Mackie & Co., 1904–10), vol. 1, pp. 130–31.

66. Massachusetts Historical Society, *Collections*, 5th ser., vol. 9, pp. 196–99.

67. Carter, *Correspondence of Gage*, vol. 2, pp. 112–13. Confirmation of Gage's be-

lief that the alteration of the council was necessary is to be found, for instance, in his letter to Barrington of 8 September 1770, *ibid.,* pp. 556–57.

68. Massachusetts Historical Society, *Collections,* 5th ser., vol. 9, p. 466.

69. *Ibid.,* p. 471.

70. During most of 1770 the Great Seal was in commission, and in the absence of a Lord Chancellor, there were only seven members of the cabinet.

71. Gage MSS., W. L. Clements Library.

Sullen Silence or Prelude to Resistance: Background to the Continental Association, 1771 to May 1774

Introduction to Chapter 6

DAVID J. TOSCANO

Almost six years of continuous agitation gave way to a period of relative calm following the repeal of all major provisions of the Townshend Acts, excluding the duty on tea, in April 1770. The agitation and extralegal action which had characterized resistance to the Stamp Act and Townshend duties greatly subsided. Some may even have suspected that the colonies had finally accepted the supremacy of Great Britain in North America. Yet many colonial leaders, such as Samuel Adams, saw the apparent tranquility in another light. Adams labeled the calm as a "sullen silence" and suggested that anyone who viewed the lack of continual colonial agitation as a ratification of British policies was sadly mistaken.[1]

In fact, colonial America was still beset with numerous problems. Some of these were domestic in origin while others arose as the result of British actions. The colonial response to these issues, while not as dramatic as in previous campaigns, was nevertheless significant in that it helped prepare the way, both politically and emotionally, for the final crisis with Great Britain in 1774 and 1775.

During this period, resistance forces strengthened themselves whenever possible. Disputes which arose between colonial assemblies and royal governors prompted legal and extralegal actions by colonists in support of their self-proclaimed rights.[2] Leaders who had arisen during the previous campaigns did their best to keep issues alive and emphasized British oppression of the colonies.[3]

The most significant development of the period involved the formation of the committees of correspondence in late 1772 and early 1773. Organization of the committees was the result of two New England developments: (1) the British response to the burning of the *Gaspée,* an armed schooner in the British Customs service, off the coast of Rhode Island in June 1772; and (2) the controversy in the summer and fall of 1772 over whether Massachusetts Superior Court justices should be paid by the Crown from revenue raised by Customs.

In March 1772, the schooner *Gaspée* began patrolling the waters off Rhode Island, ostensibly in search of American smugglers. Rhode Islanders felt no love for the British navy, and there had been frequent clashes between the two parties in the years prior to the arrival of the *Gaspée*. On 9 June, while pursuing an American vessel, the *Hannah*, the *Gaspée* ran aground near Providence. An unidentified group of over one hundred men boarded the vessel on the following night, burned it, and seriously wounded its commander. Admiral John Montagu, commander of the British fleet in North American waters, immediately reported the incident to British officials in London. The king responded in September 1772 by appointing a Commission of Inquiry to investigate the affair. This group, which included the chief justices of New York, New Jersey, and Massachusetts, the judge of the New England Admiralty District, and Governor Joseph Wanton of Rhode Island, was authorized to investigate the affair and provide evidence to local authorities, who would make the proper arrests. The accused would then be shipped to England for trial.[4]

As Rhode Islanders speculated about the consequences of the *Gaspée* incident, Massachusetts residents were confronted with a problem of their own. The British government, in July 1772, issued an order that salaries of Massachusetts Superior Court judges, heretofore paid by the province, should now be distributed by the Crown from collected Customs duties. From Great Britain's viewpoint, this new order would free the judges from popular influence and thereby render them "independent." People in Massachusetts, however, saw the Crown action differently. Prior to this order, the Massachusetts House of Representatives had been able to influence the judges through the practice of voting their salaries for only one year at a time. Consequently, the Crown action was perceived as another attempt to take power from the colonists and further centralize it in the British government.

When Bostonians heard of the order, the town meeting of 28 October 1772 chose a group, headed by Samuel Adams, to approach Governor Thomas Hutchinson for confirmation of the alarming reports. Hutchinson, however, refused to respond. The town then requested the governor to convene the assembly in order that "the Joint Wisdom of the Province may be employed." Hutchinson refused the petition and rebuked the town meeting for suggesting that the assembly be called. This response was read to the town meeting of 2 November 1772, whereupon Samuel Adams proposed formation of committees of correspondence

> to state the Rights of the Colonists and of this Province in particular . . . to communicate and publish the same to the several Towns in this Province and to the World as the sense of this Town, with the Infringements and violations thereof that have been or from time to time may be made; also requesting of each Town a free Communication of their Sentiments.[5]

Headed by James Otis, Samuel Adams, and Joseph Warren, the Boston Committee of Correspondence submitted a statement to the town meeting of 20 November alleging parliamentary and Crown infringement upon colonial rights and privileges. This statement included a protest of the recent Crown decision concerning payment of judges' salaries and a proposed circular letter to be sent throughout the province.[6]

Upon ratification by the three hundred present, the statement and accompanying letter were sent to towns throughout Massachusetts and to the other colonies. While some towns in Massachusetts at first opposed the Boston committee's initiatives, they gradually came to support the resolutions and appointed committees of their own.[7] The Boston committee did not issue a call for the establishment of intercolonial committees of correspondence; this development arose as a result of action by the Virginia House of Burgesses four months later.

During January 1773, events in both Massachusetts and Rhode Island took on crucial significance. In the Bay Colony, Governor Hutchinson felt compelled to attack the newly formed committees and to reassert parliamentary supremacy over the colonies. At first, Hutchinson saw little danger in the formation of the Boston committee. The governor quickly changed his mind as towns in Massachusetts joined Boston in a network of correspondence. In a later assessment of committee organization, Hutchinson stated:

> Thus, all on a sudden, from a state of peace, order, and general contentment, as some expressed themselves, the province, more or less from one end to the other, was brought into a state of contention, disorder and general dissatisfaction; or, as others would have it, were aroused from stupor and inaction to sensibility and activity.[8]

Worried by this development, Hutchinson attempted to reassert parliamentary supremacy in his speech to the opening session of the Massachusetts House of Representatives in January 1773. Branding the recent resolutions of the Massachusetts town meetings and committees of correspondence as "repugnant to the principles of the constitution," Hutchinson insisted that Parliament had the right to legislate for the colonies in all respects. The governor said that he knew "of no line that can be drawn between the supreme authority of Parliament and the total independence of the colonies: it is impossible there should be two independent legislatures in one and the same state."[9] The provincial council and House of Representatives, however, did not agree. These bodies stated that Parliament had no authority to tax the people without their consent given directly or by their representatives. Hutchinson's speech served only to further arouse the populace in opposition to British colonial policy and to increase the popularity of the committees of correspondence throughout the province.[10]

As Hutchinson confronted provincial organization in the committees, the Crown-appointed commission to investigate the *Gaspée* incident commenced its meetings in Rhode Island. In December of 1772, news of the king's decision to appoint this Commission of Inquiry reached New England. As its hearings commenced in January, reports circulated throughout the colonies concerning its task. The colonies had faced a similar threat in 1769, when Parliament proposed bringing Americans accused of treason to England for trial. At that time, colonial legislatures united in protest of the resolution. News of the *Gaspée* inquiry triggered a similar response. Colonial newspapers quickly labeled the commission a "court of inquisition," which was "repugnant to every dictate of reason, liberty and justice."[11]

The Virginia House of Burgesses, as they had done in 1769, again took the lead in uniting colonial opposition to British policy. On 12 March 1773, at the instigation of many of its younger members, the Burgesses appointed

> a standing Committee of Correspondence . . . whose business it shall be to obtain the most early and Authentic intelligence of all such Acts and Resolutions of the British Parliament, or proceedings of Administration, as may relate to or Affect the British colonies in America, and to keep up and maintain a Correspondence and Communication with our sister Colonies, respecting these important Considerations.[12]

This committee of eleven, which included Richard Henry Lee, Thomas Jefferson, Patrick Henry, and the Speaker of the House, Peyton Randolph, immediately transmitted copies of their proceedings to other colonial assemblies, with the request that they appoint similar committees. The Virginia resolutions were received favorably throughout the colonies, as colonial assemblies adopted the "plan of union proposed by the patriotic House of Burgesses." By the end of the year, nine assemblies had appointed committees and two others followed in early 1774.

The Rhode Island legislature was the first province to act, appointing a committee on 7 May 1773. The assemblies of Connecticut (21 May), New Hampshire (27 May), and Massachusetts (28 May) followed suit. Other legislatures which established committees in 1773 included South Carolina (8 July), Georgia (10 September), Maryland (15 October), Delaware (23 October), and North Carolina (8 December). New York appointed a committee on 20 January 1774 and the New Jersey legislature acted similarly on 8 February. The only province which refused to appoint a committee was Pennsylvania, primarily due to the influence of the Speaker of the House, Joseph Galloway.[13] Eventually, Pennsylvania joined the other colonies, by establishing a committee, but not at the initiation of the assembly. Instead, this action was taken by a mass meeting in Philadelphia called to consider the Boston Port Bill, in June 1774.

During the summer and fall of 1773, little action was taken by the committees of correspondence at the intercolonial level. In Massachusetts, the Boston Committee of Correspondence had been able to involve the town in various protests against British policies and had led the fight to unseat Governor Thomas Hutchinson and Lieutenant-Governor Andrew Oliver in the summer and fall of 1773.[14] The provincial committee, however, maintained a low profile. Nevertheless, the relative inactivity of the provincial bodies should not obscure the numerous positive functions of the intercolonial committees. Within these organizations constitutional issues were raised, discussed, and disseminated—an important development at a time when the colonies were developing a common basis of opposition to Great Britain. In addition, the creation of the committees enhanced the possibility, realized in two cases in 1774, that colonial bodies would continue resistance to policies in the event of prorogation of the assemblies by royal governors.[15] Finally, and perhaps most importantly, the legislative committees of correspondence were seen as symbols of unity; they were viewed as instruments by which liberty could be defended from British encroachments.

Colonial claims, made at the time of the formation of the committees, that they would oppose British interference of any kind in the future were put to the test with the passage of the Tea Act by Parliament in May 1773. Adoption of the law was precipitated by the disastrous financial condition of the East India Company at the time. By the end of 1772, reduction of tea consumption in America, as a result of previous nonimportation agreements and the company's expenses in supporting troops in India, had left the corporation on the verge of bankruptcy. Company directors appealed to the government for help. In early March 1773, they requested a loan of £1,400,000. The company was granted the loan but was forced in return to accept the Regulating Act of June 1773, which gave the government more control over the corporation's operations, especially in India. In the midst of the debate over the Regulating Act, Parliament passed another measure designed to help the corporation. On 10 May 1773, Parliament approved the Tea Act. This action had a dual purpose. It was designed both to help the East India Company sell its surplus tea stock, which approached 17 million pounds at the time, and to enforce the collection of a parliamentary tax in America. Import duties collected in Britain under the act would be repaid to the East India Company for all tea reshipped to America, as was the usual procedure. But the Tea Act included a major innovation which startled colonists. The new law allowed the East India Company, which had previously been required by law to sell tea bound for America at public auction, to export the commodity and establish branch offices for its sale within the colonies. By selling the tea directly to consumers through its appointed agents, the company could eliminate the middlemen, making the product cheap enough to compete with smuggled Dutch tea.[16]

The first news of the The Tea Act produced little reaction when it arrived in the fall of 1773. This was probably due to the belief by many that the new act repealed the Townshend Act duty on tea.[17] American newspapers had predicted the repeal of the tea duty as early as 1770, and by 1773 they were sure of it.[18] When this hope proved unfounded, there followed a sharp attack on the Tea Act and the company's plans to sell tea directly to the colonists. Arthur Lee, writing from London, described the new act as a "ministerial trick" of Lord North, who probably wanted to create violence to justify repressive measures intended to coerce the colonists.[19] Many Americans felt that the act was but another means by which Parliament attempted to assert its supremacy over the colonies.

The measure was also attacked by people who feared that East India Company would be able to establish a monopoly in the colonial tea market. If a monopoly could be established in tea, these people reasoned, it could be established in other commodities as well.[20] People who maintained this view ranged from smugglers to law-abiding merchants and workingmen in the cities. John Hancock wrote of the act that "we soon should have found our trade in the hands of foreigners [i.e., Englishmen]."[21] Similarly, "A Mechanic" suggested that the East India Company would soon "send their own factors and Creatures. . . . and undersell our Merchants, till they monopolize the whole Trade."[22]

Resistance to the Tea Act was focused in two areas. Colonial leaders attempted first to secure resignations from the appointed tea agents. In addition, shippers were asked to return unlanded cargos of tea to England. The city of Philadelphia took the first action aimed at nullification of the act. On 16 October 1773, a mass meeting adopted a set of eight resolutions branding the tea duty as taxation without consent. The resolutions further denounced anyone who directly or indirectly countenanced the East India Company efforts to enforce "this Ministerial Plan" as "an Enemy to his Country." Finally, the meeting appointed a committee to visit and secure the resignations of the tea consignees.[23] All of the agents acquiesed by time the tea ship *Polly* reached the city in late December.[24] Within a week of the Philadelphia resolutions, similar actions began in Massachusetts. On 21 October, the Massachusetts intercolonial committee of correspondence suggested to other colonies that East India Company tea be prevented from landing in America. Two days later, a group of Bostonians calling themselves the North End Caucus met and resolved to "oppose the vending of any tea, sent by the East India Company, . . . with our lives and fortunes."[25] The caucus, composed of many of the leaders of the Boston Committee of Correspondence, restated earlier demands made by local newspapers that the tea agents, who included the two sons of Governor Hutchinson, resign their commissions. On 3 November, a group of men headed by William Molineaux visited a meeting of tea agents, but were unable to force the consignees to resign.

The Boston town meeting was the next group which attempted to secure the resignations of the agents. Meeting on 5 November, the town adopted the Philadelphia resolutions and appointed a committee, headed by John Hancock, to visit the consignees and request their resignations. This proved fruitless, whereupon the town commissioned a second committee, headed by Hancock and Samuel Adams, to visit the Hutchinsons at Milton. Again, the town failed to obtain the resignations. By 18 November, news had circulated that the tea was on its way. On this date, the town met again, but the answer from the agents remained a firm "NO."

Since the agents had made clear their intentions not to resign, the only alternative available to those who wished to nullify the Tea Act was to block all attempts to land the tea. Consequently, the committees of correspondence of Boston, Roxbury, Brookline, Dorchester, and Cambridge met on 22 November and agreed to prevent the landing of the tea. The *Dartmouth,* first of the tea ships to reach America, arrived in Boston on 27 November. The Boston Committee of Correspondence met the next day, and on 29 November, handbills appeared which called for a mass meeting to prevent the landing of the tea. Meanwhile, the tea consignees, having heard of the arrival of the *Dartmouth,* fled along with four Customs commissioners to the protection of British troops stationed at Castle William. Mass meetings held in Boston on 29–30 November resolved that the tea must be returned to London without payment of duty and chose a group of twenty-five men to guard the *Dartmouth* and its cargo.

Tension mounted with each succeeding day. Under British law, goods became subject to seizure by the Customs service if the duty upon them was not paid within twenty-days of ship's docking. The waiting period was due to expire on 16 December. Hutchinson refused to issue papers which would allow the ship to leave Boston, and a report had circulated that tea on the *Dartmouth* and the other ships which had arrived in the interim was about to be taken to Castle William under protection of the British navy. It was feared that the consignees might then pay the duty and market the tea in secret. Consequently, on the night of 16 December 1773 a group of men disguised as Indians boarded the three ships, broke open the tea chests, and to the delight of a crowd of about one thousand watching from the wharf, emptied their contents into the bay. The group was orderly. No one plundered or injured the rest of the cargo on any of the ships.[26]

In two other port cities, Charleston and New York, colonial leaders were successful in securing the resignations of tea consignees. A committee appointed by a meeting of the "inhabitants" of New York on 24 November 1773 met with tea agents and obtained their agreement not to sell duties tea. Five days later, a mass meeting in the city adopted "The Association of the Sons of Liberty," an agreement signed in anticipation of the arrival of a tea ship. This document denounced all persons who should aid in the landing or distribution of the expected tea. A boycott was ordered against all offenders. The Association was signed by a great number of inhabitants, including "most of the principle lawyers, merchants, landholders, master of ships, and mechanics."[27] Upon receiving the news that Boston and Philadelphia had decided to return the tea when it arrived, two thousand New Yorkers met, voted approval of the Association, and resolved to prevent landing of the tea. They also agreed that a committee of correspondence be appointed to communicate with the other colonies.

In Charleston, as in the other major parts, plans to nullify the Tea Act centered around attempts to secure resignations of tea agents and refusals to land the tea. On 2 December 1773, the tea ship *London* arrived in the port. The next day, a meeting composed primarily of mechanics in the town voted that the tea agents should resign and framed an agreement designed to enlist the support of the merchants in a covenant pledging nonimportation of duties tea. The merchants, however, refused to subscribe to the document. A general meeting of the town was held on 17 December, but the townspeople were unable to arrange a nonimportation agreement. They did, however, resolve that the tea ought not to be landed or sold. Unlike Boston, the Charleston meetings were unable to organize a plan to prevent landing of the tea. Consequently, when the twenty days waiting period for payment of duties on the Charleston cargo expired on 22 December, Governor William Bull ordered the tea seized for nonpayment of duties. The tea was landed without incident, and stored in a government warehouse. It remained there for three years, when it was auctioned off for the benefit of the new revolutionary state of South Carolina.

By the time Charleston had landed the tea, news of the Boston Tea Party had spread throughout New England and to New York and Philadelphia. Tea agents at Philadelphia had resigned before the tea ship *Polly* reached the port on 26 December. Nevertheless, the town was determined to prevent the tea from landing. A mass meeting held on the next day commended Boston for not allowing the tea to be landed there and demanded that the tea ship return to London unloaded. On 28

December, the *Polly,* with a load of 696 chests of tea, began her return to England.

In New York, tea agents wrote Captain Lockyer, master of the tea ship headed for New York, informing him that they could neither receive the tea nor pay the duty on it. Their letter, dated 27 December, further advised the captain to return to sea "for the safety of your cargo, your vessel, and your person."[28] Governor William Tryon, who had felt prior to the Tea Party that tea could be landed in New York without opposition, now wrote to the Earl of Dartmouth that this could only be accomplished "under the Protection of the Point of the Bayonet and Muzzle of the Cannon, and even then I do not see how the Sales or Consumption could be effected."[29] Lockyer and his tea ship *Nancy* did not arrive in New York until April of the following year, but after meeting with a committee of the town, the captain decided to sail back to London with the unlanded tea. Another tea ship, the *London,* which also arrived in New York in April, was not as lucky. Although the vessel was not commissioned by the East India Company, its cargo nonetheless contained tea. The captain of the ship attempted in vain to conceal this fact. When this was discovered, a crowd of "Mohawks" boarded the vessel and destroyed the tea.

By the end of 1773, the Tea Act had been effectively nullified. The East India Company "found that at Boston it still had agents but no tea, at Charleston, tea (held by the customs officers) but no agents, and at Philadelphia and New York neither agents nor tea."[30] In Massachusetts, colonial leaders went one step beyond destruction of tea; they attempted to organize the boycott of all teas, whether dutied or smuggled. Boston tea dealers agreed to suspend the sale of all teas after 20 January 1774. Several other Massachusetts towns soon joined the Boston plan and by April 1774, at least forty towns had organized boycotts of dutied tea.[31] Most of these boycotts included threats of sanctions to be taken against offenders.

News of the Boston Tea Party reached London on 19 January 1774. By the end of the month, the cabinet began the deliberations which led to the Coercive Acts of 1774. At their session of 29 January, the cabinet resolved that "in consequence of the present disorders in America, effectual steps . . . be taken to secure the Dependance of the Colonies on the Mother Country."[32] Whatever their decision, it was clear that England did not look favorably upon the actions of the "Mohawks" in Boston harbor. Benjamin Franklin, writing from London in early 1774, expressed concern over the "Necessity for carrying Matters to such Extremity" and reported: "I suppose we never had since we were a people, so few friends in Britain. The violent destruction of the tea seems to have united all parties here against us."[33]

As political England debated a response to the Tea Party, activity in the colonies quieted. The Tea Act had been nullified and, outside of Boston, political agitation subsided. In early 1774, few Americans realized that Britain would retaliate so drastically against the "present Disorders." Nor did they realize that these severe measures, labeled by the colonists as the Coercive Acts, would begin the final stage in the movement for American independence.

• NOTES •

1. Pauline Maier, *From Resistance to Revolution* (New York: Knopf, 1972), pp. 220–21, gives one view of this period.

2. A number of these disputes are described in John Miller, *Origins of the American Revolution* (Boston: Little, Brown, 1942), pp. 315–23; Merrill Jensen, *The Founding of a Nation* (New York: Oxford Univ. Press, 1968), pp. 373–433; and Lawrence Henry Gipson, *The Coming of the Revolution, 1763–1775* (New York: Harper and Row, 1954), pp. 206–14. Bernhard Knollenberg, *The Growth of the American Revolution, 1766–1775* (New York: Free Press, 1975), pp. 82, 342, provides other detailed sources for these accounts.

3. Bostonians such as Samuel Adams and Joseph Warren, for example, took the occasion of the anniversary of the Boston Massacre to deliver ringing speeches which decried British infringement of colonial rights.

4 A more detailed account is in Knollenberg, *Growth of the American Revolution,* pp. 82–87.

5. "Boston Committee of Correspondence Papers," vol. 1, p. 1; *Boston Town Records 1770–1777,* pp. 92–93; quoted in Arthur M. Schlesinger, *Colonial Merchants and the American Revolution, 1763–1776* (New York: Atheneum, 1968), p. 257. The first committee was headed by James Otis, Joseph Warren, and Samuel Adams.

6. Both the circular letter and the statement by the committee are found in Merrill Jensen, ed., *Tracts of the American Revolution, 1763–1776* (Indianapolis, Ind.: Bobbs-Merrill, 1967), pp. 233–55.

7. Knollenberg, *Growth of the American Revolution,* p. 88, writes that "over a hundred towns, including nearly all of those in the vicinity of Boston, responded favorably."

8. Thomas Hutchinson, *History of Massachusetts Bay Colony* (London: John Murray, 1828), vol. 3, p. 370n; also Schlesinger, *Colonial Merchants,* p. 260.

9. Alden Bradford, ed., *Speeches of the Governors of Massachusetts, 1765–1775; and Answers of the House of Representatives to the Same* (Boston: Russell and Gardner, 1818), pp. 336–42; quoted in Jensen, *Founding of a Nation,* p. 418.

10. For more information on the development of committees of correspondence throughout Massachusetts, see Richard D. Brown, *Revolutionary Politics in Massachusetts: The Boston Committee of Correspondence and the Towns, 1772–1774* (Cambridge, Mass.: Harvard Univ. Press, 1970).

11. *Providence Gazette,* 19 and 26 December 1773; quoted in Jensen, *Founding of a Nation,* p. 428.

12. John P. Kennedy, ed., *Journals of the House of Burgesses of Virginia, 1773–1776* (Williamsburg, Va.: Univ. Press of Virginia, 1905–1907), p. 38.

13. The statements by colonial legislatures in support of the Virginia proposal for intercolonial committees of correspondence are found in *ibid.,* pp. 48–64, 143–45. A summarized· account is found in E. D. Collins, "Committees of Correspondence of the American Revolution," American Historical Association, *Annual Report* 1 (1901), pp. 251–71.

14. In June 1773, confidential letters written by Hutchinson and Oliver to Thomas Whately, former British secretary of the treasury from 1767 to 1769, were published by Massachusetts newspapers. The letters referred to leaders of the Boston town meeting as "Ignorant," described members of the Massachusetts Convention of 1768 as "ridiculous," and suggested that Parliament punish protesters of British policy.

15. Collins, "Committees of Correspondence," p. 254, writes that in 1774, the North

Carolina and New Hampshire committees called representatives of the assemblies together after prorogation. See Chapter Six in this volume for more details.

16. Jensen, *Founding of a Nation*, p. 436; Schlesinger, *Colonial Merchants*, p. 264.

17. Knollenberg, *Growth of the American Revolution*, p. 95; Gipson, *Coming of the Revolution*, p. 218.

18. Jensen, *Founding of a Nation*, p. 438.

19. Arthur Lee to Samuel Adams, 22 December 1773; *Samuel Adams Papers*, New York Public Library; quoted in Jensen, *Founding of a Nation*, p. 438.

20. Schlesinger, *Colonial Merchants*, pp. 264–76, describes the monopoly argument.

21. Hezekiah Niles, ed., *Principles and Acts of the Revolution in America* (New York: Barnes, 1876); quoted in Miller, *Origins of the American Revolution*, p. 342.

22. *Pennsylvania Gazette*, 8 December 1773; quoted in Arthur M. Schlesinger, *Prelude to Independence: The Newspaper War on Britain, 1764–1776* (New York: Knopf, 1958), p. 171.

23. *Pennsylvania Gazette*, 20 October 1773; quoted in Gipson, *Coming of the Revolution*, p. 219; Schlesinger, *Colonial Merchants*, p. 281.

24. Benjamin W. Labaree, *The Boston Tea Party* (New York: Oxford Univ. Press, 1964), pp. 98–102, 288–89.

25. Elbridge H. Goss, *The Life of Colonel Paul Revere* (Boston: Joseph George Cupples, 1891), vol. 1, p. 641; quoted in Knollenberg, *Growth of the American Revolution*, p. 96.

26. *Ibid.*, p. 100. For more information on the Tea Party, see Francis Drake, *Tea Leaves: Being a Collection of Letters and Documents Relating to the Shipment of Tea to the American Colonies in the Year 1773, by the East India Company* (Detroit: Singing Tree, 1970 reproduction of 1884 ed.).

27. Schlesinger, *Colonial Merchants*, p. 292.

28. Drake, *Tea Leaves*, pp. 358–59.

29. Tryon to Dartmouth, 3 January 1774, "The Letters and Papers of Cadwallader Colden," New York Historical Society, *Collections*, vol. 7, p. 200; quoted in Gipson, *Coming of the Revolution*, p. 221.

30. Knollenberg, *Growth of the American Revolution*, p. 102.

31. Details may be found in Schlesinger, *Colonial Merchants*, pp. 300–302; Brown, *Revolutionary Politics*, pp. 168–69.

32. The Manuscripts of the Earl of Dartmouth, vol. 2, Historical Manuscripts Commission, 11th Rep., p. 799; quoted in Knollenberg, *Growth of the American Revolution*, p. 103.

33. Letter of 2 February 1774, Franklin to Thomas Cushing, 22 March 1774, in Albert Henry Smyth, ed., *The Life and Writings of Benjamin Franklin*, (10 vols., New York: Mac-Millan, 1905–1907) vol. 6, pp. 178–80, 221.

·6·

The Continental Association: Economic Resistance and Government by Committee

DAVID L. AMMERMAN

Brit5 ritish response to the news of the Boston Tea Party, when it arrived in early May 1774, was so harsh as to surprise even those who had condemned the destruction of the tea. The Boston Port Act, first of the so-called Coercive Acts adopted by Parliament in answer to the Tea Party, arrived in Boston along with the newly appointed governor of Massachusetts Bay, General Thomas Gage. The act closed the city's harbor with a blockade to go into effect on 1 June and forbade the export of goods to any foreign port "or any province or place whatever."[1] Boston could ship no products out of the harbor and could import only provisions for the king's troops and such fuel and victuals necessary to sustain the inhabitants, as might be carried by vessels trading along the coast. Parliament had decreed that the harbor should remain closed until the king decided that the colony was prepared to obey the law and that British trade could once again enter the port safely. However, not even the king could relieve the city until full satisfaction had been made "by or on behalf of the inhabitants" of Boston to the East India Company for the destroyed tea.

Americans were even more angered by the terms of a second law, the Massachusetts Government Act, because it ordered permanent changes in the government and thus attacked the colonial political structure.[2] Parliament revised the provincial charter granted Massachusetts Bay in 1691 in order to give the British government more direct control over the province. The act provided that the council of the colony, previously elected by the lower house and the outgoing council with the approval of the royal governor, would henceforth be appointed by the king and hold office at his pleasure. Another provision allowed the governor to appoint judges without the consent of the council (even though the latter had been restructured to bring it more under the influence of the king), thereby tightening executive control over the provincial courts. The act further empowered the governor, again without consent of the council, to appoint the county sheriffs, who were in turn authorized to select jury members—an elective position under the old charter.

The Government Act curtailed the activities of the town meeting, long considered a prime source of democratic ferment by the British government, allowing only one session each year unless special permission was obtained from the provincial governor. In this, as in other provisions, the Massachusetts Government Act substantially limited popular participation in the government of the colony and enhanced the authority of the Crown and its representatives.

The third of the Coercive Acts passed by Parliament, that for the Better Administration of Justice in Massachusetts Bay, provided that the governor of the colony might, under certain circumstances, transfer a trial from Massachusetts to another colony or even to Great Britain.[3] Whenever a magistrate stood accused of a capital offense committed in the execution of official duties, the governor could remove the trial to a different location if he thought local opinion so inflamed as to cloud the court's ability to arrive at an impartial verdict. Even in cases not involving a magistrate, the governor could order a transfer of trial if the accused had been acting under the direction of a magistrate to suppress riots or to support revenue laws. The ministry anticipated that the act would protect British officials and partisans in the pursuance of official duties and thus encourage a more spirited administration of imperial measures in the colony.

The fourth, and last, of the acts resulting from British irritation over the Boston Tea Party was the Quartering Act, aimed at solving long-standing problems concerning the housing of British troops in America.[4] Previous measures had proved ineffective. New York at one point had simply refused to cooperate, and the British government had suspended the colony's legislature until it lived up to its supposed obligations. Massachusetts had provided housing for the troops but had done so at Castle William, far enough from Boston to render the troops stationed there useless in case of civil disorders in the metropolis. The Quartering Act of 1774, which applied to all the colonies, allowed officers to refuse unsuitable housing and to demand a more convenient location. In the event that local authorities did not satisfy such a request within twenty-four hours, the act empowered the governor to order any uninhabited buildings prepared for the use of the king's troops. The act did not, as has often been asserted, provide for billeting of soldiers in private homes.[5]

The Quebec Act, or Canada Act as it was sometimes called, did not develop out of British concern over the riots in Boston, but its provisions made it seem as much a part of Parliament's plan for colonial reorganization as any of the other statutes.[6] The bill extended the boundaries of Quebec to include all the area north of the Ohio River, the Northwest Territory. Inhabitants of the old French colony were to "have, hold, and enjoy, the free exercise of the religion of the Church of Rome," and the Catholic clergy was authorized to receive its accustomed dues and rights from those who professed Catholicism. Although the act established English criminal law in Canada, it permitted the continuance of French civil law, a code excluding the right to trial by jury. Moreover, since the British government deemed it inexpedient to establish an elective assembly in a province so heavily populated by foreign-speaking inhabitants, the Quebec Act provided for a legislative council consisting of seventeen to twenty-three members appointed by the king. This body, with the consent of the governor, exercised complete authority over the colony.

As news of each act arrived from Great Britain, discontent increased. Many colonial leaders saw the acts clearly as a threat not only to Massachusetts but to other colonies as well. Thomas Wharton, Sr., a moderate Quaker merchant of Philadelphia who later turned Tory, concluded that "all this Extensive Continent Considers the port Bill of Boston as striking Essentially at the Liberties of all North America."[7] From the Virginia House of Burgesses, Richard Henry Lee wrote that "the shallow Ministerial device was seen thro instantly, and every one declared it the commencement of a most wicked System for destroying the liberty of America."[8] George Washington, who had expressed serious reservations about the Boston Tea Party, asked whether it was not now "as clear as the sun in the meridian brightness, that there is a regular, systematic plan formed to fix the right and practice of taxation upon us?"[9]

Colonial suspicions of British intentions were intensified by a barrage of letters and instructions from correspondents in Great Britain. Edmund Burke informed the New York Assembly's Committee of Correspondence that the punishment of Massachusetts "had been from the Beginning defended on their absolute Necessitys not only for the purpose of bringing that refractory Town and province into proper Order, but for holding out an Example of Terrour to the other Colonies."[10] Ominous reports also came from Arthur Lee, then in London, who wrote his two brothers in Virginia warning them that if they did not unite in support of Massachusetts, all would be lost. As early as March 1774, Lee urged a general resistance or "every part will in its turn feel the vengeance which it would not unite to repel."[11]

Almost overnight, colonists convened in local, county, and provincial meetings to discuss possible means of resisting the objectionable measures. Such meetings naturally varied according to local circumstances, but they all pursued the same objective: that of forcing Britain to repeal the coercive legislation.

In debating this objective, the colonists proposed two courses of action. The more timid contended that the only proper method of protest was to draw up petitions begging the king and Parliament to rescind the acts. Such men claimed that the oppressive acts would surely be repealed if the colonists could only convince the king of the validity of colonial claims. A second, and bolder, group insisted that petitions had proved ineffectual before and would again. They argued that the only conceivable means of affecting British policy lay in economic coercion and favored an immediate ending of trade with England. Such action, they thought, would arouse opinion in England and force Parliament to grant colonial demands. Those who favored trade restrictions rejected the charge that such measures were illegal. George Washington explained that trade restrictions fell within the bounds of legality since the colonists were merely defending what was theirs by right.[12]

An overwhelming majority of Americans supported a third suggestion: the convening of a general congress. Such a meeting appealed to bold and timid alike. The former realized that concerted action must prove more effective than individual protests, while the latter craved the safety of numbers and the moderation of delay. By the end of June, nine colonies and numerous local and county meetings had endorsed such proposals for a continental congress.

Americans had long recognized the strength that union might bring to their demands for redress in Parliament. Even before the passage of the Coercive Acts, many colonists sought to effect a greater cooperation throughout the continent. Toward that end, committees of correspondence were established to encourage and direct concerted action. Such committees played an important part in promoting and arranging the general congress of 1774.

Boston, being the target of the coercive legislation, naturally initiated action for redress of grievances. Leaders in the town, however, feared that a call for a continental meeting would work to their disadvantage. Under the best of circumstances, such a meeting could not have convened before the end of summer, and Boston's port was to be closed on 1 June. Moreover, once Congress assembled, valuable weeks would pass in debate and even more time in implementation of any measures upon which the group agreed. Additional weeks would elapse before the effects of the boycott were felt in Great Britain. Such delayed assistance, no matter how well intended, might well arrive too late to benefit the city. If, as a majority of Bostonians believed, commercial coercion alone could provide effective resistance to the Port Act, then a congress would waste crucial time. Better to adopt the embargo first and talk about it later.

Within three days of the receipt of the Port Act on 10 May 1774, the citizens of Boston had taken two important steps. The Boston town meeting appointed a special committee to consult with representatives of the two neighboring ports, Salem and Marblehead, while the committee of correspondence convened a meeting with delegates from eight surrounding towns.[13]

Early on Saturday morning, 14 May, Paul Revere rode out of the Massachusetts capital carrying with him to New York and Philadelphia the resolutions of the town meeting. Mincing no words, Boston had proposed an immediate embargo, predicting that: "If the other Colonies come into a joint Resolution, to stop all Importations from *Great Britain* and Exportations to *Great Britain,* and every part of the *West Indies,* till the Act for Blocking up this Harbor be repealed, the same will prove the Salvation of *North America* and her Liberties."[14]

Even as the Boston messenger made his way south, a public meeting in Providence, Rhode Island, issued the first public call for a general congress. Meeting on 17 May, the citizens instructed their delegates in the General Assembly to propose the convening of a congress of representatives from all the colonies "for establishing the firmest union; and adopting such measures as to them shall appear the most effectual to answer that important purpose; and to agree upon proper methods for executing the same."[15]

The Boston resolutions arrived at New York on 17 May and at Philadelphia two days later, but both cities responded to Boston's plea with a noticeable lack of enthusiasm for restrictions on trade. Local Whigs had, as anticipated, proposed the adoption of an embargo in those two cities, but without success. Each city did, however, adopt resolutions endorsing a colonial congress and unified action to aid Boston.

In New York, Alexander McDougall and Isaac Sears attempted to commit the merchants to a program of commercial restrictions similar to that favored by Samuel Adams in Boston. The proposal was rejected at a meeting on 16 May, and the merchants voted instead to recommend the appointment of a committee of fifty persons to correspond with other colonies concerning the measures to be adopted.[16] Although the committee of mechanics nominated a rival committee of twenty-five at the instigation of Sears and McDougall, the fifty were elected at a public meeting on 19 May.[17] One additional name, suggested by the Sears-McDougall faction, was added to the group, making a committee of fifty-one.[18] The newly elected committee immediately drafted a reply to the dispatches received from Massachusetts. This letter, dated 23 May, rejected a decision on nonimportation as "premature," suggesting instead that a "Congress of Deputies from the Colonies in General" would strengthen American demands.[19]

Events in Philadelphia closely resembled those in New York, except that the group favoring nonimportation handled matters with greater finesse. Charles Thomson, Thomas Mifflin, and Joseph Reed—leaders of the more aggressive faction in Philadelphia—anticipated the city's reluctance to adopt the militant commercial santions of Boston and instead urged the endorsement of more moderate measures which, they correctly believed, would ultimately achieve the desired results. They enlisted the support of the immensely popular Pennsylvania Farmer, John Dickinson, in this effort. At a general meeting held 20 May, the group secured the appointment of a committee of nineteen to conduct affairs in Philadelphia and initiated a petition to Governor John Penn calling for a special session of the assembly to discuss the crisis facing the colonists.[20] The 20 May meeting authorized the committee to answer the Boston letter by recommending "prudence, firmness, and moderation."[21] That letter, drafted and signed by the committee on 21 May, rejected Boston's plea for immediate nonimportation and suggested instead that a general meeting of the colonies be convened.

Proposals for commercial coercion were more favorably received in the southern provinces. On 25 May, an express arrived in Annapolis bearing the resolutions of the Boston town meeting and a forwarding letter from the recently elected Philadelphia committee. Within twenty-four hours, about eight "Inhabitants" had adopted resolutions, appointed a committee to correspond with other communities, and written and posted letters to the several counties in Maryland as well as to the Virginia House of Burgesses. The Annapolis residents, like their Boston counterparts, called for an immediate halt to both importation and exportation. Moreover, they suggested that the embargo be incorporated into a written association, signed an oath, and advocated a boycott of trade with any colony that refused to adopt similar measures. In one area, the Annapolis meeting went even further than Boston, proposing that "the Gentlemen of the Law in this Province bring no Suit for the Recovery of any Debt due from any Inhabitant of this Province to any Inhabitant of Great Britain until the said act be repealed."[22]

Most of the Maryland counties supported the Annapolis call for an embargo. The Baltimore committee, having suspended its own deliberations in order to await the reaction of "our Friends in Annapolis," subsequently convened a county meeting which, on 31 May, endorsed the proposed boycott of trade and suggested specific dates for its implementation.[23] During the following two weeks five additional counties—Frederick, Charles, Harford, Anne Arundel, and Queen Anne—called similar meetings and approved the proposed suspension of trade.[24] Although most of these counties hedged the issue by stipulating that the proposed boycott should not go into effect until endorsed by other towns throughout America, Maryland had clearly pronounced itself ready to follow the lead of Annapolis and endorse Boston's call for an immediate suspension of trade with the mother country.

News of the Port Act, arriving directly from England, had reached Virginia about the same time that the dispatches from Philadelphia had been delivered to Annapolis. Shortly thereafter, a group of patriot leaders, including Thomas Jefferson, Patrick Henry, and Richard Henry Lee, met to work out a plan of action for the legislature. On 24 May, this group secured the unanimous approval of the House of Burgesses to set aside 1 June, the day on which the Port Act took effect, as a "day of Fasting, Humiliation, and Prayer . . . for averting the heavy Calamity which threatens Destruction to our civil Rights, and the Evils of civil War; to give us one Heart and one Mind firmly to oppose, by all just and proper Means, every Injury to American rights."[25]

Hearing that the assembly had passed this resolution, Governor Dunmore dissolved the House on May 26.[26] As the governor had anticipated, the Burgesses, since they could no longer meet in their official capacity as a legal branch of colonial government, decided to gather unofficially at the Raleigh Tavern. In part because of Dunmore's dissolution and in part because the resolutions from Boston had not yet arrived in Virginia, the legislature proceeded cautiously when it met on 28 May. Rejecting Lee's motion to issue an explicit invitation for the meeting of a continental congress, the eighty-nine delegates instead "recommended" that the provincial committee of correspondence write the other colonies concerning the "expediency" of appointing an annual congress to meet on "those general measures which the united interests of America may from time to time require."[27]

The arrival of the letter from the "gentlemen" of Annapolis on 29 May caused the Burgesses to review their unexpectedly moderate position. Peyton Randolph immediately called an emergency meeting of those Burgesses who had not left the capital, and the twenty-five members who responded to that invitation injected new life into the movement for an embargo. On the following day, a meeting of these twenty-five took a much more vigorous stand in opposition to the Boston Port Act than had any previous Virginia gathering. The participants had before them the proposals from Boston, the resolutions from Maryland, and the letter from Philadelphia—all of which had been forwarded by the committee in Annapolis one day earlier.[28] A proposal for the immediate adoption of nonimportation and nonexportation garnered considerable support, and most of the assembled Burgesses agreed that a general nonimportation was now inevitable. The proposal to interdict exports to the mother country was, however, less popular. Several members insisted that so precipitate a move would have a devastating effect on the economy of a colony that lived on its overseas sales of tobacco. In any event, so small a gathering ought not to adopt measures that would vitally affect the entire province. The meeting decided to instruct the members of the late House of Burgesses to collect the sense of their constituents and to return to Williamsburg on 1 August for a provincial convention to detail the terms of an embargo on trade.[29]

By the end of June 1774, nine colonies had endorsed proposals to hold a continental congress. During the summer, all of the American colonies except Georgia appointed delegates to attend the congress to be held in Philadelphia in September. In none of the twelve did serious opposition to the election of delegates develop. Disagreement did occur in some colonies over who should attend and how they ought to be instructed. A major source of difficulty was the obstructionism of the royal governors, which led, in some cases, to the calling of extralegal conventions. For the sake of legality, most of the colonists would doubtless have preferred to elect delegates in regular meetings of the provincial assemblies, but this was possible in only five colonies. In Rhode Island and Connecticut, where governors were locally elected, no problems arose in delegate selection. In Pennsylvania, Massachusetts, and South Carolina, the assemblies succeeded in electing delegates despite opposition from the royal governors. In every other colony, arrangements had to be made in outright defiance of the governors.

At the same time, debate continued over the wisdom of a policy of commercial coercion. Those colonists who counseled more moderate means won a few victories during the summer, but by fall, they had largely succumbed to the better organization of their opponents, which reached fruition in the First Continental Congress and Continental Association.

Rhode Island was the first colony to elect delegates to the Congress. On 13 June, the General Assembly of the province met in regular session and appointed Stephen Hopkins and Samuel Ward "to represent the people of this colony, in a general congress. . . ."[30] The Massachusetts General Assembly followed on 17 June, but only after it had barred the doors of the Assembly room in a successful attempt to prevent Governor Thomas Gage from dissolving the meeting.[31]

During this period, agitation continued in Massachusetts for implementation of trade restrictions. Encouraged by the temporizing responses of New York and Philadelphia to the proposed embargo, conservative merchants voted that those who had already signed the nonimportation agreement need not abide by it as the other ports had refused to join. Those who favored an embargo could not ignore this defection from the projected boycott and engineered a consumer boycott to keep their brethren in line. Circulation of this pledge not to purchase British goods, known as the Solemn League and Covenant, caused considerable alarm among the merchants.[32] The document's initial success initiated a major offensive by the merchants against the Boston Committee of Correspondence. In the early weeks of June, the merchants appeared in the town meeting to urge disbanding the committee, but the attempt failed.[33]

The conservatives made no further attempt to capture control of the Boston town meeting and probably ceased even to attend. News of the Government Act and the Justice Act increased the antagonism toward Parliament, and evidence of support from other colonies reinforced Boston's determination to resist. Especially reassuring were the contributions of money and produce pouring into the Massachusetts capital, which served both to ease the distress caused by the Port Act and to bolster flagging morale.[34]

In Maryland, delegates were elected to the Continental Congress by a special convention which met in Annapolis from 22–25 June 1774. The impetus for this provincial meeting came from the several counties and from local groups throughout the colony. The delegates to this provincial convention, most of whom had been elected by their respective counties, recommended commercial nonintercourse as the best means of securing repeal of the "unconstitutional" Coercive Acts. (They said, however, that nonexportation of tobacco could not be enforced unless Virginia and North Carolina also adopted that measure.) The convention promised to abide by any decisions the Congress might make and to break off all dealings with anyone or any group that disobeyed the continental body.[35]

By the end of July, six other colonies had elected delegates to the Congress. South Carolina chose its delegates at a special convention held in Charleston on 6 July. The deputies to this convention were elected by meetings of landowners in the various parishes. Resolutions declared unconstitutional the acts of Parliament taxing the colonies, altering the traditional rights of trial, and punishing Boston. The convention voted to send the delegates to the Congress without instructions, since they were undecided on the virtues of trade restrictions.[36] The South Carolina Provincial Assembly which met on 2 August unanimously approved of the elected delegates and voted to pay their expenses, before Governor William Bull could intervene.

On 13 July, the Connecticut Committee of Correspondence selected delegates according to the instructions of the General Assembly.[37] In New Hampshire, the provincial committee of correspondence disobeyed the governor and called a special convention, which met on 21 July and elected delegates.[38] New Jersey also elected its delegates at a provincial convention on 21 July, which followed local meetings in at least nine of the thirteen counties of the colony. This convention also endorsed nonimportation.[39]

The most complicated and prolonged debates over provincial policies regarding the congress and the use of economic sanctions occurred in Pennsylvania and New York. The Pennsylvania conflicts were made more complex due to the presence of a substantial Quaker population generally opposed to any kind of extralegal activity, the prolonged struggle still in progress between political factions supporting and opposing the proprietary government of the Penns, and the personal antagonism between such leaders as John Dickinson and Joseph Galloway. The issues, proposals for action, and the plans for a continental congress were seen in light of those other political issues. There was also a mixture of popular pressure and activities by established political leaders.

The main point of contention in Philadelphia concerned the proposed meeting of a provincial congress. Governor John Penn, as anticipated, refused the petition signed by nearly nine hundred persons requesting him to call a meeting of the assembly.[40] His refusal led to further demands by the people of Philadelphia. On 9 June, about 1,200 mechanics assembled in order to "cooperate with and strengthen the hand of the merchants."[41] On 18 June, a very large meeting convened in Philadelphia, under the co-chairmanship of John Dickinson and Thomas Willing. This gathering denounced the Port Act as unconstitutional, endorsed a general congress, and elected a committee of forty-three to determine the best method of appointing Pennsylvania's delegates to the Congress.[42]

Meantime, further efforts were being made to elect delegates by a more constitutional method of calling a meeting of the General Assembly.[43] After a series of negotiations in Philadelphia between the committee of nineteen (set up in May by the Mifflin-Thomson-Dickinson organization) and other city leaders, Joseph Galloway, Speaker of the House, was asked to call a special session of the Assembly to convene at the same time that elected county committees met in provincial congress.[44]

The specially organized provincial congress met on 15 July and adopted sixteen resolutions condemning the Declaratory and Coercive Acts and endorsing the Congress. They promised to accept nonimportation and nonexportation if the Congress judged such actions expedient and further pledged that if additional parliamentary oppression should necessitate the adoption of more extreme measures, they would "do all in their power to carry them into execution."[45] They also offered to settle an annual revenue to reimburse the East India Company for the tea destroyed in Boston. But their recommendations were ignored by the official General Assembly which met on 18 July. It voted in favor of the Continental Congress, appointed its own delegates, but made no promise of support for commercial restrictions, leaving the delegates uninstructed.

The bitterness of the debates that took place in New York City during the summer of 1774 made the divisions in Philadelphia seem insignificant. Fistfights broke out regularly. One side would hold a public meeting and adopt "unanimous" resolutions only to see a similar meeting by their opponents just as "unanimously" reject the same proposals. The committee of mechanics and the committee of fifty-one found it impossible to compromise. As late as 25 July, three days before the final election of delegates, Benjamin Booth, a New York merchant, predicted the "proposed Congress . . . would come to nothing, at least with respect to this Province, as we shall never agree on the Persons to be sent as Delegates."[46] Because New York's refusal to elect delegates would have served the interests of the conservatives, the Sears-McDougall faction probably agreed to accept the candidates proposed by their opponents. On 28 July, New York unanimously selected five delegates in a city-wide election. Despite claims by some that the fifty-one had "obtained a compleat victory over the Republican party," the mechanics and others who favored trade restrictions had in fact won an important concession.[47] For reasons still unclear, the New York delegation published a statement that "at present" they favored a nonimportation agreement.[48]

In Delaware, discussions concerning Congress and possible trade restrictions were less heated. The colony called a special meeting of the assembly but did not convene an extralegal provincial convention. The assembly met at New Castle on 1 August, condemned the Coercive Acts as unconstitutional and "oppressive," and selected representatives to the Congress. The delegates to Congress were instructed to use "their utmost endeavours" to frame petitions to the king and Parliament for redress and to agree to nonimportation and nonexportation "until relief shall be obtained."[49]

No colony evidenced greater unity during the summer and fall of 1774 than Virginia. Governor Dunmore's attempt to halt the movement for a congress by dissolving the House of Burgesses failed miserably, as meetings in county after county elected delegates to an extralegal convention which met in Williamsburg during the first week in August. These meetings usually declared that Parliament had no right to tax the colonies without their consent, promised support for Boston, and called for a halt to importation from and exportation to Great Britain and a suspension of civil cases in the courts until the acts were repealed. In Fairfax County, where George Washington sat as chairman, the county meeting outlined an association for enforcing nonintercourse provisions.[50]

On 1 August, delegates convened in Williamsburg and elected representatives to the Continental Congress. More significantly, they adopted the Virginia Association, a lengthy agreement outlining a plan of commercial nonintercourse for the colony and setting up the machinery to enforce it.[51] This document served as a model for the Continental Association, adopted by the Congress in October 1774.

In North Carolina, county meetings gathered and endorsed plans of action, including the Congress and in some cases nonimportation and nonexportation. The colony-wide convention met on 25 August in defiance of Governor Josiah Martin's prohibitions of "such illegal meetings,"[52] and followed Virginia's lead, adopting an almost identical plan of commercial nonintercourse.[53]

By September, all of the colonies except Georgia had met and appointed delegates to the Congress.[54] Virginia, North Carolina, Massachusetts, Maryland, Connecticut, New Jersey, Delaware, and Rhode Island had also given tangible evidence of support for commercial nonintercourse.[55]

• THE CONGRESS CONVENES •

Three distinct problems faced the members of the First Continental Congress as they gathered in Philadelphia in September 1774. They were to formulate a statement or plan that would define a viable constitutional framework binding the colonies to the British Empire, they were to decide precisely which acts of Parliament violated the rights of America, and they were to devise a means for obtaining repeal of the most objectionable of those statutes. Since the members were themselves clearly aware of the distinctions among these three tasks, they were able to prevent the rather heated arguments over constitutional issues from affecting discussion of other problems.

In fact, the First Continental Congress exhibited an extraordinary unanimity in their confrontation with Great Britain. This became apparent during the first day's meeting. Joseph Galloway, the conservative speaker of the Pennsylvania Assembly, had offered Congress the use of the State House for its meetings and made clear his determination that the offer be accepted. However, the workmen of Philadelphia had suggested that the Congress meet in Carpenters' Hall, and a number of delegates who disliked Galloway took advantage of this offer to discredit their adversary. When the delegates met at City Tavern to organize, they voted to view both Carpenters' Hall and the State House but after visiting the former decided "by a large majority" to proceed no further.[56]

After electing Peyton Randolph as president, Congress again rejected Galloway's leadership by going outside the elected membership to appoint Charles Thomson of Philadelphia as secretary. Silas Deane wrote that these decisions had proved "highly agreeable to the mechanics and citizens in general, but mortifying to the last degree to Mr. Galloway and his party, Thompson being his sworn opposite, as you may say, and by his means prevented being one of Congress for his Province."[57]

Deane's statement has often been cited as proof of the early factionalism of Congress, but the context in which the Connecticut delegate used the term "party" shows that he was speaking instead about divisions in Pennsylvania. Deane, like other delegates arriving in Philadelphia, was well aware of the conflict that had taken place in Pennsylvania between the assembly and the provincial convention. His remark clearly refers to the events in the city rather than inside Congress. Moreover, the overwhelming majorities with which the delegates chose Carpenters' Hall and elected Thomson would not have provided Deane or anyone else with much evidence concerning congressional factions. Galloway and James Duane, both of whom opposed the two decisions, referred to the "great Majority" in favor and found Thomson's election so popular that they allowed the decision to go uncontested.[58] John Adams noted in his diary that only a "very few" opposed the selection of Carpenters' Hall "and they were chiefly from Pennsylvania and New York."[59]

After resolution of procedural matters, the delegates took up the issue that most threatened to divide them—the respective rights of Britain and the colonies. A committee of twenty-four was appointed—soon to be known as the Grand Committee—and was assigned three tasks: (1) formulating a statement of American rights, (2) compiling a list of grievances, and (3) devising the "mode of redress," or a plan for securing Britain's acquiesence. At its first meeting, the Grand Committee decided to facilitate its work by dividing into even smaller groups, and the members accordingly separated into three subcommittees. Each of these groups was expected to concern itself with one of the three tasks.

As the Grand Committee began deliberations, two incidents occurred which offer further insights into the attitudes of the delegates. One of these grew out of a debate on 6 September over the suggestion that a local minister be asked to open the third meeting of Congress with prayer. John Jay and one of the Rutledges from South Carolina objected on the grounds that the delegates were too divided in religious sentiments to agree about who should be asked to give such an invocation. Samuel Adams, who was hardly known for his tolerant attitude on religious matters, sprang to his feet to insist that he was "no bigot" and could hear a prayer from any gentleman of virtue who was also a friend of his country. The delegates listened with some surprise as the Boston Congregationalist proposed that an Anglican, Jacob Duché, be invited to give the invocation.[60] This motion, coming from the Massachusetts delegation undoubtedly furthered the spirit of compromise and harmony already evident in Congress. Joseph Reed of Delaware thought the move a "masterly stroke of policy" and told John Adams that it had "a very good effect" and that the "sentiments of the people here, are growing more favorable every day."[61]

During the afternoon of that same day, the delegates were stunned by reports that the British had attacked the provincials in Massachusetts and that "troops and fleets [were] cannonading the town of Boston."[62] Though the rumor later proved false, it had a profound effect on Congress and on Philadelphia. Bells tolled in sympathy for Boston, while citizens and delegates hastened to assure the Massachusetts representatives that all America would support Boston in the reported crisis.[63] John Adams was buoyed by the realization that "every gentleman seems to consider the bombardment of Boston as the bombardment of the capital of his own province." Writing his wife, Abigail, after the rumor was contradicted, Adams predicted that "if it had proved true, you would have heard the thunder of an American Congress."[64]

The report of an attack on Boston undoubtedly affected the subsequent debates. It probably contributed to the later unanimous endorsement of the supposedly radical resolutions submitted to Congress by Suffolk County, Massachusetts, and it certainly reminded the members of Congress that almost any incident might touch off events that could lead directly to war. This reminder persuaded a few delegates that before leaving Philadelphia, Congress should suggest ways in which the colonies could defend themselves if necessary.

Among those who attempted to convince the delegates that America should arm was Virginia's Richard Henry Lee. Lee suggested that Congress encourage each colony to ready its militia and adopt measures necessary to provide this citizens' army with "ammunition and proper arms."[65] Patrick Henry wholeheartedly supported the proposal, insisting the "preparation for Warr is Necessary to obtain peace"[66] and that if nonimportation and nonexportation should fail, war was the next step. But Congress adamantly refused to recommend arms. A majority continued to hope that the situation in New England would remain stable until the nonimportation agreement could force a relaxation of British policy.

It is not surprising that when the Suffolk Resolves arrived in Philadelphia two weeks later, Congress took advantage of the opportunity to express its sympathy and determined support of the New England city. Paul Revere arrived with the resolves on 16 September, and Congress met the following day to consider them.[67] The Massachusetts representatives read the resolves, which condemned the Coercive Acts as "gross infractions of the rights to which we are entitled." The resolutions further declared that no obedience was due the acts and promised that the people would support all officials who refused to execute court orders intended to enforce them. Citizens were asked not to pay taxes to "unconstitutional authority" or "to engage in any routs, riots, or licentious attacks on properties of any person whatsoever." The resolutions also obligated each town in the county to go to the aid of any neighboring communities in case an attack was launched on any one of them.[68]

Congress endorsed the Suffolk Resolves, thereby giving the first indication of the temperment of the delegates. The members unanimously approved Massachusetts' refusal to abide by the terms of the Coercive Acts, thus condoning overt resistance to an act of Parliament. Congress further recommended the Bay Colony to "persevere" in the "same firm temperate conduct."[69] Though the delegates clearly opposed violent or aggressive measures by the towns in Suffolk County, they purposefully emphasized their support of the refusal to obey British laws. Small wonder that John Adams's diary entry for 17 September, the day the resolves were endorsed, recorded it as "one of the happiest Days of my Life."[70]

Concurrent with these general discussions by Congress as a whole, the subcommittee and the Grand Committee struggled with the problem of a statement of American rights until the end of September. They then turned a proposal over to Congress which generated so much controversy as to force an additional three-week postponement.

The attempts to formulate a statement of rights illustrate the broad areas of agreement among the delegates. The conservative Galloway, during committee debates, agreed with the radical members on fundamental constitutional issues. He admitted that it was the "essense of the English constitution" that no laws were binding unless made by the "consent of the proprietors." Consequently, Congress could, in theory, legally deny the validity of any act passed by Parliament "since the emigration of our ancestors."[71] But the Pennsylvanian hastened to add that he did not favor so extreme an assertion of right. A denial of all laws passed since the settlement of the colonies would "tend to an independency." Galloway proposed instead that Congress remedy this constitutional defect by including in its statement of rights an explicit acknowledgement of Parliament's authority in limited areas.[72] Such a statement would provide a constitutional basis for binding the colonies to the mother country and would thus remedy the defect deplored by commentators on both the left and the right—James Parker, William Bradford, Jr., James Duane, John Adams, and Joseph Galloway himself. Superficially, at least, the delegates seemed during the early meetings of the committee to be agreed on the importance of some such solution to the constitutional crisis.

Unfortunately, the consensus did not extend to more practical considerations. Whenever the delegates turned to specific proposals, they confronted the question of Parliament's right to regulate colonial trade. Galloway and Duane considered such an acknowledgement essential; others viewed it with skepticism. Few wanted to deny the validity of existing statutes affecting trade, but many opposed a blanket recognition of Great Britain's right to enact further legislation in the area. A different group, of which Galloway and Duane were the most outspoken members, insisted that Congress must accept parliamentary authority over the commerce of the empire or abandon all hope of reconciliation.[73] It was the heated nature of the debate and the nearly equal divisions on this issue that convinced the delegates to shelve the question temporarily and concern themselves instead with the "mode of redress." On 24 September, Congress dissolved the Grand Committee, voted to delay consideration of the Report on Rights and Grievances, and turned to discussion of the less controversial question of an embargo of British trade.

On 27 September, Congress voted unanimously to adopt nonimportation of British goods as one means of securing a redress of colonial grievances (which they had as yet been unable to enumerate). Eight colonies had previously endorsed the measure, and Congress had already warned colonial merchants not to order goods from Great Britain because of the probability of its adoption.[74] If any of the members privately opposed restricting trade with the mother country, they apparently had found themselves in such a minority as to make dissent not only useless but impolitic. John Jay and James Duane, known for their generally conservative outlook, stated on the floor of Congress that they supported the embargo of trade.[75] Jay expressed the general agreement of Congress when he stated that "war is, by general consent, to be waved at present. I am for negotiation and suspension of commerce."[76] It seems probable that even Galloway voted for the measure, since his opposition to so universally popular a resolution would have been noted by at least one of the delegates in a private letter or a diary. Certainly, no one raised an objection on the floor of Congress. Congress began formal consideration of nonimportation on 26 September and on the thirtieth appointed Thomas Cushing, Isaac Low, Thomas Mifflin, Richard Henry Lee, and Thomas Johnson, Jr., "to bring in a plan for carrying into effect, the non-importation, non-consumption, and non-exportation resolved on."[77]

The delegates disagreed only on the precise date for putting that program into effect. The Virginia Association, which served as a model for much that Congress did, had specified that nonimportation should begin on 1 November and nonexportation the following autumn—provided, of course, that Great Britain had not redressed colonial grievances by that time. Neither of these dates fully satisfied Congress; the first was attacked as too early and the second as too late. A number of members suggested a short delay in effecting nonimportation because they feared that too early a deadline would alienate the merchants. They argued that the cooperation of the mercantile community was essential to the success of nonimportation and contended that Congress should make every possible effort to conciliate that group. These members proposed that nonimportation begin on 1 December, rather than 1 November, in order to permit the receipt of orders sent out during the summer. Virginia at first thought this delay unnecessary. Its delegates insisted that the merchants had expected nonimportation since at least the first of June. Pennsylvania's Mifflin agreed, arguing that no "honest orders" had gone out since that date.[78] After a brief debate, the Virginians capitulated. One month's delay seemed a small price to pay for advancing colonial unity. Patrick Henry, at first a staunch supporter of the earlier date, soon conceded the point on the grounds that Congress ought not to harm even the "rascals" in America, assuming of course that there were any.[79]

The decision on 24 September to delay consideration of American rights, however, had bothered Joseph Galloway. He noted the relief with which Congress had turned to the question of an embargo, and when on 27 September the delegates unanimously approved nonimportation of British goods, he began to suspect that they might adjourn without endorsing Parliament's right to regulate trade. Consequently he decided to try a different tack. If Congress would not approve an adequate statement of Britain's authority over trade, perhaps the delegates would consider a proposal to reorganize the empire. On 28 September, the day after Congress adopted the trade embargo, the Pennsylvanian attempted to turn attention back to the constitutional issue by introducing his Plan of Union.

Galloway's proposal, in brief, called for a reorganization of the imperial ties along lines suggested by a number of Americans during the years preceding the American independence movement, most notably, Benjamin Franklin at the Albany Congress in 1754. An American Congress would be established as an "inferior branch" of the British legislature, and the colonial body would have equal authority with Parliament over such imperial issues as trade regulation and taxation. No law would be binding on the colonies unless approved by both the American Congress and the British Parliament, and the colonies would each retain control over internal matters. Each colony would have a number of representatives in the Grand Congress proportional to its wealth and population, and the king would appoint a governor general to preside over the assembly and exercise the veto power.

Historians have frequently touted Galloway's Plan of Union as the conservative alternative to the radical proposals for nonimportation, but it is apparent that the plan was a substitute not for the trade embargo but for the sidetracked statement of rights. In the first place, Galloway did not present his proposal to Congress until the debate over Parliament's right to regulate trade had bogged down, and the delegates had approved nonimportation. Moreover, in arguing for the adoption of his proposal, Galloway pointedly referred to the failure of Congress to agree on a statement recognizing Britain's authority and implied that his plan would alleviate that problem. Galloway's plan offered not an alternative to the program adopted in Congress but an addition. Probably many delegates, even those who supported it, regarded the suggestion in the same light as they considered petitions to the king—as a gesture to be supported by the more forceful method of economic coercion.

Having postponed debate on rights and grievances, the members did not relish beginning another prolonged argument over what was essentially the same issue. They considered the plan for a day and then voted six to five, with one colony abstaining, to let it lie on the table.[80] They also postponed discussion of Galloway's suggestion, and then Congress returned to the question of securing redress for colonial grievances. On 30 September, the delegates resolved that "unless the grievances of America are redressed" the exportation of all merchandise to Great Britain, Ireland, and the West Indies ought to cease.[81] This measure, like nonimportation, aroused little opposition in principle but involved the delegates in considerable debate over specific provisions.

The Virginia delegates refused to alter the timetable adopted at their colony's August convention, which had voted to delay the embargo of exports until the present tobacco crop had been marketed. No combination of inducements or threats could alter its stand. Both Maryland and South Carolina attempted to persuade the stubborn colony to change its mind, but to no avail. The Carolina delegates even proposed that Congress should go ahead without the consent of Virginia.[82] That proposal failed, not only because Congress was determined to win unanimous support for its program but because other tobacco-producing colonies considered it unfair. Maryland's Samuel Chase strongly opposed the South Carolina suggestion, noting that his colony could not think of withholding its tobacco crop unless all others did the same.[83] The delegates finally bowed to Virginia's insistent demands and agreed to continue exporting to Great Britain until 10 September 1775.

Realizing that a delay of nonexportation would substantially reduce the immediate impact of the embargo, and increasingly aware of Boston's urgent need, Congress tried to find effective proposals that Virginia would support. One suggestion was a ban on exportation of specific articles to go into effect concurrently with nonimportation. As late as 3 October, Rhode Island's Samuel Ward predicted that Congress would adopt selective nonexportation, but a few days later the effort was abandoned.

• A PLAN ADOPTED •

During the first three weeks of October, Congress worked out details of the program outlined in the early weeks of meetings. The delegates completed the Statement of Rights and Grievances, gave final form to a plan for enforcing commercial restrictions, and drafted a petition to the king. Significantly, Congress did not petition Parliament, an omission intended to suggest that the delegates did not recognize any binding tie to that branch of the British government.

On 1 October, Congress appointed Richard Henry Lee, Patrick Henry, John Adams, and Thomas Johnson to prepare a petition to the king. Two days later, Congress instructed the committee "to assure his Majesty" that the colonies could themselves make ample provision for supporting government, administering justice, and maintaining an adequate militia.[84] All these needs had previously been cited by the British government to justify taxation of the colonists. Richard Henry Lee proposed further that a militia be raised and armed in each colony to demonstrate the ability of the colonists to provide for their own defense, but Congress rejected his suggestion.[85]

A second directive, adopted 5 October, requested the committee to make clear in their address to the king that once Parliament repealed the grievances listed by Congress, all trade restrictions would be abandoned. Congress suggested a list of grievances to the committee, even though the resolution on rights and grievances had not yet been ratified. The measures referred to the committee included acts taxing the colonists for revenue, extending the power of the Courts of Admiralty, trying persons in England for crimes committed in America, punishing the colony of Massachusetts Bay, and altering the boundaries of Canada.[86]

For a few weeks, the problem of Massachusetts had slipped into the background as Congress debated its proposed statement of rights and grievances. Then, on 6 October, messengers from New England arrived with alarming news that again forced Congress to confront the possibility of military conflict. General Thomas Gage had begun building fortifications on the neck of land connecting Boston with the mainland, which, according to the town meeting, would enable him to block access to Boston "both by sea and land." The citizens feared that Gage intended to hold them hostage and had consequently decided to ask Congress for advice. So critical did the situation appear that the town meeting was prepared to recommend a mass evacuation of the city if Congress approved. Boston also asked the delegates to suggest some course of action in light of the problems plaguing the colony as a result of the prolonged absence of legally constituted government.[87]

Certainly, the situation in Massachusetts Bay at this time was difficult. The harsh punishment inflicted by the Coercive Acts and the determined but peaceful resistance of the town's citizens had rallied colonial opinion firmly behind the oppressed colony. But in order to retain this support, the town was forced to maintain her passive stance, though her situation became daily more serious. Boston's immediate need made the deliberations of Congress appear unnecessarily slow and convinced many that the city should adopt an aggressive plan of resistance. But Congress was not yet prepared to advise adoption of aggressive action, such as electing a governor other than Gage or establishing a separate governmental structure. John Adams realized this, writing to a friend in Boston that "if it is the secret hope of many, as I suspect it is, that Congress will advise to offensive measures, they will be mistaken."[88]

Nevertheless, as with the earlier Suffolk Resolves, Congress took a strong stand in support of the pleas from Massachusetts. On 7 October, Congress appointed Thomas Lynch, Samuel Adams, and Edward Pendleton to prepare a letter to General Gage informing him that "the town of Boston, and province of Massachusetts Bay, are considered by all America as suffering in the common cause." The committee was further instructed to entreat Gage to halt the building of fortifications on Boston Neck and to restrain his troops from their alleged abuses of the citizenry.[89] Sam Adams prepared the first draft of the letter to Gage. The proposed message minced no words, insisting that Gage cease his fortifications or face "Consequences of the most serious Nature." The delegates, however, refused to adopt so militant a stand and significantly modified the letter before sending it.[90] The resolution declared: "This Congress approves of the opposition of the inhabitants of Massachusetts-bay, to the execution of the late acts of Parliament; and if the same shall be carried into execution by force, in such case, all America ought to support them in their opposition."[91]

The delegates further advised the Bostonians not to attempt an evacuation of the city unless the provincial congress of Massachusetts judged it absolutely necessary. Congress also took a moderate position on the problems of government in Massachusetts Bay, arguing that if the courts could not meet in a legal and peaceable manner, the colony must get along temporarily without them. The delegates were determined, however, that conciliation not be confused with weakness, and they repeated their insistence that Massachusetts should under no circumstances submit to the Coercive Acts or accept any change of government dictated by Parliament. They further resolved that any citizen who accepted a commission under the Massachusetts Government Act should be held in detestation as a tool of the "despotism" that was aimed to destroy the liberties of America.[92]

Congress concluded its consideration of the letters from Boston on 12 October and turned again to the Statement of Rights. But once again, the delegates found themselves divided on the question of trade regulation. John Adams reported the two sides exactly even. Five colonies favored Parliament's right, five opposed, and two (Massachusetts and Rhode Island) were unable to vote because of split delegations.[93]

If Adams's later recollections are accurate, Congress finally agreed to endorse the proposals originally submitted by the Grand Committee's first subcommittee primarily because the delegates found it impossible to agree on anything else.[94] Incorporated as the fourth resolution in the Statement of Rights and Grievances, the article stated:

> The foundation of English liberty, and of all free government is a right in the people to participate in their legislative council: and as the English colonists are not represented, and from their local and other circumstances, cannot properly be represented in the British parliament, they are entitled to a free and exclusive power of legislation in their several provincial legislatures, where their right of representation can alone be preserved, in all cases of taxation and internal polity, subject only to the negative of their sovereign, in such a manner as has heretofore used and accustomed. But, from the necessity of the case, and a regard to the mutual interest of both countries, we cheerfully consent to the operation of such acts of the British parliament, as are bona fide, restrained to the regulation of our external commerce, for the purpose of securing the commercial advantages of the whole empire to the mother country, and the commercial benefits of its respective members; excluding every idea of taxation, internal or external, for raising a revenue on the subjects in America, without their consent.[95]

Once Congress had settled on a statement concerning Parliament's authority in the colonies, agreement on the statement of rights, grievances, and the means to procure redress came easily. On 14 October, nearly five weeks after the appointment of the Grand Committee to report on these matters, Congress gave final approval to a statement consisting of three separate sections. The first ten resolutions defined the rights of the American colonies. Following that came a list of those acts of Parliament which infringed upon colonial rights. The final section of the statement reaffirmed the plans for restricting trade with Great Britain until Parliament agreed to repeal the objectionable acts.[96]

Of the ten resolutions making up the first section of the Statement of Rights, only that concerning the authority of Parliament provoked serious controversy. The delegates denied Parliament's right to tax the colonists without their consent and claimed such traditional "rights of British subjects" as trial by jury and freedom of assembly. Other articles asserted the inviolability of the charter rights of each colony and of the several provincial codes, proclaimed that no standing army could be maintained in the colonies during periods of peace without the consent of the colonial legislatures, and declared that each branch of the several colonial legislatures was distinct. This last resolution condemned the exercise of legislative functions by the council in those colonies where that body was appointed by the king.[97]

The Statement of Rights and Grievances listed thirteen specific acts of Parliament, plus the practice of stationing troops in the colonies during peacetime, as intolerable. Included were the Currency Act of 1764, the Revenue Acts of 1764 and 1766, the Post Office Act of 1765, the unrepealed portions of the Townshend duties, the act of 1767 creating a Customs Board in America, the act of 1768 extending jurisdiction of the Admiralty Courts, and the Dock-Yards Act of 1772 providing in certain cases for the trial of colonial offenders in other parts of the empire. In addition, Congress demanded repeal of the acts that had occasioned its meeting: the Boston Port Act, the Massachusetts Government Act, the Justice Act, the Quartering Act, and the Quebec Act.[98] This list omitted all mention of statutes passed before 1763 but included most of the major pieces of parliamentary legislation enacted since that date. Two major exceptions were the Tea Act of 1773 and the Declaratory Act of 1766.[99]

Congress concluded its statement with a list of the "peaceable measures" adopted to procure redress. These simply restated earlier decisions made by the delegates. They included (1) the nonimportation, nonconsumption, and nonexportation of British goods; (2) an address to the people of Great Britain and the inhabitants of British America; and (3) a loyal address to the king.[100]

Having adopted these resolutions, all that remained for the delegates to do was to give their program finished form and decide upon a plan of enforcement. Work on this program had been under way since 30 September when Thomas Cushing, Isaac Low, Thomas Mifflin, Richard Henry Lee, and Thomas Johnson were appointed to draw up a final plan.[101] This committee had submitted its report on 12 October.[102] Since that time, the proposal, soon to be known as the Continental Association, had laid on the table for the delegates perusal.

Before dealing with the enforcement provisions of the Association, Congress debated the sections restating and elucidating the program of economic coercion. During the early days of October, Congress considered the advisability of extending nonimportation to include all duties articles.[103] The delegates rejected this absolute nonimportation of duties goods, but on 6 October, they did instruct the committee "that from and after the first day of December next, no molasses, coffee, or pimento from the British Plantations or from Dominica, or wine from Madeira and the West Islands, or foreign indigo, be imported into these colonies."[104] The committee itself added tea, syrups, paneles (brown unpurified sugar), and slaves to the list.[105]

By the second week in October, it seemed the Continental Association would be approved without difficulty. One unexpected obstacle remained. The South Carolina delegates refused to sign the Association because they thought the nonexportation clauses unfair. John Rutledge later explained his position at a public meeting in Charleston. He, and other members of the delegation, had favored a total nonexportation—to Europe as well as to England. But the northern colonies had rejected that proposal because they wanted to reap the profits of continued sales to Europe. Philadelphia, for example, carried on an annual export trade of £700,000, but only £50,000 of that went to the mother country. Thus Pennsylvania, like other northern colonies, would be much less affected by nonexportation than South Carolina, whose commerce, Rutledge lamented, would be "almost ruined." It's primary exports, rice and indigo, were enumerated articles and could be sold only to England. Unless Congress were to approve sale of these articles to Europe—a violation of the acts of trade and navigation—nonexportation to England would mean a total cessation of sales. Meanwhile the wheat-producing colonies could continue their trade with Europe and perhaps, if a shortage of rice resulted, even increase their profits.[106]

The South Carolina delegates kept their peace until the last week of meetings. Then, choosing the day Congress had set aside for signing the completed Association, all of the colony's delegates except Christopher Gadsden stalked out of the hall in protest. After weeks of work, it suddenly seemed that the carefully preserved unanimity would be shattered. Some of the other delegates were angry, suggesting that if the South Carolinians were determined to remain obstinate, the colony should be excluded from the Association. Gadsden tried to soften the blow by offering to take responsibility for his colony and sign the document without the consent of his fellow delegates.[107] In the end, the determination to preserve American unity prevailed. Congress invited the South Carolina delegates back into the hall and then worked out a compromise. The Association was amended in order to authorize the export of rice to Europe, and South Carolina yielded on the article of indigo.

On 20 October, the Continental Association was formally read before Congress and signed at the table in front of the hall. Every delegate present affixed his signature, and the others did so at a later time.[108] The Continental Association is one of the most important documents of American colonial history. By authorizing the establishment of local committees to enforce the embargo of trade, it provided the apparatus that would eventually develop into the government of revolution.

The Association began with a brief statement of the reasons for American opposition to certain measures of Parliament and a paragraph explaining that Congress had decided on a boycott of trade with the mother country as the "most speedy, effectual, and peaceable measure" for obtaining redress. It included fourteen separate provisions for implementing the embargo and concluded with a list of grievances whose redress Congress considered essential for a restoration of commercial ties. Most of the provisions concerning nonimportation and nonexportation were proposed and debated on the floor of Congress and have already been discussed. A number of other provisions, which did not deal directly with the implementation of the embargo, were presumably written into the Association by the committee appointed for that purpose and then adopted by the Congress without extended debate.[109] Consequently it is impossible to trace the origin of each clause of the document.

The most important sections of the Association dealt with the temporary embargo of trade, of course, but there were substantial portions aimed at permanently reducing the economic dependence of the American colonies on Great Britain. The agreement committed the colonists to "use our utmost endeavours" to increase the number of sheep in America and improve the stock so that the domestic manufacture of woolens might be advanced. It also bound the colonists to "encourage frugality, economy, and industry, and promote agriculture, arts and the manufacture of this Country." The delegates attempted to encourage republican virtue by urging their countrymen to "discountenance and discourage every species of extravagance and dissipation, especially all horse-racing, and all kinds of gaming, cockfighting, exhibitions of shews, plays and other expensive diversions and entertainments." The Association also called for a freeze on prices and especially warned peddlers and vendors against inflating profits due to the scarcity that was expected to accompany nonimportation.[110]

No provision of the Continental Association was more important than the establishment of local committees to enforce the program of commercial boycott. Committees were to be chosen in each county, city, or town by all those entitled to vote for representatives in the legislature, and they were to be responsible for observing the "conduct of all persons touching this association." Whenever a committee decided that a violation had occurred, it was authorized by the Congress to publish the name of the offender in some public place so that he might be "universally condemned" as an enemy of American liberty and ostracized. A similar isolation was to be invoked against entire towns, counties, or colonies that refused to enforce the Association.[111]

The Association also contained specific instructions for the disposition of articles imported in violation of the boycott. These provisions illustrate the determination of Congress to pacify the merchants. There was to be a period of grace from 1 December to 1 February during which the owner of imported goods could select one of three alternative means of satisfying the terms of nonimportation. He could have his goods shipped to another port, stored by the local committee until the trade boycott ended, or sold at public auction. If he chose the last alternative, the committee would arrange the auction, reimburse the importer for his costs and the charges of transportation, and then set aside the profits for the poor of Boston.[112] This provision protected the merchant whose shipment was legitimately delayed, as well as those who had sent out last-minute orders in anticipation of the coming shortage. Not until after 1 February did goods have to be returned unopened, a much more costly penalty for the importing merchant.

Congress did not adopt specific instructions on the enforcement of other provisions of the Association but instead left the committees free to adopt whatever measures they might consider necessary. The delegates did, however, authorize one other provision for making the trade boycott more effective. They instructed the existing committees of correspondence in the several colonies to "frequently inspect the Entries of their Custom Houses" and exchange information about what they found as well as "other material circumstance that may occur relative to this association."[113]

The program endorsed by the First Continental Congress was more elaborate and more comprehensive than any previously adopted by an individual town or colony; yet there was little in the Association that had not been previously suggested. In every colony, public meetings had recommended nonimportation and nonexportation and proposed means of enforcement similar to those adopted by the Congress. A number of colonies, including Massachusetts, Maryland, Virginia, and North Carolina, had established local committees similar to those recommended by the Association.

Even after adoption of the Association, Congress did not consider its work complete. For three weeks the committee had worked on the address to the king. On 21 October, a draft was submitted to Congress but rejected because of its immoderate tone.[114] Congress suggested that the committee reconsider its project and appointed a fifth member, John Dickinson. A second draft, written in large part by Dickinson, was approved by Congress on 23 October. The petition which was finally ratified did not alter any part of the program adopted by Congress but was phrased in more conciliatory language than the original draft.[115]

On 22 October, two days after completion of the Association, the delegates voted to hold another Congress on 10 May 1775, "unless grievances be redressed."[116] This date roughly approximated the length of time needed for Great Britain to respond to the measures adopted at the first meeting, and the decision attests to Congress's determination to follow through with its program.

As the delegates to the First Continental Congress left Philadelphia during the last days of October, they congratulated each other on the remarkable unanimity that had accompanied their deliberations. Unlike the Stamp Act Congress of 1765, at which two influential members had refused to endorse the resolutions adopted, every delegate at the Philadelphia meeting had signed and agreed to abide by the provisions of the Continental Association.

· GOVERNMENT BY COMMITTEE ·

All the colonies represented in Congress endorsed the Continental Association except New York, and even in the latter province, local committees saw to the enforcement of its nonimportation sections. Except in Georgia and the occupied city of Boston, purchases from Great Britain stopped entirely. The most outspoken critics of the measure were forced to admit that the boycott had the force of law throughout the colonies.[117] Another, and in the long run more significant, aspect of the Association was the provision calling for the election of committees to enforce the trade boycott. Because approval and enforcement of the Association were placed in the hands of local groups rather than provincial assemblies or congresses, these committees became the regulatory agencies of the First Continental Congress.

In almost every colony, these local committees began enforcement before any kind of provincial body met. New York City elected a committee of inspection which effectively implemented the nonimportation agreement despite the repeated refusal of the provincial assembly to endorse the program adopted by Congress. A similar situation occurred in Georgia, where the legislature also refused to act on the Association, yet the parish of St. John's promised to execute the boycott of trade and asked to be accepted by other associating communities.[118] By thus administering nonimportation, the committee system became the first step toward the creation of an American union.

Just as the committees of correspondence had aided in calling the Continental Congress, so they proved almost indispensable in organizing enforcement of the program it adopted. Some of these committees actually took over the task of implementing the Association, and in almost every other case they arranged the election of committees to do so. In New England, the towns elected committees, and the only county organizations that existed took the form of congresses made up of delegates from the several local communities. The southern colonies elected committees at county meetings, as well as in such towns as Wilmington in North Carolina, Charleston in South Carolina, and Williamsburg and Norfolk in Virginia. In the middle colonies, a hybrid system prevailed: for example, each Pennsylvania county elected a committee, as did many of the towns and districts within the several counties. In many instances, the latter groups seem to have been entirely distinct from the larger county committees.[119]

A typical election took place in James City County, Virginia. The local committee of correspondence arranged for the publication of the Association in the *Virginia Gazette* and followed it with a notice announcing

> that the above, and all other *resolutions* of the *Congress,* may be carried into *strict execution,* the several freeholders of James City county are desired to meet at eleven o'clock on Friday the 25th instant, if fair, otherwise the succeeding day, at the house of Mr. Isham Allen, in order to elect a *committee* to act *throughout* the said county, and do what is *required* of them by so respectable and august a body.[120]

Normally, the citizens, whether assembled in town or county meetings, adopted resolutions approving the Association and then proceeded directly to the election of a committee of inspection. In some southern counties, the election might be scheduled for an entire day, or even two, to accomodate those who had to travel long distances.

South Carolina was unique in that, with the major exception of Charleston, the provincial congress appointed the local committees, arguing the necessity of taking immediate action. The convention recommended that each parish and district meet as soon as possible to approve the appointed committees or to elect different ones if they so desired.[121]

The number of committee meetings varied. In many small communities—especially in the frontier areas—the committees probably did not meet at all. In larger towns and in many of the southern counties, the committees met regularly, usually once a month, as well as on special call from the chairman or members who had been authorized to convene them. Committees in seaports met more often than those elsewhere to cope with the time-consuming problems involved in implementing the nonimportation agreement. Philadelphia's committee divided the city into districts and appointed a "sub-committee of Inspection & Observation" for each. These smaller groups then designated two or three of their members to sit each day at the coffeehouse or some other central location and receive reports of incoming cargoes.[122] Similar arrangements prevailed in New York and Charleston. In Boston, of course, the British navy was enforcing a boycott under the provisions of the Port Act.

Although Congress had proposed the election of committees for the specific purpose of enforcing the Continental Association, it was apparent from the beginning that such groups might perform a variety of functions. The committees of correspondence had not always confined themselves to correspondence, and there was no reason to suppose that the new committees might not do more than inspect. Indeed, the number and size of the committees suggests an objective beyond the simple observance of a trade boycott. Whig leadership in the colonies sought to influence local opinion and strengthen its position by involving the largest possible number of freeholders in active opposition to parliamentary legislation. This effort was eminently successful. One can confidently estimate that more than 1,100 freeholders were appointed to committees of inspection in Virginia.[123] Maryland, though smaller in population, named nearly as many.[124]

The figures for Massachusetts, Connecticut, New Hampshire, and New Jersey are equally remarkable. The Bay Colony appointed at least 160 town committees, with committee members somewhere in excess of 1,600.[125] New Jersey counted more than 500, New Hampshire at least 400, Connecticut better than 650, and South Carolina just over 300.[126]

Records in the remaining colonies—New York, Pennsylvania, Rhode Island, North Carolina, and Delaware—are less informative. New York, outside its port city, was not overly enthusiastic in its support of the Association. The minimum number of persons named to committees there cannot safely be set in excess of 150.[127] At least 9 of the 11 counties in Pennsylvania established committees, with a total membership of about 500.[128] The minimum in Rhode Island can be set at 135, in North Carolina at 200 (although inadequate records make it likely that this number is only a fraction of the actual count), and in Delaware at between 40 and 60.[129]

That the Whig leadership deliberately sought to promote this extensive participation in extralegal local governments is indicated not only by the size of the committees appointed but also by their gradual enlargement. Maryland's committees, from the start larger than those in other colonies, increased dramatically in size during the latter part of 1774 and the early months of 1775.[130]

Other counties and other colonies entertained similar ideas. A broadside in Philadelphia argued in favor of appointing separate committees for the town and the county because, among other reasons, "by interesting people in most remote townships the enforcement will be more effective."[131] County committees in Pennsylvania and New Jersey often encouraged membership expansion by arranging for local districts to elect persons to represent them in enforcing the Association. In almost every colony, there were towns or counties that enlarged their committee membership despite the already total effectiveness of the nonimportation agreement.

Increased participation in government was also provided by the provincial congresses, which were much larger than the regularly established assemblies. The Boston Committee of Correspondence, in discussing plans for the colony's first congress, was "universally of Opinion that tis best to send as many Representatives as the Charter & Province Laws allow," and the provincial congress, meeting in Concord, repeatedly called on unrepresented towns to send delegates.[132] The South Carolina General Committee was larger than the assembly, in part because an early meeting of the committee had voted to create additional districts in the colony in order to ensure a more equal representation. The *South Carolina Gazette* thought that the new convention was "the most complete Representation of all the whole Colony, that ever was, and perhaps ever will be obtained."[133]

In Massachusetts, 279 persons were elected to the provincial congress of October 1774, and at least 250 of these appear to have attended.[134] Yet at the last session of the assembly held in the Bay Colony, only 129 delegates were recorded present.[135] New Hampshire sent 144 members to its convention in January 1775— more than triple the number of representatives in the assembly.[136] That same month the extralegal Pennsylvania convention met and, despite the failure of three counties to send delegates, counted almost three times as many members as the official assembly which met the following month.[137] In both New Jersey and Maryland, the membership of the extralegal provincial congresses was more than twice that of the regular assemblies, and the South Carolina Provincial Congress, with some 180 members, was over three times as large as its assembly.[138]

In addition to providing an extensive popular base for future resistance to Parliament, the committees of inspection performed a wide assortment of duties. The committees' activities affected almost every conceivable aspect of colonial life. They set the price of salt, promoted the manufacture of malt liquors, inspected Custom Houses, questioned those suspected of being Tories, and even regulated the moral standards of the inhabitants. The first and most important of their duties was of course the enforcement of nonimportation. This function proved most time-consuming during the two-month period of grace Congress had granted to merchants who might have sent orders before the Association was approved.[139]

When ships arrived in port during the months of December and January, the local committee would appoint a number of its members to investigate. If the consignee elected to sell his merchandise at auction, the subcommittee then made provisions for the sale, advertised it in the local papers, and supervised the auction. The importer rarely chose the other two options, to return or to store his goods, because of the risk of damage and uncertainty as to the Association's duration. Moreover, the committees generally favored sale because of the problems involved in supervising storage and the prevailing notion that goods already imported might as well be made available to the public. In some cases, perhaps most, importers were permitted to buy back their goods at little or no additional cost.

Before the first of February, little reason existed for anyone to oppose the nonimportation clause of the Association, and the committees had a relatively easy time enforcing it. Exactly how much merchandise came into the several ports to be sold at auction is uncertain, but some idea may be gained from the reports of those committees which kept a record of their sales. The committee in Wilmington, North Carolina, reported that during the first two months of enforcing the Association, total sales reached £9,650. New York City's committee did not estimate total value but reported the sale of goods from twenty-one different vessels and calculated the profit for the Boston poor at £347. Salem counted £109 profit for Boston, and Plymouth sent £31.[140]

After 1 February, the insistence that goods be shipped out of the colony meant a greater loss for the importer and, in spite of a reduction in the number of vessels entering port, brought increased efforts to evade the Association. Reshipment proved so expensive that some consignees elected to have their goods thrown overboard rather than sent to another port.[141] Importers made few attempts to violate the boycott forcibly, but they sometimes tried to smuggle goods into a colony or to obtain special permission from the committee.

The most notorious attempt to evade the nonimportation agreement occurred in New York City when the *Beulah,* arriving shortly after the February deadline, was refused permission to unload. Some of the Tory elements in New York had expected the *Beulah* to be an important test case; Benjamin Booth wrote that the vessel was "daily expected from London, when the matter will come to a fair trial."[142] Perhaps because of the importance of this early case, the New York committee appointed a small group to keep the vessel under observation so long as it remained in the harbor. Despite these precautions, the captain managed to transfer a portion of the shipment onto a boat from Elizabethtown, New Jersey, in order to evade the Association.[143] This infraction came to the attention of the committee in Elizabethtown, and cooperation between that group and the New York City committee resulted in the apprehension of those involved. Robert and John Murray, owners of a major portion of the cargo, confessed before the New York committee, and Elizabethtown censured Ichabod Barnet for his part in the affair.[144] Both the persistence and the intercommittee cooperation demonstrated in this instance are typical of efforts throughout the colonies.

In many parts of the colonies where the commercial aspects of the Association were of minor importance, committees were appointed for entirely different reasons. The use of tea, for example, proved a major problem in many areas, and despite its symbolic representation of British tyranny, long years of habit made it a difficult vice to control.

In some areas, the use of tea probably continued, at least in secret. But in general there can be little question that tea was an emblem of Toryism and was eschewed by most colonists. John Harrower, a recent immigrant from England, reported that he had not tasted tea during a six-month stay in Virginia and supposed the prohibition of that article to be effective throughout the colonies.[145]

Another aspect of the Association that occupied both local and provincial committees was the injunction to promote a program of economic nationalism. This provision promised not only to distress the British and lead to the repeal of the Coercive Acts but also to lessen permanently the economic dependence of the colonies on the mother country. To encourage the development of home manufacturing, many committees offered premium payments to the first person who produced certain articles needed in the locality.

Committees in every colony took steps to encourage the production of essential articles, and the proposal was considered advantageous even by many who opposed other provisions of the Association.[146] In both Pennsylvania and Virginia, the provincial conventions adopted elaborate resolutions encouraging the manufacture of a variety of articles, including woolens, cottons, flannel, blankets, rugs, hosiery, coarse cloths, all sorts of dyes, flax, hemp, salt, saltpeter, gunpowder, nails, wire, steel, paper, glass, copper products, and malt liquors.[147] The Massachusetts Provincial Congress adopted a similar list with the addition of tin plates, firearms, and buttons.[148]

One of the most ambitious programs the colonists attempted was the organization of "the United Company of Philadelphia for promoting American Manufactures." This group, set up in February 1775, was to consist of two hundred persons, each of whom would purchase a share in the company for £10. Their intention was to promote a factory for the production of linen and woolen and cotton cloth. On 16 March, they met to elect officers, and by the end of April the company was, at least temporarily, in regular operation.[149]

Almost all of the committees recognized the importance of protecting sheep as a means of reducing colonial dependence on Great Britain. Some even added their own provisions to the recommendations of Congress. In Virginia and Pennsylvania, the provincial conventions forbade the slaughter of all sheep less than four years old, and the butchers of Philadelphia, at the request of the city committee, agreed not to slaughter any sheep before the first of May.[150] The *South Carolina Gazette* reported that neither lamb nor mutton had been offered for sale in the city since the Association became effective.[151]

Among the most difficult, and pervasive, of the duties taken on by the committees of inspection was the enforcement of Congress's recommendations regarding frugality and simple living. Horse races, dances, gambling, county fairs, and all sorts of "dissipating vices" were cancelled in obedience to the Association. The Baltimore County committee, to avoid "mischiefs and disorders" and "strictly to observe the regulations of the continental congress," discouraged attendance at the approaching county fair.[152] A resolution passed in Marblehead, Massachusetts, condemned all dancing and feasting, and Portsmouth, New Hampshire, warned those who persisted in "Card & Billiards" that they must discontinue such practices in these times of "deep distress and danger."[153] The colonists accepted this interference in their social activities with little complaint.

Such a variety of activities made it necessary for the committees to employ many methods of detecting violators. Larger committees often divided themselves and assigned different groups to specific aspects of enforcement. Some of these groups might be sent to neighboring committees to exchange information or instructed to visit all persons in town and ascertain their opinions about contemporary affairs. New York City appointed a subcommittee to maintain a watch over the vessels entering the harbor, and many committees circulated copies of the Association and required all inhabitants to sign a pledge that they would obey the agreement. Especially popular in Virginia and Massachusetts, this practice found favor in various towns throughout the colonies. Groton, Massachusetts, voted to enter the names of all persons who refused to sign the document in the town records and on 12 April listed four persons for that offense.[154] Acton, also in the Bay Colony, decided that signers should include every person over sixteen.[155] Women were not normally required to sign, although some who were property holders did so.

Some committees appointed certain persons to circulate the Association for signatures, and in other cases the entire committee appealed to local citizens. In Wilmington, North Carolina, the committee voted to "go in a body and wait on all the Householders in Town, with the Association before mentioned, and request their signing it, or declare their reasons for refusing, that such Enemies to their Country may be set forth to public view and treated with the contempt they merit." The committee found one doctor, seven merchants, a planter, and two tailors who refused to sign and later published the names of the eleven as recommended by the Association.[156]

Judging from the records of committee activities, the article asking merchants not to take advantage of nonimportation to raise prices proved most difficult to enforce. To seek out violators, the committees often called upon various merchants to open their books for inspection. In Caroline County, Virginia, three subcommittees were appointed to investigate the books of certain merchants to see if they were guilty of raising prices. Six of these at first refused to cooperate, but after being publicly condemned as enemies of their country, they submitted.[157]

Enforcement of the Association varied in any number of ways from colony to colony, and even from town to town. In some places, unique "crimes" forced the committees to add new offenses to the list forwarded by Congress. Deerfield, Massachusetts, broke off all "commercial connection" with one John Williams because he appeared at the town meeting and "read the several definitions of treason, and their horrible punishments."[158] In other towns, the committees adopted special measures to ensure that every citizen adhered to the Association. Hingham, Massachusetts, sought to ensure cooperation by persuading the two town ministers to appear at a meeting and encourage all the inhabitants to comply with the provisions of the Continental Congress.[159] New Cambridge, Connecticut, was less subtle. That town appointed a special committee to interview all persons suspected of being "unsound in their political sentiments" and presumably to ostracize those whom they found guilty.[160] Punishment seems also to have varied not only from one place to another but among individuals.

The procedures adopted by the committees in investigating cases of violation also varied. New Haven County in Connecticut adopted an extraordinarily detailed set of regulations, which were then adopted throughout the province. These rules provided that any person accused of a violation should be notified of the charge in a summons issued to him and signed by at least one member of the committee. This summons explained the charges brought against the accused and asked him to appear before the committee and defend himself. Each summons had to specify a time and place for the defendant to appear and was to be served not less than six days prior to the appointed hearing. Members of the committee promised that the charge would be thoroughly heard and the accused given ample opportunity to present his case. To assure the fairest possible decision, no member involved in bringing the charge or in presenting evidence could vote to condemn the accused except "upon the fullest, clearest and most convincing Proof."[161]

The procedures endorsed by the New Haven committee, though more detailed than most, were probably not atypical. Because there was not a great deal of opposition to the Association, the committees usually did not find it necessary to proceed harshly. Many offenders were repeatedly summoned to appear before they were condemned, and in many instances persons were judged guilty and then forgiven on the basis of a simple apology.

No aspect of the committee system is more intriguing than the role that it played in arousing, or suppressing, mob violence. Virginia's Governor Dunmore contended that widespread organized defiance of Crown authority encouraged mob activity. He wrote that the committees in Virginia had assumed total authority in most counties; they watched "the conduct of every inhabitant, without distinction, and . . . send for all such as come under their suspicion into their presence; to interrogate them respecting all matters which, at their pleasure, they think fit objects of their inquiry." To stigmatize "such as they find transgressing what they are now hardy enough to call the Laws of Congress" was, according to Dunmore, "no other than inviting the vengeance of an outrageous and lawless mob to be exercised upon the unhappy victims."[162]

Dunmore's charge of mob violence was often repeated by opponents of the Association, and yet it appears that the committees more often acted to suppress lawlessness than to encourage it. The committee in Falmouth, Massachusetts, resolved to "exert their utmost endeavors to prevent all the inhabitants to this Town from engaging in any riots, tumults, and insurrections, or attacks on the private property of any person." Falmouth thought that such activities were "pernicious to the real interest . . . as well as injurious to the liberty of *America* in general."[163] The town meeting in Somersworth, New Hampshire, also viewed the committee system as a support for order in society and instructed its own group to suppress "vice and criminality." Wilbraham, Massachusetts, resolved that "the many Mobs & Riotous Practices that have been amongst us have been so far from helping the Common Cause of Liberty, that they have retarded it."[164] Thomas Ellison, a New York merchant, urged his father and brother to sign the Association because the weakness of civil government made it necessary to support the committees "to keep order, and prevent running into confusion, till these troubles can be settled."[165]

In almost every case where violence occurred, the committees opposed it. In Cumberland County, New Jersey, some members of the committee seized some tea landed at Greenwich and resolved to store it until the full committee could meet and discuss its final disposition. During the night a group of more zealous local inhabitants carried the tea away and destroyed it. The committee later held a meeting and condemned this procedure as an unnecessary act of violence.[166] An even better example of committee problems with unruly persons is found in the records of Newburyport, Massachusetts, where the group apprehended a store of East India tea and decided that it ought to be confiscated and stored. This decision aroused the ire of certain unidentified citizens who took possession of the tea and destroyed it. At the annual town meeting, the Newburyport committee appealed to the assembled freeholders for support, and the meeting voted its unanimous approval of the conduct of the committee, finding "the manner in which the Tea was taken out of their hands by no means Justifiable."[167] Such incidents occurred in almost all of the other colonies.

Nevertheless, the committees did face a serious problem in their efforts to enforce the Association and at the same time maintain local order. They were, after all, engaged in an extralegal activity that could be pursued only in defiance of the regularly established government. There was no basis in law for the proceedings of the committees, and some suggested that violent sanctions might sometimes be employed to maintain obedience to the resolutions of Congress. A county congress in Worcester, Massachusetts, condemned the use of violence "except so much as is necessary to carry the Resolves of the Continental and Provincial Congresses into Execution."[168]

As the regular local governments declined in power, the committees gradually extended their authority. In December 1774, the provincial convention in Maryland recommended that each county collect funds to buy military provisions; by the first of the year several of them had begun to do so.[169] In January 1775, the members of the committee in Fairfax County, Virginia, noted the example set by Maryland and also voted a tax for military supplies.[170] This extension of power made it increasingly necessary for the committees to insist that the inhabitants render them the same kind of obedience they had previously given the constitutionally established governments. Since this was the only way to prevent anarchy, it was little wonder that so many committees handed out their stiffest penalties to those who made slurs on the dignity of their proceedings. The committees of inspection were in the process of becoming committees of safety, and the possibility that they would take on the full responsibilities of revolutionary government was rapidly growing.

• ENFORCEMENT OF THE ASSOCIATION—NEW ENGLAND •

Enforcement of the Association was nowhere more visible than in New England. Not only did provincial and county meetings voice approval, but literally hundreds of towns endorsed the document and elected local committees to oversee its enforcement. Naturally, some opposition appeared, but in all of New England, fewer than half a dozen towns rejected the Association.

Connecticut showed overwhelming support for the Association. In November, the General Assembly voted approval of the Continental Congress and sent a letter to each of the towns in the colony recommending the election of committees to enforce the Association.[171] Of some seventy towns represented in the assembly, more than fifty either approved the Association in town meetings or elected committees of inspection to oversee enforcement. All of the six counties voiced approval, four in county congresses and two, Litchfield and Windham, in a four-county meeting held at Hartford on 15 December 1774.[172] Of the entire province, only two towns, Newtown and Ridgefield, rejected the Continental Congress and its resolutions.[173] Despite this, Fairfield County, in which the towns were located, convened a congress on 14 February 1775 and unanimously voted approval of the Association.[174] This congress, attended by representatives of every town except Ridgefield and Newtown, called on all citizens in the county and the country at large to refuse dealings with those residents who refused to endorse the Association.[175]

This sentiment spread throughout the province. The New Haven town meeting voted unanimously that "no Person in the Town should entertain the Deputies who were expected from the Towns of Ridgefield and Newtown to attend the General Assembly."[176] On 14 February, a group of gentlemen in Wethersfield escorted two Ridgefield residents out of town for defending their town's rejection of the Association. The two men were attended "with no violence," "the whole affair . . . conducted with the utmost Regularity."[177] The absence of a major port in Connecticut meant that committees there had few problems with the nonimportation clause and directed most of their efforts toward other matters.

Enforcement of the Association in Rhode Island was organized differently. There is no evidence that the towns met together in county congresses. Instead, the General Assembly and individual towns, especially Newport and Providence, provided the apparatus for effecting the program of the Continental Congress. In early December, the General Assembly approved the resolutions of Congress without debate and recommended that towns appoint committees of inspection to enforce the Association.[178] Even before the General Assembly met, at least one town, Gloucester, had appointed a committee. Newport and Providence, the two most important cities, elected committees before the end of December. Other towns followed soon after. There is no indication that any town in Rhode Island voted opposition to or worked against the resolutions of the Continental Congress in any way. As Governor Samuel Ward reported, the people were "universally satisfied with the proceedings of Congress."[179]

Though parts of New Hampshire were sparsely settled and far removed from the seaboard, that colony also took a forward stand in support of Congress and the Association. On 30 November, the colony's committee of correspondence approved the Association and sent a letter asking the several towns "immediately to appoint committees to see that the same Agreement be strictly adhered to, and faithfully executed."[180] By the time the provincial congress met on 25 January, a majority of towns had acted favorably on the Association. Governor John Wentworth testified to the effectiveness of the agreement in New Hampshire, writing Dartmouth that the measures of Congress were "received implicitly; . . . as matters of obedience, not of considerate examination."[181]

Rockingham County, with a population of about 35,000, was almost three times as large as any other in New Hampshire and the natural center of activity. The chief city in the county, Portsmouth, was also the only port of entry in the colony and therefore played a determining part in the enforcement of nonimportation. On 8 December, the town voted unanimously to endorse the Association and appointed a committee of twenty-five to see it enforced.[182] At least fifteen other towns took a similar stand before the end of February.[183]

In two counties, Hillsborough and Cheshire, conventions met to endorse the Association and recommend measures for its enforcement. Stafford County, third largest in the colony, did not hold a county meeting, but all its major towns appointed inspection committees.[184] Tiny Grafton county was also active in support of American claims.

Given the prompt and determined action taken by the towns and counties in New Hampshire, approval of the Association by the provincial assembly was a foregone conclusion. On 25 January, 144 delegates gathered at Exeter, approved the decisions of the Continental Congress, and passed a series of resolutions recommending enforcement of the Association. Among these resolutions were statements calling for the maintenance of law and order, the sanctity of private property, obedience to the Continental Association, special encouragement of domestic manufactures, and the exercise of the militia companies in case the colony was invaded by "his Majesty's enemies."[185]

No colony had so much at stake in the struggle over the Coercive Acts as Massachusetts, and none took so vigorous a stand in support of the Continental Congress. Approval of the Association in the Bay Colony was virtually unanimous. Nowhere else in the colonies were as many committees appointed as in Massachusetts.

Since the Massachusetts Provincial Congress remained in session through much of the fall and spring of 1774–75, it was among the first to ratify the Association. The delegates took the resolutions of Congress under consideration in early

December and voted their approval on the fifth. Special resolutions requested all towns which had not done so to elect committees of inspection and recommend the clauses of the Association dealing with improved manufacturing.[186]

Many towns in Massachusetts already had committees similar to those recommended in the Association. The breakdown of local and provincial government resulting from the attempted enforcement of the Coercive Acts had converted many committees of correspondence into local governing bodies. Some towns actually elected committees of observation to oversee commercial sanctions before they knew that Congress would make such a recommendation.[187] In Suffolk County, at least three towns had adopted a nonimportation covenant before Congress met, and the others acceded to the Continental Association shortly after its adoption. Records document the appointment of committees in at least fifteen towns, and it is almost certain that other communities either appointed committees or allowed existing organizations to take over the job.[188]

Enforcement of the Association in the ports of Marblehead, Newburyport, and Salem in Essex County was of particular importance since the Coercive Acts had effectively stopped importation at Boston. These ports appointed committees shortly after the Continental Congress adjourned. The effectiveness of each is well documented.[189] Other towns in Essex supported the ports, and at least fifteen communities acted favorably toward the Association.[190] In Middlesex County, over thirty towns appointed committees, more than any other county in America.[191] Hampshire County saw more than twenty-five towns elect committees.[192] Barnstable, Worcester, and Bristol convened county congresses to endorse the Association.[193] Towns in each county had either endorsed the Association prior to the congresses or acted shortly thereafter.[194] Significant support for the Association and the Continental Congress was also evident in Berkshire, Plymouth, Dukes, York, Cumberland, and Lincoln counties.

The single recorded rejection of the Association in Massachusetts came from Marshfield in Plymouth County. The citizens there not only refused the Association but, joined by persons in Scituate, signed a request for troop protection and sent it to General Gage at Boston.[195] Other towns in the county, including the port of Plymouth, were apparently united in support of Congress, and despite Marshfield's opposition, the Association was strictly enforced.[196]

The major attempt to organize opposition to the Association in Massachusetts came from Timothy Ruggles, who circulated a petition rejecting the work of the Congress. The petition pledged those who signed to support each other in resisting "unconstitutional Assemblies" and threatened the use of armed force, if necessary, to restore a proper allegiance to the king.[197] This petition, however, achieved little success.

If there was substantial opposition to the Association in New England, it does not appear in the records of the period. The extensive appointment of committees attests not only to the effectiveness of the Association but to the determination of the colonists to make known their opposition to British measures. Figures on trade, showing that importation from Great Britain to New England dropped from

£562,476 in 1774 to £71,625 in 1775, form but a small part of the story.[198] Many, perhaps most, communities that elected committees did not anticipate difficulty in enforcing the nonimportation agreement. The election of a committee symbolized a community's willingness to support the American cause and provided a basis for local government independent of the regular colonial government.

• ENFORCEMENT OF THE ASSOCIATION— THE MIDDLE COLONIES •

The Association faced its greatest test in the middle colonies and most particularly in New York. Perhaps because Congress had held its meetings in Philadelphia, opinion in that city and in Pennsylvania seemed more favorably disposed toward the Congress as the weeks passed.[199] But in New York, where the debate over sending delegates to Congress had caused considerable bitterness, there was increasing fear that the Association might be rejected.[200] This fear was not without foundation. Of all the colonies represented in Congress, only in New York did a provincial representative body refuse to endorse the Association. The supporters of Congress tried on several occasions to bring the resolutions of Congress before the assembly, but the majority consistently refused to consider them. On 26 January, a motion to take up the Association failed by eleven to ten, and in February a fuller House voted fifteen to nine against offering thanks to the New York delegation to Congress.[201] Though the assembly never actually condemned the Association, it did not nominate delegates to the Second Continental Congress and underscored its refusal to cooperate with the other colonies by sending a separate petition to the king as well as to the Lords and Commons.[202]

Despite the assembly's refusal to sanction the work of Congress, New York City went ahead with the election of a committee. Support for the Association came from all sections of the city. Just before Congress adjourned, the city importers met and pledged to avoid "any unreasonable advance" in prices and to use their efforts to prevent the creation of an artificial scarcity through the buying up of goods.[203] On 18 November, the mechanics of the city resolved to aid in carrying out the program of Congress "to the utmost of our power and ability."[204]

Problems, however, developed as the committee of fifty-one and the committee of mechanics were unable to agree on how the election might best be accomplished. After numerous meetings, the disagreements were resolved and a committee of sixty was chosen at a public meeting on 22 November 1774 to oversee enforcement of the Association in New York.[205]

Whatever the exact story behind the creation of the committee of sixty, it worked diligently in support of the Association and succeeded in halting the importation of British goods through the port of New York. At least twenty-one ships were forced to turn their cargoes over to the committee for sale during the months of December and January.[206] On 18 February, Ebenezer Hazard, of the committee of sixty, wrote: "Our committee are determined to be firm, and vigorously carry the Association into execution. This they will do, let the Assembly do what they will."[207] Governor Cadwallader Colden complained in March that the nonimportation agreement was "ever rigidly maintained" in the colony.[208]

Conflicting and scattered evidence makes it difficult to assess the reception of the Association in the other counties of New York. Albany, Suffolk, and Ulster counties responded favorably to the work of the Congress and appointed committees of inspection before the end of January.[209] In other counties, the response to the Association, prior to Lexington, was less enthusiastic. Newburgh, in Orange County, elected a committee on 27 January, but other towns in that area apparently did not do so until after the nineteenth of April.[210] Queens, Westchester, and Dutchess counties were divided over the Association, and there is no record of meetings being held in Kings and Tryon counties. Despite the mixed reaction which greeted the Association in several New York counties, no organized resistance appeared in any part of the colony.

Further light is shed on the situation in New York by the election of delegates to the extralegal provincial convention which met in April. Arrangements for the convention were made by the committee of sixty in New York City. On 15 March 1775, the city elected delegates.[211] The following day, the committee sent letters to the several counties requesting that they also appoint representatives.[212] Of the eight counties which responded to this invitation, at least three, Albany, Ulster, and Suffolk, favored the convention by clear majorities. All three appointed their delegates through existing county committees, which were made up of representatives from several towns and districts in each.

The delegates from Orange County were sent by elections in four separate towns.[213] In Westchester and Dutchess counties, opinion on the provincial convention appears to be almost evenly divided.[214] Majority opinion in Queens County[215] apparently opposed the meeting, while in two counties, Richmond and Tryon, no attempt was made to elect delegates.[216]

New Jersey's acceptance of the Association was not long in doubt. On 6 December 1774, Governor William Franklin wrote Lord Dartmouth, predicting that "the terms of Association will be generally carried into Execution even by those who dislike Parts of it."[217] Appointment of committees in New Jersey began in early December and was virtually completed by the end of January. The committee of correspondence in Essex County led the way by publishing a call for the election of committees in that county's three precincts.[218] Three other counties, Somerset, Gloucester, and Cumberland, appointed committees in December, and a fourth, Sussex, had a committee of correspondence which acted in defense of the Association as early as 23 November.[219] By the end of February 1775, the counties of Morris, Burlington, and Middlesex had approved the Association and elected committees.[220] Bergen was the only county in New Jersey which failed to marshal support for the Association. The single town meeting held in the county was at Hackensack, and the citizens there refused to appoint a committee.[221] Not until after Lexington did the county choose a committee and promise to abide by the resolutions of the Congress.[222]

Despite the opposition of Hackensack and the procrastination of Shrewsbury in Monmouth County, a large majority of the residents of New Jersey supported the Association. When the assembly met in January, it voted unanimous approval of all the resolutions of the Continental Congress and further signified its support by re-electing the same delegates to attend the Second Continental Congress in May.[223]

Pennsylvania, like New York, had been somewhat tardy in joining the patriot cause before Congress met, but the colony evidenced no hesitation in enforcing the Association once it had been adopted. Governor John Penn reported "great surprise" at the unanimity with which the colony accepted the Association and found "too general a disposition everywhere to adhere strictly to the resolutions of the congress."[224] The assembly convened in early December and on the tenth voted unanimous approval of the work done by the Continental Congress, recommending "an inviolable observation of the several matters and things contained in the Journal of the Congress."[225] During the next few months, Joseph Galloway used all of his influence to reverse this decision, but was unable to do so.

As in other colonies, the most important agency for enforcing the Association in Pennsylvania was the local committee. By the time the Second Continental Congress met in May, the city of Philadelphia and nine of the eleven counties had established committees.[226] On 14 November 1774, the city of Philadelphia elected a committee of sixty-six to enforce the Association. Most of the counties followed by year's end.[227] There is little evidence available concerning the election of committees in Pennsylvania towns, but some local communities did have separate committees.

On 23 January 1775, Pennsylvania convened its second provincial congress at the request of the committee of sixty-six in the city of Philadelphia.[228] The congress approved the Association and threatened that Pennsylvania would take steps to resist British coercion if necessary. The delegates also adopted an extensive list of resolutions designed to encourage economic independence.[229]

Pennsylvania's committee system was unquestionably effective. Philadelphia's sixty-six played the most important part in enforcing the nonimportation clause, and there is abundant testimony to its activity.[230] The primary activity of the county committees involved the promotion of local manufacturing, especially the protection of sheep.

The major opposition to the Association in Pennsylvania came from the Quakers, who took a firm stand against organized resistance to established government. They preferred "decent and respectful addresses." However, despite their wealth and influence, the Quakers were unable to prevent the Association's rigid enforcement in the province.

Not a great deal of information is available concerning the enforcement of the Association in Delaware. Two of the three counties, New Castle and Kent, chose committees which enforced the program.[231] Although Sussex County did not convene a congress at this time, there is no evidence that the county opposed the Association. Its delegates were present on 15 March when the Delaware Assembly ratified the document by a unanimous vote and later when delegates to the Second Continental Congress were elected.[232]

While it is generally true that the middle colonies were not so united in support of the Association as the New England or southern colonies, there is no question that the resolutions of Congress were enforced in that area. A letter from Delaware did not exaggerate in referring to the Association as "sacred laws."[233] Nonimportation was effective in every colony, and the number of committees appointed throughout the middle colonies indicates that the same was true for other articles of the Association as well. Even in New York, the active residents of the colony saw to the enforcement of the Association. Any opposition that existed was ineffective.

· ENFORCEMENT OF THE ASSOCIATION—THE SOUTHERN COLONIES ·

In all four participating southern colonies, Maryland, Virginia, and the Carolinas, the Association was ratified without difficulty at provincial meetings. Maryland was the first province to act. On 12 November and 8 December 1774, the provincial congress convened, endorsed the Association, and made provisions for its enforcement.[234] The later meeting took special note of the sections encouraging the production of hemp, wool, flax, and cotton. Delegates also set specific limits on the profits of merchants and elected representatives to the Second Continental Congress. Finally, the Congress recommended that each county collect a sum of money for the purchase of arms and ammunition.[235]

Meanwhile, the counties of Maryland organized enforcement committees. By the end of November, Charles, Calvert, Prince George, Anne Arundel, Frederick, and Baltimore counties had elected committees of inspection, and St. Mary's followed suit on 23 December.[236] In other counties, previously appointed committees of correspondence took over the duties of inspection. Documents show that this happened in Dorchester, Talbot, Queen Anne's, Kent, and Cecil counties.[237] Since the provincial congress made no charge to the contrary, it appears that local committees acted in every Maryland county.

Committee organization in Maryland was the exact reverse of that in New England. Instead of local committees being elected and then meeting to organize county committees, the county organizations were elected first. These were made large enough so that they could divide for enforcement of the Association in local districts. Committees did not insist that all inhabitants sign the Association, and despite the relative unanimity which prevailed in the colony, there is some indication that persons opposed to the Association were not harassed if they did not actively vent their displeasure. In Baltimore, the Reverend Mr. Edmiston admitted to the committee that his sentiments were "different from what most people think at this time" but promised "to avoid giving any just cause of offence, by propagating hereafter any opinion opposite to the decisions of the continental congress, or provincial convention."[238] There is no evidence that the committee censured him for this opinion, as would certainly have happened in Virginia and many parts of New England. In fact, most committees in Maryland were inclined, even in cases dealing with the nonimportation clause, to show leniency towards offenders provided that they promised reform.

As might be expected in a province surrounding the largest bay in the colonies, the greatest effort went into the enforcement of nonimportation. The effectiveness of this operation is unquestionable. British imports in Virginia and Maryland combined dropped from £528,738 in 1774 to £1,921 in 1775.[239] In not more than half a dozen cases did it prove necessary to censure violators of the Association, and at least half of these later issued statements of apology. More often than not, those who received goods after the nonimportation agreement became effective reported themselves to the local committee—further evidence that the chances of successful evasion were slim and punishment by public censure displeasing in the extreme.

Probably no colony outside New England gave the Association such thorough support as Virginia. The Association had been recommended by Virginia, and the resolutions of the Continental Congress simply gave further support to a program previously endorsed by the Old Dominion.[240] In a letter to Lord Dartmouth just before Christmas, Governor Dunmore described the extent of Association enforcement in Virginia. Every county, the governor explained, had elected a committee, and the feeble condition of the legal government condemned him to inaction lest further failure result in public ridicule. Dunmore found that the "Laws of Congress" were favored by the Virginians with "marks of reverence which they never bestowed on their legal Government." In fact, some of the most important officials in the colony were "the principle and most rigid Associators."[241]

In Virginia, as in most other colonies, local committees provided the most important basis for enforcing the Association. No provincial assembly met in the colony until 20 March, by which time the county committees were in effective operation. By the end of December, at least twenty-six counties had active committees and half a dozen or more elected in January.[242] H. J. Eckenrode, a historian of the period, stated that "by the middle of 1775 probably every one of the sixty counties had complied" with the resolutions of the Continental Congress.[243] Activities of these committees ranged from condemnation for card playing to levying taxes and establishing county militias. Local committees also encouraged development of domestic manufacturing.

In addition, Virginia committees made an extensive effort to ferret out opposition to the Association by a requirement that all citizens sign the document. This practice became increasingly important as the county committees assumed the functions of providing stable government. Endorsement of the Association by the Virginia Convention did not come until long after most counties had elected their Association committees. It was therefore more important as a gesture of support than as an effective factor in enforcing the agreement. On 22 March 1775, the delegates gave their unanimous approval to all the actions and resolutions of the Continental Congress.[244]

Similar to Maryland and Virginia, North Carolina convened an extralegal provincial congress to endorse the Association. Enforcement had, however, already been operating. Governor Martin urged the people to reject "all measures so subversive of order and Government" and denounced the committee as "tyrannical and arbitrary." He said they had forced people "to submit to their unreasonable, seditious, and chimerical Resolves."[245] Despite warnings from Governor Martin that those attending the congress would suffer "His Majesty's High displeasure," delegates from twenty-six counties and five towns met in New Bern on 3 April 1775.[246] This gathering coincided with the scheduled meeting of the regular provincial assembly and membership was almost identical. The purpose of calling the congress was to prevent the governor's dissolving the assembly, or if he did so, to provide the province with a semi-official representative convention.

On 5 April, the provincial congress voted unanimous approval of the Association and decided that every member present should sign a pledge of enforcement.[247] Thomas Macknight, a member from Currituck, refused to sign, pleading that he could not in good faith pledge to abide by the nonexportation agreement so long as he had debts in England.[248] After attempts at compromise failed, Congress voted by a narrow margin that Macknight was a "proper object of Contempt" and recommended that all persons break off dealing with him.[249]

In the meantime, Governor Martin asked the official provincial assembly to discourage the "illegal" provincial congress. The assembly, however, rejected Martin's request, voting instead that the provincial congress "deserve not to be called an illegal meeting, or to have the imputation of sedition cast upon them."[250] On the following day, 7 April, when the assembly voted its approval of the Continental Congress, Martin dissolved the body.[251]

Exactly how many counties in North Carolina elected committees of inspection cannot be determined. As in other colonies, most counties had previously elected local committees which sometimes took over enforcement of the Association without the formality of a second election. It is certain that at least twelve of the thirty-five counties, most of them on the coast, had special committees.[252] The most active of these was the committee operating in the chief port, Wilmington, and the surrounding county of New Hanover. Between 1 December 1774 and 1 February 1775, the committee sold almost £10,000 of imported goods without recorded objections on the part of the importers.[253]

Although records of committee action in North Carolina are less complete than in Maryland or Virginia, it is evident that the Association was effective there. British imports into the Carolinas declined from £378,116 in 1774 to £6,245 in 1775.[254] The main opposition came from the old Regulator counties, and they were in no position to undermine the document.[255]

In South Carolina, plans for a provincial congress developed soon after the return of the colony's delegates from Philadelphia. This task fell upon the general committee, a body appointed by the provincial congress the previous summer and authorized to act in its absence. The committee, which constituted the unofficial government of the province, made arrangements for the second provincial convention and enforced the Association until such time as the convention could meet. Even before the Association had been published, the general committee issued a warning to merchants against the hoarding of merchandise and forbade price increases in anticipation of trade restrictions.[256]

When the South Carolina Provincial Congress convened on 11 January, there were representatives from every part of the colony.[257] All of the resolutions of the Continental Congress were approved, and committees were appointed to enforce the Association in every parish and district except Charleston. In that city, the delegates elected to the provincial congress apparently served as a committee of inspection. The main difficulty encountered by the congress concerned the provision of the Association which exempted rice from nonexportation. After a long debate, a resolution authorizing delegates to the Second Continental Congress to work for the repeal of the provision was narrowly defeated. Arrangements were made to compensate those who might be hurt by nonexportation.[258]

As in other colonies, the congress voted special endorsement of the Association's clauses dealing with improvement of manufactures and encouraged production of all sorts of cloth. It also prohibited the slaughter of sheep for sale after 1 March.[259] All inhabitants of the colony were advised to be diligent in learning the use of arms, and militia officers were instructed to train and exercise their men at least once a month.[260] Delegates also resolved that no action on the collection of debt should proceed in the court of common pleas without express approval of the county committees.[261] Before adjourning on 17 January, the congress elected representatives to the Second Continental Congress and arranged the organization of a new general committee.[262]

The Association was enforced in South Carolina with little or no opposition. On 24 January 1775, the official South Carolina Provincial Assembly added its vote of confidence to the work of the Continental Congress, extending thanks to the delegates from South Carolina and sanctioning their reappointment by the provincial congress.[263] Throughout the spring, the committees of inspection—appointed by the extralegal provincial congress—carried into effect the resolutions of the Continental Congress and provincial convention. As in other colonies, the South Carolina county committees were assigned prerogatives normally reserved for legally established government. The general committee (a kind of executive council chosen by the provincial congress) reported to the committee of sixty in New York on 1 March: "In this colony the Association takes place, as effectually as law itself. . . . and that Ministerial opposition is here obliged to be silent."[264]

Georgia remained unsupportive of the Association. On 23 January 1775, the provincial congress adopted a modified Association but refused to approve the resolutions of the Continental Congress. The delegates, however, agreed to abide by decisions of the Second Continental Congress and elected representatives to attend that meeting.[265]

St. John's Parish made the only concerted effort in Georgia to effect the resolutions of the Continental Congress. The county had adopted the Continental Association on 1 December 1774, and when the provincial congress refused to consider the document, the delegates of the parish rejected the claim of the Congress to represent the colony.[266] St. John's subsequently sent three delegates to Charleston requesting that the South Carolina general committee exempt the parish from its 8 February 1775 decision to sever all "trade, Commerce, Dealings, or Intercourse" with the inhabitants of Georgia.[267] Noting that the terms of the Association did not provide for exceptions within a colony, the general committee rejected this petition. Since Georgia had not adopted the Association, the entire colony was subject to embargo unless the Second Continental Congress agreed to an exception.[268]

Georgia's reluctance did not seriously undermine the overall effect of the Association in the southern colonies. While the imports of British goods in that colony rose slightly from 1774 to 1775, the increase is insignificant in comparison with the figures from Maryland, Virginia, and the Carolinas. Total imports to the five colonies from Great Britain declined from £906,854 in 1774 to £8,166 in 1775.[269] Furthermore, it is clear that the gathering in Philadelphia in September 1774 added impetus to the revolutionary movement in Georgia. The second meeting of the Continental Congress found the American union completed by the addition of representatives from the thirteenth colony.

• THE COLONIES UNITED •

The significance of the widespread commitment to oppose the Coercive Acts can hardly be overstated. Much more than the Stamp Act of 1765 or the Townshend duties of 1767, the Coercive Acts crystallized American fears and grievances. They appeared to threaten the Protestant religion, the availability of land in the west, the integrity of the colonial assemblies, the right of taxation, the traditional procedures of jury trial, the civil control of the military, and the sanctity of colonial charters. There was almost no complaint voiced by the Americans in the past century that Great Britain did not manage to revive by one or more of the provisions of the Coercive Acts.

Relying upon precedents established at the time of the Stamp Act in 1765 and the Townshend duties in 1767, the colonists calmly and deliberately bound themselves to a policy of trade restrictions. Upon the unanimous endorsement of this policy by Congress, and with the prevailing belief that unanimity would bring victory, the colonists flocked to assert their support. By the time the Americans clashed with British troops at Lexington, they had established hundreds of committees instructed to enforce the Continental Association. Thousands of colonists, by accepting membership on these committees, identified themselves with the leadership of a movement which the British would soon label rebellion and move to subdue by military force. Moreover, every colony except Georgia and New York approved the Association either in its assembly or in a specially elected congress. Eleven of the thirteen colonies thus placed their political prestige on the table: they had officially objected to the Coercive Acts and committed themselves to procuring repeal. In this process, the unity at which the colonists had only aimed in the earlier crises of 1765 and 1767–70 had now been achieved.

· NOTES ·

1. The text of the Port Act is in Peter Force, ed., *American Archives,* 4th ser., (Washington, D.C.: Government Printing Office, 1837–46), vol. 1, pp. 61–66.

2. The text of the Act for Better Government of Massachusetts Bay is in *ibid.,* pp. 104–12.

3. The text of the Act for Better Administration of Justice in Massachusetts Bay is in *ibid.,* pp. 129–32.

4. The text of the Quartering Act is in *ibid.,* p. 170.

5. For a defense of the British legislation, see Jack M. Sosin, "The Massachusetts Act of 1774; Coercive or Preventative?", *Huntington Library Quarterly* 26 (1963), pp. 235–52.

6. The text of the Quebec Act is in Force, *American Archives,* vol. 1, pp. 216–20.

7. Thomas Wharton to Thomas Walpole, 10 June 1774, *Thomas Wharton Letterbook,* Historical Society of Pennsylvania.

8. Richard Henry Lee to Arthur Lee, 26 June 1774, James C. Ballagh, ed., *The Letters of Richard Henry Lee* (New York: John Hopkins Press, 1911–14), vol. 1, p. 114.

9. George Washington to Brian Fairfax, 4 July 1774, John C. Fitzpatrick, ed., *The Writings of George Washington* (Washington, D.C.: U.S. Government Printing Office, 1931), vol. 3, p. 228.

10. Edmund Burke to the committee of correspondence for the New York General Assembly, 2 August 1774, "The Letters and Papers of Cadwallader Colden," New York Historical Society, *Collections,* vol. 7, p. 232.

11. Arthur Lee to Richard Henry Lee, 18 March 1774 and Arthur Lee to Francis L. Lee, 2 April 1774, Force, *American Archives,* vol. 1, pp. 229, 237.

12. George Washington to Brian Fairfax, 20 July 1774. Fitzpatrick, *Writings of Washington,* vol. 3, p. 233.

13. Force, *American Archives,* vol. 1, p. 331 and n.; Boston Committee of Correspondence to Charlestown, Brookline, Newton, Cambridge, Roxbury, Medford, and Lynn, 11 May 1774, "Boston Committee of Correspondence Papers," New York Public Library.

14. Force, *American Archives,* vol. 1, p. 331 and n.; John P. Kennedy, ed., *Journals of the House of Burgesses of Virginia* (Richmond: The Colonial Press, 1905), vol. 13, pp. 147–48.

15. John Russell Barlett, ed., *Records of the Colony of Rhode Island and Providence Plantations in New England,* (Providence: A. C. Greene and Brothers, 1862), vol. 7, p. 280.

16. Roger Champagne, "New York and the Intolerable Acts," in the New York Historical Society, *Quarterly* 45 (1961), pp. 199–200; *Pennsylvania Gazette,* 25 May 1774.

17. William Smith, *Historical Memoirs, from 16 March 1763 to 9 July 1776,* William Sabine, ed., (New York: n.p. 1956); Champagne, *"New York and the Intolerable Acts,"* pp. 201–5.

18. *Ibid.,* p. 204; Force, *American Archives,* vol. 1, p. 295.

19. *Ibid.,* p. 296.

20. *Pennsylvania Gazette,* 8 June 1774.

21. *Ibid.*

22. John Hall et al. to Peyton Randolph et al., 25 May 1774, "Purviance Papers," Maryland Historical Society (microfilm, Colonial Williamsburg Foundation).

23. Baltimore Committee of Correspondence to Alexandria, Virginia, Committee of Correspondence, 1774, *ibid.;* Force, *American Archives,* vol. 1, pp. 366–67.

24. Resolutions from all these counties may be found in *ibid.,* pp. 366, 384, 402, 403, 410 as well as in the *Maryland Gazette* for 1774.

25. Julian P. Boyd, et al., eds., *The Papers of Thomas Jefferson* (Princeton: Princeton Univ. Press, 1950), vol. 1, p. 106n.

26. Force, *American Archives,* vol. 1, p. 350.

27. Boyd, *Papers of Jefferson,* vol. 1, pp. 107–8.

28. Virginia Committee of Correspondence to Maryland Committee of Correspondence, 31 May 1774, "Purviance Papers," Maryland Historical Society (microfilm, Colonial Williamsburg Foundation).

29. *Ibid.*

30. Bartlett, *Records of Rhode Island,* vol. 7, pp. 246–47.

31. Force, *American Archives,* vol. 1, pp. 421–22.

32. For more information on the Solemn League, see Albert Matthews, "The Solemn League and Covenant," in the Colonial Society of Massachusetts, *Publications* 18 (1915–16), p. 103.

33. For accounts of these meetings, see Coffin to Charles Steuart, 6 July 1774, "Steuart Papers," National Library of Scotland (microfilm, Colonial Williamsburg Foundation).

34. For an extensive list of the donations to Boston, see Massachusetts Historical Society, *Collections,* 2d ser., 9 (1822) pp. 158–62.

35. Force, *American Archives,* vol. 1, pp. 439–40.

36. John Drayton, ed., *Memoirs of the American Revolution Relating to the State of South Carolina* (Charleston: A. E. Miller, 1821), vol. 1, pp. 112–13, 126–30.

37. Charles J. Hoadly, ed., *The Public Records of the Colony of Connecticut* (Hartford: Lockwood & Brainard, 1887), vol. 14, p. 324.

38. Governor Wentworth to the Earl of Dartmouth, 8 June, 6 July, 13 July 1774, Force, *American Archives,* vol. 1, pp. 393–94, 516, 536, 893–94.

39. Kennedy, *Journals of the House of Burgesses,* vol. 13, p. 158.

40. Force, *American Archives,* vol. 1, p. 392.

41. *Pennsylvania Gazette,* 15 June 1774.

42. Force, *American Archives,* vol. 1, 426–27.

43. William Duane, ed., *Extracts from the Diary of Christopher Marshall, 1774–1781* (reprint of 1887 ed., New York: New York Times, 1969), p. 7.

44. Force, *American Archives,* vol. 1, pp. 426–27; Philadelphia Committee of Correspondence to the several counties in Pennsylvania, 28 June 1774, *Pennsylvania Gazette,* 6 July 1774.

45. Force, *American Archives,* vol. 1, pp. 555–64.

46. Benjamin Booth to James and Drinker, 25 July 1774, "James and Drinker Business Papers," Historical Society, Pennsylvania.

47. Benjamin Booth to James and Drinker, 28 July 1774, *ibid.*

48. Force, *American Archives,* vol. 1, p. 319; Committee of Mechanicks in New York to Boston Committee of Correspondence, 1 August 1774, "Boston Committee of Correspondence Papers," New York Public Library; Benjamin Booth to James and Drinker, 1 August 1774, "James and Drinker Business Papers."

49. Force, *American Archives,* vol. 1, p. 668.

50. *Ibid.,* pp. 597–602. Resolutions from many other meetings may be found through-out this volume as well as in the *Virginia Gazette* for 1774.

51. Force, *American Archives,* vol. 1, p. 523.

52. William Saunders, ed., *Colonial and State Records of North Carolina* (10 vols., Raleigh: Trustees of the Public Libraries 1890), vol. 9, pp. 1029–30.

53. *Ibid.,* pp. 1041–49.

54. A meeting held in Savannah on 10 August adopted a number of resolutions, but did not elect delegates. St. John's Parish supported the meeting of a congress but was unable to arouse sufficient support in other areas of the colony to justify sending a delegate to the Congress (see Force, *American Archives,* vol. 1, pp. 700, 766–67).

55. In Massachusetts the question was taken up by the assembly, but almost every major town in the colony supported the trade embargo (see "Boston Committee of Corre-spondence Papers," New York Public Library). The resolutions of Connecticut and Rhode Island towns in favor of nonimportation can also be found in *ibid., Connecticut Courant, Newport Mercury, Providence Gazette,* and several newspapers published in Boston. For the resolutions of Providence, Westerly, and Newport, Rhode Island, see Force, *American Archives,* vol. 1, pp. 333, 336–37, 343–44.

56. James Duane's "Notes on the Debates," Edmund Burnett, ed., *Letters of Members of the Continental Congress* (8 vols., Washington, D.C.: Carnegie Institute of Washington, 1921–36), vol. 1, p. 8.

57. Silas Deane to Mrs. Deane, 5–6 September 1774, *ibid.,* p. 11.

58. Duane, "Notes of Proceedings," *ibid.,* p. 8; Joseph Galloway to William Franklin, 5 September 1774, *ibid.,* p. 9.

59. John Adams, 5 September 1774, L. H. Butterfield, ed., *The Diary and Autobiog-raphy of John Adams* (Cambridge, Mass.: Belknap Press, 1961), vol. 2, p. 122.

60. John Adams to Abigail Adams, 16 September 1774, Burnett, *Letters of Continen-tal Congress,* vol. 1, p. 32.

61. Charles Francis Adams, ed., *The Works of John Adams* (10 vols., Boston: Little, Brown, 1850–56), vol. 2, p. 378.

62. Samuel Ward, "Diary," 6 September 1774, Burnett, *Letters of Continental Con-gress,* vol. 1, p. 19.

63. John Adams to Abigail Adams, 18 September 1774, *ibid.,* p. 19.

64. *Ibid.,* p. 34.

65. Christopher Collier, ed., "Silas Deane Reports on the Continental Congress," *Connecticut Historical Society Bulletin* 29 (1964), p. 3; Worthington C. Ford, ed., *Journals of the Continental Congress, 1774–1798* (Washington, D.C.: Government Printing Office, 1921), vol. 1, p. 54n.

66. Collier, "Silas Deane Reports," pp. 3–4.

67. Ford, *Journals of Continental Congress,* vol. 1, pp. 31–32.

68. *Ibid.,* pp. 32–37. See also appendix.

69. *Ibid.,* p. 39.

70. John Adams, 17 September 1774, Butterfield, *Diary and Autobiography of John Adams,* vol. 2, p. 134.

71. John Adams, "Notes of Debates," Burnett, *Letters of Continental Congress,* vol. 1, p. 22.

72. *Ibid.,* see also James Duane, "Address before the Committee to State the Rights of the Colonies," *ibid.,* pp. 23–26.

73. James Duane, "Notes of Debates," *ibid.*, p. 72.

74. Ford, *Journals of Continental Congress,* vol. 1, p. 41.

75. John Adams, "Notes of Debates," Burnett, *Letters of Continental Congress,* vol. 1, p. 53.

76. *Ibid.*, p. 50.

77. Ford, *Journals of Continental Congress,* vol. 1, pp. 42–53; John Adams, "Notes of Debates," Burnett, *Letters of Continental Congress,* vol. 1, p. 48.

78. *Ibid.*

79. *Ibid.*, p. 50.

80. Samuel Ward, "Diary," *ibid.*, p. 51.

81. Ford, *Journals of Continental Congress,* vol. 1, pp. 51–52.

82. Adams, *Works of John Adams,* vol. 2, p. 384 and n.; Drayton, *Memoirs of the American Revolution,* vol. 1, pp. 168, 170.

83. *Ibid.*, p. 168; John Adams, "Notes of Debates," Burnett, *Letters of Continental Congress,* vol. 1, p. 48.

84. Ford, *Journals of Continental Congress,* vol. 1, p. 54.

85. *Ibid.*

86. *Ibid.*, p. 55.

87. *Ibid.*, pp. 55–56.

88. John Adams to William Tudor, 7 October 1774, Burnett, *Letters of Continental Congress,* vol. 1, p. 65. John Drayton reported further that Christopher Gadsden of South Carolina had proposed an attack on Boston before Thomas Gage could be reinforced but was overruled by Congress (Drayton, *Memoirs of the American Revolution,* vol. 1, p. 165).

89. Ford, *Journals of Continental Congress,* vol. 1, pp. 57–58.

90. Harry A. Cushing, ed., *The Writings of Samuel Adams* (New York: G. P. Putnam's Sons, 1907), vol. 3, p. 159; Ford, *Journals of Continental Congress,* vol. 1, pp. 60–61.

91. *Ibid.*, p. 58.

92. *Ibid.*, pp. 59–60.

93. John Adams, "Diary," Burnett, *Letters of Continental Congress,* vol. 1, p. 74.

94. Adams, *Works of John Adams,* vol. 2, pp. 373–77.

95. Ford, *Journals of Continental Congress,* vol. 1, pp. 68–69.

96. *Ibid.*, pp. 63–74.

97. *Ibid.*, pp. 70–71.

98. *Ibid.*, pp. 71–73.

99. Both of these acts are listed as grievances in several other documents prepared by Congress. See, for example, the "Memorial to the Inhabitants of the British Colonies," *ibid.*, pp. 92, 98. During the debates on 15 and 17 October, Congress entirely dropped five of the grievances named in the Statement of Rights and Grievances: the Currency Act of 1764, the Post Office Act of 1765, the act of 1767 creating an American Board of Customs Commissioners, the Quartering Act of 1764, and the practice of stationing troops in the colonies.

100. *Ibid.*, p. 73.

101. *Ibid.*, p. 53.

102. *Ibid.*, pp. 62–63.

103. Burnett, *Letters of Continental Congress,* vol. 1, pp. 59, 61, 62, 64.

104. Ford, *Journals of Continental Congress,* vol. 1, p. 57.

105. *Ibid.*, p. 77.

106. Drayton, *Memoirs of the American Revolution,* vol. 1, pp. 168–70; John Adams,

"Notes of Debates," Burnett, *Letters of Continental Congress,* vol. 1, p. 50.

107. Drayton, *Memoirs of the American Revolution,* vol. 1, p. 169.

108. Cushing, *Writings of Samuel Adams,* vol. 3, p. 159; Ford, *Journals of Continental Congress,* vol. 1, pp. 75–81. See also A. W. Farmer [Samual Seabury], *The Congress Canvassed* (New York: James Rivington, 1774), p. 6.

109. Ford, *Journals of Continental Congress,* vol. 1, pp. 75–81.

110. *Ibid.,* p. 75.

111. *Ibid.,* p. 79.

112. *Ibid.,* pp. 78–79.

113. *Ibid.,* p. 79.

114. *Ibid.,* p. 102; Charles Stillé, *The Life and Times of John Dickinson* (Philadelphia: J. B. Lippencott, 1891), p. 145n.

115. Edwin Wolf II, "The Authorship of the 1774 Address to the King Restudied," in *William and Mary Quarterly,* 3d ser., 22 (1965), pp. 189–224.

116. Ford, *Journals of Continental Congress,* vol. 1, p. 102.

117. See, for example, Governor William Franklin to the Earl of Dartmouth, 6 December 1774, W. A. Whitehead, et al., eds., *Archives of the State of New Jersey, 1631–1800* (Newark, 1906), vol. 10, p. 503; Lieutenant-Governor Colden to the Earl of Dartmouth, 1 March 1775, E. B. O'Callaghan, ed., *Documents Relative to the Colonial History of the State of New York* (Albany: Weed, Parsons & Co., 1853–87), vol. 8, p. 543; and Governor Josiah Martin to the Earl of Dartmouth, 10 March 1775, Saunders, *Records of North Carolina,* vol. 9, pp. 1155–56.

118. Force, *American Archives,* vol. 1, pp. 1161–62.

119. The meeting in Philadelphia County in November 1774 appointed a committee to act for the county and at the same time resolved that the committees in the township be continued (*Pennsylvania Gazette,* 30 November 1774).

120. *Virginia Gazette,* 17 November 1774.

121. *South Carolina Gazette,* 20 February 1775.

122. "Philadelphia Committee of Observation Papers," Historical Society, Pennsylvania.

123. At least fifty-one of Virginia's sixty-one counties appointed committees, as did the three towns of Williamsburg, Norfolk, and Fredericksberg. Resolutions of, or references to, most of these committees may be found in the *Virginia Gazette* and in Force, *American Archives,* vol. 1. It seems probable that every county in the colony appointed committees since the Association called for condemnation of counties which failed to do so, and there are no records of such condemnations.

124. The eight counties for which records are most complete are Prince Georges, Harford, Anne Arundel, Frederick, Baltimore, St. Mary's, Charles, and Calvert. The three that definitely had committees but for which no estimate of size is known are Talbot, Kent, and Cecil. Figures for most of these may be found in the *Virginia Gazette* and in Force, *American Archives,* vol. 1.

125. The size of committees in Massachusetts ranged from three to over sixty. I have included the counties of Maine in this estimate.

126. In South Carolina, where the provincial convention appointed the local committee, I have compared the list of convention delegates with committee members and have used a total of the two to estimate the number of persons involved in enforcing the Association.

127. More communities in New York are known to have rejected the Association than

in all the other colonies combined. Only in New York City and in Albany do the committees appear to have been active prior to the engagement at Lexington.

128. The size of county committees in Pennsylvania ranged from fifteen in Berks to seventy in Chester. Nothing is known about committee activities in the two frontier counties of Cumberland and Lancaster.

129. Two of the three counties in Delaware are known to have appointed committees of inspection before the battle at Lexington. One of these, Kent, elected more than twenty, and it seems safe to assume that at least one of the others did as well. Since all three counties sent delegates to the provincial congress which endorsed nonimportation before the meeting of the Continental Congress, there seems to be no reason to suppose that any of the three refused to endorse the boycott later.

130. Prince Georges County more than doubled the membership of its committee, from eighty-four in November 1774 to one hundred seventy-one in January of the next year. The Anne Arundel committee grew from forty-four to eighty-eight in two months time, Frederick and Baltimore counties each added forty new members in January 1775, and Charles County increased the size of its committee by sixteen (Force, *American Archives,* vol. 1, pp. 1011, 1141, 1143, 1173–74, 1082).

131. *Virginia Gazette,* 17 November 1774.

132. Boston Committee of Correspondence to the Berkshire Committee of Correspondence, 24 September 1774, "Boston Committee of Correspondence Papers," New York Public Library; Force, *American Archives,* vol. 1, pp. 848, 1007–8.

133. On 8 November, the general committee voted that the January meeting be composed of six deputies from every parish, "except St. Marys, which, divided into three Districts, is to choose ten for each on Account of its great Extent and populousness; and except Charleston, the inhabitants whereof are to choose thirty" (*South Carolina Gazette,* 21 November 1774, and 23 January 1775).

134. Force, *American Archives,* vol. 1, pp. 830–34, Elbridge Gerry to Samuel Adams, 15 October 1774, "Samuel Adams Papers," New York Public Library.

135. Force, *American Archives,* vol. 1, p. 421.

136. *Ibid.,* p. 1180, vol. 2, p. 519.

137. *Ibid.,* vol. 1, pp. 1169–70, 1280.

138. Elizabeth Merritt, ed., *Archives of Maryland* (Baltimore, 1947), vol. 13; Force, *American Archives,* vol. 1, pp. 438–39, 1031, 1109–10; vol. 2, pp. 589, 685. The maximum possible attendance in the lower house of the Maryland Assembly was fifty-eight, four from each county and two from the city of Annapolis. Although the membership of the Congress came close to one hundred, it too could have been much larger. In May 1775, Harford County elected sixteen delegates, Baltimore, fifteen, and Charles County, sixteen ("Maryland Committee of Inspection Papers," Library of Congress; Charles Ridgley to John Dickinson, 19 January 1775, Logan Colonial Historic Society, Pennsylvania; *ibid.,* vol. 2, p. 668).

139. Ford, *Journals of Continental Congress,* vol. 1, pp. 78–79.

140. *South Carolina Gazette,* 3 April 1775; *New York Gazette and Weekly Mercury,* 1 May 1775; *Essex Gazette,* 4 April 1775.

141. *South Carolina Gazette,* 27 February 1775.

142. Benjamin Booth to James and Drinker, 10 February 1775, "James and Drinker Business Papers."

143. Force, *American Archives,* vol. 1, p. 1257.

144. *New York Journal,* 23 March 1775; Benjamin Booth to James and Drinker, 22

February, 2 March, 20 March 1775, "James and Drinker Business Papers."

145. Edward Miles Riley, ed., *The Journal of John Harrower* (Williamsburg: Colonial Williamsburg Foundation, 1963), pp. 56, 73.

146. Charles Yates to Samuel Martin, 5 July 1774, "Yates Letterbook," University of Virginia Library (microfilm, Colonial Williamsburg Foundation).

147. Force, *American Archives,* vol. 1, pp. 1171–72; vol. 2, pp. 170–71.

148. *Ibid.,* vol. 1, pp. 1001–2.

149. *Ibid.,* pp. 1256–57; vol. 2, pp. 140–42; Duane, *Diary of Christopher Marshall,* pp. 14, 16.

150. Force, *American Archives,* vol. 1, pp. 1171–72; vol. 2, pp. 170–71.

151. *South Carolina Gazette,* 6 March 1775. See also *ibid.,* vol. 1, p. 1051; *Pennsylvania Gazette,* 11 January 1775; *Pennsylvania Journal and Weekly Advisor,* 4 January 1775.

152. *Maryland Gazette,* 15 April 1775.

153. *Essex Gazette,* 10 January 1775; Nathaniel Bouton, ed., *Documents and Records Relating to the Province of New Hampshire from 1764 to 1766* (Nashua, N.H.: Orren C. Moore, State Printer, 1873), vol. 8, p. 445.

154. Caleb Butler, *History of the Town of Groton, Massachusetts* (Boston: T. R. Martin, 1848), p. 124.

155. Samuel Adams Drake, *History of Middlesex County, Massachusetts* (Boston: Estes and Lauriat, 1880), vol. 1, p. 199.

156. Saunders, *Records of North Carolina,* vol. 9, pp. 1150, 1152, 1166. On 13 March the committee reported that eight of the recalcitrant citizens had changed their minds and "subscribed their names within the time limited."

157. T. E. Campbell, *Colonial Caroline* (Richmond: Dietz Press, 1954), pp. 236–38.

158. *Boston Evening Post,* 20 March 1775, transcript among the Peter Force Duplicates, packed for February 1775, Library of Congress.

159. Falmouth, Massachusetts, appointed a committee to wait upon the "several Ministers of this Town, and desire them to propose a Contribution . . . for the relief of the Town of Boston" (Falmouth Resolves, 21 July 1774, "Boston Committee of Correspondence Papers," New York Public Library).

160. Carleton Beals, *The Making of Bristol, Connecticut* (Boston, 1954), p. 59.

161. *Connecticut Gazette,* 17 February 1775.

162. Governor Dunmore to the Earl of Dartmouth, 24 December 1774, Force, *American Archives,* vol. 1, pp. 1061–62.

163. *Ibid.,* vol. 2, p. 313.

164. Wilbraham Town Resolutions, 29 July 1774, "Boston Committee of Correspondence Papers," New York Public Library.

165. Thomas Ellison to his father, 29 April 1775, *Magazine of American History* 8 (1882), p. 283.

166. *Pennsylvania Gazette,* 4 January 1775; Joseph Sickler, *Tea Burning Town* (New York: Abelard Press, 1950).

167. Benjamin Labaree, *Patriots and Partisans* (Cambridge, Mass.: Harvard Univ. Press, 1962), p. 37.

168. Force, *American Archives,* vol. 1, p. 1194.

169. *Pennsylvania Gazette,* 21 December 1774; Minutes, 2 January, 23 January, 23 February 1775, Harford County, Maryland, "Committee of Inspection Papers," Library of Congress.

170. Force, *American Archives,* vol. 1, p. 1145.

171. *Massachusetts Gazette and Post Boy,* 14 November 1774; New Milford Resolutions in Samuel Orcutt, *History of the Towns of New Milford and Bridgewater, Connecticut* (Hartford: Case, Lockwood, and Brainard, 1882), p. 216.

172. Ellen D. Larned, *History of Windham County, Connecticut* (Worcester, Mass.: The Author, 1880), p. 137.

173. Force, *American Archives,* vol. 1, pp. 1215, 1216.

174. *Ibid.,* pp. 1236–38.

175. *Ibid.*

176. *Connecticut Gazette,* 3 March 1775.

177. Force, *American Archives,* vol. 1, p. 1236; *Connecticut Gazette,* 17 February 1775.

178. Bartlett, *Records of Rhode Island,* vol. 7, p. 261.

179. Bernhard Knollenberg, ed., *Correspondence of Governor Samuel Ward, May 1775–March 1776* (Providence: Rhode Island Historical Society, 1952), pp. 31–32.

180. *New Hampshire Gazette,* 2 December 1774.

181. Force, *American Archives,* vol. 1, p. 1031.

182. *New Hampshire Gazette,* 16 December 1774. Prior to the appointment on 8 December, the Association had been enforced in Portsmouth by the existing "Committee of Ways and Means" (*ibid.,* 18 November 1774).

183. Brentwood, Candia, Canterbury, Chester, Deerfield, Epson, Exeter, Hawke, Kensington, Londonderry, New Market, Kingston, Stratham, Pembroke, and Nottingham.

184. Some are listed in Force, *American Archives,* vol. 1, p. 974.

185. *Ibid.,* pp. 1180–81.

186. *Ibid.,* pp. 997–98.

187. In September, the committees of correspondence from Cambridge, Boston, Roxbury, Dorchester, Watertown, Charlestown, Mistick, Dedham, Milton, Malden, Braintree, Woburn, and Stow met and proposed that each town elect a committee of observation (*ibid.,* p. 807).

188. Bellingham, Boston, Braintree, Brookline, Canton, Chelsea, Cohasset, Dedham, Hingham, Medfield, Sharon, Stoughton, Walpole, Weymouth, and Wrentham.

189. Thomas Gage to Lieutenant-Governor Colden, 26 February 1775, "The Colden Papers," in the New York Historical Society, *Collections,* vol. 56, p. 267; *Essex Gazette,* 7 March 1775 and 4 April 1775. Also, Jackson, Tracy, and Tracy to Lane, Son, and Fraser, 11 October 1774. Kenneth Wiggins Porter, *The Jacksons and the Lees: Two Generations of Massachusetts Merchants* (2 vols., Cambridge: Harvard Univ. Press, 1937), vol. 1, p. 278.

190. Amesbury, Andover, Danvers, Gloucester, Haverhill, Ipswich, Lynn, Manchester, Marblehead, Methuen, Middletown, Newburyport (includes Newbury), Rowley, Salem, and Wenham.

191. Acton, Ashby, Bedford, Billerica, Charlestown, Chelmsford, Concord, Dracut, Dunstable, Framingham, Groton, Holliston, Lexington, Lincoln, Malden, Marlborough, Natick, Newton, Reading, Sherburne, Shirley, Stow, Sudbury, Tewksbury, Townshend, Tyngsborough, Watertown, Waltham, Weston, Westford, and Woburn. There is no conclusive proof that Concord elected a committee but the presence of representatives from a "committee" at the meeting held in September to discuss local problems indicates cooperation with other towns in the area (Force, *American Archives,* vol. 1, p. 807). Stoneham and Wilmington had made previous commitments to nonimportation (see Drake, *History of Middlesex County,* vol. 2, p. 344).

192. Amherst, Bernardston, Brimfield, Chesterfield, Conway, Deerfield, Granville,

Hadley, Hatfield, Leverett, Montague, Murrayfield, Northfield, Palmer, Pelham, Shelburne, Springfield, South Hadley, Southhampton, Sunderland, Warwick, Westfield, Whately, Wilbraham, Williamsburg, and Worthington. Monson signed a nonimportation covenant before the Continental Congress met. Belchertown signed a similar agreement and elected a committee to oversee its enforcement (see Alfred Minot Copeland, *A History of Hampton County, Massachusetts* [Boston: Century Memorial, 1902], vol. 3).

193. Barnstable met on 16 November 1774; Worcester on 27 January 1775; and Bristol on 7 April 1775.

194. Attleboro, Bristol, Berkley, Dartmouth, Dighton, Norton, Rehoboth, and Swanzey acted by February 1775. No mention of the Taunton committee has been located but since that town hosted the county committees of inspection in April it almost certainly had such an organization of its own. In Worcester, twenty-seven towns elected enforcement committees prior to the county congress. They included: Athol, Ashburnham, Bolton, Brookfield, Dudley, Fitchburg, Harvard, Holden, Hubbardston, Hardwick, Lancaster, Leicester, Leominster, Lunenburg, Mendon, Northboro, Oxford, Petersham, Rutland, Spencer, Sturbridge, Sutton, Oakham, Princeton, Uxbridge, Westboro, Winchendon, Westminster, and Worcester. The towns of Barnstable, Falmouth, Wellfleet, Yarmouth, Sandwich, and Harwich elected committees following the Barnstable congress.

195. Force, *American Archives*, vol. 1, p. 1178; Thomas Gage to the Earl of Dartmouth, 27 January 1775, Clarence Edwin Carter, ed., *The Correspondence of General Thomas Gage with the War Office and the Treasury, 1763–1775* (2 vols, New Haven: Yale Univ. Press, 1933) vol. 1, p. 391.

196. *Essex Gazette,* 13 December 1774; Samuel Deane, *History of Scituate, Massachusetts* (Boston: J. Loring, 1831), pp. 134–35.

197. Force, *American Archives,* vol. 1, p. 1057.

198. David Macpherson, *Annals of Commerce, Manufacturing, Fishing, and Navigation . . .* (4 vols., London: Nichols and Son, 1805), vol. 3, pp. 564–85.

199. Deputy Governor Penn to the Earl of Dartmouth, 31 December 1774, Force, *American Archives,* vol. 1, p. 1081; Joseph Reed to Josiah Quincy, 6 November 1774, *ibid.,* pp. 963–64; James Bowden, *The History of the Society of Friends of America* (London: C. Gilpin, 1854), vol. 2, p. 372.

200. Joseph Reed to Josiah Quincy, 6 November 1774, Force, *American Archives,* vol. 1, pp. 963–64; Lieutenant-Governor Colden to the Earl of Dartmouth, 2 November 1774, ibid., p. 957.

201. *Ibid.,* pp. 1287, 1289.

202. *Ibid.,* p. 1288.

203. *Ibid.,* vol. 2, p. 328.

204. *Ibid.,* p. 987.

205. *Ibid.,* pp. 329–30; Smith, *Memoirs,* vol. 1, p. 203.

206. *New York Gazette and Weekly Mercury,* 1 May 1775.

207. "Correspondence of Silas Deane," in Connecticut Historical Society, *Collections* 2 (1870), p. 198.

208. Lieutenant-Governor Colden to the Earl of Dartmouth, 1 March 1775, O'Callaghan, *Documents Relative to New York,* vol. 8, p. 543.

209. Ulster met on 6 January 1775, Force, *American Archives,* vol. 1, p. 1100; Suffolk appointed a committee on 15 November 1774, (*History of Suffolk County, New York* [New York: William W. Munsell and Company, 1882], pp. 62–63). Albany County elected a committee on 24 January 1775 (Force, *American Archives,* vol. 1, p. 1098). Towns in the

latter two counties had appointed committees prior to the county congresses.

210. Russel Headley, *The History of Orange County, New York* (Middletown, N.Y., 1908), p. 62.

211. Carl Beckers, "Election of Delegates from New York to the Second Continental Congress," in the *American Historical Review*, 9 (1903–1904), p. 80.

212. Force, *American Archives*, vol. 2, p. 138.

213. Goshen, Cornwall, and Haverstraw held elections on 4 April and Orange on 17 April (*ibid.*, p. 353).

214. *Ibid.*, pp. 354, 304, 356–57; Becker, "Election of Delegates," p. 84.

215. Two towns, Flushing and Newtown, elected delegates, Force, *American Archives*, vol. 2, p. 356; *New York Gazette and Weekly Mercury*, 19 December 1774.

216. Becker, "Election of Delegates," p. 85.

217. Governor Franklin to the Earl of Dartmouth, 6 December 1774, Whitehead, *New Jersey Archives*, vol. 10, p. 503.

218. Force, *American Archives*, vol. 1, pp. 1009–10; A Van Doren Honeyman, *History of Union County, New Jersey* (New York and Chicago: Lewis Historical Publishers, 1923), p. 494; F. W. Ricord, *History of Union County, New Jersey* (Newark: East Jersey Historical Society, 1897), p. 23.

219. *New Hampshire Gazette and Weekly Mercury*, 12 and 26 December 1774; *Pennsylvania Gazette*, 7 and 21 December 1774, 4 January 1775; *New York Journal or Grand Advertiser*, 8 December 1774.

220. *Minutes of the Provincial Congress and the Council of Safety of the State of New Jersey, 1774–1776* (Trenton, 1879), p. 48; *Pennsylvania Gazette*, 11 January 1775 and 22 February 1775; *New Jersey Minutes*, pp. 43–44.

221. *Ibid.*, p. 98.

222. Francis A. Westervelt, ed., *History of Bergen County, New Jersey* (New York: Lewis Historical Publishers, 1923), vol. 1, p. 101.

223. *New Jersey Minutes*, p. 71.

224. Force, *American Archives*, vol. 1, p. 1081.

225. *Ibid.*, p. 1023.

226. Northumberland and Westmoreland, the two counties which are not known to have appointed committees, were both on the frontier and sparsely settled.

227. Philadelphia County met in late November (*Pennsylvania Gazette*, 30 November 1774); Berks appointed a committee on 5 December; Bucks and Lancaster on the fifteenth; Chester on the twentieth; and Northhampton on the twenty-first (*Virginia Gazette*, 29 December 1774; *Pennsylvania Gazette*, 30 November 1774 and 21 December 1774; Force, *American Archives*, vol. 1, p. 1053; H. M. J. Klein, ed., *Lancaster County, Pennsylvania: A History* [New York and Chicago: Lewis Historical Publishers, 1924], vol. 2, p. 579; William J. Heller, *History of Northhampton County* [1920], p. 132).

228. Force, *American Archives*, vol. 1, p. 1056, 1169–72.

229. *Ibid.*, pp. 1171–72.

230. Duane, *Diary of Christopher Marshall*, p. 11. Joseph Reed to the Earl of Dartmouth, 10 December 1774, William B. Reed, *The Life and Correspondence of Joseph Reed* (Philadelphia: Lindsay and Blakeston, 1847), vol. 1, p. 88; "Letters of Eliza Farmer," *Magazine of American History* 8 (1882), p. 203; William Bradford to James Madison, 3–6 March 1775, William T. Hutchinson, ed., *The Papers of James Madison* (Chicago: Univ. of Chicago Press, 1962), p. 139.

231. New Castle met on 5 December 1774 and Kent two days later (*Pennsylvania*

Gazette, 28 December 1774).

232. Force, *American Archives,* vol. 2, pp. 126, 129.

233. Margaret Wheeler Willard, ed., *Letters on the American Revolution* (Boston and New York: Houghton Mifflin, 1925), p. 18.

234. Force, *American Archives,* vol. 1, p. 991.

235. *Ibid.,* pp. 1031–33.

236. *Maryland Gazette,* 24 November, 1 and 15 December 1774, and 5 January 1775; Force, *American Archives,* vol. 1, p. 975.

237. Elias Jones, *Revised History of Dorchester County, Maryland* (Baltimore: Read Taylor Press, 1925), p. 209; Force, *American Archives,* vol. 2, pp. 175–76; *Maryland Gazette,* 23 February and 6 April 1775; Frederick Emory, *Queen Anne's County, Maryland* (Baltimore: Maryland Historical Society, 1950), p. 227; and George Johnston, *History of Cecil County, Maryland* (Elkton, Md., 1881), pp. 320–21.

238. *Maryland Gazette,* 26 January 1775.

239. Macpherson, *Annals of Commerce,* vol. 3, pp. 564–85.

240. The Earl of Dunmore to the Earl of Dartmouth, 24 December 1774, Force, *American Archives,* vol. 1, p. 1061.

241. *Ibid.*

242. Arthur M. Schlesinger, *The Colonial Merchants and the American Revolution, 1763–1775* (New York: Columbia Univ. Press, 1918), pp. 513–15; James Madison to William Bradford, 20 January 1775, Hutchinson, *Madison Papers,* vol. 1, p. 135.

243. H. J. Eckenrode, *The Revolution in Virginia* (Boston and New York: Houghton Mifflin, 1916), p. 44.

244. Force, *American Archives,* vol. 2, pp. 165–66.

245. *Ibid.,* pp. 7–8.

246. *Ibid.,* pp. 254, 266–70.

247. *Ibid.,* p. 268.

248. *Ibid.,* p. 271.

249. *Ibid.,* pp. 269–72.

250. Saunders, *Records of North Carolina,* vol. 9, p. 1198.

251. *Ibid.,* pp. 1205, 1211.

252. Beauford, Brunswick, Chowan, Craven, Duplin, Edgecombe, New Hanover, Halifax, Onolow, Perquimans, Pitt, and Rowan.

253. *South Carolina Gazette,* 3 April 1775.

254. Macpherson, *Annals of Commerce,* vol. 3, pp. 564–85.

255. Saunders, *Records of North Carolina,* vol. 9, pp. 1160–64.

256. Force, *American Archives,* vol. 1, pp. 881–82.

257. *Ibid.,* p. 1110. *The South Carolina Gazette* (23 January 1775), claimed that the Congress was "the most complete Representation of all the good People throughout this Colony, that ever was . . . obtained."

258. Drayton, *Memoirs of the American Revolution,* pp. 169–76.

259. Force, *American Archives,* vol. 1, pp. 1114–16.

260. *Ibid.,* p. 1118.

261. *Ibid.,* pp. 1113–14.

262. The old general committee had previously determined that it would resign on the day of the second provincial congress. Convention delegates would administer provincial business until a new general committee was elected.

263. William Roy Smith, *South Carolina as a Royal Province, 1719–1776* (New

York: Macmillan, 1903), pp. 406–7.
264. Force, *American Archives,* vol. 2, p. 1.
265. *South Carolina Gazette and Country Journal,* 7 March 1775.
266. Force, *American Archives,* vol. 1, pp. 1135–36, 1162–63.
267. *Ibid.,* pp. 1161–62.
268. *Ibid.,* p. 1163.
269. Macpherson, *Annals of Commerce,* vol. 3, pp. 564–65.

·7·

The British Business Community and the Later Nonimportation Movements, 1768–1776

PAUL LANGFORD

In colonial eyes, the repeal of the Stamp Act had seemed gratifying. Nevertheless, it was not surprising that the two succeeding phases of British imperial policy in North America, represented in the Townshend duties of 1767 and the Tea Act of 1773, together with the subsequent coercive legislation of 1774, should have met with vigorous resistance across the Atlantic. Nor was it surprising that the resistance should have turned so quickly to the weapon of economic embargo. In part, this belief in the potential effectiveness of nonimportation, and even nonexportation, was a natural consequence of the well-known importance of colonial trade to the imperial economy. This importance was itself reflected in the immediate recourse to nonimportation in the wake of the Stamp Act. The extent to which Britain's commercial prosperity in the eighteenth century was actually linked to the burgeoning importance of the colonial economy is of course a matter for debate. However, it was clear to contemporaries, as it is to historians, that the connection was significant—significant enough to create powerful political leverage for the colonists.[1] The latter assumed that their indebtedness to British merchants and the dependence of British manufacturers on colonial markets would forestall any ministerial action which might upset this delicate economic balance. Thomas Hutchinson summarized these views:

> The colonies are so much in debt to the merchants in England, and that they are so necessary to the manufacturers there, as will effectively prevent any measures which may tend to destroy or lessen the debt, or lessen the consumption of the manufacturers.[2]

Extensive claims were indeed made as to the power which lay in America's hands. It was, for example, alleged in the *Virginia Gazette* that Britain had no trade that showed a balance of payments advantage to her other than that to Ireland and America. The *South Carolina Gazette* argued that six-sevenths of the English people depended on manufacturing for a living and that half of their products were

278

purchased by America. According to the *Massachusetts Gazette,* half a million industrial workers could be found in the Leeds and Halifax area alone, almost all of them directly dependent on colonial demands for their goods.[3] Such notions were wildly exaggerated, but their wide currency reinforced the fundamental fact of at least a significant dependence of British trade and industry on the American market and explains the great confidence with which the colonies set out to exploit that dependence.

Against this background, the significance of the circumstances attending the repeal of the Stamp Act can hardly be overestimated. If anything was needed to confirm the colonists' view that they had a potential stranglehold on the British economy and *ipso facto* on the British political establishment, it was amply supplied by those circumstances. As has been seen, the reasoning which convinced many, even of America's opponents, in Parliament that repeal of the Stamp Act was vital in the interests of British trade was in several respects ill-grounded and fallacious.[4] Nonetheless few contemporaries, especially in America, grasped the essential facts in this affair. It seemed clear to colonial radicals, and understandably so, that relief had been procured in 1766 by the economic sanctions employed by the merchants and dealers and that, if necessary, such relief could be similarly procured on future occasions. If the depressed trade of 1764–65 and the only briefly enforced nonimportation agreements of 1765 had procured such an immediate and effective response from British politicians, what might future campaigns of a more organized, better coordinated, and more widely enforced kind bring about?

It was anything but surprising, then, that when the imperial authorities once again resorted to what appeared repressive measures, nonimportation and allied economic sanctions should spring speedily to the colonial mind. Both the Townshend duties of 1767 and the Coercive Acts of 1774 provoked a campaign of sustained and extensive resistance in which economic sanctions were a prime weapon. The evolution of a continental nonimportation movement in the former case was somewhat erratic—with a number of false starts, much hanging back, and a good deal of backsliding—but by the spring of 1769, the key centers of New York, Boston, and Philadelphia were involved, and by the autumn of the same year, every province but New Hampshire joined them, and the movement lasted well into 1770. In the further and critical crisis of Anglo-American relations between 1774 and 1776, a major nonimportation campaign was also in operation, this time under the direction of the Continental Congress. It applied from the end of 1774 and was followed in September 1775 by a companion nonexportation campaign.[5] In each case the highest expectations were entertained in the colonies as to the likely effect of economic sanctions.

In such expectations the colonists were much encouraged from London. Thus, Bostonians were assured in 1769: "If your merchants and housekeepers generally unite with the other colonies, in not importing more goods, depend on it, you will soon be emancipated from the parliamentary yoke, and no future minister will venture to tax America."[6] Much the same pattern of hopes and promises recurred in 1774. Americans in London, such as Samuel Eliot, the visiting Boston merchant, insisted that there was "no other Hold that America can have upon the Ministry, than what arises from affecting the Trade of this Country."[7] Estimates of the period of embargo required to bring Britain utterly to her knees varied from two or three months to a year; none of the pundits seemed to think that more than a year would be necessary, and even after the introduction of nonexportation had proved unavoidable, it was thought that a further twelve or, at most, eighteen months would suffice.[8]

Despite these great expectations, results were hardly in proportion either to them or to the much cited precedent of the repeal of the Stamp Act. In the case of the Continental Association indeed, the failure of economic sanctions to change the policies of the North ministry was complete, although imports to the colonies were significantly curtailed and internal changes were effected in the colonies. Even in the earlier case, that of the nonimportation agreements of 1768–69, it was difficult to claim that they had been a great success. Admittedly, a large portion of the offending legislation—all Townshend's taxes excluding that on tea—were removed by Parliament in the session of 1770. But in truth, tea was the only significant item among the commodities affected by the Townshend Act and clearly outclassed the remainder—lead, paints, glass, and paper—in importance. Moreover, the retention of the tea duty plainly signified Parliament's refusal to budge from its basic claim to sovereignty even in matters of financial legislation. This point is confirmed by the endeavors of colonial radicals to continue the policy of embargo until a complete sweep had been made of objectionable duties. In the event, of course, these endeavors were in vain. The nonimportation campaign did not die immediately on the partial repeal of Townshend's taxes, but its death was not long delayed thereafter. Moreover, it was not altogether easy to argue that such concessions as had been extracted resulted from the pressures brought to bear by America. Well before the nonimportation agreements had really begun to bite in the spring of 1769, the Grafton administration had publicly declared its readiness to remove all but the tax on tea, largely on the grounds that Townshend's duties broke an elementary precept of economic planning in laying imposts on British exports. Action was arguably delayed rather than facilitated by American activities, which were treated as an affront to the dignity of Parliament, and when the North administration honored the undertaking of the previous year, it was in its own good time and according to its own conditions. The great lobby of merchants and manufacturers so influential in 1766 was neither as interested nor as powerful in the years of the Townshend Acts resistance. There was no dramatic reversal of imperial policy as in 1766, and little by way of reassurance and consolation for colonists anxious to register their importance at Westminster and Whitehall as in 1766. The nonimportation campaign of 1768–70 was scarcely a complete failure, but at best it was an exceedingly qualified success.

One obvious explanation for the failure or partial failure of economic sanctions after the outstanding success of 1766 merely poses further questions. Whereas in 1765–66 the business community in Britain had eagerly and effectively collaborated with the colonists and indeed organized its own initiatives by way of assistance, in the later cases such collaboration was largely lacking. In 1769 for instance, the apparent reluctance of merchants and manufacturers to assist the colonial campaign in favor of repeal of the Townshend legislation was a constant source of grievance, and one much commented on by Americans living in London. Colonial agents repeatedly bemoaned the backwardness of those who should have been the natural allies of America.[9] Even George Grenville and his friends, who were deeply cynical about the allegedly spontaneous mercantile agitation of 1766, expected an imitation of it in 1769, with a new spate of metropolitan and provincial petitions and a repetition of the lobbying which had occurred three years earlier.[10] Yet little activity materialized despite talk of a new campaign headed by the indefatigable Barlow Trecothick. There were no formal petitions or addresses from any body of merchants in 1769, and Thomas Pownall's motion for repeal of the Townshend taxes in the Commons in April was quite without supporting evidence from the merchants or manufacturers. Indeed, apart from rather desultory and informal approaches to the ministry by some of the London North American merchants, there was almost no organized activity of any kind on America's behalf. The agents, powerless to act without mercantile support and, in any case, embarrassed by the uncompromising opposition of the colonists to the bare notion of parliamentary supremacy, were totally impotent and reduced to lamenting the inactivity of the business interests.[11] Even in 1770, by which time the American embargo on imports had had sufficient time to take effect, there was little sign of organized lobbying. Only after the Bristol merchants, always the readiest to declare themselves on behalf of the American trade, had demanded action, were the London merchants prompted to draw up a petition to Parliament in February 1770, shortly before North made his by now anticipated concessions. This was the extent of British demonstration against the Townshend duties, a veritable mouse compared with the massive petitioning and lobbying movement of 1765–66.

A few years later there was naturally more activity by merchants and manufacturers in view of the extreme and evident gravity of the crisis which followed the Boston Tea Party and the Coercive Acts, but there was nothing remotely comparable with the campaign against the Stamp Act nearly a decade earlier. In 1774, for example, while the highly controversial Coercive Bills were emerging as the administration's response to the rising tide of resistance to the Tea Act in America, there was little effective lobbying by the merchants. Admittedly, March saw a meeting of the London North American merchants and a joint approach to the ministry by some of their most prominent representatives.[12] The deputation implored Lord North to hold up legislative action in order to give the Bostonians time to compensate the East India Company for their losses by the Tea Party. However, North's flat refusal to make any kind of concessions and his clear indication that the government had decided to stand firm failed to provoke any further initiatives. Indeed, according to Americans in London, an attempt to organize a concerted petition against the Coercive Acts was killed by the very merchants who had approached North. This was not surprising since London merchant John Lane himself, for example, freely confessed that he would not ask the administration to do more than repeal the tea duty and found it difficult to oppose the legislation of 1774.[13] And if there was little enthusiasm for lobbying in London, there was not the faintest flicker of interest from the provinces. "What unaccountable manoeuvre checked the vigour of their . . . operation?" inquired a mystified Lord Chatham of the merchants.[14] In early 1775, however, the formerly reluctant merchants, pressed by a mounting sense of impending disaster, intensified their activity on behalf of the colonial demands. In particular, the ministry's clear intimation in January that in view of the colonial failure to come to heel, more drastic measures would be required, extending not merely to military preparations but to a trade embargo against the Americans themselves, provoked a natural response from the London merchants. Dennys DeBerdt, son of the former Massachusetts agent, had high hopes of this response, envisaging a highly organized London petition, followed by a series of provincial petitions, and a massive inquiry in Parliament on the model of 1766.[15] Initially there seemed a possibility that such hopes would be fulfilled. The meeting of the London North American merchants at the King's Arms Tavern Cornhill—the favored venue for such assemblies for much of the eighteenth century—was extremely well attended and had no difficulty in electing a committee to draw up an appropriate petition. Every branch of the colonial trade was represented, and for good measure, the West Indies and Quebec were subsequently permitted to add their own deputies. In the end, however, the petition proved a rather "damp squib." When Alderman George Hayley presented it to the Commons on 23 January, it made a disappointing impact, though Hayley, an eminent London politician, and M.P., and a prominent merchant in the New England trade, was well suited to make the most of it. But he did not have the debate all his own way. The intervention of William Innes, M.P. for Ilchester and also an important merchant, severely damaged the impression which the petitioning merchants were endeavoring to create. He declared that "he was concerned in America a little: he thanked God was no more: he knew some that signed the Petition had said they hoped it would not succeed." Innes indeed offered to name those concerned but scarcely needed to since it was common knowledge that leading merchants like Lane were deeply opposed to significant concessions by the imperial authorities. Moreover, there were those who believed, not without justification, that despite the apparent unanimity of the meeting of 4 January, the petition was largely the device of "political" elements, like Alderman William Lee, a Virginian, and William Baker of the Rockingham party. John Lane's firm, Lane and Fraser, themselves asserted that "the whole affair of the Merchants' Petition . . . was managed by Lee, the late sheriff Baker, and one or two more, and was calculated merely to serve opposition against the Ministry, and not to serve the Colonies."[16] Lee's own comment for Josiah Quincy, Jr., on the merchants' petition to the king, submitted shortly after, is perhaps significant in this respect. "After you left us the Merchants with a good deal of dexterity were bro't to the inclosed petition."[17] In any event, the petition did not deeply impress either the ministry or the legislature and seemed but a pale imitation of its predecessor of 1766.

Further petitions were produced, but unfortunately many of them came in a form which did as much to hinder the American cause as to help it. There was, for example, the case of the Northampton stocking weavers' petition, which when it was presented to the Commons on 20 March 1775, was matched by the production of another petition from the same town offering support for the government's policy. Former Massachusetts governor Thomas Hutchinson was witness to the scene in the lower house.

> The advocate for the first alleged that he employed from 10 to 1400 people: that business grew slack, and he must stop good part of his trade. The other brought a Member of the House, who is a Banker in Nottingham, to support them. He was asked what moneys usually went through his hands upon their draft? He answered, About 2000 pounds a week. He was then asked if there had been any abatem[en]t of late? He said—No: that ever since January his payments had been more than usual.[18]

This apparent contradiction was paralleled by a still greater disagreement over the situation in the West Midlands. Birmingham had played an important part in the agitation against the Stamp Act and represented a major conglomeration of industry, especially in relation to the North American market. Moreover, the Birmingham affair came hard on the heels of the London petition, in late January, and did much to discredit that. The first petition from Birmingham was uncompromisingly behind the ministry so far as America was concerned, stating:

> That your petitioners are apprehensive that any relaxation in the execution of the laws respecting the Colonies of Great Britain will ultimately tend to the injury of the commerce of this town and neighbourhood. Wherefore they humbly request that this Honourable House will continue to exert their endeavours to support the authority of the laws of this kingdom over all the Dominions of the Crown.

The contradiction between this and the second petition demanding a lenient policy not unnaturally produced considerable controversy, with a bitter speech from Edmund Burke complaining that the other side's petition was the fraudulent fabrication of those not at all involved in colonial trade. The local complications of this case were considerable and make analysis difficult. No doubt there were extraneous and even overtly political factors at work, not the least of them being inventor Matthew Boulton's desire to curry favor with the ministry in order to obtain a renewal of his and James Watts's steam engine patent, a consideration which doubtless added to Boulton's enthusiasm for an anti-American petition.[19] But whatever the full story, there can be no question that the Birmingham imbroglio, like that at Northampton, and yet a further similar episode at Leeds, did a good deal to dent the credibility of those who attempted to repeat the campaign of 1765–66.

There were other such counterpetitions, and even where there were not, other circumstances proved embarrassing. For example, the Glasgow merchants allegedly petitioned Parliament in order to impress their colonial customers, and simultaneously "they gave Lord North to understand by their member, Lord Frederick Campbell, that they did not mean any opposition by it, but only to get credit in America." In the context of fairly general apathy among businessmen, such embarrassments were still more striking. By August 1775 Richard Champion, the Bristol merchant, had given up hope.

> Had the principal Merchants in this kingdom exerted themselves with the Spirit becoming Men who had by their Commerce contributed so much to the power and Riches of this Kingdom, the trading interest would not have been treated with such Contempt. They must now suffer many of them deservedly but the consequences much affect the whole body of the People.[20]

Coming from one of those well inclined to the American cause and generally anxious to play down the folly and ineptitude of his merchant friends and colleagues, such testimony is compelling. It is reinforced, however, by the comments of Champion's friend, Burke. "We look to the Merchants in vain," he concluded in August 1775. "They are gone from us and from themselves."[21]

In retrospect, the failure of colonial boycotts to bring about the large-scale mobilization of British business interests and, consequently, to put effective pressure on ministers and Parliament is perhaps more understandable than it was at the time. For it is clear that the Americans, especially, expected far too much of their activities, chiefly on the basis of their extraordinary success in 1766. The impact of the nonimportation campaign waged against the Stamp Act was greatly enhanced by the extensive depression in trade and industry at that time, a depression which gradually lifted thereafter. This depression was at its worst in 1767–68 when it led to popular rioting both in metropolis and countryside and arguably fueled the Wilkesite mobbing in London.[22] As one London correspondent of the *Boston Gazette* pointed out, colonial nonimportation at this time would have had disastrous results for Britain's industries.

> The Manufacturers can but barely support themselves under the present Scarcity of Provisions, & slackness of Trade, which is so great a Discouragement, that altho' Wool never was dearer in England than now, yet Clothes are 20 per Cent cheaper than ever was known: so that should your Demand cease for a Year or two; the utmost you can desire would be effected for you here without any unconstitutional Opposition on your Part.[23]

However, by the end of the decade, the economic situation was improving in what, in retrospect, can be seen as the beginning of rapid industrialization. From about 1768 until about 1777, every indication is that trade, both internal and external, was recovering and at times booming, that the financial world was riding high on a new wave of confidence, and that industrial investment and employment were both high.[24] Perhaps, unfortunately for the radicals in the colonies, the one marked interruption in this relatively smooth progress occurred at a time when political relations between Britain and America had once again grown calm. The slump of 1773 was not as enduringly serious for international trade as that of a decade earlier, though it was accompanied, perhaps initiated, by an even worse financial crash both in Holland and in Britain. There was a spectacular series of bankruptcies, a decline in commercial transactions, and widespread fears of a renewed and sustained deterioration in the business world. As it happened, 1772 and 1773 were the quietest years of the entire period between the Peace of Paris and the Declaration of Independence so far as transatlantic affairs were concerned. Had this period coincided with that of one of the nonimportation movements, prospects might have worn a quite different appearance both in the mother country and the colonies. As it was, there was no backdrop of general slump and recession to ease the work of the colonial radicals after either the Townshend duties or the Coercive Acts.

If it is easy to show that the Americans had little to help them in that respect, it is less easy to assess the precise economic effects of their activities. Virtually the only statistics of trade available are those maintained by the Customs service, and formally the responsibility of the Inspector-General of Customs, as part of the government's tax collecting operation. The ledger books summarizing these records and kept from 1695 onwards are, of course, a well-known and valuable source of information. In many ways they are remarkably detailed, listing both imports and exports between England and all her trading partners, foreign or colonial, not merely by country of origin or destiny but also by commodity and according to whether London or the outports were involved. A number of criticisms have been leveled against them, much the most important of which relates to the principle of valuation used.[25]

The statistics do at least make possible an approximate estimate of the continuing importance of North America in the domestic as well as imperial economy, an importance which was apt to be exaggerated at times, but which in general terms is undeniable. In recent years, historians have properly seen England's new empire in the North American subcontinent as the key factor in that extraordinary expansion of overseas trade in the century after 1660, which has been described as the "commercial revolution."[26] American commerce has been called the "principal dynamic element in English export trade," a claim richly deserved both by the great quantitative expansion in the colonial market in the eighteenth century and by the particular requirements of the colonies in terms of the new hardware goods on which the Industrial Revolution in Britain was to thrive. On the other hand, exaggeration is possible. In the exceptionally good year of 1764, exports to the thirteen colonies were officially estimated at some £2.8 million. Yet Germany and Holland each took over £2 million in that year, while Ireland, Spain, Portugal, and the East Indies all commanded well over a million each. Even if it were true that the alleged undervaluation of American trade in the Customs ledgers applied for that trade alone, and it is far from clear that this was the case, this suggests a limited rather than massive degree of dependence on the colonial market.[27] It was natural for merchants who derived their livelihood from Anglo-American trade either in Britain or the colonies to stress the consequence of their business, but it must be remembered that in crude terms the colonies in America accounted for at most a seventh or eighth of total exports, a large, but by no means a dominating proportion.

The official statistics provide helpful evidence on the precise effects of the colonial boycotts. In the case of the campaign of 1768–69, it is tolerably clear that nonimportation did bite into British exports despite the apparent indifference of merchants and manufacturers in England to the pressures of the colonists. The overall total of goods exported to the thirteen colonies declined from £2,276,000 in 1768, before nonimportation effectively operated, to £1,578,000 in 1769, when it did operate in a number of colonies.[28] The major trading centers of Philadelphia, Boston, and New York, essentially represented in the statistics as Pennsylvania, New England, and New York, all showed dramatic reductions in their imports, which were rather more than halved in the first two cases and more sensationally slashed from £432,000 to £74,000 in that of New York.

Such reductions were not insignificant, representing altogether about one-third, but they were hardly on the scale threatened by the Sons of Liberty, even allowing for the fact that not all goods were totally prohibited by all the nonimportation agreements. Colonial activists hoping to immobilize in London warehouses Britain's entire annual stock of £2 million worth of goods meant for the American market, can hardly have been satisfied to find that over two-thirds still succeeded in crossing the Atlantic and finding their way into colonial homes. But assumptions made about the practicality of enforcing a continental embargo by means of local action and moral pressure proved to be excessively optimistic, and there can be little question that the British industrial economy was saved a real disaster by the failure of so many colonial businessmen and purchasers to observe the nonimportation and nonconsumption agreements. The backsliding was so general and so obvious that it hardly needs highlighting, though it is possible to stress some particularly significant failures.[29]

The alleged treachery of Boston, for example, is especially important, because New England had played so prominent a part in radical agitations, generally, and in the institution of a new embargo campaign, in particular. However, Boston had a strong and entrenched block of conservatives who were well placed to make political propaganda of the shortcomings of Bostonian merchants. John Mein's *Boston Chronicle* mercilessly harried hypocritical merchants who both signed the nonimportation agreement and imported British goods with a view to making a handsome profit from shortages. There are two opinions as to the conclusion to be drawn from Mein's allegations, but the details supplied of John Hancock's misdemeanors, for instance, were too circumstantial to make Hancock's disclaimers plausible.[30] Thomas Whately was a bitter opponent of American claims and American action, but his comments to John Temple in July 1769 were not unjustified.

> As to your associations against importation, they can have little effect. Your merchants will not keep to them. Everyone would suffer if they did for want of meer necessaries, and now that the greatest parade is making about them our manufacturers feel from the demand that your agreements are evaded.[31]

In one respect it was unfair, if understandable, to pick on Boston. For New England, at least, effectively halved its consumption of British manufacturers in 1769, while other provinces actually sought to take advantage of shortages created.

Particularly in the South, the signing of impressive nonimportation and nonconsumption associations seemed to have had little impact. Admittedly, in the case of South Carolina, appearances were somewhat deceptive. There nonimportation came relatively late, and it was not altogether surprising that in 1769 imports rose from £209,000 to £306,000 only to fall to £147,000 in 1770 when the campaign actually began to bite. Paradoxically, by that time the embargo had collapsed elsewhere in the Continent. No excuses can be made for Maryland and Virginia however. Virginians, above all, were quick to imitate the example of their northern brethren in prohibiting many types of British goods, but their evasion and noncompliance were blatant and massive. The Customs figures show considerable increases in imports from £425,000 in 1768 to £488,000 in 1769 to £717,000 in 1770. These figures can only be accounted for on the assumption that Virginians were cashing in on the sacrifice made by the middle and northern colonies in 1769 and by South Carolina in 1770. Even leaders of the opposition to government in Virginia, like George Mason, were brought to confess: "There is great cause to believe that most of the Cargoes refused to be received in the other Colonies have been sent to this."[32] The account books of a London Virginia house, such as the Nortons, are ample testimony to the ruthless exploitation that was occurring.[33] As one of Norton's trading partners on the spot remarked, the Virginia Association was "a sham affair, many of the most strenuous, having sent orders to double of their usual quantity of goods."[34]

There are many plausible explanations for failure to enforce the nonimportation campaign effectively. There was no centrally directed or widely organized administration, such as was to be witnessed later, and local committees were quicker to declare their patriotism than suffer in their pockets for it. Pessimists, who pointed out the almost complete dependence of a prosperous and rapidly expanding economy on British manufactured goods, had much to support them. And cynics, apt to see among the merchants many who delighted in the patriotism of their colleagues as an opportunity to sell their wares at artificially high prices in a time of shortage and as a chance to dispose of old stock at scarcity prices, also had much to support them. As early as 1767, one journalist summarized the advantages to the businessman of a limited period of nonimportation.

> This Method of Proceeding will have this good Effect besides, viz. that you will have a good Price for all your dead Stock (by interchange with one another for Assortment) which would always have been unprofitable—you would collect in your Debts, and bring your Debts in England to a close, before you run any further into Debt; so that the Balance would hereby be bro't about in your Favour, which without some such Method must be forever against you.[35]

These benefits were necessarily short term and it was scarcely surprising in 1770, when the ministry had at any rate made some concession and when demoralization and hardship were setting in, that radicals found their demands for continued campaigning unacceptable. Understandably, New York, which had done most to limit its consumption in 1769 while other colonies went on importing, was the first to cave in, but by the end of the year the collapse was complete. And above all, both the backsliding in 1769 and the collapse in 1770 had an important economic and, perhaps still more important, psychological effect in Britain. Many, like John Temple, felt that a great opportunity had been missed, later referring to "the unfortunate and (I could wish) ever to be forgotten year 1770, when, with everything at stake, they threw up the important game when they had all the trumps in their own hands, and like a Spaniel nearly cringed, and kiss'd the rod that whip'd 'em."[36] In fact, already by 1770, British merchants and, above all, the British authorities had acquired a certain contempt for colonial nonimportation due to its apparent inefficacy in practice. Americans in London, like William Samuel Johnson, were not slow to alert their compatriots to this contempt.

> Those salutary agreements, upon which our safety and success in this country so much depend, have in many instances been shamefully broken through by some and as artfully evaded and counteracted by others, by which too much ground has been given to represent the Colonies as unstable, divided and irresolute,—to persuade the people here that they cannot exist a moment without the trade of this country, and that all the pretences of declining it are mere finesse, frivolous, and vain.[37]

Nor were those on the other side of the Atlantic unaware of the significance of their failures. As George Mason remarked, the North ministry's policy of repealing only part of the Townshend duties "was founded upon an Opinion, that the Americans cou'd not persevere in their Associations; the Custom-House Books shew'd that the Exports to Virginia in particular were very little, if at all, lessened."[38]

Nevertheless, it would be a mistake to attribute the failure of the nonimportation campaign of 1768–70 entirely to the shortcomings of the colonial merchants and populace. For there were, after all, considerable losses to British manufacturers as a result of the campaign. A loss of £700,000 worth of goods was not a vast quantity, but it was substantial in a market normally expected to stay above £2,000,000 and especially in an economy which was vulnerable to even quite marginal falls in industrial production. However, contemporaries had an admirably simple explanation for the success of British manufacturers in weathering the storm of colonial nonimportation. On both sides of the Atlantic it was repeatedly asserted that, at base, the colonial campaign had failed because British merchants and manufacturers had found extensive alternative markets for their wares. Thus, one American correspondent who was visiting England in 1770 wrote home:

> I cannot conclude, notwithstanding the Shortness of my Time, without saying something of the Manufacturing Towns, through which I have been. At Birmingham the Demand for Goods is such, that they have raised their Prices. At Manchester Goods are very scarce, noBody having them on hand there, but one House, and the Manufacturers, even in the American Trade, despairing of its being opened, have sold their Goods for other Markets, and want several Thousand Weavers who are not to be procured. At Halifax and Leeds, where Goods are not only very scarce, but have advanced 15 per Cent within these twelve Months, and difficult to be had; they say it would have been next to an Impossibility, to supply American Orders, with those they have executed already:

> People in the American Trade have had little to do, but those concerned to other Places have full Business, and I find no Place but Sheffield where Goods are to be procured merely at any Rate, where, it is said, they can be had on better Terms than formerly: Upon the Whole, I do not know how it is, but I really looked upon our Country to be of more Consequence to Great-Britain, than I find it to be![39]

Other observers were more specific about the markets which proved such alluring alternatives to the rebellious colonies. Most of them were agreed that eastern Europe was the crucial theater in this respect and that Russia in particular provided the critical upswing in demand.[40] The particular cause assigned was the Russo-Turkish War of 1768–74, which created a sudden demand for clothing and arms.[41] As the *Public Advertiser* put it: "The Russian War has caused so Great a Demand for several Branches of our Manufactures, which used to be in Demand for America, that the Manufacturers have not felt the Want of the American Trade so severely as they otherwise would have felt it."[42] Some observers, like Barlow Trecothick, also specifically mentioned the German market as linked with the Russian in this respect, and one or two even romanticized about the possibility that the government was deliberately financing employment.[43]

Such testimony, widespread as it was, and in some cases coming from fairly well-informed sources, has to be taken seriously. Even so, it suffers in retrospect from one damaging fact, that it is totally unsupported, indeed diametrically contradicted, by the evidence of the statistics. (See Chapter Nine for a more detailed discussion of these aspects.) Exports to Russia in 1768 had stood at £126,000; in 1769 they rose slightly to £158,000, and in 1770 they actually fell again to £145,000. Turkey, the other participant in the Eastern War, took £109,000 from Britain in 1768, £90,000 in 1769, and with the growing disruption of naval warfare in the Mediterranean, £22,000 in 1770. Nor does Germany fill the bill. Exports to the German states fell from £1,499,000 in 1768 to £1,338,000 in 1769 and then further to £1,273,000 in 1770. And on investigation, it is indeed the case that on the basis of the Custom House entries, almost every European market was actually diminishing. The Eastland (the Baltic states), Holland, Spain, France, even Ireland, all fell in the course of 1769 and recovered only marginally in 1770. In fact, the total European market fell dramatically from £9,709,000 in 1768 to £8,645,000 in 1769, only partially recovering to £8,910,000 in 1770. In short, at the very time that nonimportation was making small but not insignificant inroads into Britain's American markets in 1769 and early 1770, the alternative markets, far from supplying a useful opening for British industrialists, were actually in a decline, rather more rapid than that of the American market itself. Whatever imperfections may be detected in the official statistics, nothing can make them reveal the upturn in foreign markets which contemporaries assumed must lie at the heart of the failure of nonimportation.

So the mystery remains. On the one hand, it is reasonably clear that after an encouraging recovery in 1768, with observers describing exports to America as "the Greatest ever known," British industry suffered a marked setback both in colonial and European markets.[44] And yet few witnesses claimed to have observed any degree of distress in the industrial areas. Thomas Pownall testified to signs of strain among the laboring and manufacturing community in Wolverhampton and Birmingham, and one or two colonial journals eagerly reported news of economic recession from London.[45] But such reports were few and far between and unsupported in detail. On the other hand, there was ample evidence to the effect that little hardship was being suffered. A stream of reports, even in the colonial press, admitted the apparent prosperity of the British industrial and commercial scene. Thus the *Pennsylvania Chronicle* reported early in 1770 the evident well-being of British manufacturers.

> The Accounts of the flourishing State of the Trade and Manufacturers in England, being very lengthy, we must postpone them.—It appears that the Spitalfield Manufacturers of Silk—the ribbon Manufactures at Coventry—the Worsted Manufacturers in Northants and Warwicks—the Hose Manufacturers in Leics.—the Manufacturers of thin Goods, Calmanacres, etc. at Yorks, the Clothiers at Leeds, Manchester, Lancaster, all, all, are employed, and have a constant Demand for their Goods; many other Manufactures are mentioned, but Prudence at this Time prevents publishing any Particulars.[46]

And again a few weeks later, Philadelphians were assured from Liverpool:

> From the present Prospect, it will not be in the Power of the Merchants to supply the Orders they have on Hand; the Goods must come in by Degrees as they can procure them; few of the Manufacturers at Manchester, concerned in the America Trade, have any Goods by them, as they have had a good Sale for all they could make; and at many other Places, I observe it is much the same.[47]

And there was ample evidence in support. Statistics later presented to the House of Commons showed that in Yorkshire production of both narrow and broadcloths actually increased in 1769 and 1770, in the former case dramatically.[48] In the last analysis, as William Samuel Johnson pointed out, there was a simple reason for the refusal of British manufacturers to lobby the ministry in favor of concessions towards the colonies. "The manufacturers, upon application to them upon the subject of petitioning, have declared that they have no cause to complain, but, in fact, have hitherto had greater demands for goods than it was possible for them to supply."[49] Understandably there was a good deal of mystification at this state of affairs. "I cannot find any two Persons here," one correspondent of the *Pennsylvania Chronicle* noted, "who agreed in Sentiment on the Influence of the Non-Importation; there seems to be some Secret, which is yet impenetrable.—The Manufacturers are employed, and tho' there are many Goods on Hand, there is no Complaint among them; various are the Conjectures on this Head."[50]

Conjectures are equally necessary in retrospect. An obvious possibility, though one which in the nature of things must remain unsupported by anything resembling positive evidence, is that a sudden upsurge in domestic demand helped to offset the recession occurring in the overseas markets. Such a notion would fit the growing consensus among economic historians that in this early, critical stage of industrial "take-off," home consumption was becoming vitally important. It would also chime with some of the obvious features of the economic climate in 1769, notably the low food prices resulting from a good harvest, a welcome relief after the desperately bad conditions both in town and countryside in 1766–67, and the rising wages associated with a labor shortage, again contrasting markedly with the high unemployment especially of a year or so earlier.[51] In particular, the new canal building industry was making novel and heavy demands on labor in 1769, and undoubtedly there was a general air of prosperity in many sectors of the economy.[52] But for this possibility to hold, it would have needed a very sudden boom in consumer spending to explain a substantial switch of manufactured commodities from the export market, and it is surely straining credulity to envisage such a boom as suddenly and dramatically as would have had to occur in 1769 to explain the trade figures. A measure of improvement in the home market is perfectly feasible; a spectacular and extensive one is not plausible.

There remains a further explanation, one which at least has some reasonably persuasive evidence to support it. It is possible that the North America merchants in London and elsewhere were ordering goods, which kept the manufacturing centers busy, without being immediately able to pass them on to their eventual customers and, indeed, without desiring to do so. Such a policy would not, in the short run, have been as hazardous as might be imagined. For although British merchants were certain to be affected by nonimportation, throughout 1769 and 1770 they went on receiving remittances either in kind or by the usual paper transactions. Only a nonexportation agreement, which was not seriously contemplated in the late 1760s, could have cut off these remittances, and without one, colonial merchants actually went some way to reducing their debts in Britain. Just as American merchants had sometimes something to gain in this way from the embargo policy, so even their transatlantic colleagues were not entirely desolate at the prospect of a period of retrenchment, sustained by continuing remittances from their old customers. Moreover, businessmen on both sides of the Atlantic assumed throughout that a return to normal trading relations would not be long delayed. Especially in London, where the government's commitment to partial repeal of the Townshend duties was made public in the summer of 1769, there was a strong tendency to assume that nonimportation would not and could not endure long.[53] In these circumstances, there was much to be said for continuing to purchase from manufacturers at reasonable rates in the confident expectation of being able to ship warehoused goods as soon as the political climate changed. The prospect of high prices, which seemed bound to result from the scarcity consequent upon nonimportation in America, but which could only be exploited by merchants with stocks on hand and available for immediate dispatch, was extremely alluring. Moreover, the underlying tendency to fuller employment and higher prices in Britain strongly suggested that it would be wise to buy at once rather than later, when there would certainly be a mounting demand. A short-lived war scare resulting from the Falkland Islands crisis, suggesting the possibility of a new and prolonged conflict with the Bourbons, added fuel to this fire, and it is not surprising that businessmen become more rash than ever in their anxiety to safeguard immediate supplies.

There were numerous reports claiming that the great houses had indeed taken risks of this description. Thus, a London letter in the *Pennsylvania Chronicle* observed in the spring of 1770: "If the duty on tea should not be taken off, several of the houses here will be in the sudds; for in full expectation of the repeal of the tea duty, etc. they have given out their orders to a great amount."[54] Even the previous summer, the *Pennsylvania Gazette* had noted that goods continued to stream from the North into London warehouses, and there is ample corroborative evidence.[55] Two most perceptive observations in this matter came appropriately from two of the most acute and well informed Americans, loyalist Thomas Hutchinson in Boston and radical Benjamin Franklin in London. Franklin had a clear idea of what was going on in 1769, particularly after the Grafton ministry's intimation to the merchants that it would duly proceed to repeal Townshend's taxes other than the tea duty. Thus he warned the public not to be fooled by the apparent signs of full employment.

> May not that be partly owing to the public declarations of the Ministry, immediately after the late sessions of parliament, that early in the ensuing sessions the anti-commercial duties should be repealed? Has not this encouraged the employers to keep their hands at work, that they might have a stock a goods beforehand, to pour into America as soon as the trade should be opened.[56]

Hutchinson, as early as 1767, had with remarkable foresight predicted both a new nonimportation campaign against the newly passed Townshend duties and its failure as a result of mercantile antics in England. His comments are consequently worth quoting at length.

> But it may be said how can any new measures be taken without rasing new disturbances? The manufacturers in England will rise again and defeat the measures of government. This game 'tis true has been played once and succeeded, and it has been asserted here, that it is in the power of the colonies at any time to raise a rebellion in England by refusing to send for their manufacturers. For my own part I do not believe this. The merchants in England, and I don't know but those in London and Bristol only, might always govern in this matter and quiet the manufacturer. The merchant's view is always to his own interest. As the trade is now managed the dealer here sends to the merchant in England for his goods; upon these goods the English merchant puts a profit of 10 or more probably of 15 per cent when he sends them to his employer in America. The merchant is so jealous of foregoing this profit that an America trader cannot well purchase the goods he wants of the manufacturer; for should the merchant know that the manufacture had supplied an American, he would therefore having this profit in view will by one means or other secure it. They know the goods which the American market demands, and may therefore safely take them off from the manufacturer, tho' they should have no orders for shipping them this year or perhaps the next; and I dare say, it would not be longer before the Americans would clamour for a supply of goods from England, for it is vain to think they can supply themselves. The merchant might then put an advanced price upon his goods, and possibly be able to make his own terms . . . and *then the game would be over.*[57]

Hutchinson was perhaps a little fortunate in his forecasting. A continuation of the nonimportation campaign after the partial repeal of the Townshend duties would have meant that the game was far from up, and it is a fact that the initial readiness of colonial merchants, especially in Boston, to continue with the embargo caused not a little alarm and embarrassment in London. As it turned out though, Hutchinson was proved right, and those who had taken care to stock up in 1769 were amply rewarded in 1770. Indeed, with the reopened markets of 1770, there was a massive demand for goods, such as amply justified those who had made their dispositions earlier. It would have taken greater discipline than the colonists were at this time able to muster to bring business in England to its knees.

The nonimportation and nonexportation campaign of 1774 and thereafter was of course in a quite different category from that of 1768–70. For one thing, the Continental Association was rigorously enforced throughout the colonies. With a few exceptions, the nonimportation campaign, which began under the direction of Congress and local committees on 1 December 1774, and the nonexportation campaign, which commenced nearly a year later on 10 September 1775, were largely effective in America. There were a few reports in the summer of 1774 that Pennsylvania and New York would decline to take part in nonimportation, and indeed the North ministry placed great reliance in 1775 on dividing the colonies by luring the New Yorkers, perhaps rightly regarded as the most reluctant of rebels, back into the fold. However, the official statistics leave no doubt whatever that by the beginning of 1775 all but a trickle of British imports were ceasing to get through. Exports to the thirteen colonies stood at £2,644,000 in 1774 but collapsed catastrophically to £297,000 in 1775 and fell still further during the subsequent three years. Such destruction of the largest and most important of British markets was quite different from anything that had happened in 1765–66 or 1768–70. To all intents and purposes, the thirteen colonies formally disappeared as a market for British goods between the autumn of 1774 and Spring of 1775. Nonexportation, in what was becoming a war situation and with greatly superior direction and organization than had characterized earlier embargoes of any kind, was equally effective, transforming a figure of £1,900,000 for 1775 to one of £197,000 in 1776.

If it is easy to be clear about the enforcement of the embargo from the colonial angle, it does not follow that it is equally easy to be certain of the effects on the British economy. Neither manufacturers nor merchants reacted very strongly in the political sense, and such demonstrations as there eventually were in middle and late 1775 were gravely damaged by the obvious divisions among the business community. It would be surprising in these circumstances if the embargo actually had a dramatic impact on the economy, and to a great extent it is indeed the case that trade and industry continued to prosper. Generally speaking, the situation through much of 1774 was reckoned to be either very good or even booming. The nonimportation campaign was not, of course, scheduled to begin until 1 December. There were one or two reports of difficulties in the Yorkshire textile industry, but otherwise there seemed little to worry manufacturers.[58] This was not surprising in places such as Norwich, where Hutchinson noted little apprehension or disruption, but where dependence on the American market was very limited. As one of the manufacturers there observed, "it was altogether indifferent to them whether the Colonies imported goods from England or not."[59] But it was more striking in the case of Glasgow, for which the colonial trade was a staple.[60] However, by the winter of 1774–75, complaints began to be voiced as nonimportation became a fact of life for the industrialists as well as the colonists. On the other hand, such complaints were far from universal. The picture which emerges as 1775 wears on is a clear and reasonably convincing one. On the one hand, there was the inevitable grumbling from sectors which traditionally treated the thirteen colonies as their bread and butter trade. Richard Champion, one of the few observers in a position to make an authoritative assessment and interested in the political consequences, provided a helpful analysis of those industries most affected. According to him, it was the coarse woolen industry, especially duffels and serges manufactured in Yorkshire, and the iron industry, especially nail making, which were adversely affected.[61] The blanket industry was plainly hit rather badly, for reports appeared in the London and colonial newspapers which are too circumstantial to make doubts possible. There were fears from Witney of a complete cessation of orders for Indian match coating as early as December 1774, and similar alarm existed in the West Riding.[62] Dewsbury was identified as an area of serious distress, since

> the chief branch of the business of that very populous neighbourhood is making Duffil Blankets for the N American markets the total stagnation of which trade has chiefly brought on this distress. . . . All our hope of relief, while suffering the severities of a hungry and cold winter, was the revival of the demand from America. . . . I was exceedingly affected last Friday on observing the settled gloom and dejection that set on the countenances of the poor manufacturers, who brought their cloths to Mr. M's warehouse. How different from the looks they wore two years ago![63]

Such suffering, however, was located on a local rather than regional or national basis, and the general picture was quite different. Champion himself admitted: "The Manufactories of the Kingdom have not been affected in any degree to excite a clamour by the non-Importation agreement. The Trade of Yorkshire, Manchester, Norwich and the Clothing Countries near this town (Bristol) continues very brisk, even Birmingham is not greatly affected."[64] Other merchants like Bernard Eyre of London similarly remarked that while their own affairs were affected, those of industry and trade in general were not. "In regard to Business we have little or nothing to do yet there is no want of Trade, for Manufactured goods of all kinds are far from being cheap but as our greatest Employment has been in the American Trade we are at a Stand."[65] Understandably, the friends of government rejoiced that "The demand for English manufacturers still increases, so that the Opposition can raise no clamour on account of the decay of trade."[66] Against such obvious unanimity, the occasional claims by resident Americans of "the best intelligence that the manufacturers were bitterly feeling and loudly complaining of the loss of the American trade," are difficult to take seriously.[67] More especially is this so if the other symptoms of prosperity are taken into account. Most observers in 1775 were struck by the astonishing failure of the stock market to react to crisis and even war in America;[68] the London money market, normally so responsive to the faintest darkening of the political horizon, and badly shaken, for example, at the time of the Falkland Islands crisis in 1770 or at the time of the bank crisis of 1772–73, seemed sublimely unaware of the events in the colonies, indeed seemed to take positive heart from them.[69] The harvest of 1775, after a bad crop the previous year and a bitter winter in between, was especially good, and American hopes of a near famine situation, such as had occurred in the mid-1760s were disappointed.[70] And as the *Gentleman's Magazine* pointed out, the "gross produce of the excise for the year 1775, exceeds that of the preceding years almost £255,000 sterling; a plain proof that our merchants, traders and manufacturers, (notwithstanding the Americans have shut their ports,) are not in that melancholy situation that was foreboded."[71] Nor was this happy state of affairs quickly brought to a close. Benjamin Franklin had predicted that if only America stood firm until September 1776, the ensuing session of Parliament would see a massive movement of protest from the business and working community culminating in complete surrender to the colonists' demands.[72] The war, however, broke out long before that date, and this prophecy proved sadly inaccurate and irrelevant.

It was natural enough for contemporaries to account for the extraordinary prosperity of the early war years by recourse to the explanation that they had so erroneously opted for five or six years earlier. Once again it was argued that other and new markets enabled British industry to weather the storm, with obvious implications for the significance of the colonial market. Thus, one merchant house observed to its American correspondents in August 1775:

> It will surprise you not a little we dare say, when we tell you that notwithstanding our want of Trade to Our American Colonies that we never knew our Manufactures, in General, in a more flourishing state; had we at this Time orders as formerly, for America, we are certain, England cou'd not supply you so that you see, we are not so dependant on your Country for a Consumption of our Manufactures, as some People have imagin'd.[73]

As early as April 1775, Hutchinson observed that "the loss of the American trade seems to have lost all its terror: and as if it was an event really approaching, people are laying schemes for a substitute or succedanium"; six months later he confirmed, "Wherever I have been in the country there is a perfect calm, and the cessation of American trade has no effect upon the manufactures, for, by new channels, or by enlargement of old, the demand is greater now than last year."[74] The new channels were generally believed to lie in Europe. Thus, one of Ralph Izard's friends wrote from Manchester in August 1775:

> There is an amazing trade carried on in this place. The most intelligent Manufacturers here, say they feel no *great* loss *yet* in their business, from the American associations. It is, indeed, probable that they do not yet feel much, but the time must come—and even themselves acknowledge, that had the American demand been as good as *usual,* they should have been obliged to hire more hands; but the European demands have increased so much—with the decrease of the American—that they have not discharged any of their workmen, and, in fact, at present, their trade has only shifted to another channel.[75]

But more distant markets were involved, especially it seems, for Lancashire textiles. According to Lord North himself, "all the stir made by the manufacturers at the time of the Repeal of the Stamp Act, was by the contrivance of the then Ministry: that he knew the people of Manchester had been so used by the Colonies, that they chose to have no further dealing with them; that they had found out a way to get through their goods through Spain to Spanish America, more to their advantage."[76] The alleged expansion of the Spanish and Spanish American demand was also stressed in other reports, where it was paralleled by talk of growing markets in Russia, in Poland, and even in France.[77]

These claims are to some extent justified in the case of 1774–76, unlike that of five years earlier, by the official records of trade. The Spanish market did indeed show a most remarkable improvement in 1775, when exports were worth £1,205,000 as against £970,000 in 1774, the new level being sustained in 1776. Russian demands also increased by a fifth in 1774, though they fell back again thereafter, while the Eastland trade (including Poland) reveals a similar pattern. No doubt the end of the Russo-Turkish war, itself incorrectly alleged to be the cause of expanding British exports in 1768–70, was now a stimulus in eastern Europe; significantly the eastern Mediterranean generally took a growing quantity of British goods in this period—both to Turkey directly and through Italy and Venice. The figures also support the notion of increased exports to France (though only in 1774), and to other European markets, notably Germany which absorbed an increase of £1,337,000 to £1,573,000 in 1774–75 and maintained the growth thereafter. In fact, Europe as a whole registered an intriguing increase from £10,007,000 in 1774 to £10,715,000 in 1775, a figure previously exceeded only in 1764. Nevertheless, such growth was not sufficient to explain the ability of industry to cope with the American disaster. Approximately an eighth of the normal export market was wiped out by the colonial embargo, and in terms of demand for British manufactures, as opposed to re-exports, the fraction was doubtless rather greater. It would have required a gigantic expansion of the continental market to compensate for this, and such an increase was not really forthcoming.

This is not to say that there were no alternative outlets for British goods in the mid-1770s. One strong possibility is that the apparent write off of the colonial market was in some measure more apparent than real. There can be little question that commodities which could not get into the thirteen colonies officially had a way of getting into them unofficially. For example, a report in early 1775 said: "In Manchester, it is said, they are fully employed by persons who intend shipping them to Ireland, and thence smuggle them into the continent."[78] The official statistics suggest a small rather than large increase in exports to Ireland in 1775, and in view of the restrictions on Irish exports and reexports, which must have made smuggling peculiarly difficult, it is not easy to believe that large quantities of goods reached America by this route. But other channels are more convincing. For example, there was a marked improvement in exports to the British West Indies, especially Jamaica, Saint Kitts, and Antigua, and it is possible that a good proportion of the increase found its way into the thirteen colonies. Equally striking is the more than

50 percent growth in exports to Canada in 1775 (almost 100 percent by 1777) and the still more spectacular increase to Newfoundland and, above all, Nova Scotia in 1775 and 1776. The thirteen colonies were open to a certain amount of trade via the North and the West Indies, and no doubt, at least a proportion of the lost British exports continued to find its way to America by these furtive means. Even so, neither new European markets nor old but illegal colonial markets can fully account for the resilience of the manufacturing economy in 1775 and thereafter. Total exports in 1775 were well above average for the preceding decade, at £15,202,000, but the total for 1776, at £13,730,000, was worse than any year since 1758 (excluding 1769), while that for 1777, at £12,653,000, was still worse. Even allowing for a certain amount of entirely illicit trade, only a missing factor of some consequence can adequately explain the underlying prosperity of British manufacturing in these years.

That factor is provided by one single and significant source of finance and demand—the government itself. Economic historians are divided about the precise economic significance of government spending in wartime in the eighteenth century,[79] but it is indisputable that in the early years of the American war the financial resources voted by Parliament were quite sufficient to have a dramatically invigorating effect on the economy. Certainly contemporary awareness of its impact is not lacking. For William Lee it was the critical force in operation. Thus he observed in October 1776: "Trade flourishes amazingly; for the American war creates an amazing Fund for Commerce. Think what 7 or 8 millions will effect, laid out in the various manufactures and implements for the Army, with the necessary provisions, and transports, etc."[80] Military clothing and armaments made heavy demands on the textile and metal industries of the Midlands and North, and demand for both rocketed in the mid-1770s. The size of the armed forces nearly tripled in terms of manpower between 1775 and 1777,[81] while the annual budget deficit in the same period climbed to giddy heights, with dramatic effects on the government's borrowing requirements.[82] The notion of a sudden boost for British industry created by the peculiar combination of continuing commercial stability in most markets (uncharacteristic of most eighteenth century warfare) and a massive injection into the economy of public money is entirely plausible. Nor are particular illustrations wanting—for example, from the journal of Samuel Curwen. In 1776 Curwen met a frying pan maker in Birmingham who "is greatly hurt by the American quarrell, he having on hand several tons of the latter," but two days later visited a gunsmith who had just received a government order for 600 rifles. Six years later, almost at the conclusion of the war, Curwen was to meet a London contractor for hats and stockings, who not surprisingly, was "a warm opposer of American independence."[83]

The extent of this vested interest in war is difficult to quantify, but it is clear enough that it was sufficient to account for the continuing industrial prosperity and indeed development of the early years of the American war. Nor need this be surprising. In 1770, when a war emergency had briefly flared between the Bourbon powers and England, and when the administration had been compelled to undertake a rearmament program, the galvanic effect on the manufacturing economy had been intense. In 1771, duffels, the textiles which were briefly hard hit in late 1774 but which soon recovered thereafter, were virtually unobtainable because of military demands, and the same was true of woolens generally.[84] In 1771 the emergency was short-lived; in 1775 and thereafter, it was continuing. Add to this the extraordinarily good harvests of these years, not to say the calls on the labor force of recruitment for the armed services, and it is not difficult to see how government substantially assisted manufacturing industry to cope with the immediate pressures of the War of American Independence.

The significance of this stimulus to the economy enormously strengthens the importance of timing in the colonists' campaign against the mother country. Nonimportation was followed within a matter of months by a full scale mobilization of the British economy for war purposes; such strains as showed briefly in the intervening period were rapidly extinguished thereafter as the country moved into full gear. Had there been a greater lapse of time between the effective closure of the colonial market in America and the injection of funds provided by government, or rather by the taxpayer, things might have turned out differently. As it was, at least so far as manufacturers were concerned, the evil day was put off, and indeed, the cycle of prosperity actually accelerated.

Manufacturers, however, were only a part of the business community, in some respects a part less powerful and influential, certainly less forward in politics, than the merchants, and at least in theory, merchants were less able in the mid-1770s to exploit new opportunities. Manufacturers on the whole were less specialized than those who marketed their wares. No doubt many small industrialists and a few big ones, like the Elams of the West Riding, for example, tended to concentrate on American orders, but few of them did so to the exclusion of other markets, and most could manufacture their goods for any customer provided the specifications were either readily adapted to their own or provided their wares were equally acceptable to new clients. But merchants, especially in the overseas trade and in the all-important metropolis, were far more highly specialized—few more so than those in the North American trade. The association of the Molleson house with Maryland, the Lane house with New England, the Barclay house with Pennsylvania, and so on through the great majority of large commercial companies, is well known. Such merchants were in no position to adapt quickly to the transformed circumstances of 1775 and 1776. Manufacturers who sought to take advantage of new markets or government commissions did not use as intermediaries those merchants who had in the past acted for them with reference to the thirteen colonies, but turned to the appropriate and established agents.

Moreover, the very anxiety of the merchants to maintain their monopoly of transactions with the colonies ensured that the manufacturers had few damaging commitments there. With the exception of one or two extremely persistent and well-heeled industrialists, who traded to some extent directly with the colonies in order to reap the additional profits to be derived from cutting out the middleman, few manufacturers had extensive debts overseas. They expected and generally obtained fairly rapid payment from their merchants and factors and tended to advance short-term credit of a few months where the merchants themselves were compelled to offer substantially longer credit to their transatlantic customers. The collapse of the American market put a premium on the discovery of new markets for British manufacturers, but it did not in general involve great loss of property for them. For merchants there was no such consolation. Many of them actually owned property in the colonies, especially in the South, and far more had extensive debts contracted in the way of business. All merchants complained constantly about their debts, presumably like their fathers before them, but there is no reason to doubt that colonial debts, in general, were mounting in the 1760s and 1770s and the financial plight of many businesses worsening.[85] In 1766 during the Commons' inquiry into the effects of the Stamp Act, the enormous debts tied up in the thirteen colonies had been the subject of considerable interest and emphasis. Barlow Trecothick had made great play with the prospect of near bankruptcy which was likely to result in Britain from Anglo-American political breakdown.[86]

In the circumstances, it was not to be expected that the merchant houses would escape from the problems posed by the American Revolution in the same way as their manufacturing colleagues. That they did escape by and large was, like the fortune of the manufacturers, in part, at least, a matter of timing. At the time of the Coercive Acts, when there was so much complaining about the failure of the merchants to campaign on America's behalf, nonimportation had yet even to be seriously mooted, and it was not easy to believe that the trade with America would shortly be in ruins. But perhaps because there was, nonetheless, a feeling that the near future might see an interruption to business, 1774 saw a massive boom in exports to the thirteen colonies, amounting to £2,644,000. This figure was higher than any previous annual total, with the exception of the other boom years of 1771 and 1772. Americans were skeptical about the wisdom from the British point of view of indulging in such exports on credit. Thus Joseph Reed observed in September:

> The quantity of English goods imported this year is very great. Too many of your merchants, I fear, will have reason to repent their credulity in trusting their property, on so precarious an adventure. Should the sword once be drawn, and America persist in resistance, out of the five millions supposed to be due to Great Britain, I doubt whether two would be paid.

And three months later Reed again pointed out: "The very large importations of goods the last year with the quantities on hand, will enable us to bear a nonimportation agreement for a considerable time."[87] In fact, some prudent English merchants were already easing back on their shipments well before nonimportation formally began to operate.[88] But in general the merchants seized the opportunity to place new orders, and business flourished through the spring and summer of 1774, despite the clouds on the political horizon. In 1775, however, all possibility of significant exports to America had evaporated, and it is more difficult to account for the survival of the merchant houses, apparently largely undamaged by the effect of nonimportation.

In all probability the answer is again largely timing. For the essential fact was that the first nonexportation campaign attempted by the Americans was designed to come into effect almost a year after nonimportation. No doubt there were good reasons for Congress's desire to postpone launching the entire battery of economic weapons at its disposal. (See Chapter Six for further discussion of this.) For one thing, it was thought that such a deliberate and delayed escalation might tend to show the British the sense of restraint and calculation which lay behind the colonial strategy and give time for a response. Still more influential were practical politics. Particularly in the South there was a marked reluctance to sacrifice the produce of the plantations forthwith.[89] After all, it was not merely hoped but believed, in America as in England, that a short sharp dose of nonimportation would be quickly followed by a political settlement and a return to normal commercial relations. In any event, the result was to prolong the dispatch of exports from colonies well into 1775, long after imports had ceased. The result was a one-way traffic unprecedented in the history of the empire, and one which had intriguing consequences. Particularly striking was the flow of tobacco shipments across the Atlantic. Thanks to the approaching prospect of nonexportation, demand in Britain and, indeed, in Europe generally soared, and the rush to purchase and dispatch tobacco became intense in the summer of 1775. Thus, one Virginian supplier wrote in August 1775:

> With Respect to the Tobacco shipp'd you this Summer, I should imagine a very good price may be got for it, provided a Reconciliation (by Concessions from your Parliamt.) is not likely to happen. I am well informed that the last Sale to the French in Glasgow was 3¼d, and the Merchants now keep it up in Expectation of 4d at the least, so that the meanest Tob. in the same proportion ought to sell in London for 4d to 4½d.[90]

Technically, the bulk of this profit would go to the planter, since most houses sold their suppliers' tobacco without risks to themselves and acting merely as agents.[91] However, they also took a commission on sales, and in addition to this incentive for boosting supplies, they had the obvious advantage of handling and holding the considerable balances by sales. These remittances in kind would ultimately have to go toward the purchase of goods for the American market, but with the colonists themselves unable to import British manufactures in the short-term, they could be employed for the payment of long-standing debts and for judicious investment at profitable rates in the appropriate quarters.

There is ample evidence of the advantage taken in Britain from the great tobacco bonanza created by the staggered implementation of nonimportation and nonexportation. Thus, William Lee complained bitterly that Glasgow merchants were investing the tobacco crop of 1774–75 in the purchase of land. "This money is what the Virginians chiefly have supplied them with, in contemplation of the approaching troubles by treble Remittances."[92] Yet Lee himself did not scruple to share in the vast profits being made from Virginia remittances in 1775. Nor was he averse to taking a more direct part in the tobacco industry than he normally did, for if those who sold Virginia's produce on commission were making profits, they were nothing compared to those who were actually able to buy the tobacco themselves and sell it entirely at their risk. This was the case with many Scottish houses which traditionally purchased tobacco on the ground and took all the risks as well as profits involved in its marketing. It was also true of many in 1775 who saw a unique chance to make a handsome profit as a result of the political situation. Lee was among the latter, and he urged his connection in the colonies to take advantage of that situation. To Anthony Stewart in Annapolis, he wrote:

> I would by all means advise you to purchase immediately 1000 or 1500 hhds. of your very best tobacco, and ship it off in ships of about 350 or 400 hhds., by which you may make a fortune. You will say perhaps, where is the money to do this? I will tell you—draw on me at 60 or 90 days sight, when the ship sails, order insurance, and consign the tobacco to me. In this case the bills will be paid. . . . The price should not be the least obstacle; give what others do without hesitation, provided you are clear of the firmness, etc. of the Americans.[93]

Such were the economics of patriotism.

The merchants of London, Glasgow, Bristol, and Liverpool who traded in one way or another with the plantation colonies of the South naturally had interests distinct from those of their colleagues who had dealings with the North, and it was not to be expected that the latter would be feather bedded by the timing of nonimportation and nonexportation in the way that the great tobacco houses were. Merchants who dealt with the middle colonies and with New England did not expect to handle vast quantities of American produce in the way that merchants dealing with the South did, and they made their own profits chiefly by selling British goods on commission or by venturing goods in the complex triangular and coastal trades which involved North America. But thanks to chance, the timing of nonexportation turned out to be advantageous even to many of these merchants. For this there was one very straightforward reason. New York, Pennsylvania, and New England did not have tobacco or cotton, indigo or rice, but they had one commodity which was fortuitously in demand in Western Europe in 1775—grain. Britain in particular was normally self-supporting in basic foodstuffs and provided no continuing market for the great harvests of North American cereals, except on a casual and highly unpredictable basis. But the harvest of 1774 in England was quite disastrously bad and necessitated a sudden and massive demand for grain from overseas. New England, Pennsylvania, and above all New York rushed to supply this demand, since nonexportation was not due to begin until September, and poured enormous amounts of provisions across the Atlantic.[94] Colonial journals bear ample testimony to this sudden export bonanza for farmers in the temperate latitudes of North America with talk of one million bushels of wheat being imported into Bristol alone between September 1774 and September 1775, for example.[95] Thus for one year, that crucial year between the initiation of nonimportation and nonexportation, even the normally importing colonies became raw material producing provinces for the mother country.

The significance of the remittances in tobacco and in grain is beyond question and is clearly reflected in the official trade statistics. As has been seen, official exports to the thirteen colonies fell by nine-tenths in 1775 as a result of nonimportation. But with colonial exports unrestricted, the reverse traffic almost doubled. The economic effects can hardly be exaggerated. In 1774, exports to the thirteen colonies from Britain had stood officially at £2,644,000 whereas imports from America amounted to only half this figure, at £1,398,000. But in 1775 the picture was transformed. With exports collapsing to £297,000, imports rocketed to £1,946,000, a figure higher by a clear half million than any recorded since the establishment of the inspector-general's statistics in 1696. As has been seen, the precise value of such figures in calculating the balance of trade advantage between commercial partners is limited, owing to the valuation system employed by the Customs officials. But in general, it is obvious that Britain normally had a very considerable advantage over the American colonies, supplying manufactured goods far in excess of the value of imported raw materials.[96] Especially was this the case for the colonies north of the Delaware, which had none of those semitropical or tropical products which were so essential both to the British and the European reexport markets. This fundamental imbalance in terms of trade was normally financed so far as the colonies were concerned by commercial relations with third partners—the celebrated triangular trade in its manifold forms, for example—or more simply by spiralling debts. But for the one year of 1775, because of politics and chance, the situation was transformed, and Americans found themselves briefly in credit. Had an amicable settlement been reached, had the embargo quickly been terminated, in short, had relations soon returned to normal, as they had in 1766 and 1770, all would have been well; colonial merchants, having demonstrated their capacity to discharge a substantial portion of their debts, would have proceeded to incur new ones with extensive orders for British goods. But no such happy ending ensued in the mid-1770s; the great merchant houses of Britain were left holding the cash, without orders for its employment.

The consequent advantage to the mercantile interest in Britain can be seen from the recorded figures for American debts in the war period. These in the thirteen colonies were of course very large, and after the war they were to become the subject of incessant controversy and conflict between the British and United States governments.[97] But if the diplomatic problems this created are left on one side, the most striking feature of the debts recorded as undischarged during the period of the war is their relative smallness. Debts had built up rapidly in the late 1760s and the early 1770s with almost reckless colonial purchasing of British goods on credit, and there can be little question that the debt problem was genuinely a worsening one. The testimony supplied by one such as Henry Cruger of Bristol, a merchant of New York birth and colonial connections and prejudices, was politically unimpugnable and amply demonstrates the problems faced by British businessmen in this period.[98] A comparable case is that of the house of DeBerdt, which was made bankrupt on the death of the Massachusetts special agent, Dennys DeBerdt. It was left to his American son-in-law, Joseph Reed, to chastise his debtors and identify their contribution to the destruction of the family's business.[99]

Yet against the evidence of mounting colonial indebtedness on the eve of the American Revolution, there is the apparent stability of British mercantile finances in 1775 and 1776. Only the delayed implementation of nonexportation can explain the apparent contradiction. Certainly that delay produced some bizarre results. John Hancock, himself one of the worst offenders in the matter of debts, for all his eminence, in 1775 suddenly found himself in credit with his London suppliers, the firm of Hayley and Hopkins. George Hayley, the city politician and M.P., had succeeded to Trecothick's leadership of the London North American interest. Hayley had unwisely inaugurated a trading partnership with Hancock in 1767 after the firm of Harrison and Company had been bankrupted, not least by the indebtedness of Hancock himself. At that time, Hancock had had the temerity to observe that "he grieved for old Mr. Barnard (of Harrison's firm) . . . always thought they were too unlimited in their supplies to people and was fully convinc'd they must sink." Hayley and Hopkins quickly had cause to regret their readiness to take up Hancock's offer of his custom, and by July 1774 they finally arrived at the stage of refusing to honor his bills drawn on them. But nonimportation brought them a great surprise, for late in 1774 there arrived a cargo from Boston worth nearly £13,000, sufficient to put Hancock actually in credit with Hayley's firm at the onset of the Revolution.[100]

There are other examples of the stability of British mercantile finances. Pierce and Browne, who had traded with the famous Beekmans of New York since 1752, were only owed £530 when accounts were submitted in 1783, while Pomeroy's had only £1,432 due from the same house. But both these figures included substantial interest charged for the period between the last remittances in 1775 and the peace of 1783, and the actual debts were less than two thirds of these figures—remarkably low in view of the volume of business normally conducted and the amount of debt normally outstanding in the prewar period. [101] This impression is confirmed by the figures of debts drawn up in 1790 by the committee acting for creditors.[102] These figures valued American debts at fractionally under £5 million sterling. But again much of this sum consisted of interest claimed for the war period, and the actual debts outstanding at the outbreak of war were estimated at little more than £2 million. Even allowing for possible underestimates and for debts paid on the conclusion of hostilities, this figure was substantially below most contemporary assessments of what was owed in the 1760s, for example. Moreover, well over half the total sum was allocated to Virginia and Maryland alone, where a considerable proportion of it was in the form of property lost through the Revolution rather than straightforward trading debts. Property was of course vitally important, but its loss was not likely to bankrupt a merchant house in the way an undischarged business debt could, nor were most merchants dependent on it for working capital. Given these qualifications, it seems likely that the total in respect to commercial debts at the onset of war was far below the 4.5 million or so described as the normal debt to Barlow Trecothick before the Commons in 1766.[103]

The figures for particular colonies are especially striking. New York, the province which perhaps benefited most by the grain boom of 1775, apparently owed only £175,094 to British businessmen in the 1780s, half of which was interest. Pennsylvania and Massachusetts Bay owed but little more, and only in the southern colonies did this picture vary, due largely to property alienated in the Revolution. The same impression holds for individual houses listed. Two or three were evidently unfortunate or bad businessmen; Mildred and Roberts, trading with the middle colonies, and John Nutt, heavily involved in the South, both had debts of over £100,000, and the top scorer in this unhappy competition was Champion and Dickinson, who claimed £182,385. But again these figures included at least fourteen years' interest, and they were, after all, the league leaders. Otherwise most of the creditors were claiming relatively small sums in terms of the balance due at the outbreak of war. It is remarkable, for example, that a merchant house as important as Pigou and Booth, one of the great trading concerns involved in Pennsylvania, should only have claimed £6,056 (including interest) and that Trecothick's old firm and Harrison and Ainsworth should each have claimed well under £30,000. Compared with either the expressed fears of British merchants in the 1760s and early 1770s or with the expressed threats of the colonists, these debts were by no means very large. Partly, no doubt, to bring pressures to bear on their own government, and with the wisdom of hindsight, the creditor merchants blamed Parliament for its action in prohibiting trade with the thirteen colonies after 1775. For "in the course of that year very considerable remittances were made from America to the British Merchants and Others in part of payment of the very large Sums that were due from them." The parliamentary prohibitions in March 1776 "put an End to the Sources of remittances and from thence commenced their great distress and heavy losses." But this was nonsense. It was the introduction of colonial nonexportation in September 1775 which stopped the flow of remittances, and but for the time lapse between nonimportation and nonexportation, the distress and losses of the merchants would have been much worse.[104]

Some contemporary observers were well aware that it was this factor which made all the difference in the politics of 1775. As early as September 1774, William Lee reminded his transatlantic brethren that it would be necessary to stop both imports and exports simultaneously if the merchants were to be brought to support the colonies.[105] By July 1775, he was warning, "you are not to expect any really spirited exertions on the part of the people, until they feel, which they do not at present, because large remittances have been made to the merchants in general.[106] William's choleric brother Arthur Lee had also predicted the sequence of economic events in December 1774, in a letter to their eldest brother.

> Our last accounts from you signify that the non-export will not take place till the present crop is shipped. It is unfortunate that you did not adopt that measure immediately upon the receipt of the late acts, because the operation of it would have been felt by this time, and would in all probability have enforced the repeal of them this session. But now by this dangerous delay, the present parliament will be

involved like the old one, and the plea of wounded dignity will still impede a retraction. The merchants too, being in possession of one year's crop, will be enabled to pay the tradesmen, etc., and subsist themselves under a suspension of trade for at least a year, so as to prevent any clamour, and give the ministry that time to try what fraud and force can do to divest you of your liberties.[107]

A letter in Gaine's *New York Gazette* made much the same point: "If a Non-Exportation had been resolved upon the 1st of March instead of September, I think it would have had a greater Effect in alarming the Nation, and hastened your Relief."[108]

Even when nonexportation finally came in September 1775 and completed the ruin of Anglo-American commerce, it was the timing that was crucial. Merchants had hoped that a settlement would be reached before the final disaster struck. Thus, Moses Robertson, one of the Norton firm's captains in the Virginia trade, wrote from Urbanna in June 1775, "the Tea Affair seems to have blown Over and I make no Doubt but your Interest will be Established as Firm as Ever when the Exports ReOpen again." Such confidence was reinforced by the language of American merchants—for example, Lane, Son, and Fraser's customer in New England, and the Beekmans in New York.[109] But by the time it became clear that there would be no speedy settlement, it was too late to do anything. The notion of a great mercantile protest movement in the winter of 1775–76 would have been ludicrous, given the development of a war situation in America and the now unequivocal authoritarianism of government in Britain. Moreover, with manufacturing industry fully employed on government contracts or alternative markets, merchants who relied on America were hardly in a position to whip up much enthusiasm for their cause, especially as their business colleagues in other trades had little to complain of. In short, the great North American houses were left to pick up the pieces and bring about their own salvation. Despite the large debts which were a traditional feature of the American trade, and despite the particular debts which after 1775 were virtually frozen until the peace at the earliest, most merchants sufficiently benefited by the great remittances of 1775 to provide themselves with a shield against disaster. These remittances enabled merchants not merely to prosper in 1775 but to survive thereafter. After the war, it was to be pointed out by Britain's excolonial debtors that in 1775 they had committed large sums of money to England which had remained in merchant hands and for which it was reasonable to allow interest. "In all the Accounts transmitted from England," one of them wrote in 1784, "where the Money has been lying in the Merchants Hands ever since 1775 and 1776, I see no Allowance for Interest on their Part."[110] Moreover, most houses had some resources to fall back on, quite apart from the great windfall of 1775. As John Norton admitted in 1770, it was usual to hive off a portion of profits rather than reinvest them all in a trade like that with Virginia; such savings were "call'd by Traders a Nest Egg, in case of any Losses by Debts and which might happen. This Method is always pursued by prudent persons and by those I have been connected with."[111] In the crisis situation of 1776, nest eggs were much in need.

It is tempting to interpret the relative political inactivity of British merchants and manufacturers entirely in terms of the particular business conditions which formed the background to the nonimportation movements. In fact, such an interpretation would not merely be too cynical, but too crude, for businessmen may reasonably be supposed to have had more complicated and certainly more long-term considerations in mind than the immediate economic situation. One obvious factor which operated throughout the period was a purely political one—the natural relationship which at all times existed, with varying degrees of intimacy, between government and the leaders of the business community. In this respect, as in so many others, the significance of 1766 and the repeal of the Stamp Act was thoroughly misunderstood. Many, including most colonial observers, had to a great extent seen repeal as the achievement of the mercantile lobby, pressuring both administration and Parliament into accepting its demands. There was something in this thesis, though Rockingham and his friends were so well disposed towards the merchants that the task of inducing a change of policy was an easy one, at least so far as the ministry was concerned. But the truth was that the effectiveness of the repeal campaign had essentially derived from the combination of ministerial and mercantile activities. It had not been very easy to convince the House of Commons that repeal was the right policy. Only the cooperation of both elements, working in harness and carefully organizing the presentation of the pressures and arguments, could have done it. Cynical opponents of the repeal movement indeed went further. In 1766, Grenville himself alleged that the campaign was the sort of thing which any ministry could organize if it wished. "Is it difficult for Ministers to get Petitions against Taxes? I opposed the Tax upon Beer, could not I first Commissioner of Treasury have got Petitions from all the Mughouses in London."[112] This was a gross exaggeration—the flood of protest against the Grenville legislation respecting America had its origins in more than a ministerial fiat—but it was not without a grain of truth. Certainly, when the later nonimportation campaigns were launched, it was important that neither the Grafton and North administrations in 1768–70 nor the latter again in 1774–76 necessarily had quite the same readiness to cooperate with the pro-American business interests as had the Rockingham ministry earlier. The point was actually made by Lord North himself in both cases. Thus in 1768, according to Thomas Whately, North observed that "there will be no petition from the merchants, and at the same time assures that no pains has been taken by Ministry to prevent one; from whence his inference was that pains had been taken by the former Ministry to procure the petitions which led to the repeal of the Stamp Act."[113] He made a similar remark six years later to Thomas Hutchinson, insisting "that all the stir made by the manufacturers at the time of the Repeal of the Stamp Act, was by the contrivance of the then Ministry."[114] A minister who thought like this was scarcely likely to give much encouragement to business elements who sought support for a campaign in favor of liberal policies in the colonies. Nonetheless, the result was more than one crass misunderstanding by such elements. Dennys DeBerdt the younger, for example, blithely assumed that the merchants' petition of 1775, when it finally got off the ground, would inaugurate a repeat performance of the 1766 scenario, even in the legislature itself.

If this petition is heard [he wrote to America], it will lead to inquiries at the bar of the House, which will enable us to ascertain the real debt due from America; its exports and imports, and in fact, your true importance to us. This petition, you may rest assured, will be followed by others of a similar nature, from all the man-ufacturing towns, and must throw great weight into the American scale. It appears to me to be the only likely way to bring about accommodation, as it will furnish Ministry, with an excuse for repealing the obnoxious acts, and an opportunity to censure your conduct, and comply with your demands.[115]

This prediction was based on many faulty assumptions, all of them founded on the model of 1766, but none was more fallacious than the notion that North and his friends would obligingly put the weight of the treasury behind the maneuvers of the pro-American merchants, as Rockingham had done in 1766. Ministerial collab-oration with the mercantile lobby in the late 1760s and mid-1770s might not have automatically ensured success of that lobby, but it would unquestionably have made a considerable difference.

Not only did the attitudes of government act as a brake on outside activities in this way, they also did much to influence the views of businessmen. The notion that commercial interests normally found themselves in political opposition to gov-ernment in the eighteenth century is a largely incorrect one, anyway, based upon spectacular but limited evidence, like the anti-Spanish agitation of 1739, the rodomontade of the elder Pitt, and the strong tendency of the City of London, in theory the epitome of the businessman's community, to oppose government. But such symptoms were largely misleading. Pitt was a posturing bully, whose power base was never as strong as he liked to imply and whose career was advanced more by the cowardice and timidity of his rivals than by the force of popular opinion.[116] Mercantile agitations like those against Walpole and Spain in the 1730s rep-resented, at best, small sections of the business world which had vastly strengthened their political muscle by resort to discontented politicians and jour-nalists.[117] And the opposition of the City of London to government, impressive and important though it often was, was based more on the radical force of the small craftsmen, journeymen, and tradesmen—who exercised great power in the rela-tively democratic politics of the metropolis—than on the stable support of large merchant houses.[118] In general terms, the businessmen who depended on trade with colonies or foreign countries dealt in profit and power—not in patriotism or pro-grams. They had little interest in supporting political faction, and though they were quite capable of bringing pressures to bear on ministers and M.P.s, they were nor-mally cautious about the mode of doing so. Far more could be achieved by con-structive critical collaboration with government than by blackmail or bullying. Grenville himself had indeed worked well with the London merchants on many issues and was unfortunate in the picture which was painted of his relations with them once he was out of power.[119] The merchants who then turned against him were delighted to work with Rockingham and his colleagues in 1766, but it is important to bear in mind that they were working with the ministers of the Crown, not with opposition Whigs. The Rockinghams fairly prided themselves on their readiness to lend an ear to mercantile petitions, and Burke boasted that their administration "was the first which proposed and encouraged public meetings and free consultations of merchants from all parts of the Kingdom; by which means the truest lights have been received; great benefits have been derived to manufactures and commerce; and the most extensive prospects are opened for further improvement."[120] There was considerable justification for this claim, but merchants and manufacturers had collaborated with the Rockingham ministry, not with the Rockingham party, and though the latter retained extensive business connections through men such as Barlow Trecothick and Richard Champion, it had no right to complain when, as in 1775, the business community showed more interest in cultivating an amicable relationship with the court than with the opposition politicians.

Practical evidence of the importance of this relationship is not wanting. In 1769, for example, it is clear that one of the reasons for the apparent feebleness of the mercantile lobby in demanding strong action to resolve the Anglo-American dispute over the Townshend duties was the role of the government. William Samuel Johnson, as the Connecticut special agent, had a particular interest in the merchants' deliberations of 1769 and was repeatedly struck by their vulnerability to the pressures exerted by ministers. A flat and uncompromising hostility from government might indeed have provoked the merchants to take their case, such as it was, to Parliament, but the mixture of kicks and promises administered by ministers like Hillsborough, the colonial secretary, was most effective in delaying and even extinguishing any such possibility.[121] In particular, the publicly declared pledge of the Grafton ministry, in the spring of 1769, that it would repeal most of Townshend's legislation, on the grounds that it offended against the ruling principles of British commercial management, as well as the prejudices of the colonists, and on condition that the Americans did not indulge in outrages comparable to the Stamp Act riots, did much to take the wind out of the more radical merchants' sails. Again in 1770, it was an obvious and powerful argument against action independent of the court, that the ministers would soon put their promise into effect, as indeed they did. But in the meantime, the effect was created of little support for America among the mercantile interest, an impression, no doubt, which ministers were gratified to enhance. Those Americans who were aware of what was going on compared the merchants' attitude unfavorably with that of 1766, without grasping that no amount of pressure would push the great body of merchants into activities totally unacceptable to government. Thus, one Virginian, William Nelson, warned his friend John Norton:

> Allow me the Freedom of a Friend, and I will just tell you, that I like not this Cordiality and a good understanding between the Great Men and the Merchants, as I think it hath been attended with no good Consequence to the Colonies. On a former Occasion, when the Merchants stood upon their own good Sense and Importance, they procured a Repeal of the Stamp Act; but of late, the M——y seem to have cajoled them and laid them asleep; so that the Repeal We are to expect next Session must flow from the Justice and Equity of our Demand, and leaves us no ground to expose our Gratitude as before to that respectable Body of Men.[122]

In 1774–76, of course, the circumstances were quite different, since Lord North made it clear that while wishing to pursue "lenient measures," he had no intention of giving way without concessions by the colonists.[123] Whether a really grave economic crisis of the kind suffered ten years earlier would have altered North's intentions will never be known. As it was, it is clear that many merchants in the crisis of 1774–75 were anxious to stay on the right side of government and avoid getting involved in politically motivated petitions. Especially in London, agitators like William Lee strongly censured the great bulk of metropolitan businessmen who refused to follow where they led; indeed, according to Lee, most of "the principal Merchants trading to America are Abettors of the Ministry, Men who . . . ought to have America inscribed on their Carriages, Équipages, etc and gratitude on their Hearts!"[124]

Such censures raise an important and intriguing question, that of the fundamental views of the merchants. Particularly in the last years before the war, but to some extent in the years following the repeal of the Stamp Act, there were bitter comments in profusion about the hostility towards the colonies to be found even among those whose interests appeared to lie obviously in harmonious relations with them. William and Arthur Lee, of course, are not the most impartial of authorities; both of them were American radicals, and particularly intemperate ones at that. On the other hand, they had an intimate knowledge, especially in William's case, of the metropolitan business community, and their naming of names, for example, is at least interesting. According to William Lee, writing to Richard Henry in September 1774: "The merchants are almost universally your enemies . . . I do not know that you have one friend at present, but Mr. Tricothick, who is rendered incapable of business by an unlucky stroke of the palsy, 9 or 10 months ago; Mr. Bromfield, a native of Boston, in the New England trade, Mr. Johnson, a native of Maryland in that trade, and myself."[125] Lee also names particular villains—all the New England merchants excluding Bromfield (but presumably including even such as Alderman Hayley); Blackburn of Pigou and Booth; the New York and Pennsylvania merchants; the South Carolina merchants Nutt and Rolleston; and apparently worst of all, Lancelot Girt, the Virginia merchant accused of being a particular friend of the ministry and who attended meetings of the London North America merchants committee only to oppose "any sentiment or expression being introduced into our petitions that should convey to the world an idea of our taking any part with America, or hinting that we tho't them oppressed or injured."[126] Daniel Pigou himself, of the New York and Pennsylvania trades, was apparently an especially heinous traitor to the cause of America, having "declared one evening in the Committee, that he hoped the Savages will be let loose on them viz the Americans, to cut all the damned Rascals throats."[127] Similar details were attempted by Josiah Quincy, Jr., who was in London in February 1775. He listed several persons and firms as tolerable friends of America. His list included the names Molleson, Norton, Woolridge and Company, Athawes, and Lee himself, all with strong Virginia connections, together with Barclay, Mildred, and Serjeant, all engaged in trade with the middle colonies, and apparently only Dupuis and Bromfield among the New England traders. "Take out the above from the list of London merchants and where will you find a friend to America? or rather, are not the residue its bitter enemies at heart?"[128] Black lists were even published in colonial newspapers, though sometimes they clearly contradicted other evidence. Molleson, whom Quincy had deemed a friend but who made enemies in Maryland by his views, was singled out in the press "for traducing those Americans here that have honestly borne their Testimony against the iniquitous Bills by their Petition."[129] Anthony Bacon, one of the known opponents of American claims among London merchants and indeed a friend of Grenville, was similarly denounced by the *Maryland Gazette*.[130]

Colonial comments on the hostility of British merchants are of course of limited value for the judgements they make, but they are confirmed even by many British commentators, like Richard Champion, who observed in his correspondence with the Philadelphia merchant house Willing and Morris, "it is a Truth, though a melancholy one, that the generality of the American Merchants are not your best friends."[131] Moreover, they do reflect a basic fact of central importance. Between the repeal of the Stamp Act and the Declaration of Independence, large sections of the Anglo-American business community in Britain were to varying degrees alienated and disillusioned by the incipient signs of colonial rebellion. The phenomenon is a complex one, especially because businessmen were naturally less prejudiced against America and certainly less ill-informed about it than, for example, the landed gentry; moreover, they have left far less clear evidence about their changing views than other sections of the community, particularly those with a prominent part in the nation's political life. Even so, it is possible to identify some fairly marked business attitudes which altered considerably during the later 1760s and early 1770s under the pressure of worsening Anglo-American relations generally. One obvious feature was a strong sense of resentment at what was felt to be the ingratitude of the colonists. It was undeniable that the British merchants had gone to considerable lengths, and equally considerable expense, to oppose the Stamp Act and procure its repeal in 1766; many of them felt that they deserved thanks, if not recompense, but received neither. As early as June 1767, Benjamin Franklin warned his compatriots that the failure of every province but Rhode Island formally to thank the merchants for their endeavors was having a bad effect among them.[132] Even before this, a report had appeared in the *Boston Gazette* that one London captain was complaining of the attitude of New Yorkers:

> They had behaved ungrateful to the Committee, in not returning them Thanks for what they did, in getting the Stamp-act repealed, tho' it cost them £1,500 to compleat it; but on the contrary they seem to insist upon their doing more for them: They have had the Thanks of Quebec, and the little Colony of Rhode-Island, but no more; and the last Remonstrance to them was voted to be burn't, unopen'd; These Threats to a Well Wisher of America, in England, goes down very hard.[133]

There was something in such complaints. London merchants dispatched circulars in 1766 in the wake of the repeal of the Stamp Act warning Americans of the need not to rejoice overmuch, to show appropriate gratitude for the activities of their friends in London, and above all, to avoid violence and outrage, such as had marred the colonial agitation against the Stamp Act. These elicited a response of, at best, complete indifference or ignorance and, at worst, as in the case of New York, a somewhat truculent compliance, backed by demands for new exertions of mercantile pressures and lobbying in favor of novel and sweeping imperial reforms.[134] Thanks to the publicity about the London merchants' anger, there was a partial attempt to repair the damage in 1767. But the circumstances of the repair made matters worse rather than better. Thus, when William Allen of New York reported to David Barclay and Sons that the assembly of the province had instructed its agents to communicate its thanks for mercantile activities in London, he also damagingly explained:

> Some Expressions in the Committee's Letter to our Merchants recommending Submission in points that they had construed would be destructive of theyr Libertys, and the fear of disobliging them by any Reasonings on these heads, prevented them from answering their Letters, and expressing their Gratitude for their benevolent and kind Assistance afforded them in their distress. But I then thought, and now think, that they did not Judge that matter well, as it must appear in the Light of Ingratitude, when the Reasons of their not doing it would not be known.[135]

Such explanations, which distinctly smacked of insubordination, did not necessarily improve matters, and it was scarcely surprising that when the Townshend legislation produced a strong reaction in the colonies, the merchants in Britain were not quite so inclined to express their sympathy with the colonists and their plight as they had been at the time of the Stamp Act. Thus, as early as the autumn of 1768, William Samuel Johnson reported to his constituents in Connecticut: "The merchants say they had no thanks for what they did upon a former occasion, and do not seem yet to interest themselves much in our favour."[136] He was still making the same point two years later, and indeed it was made informally by well-wishers to America, such as Dr. John Fothergill, as well as being more directly conveyed via colonial journals.[137] Thus, a London correspondent of the *Boston Chronicle* warned in January 1769: "The Merchants trading to America having met with no return for the pains they took, and £1,500 expense in entertainments, etc. in obtaining the repeal of the Stamp-act, their letter not having been answered, nor their advice followed, will not again appear in its favour."[138] One year later, another London letter was still more explicit.

> I do not see there are the least dispositions to make representations to parliament for your relief, which ought to convince you, that you were more indebted to the merchants acting from a motive of principle rather than interest, in promoting the repeal of the Stamp-Act; for I assure you, there is some degree of remembrance of past transactions still remaining, which discourages us from acting so strenuously as we might otherwise be inclined to do, had our friends given us due degree of merit for our former services.[139]

Nonetheless, there was much more to mercantile irritation with the colonists than ingratitude in America or pride in Britain. Merchants and manufacturers were not the men to sacrifice their harmonious relations with important customers out of pique; the origins of their resentment go deeper than that. The truth is that they were deeply perturbed both as individuals and as a community by the fundamental trends in the thirteen colonies in the years following the Stamp Act crisis. For one thing, the apparent extremism of radical opposition to authority in America constantly alarmed them, and they were forever warning their correspondents in the colonies against opposition to government. [140] But built into their outrage at the bitterness of American politics was a far more significant fear that the colonists were endangering not merely the political authority of royal governors or the dignity of the imperial legislature but the entire imperial system under which their trade prospered. There was little opposition to reforms and adjustments which met particular demands and complaints on the part of the colonists, and there was ultimately no very deep objection to repealing a tax or duty which was found unacceptable in the colonies. But there was bound to come a time when the demands of the colonists extended to areas which not merely touched but deeply penetrated matters of fundamental interest to British businessmen.

A dawning recognition that this might be the case, that more was at issue than the specific taxation measure of a minister such as Grenville, occurred very soon after the repeal of the Stamp Act. In this context, the colonial news of the early months of 1767 was far more significant than otherwise might seem the case. The petition of the New York merchants asking further changes in the trade laws, penned in November 1766 and received in Britain in January 1767, caused considerable alarm among ministers and M.P.s. Like the Boston petition of a similar date, which was effectively suppressed in England by the action of the government, it indicated that colonial merchants, far from registering their delight at the fiscal and commercial concessions of 1766, merely regarded them as the basis for a comprehensive overhaul of imperial legislation. Even in November 1765, New York's Governor Cadwallader Colden had warned the ministry that: "The Merchants in this Place think they have a right to every freedom of Trade which the subjects of Great Britain enjoy." [141] The terms in which the New York petition was framed seemed to amply confirm this observation, and in England, the mercantile response to these new demands was one of considerable irritation and anger. [142] In London, Lord Shelburne noted that "the merchants and the Americans here seem sensible of its being the height of imprudence and are sorry." [143] In America, readers of the newspapers were warned:

> Whether the Merchants will renew their Application, I know not, being themselves much disobliged at a Petition from the New-York Merchants, complaining of the Arrangements lately made in the American Trade, about which those in England had laboured indefatigably, and with the best Intentions in the World, and do them real Services. [144]

What was at issue, of course, despite the sometimes fairly trivial points involved, was nothing less than the fundamental basis of the system enshrined in the acts of trade and navigation, generally reduced by contemporaries to the misleading but

simple description of the "Act of Navigation." In the last analysis, two groups benefited most from imperial control of colonial trade and industry. These were the
merchants, who had an effective monopoly in managing the import and reexport
of colonial produce as well as the profits of exporting goods for which there was
no competition in America, and the manufacturers, who had in America a market
protected not merely against European industry but even against the possibility of
colonial manufacturing. Throughout the late 1760s and early 1770s, it was made
increasingly clear both to merchants and to manufacturers that these highly profitable assets were in one way or another under threat. The New York and Boston
merchants in 1767 seemed to be asking for complete freedom to export colonial
produce to markets wherever there was a demand, a positive nightmare for British
merchants. As Grenville commented in 1768, "the American Factors here would
be greatly alarmed at the proposal to give the Colonies permission to export every
production."[145]

In fact, even before the controversial petitions of 1767, the London merchants
had publicly indicated their concern over some of the colonial demands reaching
Britain, especially those for direct exports to Spain and Portugal, and for a free
export of American bar iron to all markets. This concern was expressed in no uncertain terms in a letter which their committee addressed to John Hancock and was
mirrored in letters to many other customers of British merchants.

> We beg leave to recommend your avoiding hereafter any applications, which may
> be construed into the most distant means of interfering with the manufactures of
> the mother country, either by furnishing her rivals with raw materials, or by the
> public encouragement of similar manufactures among yourselves, no small
> strength having arisen to your opponents, during the late struggles from each of
> these topics.—In a word, the system of Great-Britain is to promote a mutual inter-
> est by supplying the colonies with her manufacturers, by encouraging them to
> raise, and receiving from them all raw material, and by granting the largest exten-
> sion to every branch of their trade not interfering with her own.[146]

Such reminders of the basic principles of the navigation system became more
necessary rather than less in the following years. American opposition to the Townshend Acts, for example, was in its way much more disturbing than resistance to
the Stamp Act had been. Nonimportation itself was not much to the taste of merchants and manufacturers. As Champion, a true friend of America, within the limi-
tations of that term in Britain, observed:

> The Americans have by this Measure lost many valuable Friends. Though it will
> not admit of a doubt that America was treated with severity by the Mother Coun-
> try—That arbitrary and Illegal Laws were imposed upon her, yet in her opposition
> she should have levelled her Resentment upon Administration, who really oppres-
> sed her, and not upon the Commercial and Manufacturing part of the Kingdom,
> who were always her best friends.[147]

But there were far worse worries. The actual duties of 1767 were laid on commodities which were of limited consequence to most merchants in Britain either
way. But colonial protests against indirect taxation, even if Townshend had made

it clear that the object of the duties was to raise a revenue rather than to regulate trade, suggested a deeply alarming possibility. If, for instance, Americans were to be freed from the duties on British glass imported into America, it was difficult to see why they should not be freed from the duties on their own imports from foreign sugar islands or, still more important, why they should not be freed from restrictions on trade generally.

It was this fear that American objections to taxation would ultimately extend to all the devices by which Britain tapped the economic advantages of empire which had so powerful an effect on the reasoning of almost all sections of the political community, deeply influencing even those of the Whig opposition who regarded themselves and were regarded by others as well-disposed towards the colonists' claims. But it was no less effective as an argument among businessmen. It was true, of course, that the merchants and manufacturers had no interest in nonimportation or disruption to trade and had powerful reasons for keeping their American trading partners contented. But there were limits to the compliance and conciliation which could be induced in the business community. For in the long run, it was essential for that community to keep in being the overall structure of the imperial economy and in particular the capacity of the imperial legislature to direct and enforce the regulation of the colonial economies. Once the Townshend legislation had provoked extensive opposition in America, opposition accompanied by ever more alarming colonial demands, the turning point for many businessmen in their attitudes towards the colonies began to draw near. The year 1769 perhaps witnessed this moment, for it was at this time that it was made crystal clear by many in the colonies that their demands extended not merely to the repeal of the Townshend duties but also to the elimination of the duties on molasses, wine and fruit, and other commodities. William Knox, with his semi-mercantile, semi-colonial background, was quick to see the significance of these pressures for the merchants.

> As in this demand all the Acts of trade are clearly included, the merchants must see that their interest is struck at, and that the sovereignty of Great Britain is essential to the preservation of their trade. This they ought to have seen, and perhaps did see, long ago, but their regard for self made them hope, that if they sacrificed the sovereignty now, the trade would hold out their time, and they cared not what might become of their successors. I rejoice, however, that the effects follow so quick, and that they who treacherously gave up the one will be driven to give up the other also, or else forced for their own sake to retract their former conduct and make a stand for both.[148]

Knox had extensive evidence for his view in the renewed commercial petitions which arrived in London from America at this time. Boston's demands, for example, appeared as a comprehensive attack on the economic legislation of 1764–66 and on the basic principles of the Navigation Acts, involving as they did the abolition of duties on foreign molasses imported into America, foreign sugar (a quite extraordinary demand which, if implemented, would have permitted North American merchants to import French sugar from Guadeloupe and Martinique and launch it on the British market in competition with the produce of the British sugar islands), Iberian fruit, wine, and oil imported into America. Also demanded were a whole series of new regulations, or rather absence of regulations, governing the enforcement of the Customs administration, trade with Ireland, the regulation of the fisheries, and so on.[149] This petition was dispatched to Dennys DeBerdt, the colony's special agent in London, with an additional letter stressing the need for the wholesale repeal of the Sugar Act of 1764 and the amending act of 1766. The psychological impact of such a *démarche* in London can hardly be exaggerated. There the question was how far to concede, if at all, the repeal of the Townshend duties, and the news that Americans wanted a general redrawing of imperial regulations was not calculated to have a conciliating effect. Similar resolutions from Philadelphia made a similar impact. Thus, alleged friends of the colonies in Liverpool reported back to Pennsylvania:

> The Memorial of the Merchants of Philadelphia, addressed to us, and some other Merchants in this Town, came safe to Hand, and was communicated to several of those mentioned in the Direction; but are sorry to inform you, that many of them are of unfriendly Sentiments concerning some of the chief Subjects of Complaints. Finding there was no Probability of a Concurrence in an Application to Parliament (of which indeed there is no Instance as yet from any Part of the kingdom) we took the only Step that remained for us, to forward your Views, and our Wishes, namely by transmitting to our Members of Parliament, the printed copy of your Memorial, with our Opinion of the Means and Expediency of Redress.[150]

When in 1770 the Townshend duties were in fact partially repealed, the news that some colonies were preparing to continue their resistance in order to obtain much greater concessions had an equally bad effect. Even Barlow Trecothick, one of the most favorably disposed of all merchants in London, was driven to advise his Boston friends: "Relief from such grievances as you labor under will I hope be applyed for in a regular constitutional way to Parliament, disclaiming at the same time all intentions of breaking through the Act of Navigation which has been much urged against you."[151] General Alexander Mackay, who returned to London in 1769 after commanding troops in Boston, similarly wrote to James Bowdoin of the deep psychological impact made by

> the extension of the resolutions made at your publick meetings after I left you, where it was resolved that no importation of British goods should be enterd till the dutys on sugar, wine, and molasses and indeed till all dutys were repealed. This was so deep a stroke that no man in his senses coud pretend to say a word, and allow me to say, on these grounds if any member here woud give way he woud have the whole nation against him, and many of your warmest friends said, that if any act was repealed on such grounds, it was telling you that you had only to do the same again for any purpose you pleas'd, right or wrong.[152]

In the event, of course, the attempt by American radicals to keep the nonimportation movement going in 1770 proved abortive, and not merely the great panoply of imperial control of trade, but even Townshend's tea duty remained intact. Nonetheless, enough had been said and done to put British merchants in a new and sinister frame of mind, a frame of mind which did not dispose them to leap to

America's defense when the next crisis came in 1774. Indeed, new elements of specific irritation to the merchants were added at this time. The spectacular episode which initiated the final phase of crisis, the Boston Tea Party, seemed particularly significant because it involved seizure by the colonists of mercantile (albeit East India Company) goods. Whatever the intent of the participating colonists, British merchants perceived this forcible and novel action not only as an effront to the government's authority but also a threat to British property. As Sir William Meredith, formerly an opponent of both ministers and colonial repression, but also M.P. for Liverpool, a port which was becoming savagely anti-American in these years, thus explained his conversion to a strong policy, in general, and to one of the Coercive Acts, the Massachusetts Bay Judiciary Bill, in particular:

> That he never approved the tax upon tea; and had opposed it, as he would always oppose the taxation of America. But now that the Americans had not only resisted the act of Parliament but laid violent hands on the merchants' property, it was high time to regulate the course of justice, so that our merchants might trade thither with security.[153]

Thereafter, the growing extremism of American demands and threats ensured that little would happen to mollify those who harbored deep suspicions of a fundamental challenge to British authority.

It would have taken a dramatic change in businessmen's understanding of their own and of the domestic economy's interest to make matters very different. No such change was forthcoming. On the contrary, it is clear that the economic principles of the business community at this time were profoundly conservative and traditional. The new theories about free trade, so seductive to the historian of ideas, may have been on the lips and pens of intellectuals like Adam Smith and Josiah Tucker, but they were rare indeed among merchants, who were always ready to examine a concrete and constructive proposal for reform—for example, in the free port legislation of 1766—but had no desire to dismantle the imperial system after long and profitable experience with it. When the crunch came in the mid-1770s, there can be little doubt that many merchants in England were not altogether sorry. An empire whose differences had been finally resolved by firmness and force and whose economic arrangements had been restored on a stable and lasting basis was a prospect that seemed to merit a certain degree of temporary sacrifice. It is worth quoting Knox's celebrated appeal to the merchants in 1774, not necessarily because it had a great influence on them in a direct way, but rather because it clearly expressed what many of them fundamentally believed at this time. Knox's pamphlet was designed to justify the long-standing restraints imposed upon the trade and manufactures of the colonies but, above all else, to remind British merchants that North's policies were as much in their interests as in those of the British taxpayer.

> Give up the authority of Parliament and there is an end to your trade, and to a total loss of your property. But if that authority is supported and maintained, the trade of the Colonies must remain to Great Britain and the property you intrust them with will remain secure, protected by acts of Parliament made in your behalf.[154]

Almost at the same time, Josiah Tucker was declaring the contrary, warning his readers that the North American colonies were a millstone rather than a gold mine and that actual independence, not just a free trade, would automatically bring far greater profits in its wake. In the event he was to be proved far from wrong. But in the meantime, the North American interests among merchants and manufacturers in England were hardheaded businessmen, not visionary idealists; they faced enough risks in their daily affairs without taking new ones. Like the politicians and public at large, they plumped for the certainties of the past rather than the possibilities of the future.

Whatever the good reasons which lay behind the relative lack of enthusiasm of British businessmen for the American cause by 1775, the phenomenon itself remains a striking one. Between 1766, when the merchants and, insofar as they had an independent voice, the manufacturers, were overwhelmingly on the side of extensive concessions to America, and 1776, when American agents and agitators were finding it all but impossible to enlist support among them, there was a genuine and marked change of opinion. Many of those who had been champions of America ten years before now became its bitter enemies. The transition was not an easy one, but it was surprisingly rapid and complete. Most of the cases have to be pieced together from scattered pieces of evidence, but in that of at least one merchant, there is sufficient correspondence to make the process well documented. The case was that of Charles Goore, a Liverpool merchant, with a long but not untypical career in transatlantic trade. Apprenticed to one of the best known of mid-eighteenth century tobacco merchants, Foster Cunliffe, he had direct experience of the problems of colonial business because of a long stay in Antigua. But the greater part of his business life was spent as a prominent Liverpool merchant, a station in which he built up a large and impressive tobacco trade and acquired extensive property in Virginia. In 1765–66 he was an eager supporter of the merchant lobby in its endeavors to obtain the repeal of the Stamp Act, heavily involved in the activities of the Liverpool committee, which played its part in the campaign, and personally accepting responsibility for keeping the ministry informed of the basic facts about the Africa trade, of which his own knowledge was considerable. His correspondence with the Lee family during this period was alive with enthusiasm for America's aims and interests.[155] But in the following years, like many Liverpudlian merchants, he was deeply disturbed by the mounting extremism apparent in the colonies.[156] "Certain it is they have acted indiscreetly in laying internal Taxes on the Americans," he wrote of the government; "on the other hand the Colonies assume an authority in several of their demands they have no right to."[157] This was to a colonist, but at much the same time, in January 1775, he wrote in terms which reveal the extent of his own feelings and also do much to explain why men like Sir William Meredith, to whom the letter was addressed, were converted to the cause of government at this time.

> The Coffee houses are now crowded waiting to hear the resolves of Parliament relative to American affairs—I have upwards of £5,000 amongst the Virginians,

yet I hope the British Government will not submit to their arbitrary demands, submit now and always submit for it's evident they are resolv'd to be independent—Surely if practicable its time to stop the people of Great Britain and Ireland flocking thither and to transport the Convicts to the East Indies.[158]

No merchant was more badly hit by the war than Goore; he was unable to carry on his normal trade, and at seventy-four, too old to attempt a new beginning or engage in adventure. Above all, he had invested in American land. As he himself put it in January 1776: "I am heavy in Virginians, and must wait to see the Event between the Mother Country and the Collonies. Oh dreadfull Warr!"[159] Yet he had no doubts. Meredith was again informed in June 1776, on the eve of the Declaration of Independence:

I have now only my Virginian affairs hang upon my spirits—My agent Allen dead, no courts held, nor can I trust the oldest Virginian acquaintance I have with the management of my concerns, and it will be difficult to engage a trusty Person to go over until the differences between the Government and the Colonialists be reconcil'd—The ax is laid to the root of the tree and it must be cut down or adieu to the colonies God grant such measures may be taken that his Majesty may bring the Americans to become dutiful subjects.[160]

Such were the fundamental attitudes which lay behind America's inability to secure in Britain a real measure of support for her struggle.

· NOTES ·

1. See Walter E. Minchinton, ed., *The Growth of English Overseas Trade in the Seventeenth and Eighteenth Centuries* (London: Methuen, 1969), especially the contribution by Ralph Davis, "English Foreign Trade, 1700–1774." See also Chapter Nine of this volume.

2. Peter Orlando Hutchinson, ed., *The Diary and Letters of . . . Thomas Hutchinson* (2 vols., London: Sampon and Low, 1883–86), vol. 1, p. 115–16.

3. *Virginia Gazette* (Purdie and Dixon), 6 October 1774; *South Caroline Gazette*, 4 July 1774, quoted in Philip Davidson, *Propaganda and the American Revolution, 1763–1783* (Chapel Hill: Univ. of North Carolina Press, 1941); *Massachusetts Gazette*, 20 February 1766.

4. See Chapter Three of this volume.

5. The best detailed account is still to be found in Arthur M. Schlesinger, *The Colonial Merchants and the American Revolution, 1763–1776* (New York: Atheneum, 1968).

6. *Boston Gazette*, 19 June 1769.

7. Boston Public Library, MS. 1461: 17 March 1774.

8. See for example *Virginia Gazette*, 9 June and 6 October 1774.

9. Jack M. Sosin, *Agents and Merchants: British Colonial Policy and the Origins of the American Revolution, 1763–1775* (Lincoln, Neb.: Univ. of Nebraska Press, 1965), p. 124.

10. Grenville to Whately, 8 January 1769, Huntington Library, San Marino, Cal., Grenville Letter Book.

11. See Sosin, *Agents and Merchants*, Chapter Five, for the activities of the agents and merchants in this period.

12. T. to H. Bromfield, 21 March 1774, Yale University Library, Bromfield Collection.

13. *New Hampshire Gazette*, 15 July 1774; Hutchinson, *Diary and Letters of Thomas Hutchinson*, vol. 1, p. 260.

14. William S. Taylor and John H. Pringle, eds., *Correspondence of William Pitt, Earl of Chatham* (4 vols., London: John Murray, 1838), vol. 4, p. 386.

15. William B. Reed, *The Life and Correspondence of Joseph Reed* (2 vols., Philadelphia: Lindsay & Blakeston, 1847), vol. 1, pp. 101–2.

16. Hutchinson, *Diary and Letters of Thomas Hutchinson*, vol. 1, pp. 361–62, 402.

17. Mark A. De Wolfe Howe, ed., "English Journal of Josiah Quincy, Jr., 1774–1775," *Massachusetts Historical Society, Proceedings* 50 (1916–1917), p. 493.

18. Hutchinson, *Diary and Letters of Thomas Hutchinson*, vol. 1, p. 415.

19. B. D. Bargar, "Matthew Boulton and the Birmingham Petition of 1775," *William and Mary Quarterly*, 3d ser., 13 (January 1956), pp. 26–39. See also J. Money, *Experience and Identity: Birmingham and the West Midlands, 1760–1800* (Manchester, 1977), pp. 199–201.

20. Worthington C. Ford, ed., *Letters of William Lee, 1768–1783* (3 vols., New York: Historical Printing Club, 1891), vol. 1, p. 148; G. H. Guttridge, ed., *The American Correspondence of a Bristol Merchant, 1766–1776* (Berkeley: Univ. of California Press, 1934), p. 3.

21. G. H. Guttridge, ed., *The Correspondence of Edmund Burke* (Chicago, 1961), vol. 3, p. 191.

22. On the relationship between economic strain and political disorders in these years, see Walter J. Shelton, *English Hunger and Industrial Disorders: A Study in Social Conflict during the First Decade of George III's Reign* (London: Macmillan, 1973).

23. *Boston Gazette*, 28 September 1767.

24. T. S. Ashton, *Economic Fluctuations in England, 1700–1800* (Oxford: Clarendon Press, 1959), pp. 61–62.

25. See for example, G. N. Clark, *Guide to English Commercial Statistics, 1696–1782* (London: Royal Historical Society, 1938), pp. 33 ff., and introduction to Elizabeth Boody Schumpeter, *English Overseas Trade Statistics; 1697–1808* (Oxford: Clarendon Press, 1960). An important corrective in respect to the Scottish element in trade statistics is provided by J. M. Price, "New Time Series for Scotland's and Britain's Trade with the Thirteen Colonies and States, 1740 to 1791," *William and Mary Quarterly*, 3d ser., 32 (1975), pp. 307–25.

Though the original schedules recorded the exact quantities of each commodity in question (with a bewildering variety of units of measurement), the summaries which reached Parliament and which formed virtually the sole publicly available statistics were expressed in terms of monetary value. In theory, this should have made them of great utility. In practice, all values were fixed not according to the price relevant at the time of the transaction but according to a scale essentially established in 1696 by the first inspector-general and never departed from subsequently. Contemporary experts were well aware that the result was effectively to invalidate the statistics for most purposes. On the other hand, figures representing the real value would tell the historian little about the actual volume of trade, and for the political historian, at least, volume is in some respects more important than value. As Franklin himself admitted: "The London Customs House account serves no other

320 · A DECADE OF STRUGGLE

purposes than to show the sort of goods exported to or imported from every country; and as it is kept upon the same principles or estimates as at the time it commenced, to shew whether your Exports and Imports encrease or decrease upon the whole trade, or to any country in particular." It is precisely such purposes which are those required for an assessment of the impact of the nonimportation movements (Leonard W. Labaree, ed., *The Papers of Benjamin Franklin* [New Haven: Yale Univ. Press, 1968], vol. 15, pp. 251–55).

26. Minchinton, *English Overseas Trade,* p. 106.

27. No account is taken here of the importance to Britain of America's exports, mainly of raw materials and primary products. Tobacco, indigo, rice, lumber, and provisions of many kinds all were in one way or another important to the imperial economy. But none of them directly employed British manufacturing capacity to any significant degree, and their importance was greater in terms of mercantile profits than industrial employment. It is arguable that colonial exports to Britain were far more directly important to the colonists than to the mother country.

28. For the sake of simplicity, figures are rounded to the nearest thousand.

29. Schlesinger, *Colonial Merchants,* Chapters Four and Five, examines the evidence in detail and is impressed by the extent to which nonimportation was enforced; what he does not show is that the result was an effective stranglehold on British exports.

30. The *Boston Chronicle* printing a long succession of shipping manifests clearly exposing prohibited imports, notably between August 1769 and January 1770.

31. "Bowdoin and Temple Papers," Massachusetts Historical Society, *Collections,* 6th ser. (1897), vol. 9, p. 153.

32. Robert A. Rutland, ed. *The Papers of George Mason, 1725–1792* (3 vols., Chapel Hill: Univ. of North Carolina Press, 1970), vol. 1, p. 118.

33. See Francis Norton Mason, ed. *John Norton & Sons: Merchants of London and Virginia, 1750–1795* (Richmond: Dietz Press, 1937).

34. Savage to Norton, 9 January 1771, *Brock Manuscripts,* Huntington Library, San Marino, Cal.

35. *Boston Gazette,* 28 September 1767.

36. "Bowdoin and Temple Papers," p. 284.

37. "The Trumbull Papers," Massachusetts Historical Society, *Collections,* 5th ser., vol. 9 (1885), p. 361.

38. Rutland, *Papers of George Mason,* vol. 1, p. 119.

39. *Pennsylvania Chronicle,* 20 August 1770.

40. "Bowdoin and Temple Papers," p. 293.

41. *Boston Chronicle,* 18 January 1770.

42. *Public Advertiser,* 26 July 1770.

43. William B. Reed, *The Life of Esther DeBerdt, afterwards Esther Reed of Pennsylvania* (Philadelphia: C. Sherman, printer, 1853), p. 147.

44. Rockingham to Dowdeswell, 11 August 1768, Sheffield City Library, Wentworth Woodhouse Muniments, R1-1083 (hereafter cited as WWM).

45. W. L. Clements Library, Ann Arbor, Mich., Germain Manuscripts, Pownall to Cooper, 25 September 1769.

46. *Pennsylvania Chronicle,* 30 April 1770.

47. *Ibid.,* 23 July 1770.

48. A. Anderson, *An Historical and Chronological Deduction of the Origin of Commerce* (London, 1787–89), vol. 4, p. 195.

49. "Trumbull Papers," pp. 384–85.

50. *Pennsylvania Chronicle,* 3 September 1770.

51. For the general background, see Elizabeth W. Gilboy, *Wages in Eighteenth Century England* (Cambridge, Mass.: Harvard Univ. Press, 1934).

52. W. Jones to S. Salisbury, 19 October 1769. "Salisbury Papers," American Antiquarian Society, Worcester, Mass.

53. Pownall to Cooper, 27 April 1769, Germain MSS.

54. *Pennsylvania Chronicle,* 23 April 1770.

55. *Pennsylvania Gazette,* 7 September 1769.

56. Labaree, *Papers of Benjamin Franklin,* vol. 17, p. 63.

57. *Copy of Letters Sent to Great Britain, by his Excellency Thomas Hutchinson, the Honorable Andrew Oliver, and several other persons . . .* (Boston, 1773), pp. 22–23.

58. *Massachusetts Spy,* 12 May 1774.

59. Hutchinson, *Diary and Letters of Thomas Hutchinson,* vol. 1, p. 238.

60. *Boston Evening Post,* 21 November 1774.

61. Guttridge, *Correspondence of a Bristol Merchant,* p. 47.

62. *Essex Journal,* 29 March 1775.

63. *Massachusetts Spy,* 12 May 1774.

64. Guttridge, *Correspondence of a Bristol Merchant,* p. 51.

65. Eyre to Smith and Atkinson, 21 June 1775, Atkinson Manuscripts, W. L. Clements Library.

66. Historical Manuscripts Commission, *Report on the Manuscripts of Mrs. Stopford Sackville, of Drayton House, Northamptonshire* (2 vols., London: Mackie & Co., 1904–10), vol. 1, p. 136.

67. Hutchinson, *Diary and Letters of Thomas Hutchinson,* vol. 1, p. 397.

68. Historic Manuscripts Commission, *Stopford Sackville,* vol. 2, p. 1.

69. *Correspondence of Mr. Ralph Izard, of South Carolina, from the Year 1774 to 1804* (New York: C. S. Francis, 1844), p. 76; *Essex Journal,* 29 March 1775.

70. *Essex Journal,* 17 November 1775.

71. *Gentleman's Magazine,* 1776, p. 78.

72. Hutchinson, *Diary and Letters of Thomas Hutchinson,* vol. 1, p. 397.

73. Leatham, Walker and Co. to Smith and Atkinson, 29 August 1775, Atkinson MSS.

74. Hutchinson, *Diary and Letters of Thomas Hutchinson,* vol. 1, pp. 431–32, 525.

75. *Correspondence of Izard,* pp. 116–17.

76. Hutchinson, *Diary and Letters of Thomas Hutchinson,* vol. 1, p. 182.

77. *Essex Journal,* 17 November 1775; Guttridge, *Correspondence of a Bristol Merchant,* p. 60.

78. *Maryland Gazette,* 23 March 1775.

79. See, for example, A. H. John, "War and the English Economy, 1700–1763," *Economic History Review,* 2d ser., vol. 7 (April 1955), pp. 329–44.

80. Ford, *Letters of William Lee,* vol. 1, pp. 185–86.

81. Ashton, *Economic Fluctuations,* p. 187.

82. *Ibid.,* p. 186.

83. Andrew Oliver, ed., *The Journal of Samuel Curwen, Loyalist,* (2 vols., Cambridge, Mass.: Harvard Univ. Press, 1972).

84. B. Eyre to Amorys and Taylor, 19 February, 1771, Lacaita-Shelburne Manuscripts, W. L. Clements Library; Philip L. White, ed., *The Beekman Mercantile Papers, 1746–1799* (3 vols., New York: New York Historical Society, 1956), vol. 2, p. 732.

85. See for example, Henry Cruger's Letters, "Commerce of Rhode Island," Mas-

sachusetts Historical Society, *Collections,* 7th ser., vol. 9 (1914–15), vol. 1.

86. The official record of Trecothick's evidence is at British Library (formerly British Museum), Additional Manuscripts (Add. MS.) 33030.

87. Reed, *Life of Joseph Reed,* vol. 1, pp. 80, 88.

88. Hutchinson, *Diary and Letters of Thomas Hutchinson,* vol. 1, p. 218.

89. Schlesinger, *Colonial Merchants,* pp. 398–99.

90. Mason, *John Norton & Sons,* p. 385; see also Rutland, *Papers of George Mason,* vol. 1, p. 237.

91. See the new introduction to the edition of *John Norton & Sons* published in 1968.

92. Ford, *Letters of William Lee,* vol. 1, p. 174. See also T. M. Devine, "A Glasgow Tobacco Merchant During the American War of Independence: Alexander Speirs of Elderlie, 1775 to 1781," *William and Mary Quarterly,* 3rd ser., 33 (1976) 501–513.

93. *Ibid.,* pp. 107–9.

94. See especially, Virginia D. Harrington, *The New York Merchant on the Eve of the Revolution* (New York: Columbia Univ. Press, 1935), p. 343.

95. *Essex Journal,* 17 November 1775; Gaine's *New York Gazette,* 25 December 1775.

96. The best general account of Anglo-American trade remains George L. Beer, *The Old Colonial System* (2 vols., New York: P. Smith, 1912).

97. See Charles R. Ritcheson, *Aftermath of Revolution: British Policy Towards the United States, 1783–1795* (Dallas: Southern Methodist Univ. Press, 1969).

98. *Commerce of Rhode Island,* vol. 1, passim.

99. Reed, *Life of Esther DeBerdt,* p. 147.

100. W. T. Baxter, *The House of Hancock: Business in Boston, 1724–1775* (Cambridge: Harvard Univ. Press, 1945), p. 287.

101. White, *Beekman Mercantile Papers,* vol. 3, pp. 1168, 1179. This is not to say that individual debts could not be heavy. See, for example, Edward C. Papenfuse, *In Pursuit of Profit: The Annapolis Merchants in the Era of the American Revolution, 1763–1805* (Baltimore, Johns Hopkins University Press, 1975) Chapter 2.

102. British Public Record Office, 30/8/343, ff. 170–76.

103. P. D. G. Thomas, *British Politics and the Stamp Act Crisis* (Oxford: Clarendon, 1975), p. 218.

104. Public Record Office, 30/8/343, ff. 170–76.

105. Ford, *Letters of William Lee,* vol. 1, p. 96.

106. *Ibid.,* pp. 161–62.

107. Richard Henry Lee, *Arthur Lee, LL. D. . . . with his Diplomatic and Literary Correspondence and his Papers . . .* (2 vols., Boston: Wells, 1829), p. 210.

108. *New York Gazette,* 3 April 1775.

109. Mason, *John Norton & Sons,* p. 381; Kenneth Wiggins Porter, *The Jacksons and the Lees: Two Generations of Massachusetts Merchants, 1765–1844* (2 vols., Cambridge: Harvard Univ. Press, 1937), vol. 1, p. 277.

110. *Ibid.,* p. 465.

111. *Ibid.,* p. 130.

112. C. H. Hull and H. V. Temperley, eds., "Debates on the Declaratory Act and the Repeal of the Stamp Act, 1766," *American Historical Review* 17 (April 1912), p. 572.

113. William J. Smith, ed., *The Grenville Papers* (4 vols., London: John Murray, 1852–1853), vol. 3, p. 370.

114. Hutchinson, *Diary and Letters of Thomas Hutchinson,* vol. 1, p. 182.

115. Reed, *Life of Joseph Reed,* vol. 1, p. 102.

116. See Paul Langford, "William Pitt and Public Opinion, 1757," *English Historical Review* 88 (January 1973) pp. 54–80.

117. See Richard Pares, *War and Trade in the West Indies, 1739–1763* (Oxford: Clarendon, 1936), for the best account.

118. See Lucy S. Sutherland, "The City of London in Eighteenth Century Politics," in Richard Pares and A. J. P. Taylor, eds., *Essays Presented to Sir Lewis Namier* (London: Macmillan, 1956).

119. See, for example, Sosin, *Agents and Merchants,* p. 35–36.

120. Henry G. Bohn, ed., *Works of Edmund Burke* (London: Bohn, 1854–57), vol. 1, p. 182.

121. "Trumbull Papers," *passim.*

122. Mason, *John Norton & Sons,* p. 104.

123. T. to H. Bromfield, 21 March 1774, Bromfield Collection.

124. Howe, "Journal of Josiah Quincy," p. 495.

125. Ford, *Letters of William Lee,* vol. 1, pp. 96–97.

126. *Ibid.,* pp. 130–31.

127. W. Lee to R. H. Lee, 6 April 1773, "Lee Family Papers."

128. Howe, "Journal of Josiah Quincy," pp. 466–67.

129. *Boston Evening Post,* 11 July 1774.

130. *Maryland Gazette,* 23 March 1775.

131. Guttridge, *Correspondence of a Bristol Merchant,* p. 60.

132. Labaree, *Papers of Benjamin Franklin,* vol. 14, p. 183.

133. *Boston Gazette,* 20 April 1767.

134. See Paul Langford, *The First Rockingham Administration, 1765–1766* (Oxford: Clarendon, 1973), p. 196.

135. William Allen to D. Barclay & Sons, 8 November 1767, Lewis Burd Walker, ed., *The Burd Papers: Extracts from Chief Justice William Allen's Letterbook* (Pottsville, Pa.: Standard Pub. Co., 1897–99) p. 73.

136. "Trumbull Papers," p. 298.

137. Betsey C. Corner and Christopher C. Booth, eds., *Chain of Friendship: Letters of Dr. John Fothergill of London, 1735–1780* (Cambridge, Mass.: Harvard Univ. Press, 1971), p. 286.

138. *Boston Chronicle,* 26 January 1769.

139. *Ibid.,* 8 January 1770.

140. See, for example, Henry Cruger to Jackson and Bromfield, 22 September 1768, "Lee-Cabot Papers, 1707–1773," Massachusetts Historical Society, p. 40.

141. "The Colden Letter Books," New York Historical Society, *Collections,* vol. 10, p. 62.

142. For the New York petition, see W. L. Clements Library, Shelburne Manuscripts, vol. 49, pp. 524–30.

143. Taylor and Pringle, *Correspondence of William Pitt,* vol. 3, p. 182.

144. *Pennsylvania Gazette,* 23 April 1767.

145. Grenville to Knox, 15 July 1768, Grenville Letter Book, Huntington Library.

146. *Boston Gazette,* 8 September 1766.

147. Guttridge, *Correspondence of a Bristol Merchant,* p. 22.

148. Smith, *Grenville Papers,* vol. 4, p. 456.

149. Boston Merchants' Committee to DeBerdt, 29 December 1769, "Lee Family Papers."

150. *Pennsylvania Gazette,* 20 April 1769.

151. Trecothick to Boston Selectmen, 10 May 1770, Boston Public Library, MS. 224.

152. "Bowdoin and Temple Papers," p. 171.

153. William Cobbett and Thomas C. Hansard, eds., *The Parliamentary History of England . . . to 1803* (reprint ed., New York: AMS Press, 1966), vol. 17, p. 1302.

154. William Knox, *The Interest of the Merchants and Manufacturers of Great Britain, in the Present Contest with the Colonies Stated and Considered* (London, 1774), p. 52.

155. Goore to R. H. Lee, 14 August 1766, "Lee Family Papers."

156. See, for example, *Boston Chronicle,* 10 October 1768.

157. Goore to J. McWhirter, 3 July 1775, "Goore Letter Book," W. L. Clements Library.

158. Goore to W. Meredith, 25 January 1775, *ibid.*

159. Goore to J. Newseele, 5 February 1776, *ibid.*

160. Goore to W. Meredith, 13 June 1775, *ibid.*

·8·

The British Ministers, Massachusetts, and the Continental Association, 1774–1775

IAN R. CHRISTIE

British concern with American affairs temporarily slackened after the winter of 1770–71.[1] The reasons for this are not clear and must to a large extent be inferred. They appear to include a desire to let the consequences of the partial repeal of the Townshend duties work themselves out: the ministry drew much comfort from the general collapse of the nonimportation agreements of 1769 despite the partial ban still operating on tea. Ministers may also have been anxious to keep American affairs out of Parliament, an intention based, at least partly, on the belief that the well-publicized opposition attacks on government policy in both Houses merely encouraged the troublemakers in the colonies. It is also the case that international relations raised more acute problems during the years 1770–73. Nevertheless, the ministers had a weather eye open for squalls across the Atlantic, and these were not far to seek. They did not react so sharply as might have been expected to the destruction of H.M.S. *Gaspée* by Rhode Islanders in June 1772, despite the fact that the attorney general considered it a business of "five times the magnitude of the Stamp Act." But by the end of the year, developments in Massachusetts began to arouse a deeper disquiet.

In the fall of 1772, the patriot leaders in Massachusetts exploited criticism of the imperial government's grant of salaries to the governor, the deputy governor, and the judges of the superior court to whip up popular support for a comprehensive statement of colonial rights and a list of infringements and violations, thus presenting a renewed challenge to the authority of Parliament. Both the assembly and the council upheld these popular grievances in a well-publicized controversy with Governor Thomas Hutchinson during the early months of 1773. Ministers in London took note of both these developments. On 1 February 1773, Lord Dartmouth, the colonial secretary, drew the attention of the cabinet to the agitation going on in Massachusetts over the statement of rights. However, his colleagues seem to have brushed the matter aside, and the probability is that they were then too much preoccupied by other business. The government's main concern that spring was a settlement of the affairs of the East India Company. In addition, there was a low-key but possibly menacing international crisis relating to the Baltic and to the general balance of power between Britain and France. The addresses presented to the governor by the assembly and council of Massachusetts, with their clear rebuttal of any claim by Parliament to an unlimited power over the colonies, did not reach London until the beginning of April, and by that time the parliamentary session was nearing its end. However, it appears that they struck ministers as raising questions of serious importance requiring reference to Parliament. Dartmouth delivered himself of the opinion that they were "replete with doctrines of the most dangerous nature," and by June, he was hinting at parliamentary action the following session. From statements made by Lord North a year later, it seems he took much the same view: he was then to describe the addresses as "a declaration of independence" and to have regretted that an overhaul of the government of Massachusetts had not been undertaken immediately. Thus, months before the Boston "Mohawks" tipped three shiploads of tea into the harbor in December 1773, a general feeling was growing that the affairs of the province needed regulating, though as yet perhaps no clear plan had emerged other than those already lying in the colonial department's files from the time of Hillsborough's attempt to bring a measure forward in 1770.[2] The General Court's attack upon Hutchinson and his deputy after the publication of their private correspondence further inflamed this situation.

The arrival of news of the Boston Tea Party in London in mid-January 1774 set in motion a train of action by the British administration, directed principally against the patriot resistance to parliamentary authority in Massachusetts, which was to lead inexorably to the outbreak of war in 1775. This is not to say that in the opening months of 1774, the ministers seriously contemplated such an outcome, far from it. Their policy was based on an assumption, formed from their American correspondence over the years, that a small group of conspirators at Boston were set upon destroying the imperial government's control over the affairs of America, a design which, in their minds, was clearly equated with an assertion of independence. "At Boston," North told the House of Commons on 14 March 1774, "we were considered as two independent states"; and again, a week or so later: "The people at Boston had begun many years ago to endeavour to throw off all obedience to this country."[3] To drift on would be to let the poison spread unchecked throughout the American continent. As George III expressed it in a letter to Lord North on 4 February: "All men seem now to feel that the fatal compliance in 1766 has encouraged the Americans annually to increase in their pretensions [to] that thorough independency which one state has of another, but which is quite subversive of the obedience which a colony owes its mother country."[4] However, ministers were confident that the adoption of an unyielding course, putting beyond doubt their determination to insist upon colonial recognition of parliamentary authority, would halt the movement in its tracks. General Thomas Gage, the commander in chief in America, then on leave in London, reinforced this impression in an interview with the king on 4 February, in which, so George III reported, he said: "They will be lyons whilst we are lambs, but if we take the resolute part they will undoubtedly prove very meek."[5] No doubt, also, he reinforced the impression that Boston alone was the trouble spot. Months later, when he had discovered his error, he observed: "The disease was believed to have been confined to the town of Boston, from whence it might have been eradicated, no doubt without a great deal of trouble, and it might have been the case some time ago."[6] These assessments meant that the ministers continually underestimated the opposition with which they were faced in America.

The ministers saw their task as the restoration of law and order and the elimination of a treasonable conspiracy. They assumed that the great mass of British subjects in Massachusetts and elsewhere in America would rally behind duly constituted civil authority once it was seen that this was receiving firm backing from the imperial government. They identified the patriot clique in and around Boston, William Molineux, Joseph Warren, John Hancock, Samuel Adams, and their restless confreres, as the focus of the conspiracy and considered that if they were dealt with, the agitation in other provinces would soon die down. After conversations with the colonial secretary, one government supporter in the House of Lords minuted: "Tho' the other colonys are but too deeply engag'd in this business, yet as that of the Massachusetts Bay has taken the lead, it were better perhaps to suppose that they acted from instigation and example of the disaffected there, and consider the town of Boston as the immediate object of the resentment of this country."[7] Letters from the governor of Massachusetts confirmed the ministers in their belief that active resistance was confined to a few. Writing of the charges brought against himself in the General Court, Hutchinson had observed in a dispatch of 3 July 1773: "This is all affected by half a dozen or half a score who having been negatived [for the council] show their resentment, or who hope to serve themselves or friends by my removal . . . sticking at no falsehood, ever so glaring, to gain their cause." Hutchinson wrote again in September:

> The body of the people of the province are far from a perverse disposition. They are deluded by a few men, and even among those few there are some who wish to see an end to contention upon what they call reasonable terms; but there are others and of too great influence who are against all conciliating proposals, and if every complaint of grievance should be satisfied they would immediately make as many more fresh complaints in the place of them.[8]

In hindsight, of course, the ministers' appreciation of the American situation can be seen to be defective. However, it was on the basis of this appraisal that, during the spring of 1774, they put into effect the string of legislative and administrative measures collectively known as the "Coercive" or "Intolerable" Acts. These measures responded in various ways to the uncontrovertible fact that events surrounding the Boston Tea Party constituted a violent defiance of law and order and of the acts of trade and to the fact that the machinery for law enforcement in the province seemed grossly defective. Ministers had before them reports of a riotous invasion of the premises of one tea consignee and of the terrorization of others by handbills and verbal threats. Hutchinson, they knew, could get no help from his council in restoring order, and the affair had ended in the wanton destruction of ten thousand pounds worth of private property.[9] The council had firmly staked out its position during the constitutional debates with the governor the previous year. In its address to Hutchinson, dated 25 January 1773, the council had repelled his suggestion that the cause of disorder in Massachusetts was "the unconstitutional principles adopted by the people in questioning the supreme authority of Parliament." While paying lip service to the need to suppress disturbances and preserve law and order, it had commented: "It is vain to hope that this can be done effectually so long as the cause of the uneasiness . . . exists." It had rejected the view that "supreme authority includes unlimited authority," and it affirmed that "life, liberty, property and the disposal of that property with our own consent are natural rights."[10] Lord Dartmouth, the colonial secretary, had commented at that time that these views amounted to "a declaration of independence."[11] Now, early in 1774, the East India Company had forwarded to the colonial office a report making clear that the council stood by its guns. According to the office summary:

> The Boston agents petitioned the governor and council to take charge of the tea on its arrival. The meetings of the council when this petition was taken into consideration were several times adjourned. . . . Finally . . . a committee of council . . . having been previously appointed to draw up a report of the debate, to be presented to the governor, their report was discussed and accepted. It described the origin of the disturbances to be the Act laying a duty upon tea in America, and, in regard to the petition, referred the petitioners for personal protection to the justices of the peace, and declared they had no authority to take the tea . . . out of the agents' care, while, if they advised the landing of it the duty would have to be paid or secured, and they would therefore be advising a measure inconsistent with the declared sentiments of both Houses in the last winter session of the General Court, advice which they considered to be altogether inexpedient and improper. They said they had seen with regret some late disturbances, and had advised the prosecution of their authors.[12]

The council had thus, on one hand, maintained that the riots arose out of a justifiable grievance and, on the other, suggested an expedient for relief that was no expedient at all—for the reluctance of the magistrates to intervene was well understood. The case for outside intervention seemed clear.

The general purpose of the first of the coercive measures, the Boston Port Act, was, in George III's words, "to bring the town of Boston to a due obedience to the laws of this realm."[13] The act closed the port as from specified dates in the following June and permitted removing the Customs officials. Thereafter, the town's overseas trade would be conducted with the interposition of an overland carriage of about seventeen miles to and from the port of Salem, and those activities which related directly to the waterfront would virtually come to a halt. Only vessels carrying in food supplies and fuel for the civil population and materials of any kind required by the armed services would be permitted to enter and leave. Naval patrols would ensure enforcement. The act conferred power on the Crown to terminate this state of affairs as soon as two conditions had been fulfilled: the people of Boston were to refund the cost of the lost tea to the East India Company, and they were to satisfy the government that in the future Customs officials would be able to perform their duties without hindrance.[14]

In proposing the Port Bill in the House of Commons on 14 March, North pointed out that the moral to be drawn from the recent events was "that it was impossible for our commerce to be safe, while it continued in the port of Boston, and it was highly necessary that some port or other should be found for the landing of our merchandize where our laws would give full protection." This, he declared, was "the third time the officers of the customs had been prevented from doing their duty in the harbour of Boston." He defended the case for a collective penalty on the town's inhabitants on the ground of the widespread degree of involvement in the destruction of the tea, and he observed that the authority of the empire was now at stake at Boston: "It is very clear we have none, if we suffer the property of our subjects to be destroyed." In a later debate, North's secretary to the treasury, Grey Cooper, stressed once more that the bill was "a law for the protection of trade . . . a mild measure if they obey it; if they oppose it, the result of it will only make the punishment."[15]

The Massachusetts Charter Bill, the next measure in the government's program, had as its basic object the strengthening of the executive and judicial authority in the province. By no other means could ministers see a way of preventing the rapid drift of Massachusetts into a state of independence, and if that were to happen, the rest of North America would swiftly follow. In the final debate on the Port Bill on 25 March 1774, North remarked: "If we do not mean to give up the matter in question, we must assert our right at this time, while we can, while it is in our power. Instead of our treating America like a foreign enemy, America has treated us like one: disavowing our authority, and declaring against all obedience to the laws of Great Britain." North's subordinate, Grey Cooper, declared: "The resolves at Boston I consider as direct issue against the Declaratory Act: they clearly proved a determined resolution in the Americans to oppose every law of this country; but the Bostonians alone have carried into execution what others have only resolved."[16] The printed summary of North's speech of 28 March introducing the Charter Bill accurately indicates the main points of ministerial concern:

> That an executive power was wanting in that country, and that it was highly necessary to strengthen the magistracy of it; that the force of the civil power consisted in the *posse comitatus;* and when it is considered . . . that the *posse* are the very people who have committed all these riots, little obedience to the preservation of the peace is to be expected from them. There appears to be a total defect in the constitutional power throughout. If the democratic part shews that contempt of obedience to the laws, how is the governor to execute any authority vested in him? If he wants any magistrate to act, whom he knows will be willing to execute the laws, he has not the power of appointing one, nor of removing one that will not act; the council have alone that power, whose dependence is on the democratic part of the constitution. It appears that the civil magistrate has been, for a series of years, uniformly inactive; there is something radically wrong in that constitution, in which no magistrate, for such a number of years has ever done his duty in such a manner as to force obedience to the laws. If the governor issued a proclamation, there was hardly found a magistrate to obey it; the governor of his own au-

thority can do nothing; he cannot act, or give out any order, without seven of the council consenting; the authority of that government is in so forlorn a situation, that no governor can act; and, where there is such a want of civil authority, can it be supposed that the military, be they ever so numerous, can be of the least service?[17]

To meet these difficulties, the bill conferred greatly increased powers on the governor to appoint judges and to appoint and remove justice of the peace, sheriffs, and other minor judicial officials, and it specified that he himself might act as a justice of the peace. The powers of the council to prescribe his activities in these respects were drastically curtailed. Royally appointed sheriffs were henceforth to select the panels of jurymen, who would thus no longer be chosen under the pressures of what the government regarded as a dangerous demagoguery. Strange as it seems in hindsight, there were no doubts in the minds of the ministers that, given such powers, the governor would be able to find loyal individuals who might be appointed and who would act effectively in these various capacities to maintain law and order and uphold the laws made by Parliament. Nor did the reference to military force in the passage cited signal any intention to introduce a military regime. The general restraints on the use of soldiers to suppress riots in eighteenth century Britain have already been discussed, and ministers and their agents had a lively appreciation of them in 1773–74.[18] For instance, in October 1773, Dartmouth had warned General Frederick Haldimand, the deputy commander in chief at New York: "It is the King's pleasure that his troops should not upon any requisition whatever be drawn out, without his Majesty's express command, in aid of the civil magistracy in the colonies unless in cases of absolute and unavoidable necessity, nor until it has been clearly shown that every power existing in the colony where the danger arises has been exerted without effect."[19] When news of the tea troubles began to reach Whitehall, Haldimand was advised that he should give military assistance, "on proper requisition," to civil magistrates to protect subjects and remove unlawful obstructions to commerce.[20] Dartmouth was even more explicit in a letter of the same date (8 January 1774) to Hutchinson:

> The vigilance, the firmness, and activity of the civil power are the only circumstances from which the subject can expect or derive protection in the exercise of his lawful commerce. . . . The aid of the military except in cases of actual rebellious insurrection cannot be brought forward but upon the requisition of the civil magistrate and for his support in cases of absolute necessity when every other effort has failed.[21]

Hutchinson duly replied:

> I am happy in having conformed to the rules your Lordship prescribes and upon the principles your Lordship has laid down with respect to the use of the military power. I have had no doubt that in the late outrages the civil magistrate might have been justified if, after failure of every other effort, a requisition had been made of aid from the military; but I have not one magistrate in the province who would venture upon such a measure, and I have not been satisfied that there have yet been any such rebellious insurrections as would have justified the representative

of the King in bringing forward the military power in order to suppress them. I know that these are tender points, and know the hazard to which by the English constitution the civil magistrate is peculiarly exposed whensoever he calls to his aid a military force.[22]

Almost the same day as Hutchinson had thus explained his disarmed situation in the face of a riot, North, in a speech in committee on the Boston Port Bill, had pointed out:

> The situation of the troops in that country has been such that no magistrate or civil officer of the peace has been willing to call forth their strength on proper occasion. It will become us to find out some method whereby the military force may act with effect, and without bloodshed in endeavouring to support and maintain the authority of Great Britain.[23]

It was assumed that a corps of magistrates willing and determined to do their duty would satisfy this need and that these could be found once there was an assurance that action would be taken to keep the Boston mob under control.

The prominence of the Boston town meeting as an organization for stirring up popular resistance to imperial authority provoked a dead set against this traditional New England institution. There was an assumption in London that the town meetings had strayed far beyond their province in discussing and still more in approving lines of action on matters of national or imperial concern. In his speech introducing the Charter Bill, North appealed to the understanding of his audience:

> Every gentleman will naturally see the impropriety of such irregular assemblies, or town meetings, which are now held in Boston; I would have them brought under some regulation, and would not suffer them to be held without the consent of the governor, unless upon the annual election of certain officers, which it is their province to choose.[24]

This proposal drew strong support from the back bench member Lord George Germain, not hitherto an active supporter of the ministry but who was to assume little over a year later the responsibilities of colonial secretary:

> I would not [he said] have men of a mercantile cast every day collecting themselves together, and debating about political matters; I would have them follow their occupations as merchants, and not consider themselves as ministers of that country. I would also wish, that all corporate powers might be given to certain people in every town, in the same manner that corporations are formed here; I would thus expect some subordination, some authority and order.[25]

It was on the basis of these arguments that the statutory restraint upon the assembling of town meetings on other than recognized routine occasions without the consent of the governor was built into the act.

Although rumors had been circulating early in the year among the colonial agents that the proposal for changing the composition of the council in Massachusetts, discussed during 1769 and 1770, would be renewed, North said nothing about this in his initial speech on the Charter Bill.[26] The issue was brought forward by Germain:

> I could have wished that the noble lord, when he was forming this scheme of salvation to this country, would have, at least, considered that there were other parts of the internal government necessary to be put under some regulation. I mean particularly the internal government of the province of Massachusetts Bay. I wish to see the council of that country on the same footing as other colonies. There is a degree of absurdity, at present, in the election of the council.[27]

North responded: "Every proposition the noble lord has mentioned coincides with my mind; I see the propriety of them, and I would wish to adopt them."[28] At least one of the members present at the debate went away in the belief that a separate bill for this purpose would probably be introduced.[29]

It is difficult to assess the significance of Germain's intervention. It seems likely, however, that before the debate, members of the cabinet were divided over reforming the council and preferred to see opinion in the House of Commons tested by a back bencher rather then by themselves: they did not wish to risk putting forward a measure which might not be universally approved by the general body of M.P.s who normally voted with the government. If this was so, they were probably reassured by the absence of any criticism of the idea except from those openly committed to the parliamentary opposition. During the next two weeks, two drafts of the Charter Bill were prepared; one with and one without a clause relating to the council. Possibly Dartmouth and North were the two ministers who hesitated to interfere with an electoral process built into the province's charter. But Lord Chief Justice Mansfield, the greatest legal expert of his day, advised in favor of the proposal, most members of the cabinet wanted it, and the king himself, who had shrunk from it five years before, now felt the necessity.[30] On 15 April 1774, the ministry brought the more extensive bill before the Commons. Even then, North was prepared, if the House wished, to delete the clause and have it discussed as a separate bill, and the fact that this was not done points to a general acceptance of the proposal among the ranks of the government's supporters.[31] Ministers assumed that a nominated council would give the governor that full support in maintaining imperial laws which, as both Francis Bernard and Hutchinson had pointed out over the years, had been denied by an elected council representing the popular interest: there would, said North, be "no negative voice."[32] In later debate, one supporter of the ministry observed: "How is it possible that the council should in any shape, have power, when it appears that if any person, of moderate passions towards the degree of respect or authority to this country, is chosen of the council, and is inclined to assist the governor, he has always soon after been displaced?"[33]

In general the parliamentary politicians took the Charter Act to be a measure for reestablishing a firm administration in Massachusetts capable of maintaining law and order, thus recovering control of a situation which had come to be dominated by a clique of conspirators abetted by the Boston mob. As one court supporter put it:

> Parliament has saved America from the jaws of tyranny by amending their constitution; and to say that we have no right to alter their government for such a purpose, appears to me the highest absurdity; we are perpetually altering and

ameliorating our own constitution, upon emergency; is there, then, no emergency at this present instant, when your officers are obliged to take shelter in your castle; when the magistrates refuse to execute their authority to keep the peace; when your ships are plundered, and your trade obstructed; and whenever a person endeavours to reform the constitution of that country, he incurs nought but pains and penalties?[34]

Another appealed to the House: "America, at this instant, is in a state of downright anarchy; let us give it a government."[35] And Lord George Germain embroidered more fully on the same theme:

America, at this instant, is nothing but anarchy and confusion. Have they any one measure but what depends upon the will of a lawless multitude? Where are the courts of justice? Shut up. Where are your judges? One of them taking refuge in your court. Where is your governor? All of them intimidated by a lawless rabble.[36]

Even one leading member of the Rockinghamite opposition, the Duke of Manchester (though he afterwards changed his mind) wrote in mid-April: "I had rather pass [this bill] as it is, than leave the people of Boston in such a state of democratic anarchy."[37] The small opposition vote of 64 against the bill, as compared with 239 in favor of it, reflected the overwhelming support in Parliament for what was felt to be a measure for the restoration of ordered civil government in Massachusetts.

The two remaining Coercive Acts, the Administration of Justice Act and the Quartering Act of 1774, rounded off the attempt to establish a stable and effective royal administration in Massachusetts.[38] The purpose of the Justice Bill was fully explained by North in the Commons on 15 April. The government read the situation in the province as one in which charges of the use of excessive force in putting down riots might be brought against magistrates or soldiers and for which they could be tried before local juries who were either biased or terrorized. If rioters were shot down, then soldiers and magistrates might be convicted of murder. One way to deal with this was to confer on the governor the royal prerogative of pardon in capital offenses, and this the ministry had already agreed to do.[39] But this did not exclude the possibility of supporters of the civil power having to undergo the traumatic experience of being put on trial for their lives before hostile juries, and the bill made provision for such cases to be heard before juries in another province or in Great Britain. "Unless such a Bill as this now proposed should pass into a law," North told the House, "the executive power will be unwilling to act, thinking they will not have a fair trial without it." It is possible, however, that the ministers also calculated that this measure would have a powerful moral effect on potential rebels in Massachusetts, for North continued:

I would not wish to see the least doubt or imperfection remain in the plan which we have adopted: if there does, the consequence may be that it may produce bloodshed; that the whole plan may be clear and decisive; that every part of it may be properly supported; and I trust that such a measure as this, which we have now taken, will shew to that country that this nation is roused to defend their rights, and protect the security of peace in its colonies.[40]

During subsequent discussion, Lord Carmarthen, a government supporter, stressed the problem of law and order in general and the preservation of the population from mob terrorism, declaring: "I cannot see this Act in any other light than as giving that same degree of relief to every subject in America, in the same manner as it gives protection and security to the military."[41]

The purpose of the Quartering Act was to strengthen the power of the governor or of magistrates to station troops where they were most needed to deal with expected riots. Although general in application and not confined to the province of Massachusetts, its provisions had a specific reference to the situation at Boston. To make this clear, it is necessary to refer back to the difficulties encountered there by the military in 1768. The commander in chief had then furnished a lengthy explanation to the secretary of state:

> I soon found that the council had put a construction upon the Mutiny Act for North America, which rendered it of no effect, for the purpose of marching and quartering the troops. Viz. "That whatever place in a province the King's troops should be ordered to, they could not be quartered in that place, till all the barracks in the province, however distant from it, were first filled with troops." From thence the council inferred, that no quarters could be had in the town, till the barracks in Castle Island were filled; and further, that the business of quartering did not come properly before them, till in the last instance; when not only the barracks in question, but also the publick houses should be filled with troops; which belonged to the magistrates to do, and was an affair that did not belong to them. It was in vain to set forth, that the barracks in Castle Island would be occupied by the troops expected from Ireland, or to urge the absurdity of a construction of the Act of Parliament, which annihilated the Act; as it absolutely impeded the march of troops through the province, as well as the King's right to order his troops to any town or village, as his service might require them to be ordered to.
>
> The next step to be taken was, to make application to the magistrates to quarter the troops in the publick houses. And a question arose, who were the magistrates? The select-men refused being concerned, and declared they were not magistrates, which was agreed to; and it then became necessary to apply to the justices of the peace. The difficulty then was, to find any of the justices who would act in the business of billeting. . . . This produced a resolution to assemble all the justices of the town, and I attended Governor Bernard to their meeting. . . . They desired time to consider of a measure, which they said must be very disagreeable to the people, and might be attended with bad consequences. After some days consideration, they returned for answer, that the Act did not require them to quarter troops, or words to that effect. . . .
>
> Every art and evasion has been tryed by the major part of the people of every degree, to force the troops to quit the town for want of quarters.[42]

Gage was in London during the early months of 1774—he did not leave Plymouth on his return to America until 18 April—and although this specific point is not documented, there can be no doubt that the ministers had talked fully with him about the problems of using troops to maintain order in Boston and that the Quartering Act was based on these past experiences. The previous act of 1765 had required the consent of two or more justices of the peace in a district concerned in order to requisition uninhabited houses, outhouses, barns, and other buildings for quarters if other accommodation, such as public houses, was not sufficient. The act of 1774 gave the governor himself the power to make requisitions, so that he could step in if the justices failed to act. In particular, it specified his right to take over private buildings in a locality where he wished to place troops, regardless of the existence of barracks elsewhere. This was a provision clearly intended to forestall any complaints from local authorities at Boston that the barracks on Castle Island remained empty while soldiers were billeted in the town, an arrangement which might be necessary if they were to be on the spot promptly to check rioting. To prevent prevarications of the kind displayed by the Boston justices in 1768, the act of 1774 was more peremptory in its direction that local officials must, on demand from the commander in chief in America, find billets for troops in local barracks, livery stables, taverns, and victualing houses.

Certain administrative arrangements completed the government's plan. Chief of these was the replacement of Thomas Hutchinson by General Thomas Gage as governor of Massachusetts. This appointment may have commended itself to the ministers on a number of grounds. Gage had spent a large part of his life in North America, the last twelve years as commander in chief. His wife was American, he had an extensive social acquaintance and knowledge of local conditions—at least north of the Potomac—and he was on the whole well-liked in the colonial circles in which he moved. Lord North, announcing the appointment in Parliament, commended his "great abilities and extensive knowledge of that country." Gage had shown great confidence in his belief that colonial defiance would evaporate before a show of firmness and determination. His appointment would overcome a further troublesome constitutional argument, which had revealed itself at Boston in and after 1768, concerning the respective powers of control over troops enjoyed by a colonial governor and by the commander in chief. It also gave to one and the same person the disposition of both regulars and of provincial militia in Massachusetts; the presence of units of the latter in the Castle Island barracks had appeared to Gage in 1768 likely to cause further difficulty in the quartering of regulars. The clearest advantage of all was in placing the full resources of the American military command in the hands of the civil administrator of the province that appeared to be the focal point of trouble in North America. And any possible doubt of Gage's right to call out the troops himself in his *civil* capacity in order to check rioting was dispelled in London by the considered opinion of the Crown's law officers "that the governor, by his commission, is a conservator of the peace in all cases whatsoever." Three regiments were sent across with him when he returned to America, and authority was given for three others in the middle colonies to be moved to Boston.[43]

Gage was not charged with the establishment of a military government. The policy directives sent to him make it clear that it was anticipated that he would function as head of the civil administration and that military force would only be used in its normal constitutional role of support for the civil power when absolutely necessary. Dartmouth's initial letter of instructions, before Gage left London, contained the passage:

> His Majesty trusts that no opposition will, or can, with any effect, be made to the carrying the law into execution, nor any violence, or insult offered to those to

whom the execution of it is intrusted: should it happen otherwise, your authority as the first magistrate, combined with your command over the King's troops, will, it is hoped, enable you to meet every opposition, and fully to preserve the public peace, by employing these troops with effect, should the madness of the people on the one hand, or the timidity or want of strength of the peace officers on the other hand, make it necessary to have recourse to their assistance. The King trusts however that such necessity will not occur, and commands me to say that it will be your duty to use every endeavour to avoid it.[44]

Among Gage's specific orders were the implementation of the Boston Port Act and the removal of the seat of government to Salem, where it was to remain until such time as Gage could give assurances "that the laws of this kingdom will be duly observed, and government be again administered at the town of Boston without opposition." Suspects involved in the "Tea Party," which the Crown's law officers adjudged to involve activity of a treasonous nature, were to be prosecuted in the province's courts, unless Gage considered that "the prejudices of the people" were such as to prevent conviction, "however clear and full the evidence might be."[45]

Six weeks later, Dartmouth sent Gage another lengthy dispatch, forwarding details of the remaining Coercive Acts and instructing him to put the Charter Act into operation. Once again Dartmouth laid stress on the effective functioning of the civil administration.

These Acts close the consideration of what relates to the state of your government, and it is hoped that they will have the good effect to give vigour and activity to civil authority; to prevent those unwarrantable assemblings of the people for factious purposes, which have been the source of so much mischief; and to secure an impartial administration of justice in all cases where the authority of this kingdom may be in question. . . .

It is not the mere claim of exemption from the authority of Parliament in a particular case that has brought on the present crisis; it is actual disobedience and open resistance that have compelled coercive measures, and I have no longer any other confidence in the hopes I entertained, that the public peace and tranquillity would be restored, but that which I derive from your abilities, and the reliance I have on your prudence, for a wise and discreet exercise of the authorities given to you, by the Acts which I now send you.[46]

It remains to be emphasized that throughout these months, the policy of the British ministers continued to be based on the assumption that they were merely dealing with a small knot of conspirators at Boston, who were nursing treasonable designs and who immobilized the peacekeeping authorities by the terror of the mob. Provide troops, the ministers thought, and make possible the appointment of zealous magistrates, and the civil authorities would recover control. For example, on 9 March 1774, Dartmouth sent the acting commander in chief in America, General Haldimand, a copy of a dispatch to Hutchinson giving advance notice of the proposals to close the port of Boston and move the seat of government out of the town. "It is," he wrote,

a measure which from the nature of it cannot be counteracted by any efforts of violence which the inhabitants of that town can make; but as in the present madness of the people there is no answering for events, it is to be wished that you would upon the receipt of this packet make the necessary preparations with as much silence and secrecy as possible for marching upon the first requisition to Boston with the three battalions now stationed at New York, New Jersey and Pennsylvania, or with such part of them as shall in future events be judged proper, in order to support and assist the civil officers and magistrates in the preservation of the public peace and to act as occasion shall require.[47]

Haldimand replied on 15 May, hoping the Bostonians would pay for the tea and make their submission: "I wish it may be the case, as there is no knowing how far the factious spirit of a few leading men may carry an inconsiderate multitude who have imbibed the most romantic notions of independence and liberty."[48] A letter from Hutchinson to Dartmouth of 17 May seemed to emphasize in a different way the narrow base of the Boston movement: "There are many considerate persons who seem to be waiting an opportunity to consult together upon such measures as may tend to obtain the royal favour and a restoration of the trade of the town, though they think nothing can be brought to effect until the regiments arrive."[49] And Dartmouth, in his dispatch of 3 June to Gage, pointing out his new powers under the Justice Act, commented:

> But it is a case that I trust will never occur, and I will hope that, notwithstanding all the endeavours equally flagitious and contemptible, used by a few desperate men, to create in the people ideas of more general resistance, the thinking part of them will be awakened, to such a sense of their true interests and of the miseries that await a further continuance of these unhappy disputes, as to exert their best endeavours for a preservation of the public peace, and thereby give such effect and countenance to the civil authority, as to render any other interposition, than that of the ordinary civil magistrate unnecessary.[50]

This illusion persisted. It was partly based on a misunderstanding of the situation in the colonies at the beginning of 1774 but still more on a complete miscalculation about the effect of the Coercive Acts. The ministers and their agents expected submission, not a rapid and revolutionary escalation of defiance. Not until the end of August did Gage himself fully realize that he was up against not merely Boston but almost the whole of an outraged province.[51] Although the ministers received his reports to this effect at the beginning of October, they do not seem wholly to have come to terms with this development until after the guns had gone off at Lexington and Concord.

During the last seven months before the outbreak of war in April 1775, British policy was impelled by an obstinate determination to maintain imperial authority over the American provinces on the basis of past legislation, including the Coercive Acts. Explicit American obedience now became the acid test for the future of the empire. As Dartmouth put it in a letter to a Boston correspondent, Joseph Reed: "The question then is whether these laws are to be submitted to: if the people of America say no, they say in effect that they will no longer be a part of the British Empire."[52] The alternative, as the ministers saw it, was to let the empire fall apart, in which case the discordant jumble of British communities on the eastern American seaboard, rent by interprovincial jealousies and territorial rivalries, would rapidly become the prey of any major European power ready to fish in troubled waters. The implications of this course of action appeared so horrific that it was never seriously entertained for a moment, for it seemed to lead directly to the consequence that the British communities on both sides of the Atlantic would fall under the hegemony of the Catholic Bourbon states. Considerations of international power politics were thus the ultimate factor which drove the British government down the path towards Lexington—and eventually to Saratoga and Yorktown.[53] Dartmouth voiced this concern in his instructions to Gage at the beginning of June:

> Whatever violences are committed must be resisted with firmness; the constitutional authority of this kingdom over its colonies must be vindicated, and its laws obeyed throughout the whole Empire.
> It is not only its dignity and reputation, but its power, nay its very existence depends upon the present moment; for should those ideas of independence . . . once take root, that relation between this kingdom and its colonies, which is the bond of peace and power, will soon cease to exist and destruction must follow disunion.[54]

The same preoccupation sustained British determination on receipt of Gage's news in October, that royal government in Massachusetts had collapsed, that the province was in a state of rebellion, and that nothing but overwhelming military force could right the situation. "I meet with people of no small importance very often," Thomas Hutchinson, then in London, wrote to a Boston correspondent, "who say they would most willingly break off all connection with you, if they did not suppose you would immediately fall into the clutches of France or Spain."[55]

Given these preconceptions, ministerial attitudes towards further developments in Massachusetts during the autumn of 1774 can be summed up as the perception of a growing revolutionary situation coupled with the belief that firm action would bring it under control and an increasing impatience with Gage for failing to do this. That there was violence and rebellion no one doubted. A steady stream of reports accumulated on the file. The first ministerial reaction was based on a sheaf of letters and enclosures dated late August and early September and brought across by H. M. S. *Scarborough*. Leaving Boston on 9 September 1774, this ship was bucked across the Atlantic by the equinoctial gales, and these mails were in London by 1 October. Gage's letters revealed the total refusal of people in Massachusetts to recognize any authority appointed or any action attempted under the terms of the Charter Act. His descriptions of the mass demonstrations and threats of violence by which the nominated councillors were harassed and some of them pressured into resigning were backed by graphic personal accounts supplied by the councillors themselves, and the lieutenant-governor wrote personally to Dartmouth describing his own similar experience. In Gage's dispatch of 2 September, he thus described the experiences of Abijah Willard:

> Mr. Willard was grieviously maltreated first in Connecticut where he went on business, and every township he passed through in his way home in this province had

previous notice of his approach and ready to insult him, arms were even put to his breast with threats of instant death unless he signed a paper the contents of which he did not know or regard. He went home after making me that report, but the news is that a large body was marching to his house in Lancaster to force him to some other concessions.

Shortly afterwards Willard resigned from the council. To the treasury, word came from Benjamin Hallowell, one of the American commissioners of Customs, that when riding by chance past a mass demonstration on Cambridge Common, he had had to flee for his life all the way to Boston, hotly pursued by a group who, so he was sure, designed to take his life. "Civil government is near its end," Gage wrote on 2 September, "the courts of justice expiring one after another." A clear general picture emerged of rebellious resistance, ranging from the noncooperation of those who refused to serve on juries to the offers of violence against would-be agents of the royal administration. Gage made in plain that the immediate military force a-vailable to him could do nothing and that resistance was not a matter of "a Boston rabble, but the freeholders and farmers of the country."[56]

On 4 October, after considering these dispatches, the cabinet ministers availa-ble in London decided to send a small naval reinforcement and some marines to Boston. But at this stage, although Dartmouth in his further orders to Gage agreed that the situation was alarming and the ineffectiveness of the available troops em-barrassing, he nevertheless placed unwarranted hopes on two considerations. He thought that the "anarchy and confusion" caused by the closing of the law courts could not "have long duration," and, he wrote: "I cannot but persuade myself that even in the New England government[s], where prejudice and resentment have taken such strong hold there are many friends to the constitution who would stand forth under the protection of government." Such friends were to be encouraged. Since Gage could give no "protection," this view was highly unrealistic.[57]

After that the ministers stayed their hand for some weeks. This may partly have been due to considerations regarding the Continental Congress (to be dis-cussed further below). Another reason appears to have been the failure of any further dispatches from Gage to reach London until about the middle of November 1774. These painted a picture of a province in dissolution, with the more distant counties joining in the defiance of the Charter Act and active preparations for war proceeding. "As far as it can be seen," wrote Gage, "nothing less than the conquest of almost all the New England provinces will procure obedience to the late Acts of Parliament for regulating the government of the Massachusetts Bay. . . . There is no security to any person deemed a friend to government in any part of the coun-try."[58] In a private letter to Dartmouth, and more fully in one to Hutchinson, Gage suggested suspending the Coercive Acts, at least until such time as the ministry might be in a position to enforce them. The king was horrified at the idea. In two letters of 18 November 1774, he variously commented on Gage's letters: "I am not sorry that the line of conduct seems now chalked out, which the enclosed dis-patches thoroughly justify; the New England governments are in a state of rebel-lion, blows must decide whether they are to be subject to this country or independent." Gage's suggestion was "the most absurd that can be suggested; the people are ripe for mischief upon which the Mother Country adopts suspending the measures she has thought necessary this must suggest to the colonies a fear that alone prompts them to their present violence; we must either master them or totally leave them to themselves and treat them as aliens." He confirmed his support for the existing policies.[59]

Before moving further, the ministers waited to test their strength in the newly elected Parliament, which met for the first time on 30 November 1774. Fully reassured by the debate on the address, they applied themselves once again to American affairs at a cabinet meeting on 1 December. Reviewing the material on Massachusetts up to Gage's last received dispatch of 25 September, the ministers concluded that a number of overt acts of treason and rebellion had been committed. They decided that if this was confirmed by legal advice, then a proclamation should be prepared "requiring all persons who have been guilty of the same (except such as shall be therein excepted) to surrender themselves before a certain day and to declare that such as shall not surrender themselves shall be treated as rebels and traitors." The law officers, after some delay, gave their concurrence. On 13 December, they reported that the documents submitted to them contained "the history of an open rebellion and war in the province of Massachusetts Bay." The law officers named individuals who had led crowds or formed committees in the proceedings to enforce the resignation of the nominated councillors. These persons were described as having committed overt acts of high treason.[60] "But," wrote the law officers,

> the acts of treason imputed to them are leading the rebel towns which, as we collect from these letters, possess the whole of the open country and every part of the province except the town of Boston, wholly prohibiting the exercise of his Majesty's authority and suppressing the exercise of his laws, insomuch that there exists no internal legislature or court of justice within the limits of the colony.

This general line of policy was confirmed in the light of Gage's next sheaf of dispatches, dated from 3 October to 15 November and reaching London on 2 and 3 January 1775, which provided details of the proceedings of the Massachusetts Provincial Congress.[61] A further substantial report from Gage, dated 15 December, reached London on 18 January.[62]

Just over a week later, on 27 January 1775, Dartmouth sent Gage a long letter of instructions, considered and approved in the cabinet two weeks earlier, which confirmed the policy of a military confrontation with the colonists of Massachusetts. Perhaps the most important aspect of this dispatch is its revelation of the government's continuing serious underestimation of the opposition which confronted it in this and in the neighboring provinces. Dartmouth referred first to Gage's alarmist reports received on 1 October:

> As they did not refer to any facts tending to shew that the outrages which had been committed were other than merely the acts of a tumultous rabble, without any appearance of general concert, or without any head to advise, or leader to conduct

that could render them formidable to a regular force led forth in support of law and government, it was hoped that by a vigorous exertion of that force, conformable to the spirit and tenor of the King's commands signified to you in my several letters, any further insults of the like nature would have been prevented, and the people convinced that government wanted neither the power nor the resolution to support its just authority, and to punish such atrocious offences.

Subsequent reports, he went on: "relate to facts, and state proceedings, that amount to actual revolt, and shew a determination in the people to commit themselves at all events in open rebellion. The King's dignity, and the honour and safety of the Empire, require, that in such a situation, force should be repelled by force." Troops that Gage had been authorized to collect from elsewhere were expected to amount already to a force of about four thousand men, and he was told that four more regiments, plus seven hundred marines, would shortly be on the way. Dartmouth dismissed Gage's contention that twenty thousand men would be required to recover control of New England—in effect to conquer it:

> You must be aware that such a force cannot be collected without augmenting our army in general to a war establishment, and tho' I do not mention this as an objection, because I think that the preservation to Great Britain of her colonies demands the exertion of every effort this country can make, yet I am unwilling to believe that matters are as yet come to that issue. . . . The violences so far committed have appeared to me as the acts of a rude rabble without plan, without concert, and without conduct.

A small force at that moment, he argued, would act more effectively against the rebels than a larger one would do later if it were given time to establish military discipline and a regular plan "and to prepare those resources without which everything must be put to the issue of a single action." The right course was to arrest the leaders of the provincial congress. If this action brought on hostilities, well and good: "It will surely be better that the conflict should be brought on, upon such ground, than in a riper state of rebellion."[63] Since rebellion already existed in Massachusetts, Gage could make recourse to martial law whenever he judged proper, under powers placed in the governor's hands by the charter of 1691. Over a year later, Dartmouth acknowledged in Parliament his, and by implication, his colleagues' failure to realize the strength of the forces which they had hoped by these orders to bring under control:

> I was willing to suppose, that the disorders in that country were local, and had chiefly pervaded the hearts of an inconsiderable number of men, who were only formidable because they possessed the power of factious delusion and imposition. I all along expected, that the body of the people, when they came to view the consequences attentively, would soon perceive the danger in which they were precipitating themselves, and return to their duty.[64]

These orders made an outbreak of armed hostilities certain, short of a complete surrender by the patriot leaders, for Gage could have no doubts that he was now expected to use the force at his command to put down rebellion, and it was only the length of time taken for dispatch to reach Boston—it did not arrive until

16 April—that caused the breach to be delayed for so long as it was. It is clear that in January 1775, the government was psychologically prepared for a rupture, though not, of course, for the long, drawn out war which it occasioned. Rebellion was still seen as the work of a minority, which a whiff or two of grapeshot would soon dispel. Perhaps the ministers thought in terms of Culloden, the last occasion when a civil conflict had been fought and when a backwoods army of highlanders had been cut to pieces by regulars in one decisive action.

With this policy settled, the further British moves between January and April 1775 were intended to bring both psychological and material pressure to bear on the New England provinces. This was the drift of the original Non-Intercourse Act pushed through Parliament during February and March, which interdicted the New England colonies from participation in the Newfoundland fishery or from trading with any area outside Great Britain, Ireland, and the British West Indies. An embargo on the transport of war stores from these areas to North America had already been declared the previous October. The present measure would help to check the inflow of munitions into New England from foreign sources, which had begun during late 1774.[65] Also, on 30 March, the cabinet finally approved the form of proclamation against rebellion to be issued by Gage in Massachusetts, and notice of it was sent to him on 15 April.[66] Meanwhile, the government was also maneuvering in hopes of keeping the New Englanders isolated. This attempt requires some previous consideration of the posture adopted towards the Continental Congress and the Continental Association.

The Continental Congress, and the Continental Association which emerged from it, perturbed the British government, but did not, until the spring of 1775, arouse such urgent concern as did the affairs of Massachusetts. This was partly because affairs moved more slowly, but still more, perhaps, because it took longer for information to reach London from the more distant parts of North America.

About the beginning of September 1774, Dartmouth was gloomy and sceptical about what might emerge from the meeting of the Congress. Writing to the deputy governor of Pennsylvania, he observed:

> If the object of the congress be humbly to represent to the King any grievances they may have to complain of or any propositions they may have to make on the present state of America, such representation would certainly have come from each colony with greater weight in its separate capacity than in a channel of the propriety and legality of which there may be much doubt. . . . I can only express my wishes that the result of their proceedings may be such as not to cut off all hope of that union with the mother country which is so essential to the happiness of both.[67]

Nevertheless, he was ready to snatch at any chance, however slender. On 29 August, he wrote to Lord Hardwicke, an independent member of the House of Lords who was giving increasing support to the government's American policy:

> Such a meeting is undoubtedly illegal, but *as it has been adopted with too much precipitation to be prevented or defeated by any measure that could be taken here, and will certainly take place*, I am not without hopes that some good may arise

out of it, and illegal as it is, if it should chalk out any reasonable line of accommodation, or make any moderate and temperate proposal, I should in my own private
opinion think it wise in Government to overlook the irregularity of the proceeding, and catch at the opportunity of putting our unhappy differences into some
mode of discussion that might save those disagreeable consequences which might
arise to every one of us either from open rupture and hostility with our fellow
subjects, or from the no less calamitous interruption of our commercial intercourse with them: this your Lordship perceives I throw out as my own private
opinion only, and therefore you will have the goodness to keep it to yourself as
such. I can easily admit that it might be very doubtful, whether I should find many
opinions to concur with mine.[68]

However, during the following weeks, views in London were colored by optimistic reports, written before or about the time the Congress met, which seemed
to indicate that it might act as a brake upon the New Englanders. Gage's letter of 20
July, sent over on the August packet, expressed the opinion:

When the deputies for holding the general congress assemble, the Boston faction
it's probable will pay the rest the compliment of taking their advice, and I understand it to be the opinion of most of the other colonies that Boston should begin
by indemnifying the East India Company. The virulent party at New York is routed
and we are told that Philadelphia is moderate.[69]

Deputy Governor John Penn reported from Philadelphia on the day the Congress
assembled that while American discontent was widespread, the leaders might have
great difficulty in agreeing upon a line of action:

From the best intelligence I have been able to procure the resolution of opposing
the Boston Acts and the parliamentary power of raising taxes in America for the
purpose of a revenue is in great measure universal throughout the colonies and
possesses all ranks and conditions of people. They persuade themselves there is a
formed design to enslave America, and though the Act for regulating the government of Canada does not immediately affect the other provinces it is nevertheless
held up as an irrefragable argument of that intention. General however as the resolution is to oppose, there is great diversity of opinions as to the proper modes of
opposition. Some are said to be for remonstrance alone upon a state of grievances
and claims; others are for a general, and others again for a partial non-exportation
and non-importation without any remonstrance. This perhaps may be the source
of divisions which will not be easily got over.[70]

Two days later, on 7 September, Haldimand wrote from New York: "I am not without hopes, however, that as there are some men of abilities at the congress . . . that
the measures they shall adopt will be more moderate and that they will not enter
into those illicit combinations which the warm enthusiasts would have them
adopt."[71]

The secrecy which the Congress managed to preserve with respect to its proceedings left the government with little really authentic information about its attitude until mid-December. As North was to explain in the Commons on 23 January
1775, the government had been unable to lay papers before Parliament prior to the
Christmas recess, partly "for want of necessary information" and partly "because

he understood from several persons who pretended to know it" that the address from the Congress would be sufficiently conciliatory to open the way to lenient measures.[72] These circumstances, coupled with the reassurances of the officials on the spot, caused not only Dartmouth but also other members of the administration to nurse a moderate degree of optimism and to hope that, illegal though the Congress was in their eyes, it might nevertheless restrain Boston and prevent an outright confrontation over the question of imperial authority. Secretary of State Lord Rochford wrote to Dartmouth on 5 October: "I do not despair of the American business turning out right, for if I understand Gage right, the Bostonian rebels will not meet with assistance from the other colonies."[73] Dartmouth's subordinate, William Knox, believed that the logic of the situation would force the Congress to acknowledge parliamentary control, "not only for their protection from foreign enemies, but from irreconciliable disputes and quarrels within themselves, as no other umpire can be so fit."[74] In view of the depressing correspondence in the office detailing territorial squabbles between New Hampshire and New York, Connecticut and Pennsylvania, and Pennsylvania and Virginia (to name but the most acrimonious), this last argument seemed not wholly without substance.[75]

Disillusionment began to set in in London about mid-November. On 18 November, Gage's dispatch arrived. Enclosed were the proceedings at Philadelphia approving the resolutions of Suffolk County in Massachusetts, which called for defiance of the Coercive Acts. About the same time, the ministers also learned of the intention to impose a nonimportation agreement. The American secretary's first reaction to the news about the Suffolk Resolves was that, if this was the case, a clash was inevitable. "If those resolves of your people are to be depended on," he remarked to Hutchinson, "they have declared war against us: they will not suffer any sort of treaty." This comment must be construed in the light of the information received from Massachusetts, which, in the British view, put the Suffolk Resolves firmly in context as one of a whole series of acts or gestures of rebellion: the resolution of Congress thus identified its makers with rebellion also. North had already staked out his line of action in the event of a colonial trade boycott. This time it would not be suffered with impunity. On 21 September, he told Hutchinson that if the colonies refused to trade with the mother country, then "Great Britain would take care they should trade no where else."[76] But no firm decisions could be reached until authentic reports of the proceedings of Congress had reached the government, and these did not arrive until 13 December.

Before then, however, a curious negotiation had taken place behind the scenes. On 4 December, on the suggestion of a minor official and friend of Dartmouth, Lord Hyde, chancellor of the Duchy of Lancaster, Benjamin Franklin was approached by two Quaker acquaintances, David Barclay, a banker and a merchant in the North American trade, and Dr. John Fothergill, Dartmouth's medical attendant. At their request, Franklin furnished a paper of "Hints for conversations upon the subject of terms that may probably produce a durable union between Great Britain and her colonies." In the following days, these proposals were submitted to critical comment by Dartmouth and Hyde. On a few points the respective proponents made significant concessions, but over a wide range, Dartmouth, as the spokesman for the ministry, found it impossible to concede. He insisted upon colonial provision of permanent civil lists and declined to consider a repeal of the tea duty without this condition. He refused to discuss the Quebec Act or to promise repeal of the Massachusetts Charter Act, though he expressed willingness to listen to complaints of any "disadvantages and inconveniences" which it might cause. Franklin's proposal that no troops should enter or be quartered in any colony without the consent of its legislature was dismissed as "utterly inadmissible." Dartmouth would not give up the treason statute of Henry VIII unless colonies made provision for the impartial trial of traitors. In response to the colonial complaint against Admiralty Courts, he was prepared to substitute colonial exchequer courts to hear revenue cases, and he was willing to sponsor tenure of colonial judges during good behavior, if assemblies would establish permanent salaries for them. A message therefore went back to Barclay on 13 December that Franklin's claims on behalf of America would have to be "moderated."[77]

The arrival on 13 December of news of the Continental Association and also of the comprehensive dossier of demands from the Congress—in form, a petition to the king for relief, but in effect, a demand requiring the British government to back down on all constitutional claims and exercises of power since 1763—made clear the uselessness of these pourparlers. It also put out of court a suggestion Dartmouth had aired during the previous few days, and which was to be raised again with Franklin by Lord Howe, that a British commission might be appointed to meet colonial delegates "to discuss and settle all claims, and Parliament to confirm, if approved, what they should agree upon."[78] The king bluntly rejected this idea in a letter to North of 15 December: "This looks so like the mother country being more afraid of the continuance of the dispute than the colonies and I cannot think it likely to make them reasonable; I do not want to drive them to despair but to submission, which nothing but feeling the inconvenience of their situation can bring their pride to submit to."[79]

Indeed, the petition from Congress immediately drove the government to consider means of putting pressure on the participating colonies to recede from their demands. In this same letter, the king remarked to North: "I was much pleased with your ideas concerning the suspension of bounties and other regulations which may be effected this session towards bringing the Americans to their duty." Not long afterwards, perhaps within the next day or so, George III drew up a memorandum which probably reflected ministerial ideas as well as his own:

> There is no denying the serious crisis to which the disputes between the Mother Country and its North American Colonies are growing, and that the greatest temper and firmness are necessary to bring matters to a good issue, time is undoubtedly also an ingredient as indispensible on this occasion. Had the Americans in prosecuting the ill grounded claims put on an appearance of mildness it might have been very difficult to chalk out the right path to be pursued; but they have boldly thrown off the mask and avowed that nothing less than a total independence of the British Legislature will satisfy them; this indeed decides the proper plan to be followed which is to stop the trade of all those colonies who obey the

mandate of the Congress for non importation, non exportation, and non consumption, to assist them no further with presents to the Indians and give every kind assistance to those that conduct themselves other ways, which will make them quarrel among themselves, their separate interests must soon effect this, and experience will then show them that the interference of the Mother Country is essentially necessary to prevent their becoming rivals.[80]

Key ideas here are the penalization of trade, the fostering of differences by showing favor to obedient provinces (at this time New York was still thought to be cast in this mold), and a degree of procrastination so that the many existing intercolonial feuds should have time to break down the common front which the colonies had momentarily established.

Early in the New Year, the ministers took the first steps along this road. A fully attended cabinet meeting on 13 January resolved:

Upon consideration of the association of the General Congress and the steps taken in several colonies to carry it into effect it was agreed that it would be proper to propose in Parliament that the associated colonies should be prohibited for a limited time from trading to any other ports than those of Great Britain, Ireland and the [British] Islands in the West Indies, and also restrained from carrying on the fishery.[81]

At this meeting Dartmouth's idea of a commission to be sent to America was further discussed, but thereafter it seems to have been abandoned.

By this time ministers had also determined that colonial attempts to enforce Congress's commercial policy must be resisted with force, and not necessarily only in Massachusetts. Dartmouth's outward mail of 7 January 1775 made this plain. To William Franklin he observed that the dispute must not be "finally decided." To Penn he wrote that measures of nonimportation might provoke the vengeance of Parliament, though he still hoped to find a basis for agreement on the constitutional issue.[82] His letter to Gage of three weeks later (27 January) spelled out the government's line more clearly:

The recommendation of the General Congress, that committees in the several provinces should be appointed to carry into execution the association for nonimportation, and that they should take into their possession all ships arriving in the American ports after the first of December, and should dispose of their cargoes in the manner, and for the purposes stated in the resolution, encourages acts of so illegal and arbitrary a nature that every effort must be made to protect the commerce of the kingdom and the property of the King's subjects from such outrageous insults; and if, in any such cases, the assistance be afforded with vigour and celerity, I trust not much will be hazarded in the execution, even should the attempt encourage the people to take up arms, seeing in this, as well as in the other case, their efforts of resistance must be made without plan or preparation.

In such an event as I have here supposed, it must be considered also, that any efforts of resistance on the part of the people will be the less to be feared, as the scene of action, if it should come to extremities, must be in situations, where the naval force, which will receive immediate and considerable augmentation, may be brought to act in aid of the army with full effect.[83]

This dispatch was addressed to Gage in his capacity as governor and ordered action in the immediate term in Massachusetts. But it clearly envisaged similar measures elsewhere; indeed, on 7 January, Dartmouth had already instructed the governor of New Hampshire to suppress any combinations for encouraging acts of violence in support of Congress's policy.[84] The order to suppress the committees of association could occasion no surprise. A legitimate government, under obligation to safeguard its citizens in the pursuit of their lawful avocations without molestation, could hardly do less: it could not tolerate the activities of organizations seeking to impose their own peculiar restrictions on what citizens might do. If colonists chose voluntarily not to buy British manufactures, that was not the government's affair, but if self-appointed groups pressured colonists under threat into subscribing and adhering to the Association for such a purpose, this was a very different matter: it became action incompatible with the established rule of law and an usurpation of power. The protection of subjects from such coercion, by the use of whatever force might be necessary, then became an absolute duty.

At further cabinet meetings of 16 and 21 January, a second string of policy was thrashed out, which became the basis of North's so-called conciliatory propositions. On 21 January the cabinet agreed:

> That an address be proposed to the two Houses of Parliament to declare that if the colonies shall make sufficient and permanent provision for the support of the civil government and administration of justice, and for the defence and protection of the said colonies, and in time of war contribute extraordinary supplies, in a reasonable proportion to what is raised by Great Britain, we will in that case desist from the exercise of the power of taxation, except for commercial purposes only, and that whenever a proposition of this kind shall be made by any of the colonies we will enter into the consideration of proper laws for that purpose, and in the meanwhile to entreat His Majesty to take the most effectual methods to enforce due obedience to the laws and authority of the supreme legislature of Great Britain.[85]

This decision formed the basis of the policy presented to Parliament on 20 February 1775. As it represented the furthest concession the government was prepared to make, it is instructive to consider how little it yielded to the complaints of the Congress. Ministers refused to admit as grievances colonial complaints against the maintenance of a standing army without consent of the assemblies; the overriding authority given to the commander in chief; the commander in chief's appointment as a colonial governor; the multiplication of offices in the revenue services; writs of assistance; the awards to judges out of condemnations; nominated councillors in Massachusetts and Quebec; interference by governors with assemblies' payments of their own administrative officials at their pleasure; "injurious" dissolutions of assemblies; restraints on trade; parliamentary taxation and the extension of Vice-Admiralty jurisdiction; authorization of trials away from the vicinage in cases of treason or of sabotage in dockyards; and the Coercive Acts and the Quebec Act passed in the previous session. The proposal in the cabinet minute (to adapt a famous phrase) amounted merely to "self-taxation at Parliament's command."[86] This was wholly unacceptable to the colonial leadership. One unconfirmed and perhaps dubious report suggests that, at the last minute before the submission of the policy to Parliament, at a cabinet meeting on 16 February, Dartmouth pressed for conditional abandonment not merely of the exercise but of the right of parliamentary taxation, in the hope that this would provide a basis for conciliation.[87] This is so inconsistent with his general commitment to upholding parliamentary authority, that it seems unlikely. In any case, such a concession would not have gone nearly far enough to meet colonial claims, and it was a point that no other cabinet minister, nor the king himself, would have been prepared to yield.

In the context of these cabinet discussions, the Non-Intercourse Act directed against New England can also be seen as a measure directed against Congress and the Continental Association.[88] North's conciliatory propositions fell more clearly into the second of these categories. In the first place, they held out no recognition to the Congress, and they made no concessions to its demands: George III's immediate comment on seeing the draft of the resolution the day before North introduced it in the Commons was that, "as it puts an end to Congresses, it will certainly have a good effect in this country and I should hope in at least some of the colonies."[89] In the second place, the approval of the propositions by very large majorities reaffirmed for all to see, including the colonists, Parliament's resolve to uphold its authority—on this occasion, as on others, the ministry was anxious to demonstrate to the colonists that the support for its policies was overwhelming and that sympathy in Britain for the colonial stand was minimal.[90] Third, the government had not yet quite despaired of opening the eyes of moderate men in the colonies to the disasters threatening from the brinkmanship of what it considered a small band of ingenious malevolent agitators and of retaining a degree of support for royal government in New York and perhaps in other provinces. At this moment, the plan seemed to offer a means of splitting the patriot cause without making any vital surrender of constitutional principle.

North had stressed this last theme in the debate on 2 February and in an address to the king on the American disturbances, in which first hints of some of the government's policy had been given. After outlining the proposal to control the trade of New England, he had remarked that the other colonies were not so culpable, and he hoped, might yet be brought to a sense of their duty to the mother country by more lenient means.[91] Introducing this proposition in the Commons on 20 February, he observed: "It has never been said, that all the Americans are rebels, or that all the colonies are in rebellion: it cannot I hope be said"; and again: "There are people, and I hope whole colonies, that wish for peace, and by these means, I hope they will find their way to it." In reply to charges by Isaac Barré that he was adopting the "low, shameful, abominable maxim" of *divide et impera,* he vigorously maintained that this was the right policy:

> Is it foolish, is it mean, when a people, heated and misled by evil councils, are running into unlawful combinations, to hold out those terms which will sift the reasonable from the unreasonable? . . . If propositions that the conscientious and the prudent will accept, will at the same time recover them from under the influ-

ence and fascination of the wicked, I avow the using that principle which will thus divide the good from the bad, and give support to the friends of peace and good government.[92]

Dartmouth's account, intended for colonial consumption, of the way in which the government envisaged the propositions would work confirms, but reveals more clearly than the surviving versions of North's explanations in the House of Commons, the nature of the ministers' real attempt to be flexible and to give reassurances within the constitutional guidelines which they held to be essential.[93] Dartmouth pointed out that the Commons resolution embodying North's propositions neither prescribed "what the civil establishment should be," nor demanded "any specific sum in aid of the public burthens." In both respects, matters were left at the discretion of the assemblies: the proposal, he wrote, "leaves full scope for that justice and liberality which may be expected from colonies that, under all their prejudices, have never been wanting in expressions of an affectionate attachment to the Mother Country, and a zealous regard for the general welfare of the British Empire." It would be appropriate if the colonies would offer to make contributions to the common defense, "on such terms and proposed in such a way, as to increase or diminish according as the public burthens of this kingdom are from time to time augmented or reduced in so far as those burthens consist of taxes and duties which are not a security for the national debt," and he pointed out that, under this system, the colonies would have "full security that they can never be required to tax themselves without Parliament's taxing the subjects of this kingdom in a far greater proportion." Any proposals made by the colonies, "accompanied with such a state of their faculties and abilities as may evince the equity of the proposal," would be received "with every possible indulgence," provided the colonists abandoned their practice of controverting Parliament's authority. Thus, from the British point of view, important assurances were offered that the calls on the colonists' purses would be negotiated in such a way as, in the civil sphere, to be to a considerable degree at their discretion and, in the defense area, to be tied to fluctuations in the British tax burden for the same purpose, so that there could be no occurrence of excessive, arbitrary demands. The reservation of Parliament's right was accompanied by a clear indication that its exercise would be controlled by a bargain or compact (or "treaty," to use Dartmouth's phrase to Hutchinson the previous November). These concessions were not insignificant, though of course, they fell far below the ultimatum of the colonists, expressed through Congress, that Parliament should have no power at all to lay tax burdens upon them. It was not unreasonable to hope that they might have some favorable impact on that broad middle ground of colonial opinion which the ministers believed to exist.

But even as the government adopted this line, the ice was melting beneath them. The situation in New York on which they relied was equivocal: it was true that the assembly had refused to subscribe the Association, but this had not prevented the populace from doing so, and the Opposition did its best to discredit the ministerial stand on this very point. According to one account of the debate on the address on 2 February:

Wedderburn's speech was in answer to letters read by Burke, who made no speech last night, from N. York, just arrived, which take away any hopes of their separating themselves to any purpose from the other colonies. They are only more decent, at present. In short they are probably waiting to see the turn here. Burke's use of them was, to take away hopes of disunion. Wedderburn's to shew the greater necessity and advantage of resolution and firmness at this moment, and he did it with great spirit.[94]

The ice was even thinner by the time North's propositions were put before the Commons. By 11 February, word had come that Virginia was entirely in the control of the Associators.[95] On the night before the debate, North told the king he feared another Non-Intercourse Bill would soon have to be introduced to restrain its trade and also that of Maryland and other colonies.[96] The situation on which ministers were basing their policy was shifting adversely almost daily as dispatches and intelligence reached London. Nevertheless, certain major considerations impelled them along their present course. One was the belief that they were facing a giant bluff. Among those most convinced of this was the king himself, whose words on this subject, as was usually the case, probably echoed his talks with the ministers. On 15 February, he wrote to North:

Where violence is with resolution repelled it commonly yields, and I owne though a thorough friend to holding out the olive branch, I have not the smallest doubt that if it does not succeed, that when once vigorous measures appear to be the only means left of bringing the Americans to a due submission to the Mother Country, that [then] the colonies will submit.[97]

The other was the stark realization that there was nothing else to do short of surrender. This was a course which general overriding considerations of state put out of the question.

The speeches of various politicians in the opening weeks of 1775 made clear their fears for the prosperity, power, and safety of the nation if parliamentary supremacy in America was not enforced. In the debate on Chatham's motion for withdrawing the troops from Boston, Lord Lyttelton, an independent but critical supporter of the ministry who was indignant that Gage had been left exposed with insufficient force, argued that it was plain from the resolutions of the Continental Congress that the commercial organization which underpinned the strength of the empire would break down if the government abandoned its course:

If Great Britain should give way on the present occasion, from mistaken motives of present advantages in trade, commerce, etc., such a concession would inevitably defeat its own object; for it was plain, that the Navigation Act, and all other regulatory Acts, which formed the great basis on which those advantages rested, and the true interests of both countries depended, would fall a victim to the interested and ambitious views of America. Now therefore, was the time to assert the authority of Great Britain, for if we did not, he had not a single doubt but every concession on our side would produce a new demand on theirs; and in the end bring about that state of traitorous independency, at which it was too plain they were now aiming.[98]

To Lord Townshend, master general of the ordnance, power as well as trade was in jeopardy:

> The question was not barely a question of revenue; but whether that great commercial system, on which the strength and prosperity of Great Britain, and the mutual interests of both countries vitally depended, should be destroyed, in order to gratify the foolishly ambitious temper of a turbulent ungrateful people.[99]

A speech from Earl Gower, president of the council, emphasized once again the mistaken impression still current in London that colonial opposition was narrowly based. He declared himself well informed that

> the language now held by the Americans, was the language of the rabble and a few factious leaders; that the delegates at the congress were far from expressing the true sense of the respectable part of their constituents; that in many places they were chosen by a kind of force, in which the people of consequence were afraid, unprotected as they were, to interpose; and where it was otherwise, they were borne down by faction in some instances, and perverted by the most false misrepresentations in other.[100]

The impression also persisted that British authority was indispensable to the colonies. One critical back bench supporter of the government declared:

> Though it was been asserted, America can subsist without our commerce, I believe nobody will say, she can flourish without our protection. If we abandon her to her present miserable situation, she must soon sue to us or to some other power for succour. Insecure in their lives and properties, the Americans must, ere long, experience the fatal consequences of being exposed to the depredations of marauders and lawless ruffians; they will soon cry aloud for the reestablishment of those judicial authorities that have been imprudently overturned, and which are necessary, not only to the welfare, but to the very existence of the subject among the rudest nations of the earth.[101]

And quite independently, Dunmore's letter, which did not arrive until over a fortnight after this pronouncement, presented much the same arguments for believing that a short period of anarchy would soon drive the Virginians back to a restoration of royal authority.[102] Thus, despite all the difficulties, ministerial circles believed there was a tide which would eventually work for them, provided they did not abandon the positions they had taken up in 1774.

Other letters reaching London during these months of decision kept raising false hopes that various colonies, especially New York and Pennsylvania, would draw away from the Continental Association. Gage's dispatches which arrived on 20 February and 27 March seemed to hold out better hopes even for Massachusetts. On 18 January 1775, Gage wrote that events were confirming his impression that "the frenzy . . . could not be of very long duration unless constantly supported by new events," and that time would give people opportunity for reflection. "I find," he went on, "that the people's minds are greatly cooled and many begin to want courts of justice, and that the friends of government have shown themselves openly in many places." The press had helped to put over the government's case. "The eyes of all are turned upon Great Britain waiting for her determination and it's the opinion of most people, if a respectable force is seen in the field, the most obnoxious of the leaders seized, and a pardon proclaimed for all others, that government will come off victorious and with less opposition than was expected a few months ago." On 18 February, he reported that recent news from London about Parliament's determination to uphold its authority had "cast a damp upon the faction"; he mentioned "the late instance of loyalty in the New York assembly which has had very good effects" and also reports that at Philadelphia sentiments were changing for the better.[103] A letter from Lieutenant-Governor Cadwallader Colden to Admiral Samuel Graves, reaching Dartmouth via the Admiralty on 22 April, told that "a great majority of the people and of men of the best fortunes" backed the New York Assembly's refusal to subscribe to the Continental Association.[104] Another from Joseph Galloway in Pennsylvania to William Franklin, written on 28 February, reaching London on 4 May, informed him that "the people of this province [were] altering their sentiments and conduct with amazing rapidity."[105] Galloway explained that "the Quakers, the high and low Dutch, the Baptists, Menonists, Dumplers, etc., are promoting moderate measures, insomuch that I hope with some trouble all violence will soon cease and peace and order take the place of licentiousness and sedition." Thus, up to 19 April and even after Lexington and Concord had fatally changed the colonial outlook, the ministry was still receiving hints that the firm pursuit of the policies they had adopted was the correct course and that, if their determination was made clear, the colonial leaders would lose popular support and be forced to yield. It was in the light of this logic that, during April, the second Non-Intercourse Act followed the first, extending to the southern colonies (though still excepting New York) the ban on foreign trade imposed already on New England.[106]

By the late spring the ministers' illusions were fading, and the news of the impact of Concord and Lexington made increasingly clear the extent of their error. Dunmore's letter of 14 March foretelling that a provincial congress due to meet in Virginia on 20 March would certainly set up a provincial administration to supercede the royal government reached London on 18 May. On 21 June came Governor Josiah Martin's letter of 16 March revealing that things were in such a state in North Carolina that he would need three thousand stand of arms to arm Loyalists in order to recover control of the province. Immediately after the arrival of the news of Lexington and Concord, the cabinet began planning more substantial military and naval measures in support of Gage and the southern governors.[107]

The orders which the colonial secretary issued on 1 July spelled out the government's realization that it had a general war on its hands—an undertaking for which the military preparations would require about twelve months.[108] Dartmouth notified the Admiralty that "not only the 4 New England colonies" were in "open and actual rebellion" and had seized vessels and imprisoned the crews but that "the flame" had "extended itself to most of the other colonies," where the "greatest violences had been committed, the constitutional authority of government trampled upon," and the people armed to resist measures to restore the public peace and protect commerce. The navy was ordered to police the main traffic lanes off the American coast, to enforce the Non-Intercourse Acts, and to seize munitions and contraband. Any colonial seaport arming against the government was to be treated as in open rebellion and liable to attack. To Gage, Dartmouth wrote:

> From the moment this blow [Concord] was struck and the town of Boston invested by the rebels, there was no longer any room to doubt of the intention of the people of Massachusetts Bay to commit themselves in open rebellion. The other three New England governments have taken the same part and in fact all North America (Quebec, Nova Scotia and the Floridas excepted) is in arms against Great Britain, and the people involved in the guilt of levying war against the king in every sense of that expression.
>
> In this situation every effort must be made by sea and land to subdue rebellion should the people persist in the rash measures they have adopted.

Sir Guy Carleton, governor of Canada, was ordered to begin at once raising up to three thousand troops from the local population. The governor of Nova Scotia was instructed to prepare to receive refugees and to make free grants of land to them. To Governor William Tryon, from whom word had recently come of the collapse of royal government in New York, Dartmouth wrote hoping the situation in this hitherto loyal province was not irretrievable and giving him the assurance that was to dictate British policy for the next six years:

> I am commanded by the King to say that it is his Majesty's firm resolution to exert every power which the constitution has placed in his hands to compel obedience to the laws and authority of the supreme legislature.

Although the more favorable premises on which the government's policy was based had been proved illusory, no change of course was considered. A restructuring of the empire on the terms laid down by Congress was unacceptable in London—in ministerial eyes this amounted to independence—and again in the words of George III, "blows" would decide whether the colonists were to be "subject to this country or independent."[109]

• NOTES •

1. For introductory matter in this and the following paragraph see Benjamin W. Labaree and Ian R. Christie, *Empire or Independence 1760–1776: A British-American Dialogue on the Coming of the American Revolution* (New York: Norton, 1976), pp. 155–69. The most detailed analysis of the development of British policy towards the American colonies during these two years is to be found in Bernard Donoughue, *British Politics and the American Revolution. The Path to War, 1773–1775* (London: Macmillan, 1964).

2. See Chapter Five, pp. 205–209.

3. William Cobbett and Thomas C. Hansard, eds., *The Parliamentary History of England . . . to 1803* (36 vols., London: T. C. Hansard, 1806–20), vol. 17, Cols. 1166–67, 1171.

4. Sir John Fortescue, ed., *The Correspondence of King George III* (6 vols., London: Macmillan, 1927–28), vol. 3, no. 1379.

5. *Ibid.,* (*Cf.* the Earl of Buckinghamshire's minute of 2 March 1774: "From such

accounts as have reach'd me it may be presum'd that there is no real love or true spirit in this people, and that they will submit to the superiority of this country if they think it will be exerted" [Historical Manuscripts Commission, *Report on the Manuscripts of the Marquess of Lothian,* p. 292]).

6. Gage to Dartmouth, 25 September 1774, Clarence Edwin Carter, ed., *The Correspondence of General Thomas Gage with the War Office and the Treasury, 1763–1775* (2 vols., New Haven: Yale Univ. Press, 1931–33), vol. 1, p. 377.

7. Historical Manuscripts Commission, *Lothian MSS.,* p. 291.

8. K. G. Davies, ed., *Documents of the American Revolution, 1770–1783 (Colonial Office Series),* (Shannon: Irish Univ. Press, 1975), vol. 6, pp. 180, 220.

9. *Ibid.,* vol. 4, pp. 419, 422, 426; vol. 6, pp. 239–40, 248–49, 251; vol. 7, pp. 29, 34–35; vol. 8, pp. 26, 38.

10. *Ibid.,* vol. 6, pp. 59–60, 65.

11. Dartmouth to Thomas Cushing, 19 June 1773, draft, *Dartmouth Manuscripts,* William Salt Library, Stafford.

12. Joseph Redington and R. A. Roberts, eds., *Calendar of Home Office Papers . . . 1760–1775* (4 vols., London: Longmans, 1878–99), vol. 4, pp. 176–77.

13. George III to Dartmouth, 7 March 1774, *Dartmouth MSS.*

14. 14 Geo. III, cap. 19.

15. Cobbett and Hansard, *Parliamentary History,* vol. 17, cols. 1164–67, 1185.

16. *Ibid.,* cols. 1188, 1185.

17. *Ibid.,* cols. 1192–93. As passed, the bill became the statute 14 Geo. III. cap. 45.

18. See Chapter Five, pp. 200–201.

19. Davies, *Documents of the American Revolution,* vol. 6, pp. 234–35.

20. *Ibid.,* vol. 7, p. 18.

21. *Ibid.,* vol. 8, p. 25.

22. *Ibid.,* p. 70.

23. Cobbett and Hansard, *Parliamentary History,* vol. 17, col. 1172.

24. *Ibid.,* col. 1193.

25. *Ibid.,* col. 1195.

26. Arthur Lee to Samuel Adams, 8 February 1774, in Richard Henry Lee, *Life of Arthur Lee, LL.D. . . . with his Diplomatic and Literary Correspondence and his Papers . . .* (2 vols., Boston: Wells, 1829), vol. 1, p. 240.

27. Cobbett and Hansard, *Parliamentary History,* vol. 17, col. 1195.

28. *Ibid.,* col. 1196.

29. James Harris to Lord Hardwicke, 29 March 1774, British Library (formerly British Museum), Additional Manuscripts (Add. MS.), 35611, f. 318.

30. Fortesque, *Correspondence of George III,* vol. 3, nos. 1440, 1441.

31. Cobbett and Hansard, *Parliamentary History,* vol. 17, col. 1197.

32. *Ibid.*

33. Hans Stanley, *ibid.,* col. 1304.

34. John St. John, *ibid.,* col. 1309.

35. Richard Rigby, *ibid.,* col. 1311.

36. Lord George Germain, *ibid.,* col. 1312.

37. Albemarle, *Memoirs of the Marquis of Rockingham and his Contemporaries* (2 vols., London: Richard Bentley, 1852), vol. 2, p. 243.

38. 14 Geo. III. cap. 39, and 14 Geo. III. cap. 54.

39. Cabinet minute, 7 April 1774, *Dartmouth MSS.;* Dartmouth to Gage, 11 April

1774, Carter, *Correspondence of Gage,* vol. 2, pp. 162–63.

40. Cobbett and Hansard, *Parliamentary History,* vol. 17, col. 1200.

41. *Ibid.,* col. 1209.

42. Carter, *Correspondence of Gage,* vol. 1, pp. 202, 204.

43. Cobbett and Hansard, *Parliamentary History,* vol. 17, col. 1201; Carter, *Correspondence of Gage,* vol. 1, p. 203, vol. 2, p. 168.

44. *Ibid.,* vol. 2, p. 159.

45. *Ibid.,* pp. 160–61.

46. *Ibid.,* pp. 163–65.

47. Davies, *Documents of the American Revolution,* vol. 8, p. 60.

48. *Ibid.,* p. 112.

49. *Ibid.,* p. 115.

50. Carter, *Correspondence of Gage,* vol. 2, p. 166.

51. *Ibid.,* vol. 1, pp. 369–73.

52. Historical Manuscripts Commission, *Eleventh Report,* appendix, part 5, p. 355.

53. For reflections on this subject in rather different contexts, see Ian R. Christie, "The Imperial Dimension: British Ministerial Perspectives During the American Revolutionary Crisis, 1763–1776," in Esmond Wright, ed., *Red, White and True Blue. The Loyalists in the Revolution* (New York: AMS Press, 1976), pp. 149–66, and "British Politics and the American Revolution," *Albion* (winter 1977–78).

54. Carter, *Correspondence of Gage,* vol. 2, p. 165.

55. Peter Orlando Hutchinson, ed., *The Diary and Letters of . . . Thomas Hutchinson* (2 vols., London: Samson and Low, 1883–86), vol. 1, pp. 267–68.

56. Carter, *Correspondence of Gage,* vol. 1, pp. 364–73; Davis, *Documents of the American Revolution,* vol. 7, nos. 542, 551, 566, 569; vol. 8, nos. xci, xcii, xciv, xcvii, xcviii, ci.

57. Cabinet minute, 3 October 1774, *Dartmouth MSS.;* Dartmouth to Sandwich, 4 October 1774, Davies, *Documents of the American Revolution,* vol. 8, p. 203; 17 October 1774, Carter, *Correspondence of Gage,* vol. 2, pp. 173–75.

58. Gage to Dartmouth, 12, 25 September 1774, *ibid.,* vol. 1, pp. 373–77, acknowledged by Dartmouth, 10 December, *ibid.,* vol. 2, p. 178, but referred to in the king's correspondence on 18 November (Fortesque, *Correspondence of George III,* vol. 3, no. 1557).

59. Gage to Dartmouth, 25 September 1774, Carter, *Correspondence of Gage,* vol. 1, p. 375; Fortesque, *Correspondence of George III,* vol. 3, nos. 1556, 1557.

60. Cabinet minute, 1 December 1774, *Dartmouth MSS.;* law officers' report, 13 December 1774, Davies, *Documents of the American Revolution,* vol. 8, pp. 239–40.

61. Carter, *Correspondence of Gage,* vol. 1, pp. 377–85.

62. *Ibid.,* pp. 386–88.

63. Cabinet minute, 13 January 1775, *Dartmouth MSS.;* Carter, *Correspondence of Gage,* vol. 2, pp. 179–83.

64. Cobbett and Hansard, *Parliamentary History,* vol. 18, pp. 1254–55.

65. 15 Geo. III. cap. 10. Governors had been notified of the embargo on 19 October 1774 (Carter, *Correspondence of Gage,* vol. 2, p. 176). For colonial purchasing of munitions see Davies, *Documents of the American Revolution,* vol. 7, nos. 559, 664, 669, 723, 735, 744, 753, 778, 826, 834, 865.

66. Carter, *Correspondence of Gage,* vol. 2, p. 192.

67. Davies, *Documents of the American Revolution,* vol. 8, p. 193. Dartmouth expressed similar views to Colden and to Gage, *ibid.,* vol. 7, nos. 585, 591.

68. Add. MS. 35612, fos. 48–9.

69. Davies, *Documents of the American Revolution,* vol. 8, p. 151.

70. *Ibid.,* p. 186.

71. *Ibid.,* p. 193.

72. Cobbett and Hansard, *Parliamentary History,* vol. 18, col. 174.

73. Rochford to Dartmouth, 5 October 1774, *Dartmouth MSS.*

74. Hutchinson, *Diary and Letters of Hutchinson,* vol. 1, pp. 267–68.

75. For an account of these intercolonial disputes see Lawrence Henry Gipson, *The British Empire before the American Revolution,* vol. 11 of *The Rumbling of the Coming Storm, 1766–1770* (N.Y.: Knopf, 1965), pp. 305–416, 450–54.

76. Hutchinson, *Diaries and Letters of Hutchinson,* vol. 1, pp. 284, 245.

77. For this incident see Donoughue, *British Politics,* pp. 214–15, and B. D. Bargar, *Lord Dartmouth and the American Revolution* (Columbia, S.C., Univ. of South Carolina Press, 1965), pp. 133–37.

78. Historical Manuscripts Commission, *Various Collections,* vol. 6, *Knox Manuscripts,* p. 258.

79. Fortesque, *Correspondence of George III,* vol. 3, no. 1563.

80. *Ibid.,* no. 1361, misplaced by the editor. The most likely dating is between 15 and 22 December 1774.

81. Cabinet minutes, 13 January 1775, *Dartmouth MSS.*

82. Davies, *Documents of the American Revolution,* vol. 7, nos. 857, 862.

83. Carter, *Correspondence of Gage,* vol. 2, p. 182.

84. Davies, *Documents of the American Revolution,* vol. 7, no. 858.

85. Cabinet minutes, 21 January 1775, *Dartmouth MSS.*

86. A. B. White, *Self Government at the King's Command* (Minneapolis: Univ. of Minnesota Press, 1933).

87. See the discussion in Donoughue, *British Politics,* pp. 244–46.

88. Page 340 above.

89. Fortesque, *Correspondence of George III,* vol. 3, no. 1600.

90. The government carried its resolution on 20 February 1775 by 274 votes to 88. For government concern to insure that the colonists knew Parliament was wholeheartedly in favor of the policy see Dartmouth, circulars to governors, 22 February, 3 March 1775, in Davies, *Documents of the American Revolution,* vol. 7, nos. 966, 994, and to Gage, 22 February, *ibid.,* vol. 9, p. 54.

91. Cobbett and Hansard, *Parliamentary History,* vol. 18, col. 223.

92. *Ibid.,* cols., 321, 322, 333.

93. Circular to governors, 3 March 1775, Davies, *Documents of the American Revolution,* vol. 9, pp. 60–62.

94. Add. MS. 35375, f. 143.

95. Dunmore to Dartmouth, 24 December 1774, Davies, *Documents of the American Revolution,* vol. 8, pp. 252–70; extract laid before the Commons on 15 February, Cobbett and Hansard, *Parliamentary History,* vol. 18, cols. 313–16.

96. Fortesque, *Correspondence of George III,* vol. 3, no. 1599.

97. *Ibid.,* no. 1595.

98. Cobbett and Hansard, *Parliamentary History,* vol. 18, col. 163.

99. *Ibid.,* col. 166.

100. *Ibid.*

101. *Ibid.,* col. 175.

102. *Ibid.*, cols. 315–16.

103. Davies, *Documents of the American Revolution,* vol. 9, pp. 29–30, 51.

104. *Ibid.*, p. 53.

105. *Ibid.*, p. 58.

106. 15 Geo. III, cap. 18, text circulated to governors on 15 April (*ibid.,* vol. 7, no. 1096).

107. Dunmore to Dartmouth, 14 March, Martin to Dartmouth, 16 March 1775, *ibid.,* vol. 9, pp. 78–79, 83–84; Cabinet minutes, 15, 21 June 1775, *Dartmouth MSS.*

108. Davies, *Documents of the American Revolution,* vol. 11, pp. 23, 25, 27, 28–9, 29–30.

109. Fortesque, *Correspondence of George III,* vol. 3, no. 1556.

PART 2
The Impact of the Struggle

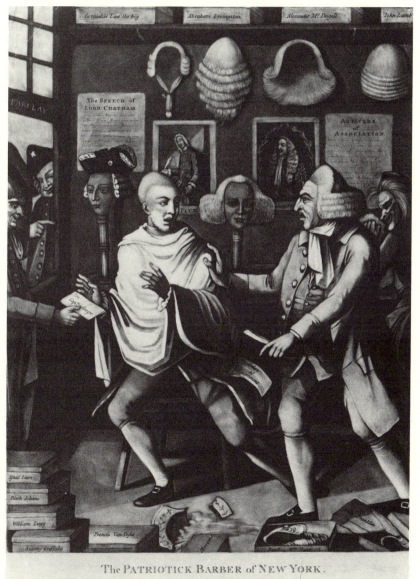

The PATRIOTICK BARBER of NEW YORK.

Plate III   London Printed for R.Sayer & I.Bennett, Map & Printsellers, N.° 53 Fleet Street as the Act directs 12 Feb.ʸ 1775.

·9·

The Impact of Commercial Resistance

WALTER H. CONSER, JR
RONALD M. McCARTHY

It was nearly self-evident to Americans of the eighteenth century that Britain's economic dependence upon the American colonies was very great—greater, perhaps, than the dependence of the colonies upon Britain. In 1765, 1768, and again in 1774, the colonies attempted to use this dependence as a weapon against Britain—as a source of leverage beyond appeal and petition that would coerce the British government into withdrawing the acts threatening to American liberties. The source of this dependence, in American eyes, was Britain's need to sell a major portion of its industrial production in the colonies and to receive from the colonies both cash remittances and the materials and foodstuffs which the nation's trade, manufacturing, and ocean-borne transportation needed. If this market was deliberately cut off, it was reasoned, Britain would soon be so affected by its loss that it would have to bow to American demands.

This conviction had its practical result in three campaigns of commercial resistance—the nonimportation and nonexportation movements, which were so much a part of the resistance against the Stamp and Townshend acts, and the Continental Association. Despite the central position of these movements in the resistance campaigns, little research has been done on their impact in the entire context of the imperial economy. Political historians in particular have not been centrally concerned with commercial resistance, sometimes even feeling that mere commercial resistance was unworthy of their patriot ancestors.[1] There has also been disagreement about whether nonimportation actually sought political ends or whether its true goal was amelioration of the economic situation.[2]

Most importantly, though, there has been disagreement over the significance and effectiveness of nonconsumption and nonimportation and their part in the process which led to independence. Did the nonimportation agreements have any effect upon British export trade or manufacturing? Did they affect British policy? Did they force or influence the repeal of the Stamp and Townshend Acts? Did nonimportation and the threat of nonexportation have any effect in 1774 and 1775,

361

when the beginning of the war was so soon to come?

To answer these questions fully would depend heavily upon research which has not yet been done and which cannot be done thoroughly for the present volume. Nor can the authorities on the colonial era be looked to for final guidance. Their conclusions often contradict each other and, in all too many cases, are based upon tradition, supposition, and partial evidence. The present effort will not offer final conclusions on the nature and effects of commercial resistance. It is intended, rather, only to outline some of the possible answers to these problems and some paths which future research may take in clearing them up.

• AMERICA AND THE ECONOMY OF THE EMPIRE •

No less an authority on eighteenth century British trade than Adam Smith recognized the very real fear of the merchants that either commercial resistance or war would take the American market away from them. In *The Wealth of Nations,* Smith wrote:

> The expectation of a rupture with the colonies, accordingly, has struck the people of Great Britain with more terror than they ever felt for a Spanish armada or a French invasion. It was this terror, whether well or ill grounded, which rendered the repeal of the stamp act, among the merchants at least, a popular measure. In the total exclusion from the colony market, was it to last only for a few years, the greater part of our merchants used to fancy that they saw an entire stop to their trade; the greater part of our master manufacturers, the entire ruin of their business; and the greater part of our workmen an end of their employment.[3]

Any inquiry into the significance of commercial resistance first requires an understanding of the system of economic relations on which it was grounded. Essentially, the political aspect of nonimportation was an attempt to use the British commercial system as a weapon against those whom it normally benefited the most. By refraining from importing the normal quantities of British goods, American merchants and Whig politicians hoped to make British merchants and manufacturers force Parliament to repeal the acts taxing and restricting trade.

This policy could have no hope of success unless American trade played a central role in the British economy. In order to see what importance the American trade had, we must review its part in the entire trade system of Britain, particularly its volume in comparison to other trade. The overseas trading system developed by England in the seventeenth and eighteenth centuries has come to be called mercantilism. By the early seventeenth century, the English had come to recognize that a commercial nation has a balance of trade with those states with which it does business. By 1650, the first steps were being taken to ensure that Britain not be harmed by a negative balance of trade.[4] Soon after, a system of trade protection began to be developed which would not only prevent the nation from becoming impoverished due to a permanent negative balance of trade but which would also enrich the nation by guaranteeing a favorable balance.

In order to create a powerful England, mercantilist policy attempted both to guarantee a favorable balance of trade and to ensure that Great Britain and its possessions enjoyed economic self-sufficiency. This was to be accomplished by the regulation of trade, industry, labor, and agriculture and by ensuring that the economic life of the colonies benefited Britain. Trade was the focal point of the mercantilist's ideas, for if trade could be controlled to the advantage of one's own country, the home industries could develop unencumbered by competition from foreign goods. By this means, it was thought that Britain could even develop a permanent advantage over its rivals, since it was believed that the total amount of trade in the world was fixed and that one party always gained at another's expense. Prosperity, in this view, could be assured only by proper manipulation of the overseas market, since the home market could never be known or used well enough to provide a basis for growth.

Given these assumptions of the mercantilists, it was natural for them to seek areas overseas in which Britain could develop a monopoly of trade. This was accomplished in two ways: by colonization and by the solicitation of trade advantages in regions not colonized, such as India and West Africa. The colonies provided the mother country with two very special advantages. Particularly in the case of the North American colonies, they acted as a population depot, a safety valve for the release of potentially unemployed or criminal people. More importantly, the colonies could serve as sources of natural resources and materials needed by the metropolitan nation but which could not be produced there. The products of America included sugar and tobacco, both for domestic consumption and for reexport; provisions such as shipbread, wheat, flour, and barreled meats; naval stores; and the like. Control of the sources of these commodities could give Britain a trading advantage over anyone else who wanted them.

The colonies were important to Britain in other ways, which became more marked as the eighteenth century progressed. In particular, the American colonies themselves, both on the continent and in the islands of the West Indies, became ever-larger markets for British manufactured goods. Vital British industries manufacturing textiles from wool, cotton, and linen; producers of ironware; and many other industries exported a major share of their production to the American market. In order to handle the shipment and exchange of these goods, communities of merchants grew up in both England and the colonies. In exchange for shipments of the manufactured goods of England, the American merchants would supply their staple products, would obtain other suitable remittances in kind, or would send cash or bills of exchange changeable into cash in England.

Since the operation of the market alone could not ensure that colonial goods would follow the desired path or that the colonies would restrict themselves to purchasing British goods, a program of legislation was undertaken to control this trade. Included in this system were regulations controlling the nationality of ships and sailors going to England or America, a structure of duties and of drawbacks (remissions of duties), and lists of enumerated goods. The enumeration provisions required that goods as vital as sugar or naval stores would go only to England or to noncompetitive markets, such as those of southern Europe. Many of these provisions of the acts of navigation and trade were not harmful to the trade of America in the least, since they tended to supply a guaranteed market for its products and to reduce the price of goods reexported from Britain to America.

By 1750, this system was reaching its final form in America. The primary economic activities there were agriculture, fishing, and trade, with manufacturing lagging far behind. The agricultural colonies all tended to develop a "staple," a particular product desirable in Britain and relatively easily grown in that part of America. The most famous of these was undoubtedly the tobacco of Virginia. South Carolina had its rice and indigo, the smaller southern colonies, naval stores and provisions, and Pennsylvania, its great quantities of flour and provisions. One by one, these products were all enumerated during the eighteenth century to ensure that Britain would have the continuing monopolistic advantage in buying them. As a result, America could never develop a positive balance of trade with Britain. The total indebtedness of America to Britain is now thought not to have been as large as previously estimated, but for the individual planter or merchant, indebtedness to English mercantile houses seems to have been more likely than a favorable balance.[5] With staples going out of America and finished goods entering, the merchant could only make a profit on the American sales or in the legally limited non-English trade to Portugal, Italy, or the foreign West Indies.

This legal structure tied America very closely to the British economy, and people in colonial economic life could hardly hope to avoid problems resulting from instability in that economy. Instabilities in the selling prices and supplies of English goods were common, while oversupply and depressed prices of American goods were always a prospect. Also, since business was habitually done on a credit rather than a cash basis, the periodic British credit crises were soon felt in America.[6]

Other problems in the system included regular attempts by merchants to avoid duties by smuggling valuable commodities such as tea and molasses and a certain amount of evasion of regulations controlling or forbidding manufacturing in America of products such as iron. Conflicts of interest between the inhabitants of the American port cities and the officers charged with enforcing these laws always existed. During most of the colonial period, either successful evasion of the acts of trade or collusion between officers and American traders had the effect of reducing the incidence of overt conflict. During the post–1763 period, however, the British government tried to bring this to an end by increasing the effectiveness of Customs enforcement.[7] Such action could only increase both the tension and the open conflict between the Customs officers (and their staffs of paid informers) and the people of the port towns. Some British Customs officers argued against the attempt to increase enforcement actions against smugglers by pointing out that enforcement was impossible in the fact of popular opposition to it, saying: "What can a Governor do, without the assistance of the Governed? What can the Magistrates do, unless they are supported by their fellow Citizens? What can the King's Officers do, if they make themselves obnoxious to the people among whom they reside?"[8] The British government did not accept this view and proceeded to attempt the enforcement of even more such acts, with or without American cooperation.

Mercantile theory gave the commerce of the colonial trading areas, which included America, a relatively prominent position. Obviously, though, British trade was not restricted solely to those areas in which advantages were guaranteed, and the trade with all parts of Europe was of large, if highly variable, proportions throughout the eighteenth century.[9] What then was the actual significance to the British economy of the colonial market? In both its long-term and its day to day effects, it appears to have been of the greatest significance. Recent research has shown that British prosperity in the 1760s and 1770s, as well as the continued growth of the British economy, were both very much supported by trade with colonial America. As W. E. Minchinton put it: "The main development in English trade in the eighteenth century was the expansion of trade with America: the growth of imports of tobacco, sugar, rice, indigo, furs, dyewoods, grain, and lumber and of exports of British manufactures, notably iron and woolens."[10]

British prosperity was doubly dependent upon American trade, first as a source of materials for domestic use and for the ever-important reexport trade and second as a consumer of ever increasing quantities of manufactured goods. A mercantilist nation concentrated its trade where possible on areas in which it could obtain unique advantages. Typically, these areas were its own colonies and parts of the world which were willing to grant trading monopolies and concessions. For Britain, these markets were Ireland, West Africa, parts of Asia including India, North America, and the British West Indies. Of these, America, comprising the last two, was the most important.[11]

The significance of this lies in the peculiar nature of these markets as outlets for the product of the expanding British industrial plant. As continental Europe began to enter its own era of industrial expansion and as Spain and Portugal, previously wealthy nations, bought less, the markets there for British manufactured goods were reduced. This in itself made the American market more important as a destination of British manufactures. The increasing agricultural wealth of America made this arrangement possible, and "the principal dynamic element in English export trade during all the middle decades of the eighteenth century was, therefore, colonial trade."[12]

Of the two markets in America, the continental colonies and the British West Indies, continental North America became the more important. British exports to these markets reached their peak in the late 1760s and early 1770s. From 1766 to 1770, exports to North America were at their highest, with £1.8 million worth of goods going to this market, as compared to £1.4 million to the West Indies.[13] This volume of trade was important because of the degree to which it underwrote both the day to day prosperity of English merchants, manufacturers, tradesmen, and workers and the long-term growth of British industry. By returning specie or raw materials for manufactured goods and as a source of reexportable products, America provided a major source of English economic growth.[14]

The nonconsumption and nonimportation agreements of 1765–66, 1769–70, and 1774–75 were intended to deny this lucrative market for export of finished goods to the British merchant and manufacturer. It was not until the nonexportation provisions of the Continental Association that the Americans attempted to withhold the sources of the reexport trade by keeping back their tobacco, provisions, and other goods. This policy was never tested in isolation from the influences of the war, which began before it was put into practice.

· ARGUMENTS FOR COMMERCIAL RESISTANCE ·

The conclusion of the Seven Years' War in 1763 saw the beginning of deep changes in the relationship between North America and Britain, changes which would ultimately lead to American independence. The political aspects of these changes have been stressed in the bulk of the present volume, but these had important and far reaching economic counterparts as well. To a great extent, these economic problems were a result of internal dislocations of the imperial economy, such as periodic recessions and credit crises. After 1763, though, there were also important changes in the legal basis of economic practice as Parliament passed acts having important economic as well as political consequences. Since the late seventeenth century, American colonial trade had been based on the acts of navigation, which had changed little during the century. They were primarily intended to regulate trade and to provide a small fund from fees to pay the officers' salaries and expenses. By 1764, however, particularly in the programs of George Grenville and Charles Townshend, the possibility that America could provide a revenue over and above this was examined. Since the source of this revenue would necessarily be trade, the mercantile sector could not avoid becoming involved.

The first economic protests of this postwar period stem from the Sugar Act and the Currency Act, both passed in 1764. In April 1764, Parliament passed an act, supported by English merchants, to forbid new issues of paper currency in the American colonies. This act was aimed primarily at the inflationary paper money practices of the middle and southern colonies, which were thought to threaten sterling remittances to England. While the act became an important grievance of the American economic community, it never spawned the sort of extralegal resistance with which this volume is concerned. Rather, the movement for its repeal (which was unsuccessful) was carried on largely by traditional constitutional means. As early as 1765, the legislatures of New York, Pennsylvania, and South Carolina moved for repeal, working through the coalition of American agents and British merchants which was so much a part of the politics of the period.[15]

The Sugar Act of 1764 was also of great significance for the continued stability of the imperial system. It was passed as an attempt to strengthen enforcement of the expiring Molasses Act of 1733, with the intention of using the increased income as a revenue. Like the act of 1733, it taxed imports of sugar and molasses from the foreign West Indies into British America. Unlike the earlier act, whose duty was so high as to prohibit the trade were it enforceable, it aimed at the strict collection of a lower duty in anticipation of raising total collections. This act was perceived as a threat by the merchants of the northern colonies even before its passage. Again, as with the Currency Act repeal movement, the attempt to gain blockage or repeal of the act was primarily constitutional. It too was unsuccessful except for encouraging a further reduction of the duty in 1766. It is distinguished, though, by the formation of merchants' committees and meetings which prepared "State of the Trade" pamphlets and remonstrances against the act. As part of this activity, a writer in the Rhode Island press in 1764 suggested a campaign of nonimportation against England. [16]

While the Currency Act and Sugar Act repeal movements went little, if at all, beyond the bounds of established procedures for redress, the Stamp Act repeal movement ushered in a decade in which these procedures were completely superseded. Much of this involved resistance movements in which new forms of political and economic leverage were sought and utilized by the American resisters. Economically, the Stamp Act resistance saw widespread agreements and associations promising to refuse to use British goods, to refuse to import them, and to encourage American manufacturing of various necessary goods. [17]

Generally, these nonconsumption and nonimportation agreements were intended to run for a period of one year, or for an even shorter time. The repeal of the Stamp Act made it unnecessary to consider extending them beyond that time. Encouraged by the apparent effectiveness of commercial resistance in the repeal of the Stamp Act, Americans again turned to the economic weapon in resisting the Townshend Revenue Acts.

From its inception in 1765, the program of commercial resistance had three major components: nonimportation, nonconsumption, and the encouragement of American manufacturing. None of these were without precedent in colonial America. Nonconsumption, in the form of the avoidance of luxuries, had long been part of proposals to reduce local indebtedness to England. Likewise, nonimportation in the form of agreements among merchants had been suggested before in an attempt to reduce merchants' inventories and raise prices. Both of these and the encouragement of manufactures, to be accomplished by not eating lamb and by wearing clothes of homespun, were either suggested or actually adopted in the protests against the Sugar Act in 1764. [18] The crucial difference between earlier attempts and the campaign of commercial resistance against the Stamp Act is that merchants were no longer trying to gain temporary localized relief nor to protest in hopes that the British would change a policy, but instead, they were attempting to *force* the British to change their policy. By these methods, the Americans wished to create a situation in England in which the ministry would have little choice but to alter the objectionable acts.

This would be accomplished, the Americans thought, because American trade played a very crucial role in the continued prosperity of England. [19] Since America was the destination of a high percentage of British manufactures, it was thought to be a market whose continuation was most necessary for British commercial health. Americans noted that Britain had restrained them from developing manufacturing (although agreeing that America probably ought not to become an industrial country) and from obtaining goods from other parts of the world in competition with British exports. They concluded from this that Britain's dependence upon America was great enough that it could be used to America's political advantage.

The closing of American ports to most British goods and the countermanding of large numbers of orders would, it was thought, hurt the British merchants and manufacturers directly and fairly quickly. In particular, those English merchants who traded heavily with North America would be hurt severely in their trade and would not be able to develop new "channels" quickly. The manufacturers would also soon see a decline in the demand for their products. If Americans ceased using "luxuries" and "superfluities" and if they made certain "necessities" (such as cheap grades of cloth) at home, the workshops of England must soon close. Besides hurting the pocketbooks of the manufacturers, this would put large numbers of workers on the streets, where they would become a potential political power themselves.

It was thought that the merchants and manufacturers of Britain would quickly turn to political action in order to work for repeal of the acts so that they could regain the American markets as soon as possible. This idea received strong confirmation in the winter of 1765–66, when the merchants of both London and the outports lobbied Parliament for repeal of the Stamp Act. This campaign was seen by the Americans as a model for the later efforts. British merchants and manufacturers both, it was thought, would argue that the losses occasioned by nonimportation were so destructive to themselves and to the national economy that the acts complained of must be withdrawn. Just as the merchants' lobby had done in 1766, they would appear in Parliament and in the press to convince the British people to give in to American demands. Their effort may even be supported, or at least made to look more crucial, by the large numbers of unemployed workers. Increased numbers of the poor would drive up the poor rates in the parishes and, being poor and hungry, might even riot in the streets for lower bread prices, as they had done in 1764.

Using these methods, domestic British political activity would unite with American political efforts to force repeal. In 1766, American agents and British merchants lobbied Parliament and the ministry and would continue to do so in the future, convincing the ministry that American trade was of greater importance than the limited revenues expected from the taxation acts. To these efforts would be added relatively institutionalized American procedures, such as legislative petitions and memorials presenting the American case. The sum of these efforts, both constitutional and extraconstitutional, would soon result in the repeal of the protested acts.

As the controversy over the proper technique of opposition to British measures grew, many of the arguments encouraging commercial resistance appeared in letters and articles in the colonial newspapers. Undoubtedly though, many of the most effective arguments never appeared in print. After all, the economically and politically active populations of places such as Philadelphia, New York, or Charleston were quite small, and much of the argumentation that preceded the adoption of commercial sanctions in these places must have been carried on face to face.

At the beginning of the Townshend Acts struggle, a Boston newspaper printed a letter expressing the developing American theory of commercial resistance:

> Let us then at once determine to lessen our demands from G. B. let us abridge our trade with those who use the very power they derive from our connection, to our destruction. We cannot be oblig'd to wear the manufactures of G. B. and who will say we are oblig'd to take them—Let us stick to this one point, which I am sure will answer all our desires, and we shall disappoint our enemies and rejoice our friends.[20]

"Philo Patria & Pacis," ostensibly writing to the English electorate, suggested that commercial resistance could force English voters to choose new members of Parliament at the next election: "Your serious attachment to the British interests, will upon the *present alarm,* render you particularly cautious in your next choice of your *Representatives,* on *whose prudent conduct* possibly the future fate of Britain may in some measure depend."[21]

That these contentions were not merely wishful thinking could be shown by reference to the repeal of the Stamp Act, when, it was believed, commercial pressure had led directly to American success. This was pointed out by another Bostonian, who included commercial resistance among the successful actions which led to repeal in 1766: "Addresses, instructions, and mobs of distressed tradesmen, on deficiency of orders from America, worked out salvation for us."[22] This view was supported by an earlier letter from a British merchant, who told a friend in Boston: "No Opposition is so reasonable because none can be so effectual, as that which procured the Repeal of the Stamp-Act, viz. the general Engagement to import no goods from England, till such a Taxation be removed or disclaimed by the Repeal of the Act."[23]

Once nonconsumption had been adopted in Boston, the community was called upon to respect the decision of the town meeting and to stay with commercial sanctions alone. As one writer put it: "No Mobs or Tumults, let the Persons and Properties of our most inveterate Enemies be safe—*Save your Money and you Save your Country.*"[24]

In Philadelphia, similar arguments were advanced in the spring of 1768, as political groups tried to encourage the city's merchants to adopt nonimportation. "A Freeborn American" wrote:

> "Nations will not think until they *feel.* A dry *remonstrance* has little *force* with those whose interest it *opposes.* They cannot *understand* such reasoning. But make it their interest to understand it, and *then* . . . rejected remonstrances become as clear as proofs of *holy writ.*" This, respectable gentlemen, you have in your power. Use it then, use it for the good of your country, stop your importations, and at *home,* I had almost said . . . they *starve.* America is their grand mart.[25]

The Americans believed that the economic position of the colonies in the economy of the empire was so central that a determined campaign to prevent Britain from benefiting from American trade must surely be capable of forcing a change in policy. But was this belief echoed in Britain? Did either merchants or politicians see American trade as being so important? Many surely did not, but at least one major student of the economy of the empire went along with American arguments in part, although his work would not be published until the War of Independence had begun.

Adam Smith was firmly convinced of the important position held by colonial trade in the development and continuation of the prosperity of Britain. He was sure that European industry as a whole had increased as a result of the colonization of America, as had Britain's in particular.[26] While he was generally of the opinion that monopolies restricted the enrichment of a nation, he felt that the sort of monopoly Britain enjoyed under the enumeration system had stimulated British prosperity. Enumeration—the requirement that many colonial products be shipped only to Britain—had helped because it had the effect of making colonial produce cheap in Britain, while it made British goods relatively expensive in America.[27]

This system had created just the effect, in Smith's view, which the Americans claimed would make commercial resistance possible. Because of the inexpensiveness and profitability of American goods, capital which would otherwise have entered other ventures was drawn to the American trade. Thus, thought Smith, the colonial trade's increase was at the expense, in part, of other branches of trade.[28] While this had benefited Britain by raising the profitability of all British trade, it presented other potential problems.[29] Because of the development of this centrality of the American trade, any blockage of it would have severe repercussions in Great Britain.[30]

While this view that American trade was a vital part of the machinery of the British Empire emerges clearly from the newspapers and pamphlets of the period, not all historians agree that the American mercantile community joined the campaigns of commercial resistance completely voluntarily and entirely for political reasons. While the present volume has stressed the political aspects of the nonimportation programs—the attempt to use commercial leverage to coerce Britain—there was also a strong economic aspect to the merchants' activity. Robert A. East has pointed out that the imperial economy had important instabilities. In particular, the British merchant tended to overship to America, while the American merchant would rather he had undershipped in order to keep inventories reasonably low and prices high. East felt that periods of raised inventories and lowered prices may have predisposed the merchants toward cooperating in methods that would reduce these problems by keeping out imports for a period of time.[31] Marc Egnal and Joseph A. Ernst feel that this desire to bring about at least a temporary remission of the economic pressures on the merchant was almost the entire cause of their cooperation in the nonimportation agreements. By this means, the colonists could sell their excess stock at a good price, reduce the pressure to be continually paying for goods lying on their shelves unsold, and even hope that some of the marginal traders would be driven out of business.[32]

Other historians have felt that the motivation of the merchants was more nearly a mixture of both economic and political elements. Leslie Thomas, for example, notes that, in the major northern ports, the nonconsumption agreements of the mechanics, country people, or other groups predate the nonimportation agreements of the large merchant bodies. An effective, or potentially effective, program of nonconsumption and the use of American manufactures would be a strong encouragement for the merchants to reduce the importation of goods which they had to pay for but possibly could not sell. Taxed articles, Thomas further notes, were often not among those to be boycotted, as listed in the merchants' agreements, and this may have been prompted by the desire to avoid the effects of nonconsumption.[33] Arthur Jensen, however, in his study of the late colonial commerce of Philadelphia, has found the participation of the Philadelphia merchants in the nonimportation agreements of 1769–70 to be more nearly political. It will be remembered that the merchants of Philadelphia entered into their agreement in the year after the merchants of New York and Boston did but that they adhered to it more strictly and for a longer time. Jensen suggested that there were two political elements entering into their decision to join the movement. The first of these was popular pressure, pressure from people and organizations of the nonmercantile community for the merchants to adopt a campaign of resistance against the Townshend Acts. This pressure was expressed in public meetings, in the newspapers, and presumably in other ways as well. The second reason which Jensen saw for their action was the merchants' own political beliefs. The merchants of Philadelphia, many of whom were Quakers, had resisted joining in popular measures, especially crowd actions and public meetings, as long as they thought there was a chance of redress through the conventional political system. When the merchants did finally join the nonimportation movement, even their private letters expressed their belief that the acts were a threat to liberty and had to be repealed.[34] They may not have wanted to take extraconstitutional action, but they surely preferred it as an alternative to sacrificing their liberty.

These considerations of the motives of the merchants in joining, or sometimes in initiating, the movements of 1765–66 and 1768–70 do not apply as strongly to the Continental Association. By 1774, the committees were almost everywhere under the control of the "popular" elements—mechanics, lawyers, and local citizens. Many of these people mistrusted the merchants and doubted their ability to carry through on a firm program. During this period, the suggestion for nonimportation came from local and county committees or conventions in many of the provinces and was finally ratified in the Continental Association. While merchants were on many of the enforcement committees of the Association, they no longer determined whether or when nonimportation would be adopted and enforced.

· ECONOMIC AND POLITICAL EFFECTS OF RESISTANCE ·

The seeming unity of action in America and evident success of the Stamp Act resistance encouraged the readoption of nonimportation in the colonies in 1768, but this unity was not echoed in the new agreements. No "Townshend Acts Congress" was ever called, nor did the mercantile cities coordinate their efforts well. (There was a suggestion of a conference of merchants in 1770, however, as part of the effort to *break* the agreements.) Nevertheless, from the spring of 1769 to the end of 1770, there were nonconsumption and nonimportation agreements in existence, and it is their effect with which we are concerned.

From the beginning, merchants, such as those in Boston, saw the Townshend Acts as a serious grievance,[35] though they interpreted them largely through the acts' effects on trade rather than their effect on liberty.[36] As with the merchants of other cities, the Boston nonimportation agreement may have been stimulated by the declining market for British goods resulting from the earlier nonconsumption agreements. It was the view of Thomas Cushing, Speaker of the Massachusetts House of Representatives, that these agreements had reduced the merchants' trade. As wrote the agent in London in April 1768: "The traders here in the English way, begin to feel the effects of the measures entered into last fall, by the people here, to promote frugality and economy."[37]

The pressures which led to the adoption of nonimportation in 1768 and 1769, whether economic, political, or ideological, did not work equally in each port city. Consequently, the various trading centers adopted agreements at different times and tried to break or modify their provisions at different times. The early confidence in the irresistible strength of nonimportation as a coercive weapon lessened as advice came from England that the ministry did not intend to repeal the acts in either 1768 or 1769, while the partial repeal in 1770 threw many groups into indecision over maintaining the agreements. Rather than seeking the cause of this in the English situation, the Americans sought it in some lack of virtue in themselves. Accusations that merchants in various cities had smuggled in British goods against the agreements were rife. These rumors were encouraged by letters from British correspondents who claimed to be secretly sending goods to some city other than the one with which they were in correspondence at the time. There was no way for the Americans at that time to judge the truth or falsity of these rumors, and they contributed to increasing distrust among the nonimporting cities.

Because current opinion is contradictory over the effectiveness of nonimportation in reducing British exports, it is useful to review statistics gathered from eighteenth century sources. James F. Shepherd and Gary M. Walton utilized the Customs 16 File of the British Public Record Office, which contains statistics on British trade to the American colonies, and addressed the question of how effective the agreements were from the point of view of total imports into America from Britain.[38]

TABLE 9.1

American Imports from Britain, 1768-1772

(£ x 1000)

Region	Year				
	1768	1769	1770	1771	1772
New England	441	228	457	1,446	1,912
Middle Colonies	1,005	325	717	1,551	979
Upper South	728	774	1,117	1,339	1,110
Lower South	399	429	261	572	635
Total	2,573	1,756	2,552	4,908	4,626

Source: James F. Shepherd and Gary M. Walton, Shipping, Maritime Trade, and the Economic Development of Colonial North America (Cambridge: Cambridge University Press, 1972), p. 163.

Table 9.1 shows not only the total effect of the nonimportation agreements in terms of their reduction of the official value of British goods entering America in each year but also the extent to which the agreements were adhered to in each area. New England, dominated by the port of Boston (but also including Portsmouth, which refused to enter into an agreement), gained a substantial reduction in 1769. Despite the vigorous and, sometimes, rowdy and threatening efforts at enforcement in 1770, imports were more nearly at their normal levels. The middle colonies were the site of two of the great ports, New York and Philadelphia. This region shows a very substantial reduction of imports in 1769, and even the increased imports of the next year are still substantially below 1768 levels. Since Philadelphia did not strongly support the movement in 1769, we can conclude that its effectiveness in New York in that year must have been very great.

Echoing Leslie J. Thomas's conclusion that the ports of the upper South, those in Virginia and Maryland primarily, did not keep their sumptuary agreements is the evidence that they actually increased their imports during 1769 and 1770. In Virginia, trading by Scottish factors and planters importing heavily for their own use reduced possibilities that the agreements could have been enforced. Burgesses President William Nelson admitted the following to the mercantile house of John Norton and Sons: "I blush on reading what you say abt the Virginians: that their Invoices rather increase than diminish. I wish such People were of any other country than of mine."[39] Despite the publicity surrounding the case of the *Good Intent* and the "trials" of importers by committees, Maryland may well have taken advantage of Philadelphia's restraint to try to capture some of its market. The great jump in imports in 1770 leads strongly to the conclusion that the goods were being sent out of the area for sale, since consumption had never been so high before. Indian trade goods became rare and expensive, and the temptation to capture some of the profits must have been felt in these ports.[40]

Evidence for the lower South, by contrast, shows that once nonimportation agreements were made, they were kept. This area, with Charleston, South Carolina, as its major port, had no agreements in effect in 1769. During this year, imports were nearly as high as those of New England in 1768. In the next year, 1770, with the nonimportation agreement in effect, imports were kept to a much lower level. Since Georgia is often accused of having imported extra British goods for sale outside the province, Charleston's agreement may have been even more effective than the numbers reveal.

This data leads to two hypotheses in particular. First, the term during which nonimportation could be kept strong in most ports was one year—whether the agreements were being kept voluntarily or by enforcement. Second, if the political consequences of nonimportation were to be maximized, coordination among the ports was necessary. This second point, at least, was noted during the Continental Association.

There were, of course, forces pulling against the ability of the port cities to maintain strict nonimportation, just as there were attempts to ensure that it would be enforced. The merchants were implicitly agreeing to a potential reduction in their profits but hoped to find alternative ways to stay in business for the year. When profits were too much reduced and when the agreements were extended for longer periods, they complained. It has already been mentioned that Indian goods were scarce, and other goods for the backcountry may have been as well, thus reducing the support of the country people for the agreements. Many merchants hoped that they could clear up balances with their English suppliers by continuing to send American goods and bills of exchange as remittances while not importing. In Philadelphia, at least, this was not possible, as exports to England fell in 1769 to £26,111 from the previous year's high of £59,406. Thus, while imports more than halved, so did potentially profitable and remittance-bearing exports.[41]

Complicating the economic picture were the fears of the merchants in nonimporting areas that those who were not keeping the agreements would capture their trade. While merchants in several ports may have been importing, Boston was the most widely distrusted after reports were circulated that the Boston merchants were smuggling in British goods under the very noses of the committee of inspection. When publisher, and opponent of nonimportation, John Mein printed reports which he maintained revealed that the largest merchants were breaking the agreements, copies of the *Boston Chronicle* containing his allegations were quickly sent to many other ports.[42] This suspicion and fear must not only have reduced the effectiveness of the agreements but must also have increased the willingness of merchants to bring them to an end. Although nonmercantile political groups in New York, Boston, and Philadelphia attempted to continue the agreements against the wishes of the merchants, once the merchants felt it imperative to end them, these groups were unable to prevent it.

In 1773, an anonymous Bostonian who signed himself "Q" offered the *Boston Evening-Post* an "Account of the Importation of Teas from Great Britain" in the form of table 9.2.

Tea was a high-profit item, all the more so because of its potential rise in value

TABLE 9.2

Boston Tea Importation, 1768-73

Year	Number of chests of tea	Number of tea Importers
1768	942	82
1769	340	35
1770	167	22
1771	890	103
1772	375	70
1773	378	61

Source: Boston Evening-Post, 15 November, 1773

should it become scarce as a result of the boycott, beginning in 1768. The temptation to import tea in spite of the agreement was strong. Despite this, declared imports fell by 64 percent in 1769 and the number of known importers by 58 percent. An even greater reduction was experienced the following year (a total of 83 percent reduction), perhaps due to enforcement by the merchants' committee of inspection. Of course, the effects of smuggling in increasing these totals cannot be known for sure. The best estimates from other sources of the rate of smuggling may or may not be helpful, since the circumstances were rather different.[43] It is to be remembered, though, that it was not the Customs service, but the nonimportation agreements which the importers wished to avoid. The Boston Committee of Inspection checked cargo manifests at the Custom House on only a few occasions before late 1769. If tea could be brought in legally and yet be hidden from the public, smuggling may not have been necessary, at least of British tea.

The Continental Association contained clauses intended to remedy some of the perceived shortcomings of the nonimportation campaign of 1768–70, as described in Chapter Six. Both the strict coordination in the time when the Association would come into effect and the enforcement procedures seem to be clear reflections of the problems of the earlier commercial resistance campaigns. Despite this, the Association had some important weaknesses as a coercive measure. First, and perhaps most importantly, nonexportation was delayed too long in its starting date. Nonexportation had not been part of earlier campaigns at all, although it had occasionally been mentioned, but during 1774, it had been brought forward regularly as a measure which would perfect commercial resistance should nonimportation fail. It was not a measure which the Americans, either merchants or planters, wanted to take and so its starting date was delayed as long as possible. Perhaps it was intended to serve as a threat for the British merchants. Josiah Quincy, Jr., while in England to organize support for the American effort against the Intolerable Acts, was told: "Had the non-exportation agreements been appointed to commence on the first of March [1775], Britain would ere this have been in popular convulsions."[44] (See Appendix G.) As it was, the Association gave British merchants nearly a year to seek alternative sources of the goods customarily imported from America.

Finally, the Americans weakened the effect of their method in 1774 and early 1775 by their talk of, and preparations for, war. While the Association did have some political effect, as will be reviewed shortly, its ability to influence some branches of British industry was weakened by the possibility of the outbreak of war. By 1775, the Birmingham iron manufacturers, who had supported the Americans in 1766, saw greater profits in war than in the renewal of American trade.[45]

· DID COMMERCIAL RESISTANCE AFFECT BRITISH POLICIES? ·

The crucial test of the policy of nonimportation was not whether New York or Charleston had received total cooperation of their mercantile community. Rather, it was whether the reduction in British imports which was achieved was sufficient to work a change in British policy toward America. The American resisters were making a complex series of wagers, particularly after the fall of the relatively well-disposed Rockingham ministry. They were betting first on the ability of the merchants to reduce imports of British products to the point where English merchants and manufacturers would feel distress. They were also betting that this commercial distress could be turned into political action, and that the British economic community would continue to be willing to bring their influence to bear on the ministry and work for an alteration of political policy. And third, they were betting that the ministry would be willing to reverse a direction which it was adopting more and more strongly with each of the acts which affected America and again allow the colonies the kind of political autonomy which they had experienced before 1763. Consequently, the factors which would decide whether the American wager on commercial resistance would be successful or not were of the greatest complexity. Success depended on the general economic situation, on what sectors of the British economy were being hurt and how much, on whether they were able to use their distress politically, on the willingness of the ministry to listen to them, on what counter-testimony the ministry was receiving from the departments, as well as many other factors.

The first crucial element in the American wager was the effectiveness of the nonimportation agreements in terms of the British export economy. A lack of success here would doom the entire effort. During the Stamp Act period, British-American trade was already suffering before nonimportation was even contemplated. Trade had been falling for a year since the postwar boom of 1764. Because of this, the nonimportation agreements of late 1765 entered a situation where economic stagnation was already of great concern. In this context, the threat of continued nonimportation, combined with the cancellations of orders received by British merchants in the final months of 1765, were an important factor in leading the British merchants to support repeal. This effect would be very difficult, perhaps impossible, to study statistically. Besides occupying parts of more than one calendar year, the nonimportation campaign was halted in the spring of 1766

TABLE 9.3

Real Value of English Exports to the
Thirteen American Colonies, 1767-71

(£ x 1000)

Year	Value
1767	15,256
1768	16,653
1769	13,936
1770	15,083
1771	18,518

Source: John G. McCusker, "The Current Value
of English Exports, 1697 to 1800," William
and Mary Quarterly, 3d. ser., 28 (1971). p. 625.

when American ports received word of the repeal of the Stamp Act. Because of this, yearly statistics do not reveal its effect. It was the practice of most American merchants trading to England to send orders in the autumn for spring goods and in the spring or early summer for fall goods.[46] Thus, British exportations for goods for spring 1766—which would normally be leaving British ports in January and February—were being reduced at exactly the time of the repeal movement in Britain. Totals for the whole year of 1766 show trade to have been lower, though only marginally. Jacob Price's "time series" shows a reduction from the 1765 level of £2,119,925 to £1,981,999 (6.5 percent) for 1766 in total exports from Britain to the North American colonies.[47] This probably does not measure the full impact, since orders deferred by the resistance were probably filled at repeal, as was done after the Townshend Acts resistance in late 1770. In any case, economic motives must have contributed to the British merchants' strong and active support for repeal.

The period of the Townshend Acts commercial resistance was somewhat different from that of the Stamp Act resistance in that trade had returned to high levels in 1768 (following the postwar slump). With the exception of 1764, 1768 was the best year yet experienced by the British export trade.[48] John J. McCusker gives the total export of Britain (in this series, England, Scotland, and Wales) to all markets in table 9.3.

Under Townshend's plan, the treasury had anticipated receiving £43,420 per annum from America in new taxes.[49] In countering this attempt, the Americans could argue that they controlled, and could therefore threaten, a large proportion of the over £16 million in export trade that Britain was enjoying. In fact, the trade to the ports of the thirteen colonies in 1768 was over two million pounds, or almost 13 percent of the total overseas trade of Britain for the year. Many historians have taken the position that the nonimportation agreements on this occasion could not have been effective simply because of the high rate of British export trade during these years. It is argued that British industry was unable to keep up with the demand for its products, particularly textiles, even without the American market. That is, that exportation from Britain to markets such as Russia, Turkey, or parts of continental Europe was increased enough to more than make up for the losses in American trade.[50] This contention does not appear to be borne out by the trade statistics for these years. Rather than exports remaining steady or rising for 1769 and 1770, they declined, and British merchants and manufacturers suffered a loss in these two years of over £4,250,000, as compared with 1768. According to McCusker's data, the thirteen colonies were directly responsible for over £1,100,000 of this reduction in trade.[51]

Why, then, did this loss not result immediately in effective political action in Great Britain? Why did it not lead quickly to repeal? A variety of factors account for this, with changed political conditions in England as important as changed economic conditions.[52] This is not to say, however, that nonimportation was merely ignored by the imperial administrators or was of no interest to them. The first secretary of state for the colonies, the Earl of Hillsborough, was particularly concerned about the activities of the nonimportation committees, as were the colonial officials with whom he corresponded.[53] Due to nonimportation, as well as other factors, British trade in 1769 was at its lowest volume in a decade.[54] By reviewing tables 9.4 and 9.5, it is possible to trace the rise and fall of these markets.[55] These tables compare the average yearly trade of England to a variety of markets for five year periods. Comparing average values for 1766 to 1770 with those for 1761 to 1765, it can be seen that increases to markets such as Canada, Ireland, Africa, Flanders, France, or Italy were more than offset by losses in the volume of trade with Germany, Holland, Spain, Portugal, and others.

Review of Schumpeter's statistics, from which these tables were abstracted, also shows that the markets which were decreasing were often markets which had been of great importance to English export economy for as long as thirty years, while many of the markets which were increasing were relatively marginal ones. At a time when average annual imports to America were second only to the captive Irish market, any credible threat to reduce them over a period of a year or more had to be taken seriously.

Some British products exported to America were affected more seriously than others. All nonimportation agreements allowed the importation of certain "necessaries" and goods used in local industry or fishing. Of the prohibited goods, the importation of certain goods was evidently considered more serious than that of others. Dry goods, for example, frequently turn up among the things which merchants were accused of importing against the agreements, as does tea. The other taxed items, however, were not taken with great seriousness, partly because they were marginal items of trade even before being taxed. The export statistics of Schumpeter reveal the fate of some of the boycotted goods in 1769 and 1770. Unfortunately, her collection of figures on the export of British products to specific destinations shows amounts only for five year intervals, which makes it impossible to judge changes in the American market for specific goods year by year. However, the total export trade of a number of goods can be reviewed to see whether they rose or fell in value exported during American nonimportation.

Among nontextile products, some show a reduction in exportation from England in 1769 or 1770. Others, such as wrought brass and copper, show mixed movement during the period. The value of candles exported fell by £1550 from 1768 to 1769 and did not completely recover in 1770. Total glass, iron, and lead exports fell substantially in 1769. Significantly less leather was exported during 1769 than during 1768, and pewter was also slightly off. Some of these commodities stayed at reduced levels in 1770, while others did not. Textile exportation also showed that certain goods were reduced in value leaving England, while others were not. Exportation of English linen, for example, was £97,996 less in 1769 than in 1768 and was even slightly lower in the next year. Some other linens and cottons of English manufacture were also off one or both years, as was the exportation of silk products. Irish linens suffered in 1769 but showed a recovery in 1770. They were reduced by £20,970 in 1769 as compared with 1768 but gained this and more back in the next year, rising to a total export of £135,374 in 1770. This supports the contention that the American boycott did contribute to reducing the exportation of British goods. Irish linen was a substitute for the more popular

TABLE 9.4

Average Annual Values of Exports from England
and Wales to Markets Whose Value Increased

(£ x 1000)

Destination	Years	
	1761-65	1766-70
Africa	399	569
Br. West Indies	1,119	1,174
Canada	294	310
Denmark-Norway	134	166
East Indies	976	1,100
Flanders	435	578
France	161	195
Ireland	1,609	2,028
Italy	551	746
Russia	66	133
Sweden	28	53
Venice	23	52
Total	5,595	7,674

Yearly average of increase: £1,079,000

Source: Elizabeth Boody Schumpeter, English Overseas Trade Statistics, 1697-1803 (Oxford: Clarendon Press, 1960), Table 5, p. 17.

TABLE 9.5

Average Annual Values of Exports from England
and Wales to Markets Whose Value Decreased

(£ x 1000)

Destination	Years	
	1761-65	1766-70
East Country	266	120
Germany	2,218	1,486
Holland	2,066	1,662
The Isles	63	58
Portugal	964	595
Spain	1,023	1,004
The Straits	195	102
Turkey	75	73
Total	6,870	5,070

Yearly average of decrease: £1,800,000

Source: Elizabeth Boody Schumpeter, English Overseas
Trade Statistics, 1697-1803 (Oxford: Clarendon Press,
1960), Table 5, p. 17.

English linen and was allowed to be imported by the Virginia Association and the nonimportation agreement of Boston.[56]

The important woolen exports also show scattered reductions in 1769. Sales of woolen hats of all sorts were reduced in 1769, with some staying off in 1770. Other woolens, such as some grades of baize, were exported from England in lesser amounts during 1769 than during 1768 but saw a large rise in 1770, often to levels higher than that of 1768. Other textiles simply increased both in 1769 and 1770.[57] This evidence would appear to support the contention of the English dry goods merchants, noted earlier, that many sorts of cloth were selling so well in 1770 as to be in short supply, so that the nonimportation agreements were not harming the producers or sellers of such items.[58] It is difficult to judge the importance of these specific items in the British export economy, especially as compared with items which do not appear in the Schumpeter tables. Further research is needed to determine just where in the economy the effect of nonimportation was felt and to what extent reductions in the exportation of particular goods was influenced by nonimportation as opposed to other factors.

Another item of interest, in part because of the American attention shown to it, is the exportation of tea. All tea was, of course, imported into England from the East. It was a staple product of the reexport trade and was enumerated by Parliament, so that it had to pass through England on its way to colonial markets. Exportation of tea grew throughout the eighteenth century, partly because of the growth of America where it was consumed in great quantity. Tea was one of the major products boycotted under the nonimportation agreements. In 1768, England exported 1,849,000 pounds of tea. This fell to 1,469,000 (off 21 percent) in 1769 and quite a bit further, to 851,000 pounds (off 42 percent), in 1770.[59] Much of this reduction was due to nonimportation and nonconsumption.

To conclude from the economic statistics about the results of nonimportation is to present a rather mixed picture of the effectiveness of the American methods. On the one hand, the total amount of British trade overseas was less in 1769 and 1770 than it had been in 1768. That year, though, was something of a boom year, and profits made then could be used to tide British industry over until the upturn that would come when nonimportation collapsed. The reduction of sales to America, though it was fairly large, does not explain the whole reduction in trade, which had also declined in other important markets. Likewise, the British textile trade, which was important to the nation and which included many of the merchants and manufacturers that the Americans wished to influence, was apparently not seriously reduced by nonimportation. Nevertheless, British politicians, viewing the state of the country's trade after more than a year of American boycotts, could only conclude that the nation's trade was down and that the Americans must have had something to do with it.

Economic considerations, of course, had always to be balanced against political ones. Britain did not wish to abandon the plans which the government had developed to change colonial administration. The desire to rationalize and to tighten control over American affairs, evident since at least 1763, and to reassert British authority where it was slipping were foremost. It was perhaps equally important, though, that Britain do something to retain the right to tax America and to avoid the appearance of giving in to commercial and political pressure. Throughout 1768 and 1769, rumors in America and in Britain that the ministry would repeal the acts proved untrue. In 1770, various motives led the North ministry to consider repeal of the bulk of the revenue portion of the acts. Intelligence from America had indicated the divisions in the agreements, and Lord North thought to take advantage of them in presenting his case for repeal. Early in 1770, according to Thomas C. Barrow, Lord North "argued that repeal was not so much a concession or an act of appeasement as it was a well-timed move to divide the colonial opposition and to end the nonimportation agreements."[60]

• THE LATER COMMERCIAL RESISTANCE MOVEMENT •

The domestic consequences of commercial resistance were at least as important as the international ones. In particular, this experience greatly influenced the form of the Continental Association. Far from being discouraged or feeling that their assessment of the strength of their method was false, resistance leaders came to feel that the shortcomings of nonimportation could be cured. Many at the First Continental Congress were willing to readopt nonimportation as a policy, only this time under the direction of popular local bodies rather than committees of merchants.

Economically, the results are not so obvious. Despite the temporary direction of economic life by public bodies, no trend toward less individualistic economic conduct resulted. Nor was American manufacturing a great success during or after nonimportation. Some Americans did brag to British merchants that they were able to clothe themselves in homespun, but important hurdles had to be cleared before American production would become successful.[61] Students of this attempt, however, have concluded that it was of real significance in transforming the American economy away from a captive colonial market toward self-sufficiency. Working against this tendency was the low cost and high availability of farming land, as well as the high value of its surplus product in relation to British goods. At the time of the nonimportation agreements, some Americans began to take up manufacturing as a way of life for the first time. Rather than continue to migrate westward in search of new land, many people in eastern Pennsylvania turned to cottage industry as an alternative livelihood. Factories were also established in New York, Boston, and Philadelphia.[62] Edmund S. Morgan has referred to this period as being, "in effect, a trial run in economic self-sufficiency."[63]

During the next three years, from 1771 through 1773, economic life went on unhampered by political concerns. Even though the nonimportation agreements had technically only been altered so that only dutied goods, such as tea, were to be boycotted, they were in fact over, and tea was imported as enthusiastically as other goods. Seventeen seventy-one, in fact, was a boom year in the transatlantic trade, as established merchants replenished their stocks and as new investors tried to join the trade on credit. Many new would-be traders tried to enter the market, often on short capital, by writing to British mercantile houses and ordering shipments. In New York, James Beekman was asked by correspondents if he would recommend that they ship to these new "friends," whom they had never heard of before.[64] Seventeen seventy-two, on the other hand, became a rather bad year, as the British credit crisis of 1772 struck at the basis of the transatlantic trade, a problem which affected 1773 as well.[65]

Late 1774 saw the beginning of the Continental Association and renewed commercial resistance, this time to the Coercive Acts of 1774. While some non-consumption agreements were formed in the towns during the summer of 1774, they had no effect on the level of total trade as the ports and the colonies waited to see what the Congress would do. The Continental Association, although ratified in the early fall of 1774, did not provide for nonimportation to begin until the end of the year. Because of this, 1775 is the first year of nonimportation under the Association. Since the war began in April 1775 and was well under way by summer, at least in the North, the true support for the policy of nonimportation as an alternative to war cannot be judged properly from calendar year statistics. If a series were available which showed the quarterly exports of England, as they were in fact collected in the eighteenth century, it would allow a more appropriate method of studying the question of the effects of nonimportation before the war became general. The areas not affected by the war, however, such as Virginia, were able to trade with Britain and seem generally to have held to nonimportation.

McCusker's statistics, which show the trade of England approximately by calendar year, demonstrate that the total current value of goods shipped from England to the united colonies in 1775 fell to £226,000. Of this figure £87,000 was sent to Boston which was occupied for nine months and £127,000 to uncooperative Georgia. In 1774, by contrast, America had accepted £2,953,000 in British goods.[66]

In our long retrospect, the events of the fall and winter of 1774–75 are so overshadowed by the preparations of both the British and the Americans for war as to obscure any effects of the Association. In England, the economic resistance attempted to influence a government little disposed to hear arguments conciliatory to America. Before the Association was fully under way, the North ministry decided on the use of troops to enforce the Massachusetts Government Act and to prevent opposition to its policies.[67] Despite the unwillingness of the government to hear them, there were complaints from the British economic community as the Continental Association began to take effect. Samuel Elam, a merchant of Leeds who sold Yorkshire woolens to American merchants, spoke up in early 1775 about the continued effects in northern England of the collapse of American trade (which had suffered since the 1772 credit crisis). Challenged to back up his statements that more and more tradesmen were being thrown on the poor rates, he collected signatures of 353 unemployed master clothiers, many from the borough of Leeds.[68]

Bristol was also hit by the onset of nonimportation in 1775. The merchants of that city petitioned Parliament as early as 18 January 1775 to plead for a settlement of the American conflict. In this petition, they reminded Parliament:

> That their total trade, to Africa and the West Indies as well as to America, depended upon the availability of re-export goods from America. This availability was to be threatened by nonexportation in the fall. The petitioners reviewed the "checks" which their trade with America had suffered from the Stamp and Townshend Acts, and would suffer again if the Americans carried through on their commercial sanctions.[69]

Bristol's American trade did suffer during the remainder of 1775. W. E. Minchinton reprints a table that shows forty-three ships bound for America from Bristol in ballast. At the same time, only a handful, three to Quebec and two to Georgia, carried cargo. Even occupied Boston consumed little from Bristol. An August cargo contained only cheese, rice, flour, currants, raisins, and beer, and it was one of few shipments to the town.[70]

The shortage of trade was not able to produce unified action by the merchants. The committees of merchants which had aided American interests in the past were in desuetude, and in any case, the interests of the merchants were not always in America's favor by this time. From the spring of 1774, when William Bollan, agent of Massachusetts, petitioned against the Coercive Acts, the major mercantile groups were uninterested in helping America.[71]

Nonexportation should have been a more credible threat than nonimportation at this time, especially if it had begun at an earlier date. By 1775, almost half of all English shipping was in the Atlantic trade routes, much of it involved in seeking sources of material for the reexport trade. At this time, 37 percent of British overseas commerce consisted of this reexport trade, which was mainly concerned with colonial and East India products.[72] If the Americans had been able to close off both export and reexport markets by nonimportation and by keeping their tobacco, naval stores, provisions, and other products out of British hands, their commercial policies would have had a better test. By early 1775, some observers in England felt that the policy may have had a chance of success. Josiah Quincy, Jr., wrote home of being told that London merchant George Hayley had received no orders from America, not even for goods to be smuggled in. By March, he was being told by Benjamin Franklin that a war would take seven years to win but that commercial resistance may be successful within the year.[73] (See Appendix G.)

Quincy had gone to England certain that the Americans must fight militarily but had become convinced that commercial resistance should be maintained until it was successful. This was not to be, and war soon intervened to alter the mode of struggle to one incompatible with the commercial coercion of Britain. Commercial measures did, of course, continue during the war, as American exports to and imports from Britain, even indirectly through the West Indies, came to a standstill in all but the occupied ports. After importing 56 million pounds of tobacco in 1775 (much of it rushed out of Virginia in anticipation of nonexportation), British imports of this commodity fell to 7.3 million pounds in 1776 and never again reached their earlier level in the century.[74] Imports of wheat and wheat flour, pitch and tar, and staves, all American products, were also large in 1775 and fell in 1776, although Britain necessarily found replacements for the American sources of these vital products in future years.[75] The reduction of trade between Britain and America was so thorough during the War of Independence that one must wonder what the effect on English policy would have been had the Americans pursued commercial resistance so strongly when there was not a war to be fought.

· FURTHER RESEARCH NEEDED ·

This review of the impact of commercial resistance has necessarily been inconclusive. Both contemporary accounts and the conjectures of historians have never been tested against the statistics. However, with the possible exception of those of Shepherd and Walton, the statistics have not been collected with a view toward the study of commercial resistance. This has been a preliminary attempt to review what the available statistics may reveal about the nature of commercial resistance, but much more has to be done. Statistics relating to exports of specific British goods to America ought, wherever possible, to be reviewed. This should be done with regards to the goods most prominently mentioned in American orders and invoices and for quarterly fluctuations, where feasible. Mercantile records on both sides of the Atlantic may be consulted to reveal who was shipping to America during nonimportation, what they were sending, and to whom. American business records, such as inventories and sales books, may also reveal whether inventories were shrinking during the nonimportation agreements or were staying steady in response to nonconsumption. Also, the question of whether colonial merchants were enriching themselves with cash sales or merely extending their lists of creditors must be addressed.

Other topics that have not been considered include the effect of commercial resistance on the British Treasury. Depending upon what goods were most successfully boycotted, revenues other than those from the taxed goods could have been threatened. Collections under the Sugar Act are one possibility, as are collections for imports bought by the British merchants for reexport to America.

The question of the effectiveness of the American commercial resistance to Britain during the decade from 1765 to 1775 is by no means settled by the recent advances in research on the economic history of eighteenth century England. Rather, the question is reopened for study in a new form, which may shed more light on this pioneering attempt at the use of economic sanctions in place of either submission or war.

• NOTES •

1. Edward McCrady, *South Carolina Under the Royal Government, 1719–1776* (New York: Macmillan, 1899), for example, criticized nonimportation as unenforceable on its 1769 basis, pp. 653, 681, and in the Continental Association, *ibid.,* p. 764.

2. Marc Egnal and Joseph A. Ernst, "An Economic Interpretation of the American Revolution," *William and Mary Quarterly,* 3d ser., 29 (1972), see the economic motive as having predominated among the merchants who adopted nonimportation. That is, all that was desired was a temporary amelioration of poor trade conditions. Arthur M. Schlesinger, *The Colonial Merchants and the American Revolution* (New York: Columbia Univ. Press, 1917), saw the policy as a political expression of a political-economic problem, the negative effects of the acts of navigation and trade on American commerce. Arthur L. Jensen, *The Maritime Commerce of Colonial Philadelphia* (Madison: State Historical Society of Wisconsin, 1963), opposes both of these "economic" interpretations, pointing out that in Philadelphia many merchants stressed political motives for economic resistance even in private correspondence.

3. Adam Smith, *An Inquiry Into the Nature and Causes of the Wealth of Nations,* 2d ed. (London: W. Strahan; and T. Caddell, 1778), vol. 2, pp. 211–12. By "rupture," Smith of course meant war but also discussed the effects of the commercial resistance.

4. The earliest uses of the term "balance of trade" and early attempts to control it are discussed by G. N. Clark, *Guide to English Commercial Statistics, 1696–1783* (London: Royal Historical Society, 1938), p. xii.

5. James F. Shepherd and Gary M. Walton, *Shipping, Maritime Trade, and the Economic Development of Colonial North America* (Cambridge: Cambridge Univ. Press, 1972), believe that the deficits in the value of commodity trade were made up in the total American economy through "invisible earnings" in shipping charges, interest, profits, etc.,

pp. 136, 165–66. Joseph A. Ernst, *Money and Politics in America: A Study in the Currency Act of 1764 and the Political Economy of the Revolution* (Chapel Hill: Univ. of North Carolina Press, 1973), doubts this, pp. 10–12, ff.

In the South, in particular, profits on the sale of English goods were often made not by an American merchant but by a British house which shipped directly to its own stores. See J. H. Soltow, "Scottish Traders in Virginia, 1750–1775," *Economic History Review,* 2d ser., 13 (August 1959), pp. 92–95.

6. The instability of the commercial system and the difficulties of merchants in adjusting to it are noted in Robert A. East, "The Business Entrepreneur in a Changing Economy, 1763–1795," *Journal of Economic History* 6 (1946) Supplement, pp. 18–19; and by Jensen, *Maritime Commerce,* pp. 100–101. A typical, if severe, credit crisis is discussed in Richard Sheridan, "The British Credit Crisis of 1772 and the American Colonies," *Journal of Economic History* 20 (1960), pp. 162–85.

7. Neil R. Stout, "The Goals and Enforcement of British Colonial Policy, 1763–1775," *American Neptune* 27 (July 1967), pp. 211–20.

8. Extract from a letter from John Swift, deputy collector, and Alex Barclay, comptroller, Philadelphia, to Commissioners of Customs, Boston, 20 December 1770 (K. G. Davies, ed., *Documents of the American Revolution, 1770–1783 [Colonial Office Series],* vol. 2, *Transcripts, 1770* [Shannon: Irish Univ. Press, 1972], p. 300).

Smuggling, that is, illegal importation of non-English tea, increased as the tea tax made the cost of British tea rise and nonconsumption did not end American desire for the product. Swift and Barclay wrote the above to the commissioners after a fight between Customs agents and port workers in Philadelphia in 1770.

9. See Elizabeth Boody Schumpeter, *English Overseas Trade Statistics, 1697–1808* (Oxford: Clarendon Press, 1960), Table 5, p. 17.

10. Walter E. Minchinton, ed., "Editor's Introduction," *The Growth of English Overseas Trade in the Seventeenth and Eighteenth Centuries* (London: Methuen, 1969), p. 30.

11. Ralph Davis, "English Foreign Trade, 1700–1774," in *ibid.,* p. 107.

12. This interpretation is heavily influenced by Davis, "English Foreign Trade," pp. 104–7; quotation from p. 106.

13. Minchinton, "Editor's Introduction," p. 30. Exports to colonial America would undoubtedly have been higher without the nonimportation agreements of 1769–70.

14. Earlier scholars felt that the colonies competed for economic growth and with the Industrial Revolution in England because they used rather than produced investment capital (see Richard Pares, "The Economic Factor in the History of the Empire," *Economic History Review* 7 [1936], p. 130). Davis and Minchinton feel otherwise. "The process of industrialization in England from the second quarter of the eighteenth century was to an important extent a response to colonial demands" (Davis, "English Foreign Trade," p. 106). "The impetus for growth in the 1750s came from an expansion of exports of English manufactured goods (notably to the American colonies) while the dynamic in the 1760s and early 1770s was due to the swelling volume of re-exports made possible by the continual expansion of imports" (Minchinton, "Editor's Introduction," p. 16).

15. Joseph A. Ernst, "The Currency Act Repeal Movement: A Study of Imperial Politics and the Revolutionary Crisis, 1764–1767," *William and Mary Quarterly,* 3d ser., 25 (1968), p. 176. Ernst reports on the continuing significance of the Currency Act of 1764 in *Money and Politics in America.*

16. Frederick Bernays Wiener, "The Rhode Island Merchants and the Sugar Act,"

New England Quarterly 3 (1930), p. 499. Even though the duty was lowered in 1766, this was the single most lucrative revenue of the period (Oliver M. Dickerson, *The Navigation Acts and the American Revolution* [Philadelphia: Univ. of Pennsylvania Press, 1951], pp. 185–86).

17. See Chapter Two of this volume for a full description.

18. East, "Business Entrepreneur," pp. 18–19; Schlesinger, *Colonial Merchants,* pp. 63–65.

19. This belief is briefly reviewed in J. E. Crowley, *This Sheba, Self: The Conceptualization of Economic Life in Eighteenth-Century America* (Baltimore: Johns Hopkins Univ. Press, 1974), pp. 134–35.

20. "M.Y.," *Boston Gazette,* 14 September 1767.

21. *Ibid.,* 21 September 1767.

22. "Pro Rege et Grege," *ibid.,* 26 October 1767.

23. *Ibid.,* 28 September 1767. Letter dated 17 June 1767. The London writer referred specifically to the resistance against providing for troops under the Quartering Act.

24. *Ibid.,* 8 November 1767.

25. *Pennsylvania Gazette,* 12 May 1768. "A Freeborn American" was evidently quoting from the letter of the Boston Merchants' Committee to the Philadelphia merchants which had been considered, but not acted on, in March (see *ibid.,* 31 March 1768).

26. Smith, *Wealth of Nations,* vol. 2, p. 193.

27. *Ibid.,* pp. 195–197.

28. *Ibid.,* p. 200.

29. *Ibid.,* p. 202.

30. *Ibid.,* p. 211.

31. East, "Business Entrepreneur," pp. 18–19.

32. Egnal and Ernst, "Economic Interpretation," pp. 21–22.

33. Leslie J. Thomas, *The Non-Consumption and Non-Importation Agreements, 1768–1770* (M. A. Thesis, Univ. of Wisconsin, 1949). See also Chapter Four of this volume.

34. Jensen, *Maritime Commerce,* pp. 79ff. Perhaps the current stress on the "ideology" of the period, the extent to which people acted on the basis of abstract political ideas, clouds rather than illuminates this problem. We cannot ignore the relationship between interests and ideas as a factor in the motivation of the resisters, in whom ideas served to shape the interpretation of interests.

35. Boston merchant John Rowe called it, "An Imposition on America in my Opinion as Dangerous as the Stamp Act," Anne Rowe Cunningham, ed., *Letters and Diary of John Rowe: Boston Merchant 1759–1762, 1764–1779* (Boston: W. B. Clarke, 1903), p. 146.

36. *Ibid.,* pp. 152–54, and ff.

37. Thomas Cushing to Dennys DeBerdt, 18 April 1768, "Letters of Thomas Cushing from 1767 to 1775," Massachusetts Historical Society *Collections,* 4th ser., 4 (1858), p. 350. Cushing refers to the Boston town meeting's nonconsumption agreement, see Chapter Four of this volume, pp. 139–140.

38. No 1767 or earlier baseline is available in this series, which was collected by the American Board of Customs Commissioners, which became active only in late 1767.

39. William Nelson to John Norton, 6 July 1770, Frances Norton Mason, ed., *John Norton & Sons, Merchants of London and Virginia, 1750–1795* (Richmond: Dietz Press, 1937), p. 138.

40. John Stuart to Governor Botetort (Virginia), 12 July 1770, Davies, ed., *Docu-*

ments of the American Revolution, vol. 2, p. 146.

41. Jensen, *Maritime Commerce,* p. 297.

42. Oliver M. Dickerson, "British Control of American Newspapers on the Eve of the American Revolution," *New England Quarterly* 24 (1954), pp. 461–63, claims that the Customs Board supported Mein in hopes of breaking the solidarity of the resistance.

43. W. A. Cole, "Trends in Eighteenth Century Smuggling," in Minchinton, ed., *English Overseas Trade,* and Hoh-Cheung Mui and Lorna H. Mui, "Smuggling and the British Tea Trade before 1784," *American Historical Review* 74 (October 1968), are concerned with the smuggling of tea from Europe into Britain. Tea was more likely to be smuggled when duties were high or some other potential for high profit existed, such as the availability in foreign markets of better grades of tea than the East India Company carried. Conditions encouraging the smuggling of tea into America were probably similar, with foreign teas being brought in, under cover, to avoid the tax. Undoubtedly, though, the period after 1768 saw tea being brought in clandestinely as much to avoid the censure of breaking the nonimportation agreement as to avoid the tax. Various English inland revenues were "drawn back" when tea was exported to America, so tea of East India Company origin was usually not very expensive in America.

44. Josiah Quincy, Jr., to Mrs. Quincy, 7 January 1775, Josiah Quincy, *Memoir of the Life of Josiah Quincy, Jr.* (Boston: Cummings, Hilliard, 1825), pp. 293–94.

45. Michael G. Kammen, *Empire and Interest: The American Colonies and the Politics of Mercantilism* (New York: Lippincott, 1970), p. 129.

46. See Philip L. White, ed., *The Beekman Mercantile Papers, 1746–1799* (New York: New York Historical Society, 1956), vols. 1 and 2, passim.

47. Jacob Price, "New Time Series for Scotland's and Britain's Trade with the Thirteen Colonies and States, 1740–1791," *William and Mary Quarterly,* 3d ser., 32 (1975), Appendix IIB, pp. 324–25.

48. See John J. McCusker, "The Current Value of English Exports, 1697 to 1800," *William and Mary Quarterly,* 3d ser., 28 (1971), Table 2, p. 621.

49. Robert S. Chaffin, "The Townshend Acts of 1767," *William and Mary Quarterly,* 3d ser., 27 (1970), p. 96.

50. See, for example, Jack Sosin, *Agents and Merchants: British Colonial Policy and the Origins of the American Revolution, 1763–1775* (Lincoln, Neb.: Univ. of Nebraska Press, 1965), p. 109ff. The Russo-Turkish War of this period is often cited in evidence and was considered at the time to have reduced the effects of the commercial resistance (*Boston Evening-Post,* 22 January 1770).

51. McCusker, "Current Value of English Exports," Table 3, p. 626. There is documentary evidence which supports the position that shortages of cloth for export existed in England which reduced the effect of the lowered American demand (see Jensen, *Maritime Commerce,* p. 185). Also, compare Shepherd and Walton's evidence compiled from American imports, page 371. The difference between the 1768 import level and the comparative reductions in 1769 and 1770 is over £838,000. These two series are not immediately comparable (e.g., as a measure of smuggling) because Shepherd and Walton utilize the official values, while McCusker introduces a factor to convert those values into an approximation of the actual value of the goods.

52. Besides Chapter Seven of this volume, see also Thomas C. Barrow, *Trade and Empire: The British Customs Service in Colonial America, 1660–1775* (Cambridge, Mass.: Harvard Univ. Press, 1967), pp. 254–56; Sosin, *Agents and Merchants,* pp. 113–26; Michael G. Kammen, *A Rope of Sand: The Colonial Agents, British Politics, and the Amer-*

ican Revolution (Ithaca: Cornell Univ. Press, 1968), pp. 185–87, 196–200, 219–23.

53. See Davies, ed., *Documents of the American Revolution,* vol. 2, letters to and from governors such as Hutchinson (pp. 32–35, 50–51, 96–99, 150–57) and Eden (pp. 46–47, 130, 171, 198), Lieutenant-Governors Bull (pp. 55–56, 219–20, 286, 297–98) and Colden (pp. 83–85, 96, 139–40, 143), and General Gage (pp. 142–43).

54. Minchinton, "Editor's Introduction," p. 17. Other factors include the steady decline of the German, Portuguese, and Spanish markets, which was not compensated for by the rise of other markets.

55. For purposes of comparison, the American market has been left out of Table 9.4, which also excludes some marginal markets not included in the Schumpeter table. Average annual exports to America from England for the period 1766–70 rose, despite nonimportation, because of the large exportations of 1767–68. This market was, to an extent, then, a balance between those that lost and those that increased.

56. Peyton Randolph to John Norton, 23 September 1770, Mason, *John Norton & Sons,* p. 147. The Boston agreement specified only that manufactures of Great Britain were to be boycotted, allowing those of Ireland. Boston merchant Samuel Abbot ordered Irish linens twice during nonimportation from his Belfast correspondent. The 1770 shipment arrived with an affidavit certifying the Irish origin of the goods (see Samuel Abbot to Samuel Hyde, 14 June 1768 and 10 April 1769; also Samuel Hyde to Samuel Abbot, 1 March 1770, enclosing the affidavit, ". . . to prevent any detention at Your place" Samuel Abbot Papers, Baker Library, Harvard Business School).

57. All figures from Schumpeter, *English Overseas Trade Statistics,* Table 7, p. 22; Table 10, p. 38.

58. Extract of a letter from London to Philadelphia, 1 November 1769, *Boston Evening-Post,* 22 January 1770. "Our manufacturers are so little sensible of the want of their usual trade with you, that people began to entertain an idea, that America never was of half the importance to us that it was generally imagined to be." The unnamed correspondent asserted that the Russian war had increased the overseas demand for British goods.

59. Schumpeter, *English Overseas Trade Statistics,* Table 16, p. 60. See also Mui and Mui, "Smuggling and the British Tea Trade," who note corresponding reductions in the total amount of tea sold by the East India Company in these years, p. 67.

60. Barrow, *Trade and Empire,* p. 243.

61. Gerard Beekman to David and William Ross, 2 May 1766, White, ed., *Beekman Mercantile Papers 1:389;* Martha Jacquelin to John Norton, 14 August 1769; William Nelson to Norton, 24 January 1770; and Martha Goosely to Norton, 8 August 1770, Mason, *John Norton & Sons,* pp. 103, 122, 143.

62. Egnal, "Economic Development," p. 249. Many of these ventures failed after a short time, but Egnal notes that "failure was often followed by the establishment of another, larger manufactory." The movement of the economy of some sections of the country was, of course, more than a question of ideology or of resistance technique. Population growth and other factors began to create a group which depended upon selling its labor rather than upon farming which was much larger than the earlier urban working class (see Kenneth A. Lockridge, "Social Change and the Meaning of the American Revolution," *Journal of Social History* 6 [Summer 1973], pp. 406–14, in which the growing scarcity of land and the impact of this upon labor is discussed).

63. Edmund S. Morgan, "The Puritan Ethic and the American Revolution," *William and Mary Quarterly,* 3d ser., 24 (1967), p. 13.

64. Fludyer, Marsh, and Hudson to James Beekman, 3 July 1771; James Beekman to

Fludyer, Marsh, and Hudson, 3 October 1771, White, ed., *Beekman Mercantile Papers,* vol. 2, pp. 739, 740–41.

65. See Sheridan, "British Credit Crisis," pp. 162–85. Credit, sometimes extended for years, was the lifeblood of all branches of the American trade (see, for example, Samuel M. Rosenblatt, "The Significance of Credit in the Tobacco Consignment Trade: A Study of John Norton & Sons, 1768–1775," *William and Mary Quarterly,* 3d ser., 19 [July 1962], pp. 383–97).

66. McCusker, "Current Value of English Exports," Table 3c, p. 626.

67. See Chapter Eight of this volume.

68. R. G. Wilson, *Gentlemen Merchants: The Merchant Community in Leeds, 1700–1830* (London: Manchester Univ. Press, 1871), p. 48. At this time, Yorkshire's share of the woolen export trade was "just under half of the national total" (*ibid.,* p. 51).

69. Walter E. Minchinton, ed., *The Trade of Bristol in the Eighteenth Century* (Bristol: Bristol Record Society, 1957), pp. 46–47.

70. *Ibid.,* pp. 48–50.

71. Kammen, *Empire and Interest,* pp. 129–30.

72. Minchinton, "Editor's Introduction," pp. 30, 26.

73. Josiah Quincy, Jr., to Mrs. Quincy, 17 January, 3 March 1775, Quincy, *Josiah Quincy, Jr.,* pp. 312, 342.

74. Schumpeter, *English Overseas Trade Statistics,* Table 18, p. 62.

75. *Ibid.,* Table 17, p. 56.

·10·

Religion and the Development of Political Resistance in the Colonies

WALTER H. CONSER, JR.

W riting to Hezekiah Niles in 1818, John Adams suggested that an important part of the meaning of the colonists' break from the Crown was to be found in the "change in their religious sentiments of their duties and obligations." While earlier chapters in this volume have emphasized the colonists' active disobedience to Crown authorities, it is equally necessary to acknowledge the transformation of attitudes which accompanied this growing political resistance. For as John Adams implied, political ideas and behavior derive from many sources, and the religious ones which form the focus of this chapter are crucial for a full understanding of the genesis and organization of the movement for American Independence.[1]

Religious leaders had regularly participated in discussions of colonial politics, and religious categories were familiar enough within the North American colonies to be acceptable within political discourse. Thus, it was not out of embarrassed misgivings but rather in the shared recognition of the very appropriateness of his comments that the Boston pastor Reverend Jonathan Mayhew, in January 1750, introduced his *Discourse on Unlimited Submission and Non-Resistance to the Higher Powers* with the observation:

> It is evident that the affairs of civil government may properly fall under a moral and religious consideration, at least so far forth as it relates to the general nature and end of magistracy, and to the grounds and extent of that submission which persons of a private character ought to yield to those who are vested with author- ity.[2]

The occasion for this sermon was the anniversary of the death of Charles I, and as the Reverend Mayhew expanded upon his theme, he reminded his listeners of the several reasons for resistance to the Crown in the seventeenth century. In so doing, he took special note of the ecclesiastical grounds for that revolution and, above all, of the senior prelates of the Church of England who had struck up a bargain "betwixt the sceptre and the surplice for enslaving both the bodies and souls of men." Such an ecclesiastical conspiracy was truly insidious, Mayhew maintained, "for people have no security against being unmercifully priest-ridden but by keeping all imperious bishops . . . from getting their foot into the stirrup at all." Pointing to this past experience, Mayhew admonished his listeners against a lax defense of their own religious liberties, especially with regard to any attempts to strengthen episcopal jurisdiction in the colonies.[3]

New England Protestants understood such exhortations to vigilance within a very specific context, that of the proposal to establish a bishop of the Church of England in America. While efforts toward this end dated back to 1703, a concentrated and renewed endeavor was begun in 1741 by Bishop Thomas Secker. Beyond that, due to the relative strength of the Anglicans in the northern colonies, New England colonists, as well as those in New York and New Jersey, often regarded the episcopacy threat as directed especially at them. Thus, while such a proposition could be attractive for Anglican clergy and laity, for Congregational and Presbyterian colonists, it could be regarded as the first step in the attempt to saddle the colonies with all the hated ecclesiastical trappings of mass, canon law, and further taxation.

Recent research has shown, however, that in these fears the American colonists were mistaken and that the British government had no intention of supporting the church hierarchy in the establishment of an American bishopric. Nevertheless, since these Congregational and Presbyterian colonists (called the dissenting denominations because of their break with the Church of England), formed the popular and religious majority in the colonies, the dimensions of their understanding of the episcopacy issue and the uses to which it could be put provide an interesting index to the eighteenth century colonial mind.[4]

A preacher such as Jonathan Mayhew could rely on his audience's familiarity with two types of argumentation in any discussion of religious liberty. One of these was the appeal to history. In the eyes of the eighteenth century New Englander, the founding of Massachusetts Bay had been entirely for the purpose of the preservation of liberty—both religious and civil. The Church of England, in this view, was one of the institutions from which their forefathers had fled. It was now bent on strengthening its power in America and, if allowed to, would surely repeat the long tale of oppression and tyranny which had been its trademark in England. The colonists cited a specific list of complaints against the sinister Anglican influence with its woeful consequences. Missionaries supposedly sent to America to convert the Indians were, in fact, concentrating their efforts in Boston and other large cities of New England in an attempt to steal away believers from already established congregations. Furthermore, the Anglicans objected whenever the dissenting clergy attempted to do any work of their own with the Indians. The colonists heard constant news of the Anglican need for new parishes to ease the overwhelming supply of new curates, but even more ominous in the eyes of the colonists was the support given to the Roman Catholics of Canada after the successful defeat of the French in 1763. While they came to America to preserve religious liberty, the colonists never forgot that it was a liberty won at the expense of civil war and the overthrow of James II, "the popish king," in 1689.[5]

Just as he could draw on history for his discussion, so too could Mayhew utilize the covenant theology so familiar to the majority of New England Protestants. Thus, in his *Discourse,* Mayhew argued that all governments were based on a covenant between rulers and ruled, just as all religious life was based on a bond of mutual relations between God and mankind. Since all governments were of divine origin, their purpose was the good of the people. Obviously, then, both rulers and ruled were under mutual obligations of service and submission. The people were to obey, while their rulers could not merely indulge their arbitrary fancies, but were bound by principles, fixed laws, and customs. Should any rulers fail to work for the public weal or overstep the bounds of law, should they attempt "to set up a monstrous hierarchy like that of Rome . . . or anything else which their own pride and the devil's malice could prompt them to," then submission was damnable and resistance wholly justified in the sight of the Lord.[6]

Mayhew's sermon has been called "the morning-gun of the revolution," and it clearly illustrates that by the 1750s a philosophical and theological basis had been constructed for resistance to unwarranted authority. This basis derived from religious sources and contemporary eighteenth century writers. It set forth the basis of legitimate government and enumerated the religious rights of freedom of conscience and the right of a parish to choose its own ministers. In the civil sphere, the rights of freedom of speech, the sacredness of contracts and the fruits of one's labor, the right to trial by jury, and the other rights of a British citizen as described in the Magna Carta were all affirmed. Finally, it justified resistance to any invasion of these rights, whether attempted by religious or civil authorities.[7]

To illustrate the development of concepts does not explain their power for motivating actions and behavior. The really effective work of the clergy during the decades from 1750 to 1776 was not merely the development of these religious categories, but, as Professor Perry Miller has argued, the imparting of a sense of crisis to the people, the renewal of the Old Testament's condemnation of impiety, and its call for a new reformed life. The efficacy of the clergy was manifested in the translation of the secular political discussion of the years 1765–75 into the religious categories so familiar to their people. All successful political movements require not only leadership but an awakened following receptive to the ideas of these leaders. Often, the leadership is more ideologically advanced than their followers, but in the American case, the result of the clergy's preaching was to narrow this gap and fire the imagination of the people to sustained action.[8]

The clergy had ample opportunities to instruct their congregations. They preached on Sabbath and midweek services, special days of thanksgiving and fasting proclaimed by the colonial assemblies, and at the annual services of the colonial councils and the ministerial associations. Furthermore, their position in the community afforded the clergy an informal kind of power as well as great social prestige. In the cities, the clergyman was recognized as a teacher, arbiter, and wise counsel. In the countryside, these attributes were set against the relative lack of newspapers and other contacts with the outside world and thereby served to establish the pulpit—along with the stump—as the primary source of information and political discussion.[9]

In addition to individual opportunities for preaching, colonial religious leaders also formed both intercolonial and transatlantic ministerial organizations. Ministerial associations had existed in America since the seventeenth century. Having met for support and to pass along information in the old days in England, the dissenting clergy merely continued and expanded these activities once they arrived in America. In 1705, for example, five of these associations located in Massachusetts Bay met and drew up a series of proposals. Designed to facilitate communication as well as to tighten discipline and church life, these resolutions formed the foundation of the Saybrook Platform (1709), the basis of colonial Presbyterianism and Connecticut Congregationalism. Though much controversy surrounded the ecclesiastical particulars of these documents, their discussion and adoption in individual colonies highlighted the dimensions of intercolonial organization and cooperation at this early stage.[10]

Only slightly less significant in assessing the nature of the religious contribution to the independence movement was the transatlantic relationship between the Nonconformists in England and the Dissenters in America. Naturally allied in their common opposition to the Anglicans, the affinity between the Nonconformists and Dissenters was purposefully expanded and developed. As far back as 1690, intermittent correspondence had been carried on between ministers in London and Boston. With increasing levels of organization occurring in England from 1714 to 1745, the committee of ministers at Boston wrote in 1750 to the Nonconformists of London requesting a deputation on their behalf be set up in England. This was done, as the English put it, in order "to Keep a Watchful Eye over the Design to introduce Bishops into America, to endeavour to prevent all Encroachments upon the Religious Rights of the people there," as well as to "Correspond with the Ministers in New England." In addition to this formal relationship, an extensive stream of books and pamphlets as well as personal letters traveled between the brethren of England and America.[11]

One of the more interesting aspects of this relationship was the manner in which the Englishmen reproached the colonists over the limits they set on religious toleration. The colonial Protestants' fear of Catholicism is but one aspect of a continuing debate from the colonial days to the present over the legitimate limits of liberty. Another example of the restrictions on religious liberty in colonial America concerned the Baptists. Nonconformists in London commented on the situation repeatedly, but still as late as 1773, the Baptist leader, Reverend Issac Backus, complained of the imprisonment of several Baptist ministers in Massachusetts for refusal to pay church-support taxes. "Liberty of conscience, the greatest and most important article of all liberty," Backus observed, "is evidently not allowed, as it ought to be in this country, not even by the very men who are now making loud complaints of encroachments upon their own liberties." As the ensuing decades of American history would amply demonstrate, liberty, whether for Baptists and Quakers or merchants and politicians, would revolve more on questions of organized power than on individual righteousness.[12]

• CHANGING TIMES, CHANGING ISSUES •

One aspect often overlooked in assessing the movement for American independence is that during the years of the French and Indian War (1754–63), the colonists continually heard from the pulpit of the threat to liberty posed by the Catholic French, of the danger of losing all their freedom, and of the need to struggle in defense of their cherished rights. Jonathan Mayhew vividly described the issue for his listeners:

> Do I behold the territories of freedom become the prey of arbitrary power? . . . Do I see the slaves of Lewis [Louis XV] with their Indian allies, dispossessing the free-born subjects of King George, of the inheritance received from their forefathers. . . . Do I see a protestant, there, stealing a look at his bible, and being taking [taken] in the fact, punished like a felon! . . . Better to die than to be enslaved by the arbitrary rule of France.[13]

The French and Indian War in combination with the threat posed by the Anglicans dramatized the many threats to colonial liberty. By reinforcing the colonists' fears about the precarious nature of their liberty, as well as reaffirming the legitimate right to resistance, these conflicts provided an on-going source for political discussion and a context for resistance well into the years when the focus would change from Louis XV to George III.

The years of the imperial crisis (1765–75) have been correctly described as a time when civil grievances were added to long-standing religious ones.[14] The episcopacy controversy continued, yet under the pressure of the political developments between Parliament and the colonies, the focus shifted to the reasons for British tyranny and appropriate means of resistance. If it had once been the case that religious and civil liberties were seen as separate and distinct, it was no more, for the nature of the British policy posed a threat to all colonial liberties, and if either civil or religious liberty succumbed, the other was sure to follow in its place.

The ideological framework of the 1750s moved easily into the struggle of the 1760s and 1770s. Its basic assumptions and outlines were to remain stable throughout this period with the largest variable being the acceptance of the necessity to separate from Great Britain. The Reverend Samuel Cooke, preaching before Governor Thomas Hutchinson in May 1770, sketched the profile of the debate for the decade between the Treaty of Paris in 1763 and the Continental Congress of 1774. The ends of civil government, as revealed in Scripture and consistent with the laws of nature and reason, Cooke contended, are ordained by God to achieve His providence. Though the particular form of government is left to the determination of mankind, rulers are bound by fixed authority and are accountable to the people in whose interests they rule. As all persons have certain inalienable and God-given rights to life, liberty, and property, so the design of government is to protect these rights and thereby preserve the public good. Yet the king and Parliament had dishonored their solemn charges by abusing their duty and denying these rights rather than protecting them. Consequently, while the particular grievances would change in response to parliamentary policy, Cooke pointed to the generally arbitrary, and therefore unconstitutional, rule by Parliament. Specifically, he pointed to the favoritism shown in appointments and also to the quartering of British troops—"in the field of battle our glory and defense . . . [but] in time of peace a very improper safeguard to a constitution which has liberty, British liberty, for its basis."[15]

In this way, the clergy took up the secular political discussion and accommodated it into the religious categories so familiar to their people. Thus, as Perry Miller argued, they effectively spread the discussion and acceptance of these ideas in a way which a purely rationalistic presentation could not have achieved. No less important though was the prescription given by the clergy to remedy these political afflictions. Whether in 1766 or 1774, the clergy consistently chastised their people for their impiety and corrupt lives and claimed, therefore, that this affliction was a trial sent by God. "Is not this people strangely degenerated, so as to possess but a faint resemblence of that godliness for which their forefathers were eminent?" asked the Reverend William Gordon. Yet if the people were leading impious lives, they need only remember the favors shown to them by God in the years past, and they need only join piety to fortitude, thereby reforming their lives, in order to beseech the Lord and ask his strength. This was the mixture of humility and exertion that provided the dynamic for the clergy's influence. For by making comprehensible the source of the affliction, the clergy fueled the colonists' resolve to resist, steeled their courage to struggle, and fortified their hopes for the future.[16]

Here again, posing the issues in familiar theological categories promoted their understanding and reception. Beyond that, this summons to action was further reinforced by the legacy of the Great Awakening of the 1740s, that religious wildfire which had called the colonists to a new reformed life. The Awakening had produced an introspective investigation into the moral and intellectual life of the colonies on a scale unprecedented in past colonial experience. Moreover, the implications of this plea for spiritual regeneration extended into other sectors of colonial society as well. Thus, while this burst of evangelical pietism was responsible for schisms within the structure of colonial religion, its appeal was nevertheless so widespread that it erased many older divisions and in some specific ways foreshadowed the rising republican nationalism of later years.[17]

This was the context in which the clergy tempered an anxious humility with the energies of righteousness and devotion. And it is within this context that we should now deal with the clergy's role as supporters and organizers of various strategies in the colonial resistance campaign. Scholars have assigned various motives to the clergy's participation on the patriot side of the Revolution. Whatever those motives may have been, it is clear that the patriot clergy included most Congregationalists and Presbyterians, while Lutherans and Roman Catholics were divided, and Anglicans were staunch Loyalists.

Resistance to threats against liberty should not be thought of as a desire for political independence, at least not until the years 1774–75 with the establishment of the continental congresses. In any case, clerical opposition to the Stamp Act—Jonathan Mayhew, his successor, Andrew Eliot, and Charles Chauncy all preached in favor of its repeal—emphasized the colonists' loyalty to the Crown. Yet they argued that the constitutional compact was the foundation of the state. Thus, the violation of the constitution justified resistance, a resistance which they proudly noted was firm and forthright. The same case was made not only in Boston, where Mayhew and Chauncy presided, but in the Massachusetts countryside as well. Reverends Joseph Emerson of Pepperell, Ebenezer Parkman of Westboro, and Jonas Clark of Lexington all took the occasion to sound the threat to liberty, praise the Lord for his mercies, and compliment their people on the judicious and spirited defense of their rights.[18]

Testimony on the effectiveness of the clergy in these campaigns can be derived from many sources. Peter Oliver, a Massachusetts judge who went into exile in the late 1770s, claimed that James Otis and the clergy had so agitated the people that "it was in vain to struggle against the Law of Otis, and the Gospel of his Black Regiment." Further assessments of the nature and intensity of the colonial resistance are provided by other observers. The commissary of South Carolina, Charles Martyn, writing to the Bishop of London, noted: "The Principles of most of the Colonists in America are independent in Matters of Religion, as well as republican in those of Government. . . . I can venture that it would be as unsafe for an American Bishop (if such be appointed) to come hither, as it is at present for a Distributor of Stamps." This perception was shared by the author of an article in an English newspaper who concluded that "the Stamping and Episcopizing of our Colonies were understood to be only different Branches of the same Plan of Power." And if the stamp and episcopacy issues appeared intertwined, this was due as much to agitation by patriot clerics as it was to the close relationship between Loyalists and the Anglican clergy.[19]

Certainly one of the most significant aspects of the resistance campaigns around the Stamp Act, Townshend Acts, and Continental Congress and Associations was the program of nonimportation and nonconsumption of British goods. These campaigns, dating from 1765 through 1774, are detailed elsewhere. However, their adoption is in part due to efforts of the clergy. In 1769, for example, the students and president of the Baptist Rhode Island College (later to become Brown University) appeared at that year's commencement dressed in American homespun in support of the nonimportation campaigns.[20] Again in 1769, the Reverend Samuel Cooper wrote to Thomas Pownall, living in London, to assess the current status of the resistance to the Townshend Acts and hinted at the significance of the struggle. "Manufactures continually increase among us," Cooper noted; "we are ambitious of being clad in our own Produce. . . . this is indeed an unnatural state—But we have been drove to it; and if the Pressure continues the state will become natural by Habit, and the Tree will break before it is made straight again." Writing again to Pownall in late 1770, the Reverend Cooper reported that the boycott had dissolved, "but its effect may long remain. The true spirit of it has been a good deal diffused thro the Country and there it. . . . flourishes."[21] Cooper and others of his clerical colleagues were in a good position to assess the dimensions of this spirit, especially as they played a significant role in its development and maintenance. Numerous accounts tell of competitions between different churches and towns to produce the greatest quantity of home manufactures. Often spinning "bees" and other church social occasions were directed to the patriot cause.[22] Peter Oliver again verified the effectiveness of the clergy when he bemoaned:

> Mr. Otis' black regiment, the clergy, were set to Work, to preach up Manufactures instead of Gospel—they preached about it & about it, until the Women and Children, both within doors and without, set their Spinning Wheels a whirling in Defiance of Great Britain. The female spinners kept on spinning for 6 days of the Week, and on the seventh, the Parsons took their Turns, and spun out their Prayers and Sermons to a long thread of Politicks.[23]

In this way, the clergy spread the ideas and the practices of nonimportation through their church life as well as their sermons. An additional focus in the clerical role became evident by the year 1774. Paralleling the growing political pressure on the colonies and the resultant radicalism of the colonists, the clergy was actively involved in the campaigns of political noncooperation that were combined with the economic resistance. In 1774, the Boston Port Act was passed. Governor Thomas Gage was asked to appoint a day of fasting and prayer, but he refused, claiming, "the request was only to give an opportunity for sedition to flow from the pulpit." The response by the Massachusetts ministerial association was twofold. First, they refused to read any proclamations in their churches from either the governor or his council, and they then designated 14 July to be observed as a day of prayer and fasting, since Gage would not do so. A similar pattern was followed by ministerial associations in New Hampshire, Connecticut, Rhode Island, and Virginia.[24]

In September 1774, the first Continental Congress met in Philadelphia. Clergymen attended as delegates and participated as counsellors and petitioners. Involved throughout in the deliberations, they went on as a group to give wholehearted support to the different resolves produced by these meetings. In addition, as this and other congresses requested that particular days be observed for purposes of fasting and prayer, the clergy again complied. As they had on numerous occasions in the past decades, the clergy spelled out the nature of the current threat and called their listeners to a spirited activism. In these ways, the years 1774–76 show the stiffening of colonial resistance in a deeper and more significant political fashion. On their own or at the suggestion of colonial assemblies, the clergy continued to support overt resistance and directly participated in numerous acts of noncooperation.[25] Consequently, though a small group, the clergy's participation in organizing resistance campaigns and drafting resolutions provided an additional source of leadership for the patriots in these critical years.

A successful political struggle is a combination of a wide variety of factors. Obviously, in the American case, the success of the various resistance campaigns was of prime importance. However, support which cannot be consolidated and organized amounts to little. The clergy played a significant role in the development of intercolonial organizations, organizations whose consequence was to bind the colonies closer together and thereby coordinate the effectiveness of this resistance. As previously noted, local and regional ministerial associations had a long history in the colonies. By the 1750s and 1760s, these organizations had assumed a regular and on-going role. Paralleling the later committees of correspondence, these ministerial associations were utilized to spread information (especially information relating to the episcopacy issue) and generally served to raise the consciousness of the people by drawing attention to grievances and enlisting support and participation on behalf of resistance. This level of organization did not go unnoticed by the Anglicans. In 1763, the Reverend Henry Caner, bemoaning the comparable lack of coordination on the part of the Anglican clergy, wrote to his Archbishop: "We are a Rope of Sand; there is no union [among us] . . . while the Dissenting Ministers have their Monthly, Quarterly, and Annual Associations, Conventions, etc., to advise, assist, and support each other in any Measures which they think proper to enter into."[26]

Though suggestions of intercolonial union had been heard in religious circles since the 1740s, a significant first step was taken in 1758 with the combination of the New York and Philadelphia Synods of the Presbyterian Church. This regional association represented over ten thousand churches in the middle colonies, Maryland, and Virginia. It was in this context, then, that the redoubtable Jonathan Mayhew wrote to James Otis in June 1766. Heartened by the recent resistance to the Stamp Act and its subsequent repeal, Mayhew wrote:

> Cultivating a good understanding and hearty friendship between these colonies, appears to me so necessary a part of prudence and good policy, that no favorable opportunity for that purpose should be omitted. I think such an one now presents. . . . It is not safe for the colonies to sleep; for it is probable they will always have some wakeful enemies in Great Britain. . . . You have heard of the communion of churches; and I am set out tomorrow morning for Rutland, to assist at an ecclesiastical council . . . while I was thinking of this . . . the great use and importance of a communion of colonies appeared to me in a strong light.[27]

Mayhew, soon to die, would never learn of the prophecy of his intuition, but in October 1766, the Reverend Ezra Stiles drew up some "Articles of Union," and in the following month, some thirty representatives from Presbyterian and Congregational churches met in New Jersey. At the next annual meeting in September 1767, more churches participated, and by 1768, this union was accomplished.[28]

Reflecting the slower tempo of political developments, organizational activity in the southern colonies proceeded in a more gradual manner. One of the more interesting facets of southern religious life during this period was the political split occurring between the clergy and laity. While the Anglican and Methodist missionary clergy were staunchly Loyalist, their parishioners were overwhelmingly sympathetic to the patriot cause. Thus, when the possibility of an Anglican bishop threatened to destroy their atypical congregational autonomy, the Anglican laity in the South quickly joined the hue and cry in defense of religious liberty.[29]

Consequently, by the late 1760s the first effective intercolonial union had been established among the clergy. It was a union which sketched out the dimensions of later political unions as well as contributing significant lessons and organizational tactics. As in the middle years of the episcopal crisis, intercolonial organization was complemented by transatlantic coordination. The significance of this transatlantic relationship lies in the long-range attempt by the colonists not only to keep abreast of political developments in England but to work to arouse dissent in their opponent's homeland as well. The purpose of this bond between Nonconformists in Britain and Dissenters in America remained fairly uniform—to alert the Americans to threats to their liberty, to act as informal lobbyists, and at least to keep an American viewpoint accessible to the Parliament through the few modes of influence open to the Nonconformists. The long-range political significance of this attempt, however, is hard to assess, for the Nonconformists still suffered under various religious strictures which limited their political influence. In addition, the active concern for the Americans was largely the special interest of men such as Thomas Hollis, and when they died or retired, there was no one to fill the gap. Thus, while Charles Chauncy could write in 1768 of twenty years of correspondence with the Nonconformists in London, it was a relationship which rested more on past accomplishments than on present struggles and held more in potential than it realized in on-going practice. This, then, is not the place to render a final judgement as to the efficacy of this tactic, but only to note that the attempt did exist and persist, and in the specific case of the episcopal issue, was of real significance.[30]

Writing in 1815, John Adams complimented the clergy for its part in the resistance against England. He agreed that the issue of an Anglican bishop had gone a long way towards awakening the colonists to the threat to their liberty and that men such as Jonathan Mayhew had exerted a salubrious influence. Yet to leave the assessment of the clergy figuring solely on the episcopacy issue shortchanges the accounting. Religion did not cause the movement for American independence, but it may have, as John Adams implied, predisposed the colonists to perceive the British policy as a threat first to religious liberty and then to civil liberty as well. Resistance was specified and orderly, the response to iniquity and sin. Thus, revolution and independence were always more than mere political changeovers; they were moral categories, fundamentally enacted as remedies for moral decay.[31]

In summary, then, the participation of the clergy figures in any judgement of the American independence movement. As ideological stimulants, they helped to unleash the energies of the colonists and direct them into the campaigns of nonviolent action. By providing intercolonial organization, these religious leaders significantly contributed to the realization of America's political independence, and by developing transatlantic communication and influence, they engaged one of the oldest means of nonviolent persuasion. As prophets or merely as partners, the clergy were of undeniable benefit and assistance in the achievement of the patriot cause.

• NOTES •

1. John Adams to Hezekiah Niles, 13 February 1818, Charles Francis Adams, ed., *The Works of John Adams* (10 vols., Boston: Little, Brown, 1850–56), vol. 10, pp. 282–84.

2. Jonathan Mayhew, "A Discourse Concerning Unlimited Submission and Non-Resistance to the Higher Powers," in John Thornton, ed., *The Pulpit of the American Revolution* (Boston: Gould & Lincoln, 1860), p. 53.

3. *Ibid.,* pp. 101–2, 50.

4. See the discussion in Frederick Mills, Sr., *Bishops by Ballot* (New York: Oxford Univ. Press, 1978), pp. 25–61.

5. See the discussion in Carl Bridenbaugh, *Mitre and Sceptre* (New York: Oxford Univ. Press, 1962), pp. 86–90, 98–100.

6. Mayhew, "A Discourse . . . " pp. 101–2.

7. The quotation is by Alice Baldwin, *The New England Clergy and the American Revolution* (Durham: Duke Univ. Press, 1928), p. 82. In addition to Baldwin's study, see Bernard Bailyn, *The Ideological Origins of the American Revolution* (Cambridge, Mass.: Harvard Univ. Press, 1967) and Gordon S. Wood, *The Creation of the American Republic* (Chapel Hill: Univ. of North Carolina Press, 1969) for a general discussion of this point.

8. Perry Miller, "From the Covenant to the Revival," in *The Shaping of American Religion,* in James Smith and A. Leland Jamison, eds., *Religion in American Life* (Princeton: Princeton Univ. Press, 1961), vol. 1, pp. 322–68.

9. See Baldwin, *New England Clergy,* pp. 4–7, 95–97, 100–101, 124 n. 11.

10. See the discussion in Charles Briggs, *American Presbyterianism* (New York: Scribners, 1885), pp. 132–33; Leonard Trinterud, *The Formation of an American Tradition: A Re-examination of Colonial Presbyterianism* (Philadelphia: Westminister Press, 1949), p. 29.

11. Quoted in Bridenbaugh, *Mitre and Sceptre,* p. 97.

12. Reverend Issac Backus, quoted in William G. McLoughlin, *New England Dissent,* (Cambridge, Mass.: Harvard Univ. Press, 1971), vol. 1, p. 551. See the discussion of the interaction of Nonconformists and Dissenters in Caroline Robbins, *The Eighteenth Century Commonwealthmen* (Cambridge, Mass.: Harvard Univ. Press, 1959), p. 225.

13. Mayhew, quoted in Baldwin, *New England Clergy,* pp. 87–88.

14. Bridenbaugh, *Mitre and Sceptre,* p. 230.

15. Reverend Samuel Cooke, "Sermon preached . . . in the Audience of Thomas Hutchinson," in Thornton, ed., *Pulpit of the American Revolution,* pp. 157–73.

16. Reverend William Gordon, "A Discourse preached December 15, 1774 . . . " in *ibid.,* p. 207.

17. See the discussion in Alan Heimert, *Religion and the American Mind* (Cambridge, Mass.: Harvard Univ. Press, 1966); William G. McLoughlin, "'Enthusiasm for Liberty': the Great Awakening as the Key to the Revolution," *Proceedings of the American Antiquarian Society,* vol. 87, pt. 1, (1977), pp. 69–95.

18. Baldwin, *New England Clergy,* pp. 90–94.

19. Peter Oliver, *Origin and Progress of the American Rebellion,* Douglass Adair and

John Schutz, eds., (Stanford: Stanford Univ. Press, 1961), p. 53; Charles Martyn is quoted in Bridenbaugh, *Mitre and Sceptre,* p. 249. The anonymous Englishman's remark first appeared in *St. James Chronicle,* 14 June 1766 and is quoted in Fred Hinkhouse, *The Preliminaries of the American Revolution as Seen in the English Press, 1763–1775* (New York: Columbia Univ. Press, 1926), p. 134.

20. In June 1775, the senior class at this time Rhode Island College requested that commencement exercises be omitted. In reply, the president of the school, the Reverend James Manning, noted, "it gives us no small satisfaction that the present members of this Institution, and particularly the respectable Senior class, are so sensibly affected with the distresses of our country in its present glorious struggle for liberty. . . . Be assured that we shall most heartily concur in this, and every other measure which has been or may be, adopted by the grand American Congress as well as the Legislature of this Colony" (for a discussion of the cases in both 1769 and 1775, see Reuben A. Guild, *Early History of Brown University Including the Life, Times, and Correspondence of President Manning, 1756–1791* [Providence: Snow & Farnum, 1897], pp. 82–87, 286–87).

21. Samuel Cooper to Thomas Pownall, 11 May 1769, in *American Historical Review* 8 (1903), p. 308; Samuel Cooper to Thomas Pownall, 12 October 1770, in *ibid.,* p. 322.

22. See the Appendices in this volume for examples of newspaper accounts of such competitions.

23. Peter Oliver, *Origin and Progress of the American Rebellion,* Adair and Schutz, eds., pp. 63–64.

24. Thomas Gage, quoted by C. H. Van Tyne, "The Influence of the Clergy, and of Religion and Sectarian Forces on the American Revolution," *American Historical Review* 19 (1913), p. 55. For another discussion see W. O. Love, *The Fast and Thanksgiving Days of New England* (Boston: Houghton, Mifflin, 1895), p. 334–35.

25. See Baldwin, *New England Clergy,* pp. 123–26.

26. Reverend Caner's remark is quoted in Bridenbaugh, *Mitre and Sceptre,* p. 184.

27. Jonathan Mayhew to James Otis, 8 June 1766, quoted in Thornton, *The Pulpit of the American Revolution,* pp. 44–45.

28. See Bridenbaugh, *Mitre and Sceptre,* pp. 273–78.

29. See *ibid.,* pp. 321–23; *idem., Myths and Realities: Societies of the Colonial South* (New York: Atheneum, 1962), pp. 30–34, 182–85; Rhys Issac, "Religion and Authority: Problems of the Anglican Establishment in Virginia in the Era of the Great Awakening and the Parson's Cause," *William and Mary Quarterly,* 3d ser., vol. 30, no. 1 (January 1973), pp. 3–37.

30. For a more general discussion of this point, see the chapters by Professors Langford and Bonwick in this volume.

31. John Adams to Jedediah Morse, 2 December 1815, Adams ed., *Works of Adams,* vol. 10, p. 185. For a general discussion of this point see Edmund Morgan, "The Puritan Ethic and the American Revolution," *William and Mary Quarterly,* 3d ser., vol. 24, no. 1, (January 1967), pp. 3–43; Rhys Issac, "Preachers and Patriots: Popular Culture and the Revolution in Virginia," in Alfred Young, ed., *The American Revolution* (Dekalb: Northern Illinois Univ. Press, 1976), pp. 125–56.

·11·

English Radicals and American Resistance to British Authority

C. C. BONWICK

American patriots enjoyed much sympathy from English radicals during the years before the war.[1] While most Englishmen were hostile, this small group of men and women offered warm understanding for the colonists in their resistance to the thrust of British policy in the last years of union and steady support for their cause during the unhappy years of war. The radicals were not merely passive observers. As the crisis in imperial relations worsened, they assumed an increasingly active responsibility for promoting the American case in the forum of public affairs. In so doing, they acted partly out of concern for the domestic well-being of the colonists but also from a belief that there were broader issues at stake; a simultaneous crisis in English politics, mainly revolving round the person of John Wilkes, suggested that liberty was in danger on both shores of the Atlantic. Under such circumstances, radicals believed it was vital that America should be preserved as a sanctuary for the protection of freedom and a haven for the victims of oppression.

English radicals' understanding of the crisis, and the colonists' part in it, was largely determined by the dictates of three premises. Overarching the other two was a theological cosmology which had specific as well as universal application and imposed its system of ethics on the resolution of political problems. Within this framework, their intellect was mainly formed by the postulates of the commonwealth tradition as formulated during the struggles of the previous century.[2] And third, the radicals were totally persuaded of the desirability and legitimacy of maintaining the imperial connection—providing, of course, that it operated on acceptable terms. Beyond these premises, other factors came into play. In particular, radicals' appreciation of the American position was further influenced by the remarkably close association many of them enjoyed with individual colonists; this suggested that the questions in dispute were not abstract but concrete.

If their American friendships inclined radicals to one side rather than the other, both the British government and the American colonists were nevertheless

required to conduct themselves within the terms of their primary criteria and conform to two principles. For its part, the British government was expected to meet
the colonists' right to genuinely representative government. For theirs, the patriots
were obliged to formulate the tactics of their resistance within the constraints of
ethically permissible action. In the first instance, the colonists were expected to
attempt the negotiation of a political solution to their complaints. Only after all
nonviolent means had been fruitlessly exhausted were they entitled to resort to
armed resistance. But though the prime justification for such imperatives was
moral, there were also strong prudential considerations which reinforced it. Improper behavior by the British government, the radicals correctly predicted, would
ultimately destroy the empire; unethical conduct by the Americans would destroy
the very liberty they were seeking to preserve. In general, the patriots did little to
betray the confidence placed in them. English radicals were highly impressed by
the manner in which the colonists attempted to resolve their dispute with the
mother country by peaceful means, but of all the methods devised to thwart the
intentions of British policy, the radicals responded most favorably to those which
were based on argument and negotiation.

Contrary to a widely held view, English radicals active during the American
Revolution were more than an eccentric group of obscure and pedantic theoreti-
cians. Several were distinguished figures in the intellectual life of the nation, and
some were prominent members of their local community. Most were members of
the three Dissenting congregations of Presbyterians, Congregationalists, and Baptists, but some belonged to the established Church and a handful were Quakers.
All were members of the broader political nation which existed outside the walls
of Parliament and Whitehall and to whose opinions shrewd politicians paid careful
respect. Several were landed gentry, and others were members of an urban middle
class. Many enjoyed the freedom of action made possible by a private income or
the financial support of friends or relatives; those who were compelled to earn their
living did so in one of the professions. Most were in Nonconformist Holy Orders,
but one or two were in commerce. Though they were overwhelmingly middle
class, many of the leading radicals were socially very well-connected and had
close connections with prominent politicians on both sides of Parliament. Among
the most important were the Quaker physician John Fothergill; the Dissenting
ministers Richard Price and Joseph Priestly; two Nonconformist laymen, Thomas
Hollis and James Burgh; Catharine Macaulay and Granville Sharp, both faithful
Anglicans; John Jebb and Theophilus Lindsey, Unitarians who left the Church
shortly before the Revolution; and Major John Cartwright, who was embarking on
a long career in reform politics, which lasted well into the following century.[3]

Intellectually, the radicals stood in the "commonwealth," or "real whig," tradition which flowed from the seventeenth century and had as its model the "ancient," or "Anglo-Saxon," constitution.[4] As a corpus of ideas, their philosophy
can be best considered as an ideology rather than an integrated political system. Its
adherents began with a concept of the universe within which Divine Providence
played a crucial, if imprecise, role in the affairs of mankind and agreed that

theological axioms were the ultimate values by which to judge public as well as private behavior. It followed that their efforts were directed towards the construction of a virtuous society, but beyond that, their views often diverged from one another. There was no single body of radical orthodoxy to which all were required to subscribe; instead, radicals shared a number of general principles but disagreed as to their relative importance and the manner of their application. In particular, men like Sharp, to whom the seventeenth-century origins were repugnant, can be incorporated into the group since they accepted its major tenets and cooperated with those who were more orthodox in subsidiary matters. Real whig political understanding was based on two intertwined foundations: the theory of natural rights and political contract as the only authority for legitimate government. It also acknowledged that theoretical postulates had to be validated by empirical evidence wherever possible. A search through the historical record of the past, and especially the evidence of classical Greece and Rome and the putative Anglo-Saxon constitution, suggested that philosophical imperatives and pragmatic requirements were often conjoined. Decay of moral virtue led to political decline, and the dynamics of human society demanded a relationship of voluntary contract between a people and their government. Such considerations could be applied in many situations throughout the world. They had especial relevance to the need for parliamentary reform in England and the relationship between Britain and her American colonies overseas.

Sentiment, emotional attachment, and a particular understanding of colonial society also contributed to radical interpretations of the dispute with America. Those who were ministers had long and close connections with their fellow sectarians in the colonies; much of their correspondence was concerned with theological and scientific matters, but as time passed, it increasingly incorporated political discussion. Thomas Hollis enjoyed a long correspondence with Jonathan Mayhew and, later, Andrew Eliot (both of Boston); Price corresponded with Charles Chauncy, Joseph Willard, Ezra Stiles, and many others; and Sharp corresponded with Benjamin Rush of Philadelphia until long after the war. Yet more important was friendship with colonists who visited England. Many Americans who lived in prewar London also associated with radicals: Arthur and William Lee of Virginia, Henry Marchant of Rhode Island, and Stephen Sayre of New York, to name only a few. All were concerned to promote the colonial interest, but one man stood out. Benjamin Franklin had a wide circle of friends, including Price, Priestley, Burgh, and Lindsey. To them, he was no impertinent colonial to be put firmly in his place by an insulting English minister; he was a brilliant scientist with a mature and subtle mind and a man to be treated on terms of complete equality. Such associations as these projected a distinctive image of American society. They also gave radicals private access to colonial argumentation and an opportunity to discuss imperial problems with active and articulate advocates of the American cause.

Knowledge of American society drawn from these sources suggested that it was culturally sophisticated and politically liberal. Priestley went to the heart of the matter when he declared that the colonists, especially in New England, were "chiefly Dissenters and Whigs."[5] Thus, the Americans were believed to be the transatlantic counterpart of what they regarded as the most desirable elements in English society. Above all, English radicals appreciated that the colonists held certain fundamental ideals and political principles in common with themselves—a feature of the Anglo-American community which Hollis and his family had sedulously cultivated for several generations. Man's natural right to liberty was accepted as enthusiastically in America as in England and the device of representative government respected as much among patriots as with commonwealthmen. Radicals were also impressed by the relative equality of colonial society; aristocratic as the Lee brothers may have been in their native Virginia, they were inescapably middle class in English terms. This assessment of the nature of American society had profound and wide-ranging implications. Radicals assumed that the patriots represented the will of the people and concluded that the Anglo-American relationship was much more equal than orthodox English opinion would allow.

A deep conviction of cultural and ideological community encouraged radicals to wish for maintenance of the imperial association. Their policy was predicated on the proposition that "national strength, security, and felicity . . . depend on UNION and on LIBERTY."[6] Both partners would derive reciprocal benefits: each would enjoy commercial prosperity, both would enjoy the liberty which was so rare in other countries, and continuing union would maintain the strategic supremacy on the North Atlantic which had been a notable consequence of the Seven Years' War. But if these desirable and substantial benefits were to be secured, the imperial constitution was required to be consistent with the principles of commonwealth ideology, and its operation was expected to be compatible with the actual distribution of power between Britain and the colonies. Articulation of these propositions into practice posed acute difficulties, both in theory and execution, but it was an exercise the radicals were eager to embark upon and one which they sustained until long after the union had been irreparably broken.

Central to the legitimate functioning of the empire was the requirement that it should depend on the voluntary consent of its members. This obligation to defer to a contractual relationship was partly justified on philosophical grounds. Price insisted that: "In general to be *free* is to be guided by one's own will; and to be guided by the will of another is the characteristic of *Servitude*. This is particularly applicable to Political Liberty.'"[7] The consent of a people was the proper origin of all civil government and was expressed through the medium of a mutual contract between the citizens and their government. In all but the smallest city-states, the compact demanded establishment of a representational system through which the will of the inhabitants could be discovered; in particular, taxation without due representative authority was illegal. Within the framework of the empire, radicals considered the function of colonial assemblies to be crucial; only through them could the obligation to secure the consent of the inhabitants to local government be discharged. The doctrine of virtual representation, advanced in England by Soame Jenyns and rejected in America by Daniel Dulany, was seen by commonwealthmen to be nonsensical when applied to a transatlantic empire. Arguments that each member of

Parliament virtually represented the entire nation, including towns such as Manchester and Birmingham that elected no member of Parliament of their own, because of a presumed community of interest, were unsatisfactory when applied to Britain; they were grotesque when extended to thirteen colonies across the ocean.

Prudential considerations massively strengthened the need to obtain consent. Parliament's insistence in the Declaratory Act of 1766 that it possessed an absolute right to legislate for the colonies "in all cases whatsoever" did not accord with the realities of the situation. Actual (as distinct from legal) power was divided between Westminster and the several colonies. Many governors discovered to their cost that colonial legislatures had over the years devised a number of very effective weapons for circumscribing their nominal power; others came to terms with reality and acknowledged that whether they liked it or not they lacked the ability to impose their authority on a reluctant population. Difficulties of enforcement within each colony were compounded at the higher level of imperial direction. As events were to prove with startling clarity, Britain would be unable to draw the full economic benefits of empire and command American assistance in the struggle with France without the willing cooperation of the colonists. Radicals appreciated these realities and constantly argued the point in public debate; as John Cartwright put it: "By adhering strictly to the principles of justice and the rights of mankind, we may firmly unite and cement together our own interests with those of our sister nations in America, and remain ourselves to the end of time, a powerful and independent state."[8]

Implicit in the theory of contractual government was a right of resistance. If an administration seemed intent on perverting its grant of power, its citizens possessed a residual power to cashier their officers, terminate the compact, and form a new government. Radicals looked back to one notable instance, the Glorious Revolution of 1688, and believed that the right was inherent in the colonies as well as in England. But the occasion and forms of resistance were also of considerable importance. A virtuous society was obliged to conduct its political affairs in a proper manner, and the right of resistance was not unqualified; it was expected to match its responses to the intensity of the provocation and was only permitted to employ violence and rebellion as weapons of last resort.

These general propositions could be readily applied to the American crisis. English radicals were convinced that Anglo-American disputes were soluble within the context of commonwealth ideology and the empire (providing the colonists conformed to their criteria of conduct), and they held firm to their belief until the course of war made separation between Britain and the United States inevitable. Though they acknowledged that the colonists were compelled to intensify their reaction to an apparently systematic challenge to their liberties, they scarcely considered the possibility of military resistance until late 1774 and constantly encouraged and assisted their American friends to use suitably limited methods. In part, their reasons were ethical, but they were also pragmatic in that they believed negotiation and political pressure could be successful—as they were during the campaign to prevent the appointment of a bishop to the colonies in the sixties.

From the time of the Stamp Act crisis onwards, the Americans developed numerous techniques for resisting the onward rush of British power. They ranged from attempts to negotiate a settlement of particular issues to refusal to cooperate with British officials and, on the eve of war, the establishment of alternative institutions of government. Some were based on localized and specific violence, but many were more narrowly political by nature. Each instrument had a specific objective. Many were directed against centers of British power in the colonies, such as the royal governors and stamp tax collectors; others were aimed at Whitehall. In all cases, radicals asked, implicitly or explicitly, whether they were morally acceptable, appropriate to the situation, and likely to achieve their purpose.

In general, English radicals preferred propaganda and negotiation. Nonimportation as a weapon of political pressure had been most successful in securing repeal of the Stamp Act in 1766, but the English side of the battle had been conducted largely by merchants and colonial agents and was carefully orchestrated by parliamentary politicians of the Rockingham group. Few of those who later became prominent radicals, apart from the Quaker John Fothergill and John Almon the bookseller, took any active part. But nonimportation was a coercive instrument of only limited effectiveness. It could be employed against those susceptible to economic pressure (as were English merchants in 1765–66), but its impact would bc substantially diminished should the patterns of international trade change (as they soon did). In any case, radicals were not greatly impressed by it; Fothergill persistently argued for an Anglo-American conference and disapproved of Massachusetts' actions in 1768, and all radicals responded more readily to political argument and rational discussion. As intellectuals, they were firmly committed to rational analysis as the best means of resolving problems and were convinced that it ought to be applied as much to public affairs as to theological controversy. Their own participation in the crisis further encouraged their faith in the importance of argumentation.

As the years passed and the conflict worsened, radicals abandoned their stance as spectators. To the very considerable extent that the empire was a single community, all of whose members enjoyed common rights and privileges, they felt obliged to conduct themselves as participants. Their duty became steadily clearer in the mid-1770s. The Stamp Act affair could be initially dismissed as an aberration, but the cumulative implications of the Townshend duties, the posting of troops to New England, the Boston Massacre of 1770, the Tea Party three years later, and the Coercive Acts of 1774 suggested there was system and purpose behind the actions of successive administrations. Similarly, the fortuitous conjunctions of the Wilkite business and the Middlesex Election debate of 1768–69 encouraged them to believe that the crisis was not confined to the colonies but affected both branches of the empire.

Under such circumstances radicals considered that the Americans urgently needed their assistance. They gave it with increasing liberality until the recognition of independence made it redundant. Necessarily, the nature of their assistance was limited in extent. The need to deploy their aid in England circumscribed their choice of methods and effectively ruled out of consideration many forms of action which were eminently feasible in America. Likewise, since almost by definition they were neither major politicians enjoying prospects of office nor great merchants capable of applying economic pressure (though they had connections with the more liberal members of both groups), two weapons of proven effectiveness were denied to them. Instead, they could lobby members of Parliament and the ministry in the hope that those in a position to do so would apply pressure on the administration. Their attempts to modify official policy directly were largely dependent on such personal contacts as they had with ministers and Opposition leaders, and for that and other reasons were only intermittent, but their activities as propagandists in the national debate were more sustained.

In the eighteenth century, the prime medium of public persuasion was the pamphlet. Radicals agreed with Franklin's judgment that: "By the Press we can speak to Nations; and good Books & well written Pamphlets have great and general Influence."[9] The debate over the American Revolution bore out their contention. Hundreds of tracts were printed on both sides of the Atlantic during a twenty-year period, among them more than a thousand in England alone and about eighty which were initially published in America and later reprinted in London or were written by colonists resident in the metropolis. Radicals contributed a full share to the discussion.

Colonial tracts were invaluable to the radical participation in American resistance. Many were sent by colonists to their English friends, and some were then reprinted and distributed among other radicals and in places where it was hoped they would be influential. Thomas Hollis, Catharine Macaulay, and Richard Price regularly received pamphlets from America. Macaulay is said to have supplied the publishing firm of Edward and Charles Dilly with pamphlets for publication, and John Almon, who was constantly on the lookout for colonial material, printed several collections of American pamphlets. Without doubt though, Hollis contributed more than any other radical to the dissemination of colonial tracts. A retiring man, he refused to take the direct part in politics that his wealth would have permitted but nevertheless believed that the private citizen had a valuable part to perform in public affairs and assumed a self-imposed responsibility of distributing libertarian tracts in America and reprinting colonial tracts in England. Most of his earlier reprints were of tracts directed against the proposed appointment of a bishop to the colonies, but later, he turned to more explicitly political pamphlets such as the *Short Narrative of the Horrid Massacre in Boston*. His most famous publication consisted of a number of Massachusetts newspaper articles which he printed in *The True Sentiments of America* under the title "A Dissertation on the Canon and Feudal Law"; only later did he discover that their author was John Adams.

Several of the tracts had considerable influence. Colonists such as John Adams and James Otis made an English reputation through their agency. The frequency with which radicals cited American pamphlets as demonstrations of the colonial position and in support of their own arguments was in itself a vindication of the usefulness of patriot propaganda. Arthur Lee's tracts, written in London, were carefully composed in order to appeal to men who accepted the doctrine of the ancient constitution and were often quoted in radical pamphlets; others to whom the commonwealthmen referred were William Smith of Philadelphia and Daniel Dulany of Maryland. But of all colonial pamphlets, one enjoyed preeminence: John Dickinson's *Letters from a Farmer in Pennsylvania*. (See Appendix B.) Published in England by Franklin in 1768, it was rapidly acknowledged as the standard exposition of American arguments. As far as radicals were concerned, there was good reason for its high reputation. Though it emphasized the seriousness of the crisis and set out the limits of parliamentary authority as the colonists saw them, it was couched in moderate terms and was, as Sharp commented, "sensible and patriotic."[10]

Another means of action open to other radicals was to cooperate with the colonists in applying pressure on the Wilkite movement in London. Arthur Lee, who like Franklin, took an expansive view of his responsibilities as an American in England, systematically campaigned to inject the American issue into it. In careful concert with Samuel Adams in Massachusetts, he sought to establish a conjunction between the English and American causes in the propaganda of the Society of Supporters of the Bill of Rights (which had been founded to promote Wilkes's interests). Its members evidently responded favorably to Lee's persuasion. When, in 1771, the Society prepared a program to which parliamentary candidates were to be invited to subscribe, the American plank was incorporated at Lee's insistence. It urged that Parliament should restore to the colonists their right of self-taxation, repeal obnoxious legislation enacted since 1763, and abolish the notorious excise which was alleged to be incompatible with the principles of English liberty.[11] Later, Wilkes's supporters subscribed to funds for the relief of New England. Whether Wilkes himself genuinely supported the colonial cause or merely exploited it to his own personal advantage must remain an open question, though his constant protestations of sympathy were accepted by Americans who knew him in London as well as by those in the colonies who knew him only by reputation. And by way of demonstrating the success of the American campaign among City politicians, two Americans, William Lee and Stephen Sayre, were elected sheriffs in 1773.

Unfortunately, the hopes placed on this method were unfulfilled, and the crisis shortly took a new turn. Wilkes was a man of little influence in high places. In Parliament, the various opposition groups were divided and incapable of coordinating a sustained attack on the ministry, and the colonial agents were rapidly diminishing in effectiveness. This left the radicals briefly in a central position in English politics as a group willing to defend the American cause. Much impressed by American conduct, they were extremely active as the dispute reached its climax.

A crucial stage was reached with the Boston Tea Party of December 1773. As soon as they learned of the affair, both sides realized that a trial of strength was unavoidable. The British government immediately retaliated with a series of Coercive Acts in the following spring, and, in turn, the Americans summoned a Continental Congress for September. News received by radicals later the same year was far from encouraging. Correspondents such as Charles Chauncy and Benjamin Rush warned their English friends that the limits of colonial tolerance were being reached. They also warned of the possibility of armed resistance; as Rush informed Sharp: "We talk with less horror than formerly of a civil war."[12] Among commonwealthmen, the suspicion grew that liberty was in danger on both sides of the Atlantic, that the government was far advanced in a sustained conspiracy, and that despotism once established in America would rapidly spread to Britain. An emissary from Massachusetts confirmed the seriousness of the situation in the winter of 1774–75. Josiah Quincy, Jr., arrived in November 1774 on a mission to persuade the administration of the justice and propriety of the colonial position. He had several long conversations with the Earl of Dartmouth, the American secretary, and Lord North himself, but to no effect. He also carried introductions to the radicals and had many long discussions with them; Theophilus Lindsey reported of a dinner with Quincy, Franklin, Price, Priestley, and other radicals in January 1775: "We began and ended with the Americans."[13]

By the spring of 1775, radicals believed that the Americans had exhausted all peaceful means of resolving the crisis. Since they were much concerned with public morality, they had always attached great importance to the manner in which the colonists had responded to the unfolding of British policy. With few exceptions, they had consistently approved of colonial tactics since the crisis had first erupted—on pragmatic grounds, as being most likely to be fruitful, as well as on ethical grounds. Most had applauded the manner in which the Townshend duties were opposed. They were especially impressed by the Bostonians' reaction to the Massacre of 1770, which demonstrated a "rare and admirable instance of patriotic resentment tempered with forbearance and the warmth of Courage with coolness of Discretion."[14] Later, the radicals warmly approved of the Continental Congress, which they regarded as a model of representative behavior when compared with the corruption and manipulation of Parliament. As time passed, the contrast between the behavior of the English and the Americans became increasingly painful. Price declared:

> In this hour of tremendous danger, it becomes us to turn our thoughts to Heaven. This is what our brethren in the Colonies are doing. From one end of North America to the other, they are fasting and praying. But what are we doing? Shocking thought! We are ridiculing them as Fanatic and scoffing at religion. We are running wild after pleasure, and forgetting everything serious and decent at Masquerades. We are gambling in gaming houses; trafficking for Boroughs; perjuring ourselves at Elections; and selling ourselves for places.[15]

Only one course of action remained open. Radicals did nothing to encourage military resistance but, as always, required it to conform to their two prime criteria: was the use of military force morally acceptable under the circumstances, and was it pragmatically necessary in order to achieve its declared objective? In the past, radicals had been critical of the use of violence. James Burgh regarded the Boston Tea Party as inexcusable, though he conceded that British actions had been provocative. John Cartwright disapproved the practice of tarring and feathering, and John Jebb hoped, as late as December 1774, that the colonists would be able to avoid bloodshed.[16] But now circumstances had changed, and they accepted that the Americans would have to stand firm as the only alternative to passive submission to an apparently arbitrary government. Even the Quaker Fothergill, who continued his efforts to achieve a reconciliation by acting as a mediator with his patient, Lord Dartmouth, advised Friends in America to submit to the "prevailing will" in the colonies. Although he did not explicitly approve the use of force, it can be assumed that he understood the implications of his advice; certainly his protégé and fellow Quaker John Coakley Lettsom applauded "the noble action of Concord."[17]

In spite of their admiration for American courage, the descent into warfare was a bitter disappointment. They had always understood the British Empire to be a community which offered benefits to all its members and whose strength was dependent on the consent of its citizens. Moreover, their acceptance of the patriots' claim to represent the true will of the American people strengthened rather than weakened their conviction that negotiation was the best and most proper means of resolving disagreements.

Acting on this belief, they continued to argue the case for imperial reformation in a series of pamphlets which had begun with Cartwright's *American Independence the Interest and Glory of Great Britain* in 1774 and came to a climax with the publication of Richard Price's *Civil Liberty* in February 1776. Their campaign was successful in stimulating a more extensive public debate, though popular opinion remained obstinately behind government policies for several years to come. And while radicals accepted the change in terms of the struggle in America, they continued their efforts to promote reconciliatory policies in Britain until long after the Declaration of Independence announced the Americans' intention to sever the British connection permanently. Pamphlets intended to influence public opinion were matched by private efforts to exploit their connections in high places. In this respect, Price and Priestley suffered from the circumstance that their friend and patron the Earl of Shelburne was a member of the smaller of the two opposition groups in Parliament, but others were somewhat more fortunate. Sharp used his social connections to apply direct persuasion on Lord Dartmouth and, if possible, on other members of the government. David Hartley, one of the few radical members of Parliament, constantly argued for reconciliation on the floor of the House of Commons and on one occasion made an ill-advised journey to Paris to negotiate with Franklin and Adams. Such efforts were fruitless. Without doubt, the outbreak of war had made their task of simultaneously promoting union and liberty immeasurably more difficult—and in retrospect, perhaps impossible. At the same time, however, it must be acknowledged that their previous efforts at achieving a peaceful solution had been equally unsuccessful. Herein lay profound irony, for their insistence on the pragmatic necessity of securing the consent of the American people to the operations of the British Empire was vindicated by the course of events. Lord North's attempt to assert British authority by coercion proved counterproductive; far from strengthening the empire, his deployment of force brought about its collapse.

In the taxonomy of political action, English radicals consistently placed the greatest emphasis on instruments of persuasion, argument, and negotiation. They insisted that colonial responses should be appropriate to the provocation offered by the British government rather than outstrip it; on the evidence of their condemnation of the violence inherent in tarring and feathering and the Boston Tea Party, it is reasonable to speculate that they would have withdrawn their support had the Americans moved more precipitously to armed resistance. Perhaps surprisingly, they were largely indifferent to specific actions such as the closing of royal courts during the crucial months before Lexington, though they were certainly aware of them through the letters of their American correspondents and were profoundly moved by the colonists' refusal to submit passively to British power. Nonimportation agreements were occasionally cited as suitable models of action by critics of the war, and the terms "committee of correspondence" and (more rarely) "congress" were sometimes used during the campaign to secure parliamentary reform, but none of these devices was ever of great consequence in England.

Several reasons can be adduced to explain the nature of their responses. Radical knowledge of colonial society and the development of American resistance was refracted through a particular and distinctive medium of communication. It was drawn from information proffered in pamphlets, correspondence, and conversation; all of which was concerned with discussion, argument, and the examination of principles rather than threats of action. Only in the last stages of the crisis was there a rapid escalation, and whatever the actuality of events in Boston and Philadelphia, English radicals continued to be more aware of a generalized resistance than particular actions. Since they were not pacifists, the outbreak of fighting seemed an appropriate response to an intolerable situation, especially as responsibility for the conflict could be assigned to the British government.[18]

This understanding of the nature of colonial resistance conformed to the radicals' existing predilections. As intellectuals they were concerned with argument and the resolution of problems by means of rational analysis. Their social position also encouraged them in the same direction. Whereas the American revolutionaries were alienated from the current processes of the British Empire, English radicals were middle class men and women who not only accepted the structure of British society in its broad outline but were also well-connected with the socially and politically powerful aristocracy. And though they were excluded from the inner circles of national decision making, they nevertheless belonged to a broader political nation which expected its views to be taken into account. Thus, in a situation in which institutions seemed corrupt and decayed and relationships were distorted, they were concerned with reform, and not with replacement or substitution.

Furthermore, the radicals regarded themselves as active participants, rather than mere observers, of a distant struggle. They firmly believed that the empire was a single community predicated on a common system of values and sharing the same grand purposes and interests. Their sense of an obligation to contribute to the defense of colonial rights was fortified by a growing recognition that a single crisis was infecting all branches of the empire and belief that it was vital to preserve America as an asylum of liberty for all men. But their potential range of action was limited. Whatever instruments of resistance were suitable in America, radicals were compelled to plan their tactics in an English context and were required to devise methods which seemed most likely to succeed in the world of British politics. A resort to nonviolent action, such as a refusal to acknowledge the authority of Parliament by a numerically miniscule minority, would have been absurd; perhaps it was this appreciation of the dynamics of English politics which influenced their understanding of American actions by obscuring the value of noncooperation as a device for obstructing royal authority. Other possible weapons also broke in their hands. The merchants, whose pressure had been so useful in obtaining repeal of the Stamp Act, withdrew their support for the colonists later in the decade and simultaneously the effectiveness of the colonial agents also declined considerably. Thus, everything encouraged them to move in one direction. Personal character, social status, and their connections to and intimate knowledge of American argument all led them to rely on persuasion through pamphlets, negotiation, and private pressure as the most appropriate methods of action for radicals to employ.

• NOTES •

1. The term "patriot" is used in a descriptive sense; it is not intended to imply any value judgment. The term "English" refers to England, not to Wales, Scotland, or Ireland.

2. For a thorough description of the transmission of this tradition, see Caroline Robbins, *The Eighteenth-Century Commonwealthman* (Cambridge, Mass.: Harvard Univ. Press, 1961).

3. Other leading radicals, notably Christopher Wyvill, entered reform politics after the onset of the revolution and are omitted from consideration.

4. Painite self-justifying natural-rights radicalism and the philosophical radicalism of Jeremy Bentham were both born in 1776 with the publication of *Common Sense* and *A Fragment on Government* respectively. They are discounted here as having their principal English influence after the conclusion of the War of Independence.

5. Joseph Priestley, "An Address to Protestant Dissenters . . ." John Towill Rutt, ed., *The Theological and Miscellaneous Works of Joseph Priestley,* (25 vols., London, 1817–31, n.p.), vol. 22, p. 486.

6. *Ibid.,* p. 498.

7. Richard Price, *Observations on the Nature of Civil Liberty,* 3d ed. (London: T. Cadell, 1776), p. 11.

8. John Cartwright, *American Independence the Interest and Glory of Great Britain,* new ed. (London: T. Woodfall, 1775), p. 26.

9. Benjamin Franklin to Price, 13 June 1782, Price Papers, Massachusetts Historical Society, Boston.

10. Granville Sharp, *A Declaration of the People's Natural Right to A Share in the Legislature* (London: B. White, 1774), p. 158n.

11. Arthur Lee to Samuel Adams, 14 June 1771, Samuel Adams Papers, New York Public Library; *London Public Advertiser,* 25 July 1771.

12. Benjamin Rush to Sharp, 1 November 1774, Hardwicke MSS, Hardwicke Court, Gloucestershire.

13. Theophilus Lindsey to William Turner, 17 January 1775, Turner MSS, Dr. William's Library, London.

14. Catharine Macaulay to the Town of Boston, 9 May 1770, Boston Public Library.

15. Price, *Civil Liberty,* p. 98.

16. James Burgh, *Political Disquisitions* (3 vols., London: Edward and Charles Dilly, 1774–75), vol. 2, pp. 322–23; Cartwright, *American Independence,* p. 57n; John Jebb to a Friend, *The Works, Theological, Medical, Political and Miscellaneous of John Jebb* (3 vols., London: T. Cadell, 1787), vol. 1, p. 87.

17. John Fothergill to James Pemberton, 17 March 1775, Betsy C. Corner and Christopher C. Booth, eds., *Chain of Friendship: Selected Letters of Dr John Fothergill of London, 1735–1780* (Cambridge, Mass.: Belknap Press, 1971), p. 446; John Coakley Lettsom to Rush, (Summer, 1775), Rush MSS, Historical Society of Pennsylvania, Philadelphia, vol. 28, p. 45.

18. In contrast, the official policy of the English Quakers, who had been sympathetic to the colonists during the early stages of the crisis, was to urge American Friends to remain true to the pacifist principles.

·12·

A Shift in Strategy: The Organization of Military Struggle

DAVID J. TOSCANO
RONALD M. McCARTHY
WALTER H. CONSER, JR.

As events described in the previous chapters of this volume indicate, colonial struggles in the years 1765 to 1775 were predominantly nonviolent in character. There is little doubt that the tactics used by the colonists during this period had a dramatic effect upon British control in the provinces. In 1775, however, the nonviolent methods were largely abandoned, and the colonists embarked upon a military struggle which would last eight years. Although the Americans made substantial political accomplishments during their nonviolent struggle, these gains were eventually defended by military force. This shift in strategy raises a crucial question: if nonviolent means operated so successfully, why then were military forms of struggle finally employed? Were there changed political considerations which contributed to the adoption of military violence? What effect did the growing divisions between patriots and loyalists, an antagonism generated by the previous decade of resistance and exacerbated by the need for discipline, unanimity, and obedience to the calls of local, provincial, and intercolonial committees, have on the decision to turn to the military? Was the decision to shift to violence a reflection of changing moral sensibilities on the part of the colonists toward England or the result of a changed set of beliefs about the nature of government, conflict, or the state? Was it perhaps based on irrational grounds, in the colonists' fears, misunderstandings, or prejudices? Or was it simply an accident of history, an action neither intended nor foreseen?

Despite the widespread attention given to the War of Independence, no one has yet written a full description and analysis of the changeover from nonviolent to military means of resistance for a single province or for the colonies as a whole. Two reasons can be offered for this lack of basic and necessary research. First, since the significance of the nonviolent years of struggle has never been stressed, no one has investigated the years 1774–76 in terms of a strategic shift in the technique of struggle. A second reason for the lack of such an inquiry may be the frequently held belief of historians that a colonial war against Britain was inevitable. In the view of these scholars, the constitutional and imperial conflicts could be resolved only through force of arms. Consequently, the question of realistic alternative forms of resistance and a subsequent shift in means of struggle has not been taken seriously. Both sets of reasons reflect a misunderstanding of the nature of the decade of nonviolent struggle and, consequently, a failure to recognize that a shift in strategy actually occurred.

In many ways, those who attempt to illuminate the nonmilitary struggle are justified in feeling that the burden of explaining the reasons for the strategic shift is not on them. In the first place, when presented with the opportunity to vote for military measures, or actually to employ them, the colonists repeatedly chose non-violent tactics. As early as 1768, resistance leaders such as Samuel Adams and James Otis counseled the use of militia and mobs to oppose the landing of troops in Boston. Their proposal, however, when presented to the Massachusetts Convention of 1768, was rejected in favor of other measures.[1] Similarly, when Patrick Henry called for war preparations in the First Continental Congress, his suggestion was rejected in favor of the Continental Association.[2]

In several areas of the colonies, it should be additionally noted, there was an expressed willingness by some Americans to use violence against the British forces well before April 1775. Incidents such as the general mobilization at Cambridge, Massachusetts, on 1 September 1774, the seizure of military stores and equipment at Fort William and Mary in Portsmouth, New Hampshire, on 14 December 1774, as well as at Leslie's Retreat at Salem, Massachusetts, on 26 February 1775 might have embroiled the colonies in a military struggle much earlier than Lexington and Concord, but these encounters were contained and military exchanges avoided. Consequently, it is as fair to ask why hostilities did not break out sooner as to inquire why they did at all.

As suggested previously, many scholars have consistently misunderstood the nature of nonviolent action. Consequently, they have been inadequately equipped to analyze the character and implications of the resistance methods used by the colonists from 1765 to 1775. The commonly held view that nonviolent and violent forms of struggle are fundamentally different in quality and purpose is not shared by the authors of this chapter. Scholars who support this perspective, either from moral conviction or from beliefs about the need for violent action in revolution, misunderstand the character of both forms of resistance. The techniques of violent and nonviolent action are, in significant ways, more similar than they are different. Both are frequently employed by pragmatists for concrete objectives. Both are active forms of opposition and struggle against an opponent—requiring organization, discipline, united action, and courage. The use of nonviolent action by the American colonists was not a reflection of a moral choice of one technique over another. Nor was the turn to violence an indication of moral failure. Advocates of colonial resistance simply did not judge the effectiveness of their actions on these grounds.

Students of history may also consider what gains made in 1774 and 1775 were later lost by the recourse to military struggle; what alternative possibilities may have occurred if nonviolent action had been retained as the major strategy? Based on evidence gathered in at least three areas—the development of economic autonomy, the growth of popular governmental institutions, and the development of a national consciousness—one could argue that nonviolent action was at least as effective as military warfare and decidedly more democratic. To test the validity of this argument, one should compare actual conditions during the nonviolent phase with those after the war. What happened to income distribution, for example, during and after the decade of nonviolent struggle? Did some colonists become wealthy war profiteers while others experienced economic hardship? What were the differences, if any, in the distribution of land or in the control of capital? In the political sphere, what were the results of a change to war leadership and the adoption of violent sanctions? Did formal or informal popular political participation decline as the war continued?

Complete answers to these questions are beyond the scope of a single chapter and depend upon a great deal of detailed research which has not yet been done. Rather than attempt a complete description and analysis of the recourse to military violence, this chapter will focus instead on possible lines of investigation toward an explanation of this shift in strategy. In the first half of this chapter, three factors crucial in explaining the shift in strategy—ideology, the formation of the militia, and the colonial committees—are investigated. Following the discussion of these aspects, several hypotheses are presented which could explain the shift to military struggle. These proposals do not and cannot totally explain the turn to military violence, but rather suggest some *possible* reasons for it. Indeed, the hypotheses are not mutually exclusive; several are interrelated, and further research is likely to indicate that some combination of these "causes" probably brought on the military conflict.

· IDEOLOGY AND THE SHIFT IN STRATEGY ·

Central to the intellectual framework of the colonial Americans was the "real Whig," or Commonwealth, tradition. With its goal of a virtuous society grounded in natural rights and canopied beneath Divine Providence, Whig ideology figured significantly in legitimating the taking up of arms against the British Crown. As Professor Bonwick argues in Chapter Eleven of this volume, the theory of contractual government, so important to Whig theorists, contained within it the right of resistance up to and including revolution.[3]

This doctrine of resistance, however, was carefully circumscribed. While the right to resist unlawful authority could even include the right of revolution, the two concepts of resistance and revolution were separate and not to be confused. Resistance, in Whig ideology, was always of a limited nature, designed to nullify specific acts or conditions, and directed against the officers of the king. Revolution, by contrast, was an open denial of the legitimacy of the entire established government and was directed against the monarch himself.[4] Secondly, neither personal insult nor private immorality could justify a revolution. Since the public good was the goal of the monarchy, only a thoroughgoing disregard for the public welfare could justify overthrowing the king. In the second of his treatises on government, John Locke concluded that justifications for popular revolution could not be found in "every little mismanagement in public affairs." "Great mistakes in the ruling part, many wrong and inconvenient laws, and all the slips of human frailty," he wrote, "will be borne by the people without mutiny or murmur." However, when "a long train of abuses, prevarications, and artifices, all tending the same way, make a design visible to the people," popular revolt is both understandable and justifiable.[5] Less than a hundred years later, Thomas Jefferson echoed the same thought. "Prudence, indeed, will dictate that Governments long established should not be changed for light and transient causes," Jefferson wrote in the Declaration of Independence in 1776, "but when a long train of abuses and usurpations, pursuing invariably the same Object evinces a design to reduce them under absolute Despotism, it is their right, it is their duty, to throw off such Governments, and to provide new Guards for their future security."

As a corollary to this second point, it followed that neither an individual nor even a group of several persons could justifiably undertake a revolution; this was a responsibility reserved for the people as a whole. Any broad appeal to an individualistic ethic was held in check by the emphasis upon the public and cumulative nature, not only of the alleged tyrannous crimes but also the contemplated recourse to revolution. In this way, the Whig theory of resistance provided a cautious revolutionary justification which, by its emphasis on the public welfare, laid an equally strong emphasis on submission in all but the most extraordinary of times.

A third and final feature of the Whig ideology concerned the description of the appropriate forms of resistance in a given conflict. In Whig theory, Professor Bonwick observes, the nature of the threat determined the character of the response. When force was employed, therefore, it should not only be morally acceptable but pragmatically necessary as well.[6] Within this ideological framework, English political theorists such as John Trenchard, Thomas Gordon, or Richard Price expected that the normal political processes should be brought to bear in all conflicts, culminating in the recourse to violent forms of resistance only as the last resort. Just as the context and meaning of resistance and revolution were different, so too were the means appropriate to the varying struggles differentiated.

The utilization of these several themes in Whig ideology can easily be seen in the colonial pamphlet and sermon literature between 1774 and 1776. Sometimes consciously reiterated, these themes often provided an implicit background of common understanding for colonial discussion of the issues of resistance and revolution. The purpose of civil government, the nature of the threat to liberty, and the traditions and sources for resisting such attacks all came under discussion. The possibility that the colonists might take up arms, or even push for independence, was also explored, but this issue was approached hesitantly and only within the context of the Whig rationale of revolution. This reluctance in working out the logic of the Whig position is well illustrated in the shift from John Adams's

Novanglus letters, written between December 1774 and April 1775, to Thomas Paine's pamphlet *Common Sense,* published in January 1776. While privately anticipating war, Adams in *Novanglus* tried to construct an intermediate position which challenged parliamentary sovereignty over the colonies while it simultaneously acknowledged allegiance to the Crown. By 1776, and with the publication of *Common Sense,* not only a summons to arms but an explicit indictment of the king and a call for independence were the terms under discussion.

The same process of analyzing alternatives within this overall ideological position can be seen in a series of sermons between 1774 and 1776. Writing in August 1774, the Reverend Ebenezer Baldwin saw two options available to colonial Americans in the face of British oppression: either the "slavery" of complete submission to British rule or the defense of American liberty "by force of arms." Elaborating upon the latter alternative and citing the proposed measures of nonimportation and nonexportation, Baldwin called for united support for any resolutions which might be decided upon by the Continental Congress. He further suggested that should any Americans refuse to comply with such resolutions, all others should "break off all trade and dealings with such selfish miscreants; and make them sensible, that without injuring their lives or property, their injured country can make them feel the weight of her vengeance."[7] Several months later, in December 1774, the Reverend William Gordon also drew attention to the available forms of colonial resistance. Though he hoped for the continuance of the "associations respecting trade and the like," Gordon noted the possibility of armed conflict: "companies [of militia] have been formed and are continually training . . . [and] they will be better prepared, than was ever before the case, to repel all invasions that may be made upon their natural and constitutional rights, even tho' supported by a British army."[8]

Concern over the likelihood of generalized military resistance grew after the battles at Lexington and Concord. Calling for Americans "to fight for our brethren, our sons and our daughters, our wives and our houses," the Reverend David Jones exclaimed: "We have no choice left to us. . . . Matters are at last brought to this deplorable extremity—every reasonable method of reconciliation has been tried in vain—our addresses to our King have been treated with neglect or contempt."[9] Once events moved to this point, Christian ministers could combine Whig ideology with older traditions, as did the Reverend John Carmichael in his sermon "A Self-defensive War, lawful." Arguing that one could only participate in "a just war, conducted in a lawful and righteous manner," Carmichael listed resistance to a foreign enemy, the suppression of riots, and opposition to "the unjust, usurped, anti-constitutional claims of mere tyranny on the essential and unalienable rights of the people" as lawful reasons for taking up arms.[10] Consistent with traditional presentations of just war theory, Carmichael argued that the cause must be matched by proper and responsible conduct on the part of the soldiers. Interestingly, while he fully expected armed engagements to ensue, Carmichael informed his military audience that they were obliged to maintain their allegiance to the king: "your drawing the sword now must not be against the person of his Majesty, but the mal-administration of his government by designing, mischief-making ministers."[11] Clearly, independence had no place in Carmichael's thinking in June 1775. Calling for allegiance to the king, he simultaneously recommended obedience to all determinations of the Continental Congress.

If Carmichael was still hesitant over the issue of independence in 1775, the Reverend Samuel West, one year later, had no more doubts. In a classic recitation of Whig resistance ideology, West's sermon of May 1776 argued that subjects are bound to obey magistrates "for conscience sake, out of regard to the divine authority, and out of obedience to the will of God." Should the magistrate countervene his office, thereby forfeiting his authority and the people's obedience, then it was up to the public, "not a few disaffected individuals, but the collective body of the state," to decide what form of opposition was appropriate. In West's view, this decision had already been made. Not only had the people "having not the civil law to regulate themselves by, become a law unto themselves," thereby preserving "good order and harmony" in the colonies, but they had also taken up arms "for the sacred cause of liberty." West closed his address with a summons of support for the American cause. We must "defend our lives, and fortunes, even to the shedding of the last drop of blood," he charged his listeners; "we must beat our plow-shares into swords, and our pruning hooks into spears, and learn the art of self-defense against our enemies."[12] West's sermon, and others like it, indicate a readiness to employ military force against the British Crown. Although this support for armed defense on the part of English radical supporters for America and the Americans themselves was not clearly evident until 1775, the ideological framework which was decades older provided a context within which any potential military hostilities could be legitimated.

· THE ROLE OF THE MILITIA ·

Speeches, pamphlets, and sermons may provide the ideological context for the shift in colonial strategy, but any serious attempt to explain the colonists' adoption of a military strategy must also trace the development of organizations and groups which served as colonial instruments of military struggle. Until the formation of the Continental Army in the summer of 1775, the most important provincial military bodies were the colonial militias. Militia organization existed in British North America since the arrival of the first settlers, but both the structure and effectiveness of the various bodies differed throughout the provinces. Pennsylvania, for example, had no formal militia before the battles of Lexington and Concord and had, in fact, never required its citizens to participate in military organization. New York had a militia law on the books, but the sparseness of its population made popular defense extremely difficult. The New England provinces and the colony of Virginia had the most effective militia organizations during the mid-eighteenth century. In New England especially, militia defense was made possible by the geographical proximity of the small towns. The villages were close enough to permit fast communication and easy cooperation among the local people.

The structure of the earliest militia organizations was largely determined by the British colonists' relations with the Indians. By the end of the seventeenth century, problems of colonial defense had been compounded by additional internal and external dangers. Some colonies, most notably South Carolina and New York, were fearful of insurrection by their African slaves, and they adapted their military laws to respond to that threat. More pressing than the African slave or Indian problems, however, were the threats arising from the advances of French and Spanish forces in North America. When Britain's rivalry with the two Bourbon empires brought military conflict to the continent, the colonists organized the defense of their settlements by mobilizing the militia. During these struggles, some colonists also took offensive action by organizing volunteer companies to conduct expeditions into the Spanish Floridas and French Quebec. While some colonials were members of both groups, the militias and volunteer companies were essentially two different organizations, each with different goals and membership.

At the outset of the French and Indian War (1754–63), then, colonial military organization—as distinct from the British army—was composed of two branches: the volunteer companies and the local militias. Each of these groups had different functions and compositions. The volunteer companies were largely expeditionary units composed of men who frequently had few ties to any particular local community. Soldiers in these companies were often drawn from the poorer segments of the population and were frequently viewed as less disciplined than the men who drilled with the colonial militia. The volunteer companies were not permanent organizations designed to defend their local communities but were, instead, temporary groupings of individuals who were interested in offensive campaigns directed against the Indians.

The second branch of the colonial military system, the local militias, were viewed by many as the first line of colonial defense. This claim was frequently exaggerated, however, since many companies had transformed themselves into social clubs of the white male citizenry, which placed more emphasis on comradship than on the exercise of the military art. In addition to their express function of providing defense, the militias often played a less obvious role as an instrument of civil order. These bodies often suppressed riots and quelled social disorders. At certain times, however, they determined that the rioters' cause was just and chose either to ignore the disorders or to join in the activity.

Britain viewed the effectiveness of colonial military organization with mild contempt and believed that her regular troops could provide a more efficient and economic defense of North America, especially in the struggles against France and Spain. During the French and Indian wars, for example, the regulars were most effective in fighting and winning the conflict. The colonials, notwithstanding provincial claims to the contrary, played a continually smaller role in the war as the fighting continued. When the final victory was accomplished in 1763, a sizeable number of the British forces remained in North America, a situation which strained relations between the colonials and the Crown in years to come.

Following the defeat of the French, the need for volunteer companies in the colonies declined. Militia organization and its orientation toward military defense persisted, but the drilling in arms that occurred often lacked enthusiasm and purpose. The militia laws which existed in the colonies were rarely enforced, and some companies had neither the men nor material to wage any kind of military struggle, whether defensive or offensive. According to the law in most provinces, men in the militia were required to drill periodically, but, in the words of one scholar of the period, "it is doubtful whether the Training Day had ever been an effective force of instruction in the art of War."[13] The poor condition of the colonial militia in the mid-1770s helps explain some of the reasons behind George Washington's misgivings about fighting Great Britain with anything but a well-disciplined, dependable, and efficient Continental Army.

From 1763 to late 1774, little discussion was given to the condition and readiness of the colonial militias. Colonists periodically issued statements which suggested that they could defend themselves and, consequently, had no need of the standing army of British regulars in the colonies. Despite such rhetoric, the colonial legislatures took few steps to ensure enforcement of militia laws or to improve the state of "the military art" in the provinces. In the latter part of 1774, however, some colonial leaders began to express concern about the state of the militia and recommend that certain actions be taken to improve its effectiveness.

Few colonists in the fall of 1774 wished for war, and fewer still believed that it would come. Colonial leaders placed their faith in the resolutions of the Continental Congress, convinced that their rights would be redressed either by petitions or through the effectiveness of colonial commercial sanctions. The First Continental Congress, in fact, explicitly rejected warlike measures in favor of "the most speedy, effectual, and peaceable measures" prescribed in the Continental Association, and committees were quickly established throughout the provinces to enforce the congressional resolutions. Some colonies, however, and especially those in New England, felt the need to prepare for "every contingency," and proceeded to organize their militias for military defense of their communities.

Historians frequently cite local, county, and provincial decisions to place their communities into "a posture of defence" as examples of preparedness for war. Colonial leaders, however, did not necessarily express aggressive intent by these decisions. Colonial militias were defensive by nature, as defense had been the only expressed goal of any of these bodies. Second, and perhaps most important, colonial leaders discouraged and, in certain important instances, physically intervened in order to prevent military engagements with British troops. Documents from the period of adoption of defensive measures indicate a colonial reluctance to proceed too quickly with measures which might appear to be warlike in intent. The development of colonial military capability and the decisions of the provinces to employ military force in their conflict with Great Britain must be viewed with the above factors in mind.

· THE ROLE OF THE COMMITTEES ·

In the fall of 1774, militia companies were still largely in the background of colonial resistance activity; the local and provincial committees were the most important instruments of American resistance to British authority at that time. By September 1774, a number of colonists and localities had gained experience with various kinds of resistance committees. Committees of merchants and of mechanics, for example, were extremely important elements of the resistance to the Stamp and Townshend acts. These groups had coordinated the enforcement of nonimportation, and encouraged noncooperation to offensive British laws. Beginning in 1769, committees of correspondence also became increasingly significant instruments of colonial resistance. In March of that year, the Virginia House of Burgesses elected a standing committee of correspondence and prompted the other twelve provinces to elect similar bodies within the next year. Several New England communities, especially in Massachusetts, selected local committees of correspondence during 1772 and 1773, in the course of that colony's dispute with Britain over the payment of judges' salaries. After news of the passage of the Coercive Acts reached the colonies in May 1774, many more towns, cities, and districts or counties throughout the provinces appointed similar bodies. Originally formed to exchange information with other localities and provinces, these organizations enhanced colonial awareness of the latest developments in the American resistance and gave encouragement to other committees, the provincial conventions, and the Continental Congress. Colonial committees became particularly important after the First Continental Congress adopted the Continental Association in October 1774. As chapters Six and Fourteen of this volume indicate, the comprehensive plan for resistance against the Coercive Acts and all other unacceptable actions of the British government which were outlined in the Association could only be enforced through the creation of an elaborate system of local, county, and provincial committees.

Most of the committees which were formed prior to the First Continental Congress in September 1774 were called committees of correspondence. With the adoption of the Continental Association, the committee structure began to change. Most of these changes occurred as committees widened the areas in which they were concerned and active. While the original committees of correspondence had primarily acted to keep the population informed about threats to their liberty and to recommend possible actions to take, these newer committees—the committees of inspection and committees of observation, for example—were charged with keeping an eye on the actions of merchants, traders, and the like in enforcing the Association. The committees of correspondence, though, remained the "master" bodies, in the sense that initiative to act stemmed from them and that the most difficult problems—enforcement, for example—were referred to them. In some areas, the Association was enforced by a subcommittee of the central committee of correspondence. This was particularly true in the cities of New York, Charleston, and Philadelphia, which kept all resistance functions under the control of a single elected committee.

The committee structure remained rather loose in many places in the early phases of the Continental Association, but the imperatives of resistance gradually encouraged committees to be more vigorous in their enforcement of Congress's resolutions and more determined in their efforts to isolate supporters of Crown policy. Additional efforts to enforce the Association, especially the changes in the character of the resistance necessitated by the militarization of the struggle against England, brought about the development of yet more kinds of committees. Throughout the later period of the nonviolent resistance and into the early phases of military struggle, however, the committees of correspondence and their successors, the committees of safety, were accorded decision-making functions. This process facilitated the transfer of power from governmental bodies legally constituted by the Crown to extralegal organizations controlled by advocates of resistance.

In 1774 and earlier, the members of the committees of correspondence were mostly notables from the town or county which the committee served. Often, they were the same men who were most likely to hold other appointments open to local leaders: representatives in the legislature, justices of the peace, and officers of the militia. Of course, before the crises of late 1774 and 1775, the designation of a man as "major" or "colonel" in the command of a militia regiment was largely honorific, often in recognition of past military or political services. Few of these officers actually exercised troops since training days seldom came in the colonies at that time.

Many of the most prominent leaders of the independence struggle were active in committees as well as in other areas of political life. Washington and Jefferson were both committeemen, only later going their separate ways, the one to pursue a military career, the other a political one. During the crisis of late 1774 and 1775, many committees of correspondence greatly expanded in size, affording opportunities for new men to serve. The committees in the cities of New York, Philadelphia, and Charleston increased manyfold as did those in rural areas. In many cases, control over the chair and often over the actions of the committees remained in the hands of one or two influential local leaders to whom others largely deferred. These local leaders, however, often had other responsibilities—acting as delegates to the provincial congresses, for example—which took them away from committee duties and allowed others to exercise more initiative than they had previously. Also, as militia and army service became regularized, men who pursued these functions were pulled away from direct influence over the committees. It is evident that there was no firm policy that would have kept military men off the committees, but a clear trend did develop to separate the military and political spheres, if only because the time required to pursue one activity may have obviated activity in the other.

As resistance activity continued into 1775, some local committees expressed a concern that their communities might be attacked by British troops or colonials loyal to the king. This concern was transformed into outright fear following the battles of Lexington and Concord. In order to reflect the belief that defense of their communities might be necessary, many committees changed their names and became known as committees of safety. Committees of safety were organized not only in the towns and counties throughout British North America but were formed by both legal and extralegal legislatures as well. The provincial congresses and conventions were more likely to organize these bodies than were the legal colonial assemblies, and they often authorized these groups to serve as executive committees of their provinces while the extralegal legislatures were not in session. The provincial committees of safety were the forerunners of military government during the war and guided the militarization of the colonies after Lexington and Concord.

• PREPARATIONS FOR MILITARY DEFENSE •

Although the colonials seemed hesitant to engage British troops militarily even after April 1775, some provinces prepared for military defense as early as October 1774. Massachusetts was the first of seven provinces which made or encouraged preparations for military defense before the battles at Lexington and Concord. When the first provincial congress met in October 1774, royal government in the province had effectively been dissolved through colonial noncooperation. General Thomas Gage's statement one month earlier that "civil government" was "near its end," accurately described the situation in the colony. One of the effects of colonial noncooperation was felt by the militia companies throughout the province. During the summer and early fall, many officers had resigned their commissions in the military bodies, willingly or under duress, forcing their companies to elect new leaders. In this way, colonial leaders were able to remove British sympathizers from positions of power and replace them with supporters of resistance activities. Such a case occurred in Worcester, Massachusetts, where the county convention met on 31 August 1774 to debate militia reorganization and procedures for countering a possible Gage foray into the countryside to open the county court. On 6 September, the day Gage was to arrive, six thousand militiamen gathered at the suggestion of the convention to "protect and defend" any town in the county threatened with invasion.[14] Gage had decided against journeying to Worcester and did not appear, but before the day was over, the county convention asked all militia officers to resign so that new commanders could be elected. The convention also recommended that one-third of the townsmen in the county be enlisted "to act at a minute's warning." Minuteman companies, as they were to be known, were formed shortly thereafter in Essex, Suffolk, and Middlesex counties.[15] The provincial congress could not ignore these developments any more than it could disregard the collapse of royal government in the province. Colonial leaders in this extralegal legislature viewed themselves as coordinators of resistance to the Coercive Acts in Massachusetts. This role required them to note any possible changes in the character of resistance organizations and to place all such innovation under their control. The emergence of defensive military preparations with militia and minutemen companies, therefore, was a development which required a response from the provincial congress.

As the need to reorganize the militia was being emphasized to the provincial congress by the deliberations and actions in Worcester, other events closer to Boston provided further impetus for such action. On 1 September 1774, Gage authorized a group of 260 soldiers to remove approximately 200 half-barrels of provincial gunpowder from storage in Charlestown. This action was successful, and the British force adjourned with the powder, as well as two field pieces seized in Cambridge, to the safety of Castle William in Boston harbor. Fearing that this was a sign that Gage intended to use military force to quell colonial resistance, thousands of men throughout eastern Massachusetts met in their communities that night to discuss possible courses of action. Many of these men proceeded to Cambridge the next morning and, leaving their weapons outside the town, elected committees to seek out and demand resignations from the three mandamus councilors who lived in that town. The crowd surrounded the Cambridge court house to hear the resignations of councilors Samuel Danforth and Joseph Lee. Danforth apologized for having acted in ways "so disagreeable to this country," whereupon the crowd voted their approval of the resignations.

After resolving their "abhorrence of mobs, riots, and the destruction of private property," the crowd requested a report from the elected committee on the status of the third councilor, Lieutenant-Governor Thomas Oliver. Oliver had been visited earlier by the committee, but had refused to resign. He argued that to do so would violate the constitution, since the lieutenant-governor was legally required to serve on the council. Instead, Oliver offered a proposal, which was accepted by the committee, whereby a provincial assembly of some kind would decide whether he should resign.

The committee was about to report Oliver's proposal to the crowd when Customs Commissioner Benjamin Hallowell, along with some associates, came through the town on his way to Boston. Hallowell was an old opponent of the resistance movement and had made many enemies when he served as a Customs officer. His presence enraged a group of demonstrators, who wanted to chase him on horseback. The leaders of the crowd, however, were able to convince all but a group of eight to give up the chase before it had gone far. Only one of the pursuers came close enough to threaten Hallowell, who soon made his way into Boston.

As men continued to arrive in Cambridge from points further south and west, news circulated that the British troops in Boston had begun military exercises. Some at the meeting now feared that the British soldiers would march into Cambridge and wanted to gather their weapons. Military hostilities might easily have begun at that time had it not been for the work of the committees of correspondence of Boston, Charlestown, and Cambridge. The committeemen were dismayed at the prospect of military confrontation and worked to dissuade the angry crowd from gathering their weapons and engaging the British.

The British troops did not march into Cambridge, and the crowd returned to the issue of Thomas Oliver. The crowd rejected the lieutenant-governor's proposal, whereupon Oliver resigned with a protest that he was forced to do so because his home was surrounded by "about four Thousand People." A military confrontation had been avoided, but the colonials remained angry with those who continued to cooperate with the Coercive Acts and fearful of the prospects of war with Gage's troops.[16]

It was after these developments that the extralegal provincial congress created a militia organization under its command. On 26 October, the congress called for the election of new officers to replace existing leaders of the provincial militia, many of whom were Tories.[17] A nine-member committee of safety, elected to meet when the congress was not in session, was given authority to summon the militia "whenever they shall judge it necessary for the safety and defence of the inhabitants of this province."[18] Three field commanders were chosen by the congress, and five commissaries were authorized to purchase ammunition. The provincial congress estimated the cost of these operations at £20,837 and hoped to finance part of this amount by calling on all tax collectors to turn monies over to a receiver general appointed by congress, rather than to the Crown-appointed provincial treasurer.[19] Despite these efforts to improve the militia and to place it firmly under the control of the newly emerging provincial government, the congress took no steps designed to create a standing army in the colony.

Before the end of 1774 colonial leaders in Connecticut, Rhode Island, and New Hampshire approved resolutions similar to those adopted by the Massachusetts Provincial Convention. In October 1774, the assemblies of both Connecticut and Rhode Island met separately to consider the problems facing British North America. Although Connecticut already had an extensive militia organization with forces estimated by the patriot governor Joseph Trumbull at twenty thousand men, the colony faced serious problems in its attempts to mobilize unified resistance of any kind.[20] Connecticut had long experienced a factional split in its political life which reflected the division of the province into eastern and western sections. Throughout the decade of nonviolent resistance, the eastern towns were consistently more active in their support of colonial goals and tactics than were their western counterparts. While the eastern towns pushed for the implementation of nonimportation in the summer of 1774, the western communities hesitated, and some even refused to subscribe to the Continental Association after its enactment in October. Moreover, the colony's militia may have had many men listed on its official roles, but individual companies had not been used since the 1760s, and many colonial leaders questioned their potential effectiveness in a military exchange with British troops. This sentiment was expressed by a meeting of town committees in New London and Windham counties on 8 September 1774. This gathering, called "to consult for their common safety," passed several resolutions which suggested that the towns revive the militia companies which had fallen into disuse since the French and Indian War, and prepare to repel any enemy.[21] On 13 October, the Connecticut General Assembly took provincial action and recommended that "the military companies" of the province "be called out and exercised in the use of arms . . . from this time until the first day of May next."[22] At the same time, the legislators suggested that towns in the colony double their stocks of powder. It is unclear how many military companies took the advice of the General Assembly, but records indicate that certain towns, such as Bolton, Waterbury, and New London, increased their stocks of powder in December 1774 and January 1775.[23]

In the last week of October 1774, the Rhode Island General Assembly appointed a committee to consider and approve petitions from five towns requesting permission to organize independent militia companies.[24] Meeting again in December 1774, the assembly revised the militia laws to permit provincial troops to aid any neighboring colony under attack and ordered cannon and ammunition to be removed from Fort George in Newport for safekeeping in Providence.[25] One motivating factor in the assembly's decision to recommend defensive military measures was undoubtedly the action taken by the British government in October 1774 to prohibit the exportation of gunpowder to the colonies. British troops in North America had firepower vastly superior to anything which could be mustered by the colonists, and colonial leaders were fearful of what might happen if His Majesty's regulars attacked unarmed citizens. This anxiety may have prompted the provincials' occasional seizures of royal gunpowder and armaments as well as their efforts to accumulate military stores in late 1774 and 1775. Samuel Ward, one of the Rhode Island delegates to the First Continental Congress, expressed the views of many patriots in a letter to John Dickinson which described the measures taken by his province. "The idea of taking up Arms against the parent State," Ward wrote on 14 December 1774, "is shocking to Us who still feel the strongest Attachment to our Sovereign . . . but if We must either become Slaves or fly to Arms I shall not (and hope no American will) hesitate one Moment which to choose."[26]

In New Hampshire, actions similar to those in Rhode Island were taken on 14 and 15 December, as Portsmouth crowds invaded the arsenal at Fort William and Mary and removed one hundred barrels of powder, sixteen cannon, and sixty muskets.[27] During the two separate raids needed to remove all the stores, the governor attempted to enlist the militia in order to quell the disorder, but the provincials refused to mobilize and permitted the crowd to finish its task. By the end of 1774, two towns in the province, Dublin (28 November) and Exeter (15 December), reported that they had provided their towns with stocks of gunpowder, and a third, Portsmouth, had organized a volunteer company known as the Portsmouth Volunteers on 28 December.[28] According to Richard Upton, an authority on this period of New Hampshire history, the meager records which exist suggest that "most of the towns in the southern part" of the province did not start organizing and drilling companies until March and April 1775.[29] The exact number of towns which drilled and the quality of militia organization are not reported by Upton.

The New England colonies were not the only areas in North America where defensive military measures were planned. In December 1774, the extralegal Maryland convention, following its approval of the Continental Association, devoted part of its session to a discussion of the state of the militia, which had largely deteriorated since 1763. Supporters of the colonial cause questioned the loyalty of some militia officers, and feared what might happen if the militia was mobilized by the governor. Consequently, they took steps to subvert royal control over the militia by calling for the formation of new companies and the election of new officers. This would place provincial military organizations firmly under popular control and lessen the danger of the militia being used as an agent of royal oppression. In a statement whose substance would be adopted by towns, counties, and provincial bodies in other colonies, the Maryland convention outlined the rationale for reorganizing the militia. Arguing that a well organized militia "is the natural strength and the only stable security of a free government," the convention suggested that "such militia will relieve our mother country from any expenses in our protection and defence, will obviate the pretence of a necessity for taxing us on that account, and render it unnecessary to keep any standing army (ever dangerous to liberty) in this province."[30]

Idealistic words notwithstanding, the effect of the convention's recommendations was not immediately apparent. Universal conscription was not enforceable by its stipulations, and no provisions were enacted to place the newly created force under a central command or to raise funds for military costs. Within a month of the passage of these resolutions, two military companies were formed in Annapolis, and one each in the towns of Severn Hundred and Elkridge Hundred, but the effect of the convention's actions, according to one historian, was minimal.[31] The resolutions, David Skaggs wrote, "resulted in the establishment of only a few companies," and the "lack of an adequate supply system insured that the milita would not be an effective fighting force."[32]

As news of the Maryland convention's resolutions spread throughout the countryside, three other provinces confronted the poor conditions of their militias. On 17 January 1775, the extralegal South Carolina Provincial Convention recommended that the population be "diligently attentive in learning the use of Arms, and that their officers be requested to train and exercise the existing militia companies at least once a fortnight."[33] The delegates at this meeting did not consider placing the colony into a "posture of defence." Nor did they suggest the formation of independent companies. These decisions would only be taken five months later, after the battles of Lexington and Concord had convinced many colonists that defensive military preparations were necessary.

The resolutions of the extralegal New Hampshire and Pennsylvania provincial congresses, both meeting in January 1775, indicated a colonial ambivalence and reluctance to organize military groups, even for defensive purposes. At a meeting of the second provincial congress on 23 January, Pennsylvanians, without extensive discussion, rejected a proposal to raise a militia.[34] Conservative supporters of the king hailed this decision as an indication that the "vulgar conduct" of their opponents had been repudiated and that Pennsylvania would now move more firmly behind British policy in the colonies. Their interpretation proved wrong, however, as Pennsylvanians continued to support the Continental Association and other measures designed to secure redress of grievances.

By the end of January 1775, Pennsylvania's position on the role of the militia in the colonial struggle was clear; New Hampshire's, however, was fraught with ambiguity. Meeting on 25 January, the second provincial congress adopted eleven articles expressing the positions of provincial leaders. "Surrounded with dangers and distresses on every side," the series of resolutions began, "it behoves us to adopt and pursue such peaceable measures as, *under God,* will be most likely to prevent those dreadful calamities with which we are threatened."[35] The delegates then voiced their approval of the Continental Association. At the same time, however, they issued a statement which recommended "that the Officers of the several Regiments strictly comply with the laws . . . for regulating the Militia."[36]

One week after both the Pennsylvania and New Hampshire provincial congresses issued their resolutions, Massachusetts colonial leaders reconvened in Cambridge. Meeting from 1–16 February, this session of the extralegal second provincial congress considered the creation of a standing army. The delegates heatedly discussed the matter but refused to take such an aggressive step and voted instead to appoint a committee to draw up articles which would regulate the conduct of any "constitutional army which may be raised in this province." The congress recommended that colonists deny any assistance which Gage requested in his military preparations and hoped that the populace would refuse to supply British forces with lumber, wagons, horses, and other military articles. Finally, the congress authorized the committee of safety to remain in session and to mobilize, if needed, "so many of the militia . . . as they shall judge necessary" to repel any armed attempt by Gage to enforce the Coercive Acts.[37]

Shortly after the congress adjourned, news reached the committee of safety of the reinforcements being sent to Boston by Great Britain. In joint session with the committee of supplies, decisions were made to purchase enough military stores for fifteen thousand men in the field and to move colonial arms to safer locations. These moves troubled Joseph Hawley, a colonial leader from western Massachusetts. Hawley, who had suggested in the fall of 1774 that "we must fight" if England refused to redress grievances, now advised against aggressive military action. Writing to Thomas Cushing on 22 February 1775, Hawley warned:

> If we, by order of our Committee of Safety, should begin the attack and so bring on hostilities before the general consent of the colonies that hostilities were altogether unavoidable . . . , there will be infinite hazard that the other governments will say we have unnecessarily and madly plunged into war, and therefore must get out of the scrape as we can. . . .[38]

Hawley's words were timely for on 26 February, four days after he wrote the letter, Massachusetts was almost "plunged into war" during a confrontation with British troops near Salem. British Colonel Alexander Leslie heard that some colonial fieldpieces had been hidden in the town, and he marched into the countryside to seize them. The local townspeople, receiving advance warning of the march, gathered at the Northfield drawbridge and raised it to prevent the British troops from crossing. Leslie was clearly baffled by this nonviolent denying tactic, and he unsuccessfully employed numerous arguments in his attempts to have the draw-bridge lowered. At one point, he even threatened to fire upon the citizens, most of whom were unarmed. But the townspeople stood firm and refused to lower the bridge. After a lengthy debate, a compromise was struck and Leslie was permitted to cross the bridge with the provision that he immediately turn around and march peacefully away from the town. Hostilities were again avoided, but another result might have occurred if, instead of a group of mostly unarmed civilians, a large force of armed militiamen had confronted the British troops.[39]

In Massachusetts, the defensive military measures taken were usually em-bodied in militia improvements. Other provinces, however, saw the development of a different type of military organization, called the volunteer company. Citizens in the New Jersey towns of Elizabeth and Freehold organized such bodies in Janu-ary and March of 1775.[40] In December 1774 and March 1775, companies were formed in the New Hampshire towns of Portsmouth and Dublin.[41] The role of these organizations in colonial politics prior to 19 April 1775 is unclear. Few records exist of their actions, and there is little indication that they did much more than periodically drill and muster. The greatest amount of information available on vol-unteer companies comes from Virginia, where a number of groups were formed prior to the commencement of hostilities. Estimates of the exact number of these *Independent Companies of Gentlemen Volunteers* existing before 19 April 1775 vary, but records indicate that at least thirteen were either established on paper or recommended by county committees before news of Lexington and Concord reached the province.[42]

The number of independent companies established in Virginia has been greatly overestimated, both in accounts written during the period and in later his-tories. As early as 26 November 1774, a young James Madison wrote William Bradford of Pennsylvania that "independent companies" were "forming and vol-untarily subjecting themselves to military discipline." While he did not give con-crete details, Madison's correspondence gave the impression of an entire coun-tryside exercising in arms. "Many publickly declare themselves ready," Madison declared, "to join the Bostonians as soon as violence is offered them or resistance thought expedient."[43] It may be true that many volunteer companies did not pub-licize their formation, but the records which do exist document the existence of only one or two companies in Virginia at the time of Madison's letter.[44] As early as September 1774, plans existed for the creation of an independent company in Fair-fax County, but these were not realized until 17 January 1775.[45]

Madison's tendency to exaggerate the extent of military preparations was shared by Virginia's Governor Dunmore. His letter to Lord Dartmouth on 24 De-cember 1774 speaks for itself: "Every county, besides, is now arming a company of men, whom they call an independent company, for the avowed purpose of pro-tecting their communities, and to be employed against government, if occasion require."[46] Dunmore's statement was misleading in two ways. First, companies had formed in very few counties before 1775, and second, those which had been organized, excepting the one in Spotsylvania County, had not been placed under the control of the county committees. When news of Dunmore's claim was published in late April 1775, numerous Virginians disputed it, and the Norfolk County committee challenged Dunmore to produce evidence to substantiate his charges.[47] The House of Burgesses, which convened again in June 1775, also questioned the governor's claim, and suggested that "not more than six or seven [had been formed] throughout the whole Colony, which consists of sixty one Counties."[48]

Robert L. Scribner suggested in his edited collection of Virginia documents that many independent companies were formed to compensate for the legal lack of military defense brought on by the expiration of the most recent militia act.[49] Virginia's extension of the militia law of 1738 had expired in July 1773, and the House of Burgesses had been unable to renew its provisions before the assembly was dissolved by the governor in May 1774.[50] Viewed in this light, the independent companies were products of the same atmosphere that generated the extralegal political bodies. Colonists felt compelled to create new institutions to meet their needs, and they proceeded to organize structures which would be subject to popular control.

Although scattered independent militia companies were formed in Virginia during the first three months of 1775, the colony was not truly placed into a state of defense until the meeting of the second Virginia convention in late March. Delegates to the extralegal convention from counties such as Fairfax, Augusta, and Cumberland had been given instructions to vote for a regularized military defense, but resolutions similar to those adopted by the Maryland convention in December were by no means assured of passage. When Patrick Henry introduced his proposals for military preparations on 23 March, he immediately touched off an "animated debate."[51] It was during this discussion that Henry rose to the podium and delivered his famous speech: "Give me liberty, or give me death."[52] For all of Henry's efforts, his motion passed by only a slim margin, sixty-five to sixty.[53]

The resolutions adopted by the Virginia convention were similar in tone to those passed three months earlier by the Maryland convention. Raising a militia, they argued, would remove the necessity of a standing army in the colonies and obviate the need for oppressive taxation. Virginia had an additional reason for raising a militia. In resolving that the colony "be immediately put into a posture of Defence," the convention argued:

> That the establishment of such a Militia is at this Time peculiarly necessary by the State of our Laws for the protection and Defence of the country, some of which are already expired and others will shortly do so; and that the known Remissness of Government in calling us together in Legislative Capacity renders it too insecure in this time of Danger and Distress to rely. . . .[54]

With this action, the extralegal Virginia convention usurped another function traditionally reserved only for legal governments: the military defense of the community. On 25 March 1775, a committee appointed to prepare a plan of military defense reported their recommendations to the conventions. The delegates quickly approved the plan, recommended that volunteer companies be formed in the counties, and suggested a structure for the proposed military organizations. No provisions were made to fund the companies, but the convention advised committees to collect money for supplies from people in their counties.[55]

As the Virginia convention concluded its deliberations, the second Massachusetts Provincial Congress reconvened in Concord. This gathering, which met from 22 March to 15 April, concerned itself first with specifying the kinds of British actions which would justify mobilization of the militia. After short deliberations, the congress voted on 25 March to prohibit the committee of safety from calling out the militia unless Gage's troops marched "out of the town of Boston, with Artillery and Baggage."[56] After resolving this question, and some others of lesser importance, nearly half of the delegates wished to adjourn the meeting. A majority of the congress, however, decided to remain at Concord until they received news which was shortly expected from England.

On 2 April 1775, two ships arrived from England with ominous news. Included in the reports from London was the text of an address by both Houses of Parliament to the king which declared that a rebellion actually existed in Massachusetts and asked him to "take the most effectual measures to enforce due obedience to the laws and authority of the supreme Legislature."[57] The colonists were informed that the king intended to act quickly to suppress the nonviolent revolt and that the cabinet had decided to send six additional regiments to Gage immediately and ten thousand additional troops shortly thereafter.

The British decisions shocked the Massachusetts Provincial Congress; it appeared that Great Britain intended to inflict the "horrors of civil war" upon North America. James Warren expressed the view of many colonial leaders in a letter to his wife. The news, wrote Warren on 6 April, left the people of Massachusetts "no longer at a loss what is intended for us by our dear Mother."[58] Proposals in the congress for quiet adjournment gave way to heated activity. After a long debate, the delegates adopted articles for the proposed Massachusetts army and approved a resolution which authorized the provincial committee of safety to enlist and pay six standing companies of artillerymen. Interestingly enough, the congress also endorsed a change in the process whereby minutemen were recruited and officers elected. The October meeting of the provincial congress had recommended that minutemen enlist by their own initiative and proceed to elect their officers. Delegates to the second congress judged these regulations to be inadequate and authorized a reversion to the method of recruiting which had been employed in earlier wars. Under the new resolutions, officers were to be appointed, rather than elected, and made responsible for enlisting eligible recruits.[59]

Despite the threatening news from Britain, the provincial congress continued to advise committees and towns against aggressive military action. Writing to all the towns in Bristol County on 6 April 1775, the delegates recommended that "the militia and especially the minute men" of the county be placed "in the best posture of defence," but that they "act on the defensive only, until further direction of this Congress."[60] Similar recommendations were sent to other towns in the colony on the following day.[61] It was only after news of the New England Restraining Act arrived on 8 April that the Massachusetts Provincial Congress agreed to ask cooperation of the other New England colonies in creating a standing army.[62] When congress adjourned four days prior to Lexington and Concord, however, still no standing force existed for defense of the province.

• THE IMPACT OF LEXINGTON AND CONCORD •

The events of 19 April 1775 at Lexington and Concord have been described in numerous works and will not be recounted again here.[63] Whatever the circumstances surrounding the exchange of gunfire, the battles impelled some colonial organizations to prepare for military defense, and others to take more aggressive military action. The New England colonies were naturally more distressed by the events in Massachusetts than were any of the other provinces. A number of towns in the region mobilized their militia and marched toward Boston to assist their neighbors in military defense. According to some inflated estimates, nearly twenty thousand militiamen had gathered in the Cambridge Common by the evening of 20 April.[64] Many of these "embattled farmers," however, lacked food or supplies for a protracted campaign and could not be expected to stay.

Colonial legislative bodies also felt the necessity of action. On 21 April 1775, the third New Hampshire Provincial Congress appointed Colonel Nathaniel Folsom to command the colony's forces in Boston and recommended that towns in the province organize minutemen. Despite the emergency the delegates to this extralegal session postponed the decision to form a standing army. One day later, the Rhode Island General Assembly, over the objections of the governor, voted to raise a fifteen hundred man army for military defense of the colony. The extralegal Massachusetts Provincial Congress and the Connecticut General Assembly were the next colonial bodies to act. Meeting in emergency session on 23 April, Massachusetts leaders resolved to raise 13,600 men as part of a continental army. Unlike the Massachusetts congress, the Connecticut Assembly felt that it could not yet commit a definite number of men to a standing army. Delegates at the assembly meeting of 26 April decided to reorganize the militia and create a minuteman organization which could march to Massachusetts if needed. They also authorized a tax for the purchase of armaments.[65] "The people of This Colony," wrote Governor Jonathan Trumbull to General Gage, "abhor the idea of taking up arms . . . and dread nothing so much as the horrors of a civil war . . . But sir," the letter continued, "they apprehend themselves justified by the principle of self defence."[66] Trumbull, in the hope that general hostilities might still be avoided, advised Gage to suspend the operations of war and requested further information about the events of 19 April.

News of Lexington and Concord spread quickly to the colonies southwest of New England. On 23 April, after hearing of the hostilities, the New York City committee of sixty called for a mass meeting on the following day. Thousands of people attended and directed the committee to organize a militia. The sixty felt that they held no authority except to enforce the Association, and they called instead for the election of a committee of one hundred and a new provincial congress. On 1 May, the slate of one hundred persons proposed by the sixty was elected. This group subsequently established an armed watch of citizens and formed seven militia companies during the month of May. No further governmental action was taken on militia organization until the provincial congress of 22 May.

Groups of citizens in Pennsylvania made more systematic attempts to organize military defense than did New Yorkers, but these efforts were partially frustrated by the conduct of the assembly. On 25 April, a mass meeting of several thousand people gathered in Philadelphia and agreed to organize themselves into neighborhood militia.[67] The "inhabitants" of the city approached the assembly in early May with a request for £50,000 in paper currency to buy military stores, and the committee of sixty-six requested reimbursement for expenses already incurred in organizing the populace. The two-week-long session was reluctant to approve these requests, but it did authorize payment of £2,000 to the sixty-six and empowered a committee on supplies to spend up to £5,000 for military defense of the province.[68] Despite the assembly's trepidation, over thirty militia companies were formed in Philadelphia by 10 May, and seven rural counties organized similar bodies by the end of the month.[69]

As news of the confrontation in New England continued to filter south, a drama with potentially similar consequences unfolded in Virginia. On 21 April 1775, a raiding party authorized by the governor seized fifteen half-barrels of powder at the colonial magazine in Williamsburg. Tempers in the town flared, and rumors circulated that a crowd would soon "repair to the palace, to demand from the Governor a restoration of what they so justly supposed was deposited in this magazine for the country's defence."[70] Happily for the governor, the town's mayor and other colonial leaders were able to quiet the potential disturbance. Rather than encourage an attack on the governor's residence, the local leaders prepared an address to the governor and requested that the powder be returned.

Reports of Dunmore's action reached Fredericksburg on 24 April and prompted the independent company there to call for a march on the capitol. The company voted to summon volunteer militia organizations from the surrounding counties and to solicit the advice of George Washington in planning a march for 29 April. Peyton Randolph, who was informed in Williamsburg of the Fredericksburg activity by three couriers, urged patience. The town, he argued, was quiet, and Dunmore had promised to return the powder if it was needed. The messengers subsequently returned to Fredericksburg and informed the gathered volunteers of Randolph's advice. Before they arrived, however, the town received news of Lexington and Concord. These reports, however electrifying they may have appeared to some, were not sufficiently dramatic to overturn Randolph's advice. On 29 April, "102 officers, committee members, and other worthies voted that the 600 men assembled should not march," and they dispatched express riders "to the troops assembled at the Bowling Green . . . to the companies from Frederick,

Berkeley, Dunmore, and such other counties as are now on the march . . . to acquaint them with the determination now taken."[71]

All of the companies which had mobilized apparently concurred with the Fredericksburg decision, except for one commanded by Patrick Henry. After a dramatic speech, Henry took command of a company of volunteers assembled at Newcastle.[72] Demanding either the return of the powder or financial compensation, he marched the company toward the capitol. Rather than risk a military confrontation, the governor approved a compromise and granted £330 as compensation for the seized powder. Henry dispersed the troops, and military hostilities were, for the moment, averted.

By the middle of May 1775, people throughout all British North America had been informed of the battles at Lexington and Concord, and while all still hoped to avoid war, some had taken the first tentative steps toward military defense of their colonies. In Delaware, the assembly chose to ignore proposals to raise a militia,[73] but two of the three counties in the province organized regiments before the end of May.[74] Three of the New England colonies were also active during this period, but on a provincial, rather than local, level. During the first week in May, the Rhode Island Assembly appointed a six member committee of safety to oversee military preparations when the assembly was not in session, and it authorized the printing of £20,000 of currency to cover military expenses. The legislature justified its formation of a committee of safety on the grounds that Governor Joseph Wanton was no longer capable of fulfilling the normal duties of his office. In late April, the governor had protested the assembly's decision to form a 1,500-man "army of Observation," arguing that such a move might prompt the Crown to revoke the colonial charter. When he refused to withdraw this protest, the legislature suspended him, appointed the committee of safety to oversee military preparations, and transferred several of the governor's functions to the lieutenant-governor and colonial secretary.[75]

On 11 May, a similar committee called the council of safety was formed at the regular session of the Connecticut General Assembly. The council was authorized to assist the governor when the assembly was not in session, and it could give orders "for defence of the Colony." At this same session, the assembly approved articles of military regulation similar to those adopted by the Massachusetts Provincial Congress in April.[76] The fourth New Hampshire Provincial Congress, acting on 20 May, voted to raise an army of two thousand men and approved a provincial tax to support military preparations.[77] Six days later, the delegates followed the examples of the three other New England colonies and established a committee of safety for the province.[78]

The experience of New York at the time of the beginning of hostilities between Great Britain and America was very different than that of the colonies to the northeast. Despite a strong Whig organization in New York City, the colony had never been centrally controlled by a resistance organization. The weakness of the committee structure, the many Loyalists or potential Loyalists, and the long frontier open to attack by Indians or troops from Canada influenced decisions throughout the colony. In addition, the weakness of the committee structure forced the committees that did exist to make decisions which many would rather have referred to the provincial convention.

This was particularly true of the northern counties. The outbreak of fighting in neighboring Massachusetts aroused fears among the Whigs in these areas that the local Tories and British officials would now oppose the Association by force of military arms. Adding to their apprehension was the loyalty of the Indians to the Crown Indian commissioner, Guy Johnson, and the possibility that he would turn the Indians against the Whigs if the county supported the military hostilities in Massachusetts. With these concerns in mind, the committee of correspondence of Tryon County, New York (along the wild northern frontier with Quebec) began to meet regularly for the first time in May 1775. Although the committee had been chosen in August 1774 to demonstrate the county's support of the resistance against the Coercive Acts, its meetings had been infrequent since that time. Tryon County committeemen decided to seek support from neighboring committees before asking for aid from New York City. In a letter of 19 May 1775, the committee informed the Albany Committee of Correspondence that a meeting in the Mohawk district had already been broken up by armed Loyalists and that any gunpowder sent to the area should be carefully shipped lest it be lost.[79] Two days later, a meeting of the "United Committees" of the various districts of the county voted to send a delegation to Albany and Schenectady "to commune . . . upon the present Situation of America in General and this County in particular" and, if they could, to get military stores.[80]

The Albany Committee of Correspondence, however, had difficulties of its own. As early as 25 April 1775, it was asked for help by the Pittsfield, Massachusetts, Committee of Correspondence, which feared that the Tories of Kinderhook, New York would attack them in retaliation for the fighting in eastern Massachusetts. The Albany committee was unsure of its authority to take action supporting military resistance by sending supplies or men and gave Pittsfield an evasive answer, assuring them that the Kinderhook people would not attack them. Although the Albany Committee of Correspondence resolved, on 29 April, to call for an election in the county to appoint a "Committee of Safety, Protection & Correspondence," fully empowered to take whatever actions became necessary to defend the county, it was neither willing nor able to support offensive military action immediately. Shortly after the recommended committee of safety was formed to supersede the previous committee of correspondence, two New Englanders came to Albany seeking aid for an attack on Fort Ticonderoga. Unable to reach a decision on its own, the Albany Committee of Safety sought advice from the New York City committee on whether or not to help the expedition. The New York City committee was also unsure of the proper course to take and did not answer until well after the fort had been taken by Ethan Allen and his men. Both groups deferred instead to the provincial congress, which was scheduled to meet in late May. When the Albany Committee of Safety received another request for aid from Allen on 13 May, it responded that action was impossible "before we have the Opinion of the Provincial or Continental Congress."[81]

The taking of Ticonderoga and Crown Point by Allen in early May 1775 served to increase, rather than reduce, the fear of the people of northern New York about British intentions. Despite this fact, the Albany Committee of Safety did little to form military companies. Some volunteer companies were organized during May, and one of these, which called itself the "Association Company," was ordered by the Albany committee, on the recommendation of the Continental Congress, to join the garrison at Ticonderoga on 26 May. Although the Albany committee maintained a watch in the town throughout most of May, because of "Suspicion of the Negroes" and fear of the Tories who were allegedly buying arms, it was unable to train troops actively until late in the month.[82]

The strength and intentions of Loyalist opponents to the struggle against Great Britain was also an issue in the neighboring province of New Jersey. On 5 January 1775, a New Jersey Tory had published a letter in Rivington's *New York Gazette* which was directed to the Essex County, New Jersey, committee. He challenged the committee system by stating: "I had rather submit to acts of Parliament implicitly, nay to the *will* of a King, than to the *caprice* of Committee-men." Shortly thereafter, on 3 January 1775, Governor William Franklin threatened the assembly, in his speech opening the session, with "Anarchy, Misery, and all the Horrors of a Civil War," if they did not abandon support for the general American resistance and humbly petition the king.[83] On several occasions following the battles at Lexington and Concord, crowds planned to attack Loyalists, who were feared and hated, but were convinced not to by the actions of colonial leaders. Elias Boudinot, a prominant Whig of the Essex County Committee of Correspondence, wrote a letter on 30 April to the committee of correspondence of Morris County to dissuade them from a planned attack on Tory Thomas Eckley, informing them that his committee had halted a similar raid on the house of pamphleteer Dr. Thomas Bradbury Chandler and that they opposed all violence against the Tories until it proved absolutely necessary.[84]

Although the Crown-supported New Jersey Assembly, which met from 11 January to 13 February 1775, did not encourage the colony to arm, citizens in towns such as Elizabeth and Freehold began military preparations on their own prior to 19 April, a move which was taken over and expanded by the county committees in May. On 26 May, the extralegal New Jersey Provincial Congress, "apprehensive that all pacifick measures for the redress of our grievances will prove ineffectual," resolved that "the inhabitants of this Province be forthwith properly armed and disciplined for defending the cause of American freedom." To organize this military defense, the provincial congress, which, unlike the congresses of many provinces, contained only nine assemblymen, directed the townships to raise a militia and passed a tax to pay for military stores.[85]

· DELIBERATIONS OF THE SECOND CONTINENTAL CONGRESS ·

As military preparations continued in many provinces and commenced in several others, the Second Continental Congress began its deliberations on 10 May 1775. Delegates to the intercolonial gathering were faced with a number of possible options. They could either submit to British rule, continue commercial resistance under the Continental Association, or organize a military force capable of repelling the British troops in America. The Congress eventually chose to form a continental army, but not before a good deal of discussion had occurred. Indeed, Congress at first refused to approve preparations for a general war and hoped the fighting would be confined to the vicinity of Boston. If British troops threatened other areas, the delegates recommended that committees and provincial militias act only in self-defense. Responding to a request from the New York City committee of one hundred for advice on what actions to take should British troops arrive in the town, Congress advised restraint. Military force, the delegates suggested in their response of 15 May, should be used only if British troops commenced hostilities.[86]

The somewhat contradictory resolutions of 26 May reflect a similar concern. Arguing that the beginning of hostilities in Massachusetts placed the provinces in a dangerous position, Congress resolved on this date that "these colonies be immediately put into a state of defence." At the same time, however, the delegates proposed negotiations for reconciliation with the Crown.[87]

A petition was eventually sent to the king, but Congress spent much more time organizing military defense of the colonies than it did debating prospects for reconciliation.[88] Progress on military measures for colonial defense, however, was slow, and this caused leaders such as John Adams extreme frustration. Writing to Moses Gill on 10 June, Adams argued that congressional actions which "hold the sword in one hand and the olive branch in the other" were dangerous, for "petitions, negotiations, everything which hold out to the people hopes of reconciliation without bloodshed is greedily grasped at and relied on—and they cannot be persuaded to think that it is so necessary to prepare for war as it really is."[89] The Massachusetts lawyer was particularly irked by Congress's response to a letter it received from the Massachusetts Provincial Congress. This correspondence, which reached Philadelphia on 2 June, requested advice on two points of critical importance to the Bay Colony. First, the provincial congress wished to know whether it should officially assume and exercise all powers of civil government in the colony. This extralegal body already enjoyed the allegiance of the people but requested advice on what official stance to take. The second critical issue which faced the provincial congress concerned the command of the army then forming around Boston. Suggesting that the military force "now collecting from different colonies is for the general defence of the right of America," the provincial congress asked that the continental gathering take "the regulation and general direction of it, that the operations may more effectively answer the purposes designed."[90] On 4 June, Congress responded to the first question and suggested that the provincial body summon an assembly of representatives to exercise the powers of government, "until a Governor of his Majesty's appointment, will consent to govern the colony according to its charter."[91] Assuming command of an army, however, was another matter, one which required more time and careful consideration.

The Continental Congress took the first tentative steps toward military preparation on 3 June when it approved a resolution to borrow £6,000 for the purchase of powder. On 14 June, Congress finally committed itself to raising troops and voted that six companies of expert riflemen be created for service in Massachusetts. These companies were viewed as part of "the American continental army" and were to be paid by the Congress.[92] One day later, George Washington was elected "to command all the continental forces, raised or to be raised, for the defence of American liberty."[93]

As Washington prepared for his journey to Boston, Congress undertook the three tasks of selecting additional military officers, raising money for an army, and constructing a rationale for military resistance. By 21 June, the first of these was completed as four major generals and eight brigadier generals were appointed to the Continental Army. One day later, several hours before news was received of "a battle" at Bunker Hill in Massachusetts, Congress agreed to finance the war by voting issuance of $2,000,000 in paper money.[94] A committee of five—John Rutledge, William Livingston, Benjamin Franklin, John Jay, and Thomas Johnson— was appointed on 23 June to draft the address which came to be known as the "Declaration of the Causes and Necessity of Taking up Arms," but its report presented on 24 June, was "referred for further considerations." It was only after two new members, John Dickinson and Thomas Jefferson, had been added to the committee that a declaration was finally approved by Congress. The declaration, which had first been drafted by Jefferson and revised by Dickinson, was adopted on 6 July 1775, three days after Washington assumed formal command of the Continental Army. In this document, Congress argued that they had done everything possible to avoid a violent confrontation:

> We have pursued every temperate, every respectful measure: we have even proceeded to break off our commercial intercourse with our fellow-subjects, as the last peaceable admonition that our attachment to no nation upon earth should supplant our attachment to liberty. This, we flattered ourselves, was the ultimate step of the controversy. . . .

> We are reduced to the alternative of choosing an unconditional submission to the tyranny of irritated ministers or resistance by force. The latter is our choice. . . .

> We . . . *declare,* that . . . the arms we have been compelled by our enemies to assume, we will, in defiance of every hazard, with unabating firmness and perseverance, employ for the preservation of our liberties; being with one mind resolved to die freemen, rather then to live slaves.[95]

• MORE PROVINCES PREPARE FOR DEFENSE •

Throughout June and July 1775, both the Continental Congress and various bodies in the individual colonies continued military preparations. By 18 July, Congress had proposed a general plan for each colony to reorganize its militia and recommended that committees of safety be appointed in each province. Many of the colonies, however, had already taken such steps in June. In the first week of that month, the extralegal New Jersey Provincial Congress continued the defensive military preparations begun in late May and elected a fourteen-man group which soon came to be known as the committee of safety.[96] On 5 June, the extralegal South Carolina Provincial Congress, worried about the preponderance of Tories in the colonial militia, recommended that volunteer military groups be organized and new officers elected.[97] One week later, the congress voted to create a thirteen-man council of safety with supreme power over the army, militia, and military affairs.[98] At its first meeting with the patriot governor, Jonathan Trumbull, on 7 June, the Connecticut "Council or Committee of War," which had been selected by the assembly in early May to act while the legislature was not in session, decided to send more troops and supplies to the army surrounding Boston. The presence of Tories was also of great concern to the organizers of resistance to British authority in Connecticut. In late fall 1774 and early 1775, mass meetings were organized by supporters of the Crown in the western communities of the colony. Although numerous in many towns, the Tories were far outnumbered in the colony as a whole, and they were largely unsuccessful in their efforts to mount any real opposition to the nonviolent resistance. The General Assembly, however, was sufficiently fearful of the Tory influence to investigate the resolutions of towns unsupportive of the Continental Association early in the session which opened 2 March 1775. In June 1775, Connecticut troops were moved closer to the New York border at the command of the council of war. There, they could not only be closer to a possible British invasion route but would be stationed near the potentially disaffected western towns. Although not militantly active, many Tories remained supportive of the Crown and were feared by the Whigs.[99]

Unlike the provinces of New Jersey, South Carolina, or Connecticut, the colony of New York was extremely reluctant to organize for military defense. Although the New York Provincial Congress was constantly pressured by the Continental Congress to form a military organization, the New York extralegal legislature refused to take decisive action. On 25 May, the Continental Congress passed several resolves calling upon New York to act. These were forwarded to the provincial congress in a letter received on 29 May and acted on the next day. New York was requested to arm and train its militia and to establish a defensive garrison for the City, "in Case any Insult should be offered by the Troops, that may land there; and to prevent any Attempts that may be made to gain possession of the City." The provincial congress complied in a vaguely worded resolution which called upon the people to obtain military arms, "and if necessary to form themselves into Companies." Organization for military defense under provincial control, however, was postponed, and the congress decided instead to appoint a fourteen-member committee to draw up a military plan. On 7 June, the provincial congress approved the action of the Albany Committee of Safety in sending two of its companies to

Ticonderoga, but it restrained the committee from sending further companies, then being raised, to the fort now held by the Americans.[100]

Some of the problems faced by supporters of military measures in New York had to do with a lack of confidence in the colonial militia. Many officers were viewed as British sympathizers, and colonial leaders believed that they would prove unreliable in any general mobilization. Although the loyalty of the volunteer companies drilling in Albany and New York, of which there were at least seven by the end of June, was unquestioned, concerns had been voiced about the condition of their armaments and quality of their training. Despite these problems, the provincial congress's committee on military "arrangement" continued its deliberations, and presented its report to the delegates on 27 June. After a short discussion, the congress approved the recommendations of the committee and began to raise companies of troops in anticipation of the formation of the Continental Army. Although the provincial congress made arrangements to purchase supplies and to pay the troops, there continued to be no arrangement for taxation of the colony, and goods were instead procured "on the public Credit."[101]

When the Crown-supported Pennsylvania General Assembly convened on 19 June, it was pressured by Philadelphia's committee of sixty-six to reconsider military organization. The committee and a lobby of officers from the volunteer companies argued that present military preparations were inadequate and proposed both the formation of a "Committee of Safety and Defence" and the adoption of a central militia plan. The assembly deliberated on these proposals until 30 June. Then, the delegates decided to endorse the formation of the local military associations, pay soldiers who defended the colony, order a stockpile of muskets for minutemen, raise £35,000 paper currency through taxation, and form a twenty-four member provincial committee of safety.[102]

Despite the arguments of the Philadelphia committee, the assembly refused to change the practice of having militia membership be voluntary and unpaid. This continued for quite some time, despite the organizing and supplying of many new companies by the Pennsylvania Committee of Safety and the expansion of the Philadelphia committee into a county committee of one hundred members. During the summer of 1775, both a committee of officers of the military association and a committee of privates were formed to press for mandatory service and for payment when on duty. Their organizers argued that poor men could hardly leave their families to take up arms and allow them to starve. Under this strong encouragement, the Pennsylvania Committee of Safety proposed a series of military regulations which did not meet the demands of the militiamen and were unacceptable to them. Finally, in November 1775, the Pennsylvania General Assembly was forced to take up the matter. Delegates at this session decided to organize and fund militia units, making either service or a compensatory fine required. In this way, Quakers or other pacifists who refused to enter the militia would be made to pay as a substitute.[103]

Military preparations on the provincial level in Delaware were virtually nonexistent in the summer of 1775, and progress remained slow in Georgia and

North Carolina. Other than agreeing on 7 June to assume its share of the costs in raising a continental army, the Delaware Assembly remained aloof from military preparations. A group of activists in the colony formed a committee of safety in September 1775, but not at the suggestion of the assembly. Georgia was only more marginally organized than Delaware. The colony's second provincial congress, which met from 5–7 July 1775, created a council of safety for the province and commissioned officers for their colonial militia.[104]

North Carolina remained relatively inactive until August 1775. Although Rowan and Wilmington counties had formed militia companies under the leadership of the local committees in 1774 and early 1775, neither the assembly nor the extralegal provincial congress, each of which met at the same time in April 1775, were willing to recommend the preparation of defensive military measures. After the fighting at Lexington and Concord, in fact, Samuel Johnson, who was authorized to call a provincial congress in case of emergency, avoided doing so and had to be pressed into it by the committees. Despite some quasi-military activities, including the carrying off of Governor Josiah Martin's cannon and the burning of a wooden fort on Cape Fear in June, the militia remained unorganized. North Carolina's delegates to the Second Continental Congress were so incensed by the lack of activity that they berated the province in a letter written to the county committees on 19 June for being "an inactive Spectator" in the "general defensive armament." After warning of the dangers represented by the slaves and Indians within the colony's borders, the delegates urged their countrymen "to follow the Example of your sister Colonies and to form yourselves into a Militia."[105] When the third provincial convention finally met on 20 August 1775, public pressure for strengthened military organization had grown. A military committee and forty-five-member committee of safety were quickly formed and the delegates pledged to raise two regiments for "the Continental Line." Public tax money, including uncollected back taxes, was appropriated to pay for these preparations.

Despite these actions, the colony remained deeply divided over military opposition to Great Britain. Governor Martin encouraged divisions within the province and even attempted to organize military opposition to the Whigs. In his efforts, Martin approached the ex-Regulators in the western backcountry, many of whom were the sworn enemies of the province's eastern leaders. Many North Carolinians of Scottish descent, who were often the butt of discrimination by easterners, were also willing to join Martin in opposing plans for a colonial militia. This Loyalist threat became serious in 1776 when a force was collected to march on Wilmington and rout the Whigs. Intercepted only eighteen miles from the town, this Tory force was defeated and scattered in the Battle of Moore's Creek Bridge on 26 and 27 February 1776.[106]

Although South Carolina was more decisive in preparing for military defense than had been her provincial neighbor to the north, the colony still faced significant problems in implementing resolutions of its extralegal provincial congresses. On 3 June 1775, the provincial congress passed a military association and proceeded to develop an organization to make their association effective. It was the task of the council of safety, appointed on 14 June 1775, to translate the wishes of the provincial convention into reality. The council of safety began its operations on 16 June, under the chairmanship of provincial congress President Henry Laurens, and signed several officers' commissions one day later. On 21 June, the council ordered the commanding officers of the province's new militia regiments to enlist men for a term of from six months' to three years' service, and recommended that the "good people of this and the neighboring colonies," give them "all necessary aid and assistance." During the remainder of June, the council of safety busied itself with military appointments, the procurement of stores, and the printing of "certificates" of public indebtedness (in lieu of currency) to pay for men and supplies.[107]

In the midst of the colony's preparations, newly appointed British Governor William Campbell arrived in Charleston to take up his duties. Although Campbell was not as effective an opponent of the Whigs as Governor Martin of North Carolina, he could call upon Tory strength in the backcountry, and his presence heightened the disunity behind the military preparations in the province. On 3 July, in an effort to mobilize support for their activities, the council of safety sent three men to discuss the colonial cause with the German settlers in the interior. The council also prepared an address to the Catawba nation of Indians, who had sent two men to discover the intentions of the colony in the struggle against the British. Supporters of the colonial cause were also fearful of the possibility of slave revolts. In a letter to the council of safety, the "parochial [county-parish] committee" of Chehaw denounced one John Burnett for "holding nocturnal meetings with the negroes." The parochial committee arrested Burnett and sent him under guard to Charleston for the council of safety to deal with. Burnett convinced the council that the meetings had merely been evangelical religious gatherings and that he had not held any since 1773. Despite Burnett's assurances and his departure to Georgia, fears remained that the Loyalists would use the slaves against the Whigs.[108]

The council of safety early recognized the need to be in control of the backcountry and ordered that several companies of "rangers" be raised in June and July. Three of these companies were ordered into the field to take possession of Fort Charlotte, deep in the backcountry near the Georgia border. Whig leader James Mayson, in charge of the force, wrote to his commanding officer, Militia Colonel William Thompson, on 18 July 1775, to apprise him of the outcome of the mission. Mayson had found only fifty-six men enlisted in the companies and had marched with them to the fort, which they seized without opposition from the British commander. While several of the rangers garrisoned the fort, Mayson and the others carried off the ammunition and military supplies to the town of Ninety Six. There, the small ranger band was confronted by two hundred armed "disaffected People from Over the River," who were soon augmented by the defection of a ranger company under the leadership of Tory Moses Kirkland. Mayson was arrested by the Tories, but later released on bail. Meanwhile, the Loyalist force carried off all of the stores, except for two field pieces, without opposition from Mayson's Whig rangers.[109]

In response to this failure, the provincial council of safety sent a delegation composed of the well-known Whig Leaders William Henry Drayton and the Reverend William Tennent into the backcountry on 23 July 1775 to talk to the people about the "unhappy public disputes between Great Britain and the American colonies." Drayton and Tennent were authorized to requisition support from the militia or rangers if they found it necessary to mobilize 1,200 men at the town of Ninety Six.[110] The Drayton-Tennent mission, like the Mayson efforts which preceded it, accomplished very little. Captain Moses Kirkland, who had acted as an officer in the council of safety's ranger regiments during the taking of Fort Charlotte but was actually a Tory, threatened the Whigs in the backcountry throughout the summer. Kirkland's efforts were supported by Governor Campbell, who continued his attempts to mobilize opposition to the provincial congress and council of safety. Henry Laurens, head of the council of safety, wrote that Campbell was "privately spiriting up the people on our Frontiers to oppose our Association & to hold themselves in readiness to act in Arms against the Colony."[111]

Despite the alarm, the crisis with the Loyalists of the backcountry districts did not actually result in fighting at that time. The new provincial military bodies—the militia, rangers, and volunteer companies—were not, however, easily disciplined by the council of safety. In September, an attempt by the council of safety to tighten the conditions of military service and put volunteer companies under full discipline was loudly protested by the men involved. "We judged it necessary," said Henry Laurens of the action, "to Issue an Order for compelling many delinquents to do equal duty with their fellow citizens in the militia." This decision, he continued, raised "a general clamour." The council of safety received several petitions from the volunteer companies which protested the new regulations. A special grievance was the new practice, so reminiscent of British practice, of giving militia officers precedence over officers of the volunteer companies—allowing a militia officer to give orders to a volunteer company officer of the same rank. Although the council of safety did not change the order, it made diligent attempts to conciliate the companies by explaining the reasons for the orders and was able to gain pledges of solidarity from some of them.

In the autumn of 1775, although no fighting had yet occurred in the province, Henry Laurens felt that South Carolina was unprepared for war. In a letter to the South Carolina delegates to the Continental Congress, Laurens requested that the Continental Congress form an "Army of Observation" in South Carolina of the type he believed North Carolina to have. He also suggested that the Congress in Philadelphia pass a general militia law that would settle many questions about military discipline and duties that the South Carolina Council of Safety had been unable to resolve itself.[112]

· POLITICAL PROBLEMS OF MILITARY RESISTANCE ·

Like many other colonial leaders, Laurens was extremely conscious of difficulties involved in preparing the colonies for military defense of British North America. Although the provinces had firmly committed themselves to this strategy by the end of the summer 1775, significant military and political problems remained. By September, most of the colonies had resolved to reorganize their militia and had begun recruitment for the Continental Army, but passing resolutions and mobilizing an effective fighting force often proved to be two different matters. The fact that extralegal provincial congresses in colonies such as Pennsylvania, Maryland, and New York reorganized their militia companies a number of times before the end of 1775 indicates that preparations for military defense had not proceeded as smoothly as had been expected. Moreover, the provincial congresses had a difficult time evolving a relationship between the militia units and the Continental Army. The Second Continental Congress provided quotas of troops to be raised in each colony, and leaders in individual provinces wondered whether the emphasis placed on a continental body would hurt the already limited effectiveness of the militia.

As noted earlier, certain political problems also emerged with the shift to military struggle. One of the major difficulties involved the coordination of this new type of resistance. During the ten years prior to Lexington and Concord, a new class of leaders had emerged, many of whom had little expertise in military affairs. With the decision of the Second Continental Congress to form an army and the moves by provincial congresses and local committees to organize for military defense, these leaders were confronted with the choice of whether to apply for military commissions, or to remain as members of a committee. Some opted for the first alternative and left the committees, sometimes in frustration over the difficulties involved in making them work once military hostilities had commenced.[113] This created a void in leadership in the political committees and encouraged the new local and provincial decision-makers to defer to higher authorities such as the Continental Congress. The power of military officers increased as well. Although certain military leaders, most notably George Washington, had been active in political affairs, many had little experience in this area and were unsure of the extent of their power to determine the course of the resistance. The committees periodically attempted to reassert control of the military resistance, but were frequently at odds with the numerous military associations and volunteer companies which had formed to protect the communities.

As support for military resistance grew, the belief which the colonists had formerly placed in the nonviolent technique declined. The Continental Association remained, but the document was radically amended in late 1775 and thereafter lost its character as an instrument of nonviolent coercion. In addition, supporters of the colonial cause treated Loyalists differently after military hostilities had commenced. During the previous ten years, colonists who disagreed with the nonviolent resistance campaigns were the subject of social and economic boycott. While some had been threatened, few were actually attacked. After Lexington and Concord, however, fear of Loyalist opposition grew, and the committees made preparations designed to threaten use of violence against the Tories to intimidate them into submission. The township of Shrewsbury, New Jersey, for example, upon organizing a militia on 19 June 1775, passed several resolutions which implied that this body would be used against opponents of colonial resistance.[114] As military preparations continued throughout the provinces and as the formal break with Great Britain drew increasingly near, conflicts with the loyalists escalated. By late 1775, in fact, many Whigs had concluded that "moderation" with respect to the Tories "was no longer compatible with safety."[115]

· HYPOTHETICAL REASONS FOR THE SHIFT IN STRATEGY ·

The previous sections of this chapter describe the shift in the colonists' strategy, but they do not explain *why* such a change occurred. Based on the evidence presented to this point, however, it is possible to advance several hypotheses which may aid our understanding of this transformation. These propositions cannot, of course, totally explain the shift to military struggle, but they may be useful to those interested in exploring this area in greater detail.

Hypothesis One: Changes Within the Movement and "the Last Resource"

One might argue that the shift to military struggle was caused by changes in organization and goals which occurred within the American resistance movement during the years 1774–76. These times saw important qualitative alterations in the American struggle, which inevitably influenced colonial perceptions of their status in the British Empire. Supporters of this view might suggest that the weakening and breaking of the imperial bond caused by ten years of resistance allowed, even encouraged, the colonists to take action that their previous allegiance to the king had forestalled. The earlier movements against the Stamp and Townshend Acts had been designed to counter action by the ministers, and Parliament, not the king, had been the colonial opponent. It was a commonly held belief that if colonial protests could reach the ear of the king, George III would surely grant redress to his subjects in need. Many colonists felt that the only reason he did not do so was the "ministerial plot"—the combination of anti-American and power-hungry syncophants who kept American petitions and grievances away from the king. When it was discovered that King George was not sympathetic to the colonies and that he was actually antagonistic toward them and in favor of using harsh measures, their attitude changed. One might argue that once the king was no longer felt to be a trustworthy sovereign, but a tyrant and usurper, it was legitimate to fight against him and the British army.[116]

As the colonists gained a new view of their sovereign, they may also have developed concerns about the most appropriate means of resistance. There is some support for the idea that the colonists believed in the existence of a natural and justifiable progression of measures to be used against the actions of government. At the bottom of this scale were legislative petitions and memorials to Parliament. If protest did not gain redress, it was legitimate to organize for measures which would unite various groups in resisting the ministry by nonmilitary means. These included the sending of circular letters to other colonies and the development of nonimportation and, later, nonexportation pacts. If all these measures were tried, but Britain still did not relent and, instead, answered colonial actions by sending troops to punish the Americans, the next step was to use military violence. This was a big step. In George Washington's words, it was "the last resource," a measure which he saw as necessary in view of the dire position of unarmed provinces threatened by the British army.[117] Throughout the earlier years of the struggle, whenever the suggestion to use violence had been made, it had been rejected because conditions did not permit the use of "the last resource." In 1775, however, the time came when committed patriots concluded that the only measures left to them were military ones. Reluctantly, they formed the Continental Army and brought it into battle with the British, believing that no other path remained open to them.

One might argue that as support for the idea of independence from Great Britain broadened throughout the colonial society during 1775 and early 1776, the Americans felt that they could no longer continue nonviolent means of struggle. While nonimportation and allied actions had been thought excellent methods with which to pursue redress of grievances, they were now regarded as ill-suited to the task of gaining independence. They may have been perceived in this way because they were essentially viewed as noncoercive methods, that is, ones which left the final decision in the hands of the British. Colonists may also have felt that these nonviolent methods were insufficiently powerful to force the British to grant independence or would take longer than military means.

Hypothesis Two: Inadequacy of the Nonviolent Technique

It might be argued that while the provincial leaders had successfully relied on the methods of noncooperation and nonimportation in the past to induce changes in British policy, these were unable to effect change under the conditions existing in 1774 and after. In the years prior to the adoption of the Coercive Acts, neither the king nor any significant portion of the British populace had been in favor of enforcing the parliamentary regulations at any cost. By late 1774, however, both the king and the landed gentry were not only in favor of enforcement by British officials in the colonies but proposed coercive action by the army as well. Moreover, the British economy was not badly hurt by the nonintercourse agreements during this period of stability at home, and the protests of merchants were rejected or ignored in Parliament. In this situation, one might claim that the use of commercial sanctions for a third time could not work because they no longer had any leverage. If the provincial leaders hoped to defend the colonies against British troops and gain the goal of preserving their liberties in the face of repressive measures, it was thought that they had to take up arms. There was no longer any possibility that the ministry would either listen to reason or give in to avoid commercial losses and accommodate to colonial wishes. One might reasonably conclude, therefore, that the British were going to stand firm and the Americans would have to escalate their methods in order to win.[118]

One factor which may have contributed to this colonial perception was the fear and insecurity engendered by the presence of British troops throughout North America. It had long been a belief of both colonial and British constitutional thinkers that a standing army was a prime threat to liberty. When the standing army took on the character of an occupation force as well, or at least showed that potential, the fears of the people magnified. As the French war of 1754–63 receded further into the past, many colonists became more convinced that British troops were unnecessary for their protection, but rather served some other purposes. The tensions caused by the presence of the troops sometimes exploded into antimilitary violence, such as that which occurred in Boston and New York late in the winter of 1770. Consequently, with marches into the countryside in the fall of 1774 to seize colonial gunpowder and military stores, as well as frequent military demands of the local communities for food, lodging, and even money, the colonials came to view British troops as armed aggressors. As these fears grew, people felt compelled to arm themselves against the threat, both as individuals and as communities. The militia groups were reactivated and trained, and the towns bought powder and shot, just in case. There need not have been any intention to use them to oppose political policies, such as the Coercive Acts, but the people wanted to be ready and to feel more secure. They felt that the capacity for self-defense by military means was the only way to promote collective security.[119]

A second factor contributing to the colonial perception concerned potential retaliation against the British army. The colonists had been both willing and able to use nonviolent action against Britain as long as the price they had to pay for it was self-inflicted (such as economic hardship). When Britain threatened in late 1774 and early 1775 to use her military might to punish the colonists for their nonviolent opposition, however, they may no longer have felt able to use the same technique. "If we are not subject to the supreme authority of parliament," John Adams warned the colonies in February 1775, "Great-Britain will make us so." At that point, Adams continued, "all other laws and obligations are given up, and recourse is had . . . to the law of brickbats and cannon balls, which can be answered only by brickbats and balls."[120] Although the colonials had seen how nonviolent tactics could be used against the policies of the ministry when no troops were used to enforce them, perhaps they did not feel that the technique could maintain their freedom and gain them redress in the face of Britain's military strength. If Britain sent an army of occupation to the colonies which arrested leaders, demanded to be quartered, and threatened the populace, the Americans would have to answer with an army of their own. They could not see how any other methods than military ones could work against an army, since their nonviolent methods could not prevent occupation and seizures. After the Declaration of Independence, it was perceived as particularly necessary to have an army since they now had newly formed home governments (both on a local and national level) to protect against the military maneuvers of Lord Howe. In short, they may have perceived that military means must be answered in kind.

Hypothesis Three: A Violent Party

The war might have occurred because of the efforts of a small faction of colonial radicals—possibly including Samuel Adams, John Lamb, and Patrick Henry—who believed that the only way in which British control could ultimately be defeated was through violence. They were perhaps among those who felt from the beginning of colonial resistance activities that independence and violent revolution were necessary. While members of this faction were willing to go along with or even organize "more moderate" methods if they served to stimulate popular unrest, to create organizations useful in aiding the violent struggle once it got started, or to antagonize the British, they believed that independence could only be achieved through military struggle. One could claim that these leaders frequently took the occasion of the movements against the various revenue acts to stimulate incidents which would force the British troops to retaliate and hoped that the British military would enrage the people and induce them to resist. In an effort to achieve their goals, they sent mobs into the streets in 1765, 1768, and 1770, later encouraged the countryside to raise and train militia and to keep military stores, and pushed for the formation of a continental army by Congress. Likewise, if we review the events leading up to the battles of Lexington and Concord, particularly 18 April when the riders were sent out in the night, we find that armed men from all over eastern Massachusetts were called out to meet the British not by their elected officials but by the committee of safety. Supporters of this hypothesis might argue that this party's advocacy of violence was not based on an analysis of what the political situation required, nor an understanding of colonial desires, but in their *belief* in the need for anti-British violence in order to make their own goal of independence one which would be adopted by other Americans.

Hypothesis Four: A *Fait Accompli*

The decision to use military means may not have been a decision at all but resulted from a fait accompli *presented to the Second Continental Congress by the battles at Lexington and Concord, Bunker Hill, and the seizure of Ticonderoga.* The first Continental Congress strongly opposed military preparations, and the Second Congress moved towards preparation of colonial military defense only after 19

April 1775. While militia groups had been strengthened by the committees under the Association in 1774 and 1775, there was no clear idea of how, when, or under what conditions these militia bodies might be used. If anyone had the legal authority to call upon these militia or minutemen forces, it would have been either the assemblies or local government, but by 1775 these bodies were in the turmoil of change. This turmoil was reflected in the battles of Lexington and Concord. The day of 19 April 1775 has often been characterized as a day of egregious blunders on both sides.[121] Once the fighting broke out in Massachusetts, however, rational decision-making was shunted into the background as the country prepared for a war that now seemed inevitable.

Hypothesis Five: The Military as a Symbol of Sovereignty

As the resistance against the Coercive Acts progressed and as more and more functions of government were assumed by sections of the new extralegal governments, it became clear to colonial leaders that these bodies were becoming sovereign in North America. While this sovereignty existed in fact, it was not legally recognized. Even if committees of observation functioned as courts, for example, they still did not have the majesty and tradition of the established tribunals. *One might argue that members of the new provincial governmental bodies wanted to develop the external trappings that would illustrate their authority to the world and that the use of military force would further this goal.* One of the major characteristics of a state is the ability to tax its people and to establish with that tax money a military body, whether army or militia. Modern social scientists and political philosophers claim that the state is the only institution in which the means of violence should be concentrated and its use legitimated. It follows from this that one of the formal signs of statehood is the ability to use violence legitimately.[122] The colonials, inheritors of the European tradition, felt much this way. Once they realized their sovereignty, they wanted to demonstrate their power to whomever was watching. They may not have wanted to fight the British, but much of the discretion was taken out of local hands. After the spring of 1776, when the Continental Army incorporated the new provincial military units and the Second Continental Congress authorized George Washington to recommission any army officer in their name rather than in terms of the "revolutionary organization of his own colony," the local provinces no longer had as much influence.[123]

Hypothesis Six: Misunderstanding of the Nonviolent Technique

From the evidence in this and previous chapters, a case might be made that the colonists' limited awareness of the strength of their means of struggle, how it would best be used, and how to distinguish success from failure led them to abandon prematurely the nonviolent strategy. When the nonimportation agreements against the Townshend Acts ended in 1770, for example, the Americans had nullified or forced repeal of all sections of the acts except the tax on tea, which was minor in terms of its amount. Many colonists, however, considered the campaign to have failed outright, both because the tea tax was retained and because Parliament had not repudiated the right to tax America. There was little idea of a partial victory or of weighing the gains achieved against the energy expended. Victory was seen by many as all or nothing, and they felt that what they had achieved was as good as nothing in the face of what was left undone. It is possible, of course, that this attitude was partially encouraged by the manner in which the agreements were terminated. No clear line of demarcation could be used to see the end of the campaign, as would exist in a military armistice. On the other hand, participation in organized violence is in some ways its own reward, and the standards by which success or failure are judged are different than is usually applied in nonviolent struggles. In this sense, the Boston Tea Party was considered a great success because of its visibility and because no one was punished for it, even though its only real accomplishment was stimulating passage of the highly repressive Boston Port Act. This differential assessment of success and failure may have led the American leaders to feel that military struggle would be a better choice and to move toward initiating it in 1775 and 1776.

It is very difficult to determine the precise reasons for the colonists' shift to the use of military measures against the British. Some of the evidence outlined above may suggest avenues for fruitful inquiry, but the editors believe that definitive conclusions are premature at this time and await the future efforts of skillful scholars sensitive to the issues raised in this volume. What actually went on in the "minds and hearts" of the colonists during the decade, 1765–75, will always be difficult to access. The historical record is present for serious examination, and it is hoped that people will remain open to the wealth of information contained within it.

• NOTES •

1. John C. Miller, "The Massachusetts Convention: 1768," *New England Quarterly* 7 (September 1934), pp. 449, 466.

2. See Chapter Seven of this volume and the article by Roger Champagne, "The Military Association of the Sons of Liberty," *New York Historical Society Quarterly* 61 (1957), pp. 338–50.

3. See Chapter Eleven in this volume.

4. See the discussion in Pauline Maier, *From Resistance to Revolution* (New York: Knopf, 1972), Chapter Two.

5. John Locke, *The Second Treatise of Government,* ed., with an intro. by Thomas P. Peardon (Indianapolis: Bobbs-Merrill, 1952), p. 126.

6. See Chapter Eleven in this volume.

7. Reverend Ebenezer Baldwin, "An Appendix Stating the Heavy Grievances the

Colonies Labor Under" (New Haven, 1774), pp. 77–80.

8. Reverend William Gordon, "A Discourse Preached on the Morning of December 15, 1774" (Boston, 1775), pp. 26–29.

9. Reverend David Jones, "Defensive War in a Just Cause Sinless, A Sermon Preached on the Day of the Continental Fast" (Philadelphia, 1775), pp. 18–21.

10. Reverend John Carmichael, "A Self-defensive War, Lawful" (Philadelphia, 1775), pp. 8, 21–23.

11. *Ibid.*, p. 30.

12. Reverend Samuel West, "A Sermon Preached Before the Honorable Council and the Honorable House of Representatives of the Colony of Massachusetts-Bay in New England, May 29, 1776" (Boston, 1776), pp. 16–17, 27, 50, 54.

13. Lee Nathaniel Newcomer, *The Embattled Farmers* (New York: Russell and Russell, 1971), p. 51.

14. Neil R. Stout, *The Perfect Crisis: The Beginnings of the Revolutionary War* (New York: New York Univ. Press, 1976), p. 183.

15. Proposals for formation of minuteman companies were actually revivals of an old concept. In the French and Indian wars, for example, a portion of each militia company was required to be ready to act "at a minute's warning" (see John Shy, *Toward Lexington: The Role of the British Army in the Coming of the American Revolution* [Princeton: Princeton Univ. Press, 1965]).

16. *Boston Evening-Post*, 5 September 1774; Lieutenant-Governor Thomas Oliver to Earl of Dartmouth, 3 September 1774, Benjamin Hallowell to Grey Cooper, 5 September 1774, in K. G. Davies, ed., *Documents of the American Revolution, 1770–1783 (Colonial Office Series)* (Shannon: Irish Univ. Press, 1975), vol. 8, pp. 182–84, 187–91. See also Dirk Hoerder, *People and Mobs: Crowd Action in Massachusetts During the American Revolution* (Inaugural-Dissertation, Freie Universität Berlin, 1971), pp. 485–90. This was not the last time that colonial leaders narrowly avoided hostilities with the British. Again on 18 September 1774, the colonial militia was mobilized when British troops were reported to be gathering. This turned out to be a false alarm, as the 38th regiment was merely conducting an inspection (see Stout, *The Perfect Crisis*, p. 182).

17. William Lincoln, ed., *The Journals of Each Provincial Congress of Massachusetts in 1774 and 1775 and the Committee of Safety* (Boston: Dutton and Wentworth, 1838), pp. 33–34 (hereafter cited as *Mass. Cong. Journals*). For proceedings of this session, see also Peter Force, ed., *American Archives*, 4th ser. (Washington, D.C.: Government Printing Office, 1836–1846), vol. 1, pp. 841–50.

18. *Mass. Cong. Journals*, vol. 1, pp. 31–35.

19. Bernhard Knollenberg, *The Growth of the American Revolution, 1766–1775* (New York: Free Press, 1975), p. 431, indicates the difficulties in securing compliance with this resolution.

20. Stout, *The Perfect Crisis*, p. 185.

21. Oscar Zeichner, *Connecticut's Years of Controversy: 1750–1776* (Williamsburg, Va.: Institute for Early American History and Culture, 1949), p. 178–80; *New London Gazette*, 19 September 1774.

22. Charles Hoadly, ed., *The Public Records of the Colony of Connecticut* (Hartford: Case, Lockwood, Brainard, 1889), vol. 14, p. 337.

23. Oscar Zeichner, *Connecticut's Years of Controversy*, p. 188.

24. Requests were received from E. Greenwich, Newport, Warwick, Coventry, and Providence (John R. Bartlett, ed., *Records of the Colony of Rhode Island and Providence*

Plantations in New England [Providence: A. Crawford Greene, 1862], vol. 7, pp. 257, 260, 261).

25. *Ibid.*, pp. 269–71.

26. Bernhard Knollenberg, ed., *Correspondence of Governor Samuel Ward, May 1775–March 1776* (Providence: Rhode Island Historical Society, 1952), p. 31; quoted in idem., *Growth of the American Revolution*, pp. 176–177.

27. Richard Frances Upton, *Revolutionary New Hampshire* (Port Washington, N.Y.: Kennikat, 1970), pp. 22–23.

28. *Ibid.*, p. 40.

29. *Ibid.*, p. 41.

30. *Proceedings of the Conventions of the Province of Maryland* (Annapolis: Frederick Green, 1775), p. 7; quoted in Skaggs, *Roots of Maryland Democracy, 1763–1776* (Westport, Conn.: Greenwood, 1973), p. 157, and in Robert L. Scribner, ed., *Revolutionary Virginia: The Road to Independence* (Charlottesville: Univ. Press of Virginia, 1975), vol. 2, p. 187. A committee in Fairfax County, Virginia, on 17 January 1775, drew upon the Maryland resolutions in constructing their own, as did Augusta County (22 February 1775) and the Virginia Provincial Convention of 23 March 1775 (for details, see *ibid.*, vol. 2, p. 367).

31. Skaggs, *Roots of Maryland Democracy*, p. 158.

32. *Ibid.*, p. 157. Skaggs cites one town (Annapolis) in which people voted to contribute money for the purchase of arms (*ibid.*, p. 158).

33. Force, *American Archives*, vol. 1, p. 1118.

34. Richard Alan Ryerson, *The Revolution Is Now Begun: The Radical Committees of Philadelphia, 1765–1776* (Philadelphia: Univ. of Pennsylvania Press, 1978), p. 102.

35. Force, *American Archives*, vol. 1, pp. 1181–82.

36. *Ibid.* This was the ninth of eleven resolutions.

37. Lincoln, *Mass. Cong. Journals,* p. 90. Proceedings of the entire first session of the Second Provincial Congress are described in pp. 77–108.

38. Joseph Hawley to Thomas Cushing, 22 February 1775, *ibid.*, pp. 748–50, quoted in Knollenberg, *Growth of the American Revolution*, p. 182.

39. For reports of the incident, see Page Smith, *A New Age Now Begins* (New York: McGraw Hill, 1976), vol. 1, pp. 465–68; Lawrence Henry Gipson, *The British Empire Before the American Revolution*, vol. 12, *The Triumphant Empire: Britain Sails into the Storm, 1770–1776* (New York: Knopf, 1965), p. 318.

40. Larry R. Gerlach, *Prologue to Independence: New Jersey in the Coming of the American Revolution* (New Brunswick, N.J.: Rutgers Univ. Press, 1976), p. 255.

41. Upton, *Revolutionary New Hampshire*, p. 40.

42. Testimony given to the House of Burgesses in June 1775 documents the formation of companies in Prince William (24 September 1774), Spotsylvania (15 December 1774), Westmoreland (February 1775), Caroline (February or March 1775), and King George ("since the Virginia convention") counties (for details, see John P. Kennedy, ed., *Journals of the House of Burgesses of Virginia, 1773–1776* [Richmond: E. Waddey Co., 1905], pp. 231–37). Scribner, *Revolutionary Virginia*, vol. 2, pp. 242, 286, vol. 3, pp. 50–51, contains additional resolutions indicating the actual or recommended formation of companies in the counties of Fairfax (7 January 1775), Isle of Wight (13 February 1775), and Albemarle (18 April 1775), *Revolutionary Virginia*, p. 41, suggests that the Caroline company was not formed until 13 April 1775.

Further indication of companies' formation is provided by an investigation of

Washington's correspondence. In a letter written on 6 January, Washington states that companies had formed "in this county [Fairfax], Prince William, Loudoun, Fauquier, Berkley and many others round about." (quoted in Knollenberg, *Growth of the American Revolution*, p. 177). Washington does not provide the dates on which the companies were formed. Entries in his diaries (John C. Fitzpatrick, ed., *The Diaries of George Washington, 1748–1799* [Boston: Houghton Mifflin, 1925], vol. 2, pp. 70–188), suggest that a company was also formed in Dumfries in early 1775.

The House of Burgesses notes that Hanover County formed an independent company in November 1774 but said that "it was not embodied" until April 1775. The Burgesses noted further that independent companies were formed in Norfolk (some years ago) and in Williamsburg (fall 1774), but these bodies appeared to be sanctioned by the governor (see Kennedy, *Journals of the House of Burgesses, 1773–1776*, pp. 231–37).

43. Madison to William Bradford, 26 November 1774, William T. Hutchinson and William M. E. Rachel, eds., *The Papers of James Madison* (Chicago: Univ. of Chicago Press, 1962), vol. 1, p. 129.

44. Prince William and Hanover, see footnote 29.

45. On 21 September 1774, George Mason convinced George Washington and the county executive committee of twenty-five to adopt a plan for the creation of the "Fairfax Independent Company of Volunteers." Mason believed that a military organization was necessary "in this time of extreme Danger, with the Indian Enemy in our Country, and threat'ned with the Destruction of our Civil-rights, and Liberty." (Robert A. Rutland, ed., *The Papers of George Mason* [3 vols., Chapel Hill: Univ. of North Carolina Press, 1971], vol. 1, pp. 210–11). Mason also believed that the Fairfax company would be the first of its kind on the continent. For his views on this, see Helen Hill Miller, *George Mason: Gentleman Revolutionary* (Chapel Hill: Univ. of North Carolina Press, 1975), pp. 110, 112, 114.

46. Governor Dunmore to Dartmouth, 24 December 1774, quoted in Scribner, *Revolutionary Virginia*, vol. 3, p. 40.

47. *Ibid.*, p. 89.

48. Kennedy, *Journals of the House of Burgesses, 1773–1776*, p. 255. Charles Randall Lingley, *The Transition in Virginia from Colony to Commonwealth* (New York: Columbia Univ., 1910), p. 107, estimates that thirty volunteer companies had been formed by June 1775, but provides no precise dates on which they were organized.

49. Scribner, *Revolutionary Virginia*, vol. 3, p. 76.

50. For details, see *ibid.*, vol. 1, pp. 105, 204–5, 206.

51. *Ibid.*, vol. 2, pp. 223–25.

52. An approximate text of this speech, and the events surrounding it, may be found in William Wirt, *The Life of Patrick Henry* (Hartford, Conn.: S. Andrus and Son, 1846), pp. 141–42.

53. Scribner, *Revolutionary Virginia*, vol. 2, p. 369.

54. The complete text of the resolution is printed in *ibid.*, p. 366.

55. *Ibid.*, pp. 374–75.

56. Quoted in Knollenberg, *Growth of the American Revolution*, p. 182.

57. This motion was adopted by Commons on 2 February and by the Lords on 6 February. For a complete version of the motion, as well as the parliamentary debates surrounding it, see Force, *American Archives*, vol. 1, pp. 1542–87.

58. James Warren to Mercy Warren, 6 April 1775, quoted in Knollenberg, *Growth of the American Revolution*, p. 182.

59. For some of the difficulties, see Allen French, *The First Year of the Revolution*

(Boston: Houghton Mifflin, 1934), pp. 40–43.

60. Lincoln, *Mass. Cong. Journals,* p. 130.

61. Towns included Boston, Milton, Roxbury, Dorchester, Cambridge, Newton, Watertown, Lynn, Malden, Woburn, Charlestown, and Marlborough (*ibid.,* pp. 134, 135).

62. *Ibid.,* p. 135. This resolution passed, 96–7.

63. See, for example, Frank W. Coburn, *The Battle of April 19, 1775* (Lexington, Mass.: The Author, 1912); Allen French, *General Gage's Informers* (Ann Arbor: Univ. of Michigan Press, 1922); Knollenberg, *Growth of the American Revolution,* pp. 191–96, 264–68.

64. Donald Higginbotham, *The War for American Independence* (New York: Macmillan, 1971), p. 65.

65. Hoadly, *Records of Connecticut,* pp. 415–34.

66. Governor Joseph Trumbull to General Gage, 28 April 1775, Force, *American Archives,* vol. 2, pp. 433–34.

67. *Ibid.,* pp. 399–400.

68. Merrill Jensen, *The Founding of a Nation* (New York: Oxford Univ. Press, 1968), p. 597, says that, despite their authorizations, the assembly "had no money and made no effort to raise any."

69. Ryerson, *The Revolution is Now Begun,* p. 118. The counties which organized companies included Berks, in which two were formed, Lancaster, Bedford, Chester, Westmoreland, Northampton, and Cumberland.

70. Quoted in Scribner, *Revolutionary Virginia,* vol. 3, p. 5.

71. *Ibid.,* p. 7; Spotsylvania Council, 29 April 1775, in *ibid.,* vol. 2, p. 71.

72. Estimates of the actual number of volunteers assembled range from 150 to over 5,000 (see *ibid.,* vol. 3, p. 8).

73. On 13 and 20 March, 1775, the Delaware Assembly received petitions from Kent County requesting that a colonial militia be formed, but took no action on the proposals (see John Neuenschwander, *The Middle Colonies and the Coming of the American Revolution* (Port Washington, N.Y.: Kennikat, 1973), p. 77.

74. On 3 May, New Castle County levied a defense tax and began recruitment for a local militia. Kent County began military preparations three weeks later. Sussex County did not act until 20 June, when a county meeting voted to establish a committee of correspondence and public safety (*ibid.,* p. 80).

75. Bartlett, *Records of Rhode Island,* p. 322.

76. For proceedings of this session, see Hoadly, *Records of Connecticut,* pp. 12–31.

77. Upton, *Revolutionary New Hampshire,* p. 212.

78. *Ibid.*

79. *The Minute Book of the Committee of Safety of Tryon County, The Old New York Frontier* (New York: Dodd, Mead, 1905), pp. 4–8.

80. *Ibid.,* pp. 12–14.

81. *Minutes of the Albany Committee of Correspondence, 1775–1778* (Albany: Univ. of the State of New York, 1923), vol. 1, pp. 13–16, 20–21, 31–32. Kinderhook was the home of several Tory militia officers (see Rich J. Ashton, *The Loyalist Experience: New York, 1763–1789* [Ph.D. diss., Northwestern Univ., 1973], pp. 103–5).

82. *Albany Committee of Correspondence Minutes,* vol. 1, pp. 24, 33, 40–43, 55.

83. Larry R. Gerlach, ed., *New Jersey in the American Revolution, 1763–1782: A Documentary History* (Trenton, N.J.: New Jersey Historical Commission, 1975), pp. 104, 110. See also proposed, but evidently never formed, Loyalist association, pp. 115–17.

84. *Ibid.,* pp. 132–33.

85. John A. Neuenschwander, *Middle Colonies,* pp. 62, 120–21. Volunteer companies were formed in the counties of Essex, Middlesex, Monmouth, Morris, Somerset, and Bergen during the month of May (see Gerlach, *Prologue to Revolution,* p. 259).

86. Worthington C. Ford, *Journals of the Continental Congress, 1774–1798* (Washington, D.C.: Government Printing Office, 1904–1937), vol. 2, pp. 49, 52.

87. *Ibid.,* pp. 64–66.

88. The petition, which was prepared primarily by John Dickinson, was approved by Congress on 5 July 1775. King George III, however, refused to receive it (see Edward Cody Burnett, *The Continental Congress* [New York: Macmillan, 1941], pp. 85, 87, 115, 116).

89. John Adams to Moses Gill, 10 June 1775, quoted in Jonathan G. Rossie, *The Politics of Command in the American Revolution* (Syracuse: Syracuse Univ. Press, 1975), p. 9.

90. Ford, *Journals of the Continental Congress,* vol. 2, pp. 76–78.

91. Quoted in Burnett, *Continental Congress,* p. 73.

92. Two companies were to be raised in Pennsylvania, Maryland, and Virginia. A few days later, Pennsylvania's quota was raised to six.

93. Ford, *Journals of the Continental Congress,* vol. 2, p. 91. Washington's appointment was greeted with varying degrees of enthusiasm. For the considerations involved, see Louis Clinton Hatch, *The Administration of the American Revolutionary Army* (New York: Longmans, Green, and Co., 1904) pp. 5-11, and Burnett, *Continental Congress,* pp. 76–78.

94. Ford, *Journals of the Continental Congress,* vol. 2, pp. 105–6.

95. For the complete text of the Declaration, see Force, *American Archives,* vol. 2, pp. 1867–69.

96. Donald L. Kemmerer, *Path to Freedom: The Struggle for Self-government in Colonial New Jersey, 1703–1776* (Cos Cob, Conn: John E. Edwards, 1968), p. 332.

97. Edward McCrady, *The History of South Carolina in the Revolution, 1775–1780* (New York: Macmillan, 1902), p. 13.

98. *Ibid.,* p. 5.

99. Hoadly, *Records of Connecticut,* vol. 14, pp. 392, 413–34, vol. 15, pp. 84–87, 89; Zeichner, *Connecticut's Years of Controversy,* pp. 183–88, 199; Christopher Collier, *Roger Sherman's Connecticut: Yankee Politics and the American Revolution* (Middleton, Conn.: Wesleyan Univ. Press, 1971), pp. 103–4.

100. Roger Champagne, *Alexander McDougall and the American Revolution in New York* (Schenectady, N.Y.: Union College Press, 1975), pp. 82–92.

101. *Ibid.;* Berthold Fernow, ed., *Documents Related to the Colonial History of the State of New York,* vol. 15, *State Archives,* vol. 1 (Albany: Weed, Parsons, and Co.: 1887) [reprinted as *New York in the Revolution* (Cottonport, La.: Polyanthus, 1972)], pp. 4–5, 7, 11–12, 14–17; Bruce Bliven, Jr., *Under the Guns: New York, 1775–1776* (New York: Harper and Row, 1972), pp. 21–22.

102. Ryerson, *The Revolution Is Now Begun,* p. 122.

103. *Ibid.,* pp. 117–19; Neuenschwander, *Middle Colonies,* pp. 57, 81, 103.

104. Kenneth Coleman, *Colonial Georgia: A History* (New York: Scribners' Sons, 1976).

105. Rowan County had formed a militia company by late September 1774, and Wilmington County had taken similar action by the following January. Mecklenburg County issued a similar call before June 1775. For details of these actions and for the letter of the congressional delegation, see William L. Saunders, ed., *The Colonial and State Records of North Carolina* (10 vols., Raleigh, N.C.: Josephus Daniels, 1890), vol. 10, pp. xxix, 20–

23; Hugh T. Lefler and Albert R. Newsome, *North Carolina: The History of a Southern State* (3d ed., Chapel Hill: Univ. of North Carolina Press, 1973), pp. 203–7; and Hugh T. Lefler and William S. Powell, *Colonial North Carolina* (New York: Scribners' Sons, 1973), pp. 267–70.

106. Saunders, ed., *Records of North Carolina*, vol. 10, pp. 9–10; Lefler and Newsome, *North Carolina*, pp. 208–13.

107. "Journal of the Council of Safety for the Province of South-Carolina, 1775," *Collections of the South Carolina Historical Society* 2 (1858), pp. 22–37, 50, 70; "Miscellaneous Pages of the General Committee, Secret Committee and Provincial Congress, 1775," *South Carolina Historical and Genealogical Magazine* 8 (1907), pp. 149–50.

108. "Journal of the Council of Safety," pp. 22–37, 43, 50–51.

109. "Papers of the First Council of Safety of the Revolutionary Party in South Carolina, June–November, 1775," *South Carolina Historical and Genealogical Magazine* 1 (1900), pp. 44–47.

110. "Journal of the Council of Safety," p. 58 (23 July 1775).

111. "Papers of the First Council of Safety," pp. 285–90.

112. *Ibid.*, pp. 287–88.

113. Ryerson, *The Revolution Is Now Begun,* mentions more than one prominent member of the Philadelphia committee who found military service more attractive than politics, e.g., Thomas Mifflin and John Reed, pp. 125–26. The New York City committee also lost members this way, especially Issac Sears, who rode off to Connecticut to raise a volunteer company in May and then later destroyed Tory printer James Rivington's press with a band of followers. Alexander McDougall, according to his biographer Roger Champagne, left the provincial congress and New York committee specifically over his frustration with the slow pace of politics (see Champagne, *Alexander McDougall*, pp. 95–96, 108–9). John Lamb sought an artillery commission from the provincial congress on 2 June 1775, later received it, and became an artillery general (Fernow, *Documents Relative to New York,* p. 6). Massachusetts lost the services of key resistance leader Dr. Joseph Warren permanently when he fell at the Battle of Bunker Hill on 17 June 1775 (John Cary, *Joseph Warren: Physician, Politician, Patriot* [Urbana, Ill.: Univ. of Illinois Press, 1961], p. 221).

114. Gerlach, *New Jersey,* pp. 109, 132–34, 148, 171.

115. Zeichner, *Connecticut's Years of Controversy,* p. 199.

116. See the discussion in Pauline Maier, *From Resistance to Revolution,* Chapter Seven.

117. George Washington to George Mason, 5 April 1769, Worthington C. Ford, ed., *The Writings of George Washington* (14 vols., New York and London: G. P. Putnam, 1889), vol. 2, p. 263.

118. The inability of these methods to succeed is roughly Jack Sosin's position in *Agents and Merchants: British Colonial Policy and the Origins of the American Revolution, 1763–1775* (Lincoln, Neb.: Univ. of Nebraska Press, 1965), pp. 224–25.

119. Bernard Bailyn, *The Ideological Origins of the American Revolution* (Cambridge, Mass.: Harvard Univ. Press, 1967), pp. 61–63, discusses the threat of standing armies as the provincials viewed it.

120. John Adams, "Novanglus," 6 February 1775, in Robert J. Taylor, ed., *Papers of John Adams* (Cambridge, Mass.: Harvard Univ. Press, 1977), vol. 2, p. 251.

121. See, for example, Edmund Morgan, *The Birth of the Republic* (Chicago: Univ. of Chicago Press, Phoenix Books, 1956), pp. 1–3.

122. See Max Weber, "Politics as a Vocation," in Hans Gerth and C. Wright Mills,

eds., *From Max Weber* (New York: Oxford Univ. Press, 1958), pp. 77–128.

123. Gipson, *British Empire,* vol. 12, *The Triumphant Empire: Britain Sails into the Storm, 1770–1776,* pp. 322–23.

·13·

British Attitudes to the American Revolution

J. H. PLUMB

The political state of England in 1779 was a sorry mess, and for nearly two decades every ministry had proved itself totally incapable of dealing with the American question. During the 1760s, harshness alternated with weakness, repression was followed by conciliation as one Whig ministry rapidly followed another. The House of Commons was composed of small Whig factions struggling for power, and George III's faith in Lord North derived from the fact that North in 1769 had brought to an end the confusion of a decade and created a stable ministry, solidly Whig at the core, but supported by many Tories and independents. Of course, North had not been able to secure the support of all the Whig groups, and the important group, led by the Marquis of Rockingham, whose formidable spokesman was Edmund Burke, stayed outside the government as did Lord Chatham (William Pitt) and his supporters. Not until rebellion flared up was North's American policy much more consistent than his predecessor's. As rebellion turned to war and the war itself grew long and difficult, many of North's erstwhile supporters began to have doubts of the wisdom of his policy. Criticism grew in volume. And criticism mattered. Public opinion was important in a crisis, even in the oligarchical structure of British politics. Since the accession of George III in 1760, the feeling that a Parliament of landowners, dominated by the aristocracy, was becoming out of touch with the true needs of the nation had steadily strengthened. Criticism of the parliamentary system as well as of North's American policy had become widespread. There had developed an ever-increasing band of radicals whose radicalism was social, legal, religious, though not, of course, economic. They believed in a wider democratic franchise, toleration of religious belief, and the rationalization of law and administration. They were irritated by anachronism: that little girls and boys should be hanged for theft or that a duchess should draw a fat salary as a housekeeper for a nonexistent palace infuriated them. These views were particularly powerful amongst the radical intellectuals and publicists, Joseph Priestley, Richard Price, Tom Paine, and Junius, that savage critic

461

of George III who still retains his anonymity. Their books and pamphlets were read as eagerly in the provinces as in London, and they had helped to make the American question a dominant issue, not only for members of Parliament, or even for parliamentary electors, but for all who could read. They appealed particularly to that mass of Englishmen who were politically dispossessed by the quaint franchises of the unreformed House of Commons, and who, therefore, felt a natural kinship with the Americans in revolt. Their attitude to America was based on their hopes for their own society, and they felt a community of interest with the rebelling colonists both in ideas and in political aspirations. Historians have underestimated the extent of British sympathy for America which flourished in the 1760s and early seventies, just as they have overlooked the reasons for its decay once rebellion turned to war.

First, it is necessary to look more closely at those who sympathized, the manner of men they were. This radical sympathy for America is nowhere reflected so sharply as in Sylas Neville's *Diary*. Like Lord Pembroke's papers, the *Diary* is a comparatively recent discovery and one that has certainly passed almost unnoticed by the political historians of George III's reign. For those who believe that radical public opinion mattered little in the eighteenth century, it is an uncomfortable document.

Neville kept his diary from 1767 to 1788, during his early manhood. He was born in 1741 and died in 1840, just a few months short of his century. His diary is remarkable for the bitterness with which he refers to George III and his ministers. Here are a few of his sentiments culled from 1767:

> No person is a true friend of liberty that is not a Republican.

> The evils of which monarchy is productive should deter any wise nation from submitting to that accursed government.

> The Gazette says 10,000 people a year go from the North of Ireland to America and 40,000 in all. May they flourish and set up in due time a glorious free government in that country which may serve as a retreat to those Free men who may survive the final ruin of liberty in this country; an event which I am afraid is at no great distance.

Such comments would have done credit to a Boston radical, but these were not peculiar to Neville and his friends: strong, blunt sentiments such as these found their echoes elsewhere.

William Turner of Wakefield in Yorkshire urged his son to emigrate:

> Through the folly and wickedness of the present, you of the rising generation have indeed a dark prospect before you. . . . Your best way will be to gather as fast as you can a good stock of the arts and sciences of this country; and if you find the night of despotism and wretchedness overwhelm this hemisphere, follow the course of the sun to that country where freedom has already fixed her standard and is erecting her throne; where the sciences and arts, wealth and power will soon gather round her; and assist and strengthen the empire there.

Neville was also in touch with many like-minded men and women; some were well-known London radicals such as Mrs. Catherine Macaulay, the historian; Caleb Fleming, the unitarian minister of Pinners Hall; and Thomas Hollis, whose lavish patronage of liberal ideas helped to keep republican sentiment alive in the middle decades of the eighteenth century.[1] These ardent radical intellectuals certainly fortified Neville's attitude. Fortunately, however, radical intellectuals were not the only characters in Neville's diary to share his sentiments. People who but for him would have merged into the nameless millions of history echo his republican sentiments as well as his hatred for George III's government—Kearsey, Bacon, and Mrs. Winnick and their friends who entertained him with tea and radical politics. Obviously, in the sixties there were little knots of republicans and radicals scattered throughout London and its suburbs.

Even more impressive, however, are the chance conversations that Neville had, or overheard, which indicate the width of public criticism and the frequency with which it was expressed. Viewing the Raphael cartoons at Hampton Court, Neville heard a man tell his wife that they would soon belong to the people of England, and at Terry's Coffee House in August 1767, he got into conversation with a stranger who said that he "wished N. America may become free and independent, that it may be an asylum to those Englishmen who have spirit and virtue enough to leave their country, when it submits to domestic or foreign Tyranny."

Sympathy for America and tenacious adherence to liberal and radical sentiments reached down to the grass roots and was not merely a cause for opposition politicians, dissenting intellectuals, and self-interested merchants, as recent American and British historians have stoutly maintained.[2] Fortunately, Neville's diary is not the only new source that illuminates the strength and intensity of pro-American feeling amongst those classes of society that wielded next to no formal political power and whose voice received little notice at the center of affairs.

At Birmingham, then a rapidly growing manufacturing town, a group of professional men, manufacturers, and dilettantes had come together for the purpose of discussion and mutual improvement. They had been fascinated by the ideas of the Enlightenment, as indeed had many similar intellectual elites from Philadelphia to Marseilles.[3] The importance of such groups—and particularly the British ones that are to be found in most large provincial towns—is that they represent people not outside the mainstream of economic and social development but right in the heart of it. This is certainly true of the West Midlands group, largely based in Birmingham. Their names are well known: James Watt, the inventor; Matthew Boulton, the manufacturer; Erasmus Darwin—grandfather of Charles—poet, philosopher, doctor; Joseph Priestley, chemist and publicist; Dr. Small, the tutor of Thomas Jefferson; Thomas Day and Richard Edgeworth, both educationalists and both weirdly eccentric; and, perhaps the most interesting of the rest, Josiah Wedgwood, the potter.

Wedgwood, a man of vast intellectual appetite and broad human sympathy, makes a strong contrast to Neville. Everything that Wedgwood did succeeded, and he rose from obscurity to international renown. He was happily married, blessed with brilliant children, prosperous, secure, the admired and admiring friend of many distinguished men in all walks of eighteenth-century life. He was a supremely successful man of affairs. He and his friends would have been thoroughly at home in the purposeful, expanding world of Benjamin Franklin's Philadelphia. They would have shared its eupeptic self-confidence in its expanding commerce, and discovered the same ideas about politics and government, science, education, and the arts as their own, amongst its intellectual leadership. As with Philadelphia's elite so with the Lunar Society; its members felt the future in their bones. They were ready for a new world, freer from tradition, closer to the rational principles upon which they modeled their industry and commerce. After all, reason and its application, they believed, had brought their success in life. Of course, as in Philadelphia, not all translated their intellectual liberalism into radical politics. Matthew Boulton supported Lord North although his friends teased him endlessly on that score; Thomas Day, a dedicated follower of the philosophy of Jean-Jacques Rousseau, found it difficult to support the Americans so long as they maintained slavery. In general, however, the members of the Lunar Society felt as Wedgwood did.

Wedgwood's views on the American problem were conveyed in his letters to Richard Bentley, his partner, whose judgement in politics as well as in the arts, sciences, and social intercourse he revered.[4] Wedgwood and Bentley were, of course, wholehearted supporters of the American cause. They thought coercive measures wicked, preposterous, and doomed to disaster. Wedgwood sent for Dr. Price's *Observations on Civil Liberty*. He wrote back enthusiastically: "I thank you for Dr. Price's most excellent Pamphlet: those who are neither converted, nor frightened into a better way of thinking by reading his excellent and alarming book may be given up as hardened sinners, beyond the reach of conviction."[5] And he asked for more copies so that he could distribute them in the right places. Later, Bentley sent him Paine's *Common Sense* and many other pro-American pamphlets to fortify, if fortification were needed, his strong sympathies for America and to help in Wedgwood's work of conversion of others. Wedgwood willingly subscribed £20 towards alleviating the miseries of American prisoners captured by the British. "Gratitude to their country men for their humanity to G[eneral] Burgoine and his army is no small motive for my mite."[6]

Wedgwood and Bentley's views chimed not only with those of their immediate friends but were echoed in the correspondence of other industrialists. In Bristol, Manchester, Birmingham, and Leeds, indeed wherever the middle-class manufacturers were to be found, sympathy for the American attitude abounded.

Of course, it is not surprising that many of the leaders of the Industrial Revolution should have been so strongly pro-American: they too wanted a social revolution, an end to the system of oligarchy and patronage which created not only a sense of keen injustice but also real practical obstacles to their industrial activities. Whatever they wanted—a canal, improved roads, efficient lighting or paving of streets, more education, better law and order, or a new water supply—they had to struggle to get for themselves, and not only struggle but pay. Neither local nor central government in Britain provided initially the slightest aid, and it is no wonder that the whole oligarchical, unrepresentative structure of eighteenth-century English society should become an anathema to them. What is surprising is that these social elites, which were beginning to wield so much economic power, proved in the end to be so weak an ally for the American cause.

This was only partially due to the nature of the British political system which put all effective power into the hands of the landowning classes, for many of the industrialists had contacts with politicians, particularly those Whigs, led by the Marquis of Rockingham, who were in opposition to Lord North. The widespread sympathy for America failed to be effective for a more profound reason: the change in the nature of the conflict itself.

In the 1760s, even in the early seventies, friendly support for America could be indulged with a clear conscience. The policy of successive ministries lacked consistency; many acts, particularly the Stamp Act, seemed to be as inimical to British commercial interests as American; both British and American merchants appeared to be the victims of these arbitrary acts, so resentment could be shared in common. But American resentment hardened, developed a program, and became a revolt, violent, bloody, bitter, that, as Chatham had foreseen, turned itself into a European war. Doubts began to cloud sympathy and many consciences became uneasy. It required political and moral convictions of a thoroughly radical kind to support unquestioningly the right of the Americans to obtain their independence by any means whatsoever, *once rebellion had started to transform itself into war*.

Indeed, this is sharply reflected in Wedgwood's correspondence. On 6 February 1775, he wrote to Bentley:

> Doctor Roe had been at Manchester about a week before—exceeding hot & violent against the Americans, Dr Percival told me he quite frothed at the mouth, and was so excessively rapid in his declamations, and exclamations, that nobody could put in a word 'till his story was told, & then away he flew to another House repeating the same Rigmorow over again. . . . And away he flew to promote the same good work at Leeds, Hallifax & c—& I find . . . from these Towns, that his labor has not been in vain. . . . Many were surpris'd to find him so amazingly alter'd in his sentiments, but nevertheless his harangues, & even those simple queries have had a very considerable effect amongst many, Dissenters & others.
>
> I do not know how it happens, but a general infatuation seems to have gone forth, & the poor Americans are deemed Rebels, now the Minister has declared them so, by a very great majority wherever I go.

Although Roe might have swung over many moderates in one of the most radical areas in Britain, the sympathy for America remained both extensive and vociferous. At a meeting at Stafford to adopt a Loyal Address in support of the policy of George III towards America, Mr. Wooldridge produced a counterpetition and proposed it so vigorously that, according to Wedgwood, "the gentlemen were cut down and could not answer it"; nevertheless, most of them signed the Loyal Address. It is true that Wooldridge and his friends, not to be outdone, advertised their counterpetition in the local press, and signatures were canvassed in Birmingham,

Lichfield, Walsall, and Hanley. Yet Wooldridge's and not Roe's proved to be the losing game.

The contrast between the effectiveness of merchant radicals in America and merchant radicals in England became quickly apparent. War strengthened the former, weakened the latter. The taking of New York by the British army brought the mob out into the streets. "Our people at Newcastle," wrote Wedgwood, "went wild with joy," and he was relieved that those stalwarts who refused to illuminate their houses to celebrate the victory were not attacked.[7] Elsewhere, too, the mob roared their delight at a British triumph. War had inflamed the natural xenophobia of the semiliterate, as indeed it did in America, but whereas in America mob support, the hopeless anger and despair of the dispossessed, strengthened radical and revolutionary attitudes to government and society, in England the reverse process took place. British mobs became increasingly patriotic, for the Americans could so easily be blamed for the economic tribulations which the working classes had to endure. When Wedgwood as early as 1774 came across an armed mob of four hundred working men who had been out machine-breaking, they blamed the loss of their livelihood on the decline of trade due to the American troubles.

This, of course, was scarcely half-true, but it was good grist for the patriot's mill. And once war began it changed many minds. Indeed, nothing illustrates this better than the case of Bristol, where the earlier opposition to the American policy of Lord North's government was gradually overwhelmed; in 1775, the mayor, corporation, and clergy sent a Loyal Address to George III and in 1777 so did the Merchant Adventurers, expressing support of North's policy.

Also, many Bristol merchants, who like Richard Champion worked for the American cause (short of independence) and supported wholeheartedly Burke and the Rockingham Whigs, feared an open alliance with the radicals when the real test of war came. "The Leaders," he wrote of the radicals,

> are in themselves so little adequate to the task they have assumed, and conduct themselves with such a wildness of popularity, and so little attention to common sense, that with respect to the great point in view, the removal of the dangerous Faction at Court, which threatens destruction to the Liberties of the whole Empire, it can have no effect.[8]

Many British merchants feared not only the victories of the radicals but also that American independence would lead to a ruin of trade, and their fear was enormously strengthened when Congress entered into an alliance with France. Indeed, the effect of this alliance on the British attitude towards the revolution has been consistently understressed. The distinction between what happened in America and in Britain is of exceptional importance. In America, radicals were able to exploit patriotic sentiment and so wrest the leadership from the more doubtful and conservative northern merchants or southern planters. Loyalists, supporters of conciliation, could be regarded as traitors, and treated as such.[9] By such means, the radical theories of natural rights, of the equality of men, the belief that all men had a right not only to life, liberty, and the pursuit of happiness but also to overturn and abolish governments which did not grant them became essentially American: here radical attitudes and patriotism were united by the call of war.

In England, war *divided* radicalism and patriotism and tainted the support of America with sedition. Tom Paine became not a hero but an anathema, the symbol of a violent, radical traitor. No one had been more constant in his sympathy towards America than Wedgwood, but war brought him doubts. In the summer of 1779, the extension of the war had so denuded Britain of regular troops that the government encouraged its supporters to raise subscriptions or regiments or both in their counties. On 7 August 1779, Wedgwood attended a meeting of the lord lieutenant, sheriff, and gentlemen of Staffordshire: "The meeting was thin but respectable in number," Wedgwood reported:

> and its proceedings enlightened only by a trenchant speech by Mr Eld, a man of eighty who, after complimenting the soldiers on their bravery, went on to say,
>
> "In the times of our prosperity & exultation we, the gentlemen of this county, thought ourselves of consequence enough to address the throne, &, with offers of our lives & fortunes, call'd upon our sovereign to pursue the coercive measures already begun in America. In these days of our humiliation & despondency, which shd be a time for learning wisdom, I wish we c[oul]d now think ourselves of importance enough to address his majesty once more, & humbly beseech him to grant such terms to his late subjects in America as *freemen may accept*. I have heard of none such being hitherto offer'd to them. Submission without terms—Unconditional submission! are offers for slaves, & those who accept them must be such. I hope & trust we are none of us in love with slavery." Mr Eld broke off rather abruptly, & without speaking to the specific business of the day, as I wish'd him to have done. He said ma[n]y good things, & said them well, & with great energy for an old man of 80.[10]

Wedgwood wished Eld to say more because he was troubled. He read all the arguments that he could about not subscribing, yet they did not carry conviction with him. They broke down because in the last resort they conflicted with his patriotism.

> I am not at present fully convinced by them, that it is better to fall a prey to a foreign enemy rather than defend ourselves under the present ministry. Methinks I would defend the land of my nativity, my family and friends against a foreign foe, where conquest and slavery were inseparable, under any leaders—the best I could get for the moment, and wait for better times to displace an obnoxious minister, and settle domestic affairs, rather than rigidly say, I'll be saved in my own way and by people of my own choice, or perish and perish my country with me. If subscribing would certainly rivet the present ministry in their places, and non-subscribing would as certainly throw them over, the nation at large being in no hazard at the same time from a foreign foe, I should not hesitate a moment what to do, but none of these propositions seem clear to me.[11]

Here we see how "hazard from a foreign foe" was circumscribing Wedgwood's radical attitude. Radicalism was becoming unpatriotic; what in America gave radicalism its opportunities, in England inhibited them.

The upsurge of patriotic sentiment that Wedgwood experienced was typical of many men of similar views. Even Major Cartwright, one of the most dedicated supporters of the American revolution, who, indeed, sacrificed his military career and chance of marriage by his refusal to serve against the Americans, nevertheless took to organizing and drilling the militia in Nottinghamshire in case invasion by the French became a reality. Although such radical leaders as Cartwright continued to demand not only independence for America but also linked it with the need for the reform of Parliament and an extension of the franchise, their support in Britain contracted rather than expanded once the country was involved in a large-scale war.

This also proved true of radicalism's best organized and strongest supporters, the freemen of the City of London. In the middle seventies they left Lord North's government in no doubt of their sympathy for the American independence movement. In 1773, they chose two Americans, Stephen Sayre of Long Island and William Lee of Virginia, as sheriffs; in 1774, they insisted on their parliamentary candidates signing pledges to support a bill which would have given America the right to elect its own Parliament and tax itself. Naturally the Coercive Acts were denounced; even as late as 1778, they refused to give public support to the war. Yet even amongst men as tough-minded as these, there is a marked decline in their pro-American activity after 1776. The war constricted their sympathy and restrained them from an all-out attack on the institutions by which they were being governed.

In spite of the widespread radical sympathy that had existed for ten years or more, little had been done to channel it into an effective political party capable of action. It was this lack of organizational structure that permitted patriotic sentiment to corrode radical fervor and inhibit action. Yet the impotence of the radicals, particularly between 1774 and 1776, must not be exaggerated. They had captured more or less effective control of the Corporation of the City of London, and they even had one or two representatives in Parliament. And it should be remembered that in many ways the City Corporation was the most powerful single institution in Great Britain after Parliament. Although war certainly weakened the radicals' attitude and their influence, their ineffectiveness cannot be entirely explained either by the upsurge of patriotism or the incompetence of their political organization; a contributory cause, and an important one, arose from their total inability to carry any major Whig politician with them.

Lord Brougham, a radical himself and a politician with long parliamentary experience, wrote early in the nineteenth century: "Is any man so blind as seriously to believe that, had Mr Burke and Mr Fox been ministers of George III, they would have resigned rather than try to put down the Americans?"[12] And it should be remembered that Charles James Fox spoke in favor of the Declaratory Act as late as 1778. The Whigs brought neither consistent action nor consistent policy to the American situation. In 1774, when radical agitation was at its strongest, the Whig leaders in opposition to the government showed the utmost reluctance to concentrate their energies on the problem of America.[13] The Duke of Richmond said he was sick of politics and Edmund Burke had to convince the Marquis of Rockingham of "the necessity of proceeding regularly, and with your whole force; and that this affair of America is to be taken up as business."

Here was no realization of the profound social causes at work both in America and Britain, no sense of the future, nor of the need to reform political institutions as well as change ministries. The American problem was a useful weapon for Rockingham with which to attack North's administration, but he and his friends did not welcome the wider political and social implications of the American revolt. And yet without some effective leadership in Parliament, radicalism was hamstrung. Dissatisfaction with the oligarchical and aristocratic structure of British political and social life was widespread, but the frustration was neither deep enough nor savage enough to create an organization bent on forcing change.

Lacking political leadership in Parliament, smeared with antipatriotism, the widespread radical sentiments of the late sixties and early seventies failed, except in the City of London itself, to become a powerful factor in the American revolution.

In the end, neither the attitude of politicians nor radicals, not even the voice of merchants or industrialists, and least of all the pressure of the mob proved significant. Rather, the acceptance by Britain of America's independence was secured by those country gentlemen who had decided every major political issue in Great Britain since the Reformation. The country interest, the independent members who sat in Parliament as Knights of the Shire, who never spoke in debates and usually voted with the government, finally rebelled, for the very same reason that they had given their initial support to George III and Lord North—taxation. Self-interest, the need to lighten their own taxes, and to relieve themselves of the costly burden of defending America, had combined with their traditional respect for the Crown and the sovereignty of Parliament to make them tolerant of the ramshackle confusion, the endless contradiction of what passed for American policy in the sixties and seventies. What broke their spirit was defeat at Yorktown and, more especially, the cost of defeat. They could not face the prospect of a protracted war of uncertain outcome.

Patriotic sentiment deeply influenced all British attitudes to the American independence movement—perhaps more than any other factor. It was only to be expected that sympathy towards America should be rarest amongst those who were content with the fabric of British society—the aristocrats, gentry, government officers, admirals, generals, lawyers, and ecclesiastics—and that it should be strongest amongst those new men—the industrial and aggressive commercial classes—to whom the future belonged. The extent of that sympathy was much wider, and the identity of their interests with America much closer than has been generally believed. Radical sentiment was very widespread in the late sixties and early seventies, but its ineffectiveness became ever more apparent once the American Revolution had become a European war: by that fact a terrible dilemma was created for the radicals and this, as much as anything, weakened resolve and helped to inhibit action—in such marked and vivid contrast with the developments of radicalism in America itself.

And this proved to be more than a transitory handicap to the development of radicalism in Britain, for although radicalism, especially in its demands for parliamentary reform, began to climb back to respectability under the aegis of William Pitt and William Wilberforce, the revolutionary wars with France reimposed, even more markedly, the stigma of disloyalty upon it. Demands for political and social equality became seditious: the ancient institutions—monarchy, aristocracy, landed gentry—were sanctified by patriotic gore. And this sanctification took place when the archaic institutions by which Britain was governed—an extraordinary hodgepodge of feudal custom, medieval charted rights, and Tudor legislation—were becoming even more inadequate to meet the needs of the rising tide of industrialism. So when reform came in the nineteenth century, it was piecemeal, *ad hoc,* never radical in any fundamental sense. A radical attitude to political institutions and social organization was in England always tainted with disloyalty. And, perhaps, it should be stressed once again that eighteenth- and early nineteenth-century British radicalism demanded no more than political and social equality, no more, in fact, than Americans were guaranteed by their Constitution. Such ideas, however, were no longer regarded as British; they were alien, Jacobin, Yankee, or French.

Of course, traditional institutions were strengthened by other factors apart from the alienation that took place between radicalism and patriotism at the time of the American and French revolutions; the possession of empire, particularly in India, fortified aristocratic and patriotic attitudes as well as the monarchy. Nevertheless, the American War for Independence was almost as much a watershed in the development of British society as of American, for it rendered feeble a widespread middle-class intellectual radicalism that was beginning to take root in many of the socially and commercially aggressive sections of British society. Its failure to develop and grow, its relegation to political insignificance; its exclusion from the heart of British society was to taint its middle-class radicalism with oddity, eccentricity, social neurosis, and so justify the continuing anti-intellectualism of the British establishment. And the corollary was to link patriotism with George III, with monarchy, no matter how stupid, with aristocracy, no matter how incompetent. As a future of social equality and equal opportunity opened for America, Britain became more firmly saddled with its feudal past.

• NOTES •

1. For a discussion of the influence of these dissenting radicals, see Caroline Robbins, *The Eighteenth-Century Commonwealth Man* (Cambridge: Harvard Univ. Press, 1959), pp. 320–77, an invaluable book on an obscure and difficult subject that still needs further detailed study.

2. John C. Miller, *Origins of the American Revolution* (Boston: Little, Brown, 1943), p. 201, writes, "although it must be recognized at the outset that some factions of the Whigs, such as John Wilkes, John Horne Tooke, Joseph Priestly, Richard Price, and Catherine Macaulay, adopted a liberal, conciliatory position in the dispute between Great

Britain and the colonies, it cannot be claimed—as has so often been done—that they represented English public opinion." See also Eric Robson, *The American Revolution in Its Political and Military Aspects, 1763–1783* (London: Oxford Univ. Press, 1955), pp. 36, 80.

3. Groups which, I might add in passing, are badly in need of more detailed research, and one can only wish that many European cities had received the same scholarly attention that Carl and Jessica Bridenbaugh have given Philadelphia in *Rebels and Gentlemen: Philadelphia in the Age of Franklin* (New York: Reynal & Hitchcock, 1942).

4. See Neil McKendrick, "Josiah Wedgwood and Thomas Bentley: The Inventor-Entrepreneur Partnership in the Industrial Revolution," *Transactions of the Royal Historical Society,* 5th ser., 14 (1964), pp. 1–34.

5. Wedgwood to Bentley, 24 February 1776, *Barlaston Manuscripts.*

6. Wedgwood to Bentley, 22 December 1777, *ibid.*

7. Wedgwood to R. Wedgwood, to Mr. Holland of Bolton, Lancs., (n.d., ca. November 1776), *ibid.*

8. G. H. Guttridge, ed., *The American Correspondence of a Bristol Merchant, 1766–1776* (Berkeley: Univ. of California Press, 1934), p. 2.

9. Philip Davidson, *Propaganda and the American Revolution, 1763–1783* (Chapel Hill: Univ. of North Carolina Press, 1941), pp. 139–52.

10. Wedgwood to Bentley, 7 August 1779, *Barlaston MSS.*

11. *Ibid.*

12. Lord Brougham, *Historical Sketches of Statesmen Who Flourished in the Time of George III* (London, 1839), vol. 1, pp. 303–4.

13. G. H. Guttridge, *English Whiggism and the American Revolution* (Berkeley: Univ. of California Press, 1942), pp. 76–77.

·14·

Resistance Politics and the Growth of Parallel Government in America, 1765–1775

RONALD M. McCARTHY

American resistance to the laws, policies, and actions of the British government during the 1765–75 decade was no mere "prelude" to the Revolution or to the War of Independence. To dismiss these struggles in that way ignores the special nature and the outcomes of the means of struggle used by the colonists in the three major conflicts of the decade, assuming instead that these campaigns were merely preparations for military struggle. As the several chapters discussing these movements have shown, the colonists were often aware that they were substituting other means of struggle for military action or mass violence and that the means chosen were intended to force Britain to alter political policies by means other than resort to arms.

The narrative chapters above provide the information for judging whether these means of struggle achieved their intended effects. Clearly, British policy was often thwarted, the ability of the imperial government to control events in America was limited, and specific attempts to tax America were abandoned. At the same time, American methods did not achieve the degree of success for which many colonial resisters hoped. Especially, Britain continued to attempt to levy new taxes and to change the political institutions of the North American colonies and their relation to the imperial central government. These are not, however, the sole consequences of importance.

Beyond the intended effects of these struggles, and in many ways more important than them, were the *unintended* political effects which moved America toward independence from Britain. The autonomous provincial governments forming everywhere in the colonies in defiance of British controls *before* fighting began in 1775 cannot have been a result of that warfare, although they continued to develop during the war. There must have been other sources of their development. Clearly, this ability to govern themselves successfully—to keep the public peace, to enact and carry out policies, to settle public and private disputes, even to tax the inhabitants—was far more the basis of independent self-government than was the colonists' ability to raise an army. The formation of these political and governing bodies was made possible by the technique of opposition pursued from 1765 to 1775. Indeed, this was a direct outcome of that *type* of struggle.

This chapter explores the process through which this lengthy struggle created the conditions for independence. The imperial structure is described both as one of the sources of this conflict and the context within which it was fought. Colonial institutions affected by the conflict, especially those under joint imperial and local control, are explored with regard to their role in influencing the form and outcomes of the conflict. In particular, the *means of struggle* which the colonists used is reviewed here, especially the extensive use of nonviolent action. Finally, the central contribution of nonviolent action to the construction of self-directed parallel governing institutions in the colonies is discussed.

• EMPIRE AND CONFLICT IN THE EIGHTEENTH CENTURY •

It is evident from an examination of the historical record that the majority of the British colonies that became the United States in 1776 enjoyed de facto political independence from Great Britain during the spring of 1775. Those colonies which had not realized de facto independence had at least gone far toward achieving it. The significance of this virtual self-rule can be seen most clearly by reviewing the specific developments through which the colonists progressively created autonomous parallel governing institutions in the colonies. Viewed from this perspective, the decade of struggle is divided into two vital periods. The first, and longer phase, beginning in the summer of 1765 and continuing through the summer of 1774, formed the political *basis* for independence. This basis included: (1) the development and acceptance of ideas which justified resistance even when the operation of established institutions of government was threatened; (2) the development of organizations for resistance which unified an aroused people into a mass, but relatively structured and orderly, movement; and (3) the development of means of struggle by which the movement attempted to defeat British policies and nullify British laws. These aspects were not linked in the sense that one followed upon another causally or in time, but they proceeded together in coming to fruition. Ideology, for example, would not have needed to face its own challenges if effective action had not occurred, while both required increasingly effective means of organizing the community for struggle against Britain.

The brief second phase of the development of parallel government began in some areas in the summer of 1774 with the first resistance to the Coercive Acts, and in other areas with the implementation of the Continental Association in the autumn. The political basis for independence, developed in the first phase, was quickly built upon as new bodies, such as local committees and provincial congresses, were formed and empowered, creating a condition of de facto independence in 1775. De facto independence consisted of two components: (1) the ability of the American communities to dispense totally with royal direction of their political institutions, and (2) their simultaneous capacity to reconstruct or replace the British institutions with self-created bodies able to fulfill the functions of government.

The political process by which this de facto independence came about was very much a result of Americans' increasingly sophisticated use of nonviolent action. In order to understand this process another look at the events of the decade from 1765 to 1775 is necessary, noting in particular the ways in which the resistance produced concrete changes in the political scene within the towns, counties, and provinces at the same time that the populace struggled against the policies of Britain.

First, however, it is important to examine the background to these changes, the imperial milieu in which they occurred. This milieu provided both the sources of the conflicts which rent it and the model against which internal alterations can be seen. The first British Empire was developed by Great Britain during the seventeenth and eighteenth centuries. It stretched from America to India, including ultimately not only the thirteen American colonies but also Canada, many islands in the West Indies, portions of Africa and India, as well as the whole of Ireland. Not only colonies but individual forts and trading concessions and the holdings of incorporated firms, such as the East India Company, made up the empire. In consequence, the thirteen colonies were by no means alone in the center of British imperial thought in the eighteenth century. Nor was America a single administrative area, being made up instead of colonies as diverse as Newfoundland and Jamaica, as old as Virginia and as new as Canada, conquered from the French only in 1761. At the end of the war with France in 1763, Britain's colonial holdings in the New World had increased dramatically in land area and in potential wealth. This, along with serious administrative problems which had cropped up during the war, forced the government to turn more attention to its American possessions.[1]

The structure of imperial government which administered this far-flung empire had grown up over the course of a century and a half before the 1760s. It was not developed according to any plan but in response to the need to apply the institutions of the British government—especially the Crown offices and Parliament—to new conditions. Administrative and commercial problems had influenced the form the imperial bureaucracy took, until it contained a variety of boards, departments, and agencies, many with overlapping and unclear jurisdictions. From the time of the first settlement of America, the Privy Council involved itself in American affairs, including having the ability to reject or "disallow" statutes made by colonial assemblies. As the commercial interests of Britain in the colonies increased, the Board of Trade and Plantations, originally a committee of the Privy Council, took independent interest in colonial affairs. Among its responsibilities was ensuring that growing colonial commerce and colonial statutes did not interfere with or restrict British trade to America. Throughout most of the eighteenth century, colonial governors and assemblies corresponded with the London government through the Board of Trade. The Board, in turn, would refer matters to the Privy Council, or, if of sufficient importance, to the secretary of state for the southern department.[2]

Following 1763, the organs of British government which dealt with America changed somewhat. Of course, these institutions had always undergone change as the conditions under which they operated altered. Following 1763, this change was fairly steady and often deliberate. Some of the planned alterations are discussed in the Introduction to Chapter Four. Very important among them was the creation in 1767 of the office of secretary of state for the colonies, held by the Earl of Hillsborough until 1772 and the Earl of Dartmouth from 1772 until 1775. Governors in conflict with their colony's legislature, Customs officers with a grievance, and other officials thwarted in their attempts to rule America efficiently could complain directly to this department. The secretary in turn could, after consultations with the ministry of which he was a part, operate with a relatively free hand to instruct and support the governors and officials. As earlier chapters have shown, the person and office of the colonial secretary were often involved in the struggles of the late 1760s and early 1770s.[3]

Also of great importance was the increased extent to which Parliament interested itself in colonial affairs during the late 1760s and 1770s. Before that time, it was not the habit of the ministry to involve Parliament directly in consideration of American business. Previous to 1760, most American matters were either administrative or military in nature, and thus were dealt with by the department most affected.

In the 1760s, the ministry became much more prepared to seek parliamentary remedies for its American problems, notably, of course, its taxation problems. Still, the traditional channels of administration were regularly used. During 1767, for instance, the Massachusetts Indemnity Act came before the Privy Council for routine consideration. This act angered the ministry greatly, for with it the Massachusetts legislature had voted not only to indemnify those who had suffered losses in the riots of August 1765 but to pardon the rioters as well. The ministry discussed bringing this to the consideration of Parliament, but instead it was dealt with through the Privy Council's right to review colonial statutes. This act was disallowed by the Privy Council as being null and void from its inception for usurping the king's right of pardoning criminals.[4] This solution was deemed sufficient. In later years, however, administrative solutions to American problems became harder to find, and Parliament was more likely to become involved. After the Boston Tea Party, the ministry considered acting against the perpetrators without new laws by closing the port of Boston through an order in council and through bringing those accused of participation to England to be tried for treason. Informed by their legal staff that the latter charge could not be supported and that the port could not be legally closed in that manner, the ministry turned to Parliament for aid, bringing in the Coercive Acts in March 1774.[5]

Domestic colonial government also reflected its history both in its variety and in the elements of independence and of dependence upon Britain that it possessed.

Among the thirteen colonies, there were three different forms of government: proprietary colonies, corporate colonies, and royal provinces. All possessed the common features of having a governor, council, and elected legislature, as well as independent local courts. In proprietary colonies, such as Pennsylvania, the governor was chosen by the "proprietors," the family that nominally owned the colony. In the more numerous royal provinces, like Virginia or South Carolina, the governor, council, and many officials were chosen and instructed by the Crown—in other words, the ministry.

Rhode Island and Connecticut were insulated from direct royal interference through charters specifying the rights and liberties of the inhabitants, among which were the choice of the governor and council by election. Massachusetts also possessed a charter, but not the right to elect the governor, who was chosen by the Crown. The colony did elect the council, however, in a yearly choice made by the House of Representatives. Many of these differences—significant for the development of the individual colonies as they were—faded as the ministry and Parliament increasingly passed laws or made decisions which treated the colonies as if they were a whole. At the same time, these distinctions represented a variety of differing political resources in the resistance struggles of the colonies, as each asserted its most basic rights.

The legislatures of the colonies, especially the lower houses or assemblies which were chosen by the voters, had come to view themselves as possessing powers very much like those of Parliament. This included not only the right to tax within the borders of their colony but to establish electoral districts and courts. The British government never accepted that view. Rather, the legislatures were seen, in Lawrence Henry Gipson's words, as "overseas ordinance-making municipal corporations;"[6] something analogous to a city council. The ministry saw no contradiction in asserting that it had the power to instruct the governors of the colonies and make its own policies superior to those of the colonial legislatures. The controversy over the Massachusetts circular letter of 1768, calling on the colonial legislatures to protect the Townshend Acts, is a case in point.

An even more serious conflict arose in South Carolina the next year. Support was very strong in South Carolina for British politician John Wilkes. Wilkes, jailed at the time for libel against the king, stood as a symbol of liberty in the colonies. In South Carolina, clubs and committees were formed to support the defense of Wilkes and constitutional liberties in general. On 8 December 1769, the Commons House of Assembly voted to provide Wilkes's defense fund with £1500 sterling as a gift from the people of the province. In response, the Privy Council instructed William Bull and all succeeding governors of that colony to no longer allow the legislature to appropriate special funds on its own authority. This had long been the practice in South Carolina, and the assembly considered the instruction a direct interference with their rights as a legislature. At every session from 1770 until the collapse of the royal government, the struggle raged between the governor and the assembly as the assembly refused to pass money bills while the instruction was in force. In fact, it passed no bills at all until 1773 and only very few thereafter. Unable to act as a constitutional legislature because of this conflict, the Commons House developed a system of standing committees to deal with business that could not come before regular sessions, as will be discussed below.[7]

Conflicts of this kind, both before the 1760s and after the independence movement began, acted as a check upon the powers of the governor and the ability of the British government to carry out its own policies in America. Matching this tradition of legislative independence were traditions of independent courts, with their own native interpretations of the common law of England and the laws of their own colonies, and of independent local governments. While these, of course, did not add up to constitutional "independence" from Britain before 1775, they do point up the areas of dissimilarity and of conflict between American and British understandings of the nature of the constitution under which they operated. Officials and others who assumed that the two systems were relatively the same, that the colonial constitution was only a partial and imperfect reflection of the British, or that decisions made in accordance with British practices would automatically be accepted in the colonies found that when they acted on those assumptions, the results were often very different than expected.

· COLONIAL GRIEVANCES AND POLITICAL CHANGE ·

Knowledge of the institutional structure of the British Empire and the elements of control and conflict which it afforded can be used to understand the process by which the empire disintegrated by looking at the immediate issues of the struggle in North America and the means by which it was pursued. Neither intellectual discussion of the wrongs of British actions nor generalized feelings of discontent could possibly alone have destroyed the forces holding the empire together. These forces—custom, authority, tradition, economic and cultural ties—operated in all the colonies to prevent disputes from destroying the structure rather than being settled within it. Nevertheless, in the decade of 1765 to 1775, the colonists developed means of struggle which, despite those strong forces, dismantled the structure. This did not result merely from the working out of ideas, but required means of struggle capable of successfully opposing the acts that the colonists rejected and of opposing the attempts by the imperial government to enforce its policies.

The choice of means, of specific collective actions that would express colonial grievances and attempt to make the government redress them, had a major impact upon the course of the struggle. To a very large extent, the means that were used determined, or at least strongly conditioned, the outcome of the struggles. Not only the question of which side in the conflict was successful, which took nearly twenty years to determine finally, but also the form of the final settlement was influenced by the available means of struggle. In America in the spring of 1765, there was no single causal factor which inexorably resulted ten years later in the reconstruction of political institutions. Rather, the changes in political relation-

ships, internal organization, beliefs, and political goals produced by the three resistance struggles helped shape the eventual outcome, including the reconstruction
of political institutions. This is not to say that the people who acted in this struggle
simply set the process in motion and had no control over its course. It is to say that
the particular type of resistance used by the Americans acting together was a powerful new factor in the situation. This factor must be considered along with the
colonists' interpretation of their situation, their objectives, and the existing tendencies in the North American and imperial structures in an attempt to understand
this decade of conflict.

The conflict of the years 1765 to 1775 was in large measure a conflict over the
use of political power, as historians have often stressed. This is not to slight the
very important conflicts over economic power which appeared in the merchants'
attempts to mitigate the economic domination of England. Nevertheless, one of
the keys to understanding the independence movement lies in the question of who
was to utilize the power found within the imperial institutions. The imperial "constitution" described above was not an ideal structure of abstract rights and powers,
but a set of institutions for making and implementing decisions, settling disputes,
controlling economic life, and controlling conflict. In this light, many of the actions of the British ministries in taxing the colonies, shifting army regiments, altering and moving courts, and establishing new authoritative institutions were attempts to alter this "constitution" to Britain's benefit. England's dominion over
the colonies implied the power to make such alterations. American resistance up
to the autumn of 1774 was an effort to restrain and resist these changes, lessen
their scope, or prevent them from taking place. At the end of 1774 and throughout
1775, the focus of American resistance shifted to an assertion that if alterations
were made, they were to be ones primarily aimed at benefiting Americans.

The conflict over the constitution under which Americans were going to live
was foreshadowed near the end of the French and Indian War when Prime Minister
William Pitt tried, in 1760, to tighten administration of the Customs in North
America. The British government also decided to keep a large postwar force of
troops there, despite the fact that relatively few were to be used against the Indians,
who remained a threat on the frontier. The first major issue that became an object
of struggle between Britain and America was, of course, the taxation issue. The
first of the tax levies, the Sugar, or American, Act of 1764, was greeted with alarm
by the colonists, but not with open resistance. In the northern colonies, merchant
groups organized and sent memorials to Britain explaining why the act should not
be passed. The legislatures of some of the northern colonies also opposed the act
and sent petitions and memorials to Britain requesting the ministry not to impose
it, as well as instructing their agents in London to lobby against it in Parliament.
These efforts did not cause any alteration of the Sugar Act. Although the rate of tax
was reduced in 1767, the Sugar Act was a grievance for the rest of the colonial era.
The next taxation act, the Stamp Act of 1765, was, however, greeted with open
resistance.

How are we to explain the fact that one of these acts was strongly resisted and the other not? How are we to explain that throughout the period, some acts of the British government were resisted, others complained about but not resisted, and still others either ignored or accepted? At first glance, it looks as if only the taxation acts were capable of uniting American attention on a single point. A more careful view, however, shows that this is not entirely true. There was also intercolonial resistance to other acts of the ministry which were thought to be unacceptable uses of authority and an even greater number of examples where only a single province was primarily involved. An example of the former was the widespread support for Massachusetts at the time of the circular letter controversy in 1768. Many of the colonial assemblies then reaffirmed not only the right of Massachusetts to send such a letter but their own right to consider it. Likewise, the initial grievance that provoked the writing of the *Farmer's Letters* was not the Townshend Act taxes, but the suspension of the New York Assembly. One grievance often stressed by the port cities in the early years was the restraint that the new statutes placed on trade, a grievance not expressed by the country districts.

Certain grievances were thus shared by many colonies, while others were not. Likewise, some grievances lent themselves to long-term opposition, while others were in the public eye for a shorter time. A distinction, then, can be made between "complaint issues" expressed in organized opposition, and the "general grievance issues" that people felt. Many individual grievances were not important enough or did not affect a wide enough area to serve as complaint issues to be adopted by an organized movement, but they were resented and remembered when the time came for the break with England. From this point of view, taxation was of importance as a grievance because it directly affected so many people over the course of several years and because so many in the colonies agreed that the taxes were unprecedented and dangerous. From the first, though, the question of liberty and the question of what were proper and improper uses of power were on the minds of Americans. The argument was not that Parliament *ought* not to take American money, but that it *could* not, without ignoring the American right to self-taxation through the colonial assemblies. Other issues, such as the right to a jury trial and the payment of officials with funds controlled by Whitehall, further point up the constitutional nature of the struggle.

The resistance movements against the revenue acts formed the core of the struggle up to 1774 because these acts served as the central issue around which intercolonial resistance was organized. In the early stages of the struggle, organized merchant leadership was already available, and the merchants saw taxation and trade restrictions as their main grievances. Likewise, direct action could concentrate upon the repeal of the Stamp Act or Townshend duties as concrete goals, perhaps implicitly assuming that a Parliament forced to repeal those duties would acquiesce in altering the entire plan to raise a revenue in America and tighten imperial control. Through such a process, taxation issues were used to establish the arena in which broad constitutional issues could be decided. The test from 1765 on was whether Britain could control America through new or existing institutions or whether the American colonists could force Britain to back down and thereby acquiesce in a relatively autonomous status for the colonies.

· HOW THE CONFLICT WAS WAGED ·

In the spring of 1765, ships carrying news from England first informed the port cities of Boston, New York, Philadelphia, and Charleston that Parliament had passed Prime Minister George Grenville's Stamp Act. This news quickly spread throughout the colonies in the weekly newspapers of these cities and those of Williamsburg, Providence, and the other trading towns. At first, there was little discussion in the press of what to do about the act. Even in the mercantile towns most afraid of the act's effects, there was no plan immediately available to oppose the Stamp Act's being implemented. In fact, as Pauline Maier pointed out, there was great confusion about how to proceed.[8]

Many counseled that the act had to be obeyed as long as it was in force; until the legislatures could convince Parliament through lawful petitions to repeal the act, Americans would have to use the stamped paper and pay the taxes. Many others, who believed that America's rights had been cruelly violated and that the act might have a terrible economic effect, were not always convinced that obedience was the best course. Many must have felt, as their actions so clearly showed, that the Stamp Act had to be prevented from operating. The problem which was presented to them was how to go about it. What precedents were there which could give them a clue as to how to act? There was always the military precedent, the precedent of revolt, and English history had plenty of glorious examples of those who had fought rather than obeyed oppressive orders of the magistrates and kings. At the same time, there were also precedents in English history of refusal to obey improper orders even if the resisters were punished.

There also existed precedents that were closer to home. No province had been without crowd actions during its history. Crowds had collected not only in the cities but in rural areas to prevent officials from acting. They had rescued accused criminals from jail, stopped Customs officers from seizing ships, interfered with royal white pine officers, and the like. In very recent experience, there was also the precedent of groups which had come together to protest the Sugar Act, in part outside constitutional channels and not working solely through the assemblies. Most of the members of these groups had been merchants, but in New Jersey and Philadelphia, tradesmen had also protested the Sugar Act.

These precedents were available to those people and groups who wanted to stop the Stamp Act. Some were more acceptable to them than others. No one thought that the situation warranted taking up arms unless Americans were attacked. In any case, that is not something a community does easily without support and preparation. On the other hand, the problem was not just one of how to protest the act. The people of the commercial towns did not want to wait quietly and hope that Parliament would repeal the act if humble applications were made. They wanted to prevent the act from ever being enforced, to keep the stamped paper from ever being used, and the collectors from ever taking any of the colonists' money back to England. The means which they used to do this, and to oppose the later acts as well, are described in the earlier chapters of this volume. Here, we want to look at the individual methods themselves and see how they can be divided into a series of types, and examine the way in which they operated.

One of the most important sets of decisions made during the Stamp Act struggle was the decision to limit the amount of violence used against opponents, while at the same time pursuing collective, extralegal methods of struggle. After the riots of August and early November 1765, most of those who opposed the Stamp Act came to feel that violent action by crowds was not the correct way to defend their rights. Nevertheless, they did not repudiate all crowd actions in the struggle; neither did they insist that only legal means could be pursued. Nor did they concur that only the "cooler" heads, to be found presumably in the assemblies, could have a hand in the protests.[9] This decision, to limit violence but pursue popular struggle, resulted, as various means were tried, in an extensive use of nonviolent action as an alternative to violent means.

One way of looking at actions in social and political conflict is to deliberately ignore the context in which we know them (here the individual resistance campaigns in the different colonies), and look for similarities or differences among the actions themselves. One important distinction is between actions which use institutions that already exist in the government to protest against the impact of government and those which use other types of institutions. In our case, the British Empire of the eighteenth century contained many procedures that people could use if they wanted a governmental decision revised or even withdrawn. They could contact ministers, lobby or petition, or take some kinds of decisions into the courts. We can broadly call the use of governmental institutions to oppose the actions of government the "constitutional" technique of action. This type of activity depends upon the availability of governmental institutions and procedures which can be used by those with a grievance, especially one brought on by governmental action, to have the situation changed.

Resisters have often sought out means of action that do not operate directly through the institutions already established for handling conflict. There are, of course, many objections to its policies that a government does not want to hear and will not act on. Likewise, officials and others with close institutional ties to government are in a position to get the attention of decision-makers, while outsiders find their access blocked. Economically powerful groups can afford to use their resources to pursue their interests in the courts, while the poor cannot. For these and other reasons, "outsiders" have found it necessary to take actions outside the system in order to make up for the lack of effective access. Where extraconstitutional means are used, the activists are not trying to "convince" the government to alter a policy while concurrently obeying the policy and only protesting "through channels," but deliberately develop actions that go outside and beyond those channels. Rather than insisting upon a court test of a policy or law or trying to reason with legislators to repeal an act, the activists create disruptions, protest against it in the streets, or bring economic or moral pressure to bear on the policy's supporters.

These extraconstitutional forms of action fall generally into three types: violent action, nonviolent action, and the destruction of property.[10] The distinction between violent and nonviolent techniques of action was discussed in Chapter One. According to this distinction, violence is a form of action which inflicts physical harm on persons or threatens to do harm to them. The distinction between violence and the simple destruction of property without violence is not always made clearly and, in fact, is not always accepted. Conceptually, it is an important distinction to make, for it separates harm done to persons from harm done only to things and insists that they are two different categories. A significant number of actions taken in the American resistance movements did indeed damage property, houses, or goods but did not threaten the lives or safety of persons. The most prominent of these was the Boston Tea Party. Many accounts of the action on the evening of 16 December 1773 stress that no harm was done or threatened to persons and that the destruction of the tea was done with no violence whatsoever.[11]

The first of these techniques of action, the constitutional technique, depends upon the existence of means for settling disputes and for the redress of grievances which are provided for within the institutional structure of society. The government need not be a party nor are only its institutions involved. Corporations, schools, churches, even families are other examples of institutions that have to develop some means of settling internal disputes in order to survive. (*Force majeure* is of course such a means.) Very often, though, it is the institutions of government that are intimately concerned with the settling of conflict. Courts are expressly designed for such a purpose, and legislative and administrative bodies are also often involved in disputes within the society, both where the government is a party and where it is not.[12]

The British constitution of the eighteenth century contained a variety of institutions which were available to Americans trying to settle their grievances with the central government or with other colonies. Some procedures, such as appeal of colonial court decisions to the Privy Council, were primarily for the use of individuals. Others were for use by a colony as a whole, expressing itself through its legislature. One mechanism provided for Parliament, under certain conditions, to review the arguments sent to it by American colonial legislatures in the form of petitions or memorials. These petitions, after being passed by the assembly and, generally, approved by the governor and council as well, were sent to the agent of the colony in London. The agent in turn delivered them to the ministry, which would introduce them in Parliament if it saw fit. It was an important part of the agent's commission to see that these memorials were understood and given due consideration by Parliament. The agents were also expected to lobby the members of Parliament to induce them to grant the request made in the petition.

In the decades before 1765, the system contained in these institutions had largely succeeded in adjusting quarrels between the colonies and the government in London or between individual colonies. The British government had been able to control the American colonies so far as was necessary without resort to military force. American lobbyists, on the other hand, had occasionally managed to prevent Parliament from taking actions which they had found objectionable, or they had gained concessions they needed. These concessions were not always ones which benefited the colonies as a whole, but may have been ones which aided only special interests, such as a bounty on a certain product which primarily benefited its producer.

There were, of course, cumbersome elements to the system. It was very difficult for Americans to get a "day in court" in Britain, and some individuals spent years trying to redress private wrongs. Beyond this, the decisions of American courts or legislatures simply did not have the force of law in Britain. Often, the Privy Council would let stand a statute which it objected to but had reviewed favorably before realizing its objectionable features, but there was nothing requiring it to do so.[13] Also, many of the "constitutional" arrangements were not legally binding but merely traditional. The rights of the agents to seek access to Parliament and Parliament's long-standing restraint from taxing America directly came, in the 1760s, to be seen by the ministry to be neither rights nor even strongly held privileges of the colonies, but rather nonbinding arrangements.[14]

The British constitution as it related to imperial administration was going through concrete changes of structure at this time. As this occurred, the institutions and procedures by which conflicts between the central government and the colonies could be clarified and adjusted became outmoded. Likewise, during the years of the resistance to the decisions of Parliament in the American colonies, these institutions underwent strains which they were not equipped to take. These institutions and procedures were intended to adjust details of a system's operation and were not necessarily capable of transmitting or handling challenges to the legitimacy of portions of the system. One effect of this was an increasing rigidity of British policy, and with it, an increasing inability of the Americans to gain serious considerations of their arguments in Whitehall and in Parliament. Access through the agents, for example, was greatly curtailed. Their advice was refused by the ministry, they were denied access to the chambers of Parliament, and the rules for the admission of petitions were more strictly enforced, if not even altered.[15]

From the point of view of Americans trying to protect their rights, the growing unresponsiveness of the ministry was a sign of the failure of these constitutional means of redress. Those constitutional procedures failed to correct the grievances, were unavailable for specific needs, and were restricted by the refusal of Parliament and the ministries to recognize American grievances. Therefore, it became necessary for the colonists to look to other methods of action for relief. In 1763 and 1764, as mentioned earlier, merchants in some of the northern cities worked together to prepare arguments against the proposed Sugar Act. They wrote both pamphlets and petitions objecting to the bill as economically unsound, claiming that the economy depended upon cheap supplies of sugar products and would be damaged if prices were raised through a tax. These petitions were endorsed by some of the legislatures and were sent with the pamphlets to the agents in London, to be presented to the ministry. At that time, the agents were successful at least in presenting the petitions (although they were too late to have any effect). The government had not objected to the colonial attempt to block the act.[16] In the petition campaign which took place after the Stamp Act was proposed, things were rather different. The petitions of all the assemblies except that of Massachusetts were not even accepted for presentation in Parliament because of their content. They argued that Parliament should not pass the Stamp Act because it had no right to tax unrepresented Americans, not solely because of the economic damage. The petition of Massachusetts, which did not press claims based on rights, was reportedly accepted, but not heard in opposition to the Stamp Act before passage—not, in fact, until the repeal debate in 1766.[17]

The institutional arrangements imbedded in the British constitution of that time were capable of responding to certain conflicts but not to others. In the case of American opposition to taxation acts of the 1760s, Parliament and the ministry were willing to hear objections that the acts they had passed were economically impractical or inexpedient. Those same bodies were unwilling to entertain challenges to their legitimacy to pass such acts, a question which—in their view—the Declaratory Act settled. For the majority of the period under study, the American legislatures did not totally abandon the attempt to use constitutional remedies to oppose parliamentary legislation or policies, or actions of British officials to which they objected.

It was only in 1774 and 1775 that the Americans ceased to attempt the traditional method of legislative petition, when the colonial legislatures and courts were disbanded and replaced by new institutions. The new institutions, the provincial congresses and the committees, were completely outside of the existing constitutional structure. These bodies were organized largely in response to decreasing colonial expectations that constitutional methods could succeed in redressing their grievances. That perception drove the Americans further in search of alternative means. Over the course of the campaigns against the Stamp Act, Townshend Acts, and Tea and Coercive Acts, the American colonies developed an impressive array of methods of nonviolent action.

As described in Chapter One, the methods of nonviolent action may be grouped into three classes: *nonviolent protest and persuasion, noncooperation,* and *nonviolent intervention.* Each of these classes contains a large number of different methods for the group to use. Often, the group will have no prior experience or knowledge of the range of actions open to it and will actually devise the different methods anew as its members look for ways of acting against their opponent. This occurred quite often in the American experience of the 1760s and 1770s, as was shown in the chapters recounting the resistance campaigns of those years. Consequently, a wide variety of different methods of action from all of these classes was used all over the colonies. If we remove these various individual forms of action from their own context and compare them instead by their characteristics as methods of action, we can see how wide a range of methods was developed.

The methods of nonviolent protest and persuasion used were widely varied. Occasionally, they were actions of individuals, but far more often, they were undertaken as actions of a group. All sorts of groups and organizations took part, not only town meetings and legislatures but occupational groups, churches, colleges, and people drawn simply from the general populace. The methods they used include protest marches and demonstrations, crowd "visits" to the homes of importers, demonstrative funerals—both genuine and mock—and a wide variety of extralegal protest meetings. Likewise, letters and petitions from various groups were drafted and addressed to other organizations and committees: from town to town or province to province, to encourage firmness in the cause; from merchant committee to merchant committee, to encourage and gauge support; and from provincial legislatures to Parliament, protesting the duties. Early on, many of the petitions from the legislatures of the colonies to Parliament were merely applications to the Parliament for relief and were sent in the firm hope that the government, on hearing of the difficulties of the colonists, would gladly reverse its action. In the petition drive against the Sugar Act before its passage, a correspondent to the *New York Gazette* of 20 October 1763 expressed this faith. He wrote: "there can be no Doubt that upon a proper Representation to his Majesty and his Ministry, we shall have every just Cause of Complaint removed."[18] As Parliament refused to act upon the grievances expressed in the petitions, these remonstrances became increasingly strong expressions of deeply felt protest, intended not merely to memorialize Parliament or the king with rational argument, but to impress the determination of the colonies upon British minds.

New Hampshire, not a colony to act hastily against royal authority, showed this feeling of protest in 1770. The legislature had prepared a letter to the king protesting the Townshend Acts (probably in August 1768), and voted to send it only in 1770, after realizing that the Townshend Acts were not to be repealed in full. In the covering letter, the legislature's committee told their agent, Barlow Trecothick, that they had little faith in the effect of the remonstrance, saying: "That if it has no other effect, it may at least demonstrate that we have Sensibility to feel the Oppression . . . and hope it may serve as a Remembrancer that we acted in Concert with our neighbors, to obtain a Removal of the Burdens under which we groan."[19]

Symbolic action of protest and persuasion was of the greatest importance in informing the people of resistance issues and for disseminating information. Broadsides containing the names of importers to be boycotted, announcing meetings, criticizing the movement's opponents, or rebutting their ideas became very common. Effigies and mock figures of opponents held them up to ridicule and made everyone aware of who among them were supporters of the Crown. Often, they were hanged from trees or mock scaffolds, or buried as the corpse of Liberty. In Boston in 1770, effigies were placed in front of the shops of those who persisted in importing despite the nonimportation agreements in order to warn potential customers away from the shop. This was not done only to those who had signed the agreement and broken it but also to those who had never signed it and who did not intend to stop importing. Other symbolic acts used were various kinds of celebrations, sermons, public speeches, and ceremonies. They were used both to show the strength of the people's feelings and to keep interest in the resistance high by showing what great support it had. At times, protest ideas even entered the courtroom. In the Boston Massacre trial in the fall of 1770, defense attorney Josiah Quincy, Jr., used his argument to the jury to remind the townspeople of John Dickinson's warning in the *Farmer's Letters* against the use of violence. Although Quincy was counsel for the accused soldiers, he used the occasion of the trial for a public discussion of the place of violent action in the movement against the Townshend Acts.[20]

One of the most important uses of nonviolent protest and persuasion lay in the development of a whole system of iconography and symbolism. At first, many of the symbols utilized were borrowed from England. John Wilkes, in his struggle against general warrants, provided the colonists with the cry, "Wilkes and Liberty" and the number forty-five. (Wilkes was imprisoned for libelling the king in issue number forty-five of the *North Briton*.) The colonists also used the ancient symbol of the freeman, the Phrygian cap and pole, for example, on Paul Revere's Liberty Bowl of 1768. This tied Americans to generations of the Whig political tradition of Britain and helped to justify their disobedience of authority by connecting it to the principled disobedience of others. Soon the Americans started developing their own set of symbols and using the old ones in new ways, often with regional variations appropriate to the different experiences which the various colonies had. To the number forty-five were added new numbers with a significance derived from the present struggle. Both Massachusetts and South Carolina honored numbers derived from the number of legislators who had supported the Massachusetts circular letter of 1768. In Massachusetts, this number was "the glorious ninety-two," after those who had voted not to rescind, and in South Carolina, twenty-six, after the number who had voted to uphold their right to respond to the letter. Celebrations held in South Carolina included a procession in which twenty-six lights were carried.[21] Dates were also added to the developing symbolism, such as 14 August, when the Sons of Liberty in Boston first came out in opposition to the Stamp Act in 1765, and 8 March, when the Stamp Act was repealed. Symbols that could be shown outwardly without verbal explanation were also used, such as the wearing of homespun during times of nonconsumption to show that one was not importing or buying British cloth. Many towns designated a particular tree, sometimes a very large or old one, as a Liberty Tree, while others raised a Liberty Pole.[22]

Methods of nonviolent protest and persuasion could be—and were—directed not only at the imperial government in Britain but equally at people in America. One of the most dramatic examples of crowd actions intended primarily to affect Americans was the crowd "visits" to importers during the late 1769 and early 1770 crisis in the nonimportation movement in Boston. At this time, a group of signers of the agreement who had pledged not to sell any goods imported after the deadline were found to be selling stored dry goods. At first these signers were reluctant to comply with the merchants' committee's demand that they cease. In attempting to convince these importers to return to the fold, "The Body" voted to visit them en masse, "*orderly* and *peaceably*." They also voted that only five persons would be chosen to speak to the importers, not the entire crowd. The *Boston Evening-Post* claimed that there were a thousand people at the meeting, a large crowd in the streets of an eighteenth century port town.[23]

Symbolic actions were not always as dramatic as these, but they did not need to be. To the opponents of the resistance, whether officials or ordinary citizens, a sign, symbol, or act as commonplace as the repetition of a number, the celebration of an anniversary, or the holding of a day of fasting and prayer could act as constant reminders of the strength of the resisters. In much the same way, the movement was strengthened by convincing the faint of heart to be strong and by reminding the supporters of the campaign that they were not alone. In this way, the methods of nonviolent protest and persuasion could affect three groups: opponents of the resistance in America and overseas, supporters of the resistance, and the uncommitted, who were urged to support, or at least not to oppose, the struggle.

The first attempt to include nonviolent forms of action in the effort to prevent the Stamp Act from being enforced in America used only methods of protest and persuasion, especially crowd actions. These included the parades and processions and mock funerals of liberty of early November 1765. The Stamp Act went into effect on 1 November 1765. This made it clear that symbolic actions alone could not be effective. In 1765, as at the inception of each later campaign, the colonial opposition faced the problem of how to act effectively, first to nullify the act where possible, then to force its repeal. Violent action was of course considered, but the experience of the early Stamp Act resistance led to its almost complete rejection. Not only large-scale violence against troops or government officers was abandoned, but also actions against persons were largely halted in even the most tumultuous cities. This rejection occurred in part because violent attacks on persons involved the innocent along with the guilty and allowed persons with a private interest or grudge to use the public arena in an attempt to settle it. Likewise, violence was rejected because it appeared to present as severe a threat to liberty and order as the acts did, and several of the places that experienced violent or disruptive crowd actions moved quickly to control them and prevent a repetition.

The first adoption of noncooperation as a means of resolving the problem of how to act effectively was limited: refusal to use the required stamped paper or to cooperate with any institution which complied with the law requiring their use. This was particularly easy during 1765 because the stamps were simply unavailable—stored away or under guard—in most colonies. But the precedent was established of refusing to do what was ordered or expected. This was elaborated later in a great variety of ways during each of the separate campaigns of resistance. By 1768, as the actions against the Townshend Acts were getting under way, noncooperation in the form of nonimportation had become the main thrust of the resistance. The colonists concentrated on "withholding from Great Britain, all the advantages she has been used to receive from us."[24] This class of methods of nonviolent action may be broken down further into methods of social, economic, and political noncooperation.

The methods of *social* noncooperation were primarily ones which penalized a person for failing to act as supporters of the movement wished. Primarily, of course, this social noncooperation involved the social boycott of a person whom the movement wished to sanction. This was often combined with economic boycott as well. When fully applied, this was a strong weapon against domestic opponents. Opponents of the movement felt themselves isolated, especially in the smaller communities. Continued "discountenancing" was often combined with other reminders of popular displeasure in the forms of delegations, crowd visits, and publication of names. This combination induced many people who had wavered or not complied with the resistance program to conform to the nonimportation agreements and other aspects of the resistance. The social boycott as a sanction against those who broke the united front of economic resistance was a specific provision of the Continental Association of 1774. The Continental Association lacked the machinery of a state and therefore the capacity to enforce laws as a state does, by jail, fines, and the like, as administered by courts. The Association was instead enforced by the boycott. Arthur M. Schlesinger believed that a pair of New York merchants who sent a cargo back to England, despite the expense and loss of doing so, "feared the blast of the boycott" even more than the economic loss.[25] The boycott was also used to bring around those who opposed the Association to the views of the committees which enforced it, Pauline Maier argued.[26] Since the social boycott could be lifted, and the offender returned to the good graces of the community, the possibility of trading good behavior for ending the boycott was held out to those stigmatized.

Other methods of social noncooperation used during the three campaigns include the suspension or extreme limitation of some social activities or the refusal to go where opponents of the resistance who were particularly notorious were present. Some colleges gave commencements with much less than the usual pomp in years when liberty was most threatened. The students at the College of Rhode Island (now Brown University) graduated in homespun in 1769. Harvard College curtailed commencement festivities in 1774, even to the point of doing away with the public presentation of degrees.[27] These graduations were usually occasions of great ceremony for the governor and the colonial social elite. Restricting them made the displeasure of the people involved very clear. In Boston in 1773, the people who were normally expected to attend the governor's banquet at election time announced their refusal to go if the Customs commissioners attended. The town of Boston also refused to allow use of Faneuil Hall, the banquet's usual site, for the occasion. Governor Hutchinson reported that he dined elsewhere with "the obnoxious persons."[28]

Nonfraternization with officials, as in this case of refusal to dine publicly with the Customs commissioners, was sometimes practiced in other ways. Anne Hulton, sister of Commissioner Henry Hulton, recorded how small her circle of Boston acquaintances was.[29] Nonfraternization with the troops was also practiced on occasion. When, in 1768, two regiments arrived in Boston to garrison the town, the Reverend Andrew Eliot wrote that the popular mood was against cooperating with them at all, "to treat them, the troops, with civility, but to provide nothing."[30] During the next two years, though, the troops appear to have taken part in the life of the town in many ways that went beyond their strictly military duties. The soldiers were withdrawn from Boston in 1771, but returned in 1773. At this time, some Bostonians tried to convince some of the troops to practice noncooperation by deserting. A broadside put up in the streets of Boston in June 1774 encouraged the soldiers to slip away, saying, "you may have Liberty and by a Little Industry may obtain Property. . . . The Country People are Determined to Protect you and Screen you."[31]

The importance of economic noncooperation cannot be exaggerated. It was the primary sanction against the British government for a decade before the war. It was also the action toward which most other resistance activities were oriented. Primarily, the method used was nonimportation, a type of economic boycott consisting of refusal to import goods from the British Isles or from the British West Indies. The object of the action was to reduce the flow of English-made goods from those sources so that England's economy would suffer. (The products of England, the most industrialized part of Great Britain, were clearly the main object of nonimportation.) If this were done, the thinking went, exporters, manufacturers, tradesmen, and factory workers would be thrown out of work, and their distress would force Britain to repeal the acts to which the colonies objected. Both the organization and effectiveness of this policy have been discussed at length in this volume. It is important here to see that the use of this particular economic weapon (and even to some extent its shortcomings), decisively contributed to shaping the organization of the resistance. The development of committees among the merchants and working people of the various towns, the expansion of groups that enforced the boycotts so that they included nonmerchants, and the development of political bodies to enforce the boycott all greatly contributed to the ultimate ability of the Continental Association to transform itself from a resistance plan to an alternative government.

The nonimportation campaigns were the center of the commercial resistance throughout the decade. The policy had weaknesses, however, even when enforced by the committees. Several merchants in each port refused to sign the nonimportation agreements, some ports joined the movement only reluctantly, and few merchants wished to forgo an income for long periods of time. Nonconsumption, collective refusal by groups other than the merchants to *use* certain British goods, was a method by which the general population could support nonimportation (see Chapter Four). Nonconsumption particularly involved not buying British-made luxuries from the merchants or goods for which substitutes could be found in America. Another aspect of nonconsumption was to use American-made products created from American resources such as wool and flax. This also involved not selling those resources overseas, and refraining from eating lamb so that the stock of shearable sheep could be increased.[32]

During the Stamp Act resistance, some merchants refused to pay debts owed to English merchants in order to increase the pressure of nonimportation on them. This method was not pursued in later campaigns, as the merchants of America used the reduction in imports to sell off inventories and reduce their heavy balances in England. This lessened the effect of the resistance agreements upon the British merchants by allowing them to have a cash income while not needing to incur further debts of their own with suppliers.[33] Another method of economic noncooperation used against the British was the refusal of carpenters to accept jobs building barracks for soldiers, a method used in Boston on more than one occasion. In 1768 and 1769, this refusal to work was combined with the refusal of the Massachusetts Council to supply funds to pay for barracks for the troops, as required by the Quartering Act. As a result, the British troops in Boston were never quartered in a single barracks, but, instead, were scattered all over the town of Boston. This may have reduced their effectiveness as an occupying force. However, by spreading the troops into many areas, it also contributed to the antagonism between the soldiers and inhabitants which culminated in the Boston Massacre.

The final method of economic noncooperation, mandated by the Continental Association, was nonexportation. Under this plan, the colonies would no longer send the produce they normally exported to England as long as the Coercive Acts were in force. It was decided at the First Continental Congress that this would not begin until September 1775, rather than commencing at the same time as nonimportation (1 December 1774). Consequently, nonexportation did not begin until after the war had started, and that weapon was not tested in its own right to determine its capacities.

Political methods of noncooperation were also important as sanctions against the British and as means of increasing the organizational strength of the movement. Often, these methods of political noncooperation included a denial of the legitimacy of commands or acts of the British officials, and that denial in turn served as a justification for disobedience. One of the methods of political noncooperation used was the continued advocacy by colonists of extralegal resistance after the ministry or the governor had threatened punishment for doing so. The North Carolina legislature in 1769 perceived the ministry's threat to revive an ancient law allowing colonial treason cases to be tried in England to be very dangerous. When the legislature protested to London, the governor dissolved the assembly.[34] Often, political noncooperation took the form of persisting in a course of action once begun, despite commands to desist. All of the colonial assemblies which upheld their right to act upon the Massachusetts circular letter in 1768 committed this sort of political disobedience.

Use of political noncooperation began during the Stamp Act struggle. At this time, the disobedience consisted of refusal to cooperate with existing institutions if they were thought to be operating illegitimately. During the months before 1 November 1765, groups of lawyers and merchants announced that they would simply not carry on business with the required stamps. While lawyers and merchants refused to use the stamped paper or patronize institutions which used it, judges and Customs officers refused to break the law by operating without stamps. The stalemate forced the courts and Customs Houses to close down by denying them any clients.[35] This method of refusing to use existing institutions was also of great importance during the period of the Continental Association. In Maryland, for example, the committees which enforced the Association requested that both lawyers and litigants refuse to use the courts when they were open. In this way, opponents of the Association who wished to bring actions into these courts would be unable to do so, and royal authority to settle disputes through the courts was destroyed.[36] In Massachusetts in 1774, jury panels in several counties refused to serve in a courtroom where Chief Justice Peter Oliver, under impeachment by the legislature for accepting a royal salary grant, was presiding, thus protesting the unconstitutional salaries and punishing Oliver for being the only justice to accept a salary.[37]

At other times, Americans refused to dissolve meetings of bodies as demanded by authorities until their work was done. The Virginia House of Burgesses reconstituted itself extraconstitutionally in 1765 after the governor ordered it to dissolve. The North Carolina legislature, as mentioned above, also reconstituted itself "on its own authority" when dissolved in 1769.[38] Other legislatures, South Carolina and Massachusetts among them, "refused to hear" the person sent to prorogue the meeting until their work was completed.[39] In the fall of 1774, the Salem, Massachusetts, Committee of Correspondence was ordered by Governor Gage to call off a town meeting assembled to elect delegates to the extralegal county convention. Although the towns of that colony had always had the right to call a town meeting whenever they wished to, the Massachusetts Government Act required that they meet only once a year, to elect representatives and town officers. Consequently, an acquiescence in Gage's order would be an admission that the act was binding and that Gage had the right to order the meeting called off. The committee refused to do so, informing Gage that they would not interfere with the people's right to assemble. Subsequently, the members of the committee were arrested by order of Gage after the town had met and held its election. They were threatened with prosecution for breaking the provisions of the Massachusetts Government Act. Of the seven members of the committee, five refused to post bail in the case. They argued that since the act was unconstitutional, they could not recognize the authority of the governor to arrest them or of the court to try them for breaking it. The matter was decided when Gage proved unwilling to try them under the act and released them and quashed the indictments.[40]

On several occasions, the colonial resistance faced the problem of British or colonial officials who wished to shut down an institution that the Americans preferred to remain in operation. Methods were then needed to convince these officers to comply with the resisters' demands. These methods have certain characteristics of nonviolent intervention but remain political noncooperation as long as the institution works contrary to the expectations of the government. The first experience occurred in the winter of 1765–66, during the Stamp Act resistance. After the act took effect on 1 November 1765, the courts and Customs Houses in most cities were closed by the refusal of people to use them and by the unavailability of the stamps. With the absence of stamps, people began to realize that they could more effectively nullify the act if they continued activities for which the stamps were required, but without using the stamps. Government opposition to these attempts, especially at the local level, was almost certain. The royal officials did not want to break the law themselves or tolerate the defiance of others. Under the provisions of the Stamp Act, officials, including governors, who did not faithfully execute the act were subject to prosecution and fines at the Admiralty Court in Halifax, Nova Scotia.

The first major institution to begin operation without the use of stamps was the press. Many newspapers continued to appear on or around their usual publication date immediately after 1 November. At first, some of the papers included the disclaimer that no stamps were available. Some attempted to disguise their identity, and a single edition of an anonymous paper, the *Constitutional Courant*, came out. Soon, though, the newspapers simply continued to publish "normally," as if there were no Stamp Act.

It was not as simple to get the courts to reopen and to operate without the tax stamps. Not only were many of the judges either royal appointees or supporters of the Crown themselves, but lawyers and litigants were naturally afraid lest the decisions made by courts acting illegally not be binding later. In Massachusetts, there was no great difficulty in reopening the probate courts, which were presided over by a member of the local elite.[41] There, as elsewhere that winter, each session of the superior courts was adjourned without taking any action. In South Carolina, Chief Justice Charles Shinner adjourned the court at each scheduled session until 4 March 1766. On that day, three recently appointed justices, who had previously refused to attend court under the Stamp Act, appeared and agreed to hear arguments that the court should be reopened. A case was also heard at that time. At the next session, on 1 April, the three judges in favor of reopening the court outvoted the Crown-appointed chief justice in passing down a decision on the case. The matter stopped there, however. Even though the justices were willing to act in disregard of the Stamp Act, Clerk of Court Dougal Campbell was not, and he refused to serve any papers under the order. Although the legislature tried to punish the clerk and fined him, he neither was removed from office nor did he acquiesce. The courts of South Carolina remained ineffective until repeal of the Stamp Act, and the clerk's fine was later remitted by the Privy Council.[42]

Generally, the Customs establishment was more easily induced to resume relatively normal operation. In some ports, the Customs House began clearing ships shortly after the act took effect. It was, of course, the shipowners who took the financial risk of sailing without properly stamped papers, not the officers. Some customs officers, such as those in Philadelphia, backdated the papers to make them appear legal. Others devised forms for the captain to carry explaining that no stamps were available. The officers at Boston used the excuse that they feared for the safety of Customs revenues held in the Custom House. Charles Steuart, surveyor general of Customs in the southern part of America, wrote to the Customs commissioners in London on 7 December 1765, explaining that he had advised his subordinates to clear the ships. He expressed concern that the sailors who would be unable to find work would threaten the safety of the funds held in the Customs offices.[43]

This method of defiantly continuing to operate institutions while refusing to comply with the provisions of the law played an important role in the nullification of the Stamp Act by ensuring that, although the act was legally binding, it was not enforceable. In effect, such nullification of an act of Parliament was an attempt by the colonial resisters to assert in action that the only constitution they would recognize was the one that already existed. They were further saying that they would not tolerate changes in the form of government. Historian David S. Lovejoy noted the effect that nullification had: "Parliament repealed the Stamp Act not because it was unconstitutional, as the colonists claimed, but for the sake of expedience, since it was economically unwise and, probably more importantly, since the colonists generally refused to obey it."[44]

The Townshend Revenue Acts and the Coercive Acts presented resisters with a new type of problem. For various reasons, the Townshend Acts were not easily opposed by the kind of noncooperation, especially the "business as usual" way of acting, that had characterized the Stamp Act resistance. The Townshend Acts developed a system of enforcement and provided for eventual internal changes to be made in American government. These changes would extend the kinds of independent actions which royal officials could take without the support of the colonists. The American Board of Customs Commissioners afforded much greater control over the actions of local Customs officers than was possible when the London board alone supervised American collections. At the same time that local influence over the officers decreased, their powers grew. In particular, it was the Customs officers who directly enforced the Townshend Revenue Acts by performing the tax collections.

When those provisions of the Townshend Acts allowing colonial officials to be paid from royal grants were put into effect in 1771 and 1772, the legislatures, in particular, feared that the executive portion of the government would be strengthened out of proportion to the legislative. In addition to resenting the loss of yet another traditional right, that of paying their own officials, the colonies feared the growth of Britain's independent power in America. When these salary offers were first made to Massachusetts officials in 1772, a wave of protest broke out. This stimulated the establishment of the committees of correspondence in that colony and provided the issues for their first important actions.[45]

In 1774, the Massachusetts Government Act created a similar problem. This act again attempted to strengthen the executive (the governor and council), while weakening the legislature and the town meetings. The problem for those who wanted to oppose these acts was again similar to that of the 1772 opponents of the royal payment of judges' salaries: how could resistance groups with only limited constitutional control make officials act as the resisters wished? If they could not, how could the functions which these officials performed be taken care of in other ways or abolished? The problem was one of making concrete changes in a situation when neither protest nor noncooperation was capable of doing so. Up to this point, the protestors could ask themselves how their particular positions in existing institutions could be used to afford them the power to control what the institutions were going to do. Now, the problem of change, whether temporary or permanent, brought about by forceful action arose. This was, in short, the problem of possible political intervention.

• FROM NONCOOPERATION TO INTERVENTION •

The actions taken in 1765 and 1766 to reopen the courts and customs houses were attempts to induce existing institutions to act as they had usually done, but in violation of the statutes. In contrast, political intervention involved new relationships to the institutions insofar as it asserted new popular authority and constructed new institutions to replace those which were no longer responsive. This meant the formation of a set of related or interlocking parallel institutions (parallel in function, that is, to the legal institutions) which eventually attempted to replace the existing ones by taking over their functions or by creating new ones. This method of action is called parallel government. The concept of parallel government is discussed at greater length below. First, let us focus on some of the methods of nonviolent intervention that may precede parallel government.

Some of the actions of the resistance movements prior to 1770 included methods of intervention which were not political. Some actions taken against importing merchants to force them to cease violating the nonimportation policy can be interpreted as psychological intervention. Having crowds follow these merchants through the streets or the placing of effigies or signs at their shop doors to turn people away from the shops were forms of nonviolent harassment. This constituted a method of intervention to the extent that people, whether merchants or potential customers, were dissuaded or even prevented from doing things they would otherwise have done. People in Massachusetts also sometimes used methods of intervention which physically blockaded a place. In 1768, when soldiers wished to use the Boston Manufactory House as a barracks, the people who lived and worked there jammed inside and refused to come out, daring the soldiers to show their true colors by removing the occupiers by force.[46] In the western part of that colony in 1774, crowds prevented county courts from opening a session by blocking the courthouse and its approaches so that the judges could not get in.[47]

By far the most significant methods of intervention, though, were those that helped create new institutions, replaced currently legal ones, adopted new functions, or operated under new authority. In the years from 1765 to 1772, extralegal bodies met and acted largely on an *ad hoc* basis. They met once or a number of times, but, having completed the business for which they were formed, then dissolved. The Stamp Act Congress, which met in New York in October 1765, was such a body, dissolving upon the completion of its work and leaving behind neither an executive committee nor plans to meet again. When various extralegal bodies became both continuous and self-sustaining, an important step was taken in developing alternative social and political structures. The only way that British institutions could be replaced as they lost legitimacy in the eyes of the colonists was to shift popular recognition of legitimacy to new bodies. In part, this shift owed a great deal to the heightened political awareness which segments of the population gained. The shift also developed from the tendency of the committees, which had been impermanent in the past (as those which enforced the nonimportation associations), to survive beyond the immediate conditions which had given rise to them.

The first really significant step in the creation of on-going parallel institutions was the creation of the committees of correspondence in 1772 and 1773. At the instigation of Boston's newly organized committee of correspondence, the towns of Massachusetts began to form standing committees of correspondence in the fall of 1772. These committees were voted into existence by the town meetings primarily for the purpose of consulting with the other towns, especially Boston, about grievances that affected the whole colony. They were not limited, of course, to merely sending and receiving letters. The Plymouth town meeting called upon its committee of correspondence to advise the town not only about the content of threats to their liberty but about ways that the town could act to seek redress—in short, how to resist if necessary.[48] The colonies outside New England did not have town government. With the exception of the major ports, which still had or could easily reorganize committees left over from the Townshend Acts resistance, few local committees came into existence before the autumn of 1774. The Virginia House of Burgesses, though, devised a scheme for forming standing committees of correspondence in the provincial legislatures. This move established a committee which would not expire and become ineffective when the legislature was not in session. Consequently, a colonial governor could not prevent the committee of correspondence from working by proroguing or dissolving the legislature. Within a year after the Virginia House of Burgesses organized its standing committee of correspondence in 1773 and recommended the plan to the other assemblies, ten more such committees were in existence.

The notion of a system of committees as part of a legislative body was hardly new. The significance was that they were now viewed as permanent bodies which outlasted the legislative session or the life of the town meeting which formed them. Not all of the credit for the formation of the system can go to Massachusetts and Virginia, though. South Carolina, in the on-going power struggle between the governors and the Commons House of Assembly, developed one of the earlier systems for carrying on government in the absence of an effective constitutional legislature. In that colony, the Commons House had long used a system of temporary and permanent legislative committees to handle regular work, such as reporting on bills. After the donation to the Wilkes Fund, described above, the legislature and the governor came into conflict over the right of the Commons House to appropriate funds without the province treasurer's consent. At nearly the same time, the assembly found that its statutes establishing court districts in the backcountry were being disallowed by the Privy Council. The ensuing conflict and the refusal of the Commons House to pass money bills unless it could do so freely resulted in a total blockage of legislative work for several years. In order to circumvent its inability to act constitutionally, the Commons House sought extralegal ways of getting legislative work done and developed a series of standing committees authorized to act even when the House was not in session. The committee on taxes, for example, issued certificates of public credit in 1774, to be honored when taxes could again be collected, in order to pay the assembly's bills. Also, the House could avoid being accountable to the governor by acting as a committee of the whole rather than officially as the Commons House of Assembly. In South Carolina, as in other colonies, the committee of correspondence remained active whether the Commons House was in session or not, and it was available at all times in case action had to be taken.[49]

The significance of the committees in the provinces and in the towns increased with the meeting of the First Continental Congress. The Congress lifted itself above the *ad hoc* level as a temporary consultative body by agreeing to reconvene in the spring of 1775 and by the development of its comprehensive resistance program, the Continental Association. As Professor Ammerman discusses in Chapter Six, the Continental Association was enforced by local committees, many of which grew out of the committees of correspondence where they were already in existence. Others grew out of established city committees, such as the General Committee of Charleston and existing committees in Philadelphia and New York. These enforcement committees were complemented on the colony-wide level by the provincial conventions and congresses. In the fall and winter of 1774–75, these bodies quickly adopted more and more of the functions previously performed by the legislatures, executive officials, magistrates, and courts of the crown regime. These committees thus became an effective parallel government. This method of nonviolent political intervention, the replacement of old institutions with new, is of such central importance to the triumph of the resistance in 1774 and 1775 that it will be discussed in greater depth below.

Interpretation of the political significance of the use of nonviolent action in the first of the two major stages of the resistance, from 1765 to 1774, shows that this period contained the vital preparation for the destruction of British authority and control. During the second stage of the resistance, in 1774 and early 1775, authority was relocated into indigenous and more popular institutions which replaced imperial British ones. This falls in line with the summary of these changes presented at the beginning of this chapter. During this time, many Americans learned to break decisively the habit of obedience to the Crown, learned means of using disobedience as a powerful sanction, and created, as a result of these, a changed political and social life in the colonies—changes that allowed the final resistance struggle to break the connection with England. To an important extent, these changes were the result of the Americans' choice and use of weapons before 1775. In choosing economic and political forms of noncooperation as sanctions against British power, they avoided directly confronting the full weight of that power, the army, until their strength had grown through increased organization and unity.

The choice of the resisters to use certain means of opposing objectionable acts of the British government had consequences far beyond the winning or losing of the particular campaign against the issues then at hand. The means of struggle also altered the conditions under which the conflict took place. A particular example of this is the influence of the resistance campaigns upon patterns of political leadership, and the significance of that influence for the future American experience. In most of the colonies of eighteenth century America, the wealthy, particularly the landed rich, had succeeded in controlling political life so that the only important participation was their own. In colonies which had relatively wide suffrage, such as Massachusetts, methods of assigning leadership functions in the legislature had ensured that the class of persons from whom the leaders came would be restricted. In other colonies—North Carolina, South Carolina, and Pennsylvania, for example—the backcountry—through increasingly populated—remained either unrepresented or significantly underrepresented. At the same time, urban representation was restricted to the wealthy because the workers and tradesmen could not meet the high property requirements for suffrage and, importantly, for membership in the legislature. New York was particularly notorious for control of the legislature by the owners of several large estates. Since much of the colony consisted of large estates on which the farmers were only tenants, the rich families already had a stock of clients available to vote for them at any election.[50]

The events of the independence movement did not overthrow the system of leadership by a wealthy elite. However, the course of the movement did much to alter that system and to set the stage for the conflicts over democracy of the early republic. First, of course, the portion of the old elite which remained loyal to Britain during the 1760s and 1770s and supported imperial policies was swept from political influence and power. This was particularly true of those who continued to hold offices in the royal provinces into 1774 and 1775. Many of these people, though still in office, saw their political influence in their colony destroyed long before the end of colonial government. In Massachusetts, the careers of those who voted to rescind the Massachusetts circular letter in 1768 were destroyed by that vote. The biographer of Israel Williams, the western Massachusetts "River God," noted that the powerful Williams was finished as a political figure after opposing the circular letter. His little remaining public influence was spent in preventing his town of Hatfield from taking part in the Convention of September 1768.[51]

In Maryland, challenges to the old elite, the "gentry," clearly began with the movement of the lower classes into resistance politics in 1765. Thereafter, the "swamp men and shingle makers" were a force in both resistance and constitutional politics.[52] Philadelphia was too stratified for existing elites to be removed, although several Crown supporters suffered losses in their political fortunes, among them the powerful Joseph Galloway. In addition, the "mechanics" became a force in provincial politics, organizing both in election campaigns and during nonimportation as a pressure group.[53]

The removal of these old elites was very significant because they had been, by and large, the persons most successful under the old order at currying power from British-dominated institutions. With their loss, the British were deprived of a measure of control in the colonies where there had been a progovernment elite. The places of the old elite did not remain empty, of course, as long as there were offices to be filled. They were at times replaced by new leaders who arose, but more often by their rivals in contending leadership factions. In other words, when a section of the elite was removed, the system of leadership by the wealthy was not destroyed along with them. In some places though, these new leaders had to be more aware of the desires expressed by the average citizen than had ever been necessary before. In cities where nonconsumption and nonimportation agreements were made not exclusively by the merchants but by the tradesmen as well, the tradesmen formed committees of their own. These committees were not merely content to back up the actions of the merchants and to follow along but attempted to influence the decisions of the merchants and the city committees and joined in electoral politics as well. In the cities of Charleston, Philadelphia, and New York, decisions about the course of the resistance campaigns were influenced by the actions of the tradesmen as well as those of the merchants. As was shown in Chapter Four, meetings and demonstrations by workers in both of those cities restrained the merchants from abandoning the agreements in 1770.

In Charleston, South Carolina, a body of working people organized for the first time during the 1760s and began to take part in electoral politics. Although high property qualifications for the holding of office (significantly higher than those necessary to vote) prevented tradesmen from taking office, if the working people who had the franchise voted together, they represented a formidable bloc of votes in elections for the city's representatives. After 1766, when the tradesmen began to meet regularly at Liberty Tree, some politicians, notably Christopher Gadsden, began to court the tradesmen's votes. Another means of widening political partici-pation was also used in Charleston. Pauline Maier pointed out that the city had no municipal government and that an extralegal, but effective, local government was formed around the nucleus of meetings of the mechanics' committee. During 1768 and 1769, these meetings gradually took in wider segments of the politically active population. This was, in Maier's opinion, an attempt to "create in the resistance organization a surrogate for the New England town meeting."[54]

Actions and organizations of this sort did not end the system of leadership by elites, but they did put new constraints upon elites and began to expand the class background from which leaders could emerge. The city committees in particular, after 1768, showed the wider social sources from which activists could be drawn.[55] It is possible to try to explain the participation of tradesmen, particularly those from the less prosperous trades, by contending that these people were essentially pawns of dissenting segments of the elite, trying to improve their own positions by extralegal means. Or, more benignly, a theory of leadership may be put forward which sees only a very few persons as capable of directing action, while the followers were merely an amorphous mass with neither will nor wishes of their own. Either of these positions can be supported by the fact that most of the resistance leaders came from a relatively wealthy elite. These included not only legislative leaders but members of the committees as well. In fact, some committees, for which occupation was a criterion for membership, deliberately reserved more places for the wealthy than they did for "mechanics."

We must be careful, though, not to commit a common fallacy in the use of the term "elite" by equating leadership position and material wealth. That is, many of those who use the term "elite" begin with the assumption that it refers to one of these, often only to wealth, but in using the term to describe both leadership and wealth they treat them as one. We ought to look more closely at the social origins of those who became leaders before assigning them to the "elite." Many of these leaders, such as Christopher Gadsden and John Hancock, were men of wealth. Other important leaders were not, however. Samuel Adams certainly was not. Nor, despite his later success, was John Adams. In Boston, where the elite of wealth was represented by the rich merchants, there was great participation in the resistance campaigns by the professional middle class. Lawyers, such as John Adams and Josiah Quincy, Jr., played a major role, as did physicians, notably Doctors Thomas Young and Joseph Warren. With the exception of John Adams, recognition of these men as leaders demonstrates that we must not look only at office holders in defining who were the leaders of the struggle. Joseph Warren served on many Boston town committees, especially those concerned with the resistance, yet he was not an official. Quincy (whose letters are reprinted in Appendix G), held no office at all. His participation in the resistance was particularly important, though, as he opened up lines of communication between the Boston resistance leaders and those as far south as Charleston.

The participation of members of the middle class, as well as those persons' strong ties among the farmers and working people, from whom they often had found their own origin, was well recognized by the historians in the early part of this century. It is only within recent years that historians have sought to locate the sources of leadership primarily among the elite of wealth. In addition to these middle class leaders, there were known leaders from among the tradespeople. Many of these people were probably not numbered among the first rank of leaders but, nonetheless, took responsibility for action. Each city had printers who worked primarily for the people who were members of the resistance groups. They printed the handbills, broadsides, and pamphlets for resistance meetings and organizations and edited the newspapers in which correspondence supporting the Whig point of view was set forth. Some projects, such as the printing and reprinting of the *Constitutional Courant* in 1765, were undertaken by the printers themselves, apparently without direction or control by other leaders.

We also do a disservice to the role of nonelite leaders as well as to the mass of people who acted without requiring the direction of leaders if we ignore the many actions which took place to further the cause of the movements which were not done at the behest of any centralized leadership. This is especially true in the countryside, where the commands of central urban leaders could not have been binding in any case. Many of these actions are not available to the historian because they were not recorded, but we do know that the country towns of many of the colonies were the site of both protest meetings and symbolic actions, such as the church-sponsored spinning parties described in Appendix C. Where these actions existed, other resistance activities must also have taken place.

Even though the committees of the urban centers were primarily staffed by members of wealthy groups, especially merchants and planters, there is no evidence that the wealthy alone controlled the actions of these committees. In fact, there is substantial evidence that indicates that the merchants did not wish for the continuation of nonimportation for more than a year during the Townshend Acts resistance and that they very much wanted nonimportation to end long before it did. During the Continental Association, the merchants in some ports were very much opposed to the resumption of nonimportation for fear of the economic consequences to themselves. Nevertheless, commercial resistance was resumed and many merchants served on the committees.

If the intentions of a major group of leaders do not explain the continuation of resistance activity, where can we look for the answer to our questions about how such decisions were made? It is necessary to recognize the reciprocal influences which existed between the leaders and followers in the movement. The explanation may lie there. This is true not only of the movement we are reviewing but, although often unrecognized, of all power relationships.[56] At times in the course of the campaigns, the leadership's major concern was the creation of a public perception that the act being protested was unjust and one which could and should be resisted. At other times, the leadership was concerned with influencing people to accept the means of action which they recommended to oppose the act. Often though, leadership and followers were clearly not of a single mind as to what should be done. In Philadelphia, New York, and Boston, the early months of 1770 included an effort on the part of a segment of the merchant class to end economic resistance. As time passed, this move gained support among the merchants who were members of the committees which oversaw the agreements (although certainly not in the form of a coalition between the Tory merchants and their opponents). In each case, the wishes of the populace were made known and consulted before action to end the agreements was taken. In all these cities, economic resistance clearly outlasted the desires of the merchants' committees to continue it. This can only be explained by recognizing that the wishes of those normally seen as followers had a major impact on the actions taken by the leadership.[57]

These alterations in the political role of the nonelite elements of the population resulted in few actual structural changes prior to the coming of the Continental Association, especially in the assemblies and among the executives of the colonial governments. Ideology, the set of ideas which people utilized to interpret the political situation in which they found themselves, did undergo important changes as new issues came to the fore. The question of ideology and the changes which colonial consciousness of political issues underwent have been thoroughly discussed by Professors Bernard Bailyn and Pauline Maier and need not be reviewed here.[58] Essentially, from 1765 to 1775, they see not only that public discussion of political issues altered, in part by becoming more able and discriminating, but that the vital issues themselves changed in some ways. For the present discussion, the question is not that of what issues motivated the Americans to resist Britain, but how they understood the kind of resistance in which they were engaged.

In some vitally important ways, what Professor Bailyn called the "transformation" of American ideology did *not* create the resistance activities we have reviewed, *but was created by them*. This was in large part because, although political disputation was by no means a new phenomenon for the people of 1765, the practical problems of resistance were. Some of the major texts of the eighteenth century American Whigs were the writings of the seventeenth century British Whigs. These writers, particularly those of the period of the Commonwealth and of the Glorious Revolution, were centrally concerned with the conditions under which lawfully constituted but unconstitutionally used power could be justly opposed. In fact, while the colonies had been too young to be involved in the Commonwealth, many had taken part in the Glorious Revolution or in revolts against their proprietors thereafter.[59] Many Americans, consequently, were intellectually comfortable with discussions of resistance to authority when it acted irretrievably amiss. As Thomas Hutchinson said of the people of Massachusetts in his *History of the Province of Massachusetts-Bay,* "in general [they] were of the principles of the ancient whigs, attached to the revolution, and to the succession of the crown in the house of Hanover."[60] The problem, however, for such "ancient whigs" in 1765 and after, was that many of the insights gained in the struggles against Charles I and James II applied only in the most general way.

The result of the attempt to apply Whig political thought to American conditions was to force changes in that doctrine. The old Whigs were most concerned with justifying total resistance to a government which had completely lost its authority. One major problem of the Americans, particularly before 1774, was that they did not completely reject the authority of the imperial system which had imposed the taxation acts and other restraints on them. In the case of the Stamp Act, it was believed that Parliament and the ministry had used their power improperly, even unconstitutionally. Members of Parliament had failed to recognize this or had been duped by bad advice. The authority of Parliament and the Crown was not destroyed, but misused. For this and other reasons, military struggle initiated by the Americans could not be seen intellectually as a realistic alternative. Also, colonial resisters during the resistance campaigns, as well as for a time after the outbreak of the war, intended that Britain would recognize its policy as wrong and alter it. Consequently, the colonists devised a combination of actions which nullified the application of the acts in America, while putting pressure on Britain commercially and politically to revise them. How to apply this pressure was a practical problem. How to justify this kind of resistance was an intellectual one, which followed the development of these resistance methods themselves.

What was the colonists' understanding of the technique of nonviolent struggle which they were using? In many ways this understanding was a completely pragmatic one. That is, colonial resistance planners did not attempt to enshrine commercial resistance and noncooperation with government as the best possible responses under all circumstances. Rather, these were seen practically as the best available means under the existing circumstances.

Part of the problem was to restrain crowds and individuals from committing violence to persons in the course of the resistance. Articles and letters in the newspapers, not learned arguments in pamphlets, reminded people that, as things stood, this was the most effective way to act (see Chapter Nine). Not only are there records of members of crowds and leaders attempting to restrain the crowds from violence, but parades and large-scale crowd "visits" could have been an express alternative to nighttime raids by affording people an opportunity to express their anger and resentment without destruction. Tory James Murray was protected from an angry crowd in Boston in 1769 by several Sons of Liberty who called out to the crowd: "No violence, or you'll hurt the cause."[61] Especially in those places most threatened by violence—either their own or, as they saw it, that of the officers or soldiers—attempts were made to understand the role of possible violence in the movement and reasons to avoid it. Boston was such a place. One of the episodes reported there concerned Bostonians, fear of what the troops would do when they landed in the town in 1768 (see Introduction to Chapter Four). Governor Bernard reported to his superior, the Earl of Hillsborough, that serious consideration had been given in September 1768 to arming a force to seize Castle William in the harbor. Bernard told Hillsborough that this had not been done because the province was at the time petitioning Parliament for redress of grievances and that it was therefore not a proper response.[62]

It is difficult to assess the colonists' appreciation of their methods of action partly because they *were* chosen for their pragmatic effectiveness and their relation to existing concepts of correct action in resistance. The decision to reject some forms of violence and severely limit the use of others was consequently combined with, as John Dickinson put it in his 1768 *Farmer's Letters,* a view of those methods *proper* to the defense of liberty (see Appendix B). Although, currently, it may seem disingenuous of the colonists to have argued this way, it was contended that the resistance methods used were proper in part because they were legal and fitting to the British constitution. Nevertheless, Whigs were often reproached with the observation that their methods were in fact violent: that they held illegal and noisy meetings, damnified honest men in the eyes of their neighbors through the boycott, countenanced tarring and feathering, and openly carried on illegal and conspiratorial associations in restraint of trade and the liberties of their opponents. Massachusetts attorney Daniel Leonard, writing in the *Boston Post Boy* as "Massachusettensis" in early 1775, made many such accusations. John Adams answered, as "Novanglus," in the Whig *Boston Gazette.* In his polemical replies, Adams pointed out that the leaders of the Whigs had actually done everything in their power to restrain violent actions during the movement. To the accusation that tarring and feathering had been countenanced, Adams answered that the most notorious case, John Malcolm's, had been as much opposed by the Whig leaders as by anyone and was the result of private grudges.

Adams attempted, complete with quotations from Whig classics of the seventeenth century, to show that Leonard was not justified in calling the actions of those who had opposed the Coercive Acts violent. Meetings are not violent just because they are full and rowdy, nor is it violent—here citing Algernon Sydney—to oppose the magistrates when they act illegally themselves.[63] For Adams as for others of the period, the enforcement through the boycott of associations voluntarily joined was neither violent nor improper, and this was made the keystone of the search for unity of action among all the American colonies.

The experience of the resistance campaigns against the Stamp Act and the Townshend Acts and the individual struggles which had gone on in many of the colonies over local issues had, by 1774, taught American resisters much about the uses of their technique of action. Their uncertainty in 1774 was not over whether to resist the Coercive Acts (even though only one colony—Massachusetts—was directly affected); the question at that time was over methods of organizing the campaign that would ensure maximum unity and participation and, thus, the greatest effect. The previous use of commercial resistance had demonstrated that a series of independent nonimportation agreements covering different time periods and with different provisions resulted in a weaker movement than one with greater unity of action promised to. People also realized that weak enforcement of the agreements during the 1769–70 period had reduced their ability to succeed. This was to be remedied in the Continental Association of 1774 by increasing the numbers of committees until all geographical areas were covered.

The active conflict over the Coercive Acts began with the Americans having two important sources of strength as a result of their nine years of intermittent conflict with British government policy: extensive experience in the use of the nonviolent technique of struggle and a mode of organization capable of making it effective for them. These along with the ideas explaining and justifying the colonists' actions constituted the foundation upon which the political reality of independence could be laid in the coming months. Structurally, this foundation included the following components: (1) committees that could be reactivated or reformed when required and which were capable of carrying out new tasks as well as performing old ones, (2) procedures which could be repeated for selecting members of such bodies, and (3) means to form new bodies should the need arise. Consequently, future action did not depend upon the commitments of certain individuals. The resistance groups could now survive and act, even if many persons who manned the groups at any given time later came to oppose their activities. As Ryerson has shown with regard to Philadelphia, continuity of action could be maintained over time by the committees of that city despite changes in membership.[64]

These organizational advances represented the foundation of new institutions within the colonies which did not depend for their legitimacy upon British authority or recognition. When these institutions were combined with a wide and growing willingness to deny the authority of Parliament and the Crown to make decisions binding in America, the result was the firm establishment of the infrastructure of independence.

• THE RISE OF PARALLEL INSTITUTIONS •

An understanding of the developments which produced American independence need not rest upon the view that the independence movement, even as late as 1775, was a planned attempt to create conditions under which America could be and so could declare itself to be independent of British authority. There was great disagreement right up until 4 July 1776 (and after as well) over whether or not the thirteen colonies could or should be independent from Britain. Essentially though, long before this, as the various authors in this volume have shown, the actions of those Americans who resisted British authority to tax the colonies, to control their legislatures, and to punish them for disobedience had already destroyed this authority and created new institutions which replaced it. These institutions were the true basis of independence, and the arguments of 1776 were aimed primarily at whether or not to recognize this fact.

The replacement of British imperial institutions as the politically authoritative bodies with the parallel political institutions which arose during the period of the Continental Association was an unintended consequence of resistance activity. The intended effect of resistance measures, such as the nonimportation agreements and associations, was to prevent Britain from enforcing the objectionable acts and to induce Parliament to repeal them. In order to implement the provisions of these agreements, the colonists found it necessary to form committees whose purpose it was to find out who was or was not cooperating with the nonimportation agreements and to recommend sanctions against those who broke them. The organization and operation of these committees in turn required the cooperation of significant numbers of people. Consequently, resistance by nonviolent struggle not only had its intended political and economic effects but lasting unintended organizational effects as well.

The Americans secured British concessions to their resistance campaigns against the Stamp and Townshend Revenue Acts through what Gene Sharp calls the mechanism of accommodation.[65] The British altered their policies in 1766 and 1770 to repeal most of these acts, but they did not do so because American adamance or arguments had *convinced* them of the rightness of the American position. Parliament and the ministry *never* admitted that the American claims to the right to be taxed solely through their own legislatures were valid. Neither were the American methods sufficiently strong to *coerce* the British, giving the British government no choice whether to keep or to repeal the acts. Rather, the Americans acted in such a way that the ministry could see and compare the costs and benefits of continued efforts to enforce the acts and those of backing down. The cost to the British of American commercial resistance, of their own limited nonmilitary sanctions, of the necessity to keep British troops in some of the American cities, and the like could be weighed against the advantages of showing firmness, of trying to break down the agreements, and of refusing to change policy under pressure.

British officials could also consider the policy of acceding to a portion of the American demands in order to break the resistance front and avoid having to accede to all. The imperial government saw in the first months of 1770 that there were internal strains within the nonimportation agreements which could be exploited. Speaking on the subject of repeal of portions of the Townshend Revenue Acts, Lord North, according to Thomas C. Barrow, "argued that repeal was not so much a concession . . . as it was a well-timed move to divide the colonial opposition and to end the nonimportation agreements."[66] In effect, the avoidance of military struggle by both Britain and America during this period forced the British to adopt a greater degree of rational calculation of costs and returns than could have been expected if the Americans had challenged Britain's military might. Not only would army leaders have then been involved in the making of decisions, but elements of national self-assertion, honor, grandeur, and the like would have become more intimately involved.

When the first of the Coercive Acts, the Boston Port Act, was passed on 31 March 1774, it was a forgone conclusion to many observers that the American colonies would resist it by primarily commercial means. As early as that very date, a British "friend of the colonies," reporting passage of the act, commented: "I suppose there will be a general Congress from the Colonies. . . . A determination to stop the exports of your country, and not import any *British* manufactures, will in two years restore you to liberty, and draw poverty and ruin on the mother country."[67] As early as the Tea Act resistance, the New Hampshire Assembly had recognized the possibility of such a union: "A union of all the Colonies appears to be the most likely method, under God, of obtaining a repeal of all those acts, which are so subversive of the freedom of the British colonies."[68] In short, there was recognition from the beginning of the final phase of struggle that a plan which bound all of the colonies together in resistance was essential to assure success. Such a resistance plan had also to be able to gain the support of all the persons in each colony, even if that support had to be enforced. On the basis of such considerations, the Continental Association was formed.

The colonists had not planned that the committees organized to supervise and to enforce the Association would join with existing social and economic institutions which denied British authority in the colonies to become a new government. For a period of time, two competing sets of governing institutions existed: (1) the provincial executives and officials and the royal military and Customs establishments; and (2) the new institutions of the Continental Association, represented by the committees of inspection and correspondence and the provincial congresses. These new institutions constituted a "parallel" government.

The concept of parallel government contends that during conflicts in which the legitimacy of existing governments or governing institutions is challenged, authority—the recognition by a populace of an institution's *right* to command their obedience in a certain matter—may be shifted to new institutions.[69] This may be done temporarily. People may develop a new organization to perform a specific function when an existing body has lost authority, but they may later return their allegiance to the existing institution. Or, parallel government may become permanent. The existing governmental bodies may be abandoned in favor of others. While the process is going on, both sets of institutions may exist at once, each attempting to gain recognition and support from the populace. Different sections of the population may support opposing sets of institutions, while others may be torn between the two or may be indifferent or hostile to both.

The contest will be decided by the ability of each set of institutions to gain the *obedience* of the people at large. That is, in the process of attempting to govern, each institution issues commands which constitute claims upon the obedience and cooperation of the people. The authority of a government can be measured by the ability of its institutions to have their commands carried out by a sufficiently large number of persons that they become effective. This implementation of commands cannot depend solely upon the ability of the institutions to enforce obedience. The attempt to enforce obedience on the large scale, rather, is an attempt to substitute punishments for effective authority. In any case, enforcement itself requires the organization and cooperation of those who carry out the sanctions. Rather, the institution must appeal to people to support and obey it. This appeal may be made on the basis of tradition, law, natural justice, self interest, beliefs, or on many other grounds. In essence, the appeal is to support one body and ignore the other, since only one of the two rival "governments" can ultimately be authoritative.

An institution of parallel government in such a situation need not have been planned. Members of such institutions may not realize that their request for obedience and appeals for the acceptance of the authority of their body are potentially destructive to the authority of the other institution. Even the persons who initiate and operate the new institution may not realize that they are forming an organ of government. Parallel governments emerge as bodies arise which are capable of implementing a program of action by commands which are obeyed by some portion of the populace to the exclusion of obedience to demands from any other body. In fact, some institutions of the existing regime may continue to function, even under their old authority, insofar as their functions are not in opposition to more authoritative new counter-institutions. (A "benign" institution such as the post office is an example.) In other cases, some orders of an institution may be obeyed or some of its functions retained, while others are challenged. In effect, the situation occurring in the development of parallel government is a contest between institutions to determine which authority will survive and which will not.

How does this concept of parallel government apply to the resistance to Britain by the Continental Association? It applies if, and only if, it can be shown that bodies arose which were capable of issuing commands (or recommendations) for action which were followed by major segments of the population, to the exclusion of the commands or expectations of governmental bodies which already existed and which also claimed authority. The true measure, of course, would be in cases where directly opposing commands were given by both old and new bodies and those of one were obeyed in preference to those of the other.

Another measure of whether a new institution or set of bodies constitutes "parallel government" is that these bodies must show evidence of becoming "institutionalized"—regular and lasting bodies with their own procedures and personnel, as well as sources of support. By parallel government, we do not refer to obedience of commands of *ad hoc* bodies established only to conduct resistance. Rather, a pattern of action is required which demonstrates that the new bodies are potentially capable of lasting and of becoming broadly accepted as authoritative throughout the population. To illustrate, an *ad hoc* resistance group may be able to issue an order to its supporters to perform an action which will further the resistance movement—not to import foreign goods, for example. That same group, however, may not be able to control their activity in any other area. On the other hand, a parallel governing institution, or a set of them, will tend to take over broader areas of authority and governmental functions, perhaps moving into the range covered by the civil courts, or performing legislative functions, such as taxation or the regulation of commerce. Parallel government exists when there is a conscious or unconscious attempt to remove sovereign authority from the hands of the previous regime and to concentrate it in the "new" government, which for a time exists alongside the old.

One of the major sources of the need for parallel institutions during the Continental Association was the inability of constitutional bodies to perform a major role in the resistance. During the earlier campaigns, the legislatures had often supplied both leadership and a forum for the discussion of resistance issues, as well as being themselves the source of petitions, resolutions, and circular letters. By the summer of 1774, it was the firm policy of the royal governors simply to prevent a legislature from meeting if they knew or suspected that it would take action to further the resistance against the Coercive Acts. It was a common occurrence during the summer of 1774 for legislatures to be dissolved for discussing participation in the First Continental Congress or for voting to send delegates to Philadelphia. Other legislatures were not called into session at all lest they take such action. In attempting to find a way out of the problem presented by not being able to act officially, the legislatures often suggested the formation of extralegal assemblies in their place.

Governor William Franklin of New Jersey kept the assembly out of session after their meeting of February 1774, refusing a request to call a session in August of that year. In his address to the next session in January 1775, Franklin reprimanded the members for the actions taken at the county meetings and the provincial congress. The assembly replied that they had no choice but to call the extralegal meetings, since the assembly had not been allowed to meet.[70] In July 1774, the legislature of New Hampshire was prorogued by the governor before it was able to elect any delegates to represent the province in the First Continental Congress. No longer able to act officially and yet unwilling to take upon themselves authority to act without consulting the wishes of the towns, the legislators reconvened in a tavern in Portsmouth and requested that each town send a delegate to a special meeting to consider this question. The result was the first provincial congress of New Hampshire on 21 July 1774. The meeting, held at Exeter, attracted eighty-five delegates and quickly voted to sent two representatives to Philadelphia to take part in "the General Congress." They also appointed a committee of five to instruct the delegates regarding the attitude of the province on matters likely to come up in Philadelphia and be ready to appoint a replacement for either of the delegates should one be unable to go to Philadelphia.[71]

Very early in 1774, South Carolina had already begun to shift away from depending upon the Commons House of Assembly for leadership. This continued on 20 July 1774, when the Charleston city committee (which had been organized to enforce the nonimportation agreement during the Townshend Acts struggle and which had remained active) expanded itself into a "general Committee" of ninety-nine members drawn from all over the province. In that colony, under the existing constitutional procedures, regular legislative leadership in resistance questions was quite impossible. The governor would simply not allow the assembly to remain in session if its members attempted to respond to the appeals sent to them by the committees of correspondence of the other colonies. As has been seen, during the years of overt conflict between the governors and the Commons House over money bills, the House had evolved procedures for considering business without acting officially. In order to do this, though, it was necessary that they remain in session. In March 1774, when the Commons met and began to consider correspondence from other colonies, it was immediately prorogued by the governor and kept out of session until August. By this time, extralegal meetings had completely taken over the functions of the assembly. When the Commons House finally met officially, all it could do was confirm the earlier selection of delegates to the Continental Congress by an extralegal assembly. The members were forced to act in secret to accomplish even this, and the House was immediately dissolved again by Lieutenant-Governor Bull.[72] The Commons House of Assembly did not meet again.

Governor Gage of Massachusetts, after keeping the House of Representatives out of session for the greater part of 1774, allowed warrants to be prepared for a meeting to be held at Salem on 5 October 1774. It had not met since May of that year, when the members appointed delegates to the Congress and the House was immediately dissolved by Gage—dissolved, in fact, while in the process of voting on its delegation to go to Philadelphia. When the towns elected members to the new session of the House, plans had already been made to replace the House with a provincial congress. Gage attempted to avoid the issue by revoking permission for the House to form and refusing to meet them to open the session officially. The members spent three days in Salem waiting to see if the governor would act and, when he did not, declared that they had no choice but to join the delegates waiting in Concord and form a provincial congress, which they did on 8 October.[73]

The disappearance or impotence of institutions legal under the existing constitution gave great impetus to the development of extraconstitutional bodies, but it was not their only source. During the spring, summer, and early fall of 1774, many such bodies appeared throughout the colonies. These took the widest variety of forms. Some were already becoming permanent and, indeed, were direct continuations and expansions of older bodies, such as the existing city committees of Charleston, Philadelphia, and New York. Others met for specific purposes and disbanded, but they were renewable later, as were the provincial congresses. Still others met on an *ad hoc* basis to consider resolutions supporting the resistance and broke up when their job was done, as did the county conventions of Massachusetts and town and county meetings in other provinces.

The crucial period for the formation of extralegal political bodies came after the Continental Congress drew up the Continental Association in October 1774, and then disbanded, allowing resistance to be carried on from there under the direction of essentially local bodies. The establishment of the committees which enforced the Continental Association was the culmination of the period of political mobilization which had begun with the Stamp Act resistance. This mobilization consisted of a discontinuous but ever increasing expansion of the social groups responsive to and involved in resistance politics. R. A. Ryerson identified four "phases" of this process as they relate to the formation, membership, and following of the Philadelphia general committee. These were: (1) the formation of a relatively small group of resistance leaders; (2) the development of institutions capable of acting on the existing government to attempt to force policy change and later of acting as "alternative executors of political authority" when change was not forthcoming; (3) the development of "virtually unanimous" public opinion behind a concept of provincial autonomy; and (4) the ability to recruit new leaders rapidly who would extend the tasks of resistance bodies and their degree of representativeness.[74]

The second "phase" of this fourfold scheme corresponds directly to the method of nonviolent action which we have been calling, after Sharp, "dual sovereignty and parallel government."[75] Chronologically and conceptually, Ryerson has combined the earlier bodies which carried on the resistance from 1765 to 1774 with those which created actual independence in 1774 and 1775. This is legitimate in the case considered, Philadelphia, because of the close continuation of the city's committee from its founding during the Townshend Acts resistance through the end of the period. This identity of resistance bodies over time is less true in nonurban areas, although the whole process and final outcome were not greatly different. In many ways, Ryerson's position is similar to that expressed here in viewing the progression leading from resistance to parallel or "alternative" politically authoritative institutions as the thrust of the independence movement before the war. This process finally combined mobilized leadership with an active following, the ideology of autonomy, and the rejection of unresponsive Crown authority during the Continental Association.

Section Eleven of the Association provided for the election in each town or city and in each county of a committee to supervise nonimportation. This program of enforcement, described in Chapter Six, was adopted to a greater or lesser degree in all colonies but Georgia. In many areas, similar committees had already met and had begun to concern themselves with the resistance which was sure to follow upon the meeting of the Continental Congress. When the Continental Association was adopted, it provided a basis upon which the committees could begin to regularize themselves and become lasting parts of the political structure. With this ability to enforce the decisions of Congress coming into play, the structure established by the Association began to take on the characteristics necessary to make binding claims upon the actions of the people of the several colonies. According to Lawrence Henry Gipson: "The measures it [Congress] had adopted were held by the patriots to be nothing less than the supreme law of the land, taking precedence over any measure or pronouncement of the individual colonial assemblies, not to mention the laws of Parliament relating to America."[76]

There were two essential trends which proceeded side by side in this process. Indeed, in some ways the two events are one, for one follows necessarily from the other. The first was the proliferation of local enforcement bodies of the Association, from the local committees up through the provincial congresses, and their rapid broadening of the areas in which they were competent to interest themselves. The second was increased refusal to recognize the authority of the Crown and its officers to order any particular action to be taken or not to be taken. Especially as the most vital organs of constitutional government in the countryside, the courts, were being closed or boycotted in most places, the standing government and its organs were atrophying to the point where the orders of the governor and the established procedures were of no effect. Parallel institutions and procedures were quickly developed to replace basic functions where they were being abandoned by the royal government, and themselves claimed at least portions of the authority the Crown was losing.

Local committees—those of the towns, townships, or counties, depending upon the basic organization of the particular colony—were of essential importance in this process. Unlike the provincial conventions, these were not deliberative bodies; they did not decide resistance policy but rather administered it or carried it out. There are two particular ways in which they were essential to the progress of parallel government. First, they provided a nearby institution through which the influence of that portion of the population interested in the resistance could make itself felt. This is typically shown by the experiences of the Philadelphia and, particularly, the New York city committees. In both cities, there were segments of the population, especially after 1769, which were very influential and which did not want the committees to support nonimportation. In New York, even more than in Philadelphia, these individuals formed the bulk of the membership of the committee but found themselves unable to control its actions, for public pressure to support the resistance was too great to withstand.[77]

Second, and more blatant, the committees of the localities were the bodies which held the power to enforce the Association through the threat, or the actual practice, of boycotting those who opposed or broke the terms of the Association. This has been discussed earlier with respect to the actions of committees which did actually punish such persons. In some areas, an attempt was made by those who still supported the royal government in 1774 and 1775 to prevent the committees from being formed and thus to make the Association effective in their area. Again in New York, this time in the rural areas of the province, Tories who opposed the committee system acted against it. Perhaps realizing, following the experience of their brethren in that city, that if committees were formed, there would necessarily be increased pressure for them to be made effective; the Loyalists of at least five counties succeeded in preventing a county committee from being formed. Bernard Mason pointed out that the system which the Association envisaged, a hierarchy of committees checking and supporting each other, was ineffective in those counties. "The Whigs managed to maintain intact the ranks of the intercolonial opposition to the North ministry but their activity faltered because they did not have a viable county committee network."[78]

To claim that these new institutions—the committees of inspection and correspondence and the provincial congresses—began to take on governmental functions is not to claim that the things they did were the same as or comparable to the functions of a government of today. The object of most of their activities was furtherance of the resistance to the Coercive Acts, and, consequently, they stressed those functions which mobilized forces and preserved internal discipline to do just that. In the process, they began to carry out the activities of a normal government. Typical among these functions were those of taxation, establishment of courts, legislation, and, finally, the adoption of an executive.

As described earlier, courts under royal authority were not allowed to operate. Either the justices failed to appear or crowds prevented the courts from opening and doing business. Consequently, the large number of state functions normally performed by the courts could not be guaranteed. It may seem a minor matter that suitors refused to bring action in courts under royal authority or that the merchants who felt themselves wrongly boycotted brought their cases before the enforcement committees. These were actually of the utmost importance. Instead of the functions of courts being totally abandoned, some were adopted by the committees established under the Continental Association. If the resolves passed by the Continental Congress were in any sense "law," as claimed above, they needed courts to apply and interpret them. The committees became these courts and took upon themselves the power to settle disputes arising from the application of these laws. The ability to settle disputes authoritatively in courts is as much a sign and symbol of independence as is the ability to legislate or to wage war.

· THE FORMATION OF AUTONOMOUS POLITICAL INSTITUTIONS ·

Max Weber defined the state as a political body possessed of the sole ability to use violence legitimately within a territory.[79] As we have seen in this book, violence is not the only way in which a political community can forcefully act to carry through policies, enforce expected behavior, punish opponents, and so on. The possibility that these coercive actions could be taken by a community that did not also control the legitimate use of organized violent coercion is undoubtedly a marginal one, but we are in fact dealing here with a marginal (or transitional) case. The ability of a political association or institution, or a set of them, to make a valid claim of being the sole body legitimately authorized to use sanctions in enforcement of political goals may be used to establish a behavioral *test* of the existence of a state. However, only certain offices are authorized to mobilize or make direct use of the coercive capability. This includes those executive officials who can give direct orders to police or army, but there may be cases where such roles do not yet exist. Other officers who can use the state's coercive capabilities are found in the legislatures or the courts. Under the provisions of the Continental Association, the committees of inspection became, among other things, courts during 1774 and 1775 because they were capable of trying people for breaking the Continental Association, of punishing them when they were found to have done so, and of releasing them from punishment when they agreed to comply. For example, occasionally merchants were accused of having imported goods in contravention of the Association or of having raised prices excessively to take advantage of shortages created by nonimportation. It was the function of the local committee to look into the case, to collect and consider evidence, and to determine whether or not the person was to be found guilty and punished by the economic and social boycott. The merchant could offer evidence to show that he had not breached the Association. On occasion, appeals could be taken to a higher tribunal, such as the provincial congress.[80] By deciding whether the social and economic boycott was to be brought against a person or not, the committees operating as courts disposed of or utilized the public force.

Another area in which the political bodies which arose under the resistance to the Coercive Acts began to adopt governmental functions was in taxation. Just as taxation had been viewed since 1765 as a function solely to be undertaken by the people's representatives in assembly, now it became a function of the provincial congresses which were replacing the legislatures. This extraconstitutional taxation began in some provinces at the time of election of delegates to the Continental Congress. In those provinces where the governor refused to allow the legislature to meet to consider sending a delegation, the body which chose the delegation also found it necessary to devise a method for paying their expenses. This was true of South Carolina, where a July 1774 meeting of delegates was called by an earlier Liberty Tree meeting. This meeting voted that if the money was raised, the Commons House would reimburse or guarantee it, which the House later did. New Hampshire went beyond this when the representatives of the towns met on 21 July 1774 to choose their delegates to the Congress. This meeting voted not only to raise money by a tax on the towns but to appoint a treasurer, John Giddinge, who would receive all funds for the expenses of the delegates.[81]

When the Massachusetts Provincial Congress met at Concord in October 1774, it carried still further the process of placing taxation into the hands of the extralegal bodies. It was decided that none of the constitutional officers could be allowed to continue his function and that the provincial congress must be able to raise taxes and dispose of public funds as it saw fit. Consequently, it resolved that Henry Gardner should be appointed "Receiver-General" and that the constables of the towns should pay all of the tax money they collected to him, and not to the constitutional provincial treasurer, Harrison Gray.[82] The provincial congress, of course, had no power to enforce this command, and its validity depended completely upon the recognition by the towns of its legitimacy and of their acting accordingly.

The situation did evidently remain somewhat confused. Although many towns did send tax collections to Gardner, others withheld them altogether. On 28 February 1775, the Suffolk County Committee of Correspondence asked the selectmen of the town of Medway to send withheld tax monies to the county treasurer, rather than the provincial treasurer. When Gray fled to England after the British evacuation in March 1776, his account books were greatly in arrears because of his inability to collect the province taxes from the towns. Gray himself testified to the effectiveness of the tax refusal in an undated letter of early 1775, in which he informed merchant John Erving that the provincial bonds that Erving held could not be paid when due. Complaining that the provincial congress had illegally appointed its own treasurer, Gray wrote: "The public Treasury has been robbed of the funds which were laid for the support of the public faith in consequence whereof the Treasurer is unable to discharge either the principle or Interest of the Government securities presented to him for payment by the Honble John Erving Esq."[83]

Many of the towns in Massachusetts did vote in town meeting to send their taxes to Gardner and the provincial congress, which used them for a variety of purposes, including the reorganization and rearming of the militia. As noted earlier, an important sign of the development of parallel government lies in the willingness to obey commands of new institutions to the exclusion of the old. Governor Gage attempted to test this himself by ordering, in a proclamation on 10 November 1774, that no one should follow the commands of the provincial congress, which had no legal existence under the constitution.[84] He was unsuccessful in this attempt.

The provincial congresses were also more representative, at least formally, than the assemblies had been under the colonial system. They were certainly often larger than the assemblies had been, reflecting the movement into politics of new social groups, such as the tradespeople, and the growth of the country areas. In the late colonial period, the backcountry areas of many colonies, especially the Carolinas and Pennsylvania, had grown enormously. They had, however, gone without representation in the assemblies. This was often because the Privy Council would not allow the colonies to create new electoral districts or change the size of the legislature on their own. This was a privilege reserved to the king, but the crown refused to act upon it. During the formation of the provincial congresses, provision was made, either formally or informally, for these areas to be represented. The South Carolina Provincial Congresses and the constituent meetings which preceded them quickly adopted an enlarged schedule of representation as compared with the Commons House of Assembly. The first such constituent meeting of 6 July 1774 was attended by 104 delegates, many from the backcountry, as compared with 48 in a typical House. Although the meetings of delegates did not adopt the name "Provincial Congress" until January 1775, they acted as an extralegal legislative body from the spring of 1774 on.[85] Other colonies experienced similar alterations in the size and representativeness of provincial congresses as compared with the legislature.[86]

The two remaining functions of government gradually adopted by the extralegal committees and provincial congresses were the legislative and executive. Legislative functions were adopted from the very beginning of the meetings, largely because the bulk of the leadership of the provincial congresses were experienced assemblymen. Although their actions were expressed as "resolves" or suggestions rather than statutes, it was intended that, acting through the network of Association enforcement committees, they would gain the force of law by their ability to gain the obedience of the populace. In particular, the committees and provincial congresses tried to ensure that they would be the *sole* authoritative body concerned with the resistance. This attempt in New York led to a lengthy period of conflict between the city committee on one hand and the mechanics committee on the other. Although the city committee as an institution survived the conflict to remain the only body capable of directing resistance, its membership changed drastically in response to the pressure from those who wanted more adamant action against Britain than the original committee was willing to support.[87]

In some areas, it is evident that opposition to the official committees came not only from the Loyalists who attempted to prevent them from forming or, rarely, organized their own counter-committees, but from those who wanted resistance but felt that it was not being carried far enough. Though such groups existed, they did not leave records and remain only in the reflections they left in the records of official bodies. Thus, there must have been some opposition in the province of Maryland to the course being taken by the committees after the beginning of the Continental Association. The third provincial convention there included among its resolves one which stated that *only* the committees should interpret the Association, implying that some individuals or nonofficial groups must have attempted to do so.[88] While this process may well have ensured that some entrenched interests remained in power, it also ensured that the resistance would ultimately follow one main course of action, under one organization. The significance of this was shown when the committees began to form themselves into de facto governments.

An example of a county committee which took action to preserve its authority against a more conservative local committee occurred in Virginia in early 1775. William Allason, a Virginia merchant who was not a supporter of the Continental Association, was one of the twenty elected to the Falmouth town committee in January 1775. The county committee did not approve of the composition of the town committee and called an early February meeting of some 150 members of several county committees to judge the affair. Allason and several others were tried by this meeting for breaking the Association and the resolves regarding elections passed by the county committee. At the same time, it was necessary to control spectators who wished to do violence to the Falmouth committeemen. Fearful of violence and condemned to be branded as enemies of their country, "agreeable to the method of advertising laid down by the Congress," the Falmouth committee recanted and resigned.[89]

At the beginning of resistance under the Continental Association, it was not necessary that a central executive body should exist in each province, since most problems of administration were handled by the local committees. Consequently, the committees became the first organs of executive power to be found during the Association period. Soon, however, the provincial conventions in some areas perceived that a body was necessary which would continue *between* sessions and deal with administrative problems and questions regarding the proper interpretation of the Continental Association. In many areas, this committee of the provincial congress was called the committee or council of safety.

Pennsylvania adopted a committee of safety in the legislature, which was continuing to meet during late 1774, in order to wrest executive power from the governor. The powers of this body were challenged by the provincial convention, which feared that the assembly would not support the resistance actions which it had taken, particularly to the extent that they tended to replace the authority of old institutions including that of the assembly. The city committee of Philadelphia consequently acted to take the executive power into its own hands. The city committee claimed, among other powers, the right of calling provincial conventions when it felt that consultation with popular representatives was needed. This was a power directly analogous to the colonial governor's right of calling sessions of the assembly. It was this committee which was granted, according to Charles H. Lincoln, executive powers by the provincial convention.[90]

The Massachusetts Provincial Congress voted a committee of safety into existence on 27 October 1774. This committee consisted of eleven members and was active between sessions of the provincial congress. Its duties were not carefully specified, although oversight of the reorganization and training of the colony's militia was among them.[91]

• PARALLEL INSTITUTIONS AND AUTHORITY •

It is not necessary to multiply examples further to show that the bodies which the American towns, counties, and provinces set up to resist the Coercive Acts in 1774 very quickly began to challenge the constitutional officers for authority and to replace both the officers and institutions of the British empire in the thirteen colonies. This represents the significant set of actions which transformed the previous series of resistance campaigns into an attempt to gain independence. As we saw, many of the *kinds* of bodies and activities found in 1774 also existed as far back as the Stamp Act resistance. In that campaign, there was a strong refusal to recognize certain uses of royal authority, the development of committees to organize and supervise resistance, and the attempt to force institutions to accede to the needs and wishes of the colonial populace, not their British masters.

During the Stamp Act resistance, though, and during the campaign against the Townshend Revenue Acts, no permanent alternative institutions arose. It is true that there were far-reaching and important changes in American institutions during this period, as the assemblies and the people whom they represented became less and less willing to give in to the demands of British authority. After the passage of the Coercive Acts and after it became evident in America that even more militant means would be called for this time, the ground was laid for the final rejection of that authority. That both the American colonies and the British ministry acted adamantly in 1774 and 1775 was most appropriate to the importance of the struggle. By late 1774, the ministry had finally concluded that only the firmest counteractions could meet the seriousness of the challenge the colonies posed. American resisters, for their part, realized that the Coercive Acts, though directed only against Massachusetts, represented a more serious threat to alter the political conditions under which they lived than any previously proposed by Townshend or Grenville.

It can easily be seen that the Continental Association's plans of action intended to affect Britain were not great advances over methods previously used. Nonimportation, a part of the colonial arsenal since 1765, did take effect fairly soon after the plan was put into effect. Nonexportation, though, which had been widely discussed throughout the summer of 1774, did not take place until nearly a year later. It also contained an important exception, the rice crop of the Carolinas, which surely would have caused conflict within the Association had nonexportation ever taken place under non-wartime conditions. The innovative and ultimately crucial component of the Continental Association as a resistance plan was the decision to establish a network of enforcement groups in each colony which would be totally beyond British control. These committees and the provincial congresses together established for the first time a set of institutions which the British could not control by constitutional means. The governors could not order them prorogued or disbanded nor could the ministry punish the colonies which adopted them by restricting their constitutional rights or privileges, since the constitutional bodies were no longer the major holders of authority.

It was not long after these bodies first began to organize and to move to challenge the constitutional officers for authority that the fighting at Lexington and Concord took place and the war began. Necessarily, the conduct of warfare altered the conditions under which the colonial governments acted. Major concerns shifted from the enforcement of commercial resistance measures to the recruitment, supply, and use of the Continental Army. With this shift in emphasis came an alteration of the bodies most necessary to carry on the resistance. Now, instead of broadly based deliberative assemblies, the central executive committees became more important since they could act quickly to respond to wartime crises without consulting the wishes of countervailing mass interests. They could also act as a civilian liaison with the military and its structure of command, upon whom the burden of resistance now fell.

Despite the alteration of political conditions brought on by the war and the changes that several years of war brought about in the perception of what had gone before, the achievements of the political bodies which operated during the essentially nonviolent period of resistance from the spring of 1774 through the spring of 1775 were of the greatest importance. As can be seen from the present chapter, as well as chapters Six and Twelve, indicators of change which include all the colonies are difficult to propose, partly because of the internal differences among them. Some such indicators can be proposed, however. In many of the colonies, the influence of the governor over the course of events was at an end. Several of the governors were powerful and influential figures—Wentworth of New Hampshire and Lord Dunmore of Virginia come to mind. Nevertheless, they could not restrain the continuation of the resistance. While several colonies went the route of choosing provincial congresses, the legislatures of some—Rhode Island, Connecticut, and Pennsylvania—themselves pressed forward with the resistance. The councils either disappeared from the scene or were annexed by the revolutionary legislature. The courts were either totally inoperative or under the control of the provincial congresses and local committees. In areas where town government existed, it was either augmented or replaced by the committees mandated by the Continental Association. In many areas where town or local government did not exist, it was created for the first time by the organization of the committees as authoritative bodies. These committees acted not only as overseers of the resistance but as courts, in that they could decide whom the resisters would punish and settle disputes arising under the Association. Among those colonies which proceeded to establish a new constituent assembly, it was often more broadly chosen and with a wider membership than in the constitutional legislature. And finally, many of these legislatures set up committees with executive powers to act while the assembly was out of session.

All of these characteristics added up to a system of de facto independent government which successfully challenged the political authority of Britain in the center of the American continent and replaced it. For the first time in the European settlement of North America, wholly indigenous and independent political bodies, which owed no allegiances outside of their own borders, had arisen. No longer could imperial authority direct the actions or policies of the people of these states, who had now taken it upon themselves to direct their own destinies.

· NOTES ·

1. See George L. Beer, *The Old Colonial System, 1600–1754* (New York: Peter Smith, 1933); Lawrence Henry Gipson, *The British Empire Before the American Revolution* (15 vols., New York: Knopf, 1958–76), vol. 9, *The Triumphant Empire: New Responsibilities Within the Enlarged Empire, 1763–1766,* pp. 5–21.

2. The Privy Council was a committee of notables which performed various administrative tasks, among them the review of colonial legislation. Most of the colonies were required to send their laws to the Privy Council as they were passed. The Council, acting on the advice of attorneys and the Board of Trade, could "disallow" these laws if reason to do so were found—for example, if they restricted British commerce or infringed upon the rights of the Crown (see Charles M. Andrews, "The Royal Disallowance," *Proceedings of the American Antiquarian Society,* new ser., 24 [October 1914], pp. 342–62).

3. M. A. Thompson, *The Secretaries of State, 1681–1782* (Oxford: Clarendon Press, 1932), pp. 54–56; Margaret Marion Spector, *The American Department of the British Government, 1768–1782* (New York: Columbia Univ. Press, 1940), p. 20. Gipson believes the process of organizing this department to have been part of the rationalization of British administration, done to ease the load of work of the secretary of state for the southern department (Gipson, *British Empire,* vol. 11, *The Triumphant Empire: The Rumbling of the Coming Storm,* pp. 226–28).

4. James Munro, ed., *Acts of the Privy Council of England, Colonial Series* (6 vols., London: His Majesty's Stationery Office, 1912), vol. 5, pp. 86–87.

5. Benjamin W. Labaree and Ian R. Christie, *Empire or Independence, 1760–1776: A British-American Dialogue on the Coming of the American Revolution* (New York: Norton, 1976), pp. 184–87.

6. Gipson, *British Empire,* vol. 9, *New Responsibilities Within the Enlarged Empire,* p. 18. See also Andrews, "Royal Disallowance," p. 243, where colonial legislatures are described from the viewpoint of the Privy Council as "inferior law-making bodies," not Parliaments.

7. Jack P. Greene, "Bridge to Revolution: The Wilkes Fund Controversy in South Carolina, 1769–1775," *Journal of Southern History* 29 (February 1963), pp. 19–52; George E. Frakes, *Laboratory for Liberty, The South Carolina Committee System, 1719–1776* (Lexington: Univ. of Kentucky Press, 1970), pp. 112–14; Edward McCrady, *The History of South Carolina Under the Royal Government, 1719–1776* (New York: Macmillan, 1899), pp. 662–63; Leonard W. Labaree, *Royal Instructions to British Governors, 1670–1776* (reprint ed., New York: Octagon Books, 1967),vol. 1, pp. 208–9.

8. Pauline Maier, *From Resistance to Revolution* (New York: Knopf, 1972), pp. 52–53.

9. See *ibid.,* pp. 61–76, for the decision to limit the amount of violence used in the Stamp Act resistance. Roger Champagne, "The Military Association of the Sons of Liberty," *New York Historical Society Quarterly* 41 (July 1957), pp. 338–50, points out that the Sons of Liberty organizations in several colonies pledged military support to any colony—especially New York—punished by the British army for anti-Stamp Act rioting.

10. These types of action in conflict are described in Gene Sharp, *The Politics of Nonviolent Action* (Boston: Porter Sargent, 1973), pp. 65–67.

11. R. S. Longley, "Mob Activities in Revolutionary Massachusetts," *New England Quarterly* 6 (March 1933), p. 123, noted that the Tea Party "Mohawks" touched only the tea and did no harm to persons. Longley claimed that "only a fear of attracting attention from the main business of the mob prevented the usual tarring and feathering," an interpretation not supported by any evidence the author presents. Exactly who would have been thus mistreated, since the ship owners and masters were trying to be cooperative and the consignees were out of reach at the castle, is not clear (see also Benjamin W. Labaree, *The Boston Tea Party* [New York: Oxford Univ. Press, 1964], pp. 144–45).

12. In the United States, the adoption of the doctrine that the Supreme Court could

rule on binding interpretations of the Constitution has led to a wide acceptance of the Court as an institution capable of settling, or going a long way to settle, even basic disputes. The program of litigation carried on by black groups that culminated in the 1954 *Brown v. Board of Education* decision and its result is an example of the strengths and weaknesses of Supreme Court decisions.

13. Andrews, "Royal Disallowance," p. 348, noted that the Privy Council at least once disallowed a statute it had previously upheld.

14. See the attitude toward the South Carolina Commons House of Assembly's practice of raising money for special purposes without the consent of the governor and council (Greene, "Wilkes Fund," pp. 22–23, 25).

15. Michael G. Kammen, *A Rope of Sand: The Colonial Agents, British Politics, and the American Revolution* (Ithaca: Cornell Univ. Press, 1968), pp. 230–33, for example. Another example of the growing rigidity of the British government in its relations to America is the position taken in 1766 and after that the Declaratory Act settled once and for all the question of whether Parliament could tax the colonies. See Lord North's statement, in opposition to hearing the petition of the General Assembly of New York in March 1769, that this right could not be questioned since Parliament had passed "a law declaratory of its right to tax America" (Alan Valentine, *Lord North* [Norman, Okla.: Univ. of Oklahoma Press, 1967], vol. 1, p. 175).

16. Frederick Bernays Wiener, "The Rhode Island Merchants and the Sugar Act," *New England Quarterly* 3 (July 1930), pp. 471–79, 486–96.

17. Thomas Hutchinson, *The History of the Province of Massachusetts-Bay* (London: John Murray, 1828), vol. 3, pp. 114–15.

18. Quoted in Wiener, "Rhode Island Merchants," pp. 473–74.

19. Nathaniel Bouton, ed., *Documents and Records Relating to the Province of New Hampshire from 1764–1776* (Nashua, N.H.: Orren C. Moore, State Printer, 1873), vol. 7, p. 250. On the earlier preparation of the memorial, see *ibid.,* pp. 187–88.

20. Josiah Quincy, *Memoir of the Life of Josiah Quincy, Jr.* (Boston: Cummings, Hilliard, 1825), pp. 51–52.

21. McCrady, *History of South Carolina*, pp. 609–10, 613, 614; Hutchinson, *History of Massachusetts-Bay,* vol. 3, p. 197; Greene, "Wilkes Fund," pp. 27–28.

22. Arthur Schlesinger, "Liberty Tree: A Genealogy," *New England Quarterly* 25 (December 1952), pp. 435–54. Schlesinger claimed that the device of a pole surmounted by a Phrygian cap is a later "Gallic innovation" (p. 454). This is mistaken, as the device appears in various political cartoons of the period and on Paul Revere's "Liberty Bowl," 1768.

23. *Boston Evening-Post,* 22 January 1770 (italics in original). The meetings described took place on 17 and 18 January. Thomas Hutchinson later demanded of the crowd, which was "visiting" his merchant sons, that it disperse. He admitted that the crowd was not acting "in a Tumultuos manner" (*ibid.,* 29 January 1770).

24. John Dickinson, *Letters of a Farmer in Pennsylvania to the Inhabitants of the British Colonies* [1767–1768] (reprinted ed., St. Clair Shores, Mich.: Scholarly Press, 1969), p. 35.

25. Arthur M. Schlesinger, *The Colonial Merchants and the American Revolution, 1763–1775,* Columbia Univ. Studies in History, Economics, and Public Law (New York: Columbia Univ. Press, 1918), p. 491.

26. Maier, *From Resistance to Revolution,* pp. 282–83.

27. "In 1769, the President and first graduating class of Brown University appeared at Commencement exercises in garments made of wool grown in Rhode Island. The Harvard

graduates followed their example the next year" (Milton T. Rollas, *Household Manufactures in the United States, 1640–1860* [Chicago: Univ. of Chicago Press, 1917], pp. 53–54; *Boston Evening-Post*, 6 June, 13 June 1774; Anne Rowe Cunningham, ed., *Letters and Diary of John Rowe: Boston Merchant, 1759–1762, 1764–1779* [Boston: W. B. Clark, 1903], p. 280).

28. Hutchinson, *History of Massachusetts-Bay*, vol. 3, pp. 393–94; *Report of the Record Commissioners of the City of Boston, Containing the Boston Town Records, 1770 through 1777*, 18th Report (Boston: Rockwell and Churchill, City Printers, 1887), p. 139.

29. Anne Hulton, *Letters of a Loyalist Lady: Being the Letters of Anne Hulton, Sister of Henry Hulton, Commissioner of Customs at Boston, 1767–1776* (Cambridge, Mass.: Harvard Univ. Press, 1927), p. 18.

30. Andrew Eliot to Thomas Hollis, 17 October 1768, *Collections of the Massachusetts Historical Society*, 4th ser., vol. 4 (1858), p. 432.

31. John Shy, *Toward Lexington: The Role of the British Army in the Coming of the American Revolution* (Princeton, N.J.: Princeton Univ. Press, 1965), p. 413.

32. See Chapter Two of this volume and Schlesinger, *Colonial Merchants*, pp. 64, 76, 427.

33. Schlesinger believed that this reduced the effectiveness of the Association in the attempt to force British merchants to support repeal of the Coercive Acts (*ibid.*, p. 539). Merchants were very concerned with maintaining their credit in Britain, which could only be done if they continued to pay at least part of their debts.

34. Joseph A. Ernst, *Money and Politics in America: A Study in the Currency Act of 1764 and the Political Economy of Revolution* (Chapel Hill: Univ. of North Carolina Press, 1973), p. 229.

35. See Chapter Two of this volume.

36. John Archer Silver, *The Provisional Government of Maryland (1774–1777)*, Johns Hopkins Univ. Studies in Historical and Political Science, 13th ser., vol. 10 (Baltimore: Johns Hopkins Press, 1895), p. 12.

37. The juries of some court sessions in Massachusetts refused to be sworn if Peter Oliver, who was being impeached by the House of Representatives for taking the salary grant, was on the bench (Stephen E. Patterson, *Political Parties in Revolutionary Massachusetts* [Madison: Univ. of Wisconsin Press, 1973], pp. 98–100). The American Political Society of Worcester, a Whig political club, agreed amongst themselves to pay any fine laid upon the town's members of the Worcester County grand jury of April 1774 for refusing to be empanelled in Oliver's presence. Oliver did not attend court (William Lincoln, *History of Worcester, Massachusetts* [Worcester, Mass.: Charles Henry, 1862], pp. 774–75).

38. The Virginia Burgesses convened extralegally after dissolution by the governor and adopted the Virginia Association in 1769 (Jack P. Greene, *The Quest for Power: The Lower Houses of Assembly in the Southern Royal Colonies, 1689–1776* [Chapel Hill: Univ. of North Carolina Press, 1963], p. 376; Ernst, *Money and Politics*, p. 229).

39. The South Carolina Commons House tricked Lieutenant-Governor Bull by meeting very early in the morning to vote support for the delegates to the First Continental Congress (Frakes, *Laboratory for Liberty*, p. 123; McCrady, *History of South Carolina*, pp. 745–46). The Massachusetts House locked the door to its chamber when choosing delegates to the Continental Congress. The secretary of the colony was forced to shout the governor's message of dissolution from outside (Patterson, *Political Parties*, p. 86; Gerald H. Clarfield, "The Short Unhappy Civil Administration of Thomas Gage," *Essex Institute Historical Collection* 109 [April 1973], p. 144).

40. Descriptions of this event are found in Patterson, *Political Parties,* p. 107; Clarfield, "Thomas Gage," p. 145–50; and James Duncan Phillips, *Salem in the Eighteenth Century* (Boston: Houghton Mifflin, 1937), pp. 330–31.

41. Hutchinson, *History of Massachusetts-Bay,* vol. 3, pp. 141–44.

42. McCrady, *History of South Carolina,* pp. 573–75. Lieutenant-Governor William Bull was strongly criticized by the Commons House for not suspending Clerk of Court Campbell. Bull defended his actions to the Privy Council which approved of them. At that time, the Privy Council suspended Campbell's fine, although no formal appeal of it had been made (Munro, ed., *Acts of the Privy Council: Colonial Series,* vol. 4, pp. 770–71).

43. Arthur L. Jensen, *The Maritime Commerce of Colonial Philadelphia* (Madison: State Historical Society of Wisconsin, 1963), pp. 159–60; Neil R. Stout, "Captain Kennedy and the Stamp Act," *New York History* 46 (January 1964), p. 52; Thomas C. Barrow, *Trade and Empire: The British Customs Service in Colonial America 1660–1775* (Cambridge, Mass.: Harvard Univ. Press, 1967), pp. 199–200; Charles Steuart to Commissioners of Customs, Philadelphia, 7 December 1765, *Maryland Historical Magazine* 4 (June 1909), p. 137.

44. David S. Lovejoy, "Rights Imply Equality: The Case Against Admiralty Jurisdiction, 1764–1776," *William and Mary Quarterly,* 3d ser., vol. 16 (October 1959), p. 472.

45. Richard D. Brown, *Revolutionary Politics in Massachusetts: The Boston Committee of Correspondence and the Towns, 1772–1774* (Cambridge, Mass.: Harvard Univ. Press, 1970), p. 48ff.

46. Hutchinson, *History of Massachusetts-Bay,* vol. 3, p. 217.

47. Patterson, *Political Parties,* p. 99; George Henry Merriam, *Israel Williams, Monarch of Hampshire, 1709–1788* (Ph.D. diss. Clark Univ., 1961), p. 114.

48. When Plymouth, Massachusetts, formed its town committee of correspondence in 1772, it was charged with determining what threats to liberty existed and with recommending to the town meeting what measures ought to be taken to obtain redress (James Thacher, *History of the Town of Plymouth,* Peter Gomes, ed., [reprint ed., Yarmouthport, Mass.: Parnassus Imprints, 1972], p. 196).

49. The South Carolina committee system, as it developed in the legislature, has been studied in depth in Frakes, *Laboratory for Liberty,* see pp. 113–18.

50. Robert Zemsky, *Merchants, Farmers, and River Gods* (Boston: Gambit, Inc., 1971), pp. 28–38, 216–29; Carl L. Becker, *The History of Political Parties in the Province of New York, 1760–1776* (reprint ed., Madison: Univ. of Wisconsin Press, 1968), pp. 8–10, 11–14; Elisha P. Douglass, *Rebels and Democrats* (Chicago: Quadrangle Books, 1965), pp. 33–36, 46–47, 216–17, 242–43. For a general summation of the (often contradictory) course of social change in America during the eighteenth century and its impact upon elites see Kenneth A. Lockridge, "Social Change and the Meaning of the American Revolution," *Journal of Social History* 6 (Summer 1973), pp. 403–39.

51. Merriam, *Israel Williams,* pp. 92–94.

52. David Curtis Skaggs, "Maryland's Impulse Toward Social Revolution: 1750–1776," *Journal of American History* 54 (December 1967), pp. 777, 779. Skaggs quotes Loyalist Jonathan Boucher's characterization of the backcountry people.

53. John J. Zimmerman, "Charles Thomson, 'The Sam Adams of Philadelphia,'" *Mississippi Valley Historical Review* 55 (December 1958), pp. 471, 474–77, 479–80.

54. Maier, *From Resistance to Revolution,* p. 118.

55. Richard Alan Ryerson, "Political Mobilization and the American Revolution: The Resistance Movement in Philadelphia, 1765 to 1775," *William and Mary Quarterly,* 3d

ser., vol. 31 (October 1974), pp. 568–71, 585–87.

56. Kurt H. Wolff, ed., *The Sociology of Georg Simmel* (New York: Free Press, 1950), pp. 182–83, 185–86; Sharp, *Nonviolent Action,* pp. 12–16, 49 nn. 8, 9, p. 53 n. 47.

57. See Chapter Four of this volume; Jensen, *Maritime Commerce,* pp. 187–95; Schlesinger, *Colonial Merchants,* pp. 219–20, 225–27. Popular action restrained abandonment of nonimportation but did not prevent it.

58. Bernard Bailyn, *The Ideological Origins of the American Revolution* (Cambridge, Mass.: Harvard Univ. Press, 1967); Maier, *From Resistance to Revolution,* Introduction, Chapters One and Two.

59. Theodore B. Lewis, "A Revolutionary Tradition, 1689–1774: 'There was a Revolution Here as Well as in England,'" *New England Quarterly* 46 (September 1973), pp. 424–38.

60. Hutchinson, *History of Massachusetts-Bay, vol. 3, p. 103.*

61. Murray was considered a supporter of the people who had beaten James Otis (see Introduction to Chapter Four of this volume). Nina Moore Tiffany, ed., *The Letters of James Murray, Loyalist* (reprint ed., Boston: Gregg Press, 1972; original ed., Boston: the Author, 1901), pp. 159–60.

62. Governor Frances Bernard to the Earl of Hillsborough, 16 September 1768, copy endorsed by John Speed, Palfrey Papers, Houghton Library, Harvard Univ., Cambridge, Mass. The Reverend Samuel Cooper of Boston wrote to ex-Governor Thomas Pownall, then in England, informing him that the Convention of 1768 was never intended to undertake military defense of the town or to overthrow the government, but was intended "to calm the People, to prevent Tumults, to recognize the Authority of Government by humble Remonstrances and Petitions, and to lead the People to seek redress only in a Constitutional Way" ("Letters of Samuel Cooper to Thomas Pownall, 1769–1777," *American Historical Review* 8 [January 1908], p. 302).

63. Charles Francis Adams, ed., *The Works of John Adams* (10 vols., Boston: Little, Brown, 1850–1856), vol. 4, pp. 74–77, 81–82.

64. Ryerson, "Political Mobilization," pp. 565–88.

65. Sharp, *Nonviolent Action,* pp. 733–38.

66. Barrow, *Trade and Empire,* p. 243.

67. Peter Force, ed., *American Archives,* 4th ser., (Washington, D.C.: M. St. Clair Clarke and Peter Force, 1837), vol. 1, pp. 230–31. The letter is headed "A Gentlemen in London to a Friend in Annapolis, MD." The original source is not given.

68. Bouton, ed., *Documents of New Hampshire,* vol. 7, pp. 333–34. Of course, the term "union" did not specifically mean the holding of a congress.

69. Sharp, *Nonviolent Action,* pp. 416, 422–23, 633, 744–45.

70. Edgar J. Fisher, *New Jersey as a Royal Province, 1739–1776,* Columbia Univ. Studies in History, Economics, and Public Law, vol. 41, no. 7 (New York: Columbia Univ. Press, 1911), pp. 447–48.

71. *New Hampshire Gazette,* 29 July 1774; Bouton, ed., *Documents of New Hampshire,* vol. 7, pp. 369, 399–401.

72. Frakes, *Laboratory for Liberty,* pp. 120–23.

73. William Lincoln, ed., *Journals of Each Provincial Congress of Massachusetts in 1774 and 1775 and of the Committee of Safety* (Boston: Dutton and Wentworth, 1838), pp. 3–6 (hereafter cited as *Mass. Cong. Journals*).

74. Ryerson, "Political Mobilization," p. 566, sees these four aspects as "four phases of the process of mobilization."

75. Sharp, *Nonviolent Action,* p. 423.

76. Gipson, *British Empire,* vol. 12, *The Triumphant Empire: Britain Sails into the Storm, 1770–1776,* p. 313.

77. Jensen, *Maritime Commerce,* pp. 187–95; Bernard Mason, *The Road to Independence: The Revolutionary Movement in New York 1773–1776* (Lexington: Univ. of Kentucky Press, 1966), pp. 26–30, 37–38.

78. *Ibid.,* pp. 42, 44–45.

79. H. H. Gerth and C. Wright Mills, eds., *From Max Weber: Essays in Sociology* (New York: Oxford Univ. Press, 1946), pp. 77–78.

80. Maier, *From Resistance to Revolution,* pp. 281–83; Schlesinger, *Colonial Merchants,* pp. 487–88.

81. Frakes, *Laboratory for Liberty,* pp. 122–123; *New Hampshire Gazette,* 29 July 1774.

82. Lincoln, ed., *Mass. Cong. Journals,* pp. 38–39.

83. Suffolk County, Mass. Committee of Correspondence to Medway Selectmen, 28 February 1775 (Ms. Collection, Boston Public Library); Samuel Eliot Morison, "The Property of Harrison Gray, Loyalist," *Publications of the Colonial Society of Massachusetts, Transactions, 1911–1913,* vol. 14, p. 327 n.; Harrison Gray to J[ohn] Erving, n.d., [attributed, "circa Mar. 1775"] (Ms. Collection, Boston Public Library). Many town meetings took action during the crisis period to keep their taxes out of the provincial government's hands and later to transfer them to Gardner as receiver general. Dudley voted on 28 November 1774 that the constables ought to "keep the province money in their hands until further orders" and on 2 January 1775 to pay that money to Henry Gardner (*Town Records of Dudley, Massachusetts* [Pawtucket, R.I.: 1894], vol. 2, pp. 155–58). Concord and Framingham, on the other hand, complied quickly with the request of the provincial congress, on 28 November and 8 November 1774, respectively (Lemuel Shattuck, *A History of the Town of Concord* [Boston: Russell, Odiorne, 1835], p. 92; J. H. Temple, *History of Framingham, Massachusetts* [Framingham, Mass.: The Town, 1887], pp. 267–68). Canton, which had refused to consider a town meeting article to pay the town's share of the expenses of the delegates to the Continental Congress, on 11 July 1774, voted on 16 February 1775 to pay the town's tax money to Henry Gardner (Daniel V. Huntoon, *History of the Town of Canton, Norfolk County, Massachusetts* [Cambridge: John Wilson and Son, 1893], pp. 335, 345–46). The Northampton town meeting refused to take any action at all when the resolves of the provincial congress reached them (James R. Turnbull, *History of Northampton, Massachusetts* [Northampton, Mass.: Gazette Printing Co., 1902], p. 353).

84. Force, ed., *American Archives,* vol. 1, pp. 973–74; Patterson, *Political Parties,* pp. 111–12. In the 10 November proclamation, Gage accused the provincial congress of intending "to assume to themselves the powers and authority of government" and commanded the sheriffs and constables to obey "the well known established laws of the land."

85. Frakes, *Laboratory for Liberty,* p. 122; McCrady, *History of South Carolina,* pp. 757–60; William E. Hemphill, ed., *Extracts from the Journals of the Provincial Congresses of South Carolina, 1775–1776* (Columbia, S.C.: South Carolina Archives Dept., 1960),p. xvi.

86. Patterson, *Political Parties,* p. 110. A meeting of the Massachusetts House of Representatives could expect to seat about 150 members, the first congress contained 293. The size of the Maryland conventions varied and were often nearly 100 members in size (*Proceedings of the Conventions of the Province of Maryland* [Baltimore: Lucas and Deaver, 1836]. pp. 3, 6, 7, 11, 19).

87. Mason, *Road to Independence,* pp. 27–30, 38–40.

88. *Proceedings of . . . Province of Maryland,* p. 7.

89. D. R. Anderson, ed., "The Letters of William Allason, Merchant of Falmouth, Virginia," *Richmond College Historical Paper* 3 (June 1917), Allason to Thomas B. Martin, 6 February 1775, pp. 162–64.

90. Charles H. Lincoln, "The Revolutionary Movement in Pennsylvania 1760–1776," *Publications of the University of Pennsylvania,* Series in History, vol. 1 (Philadelphia: Univ. of Pennsylvania, 1901), pp. 185–88.

91. Lincoln, ed., *Mass. Cong. Journals,* p. 35.

PART 3
Appendixes

·A·

Examination of Benjamin Franklin on the Stamp Act, 12–13 February 1766

On 12–13 February 1766, Benjamin Franklin appeared before the House of Commons to answer questions regarding the policy of taxation in the colonies. His clear and moderately worded answers gained him a measure of respect from England, while reprints of the transcript of his interrogation became an important contribution to the constitutional controversy at the time. The transcript as printed here is taken from *The Life and Writings of Benjamin Franklin,* edited by Albert Henry Smyth ([10 vols., New York: Macmillan, 1905–1907], vol. 4, pp. 412–48).

Q. What is your name, and place of abode?

A. Franklin, of Philadelphia.

Q. Do the Americans pay any considerable taxes among themselves?

A. Certainly many, and very heavy taxes.

Q. What are the present taxes of Pennsylvania, laid by the laws of the colony?

A. There are taxes on all estates real and person, a poll tax, a tax on all offices, professions, trades and businesses according to their profits; an excise on all wine, rum, and other spirits; and a duty of Ten Pounds per head on all Negroes imported, with some other duties.

Q. For what purpose are those taxes laid?

A. For the support of the civil and military establishments of the country, and to discharge the heavy debt contracted in the last war.

Q. How long are those taxes to continue?

A. Those for discharging the debt are to continue till 1772, and longer, if the debt should not be then all discharged. The others must always continue.

Q. Was it not expected that the debt would have been sooner discharged?

A. It was, when the peace was made with France and Spain—But, a fresh war breaking out with the Indians, a fresh load of debt was incurred; and the taxes, of course, continued longer by a new law.

Q. Are not all the people very able to pay those taxes?

A. No. The frontier counties, all along the continent, having been frequently ravaged by the enemy and greatly impoverished, are able to pay very little tax. And therefore, in consideration of their distress, our late tax laws do expressly favour those counties, excusing the sufferers; and I do suppose the same is done in other governments. . . .

Q. What may be the amount of one year's imports into Pennsylvania from Britain?

A. I have been informed that our merchants compute the imports from Britain to be above 500,000 Pounds.

Q. What may be the amount of the produce of your province exported to Britain?

A. It must be small, as we produce little that is wanted in Britain. I suppose it cannot exceed 40,000 Pounds.

Q. How then do you pay the balance?

A. The balance is paid by our produce carried to the West-Indies, and sold in our own islands, or to the French, Spaniards, Danes, and Dutch; by the same carried to other colonies in North-America, as to New England, Nova-Scotia, Newfoundland, Carolina, and Georgia; by the same, carried to different parts of Europe, as Spain, Portugal, and Italy. In all which places we receive either money, bills of Exchange, or commodities that suit for remittance to Britain; which, together with all the profits on the industry of our merchants and mariners, arising in those circuitous voyages, and the freights made by their ships, center finally in Britain to discharge the balance, and pay for British manufactures continually used in the province, or sold to foreigners by our traders. . . .

Q. Do you think it is right that America should be protected by this country and pay no part of the expence?

A. That is not the case. The Colonies raised, cloathed and payed, during the last war, near 25,000 men, and spent many millions.

Q. Were you not reimbursed by parliament?

A. We were only reimbursed what, in our opinion, we had advanced beyond our proportion, or beyond what might reasonably be expected from us; and it was a very small part of what we spent. Pennsylvania, in particular, disbursed about 500,000 Pounds, and the reimbursements, in the whole, did not exceed 60,000 Pounds. . . .

Q. Do you think the people of America would submit to pay the stamp duty, if it was moderate?

A. No, never, unless compelled by force of arms. . . .

Q. What was the temper of America towards Great Britain before the year 1763?

A. The best in the world. They submitted willingly to the government of the Crown, and paid, in all their courts, obedience to acts of parliament. Numerous as the people are in the several provinces, they cost you nothing in forts, citadels, garrisons, or armies, to keep them in subjection. They were governed by this country at the expence only of a little pen, ink and paper. They were led by a thread. They had not only a respect, but an affection for Great-Britain; for its laws, its customs and manners, and even a fondness for its fashions, that greatly increased the commerce. Natives of Britain were always treated with particular regard; to be an Old-England man was, of itself, a character of some respect, and gave a kind of rank among us.

Q. What is their temper now?

A. O, very much altered.

Q. Did you ever hear the authority of parliament to make laws for America questioned till lately?

A. The authority of parliament was allowed to be valid in all laws, except such as should lay internal taxes. It was never disputed in laying duties to regulate commerce. . . .

Q. In what light did the people of America use to consider the parliament of Great-Britain?

A. They considered the parliament as the great bulwark and security of their liberties and privileges, and always spoke of it with the utmost respect and veneration. Arbitrary ministers, they thought, might possibly, at times, attempt to oppress them; but they relied on it, that the parliament, on application, would always give redress. They remembered, with gratitude, a strong insistence of this, when a bill was brought into parliament, with a clause, to make royal instructions laws in the colonies, which the House of Commons would not pass, and it was thrown out.

Q. And have they not still the same respect for parliament?

A. No, it is greatly lessened.

Q. To what cause is that owing?

A. To a concurrence of causes; the restraints lately laid on their trade, by which the bringing of foreign gold and silver into the Colonies was prevented; the prohibition of making paper money among ourselves; and demanding a new and heavy tax by stamps; taking away, at the same time, trials by juries, and refusing to receive and hear their humble petitions. . . .

Q. Have you not heard of the resolutions of this House, and of the House of Lords, asserting the right of parliament relating to America, including a power to tax the people there?

A. Yes, I have heard of such resolutions.

Q. What will be the opinion of the Americans on those resolutions?

A. They will think them unconstitutional and unjust.

Q. Was it opinion in America before 1763, that the parliament had no right to lay taxes and duties there?

A. I never heard any objection to the right of laying duties to regulate commerce; but a right to lay internal taxes was never supposed to be in parliament, as we are not represented there.

Q. On what do you found your opinion, that the people in America made any distinctions?

A. I know that whenever the subject has occurred in conversation where I have been present, it has appeared to be the opinion of every one, that we could not be taxed by parliament where we were not represented. But the payment of duties laid by an act of parliament, as regulations of commerce, was never disputed. . . .

Q. But in case a governor, acting by instruction, should call on an assembly to raise the necessary supplies, and the assembly should refuse to do it, do you not think it would then be for the good of the people of the colony, as well as necessary to the government, that the parliament should tax them?

A. I do not think it would be necessary. If an assembly could possibly be so absurd, as to refuse raising the supplies requisite for the maintenance of government among them, they could not long remain in such a situation; the disorders and confusion occasioned by it must soon bring them to reason.

Q. If it should not, ought not the right to be in Great Britain of applying the remedy?

A. A right, only to be used in such a case, I should have no objection to; supposing it to be used merely for the good of the people of the Colony.

Q. But who is judge of that, Britain or the Colony?

A. Those that feel can best judge.

Q. You say that the Colonies have always submitted to external taxes, and objected to the right of parliament only in laying internal taxes; now can you shew, that there is any kind of difference between the two taxes to the Colony on which they may be laid?

A. I think the difference is very great. An external tax is a duty laid on commodities imported; that duty is added to the first cost and other charges on the commodity, and, when it is offered for sale, makes a part of the price. If the people do not like it at that price, they refuse it; they are not obliged to pay it. But an internal tax is forced from the people without their consent, if not laid by their own representatives. The stamp act says, we shall have no commerce, make no exchange of property with each other, neither purchase, nor grant, nor recover debts; we shall neither marry nor make wills, unless we pay such and such sums; thus it is intended to extort our money from us, or ruin us by the consequences of refusing to pay it. . . .

Q. Can any thing less than military force carry the stamp act into execution?

A. I do not see how military force can be applied to that purpose.

Q. Why may it not?

A. Suppose a military force sent into America, they will find nobody in arms; what are they then to do? They cannot force a man to take stamps who chuses to do without them. They will not find a rebellion; they may indeed make one.

Q. If the act is not repealed, what do you think will be the consequences?

A. A total loss of respect and affection the people of America bear to this country, and of all the commerce that depends on that respect and affection.

Q. How can the commerce be affected?

A. You will find, that if the act is not repealed, they will take very little of your manufactures in a short time.

Q. Is it in their power to do without them?

A. The goods they take from Britain are either necessaries, mere conveniences, or superfluities. The first, as cloth, &c. with a little industry they can make at home; the second they can do without, till they are able to provide them among themselves; and the last, which are much the greatest part, they will strike off immediately. They are mere articles of fashion, purchased and consumed because the fashion in a respected country; but will now be detested and rejected. The people have already struck off, by general agreement, the use of all goods fashionable in mournings, and many thousand pounds worth are sent back as unsaleable.

Q. Is it in their interest to make cloth at home?

A. I think they may at present get a cheaper from Britain, I mean of the same firmness and workmanship; but, when one considers other circumstances, the restraints on their trade, and the difficulty of making remittances, it is their interest to make every thing.

Q. Suppose an act of internal regulations connected with a tax; how would they receive it?

A. I think it would be objected to.

Q. Then no regulation with a tax would be submitted to?

A. Their opinion is, that, when aids to the Crown are wanted, they are to be asked of the several assemblies, according to the old established usage; who will, as they always have done, grant them freely. And that their money ought not to be given away, without their consent, by persons at a distance, unacquainted with their circumstances and abilities. The granting aids to the Crown is the only means they have of recommending themselves to their sovereign; and they think it extremely hard and unjust, that a body of men, in which they have no representatives, should make a merit to itself of giving and granting what is not its own, but theirs; and deprive them of a right they esteem of the utmost value and importance, as it is the security of all their other rights. . . .

Q. But suppose Great-Britain should be engaged in a war in Europe, would North-America contribute to the support of it?

A. I do think they would as far as their circumstances would permit. They consider themselves as a part of the British empire, and as having one common interest with it; they may be looked on here as foreigners, but they do not consider themselves as such. They are zealous for the honour and prosperity of this nation; and, while they are well used, will always be ready to support it, as far as their little power goes. . . .

Q. Do you think the assemblies have a right to levy money on the subject there, to grant to the Crown?

A. I certainly think so; they have always done it.

Q. Are they acquainted with the declaration of rights? And do they know, that, by that statute, money is not to be raised on the subject but by consent of parliament?

A. They are very well acquainted with it.

Q. How then can they think they have a right to levy money for the Crown, or for any other than local purposes?

A. They understand that clause to relate to subjects only within the realm; that no money can be levied on them for the Crown, but by consent of parliament. The Colonies are not supposed to be within the realm; they have assemblies of their own, which are their parliaments, and they are, in that respect, in the same situation with Ireland. When money is to be raised for the Crown upon the subjects in Ireland, or in the Colonies, the consent is given in the Parliament of Ireland, or in the assemblies of the Colonies. They think the parliament of Great-Britain cannot properly give the consent, till it has representatives from America; for the petition of rights expressly says, it is to be by common consent in parliament, to make a part of that common consent. . . .

Q. If the stamp act should be repealed, would it induce the assemblies of America to acknowledge the rights of parliament to tax them, and would they erase their resolutions?

A. No, never.

Q. Are there no means of obliging them to erase those resolutions?

A. None that I know of; they will never do it, unless compelled by force of arms.

Q. Is there a power on earth that can force them to erase them?

A. No power, how great soever, can force men to change their opinions. . . .

Q. What used to be the pride of the Americans?

A. To indulge in the fashions and manufactures of Great-Britain.

Q. What is now their pride?

A. To wear their old cloaths over again, till they can make new ones.

·B·

Letter Three of John Dickinson's
Letters from a Farmer in Pennsylvania

This letter, the third of John Dickinson's famous series, was first published in the *Pennsylvania Chronicle* on 19 December 1767. The letters were soon reprinted in nearly every newspaper in the colonies and, after the series was complete, in pamphlet form both in America and in Great Britain. In the essay printed here, Dickinson carefully distinguishes among the various means of opposition to unjust acts of a government which the citizens may justifiably take. Although couched in the terms under which political discourse was carried on at the time and therefore somewhat foreign to twentieth century ears, Dickinson's argument carefully explores the dual problems of how a community may act effectively to advance its own rights and interests and how it may at the same time preserve values and political relationships of great importance. In speaking of "the cause of liberty," Dickinson is very concerned to provide his readers with means of opposition which are consistent with the ends the resistance hopes to achieve. At the same time, Dickinson realizes that ineffective actions must be superseded by effective action, and he recommends to his readers that loyal petitions which are ignored by the government must be followed by more forceful actions. Specifically, Dickinson recommends noncooperation, withholding from the opponent the support which the American colonies normally afford. "This," Dickinson argued, "consists in the prevention of the oppressors reaping advantage from their oppressions, and not in their punishment."

John Dickinson continued to be a leader of the campaigns of resistance to Britain, both in his native colony of Pennsylvania and in national affairs beginning with the organization of the First Continental Congress in 1774. A conservative, Dickinson opposed measures which led to irreparable breaches in the imperial political system. At the same time, he believed that the American colonies must be firm in their measures, once having decided to act, and he supported nonimportation in 1770 even after the Philadelphia merchants wished to terminate their agreements. Dickinson was also a central figure in the debate over independence in

1776, opposing a too hasty declaration, but staunchly supporting independence once it came.

This letter is printed in John Dickinson, *Letters from a Farmer in Pennsylvania to the Inhabitants of the British Colonies* (New York: Outlook, 1903).

Beloved Countrymen,

I rejoice to find, that my two former letters to you, have been generally received with so much favour by such of you whose sentiments I have had an opportunity of knowing. Could you look into my heart, you would instantly perceive an ardent affection for your persons, a zealous attachment to your interests, a lively resentment of every insult and injury offered to your honour or happiness, and an inflexible resolution to assert your rights, to the utmost of my weak power, to be the only motives that have engaged me to address you.

I am no further concerned in any thing affecting America, than any one of you, and when liberty leaves it I can quit it much more conveniently than most of you: but while divine providence, that gave me existence in a land of freedom, permits my head to think, my lips to speak, and my hand to move, I shall so highly and gratefully value the blessing received, as to take care that my silence and inactivity shall not give my implied assent to any act degrading my brethren and myself from the birthright wherewith heaven itself "*hath made us free.*"

Sorry I am to learn, that there are some few persons, shake their heads with solemn motion, and pretend to wonder what can be the meaning of these letters. "Great-Britain, they say, is too powerful to contend with; she is determined to oppress us; it is in vain to speak of right on one side, when there is power on the other; when we are strong enough to resist, we shall attempt it; but now we are not strong enough, and therefore we had better be quiet; it signifies nothing to convince us that our rights are invaded, when we cannot defend them, and if we should get into riots and tumults about the late act, it will only draw down heavier displeasure upon us."

What can such men design? What do their grave observations amount to, but this —"that these colonies, totally regardless of their liberties, should commit them, with humble resignation, to *chance, time* and the tender mercies of *ministers.*"

Are these men ignorant, that usurpations, which might have been successfully opposed at first, acquire strength by continuance, and thus become irresistible? Do they condemn the conduct of these colonies, concerning the *Stamp-act*? Or have they forgot its successful issue? Ought the colonies at that time, instead of acting as they did, to have trusted for relief, to the fortuitous events of futurity? If it is needless "to speak of rights" now, it was as needless then. If the behaviour of the colonies was prudent and glorious then, and successful too; it will be equally prudent and glorious to act in the same manner now, if our rights are equally invaded, and may be as successful. Therefore it becomes necessary to enquire, whether "our rights *are* invaded." To talk of "defending" them, as if they could be no otherwise "defended" than by arms, is as much out of the way, as if a man having a choice of several roads to reach his journey's end, should prefer the worst, for no other reason, than because it is the worst.

As to "riots and tumults," the gentlemen who are so apprehensive of them, are much mistaken, if they think, that grievances cannot be redressed without such assistance.

I will now tell the gentlemen, what is "the meaning of these letters." The meaning of them is, to convince the people of these colonies, that they are at this moment exposed to the most imminent dangers; and to persuade them immediately, vigourously, and unanimously, to exert themselves, in the most firm, but most peaceable manner for obtaining relief.

The cause of liberty is a cause of too much dignity, to be sullied by turbulence and tumult. It ought to be maintained in a manner suitable to her nature. Those who engage in it, should breathe a sedate, yet fervent spirit, animating them to actions of prudence, justice, modesty, bravery, humanity, and magnanimity.

To such a wonderful degree were the antient *Spartans,* as brave and as free a people as ever existed, inspired by this happy temperature of soul, that rejecting even in their battles the use of trumpets, and other instruments for exciting heat and rage, they marched up to scenes of havock and horror, with the sound of flutes, to the tunes of which their steps kept pace—"exhibiting, as *Plutarch* says, at once a terrible and delightful sign, and proceeding with a deliberate valour, full of hope and good assurance, as if some divinity had insensibly assisted them."

I hope, my dear countrymen, that you will in every colony be upon your guard against those who may at any time endeavour to stir you up, under pretences of patriotism, to any measures disrespectful to our sovereign and our mother country. Hot, rash, disorderly proceedings, injure the reputation of a people as to wisdom, valour and virtue, without procuring them the least benefit. I pray God, that he may be pleased to inspire you and your posterity to the latest ages with that spirit, of which I have an idea, but find a difficulty to express: to express in the best manner I can, I mean a spirit that shall so guide you, that it will be impossible to determine, whether an *American*'s character is most distinguishable for his loyalty to his sovereign, his duty to his mother country, his love of freedom, or his affection for his native soil.

Every government, at some time or other, falls into wrong measures; these may proceed from mistake or passion.— —But every such measure does not dissolve the obligation between the governors and the governed; the mistake may be corrected; the passion may pass over.

It is the duty of the governed, to endeavour to rectify the mistake, and appease the passion. They have not at first any other right, than to represent their grievances, and to pray for redress, unless an emergency is so pressing, as not to allow time for receiving an answer to their applications which rarely happens. If their applications are disregarded, then that kind of opposition becomes justifiable, which can be made without breaking the laws, or disturbing the public peace. This consists in the prevention of the oppressors reaping advantage from their oppressions, and not in their punishment. For experience may teach them what reason did not; and harsh methods, cannot be proper, till milder ones have failed.

If at length it becomes undoubted, that an inveterate resolution is formed to annihilate the liberties of the governed, the English history affords frequent examples of resistance by force. What particular circumstances will in any future case justify such resistance, can never be ascertained till they happen. Perhaps it may be allowable to say, generally, that it never can be justifiable, until the people are FULLY CONVINCED, that any further submission will be destructive to their happiness.

When the appeal is made to the sword, highly probable it is, that the punishment will exceed the offence; and the calamities attending on war outweigh those preceding it. These considerations of justice and prudence, will always have great influence with good and wise men.

To these reflections on this subject, it remains to be added, and ought for ever to be remembred; that resistance in the case of colonies against their mother country, is extremely different from the resistance of a people against their prince. A nation may change their King or race of Kings, and retain their antient form of government, be gainers by changing. Thus Great-Britain, under the illustrious house of Brunswick, a house that seems to flourish for the happiness of mankind, has found a felicity, unknown in the reigns of the Stuarts. But if once we are separated from our mother country, what new form of government shall we accept, or when shall we find another Britain to supply our loss? Torn from the body to which we are united by religion, liberty, laws, affections, relations, language, and commerce, we must bleed at every vein.

In truth, the prosperity of these provinces is founded in their dependance on Great-Britain; and when she returns to "her old good humour, and old good nature," as Lord Clerendon expresses it, I hope they will always esteem it their duty and interest, as it most certainly will be, to promote her welfare by all the means in their power.

We cannot act with too much caution in our disputes. Anger produces anger; and differences that might be accommodated by kind and respectful behaviour, may by imprudence be changed to an incurable rage.

In quarrels between countries, as well as in those between individuals, when they have risen to a certain heighth, the first cause of dissention is no longer remembred, the minds of the parties being wholly engaged in recollecting and resenting the mutual expressions of their dislike. When feuds have reached that fatal point, all considerations of reason and equity vanish; and a blind fury governs, or rather confounds all things. A people no longer regards their interest, but the gratification of their wrath. The sway of the Cleon's, and Clodius's [Cleon was a popular firebrand of Athens and Clodius of Rome; each of them plunged his country into the deepest calamities], the designing and detestable flatters of the prevailing passion, becomes confirmed.

Wise and good men in vain oppose the storm, and may think themselves fortunate, if, endeavouring to preserve their ungrateful fellow citizens, they do not ruin themselves. Their prudence will be called baseness; their moderation, guilt; and if their virtue does not lead them to destruction, as that of many other great and excellent persons has done, they may survive, to receive from their expiring country, the mournful glory of her acknowledgment, that their councils, if regarded, would have saved her.

The constitutional modes of obtaining relief, are those which I would wish to see pursued on the present occasion, that is, by petitioning of our assemblies, or, where they are not permitted to meet, of the people to the powers that can afford us relief.

We have an excellent prince, in whose good dispositions towards us we may confide. We have a generous, sensible, and humane nation, to whom we may apply. They may be deceived: they may, by artful men, be provoked to anger against us; but I cannot yet believe that they will be cruel or unjust; or that their anger will be implacable. Let us behave like dutiful children, who have received unmerited blows from a beloved parent. Let us complain to our parents; but let our complaints speak at the same time, the language of affliction and veneration.

If, however, it shall happen by an unfortunate course of affairs, that our applications to his Majesty and the parliament for the redress, prove ineffectual, let us then take another step, by withholding from Great-Britain, all the advantages she has been used to receive from us. Then let us try, if our ingenuity, industry, and frugality, will not give weight to our remonstrances. Let us all be united with one spirit in one cause. Let us invent; let us work; let us save; let us at the same time, keep up our claims, and unceasingly repeat our complaints; but above all, let us implore the protection of that infinite good and gracious Being, by whom kings reign and princes decree "justice."

"Nil desperandum."
Nothing is to be despaired of.

A Farmer

·C·

Excerpt from the *Boston Newsletter*,
6 July 1769

Ipswich, June 22, 1769

Yesterday morning, very early, the young ladies in that parish of this town called, Chebacco, to the Number of 77, assembled, at the house of the Reverend Mr. John Cleveland, with their Spinning Wheels, and tho' the weather, that day, was extremely hot, and divers of the young ladies were but about 13 years of age, yet by six o'clock in the afternoon, they spun, of linen yard 440 knots, and carded and spun of cotton 730 knots, and of Tow [i.e., flax] 600, in all 1770 knots, which makes 177 ten knot skeins, all good yarn, and generously gave their work, and some brought cotton and flax with them, more than they spun themselves, as a present; and several of the people were kind and generous upon this occasion. And it may be worthy of noting, that one spun of good linen yard 53 knots, and another of cotton 60 knots, it being carded for her. After the music of the wheels was over, Mr. Cleveland entertained them with a sermon on Prov. 14.1 "every wise woman buildeth her house; but the foolish plucketh it down with her hands":—which he concluded, by observing how the women might recover to this country the full and free enjoyment of all our rights, properties, and privileges, (which is more than the men have been able to do); and so have the honor of building, not only their own, but the houses of many thousands, and, perhaps, prevent the ruin of the whole British empire, viz., by living upon, as far as possible, only the produce of this country; and to be sure to lay aside the use of all foreign teas. Also by wearing as far as possible, only clothing of this country's manufacturing—their behaviour was decent, and they manifested nothing but pleasure and satisfaction in their countenances at their retiring as well as through the whole proceeding of the Day.

·D·

Virginia Association, August 1774

At a very full Meeting of Delegates from the different Counties in the Colony and Dominion of *Virginia,* begun in *Williamsburg* the first day of *August,* in the year of our Lord 1774, and continued by several adjournments to *Saturday,* the 6th of the same month, the following Association was unanimously resolved upon, and agreed to:

We, his Majesty's dutiful and loyal subjects, the Delegates of the freeholders of *Virginia,* deputed to represent them at a general meeting in the City of *Williamsburg,* avowing our inviolable and unshaken fidelity and attachment to our most gracious Sovereign; our regard and affection for all our friends and fellow-subjects in *Great Britain* and elsewhere; protesting against every act or thing which may have the most distant tendency to interrupt or in any wise disturb his Majesty's peace, and the good order of Government within this his ancient Colony, which we are resolved to maintain and defend at the risk of our lives and fortunes; but, at the same time, affected with the deepest anxiety and most alarming apprehensions of those grievances and distresses by which his Majesty's *American* subjects are oppressed; and having taken under our most serious deliberation the state of the whole Continent, find that the present unhappy situation of our affairs is chiefly occasioned by certain ill advised regulations, as well of our trade, as internal polity, introduced by several unconstitutional Acts of the *British* Parliament, and, at length, attempted to be enforced by the hand of power.

Solely influenced by these important and weighty considerations, we think it an indispensable duty which we owe to our country, ourselves, and latest posterity, to guard against such dangerous and extensive mischiefs, by every just and proper means.

If, by the measures adopted, some unhappy consequences and inconveniences should be derived to our fellow-subjects, whom we wish not to injure in the smallest degree, we hope, and flatter ourselves, that they will impute them to their real cause, the hard necessity to which we are driven.

That the good people of this Colony may on so trying an occasion continue steadfastly directed to their most essential interests, in hopes that they will be influenced and stimulated by our example, to the greatest industry, the strictest economy and frugality, and the exertion of every publick virtue; persuaded that the merchants, manufacturers, and other inhabitants of *Great Britain,* and above all, that the *British* Parliament will be convinced how much the true interest of the Kingdom must depend on the restoration and continuance of that mutual friendship and cordiality which so happily subsisted between us, we have, unanimously, and with one voice, entered into the following Resolutions and Association, which we do oblige ourselves by those sacred ties of honour and love to our country, strictly to observe; and farther declare, before *God* and the world, that we will religiously adhere to and keep the same inviolate in every particular, until redress of all such *American* grievances as may be defined and settled at the general Congress of Delegates from the different Colonies shall be fully obtained, or until this Association shall be abrogated or altered by a general meeting of the Deputies of this Colony to be convened as is herein after directed. And we do, with the greatest earnestness, recommend this our Association to all gentlemen, merchants, traders, and other inhabitants of this Colony, hoping that they will cheerfully and cordially accede thereto:

1st. We do hereby resolve and declare, that we will not, either directly or indirectly, after the first day of *November* next, import from *Great Britain* any goods, wares, or merchandises whatever, medicines excepted; nor will we, after that day, import any *British* manufactures, either from the *West Indies* or any other place; nor any article whatever which we shall know, or have reason to believe, was brought into such countries from *Great Britain;* nor will we purchase any such articles so imported of any person or persons whatsoever, except such as are now in the country, or such as may arrive on or before the first day of *November,* in consequence of orders already given, and which cannot now be countermanded in time.

2d. We will neither ourselves import, nor purchase any slave or slaves imported by any other person, after the first day of *November* next, either from *Africa,* the *West Indies,* or any other place.

3d. Considering the article of tea as the detestable instrument which laid the foundation of the present sufferings of our distressed friends in the town of *Boston,* we view it with horrour; and therefore resolve, that we will not from this day, either import tea of any kind whatever; nor will we use, or suffer even such of it as is now on hand to be used in any of our families.

4th. If the inhabitants of the town of *Boston,* or any other Colony, should by violence or dire necessity be compelled to pay the *East India* Company for destroying any tea which they have lately by their agents unjustly attempted to force into the Colonies, we will not directly or indirectly import or purchase any *British East India* commodity whatever, till the Company, or some other person on their behalf, shall refund and fully restore to the owners all such sum or sums of money as may be so extorted.

5th. We do resolve, that unless *American* grievances are redressed before the 10th day of *August,* 1775, we will not after that day, directly or indirectly, export tobacco, or any other article whatever to *Great Britain;* nor will we sell any such articles as we think can be exported to *Great Britain* with a prospect of gain to any person or persons whatever, with a design of putting it into his or their power to export the same to *Great Britain,* either on our own, his, or their account. And that this resolution may be the more effectually carried into execution, we do hereby recommend it to the inhabitants of this Colony to refrain from the cultivation of tobacco as much as conveniently may be; and in lieu thereof, that they will, as we resolve to do, apply their attention and industry to the cultivation of all such articles as may form a proper basis for manufactures of all sorts, which we will endeavour to encourage throughout this Colony, to the utmost of our abilities.

6th. We will endeavour to improve our breed of sheep, and increase their number to the utmost extent; and to this end we will be as sparing as we conveniently can, in killing of sheep, especially those of the most profitable kind; and if we should at any time be overstocked, or can conveniently spare any, we will dispose of them to our neighbours, especially the poorer sort of people, upon moderate terms.

7th. *Resolved,* That the merchants and other venders of goods and merchandises within this Colony ought not to take advantage of the scarcity of goods that may be occasioned by this Association, but that they ought to sell the same at the rates they have been accustomed to for twelve months last past; and if they shall sell any such goods on higher terms, or shall in any manner, or by any devise whatever, violate or depart from this resolution, we will not, and are of opinion that no inhabitant of this Colony ought, at any time thereafter, to deal with any such person, their factors or agents, for any commodity whatever; and it is recommended to the Deputies of the several counties, that Committees be chosen in each county by such persons as accede to this Association, to take effectual care that these Resolves be properly observed, and for corresponding occasionally with the general Committee of Correspondence in the City of *Williamsburg,* provided, that if exchange should rise, such advance may be made in the prices of goods as shall be approved by the Committee of each county.

8th. In order the better to distinguish such worthy merchants and traders who are well-wishers of this Colony, from those who may attempt, through motives of self-interest, to obstruct our views, we do hereby resolve that we will not, after the first day of *November* next, deal with any merchant or trader who will not sign this Association; nor until he hath obtained a certificate of his having done so from the County Committee, or any three members thereof. And if any merchant, trader, or other person, shall import any goods or merchandise after the first day of *November,* contrary to this Association, we give it as our opinion that such goods and merchandise should be either forthwith reshipped, or delivered up to the County Committee, to be stored at the risk of the importer, unless such importer shall give a proper assurance to the said Committee, that such goods or merchandises shall not be sold within this Colony during the continuance of this Association; and if such importer shall refuse to comply with one or the other of these terms, upon application and due caution given to him or her by the said Committee, or any three members thereof, such Committee is required to publish the truth of the case in the Gazettes, and in the county where he or she resides; and we will thereafter consider such person or persons as inimical to this country, and break off every connection and all dealings with them.

9th. *Resolved,* That if any person or persons shall export tobacco, or any other commodity, to *Great Britain,* after the 10th day of *August,* 1775, contrary to this Association, we shall hold ourselves obliged to consider such person or persons as inimical to the community, and as an approver of *American* grievances; and give it as our opinion that the publick should be advised of his or their conduct, as in the eighth article is desired.

10th. Being fully persuaded that the united wisdom of the general Congress may improve these our endeavours to preserve the rights and liberties of *British America,* we decline enlarging at present; but do hereby resolve that we will conform to and strictly observe, all such alterations or additions assented to by the Delegates for this Colony, as they may judge it necessary to adopt, after the same shall be published and made known to us.

11th. *Resolved,* That we think ourselves called upon, by every principle of humanity and brotherly affection, to extend the utmost and speediest relief to our distressed fellow-subjects in the town of *Boston;* and, therefore, most earnestly recommend it to all the inhabitants of this Colony to make such liberal contributions as they can afford, to be collected and remitted to *Boston,* in such manner as may best answer so desirable a purpose.

12th. And lastly, *Resolved,* That the Moderator of this meeting, and, in case of his death, *Robert Carter Nicholas,* Esquire, be empowered, on any future occasion that may, in his opinion, require it, convene the several Delegates of this Colony, at such time and place as he may judge proper; and in case of the death or absence of any Delegate, it is recommended that another be chosen in his place.

· INSTRUCTIONS FOR THE DEPUTIES APPOINTED TO MEET IN GENERAL CONGRESS ON THE PART OF THIS COLONY ·

The unhappy disputes between *Great Britain* and her *American* Colonies, which began about the third year of the reign of this present Majesty, and since continually increasing, have proceeded to lengths so dangerous and alarming, as to excite just apprehensions in the minds of his Majesty's faithful subjects of this Colony, that they are in danger of being deprived of their natural, ancient, constitutional, and chartered rights, have compelled them to take the same into their most serious consideration; and being deprived of their usual and accustomed mode of making known their grievances, have appointed us their Representatives to consider what is proper to be done in this dangerous crisis of *American* affairs.

It being our opinion that the united wisdom of *North America* should be collected in a general Congress of all the Colonies, we have appointed the Honourable *Peyton Randolph,* Esquire, *Richard Henry Lee, George Washington, Patrick Henry, Richard Bland, Benjamin Harrison,* and *Edmund Pendleton,* Esquires, Deputies to represent this Colony in the said Congress, to be held at *Philadelphia,* on the first *Monday* in *September* next. And that they may be the better informed of our sentiments touching the conduct we wish them to observe on this important occasion, we desire that they will express, in the first place, our faith and true allegiance to his Majesty King *George* the Third, our lawful and rightful Sovereign; and that we are determined, with our lives and fortunes, to support him in the legal exercise of all his just rights and prerogatives; and however misrepresented, we sincerely approve of a constitutional connection with *Great Britain,* and wish most ardently a return of that intercourse of affection and commercial connection that formerly united both countries, which can only be effected by a removal of those causes of discontent which have of late unhappily divided us.

It cannot admit of a doubt, but that *British* subjects in *America* are entitled to the same rights and privileges as their fellow-subjects possess in *Britain;* and, therefore, that the power assumed by the *British* Parliament, to bind *America* by their statutes, in all cases whatsoever, is unconstitutional, and the source of these unhappy differences.

The end of Government would be defeated by the *British* Parliament exercising a power over the lives, the property and the liberty of *American* subjects, who are not, and from their local circumstances cannot, be there represented. Of this nature we consider the several Acts of Parliament for raising a revenue in *America;* for the extending the jurisdiction of the Courts of Admiralty; for seizing *American* subjects, and transporting them to *Britain* to be tried for crimes committed in *America;* and the several late oppressive Acts respecting the town of *Boston* and Province of the *Massachusetts Bay.*

The original Constitution of the *American* Colonies possessing their Assemblies with the sole right of directing their internal polity, it is absolutely destructive of the end of their institution that their Legislatures should be suspended, or prevented, by hasty dissolutions, from exercising their Legislative powers.

Wanting the protection of *Britain,* we have long acquiesced in their Acts of Navigation restrictive of our commerce, which we consider as an ample recompense for such protection; but as those Acts derive their efficacy from that foundation alone, we have reason to expect they will be restrained so as to produce the reasonable purposes of *Britain,* and not be injurious to us.

To obtain redress of these grievances, without which the people of *America* can neither be safe, free, nor happy, they were willing to undergo the great inconvenience that will be derived to them from stopping all imports whatsoever from *Great Britain,* after the first day of *November* next, and also to cease exporting any commodity whatsoever to the same place, after the 10th day of *August,* 1775. The earnest desire we have to make as quick and full payment as possible of our debts to *Great Britain,* and to avoid the heavy injury that would arise to this country from an earlier adoption of the non-exportation plan, after the people have already applied so much of their labour to the perfecting of the present crop, by which means they have been prevented from pursuing other methods of clothing and supporting their families, have rendered it necessary to restrain you in this article of non-exportation; but it is our desire that you cordially co-operate with our sister Colonies in general Congress, in such other just and proper methods as they or the majority shall deem necessary for the accomplishment of these valuable ends.

The Proclamation issued by General *Gage,* in the Government of the Province of the *Massachusetts Bay,* declaring it treason for the inhabitants of that Province to assemble themselves to consider of their grievances, and form Associations for their common conduct on the occasion; and requiring the Civil Magistrates and officers to apprehend all such persons, to be tried for their supposed offences, is the most alarming process that ever appeared in a *British* Government; that the said General *Gage* hath thereby assumed and taken upon himself powers denied by the Constitution to our legal Sovereign; that he, not having condescended to disclose by what authority he exercises such extensive and unheard of powers, we are at a loss to determine whether he intends to justify himself as the Representative of the King, or as the Commander-in-chief of his Majesty's forces in *America.* If he considers himself as acting in the character of his Majesty's Representative, we would remind him that the statute, twenty-fifth, *Edward* the Third, has expressed and defined all treasonable offences, and that the Legislature of *Great Britain* hath declared that no offence shall be construed to be treason but such as is pointed out by that statute, and that this was done to take out of the hands of tyrannical Kings and of weak and wicked Ministers that deadly weapon which constructive treason had furnished them with, and which had drawn blood of the best and most honest men in the Kingdom; and that the King of *Great Britain* hath no right, by his Proclamation, to subject his people to imprisonment, pains, and penalties.

That if the said General *Gage* conceives he is empowered to act in this manner, as the Commander-in-chief of his Majesty's forces in *America,* this odious and illegal Proclamation must be considered as a plain and full declaration that this despotick viceroy will be bound by no law, nor regard the constitutional rights of his Majesty's subjects, whenever they interfere with the plan he has formed for oppressing the good people of the *Massachusetts Bay;* and, therefore, that the executing, or attempting to execute, such Proclamation, will justify resistance and reprisal.

·E·

Suffolk Resolves, 14 September 1774

At a Meeting of the Delegates of every Town and District of the County of *Suffolk,* on *Tuesday,* the 6th of *September,* at the house of Mr. *Richard Woodward,* of *Dedham;* and by adjournment at the house of Mr. *Vose,* of *Milton,* on *Friday,* the 9th instant,

JOSEPH PALMER, Esquire, being chosen *Moderator,* and WILLIAM THOMPSON, Esquire, *Clerk,*

A Committee was chosen to bring in a Report to the Convention; and the following, being several times read, and put, paragraph by paragraph, was unanimously voted, viz:

Whereas the power, but not the justice, the vengeance, but not the wisdom, of *Great Britain,* which of old persecuted, scourged, and excited our fugitive parents from their native shores, now pursues us, their guiltless children, with unrelenting severity. And whereas, this then savage and uncultivated desert, was purchased by the toil and treasure, or acquired by the blood and valour of those our venerable progenitors; to us they bequeathed the dear-bought inheritance; to our care and protection they consigned it; and the most sacred obligations are upon us to transmit the glorious purchase, unfettered by power, unclogged with shackles, to our innocent and beloved offspring. On the fortitude, on the wisdom, and on the exertions of this important day, is suspended the fate of this new world, and of unborn millions. If a boundless extent of Continent, swarming with millions, will tamely submit to live, move, and have their being at the arbitrary will of a licentious Minister, they basely yield to voluntary slavery, and future generations will load their memories with incessant execrations. On the other hand, if we arrest the hand which would ransack our pockets; if we disarm the parricide which points the dagger to our bosoms; if we nobly defeat that fatal edict which proclaims a power to *frame laws for us in all cases whatsoever,* thereby entailing the endless and numberless curses of slavery upon us, our heirs, and their heirs forever; if we successfully resist that unparalleled usurpation of unconstitutional power, whereby our

545

capital is robbed of the means of life; whereby the streets of *Boston* are thronged with military executioners; whereby our coasts are lined and harbours crowded with ships of war; whereby the Charter of the Colony, that sacred barrier against the encroachments of tyranny is mutilated, and, in effect, annihilated; whereby a murderous law is framed to shelter villains from the hand of justice; whereby that unalienable and inestimable inheritance which we derived from nature, the Constitution of *Britain,* and the privileges warranted to us in the Charter of the Province, is totally wrecked, annulled, and vacated, posterity will acknowledge that virtue which preserved them free and happy; and while we enjoy the rewards and blessings of the faithful, the torrents of panegyrists will roll our reputations to the latest period, when the streams of time shall be absorbed in the abyss of eternity.— Therefore we have resolved, and do resolve,

1. That whereas his Majesty King *George* the Third, is the rightful successor to the Throne of *Great Britain,* and justly entitled to the allegiance of the *British* Realm, and agreeable to compact of the *English* Colonies in *America;* therefore, we the heirs and successors of the first planters of this Colony do cheerfully acknowledge the said *George* the Third to be our rightful Sovereign; and that said covenant is the tenure and claim on which are founded our allegiance and submission.

2. That it is an indispensable duty which we owe to *God,* our country, ourselves, and posterity, by all lawful ways and means in our power, to maintain, defend, and preserve these civil and religious rights and liberties for which many of our fathers fought, bled, and died, and to hand them down entire to future generations.

3. That the late Acts of the *British* parliament for blocking up the harbour of *Boston*; for altering the established form of Government in this Colony; and for screening the most flagitious violators of the laws of the Province from a legal trial, are gross infractions of those rights to which we are justly entitled by the laws of nature, the *British* Constitution, and the Charter of the Province.

4. That no obedience is due from this Province to either or any part of the Acts above mentioned; but that they be rejected as the attempts of a wicked Administration to enslave *America.*

5. That so long as the Justices of our Superiour Court of Judicature, Court of Assize, &c., and Inferiour Court of Common Pleas in this county, are appointed, or hold their places by any other tenure than that which the Charter and the laws of the Province direct, they must be considered as under undue influence, and are therefore unconstitutional officers, and as such, no regard ought to be paid to them by the people of this county.

6. That if the Justices of the Superiour Court of Judicature, Assize, &c., Justices of the Court of Common Pleas, or of the General Sessions of the Peace, shall sit and act during the present disqualified state, this county will support and bear harmless all Sheriffs and other Deputies, Constables, Jurors, and other Officers, who shall refuse to carry into execution the orders of said Court; and as far as possible to prevent the many inconveniences which must be occasioned by a sus-

pension of the Courts of Justice, we do most earnestly recommend it to all creditors that they show all reasonable and every generous forbearance to their debtors, and to all debtors to pay their just demands with all possible speed; and if any disputes relative to debts or trespasses, shall arise which cannot be settled by the parties, we recommend it to them to submit all such cases to arbitration; and it is our opinion that the contending parties, or either of them, who shall refuse so to do, ought to be considered as co-operating with the enemies of this country.

7. That it be recommended to the Collectors of Taxes, Constables, and all other Officers, who have publick moneys in their hands, to retain the same, and not to make any payment thereof to the Provincial County Treasurer, until the Civil Government of the Province is placed upon a constitutional foundation, or until it shall otherwise be ordered by the proposed Provincial Congress.

8. That the persons who have accepted seats at the Council Board, by virtue of a mandamus from the King, in conformity to the late Act of the *British* parliament, entitled "An Act for the regulating the Government of the *Massachusetts Bay*," have acted in direct violation of the duty they owe to their country, and have thereby given great and just offence to this people; therefore, resolved, that this county do recommend it to all persons who have so highly offended by accepting said departments, and have not already publickly resigned their seats at the Council Board, to make publick resignation of their places at said Board, on or before the 20th day of this instant *September*; and that all persons refusing so to do, shall, from and after that day, be considered by this county as obstinate and incorrigible enemies to this country.

9. That the fortifications begun and now carrying on upon *Boston Neck,* are justly alarming to this county, and give us reason to apprehend some hostile intention against that town; more especially as the Commander-in-chief has, in a very extraordinary manner, removed the powder from the Magazine at *Charlestown,* and has also forbidden the keeper of the Magazine at *Boston* to deliver out to the owners the powder which they had lodged in said Magazine.

10. That the late Act of Parliament for establishing the Roman Catholick religion and the *French* laws in that extensive country now called *Canada,* is dangerous in an extreme degree to the Protestant religion, and to the civil rights and liberties of all *America*; and therefore, as men and Protestant Christians, we are indispensably obliged to take all proper measures for our own security.

11. That whereas our enemies have flattered themselves that they will make an easy prey of this numerous, brave, and hardy people, from an apprehension that they are unacquainted with military discipline; we, therefore, for the honour, defence, and security of this county and Province, advise, as it has been recommended to take away all commissions from the officers of the militia, that those who now hold commissions, or such other persons be elected in each town as officers of the militia, as shall be judged of sufficient capacity for that purpose, and who have evidenced themselves the inflexible friends to the rights of the people; and that the inhabitants of these towns and districts who are qualified, to use their utmost diligence to acquaint themselves with the art of war as soon as possible,

and do, for that purpose, appear under arms at least once every week.

12. That, during the present hostile appearances on the part of *Great Britain,* notwithstanding the many insults and oppressions which we most sensibly resent, yet, nevertheless, from our affection to his Majesty, which we have at all times evinced, we are determined to act merely upon the defensive, so long as such conduct may be vindicated by reason and the principles of self-preservation, but no longer.

13. That, as we understand it has been in contemplation to apprehend sundry persons of this county, who have rendered themselves conspicuous in contending for the violated rights and liberties of their countrymen, we do recommend, should such an audacious measure be put in practice, to seize and keep in safe custody every servant of the present tyrannical and unconstitutional Government, throughout the county and Province, until the persons so apprehended be liberated from the hands of our adversaries, and restored safe and uninjured to their respective friends and families.

14. That until our rights are fully restored unto us, we will, to the utmost of our power, and recommend the same to the other counties, withhold all commercial intercourse with *Great Britain, Ireland,* and the *West Indies,* and abstain from the consumption of *British* merchandise and manufactures, and especially of *East India* teas and piece goods, with such additions, alterations, and exceptions only, as the Grand Congress of the Colonies may agree to.

15. That, under our present circumstances, it is incumbent on us to encourage arts and manufactures among us by all means in our power; and that * * * * * * * * * * * be and hereby are appointed a Committee to consider of the best ways and means to promote and establish the same, and to report to this Convention as soon as may be.

16. That the exigencies of our publick affairs demand that a Provincial Congress be called to concert such measures as may be adopted and vigorously executed by the whole people; and we do recommend it to the several towns in this county to choose members for such a Provincial Congress, to be holden at *Concord,* on the second *Tuesday* of *October* next ensuing.

17. That this county, confiding in the wisdom and integrity of the Continental Congress, now sitting at *Philadelphia,* will pay all due respect and submission to such measures as may be recommended by them to the Colonies, for the restoration and establishment of our just rights, civil and religious, and for renewing that harmony and union between *Great Britain* and the Colonies so wished for by all good men.

18. That whereas, the universal uneasiness which prevails among all orders of men, arising from the wicked and oppressive measures of the present Administration, may influence some unthinking persons to commit outrage upon private property, we would heartily recommend to all persons of this community not to engage in any routs, riots, or licentious attacks upon the properties of any person whatsoever, as being subversive of all order and government; but, by a steady, manly, uniform, and persevering opposition, to convince our enemies that in a

contest so important—in a cause so solemn, our conduct shall be such as to merit the approbation of the wise, and the admiration of the brave and free of every age and of every country.

19. That, should our enemies, by any sudden manoeuvres, render it necessary to ask the aid and assistance of our brethren in the country, some one of the Committee of Correspondence, or a Selectman of each town, or the town adjoining where such hostilities shall commence, or shall be expected to commence, shall despatch couriers with written messages to the Selectmen or Committees of Correspondence of the several towns in the vicinity, with a written account of such matter, who shall despatch others to Committees more remote, until proper and sufficient assistance be obtained; and that the expense of said couriers be defrayed by the county, until it shall be otherwise ordered by the Provincial Congress.

·F·

Continental Association,
October 1774

W e, his majesty's most loyal subjects, the delegates of the several colonies of New-Hampshire, Massachusetts-Bay, Rhode-Island, Connecticut, New-York, New-Jersey, Pennsylvania, the three lower counties of New-Castle, Kent, and Sussex, on Delaware, Maryland, Virginia, North-Carolina, and South-Carolina, deputed to represent them in a continental Congress, held in the city of Philadelphia, on the 5th day of September, 1774, avowing our allegiance to his majesty, our affection and regard for our fellow-subjects in Great-Britain and elsewhere, affected with the deepest anxiety, and most alarming apprehensions, at those grievances and distresses, with which his Majesty's American subjects are oppressed; and having taken under our most serious deliberation, the state of the whole continent, find, that the present unhappy situation of our affairs is occasioned by a ruinous system of colony administration, adopted by the British ministry about the year 1763, evidently calculated for inslaving these colonies, and, with them, the British empire. In prosecution of which system, various acts of parliament have been passed, for raising a revenue in America, for depriving the American subjects, in many instances, of the constitutional trial by jury, exposing their lives to danger, by directing a new and illegal trial beyond the seas, for crimes alleged to have been committed in America: and in prosecution of the same system, several late, cruel, and oppressive acts have been passed, respecting the town of Boston and the Massachusetts-Bay, and also an act for extending the province of Quebec, so as to border on the western frontiers of these colonies, establishing an arbitrary government therein, and discouraging the settlement of British subjects in that wide extended country; thus, by the influence of civil principles and ancient prejudices, to dispose the inhabitants to act with hostility against the free Protestant colonies, whenever a wicked ministry shall chuse so to direct them.

To obtain redress of these grievances, which threaten destruction to the lives, liberty, and property of his majesty's subjects, in North America, we are of opinion, that a non-importation, non-consumption, and non-exportation agreement, faithfully adhered to, will prove the most speedy, effectual, and peaceable measures: and, therefore, we do, for ourselves, and the inhabitants of the several colonies whom we represent, firmly agree and associate under the sacred ties of virtue, honour and love of our country, as follows:

1. That from and after the first day of December next, we will not import, into British America, from Great Britain or Ireland, any goods, wares, or merchandise whatsoever, or from any other place, any such goods, wares, or merchandise, as shall have been exported from Great-Britain or Ireland; nor will we, after that day, import any East-India tea from any part of the world; nor any molasses, syrups, paneles, coffee, or pimento, from the British plantations or from Dominica; nor wines from Madeira, or the Western Islands; nor foreign indigo.

2. We will neither import nor purchase, any slave imported after the first day of December next; after which time, we will wholly discontinue the slave trade, and will neither be concerned in it ourselves, nor will we hire our vessels, nor sell our commodities or manufactures to those who are concerned in it.

3. As a non-consumption agreement, strictly adhered to, will be an effectual security for the observation of the non-importation, we, as above, solemnly agree and associate, that, from this day, we will not purchase or use any tea, imported on account of the East-India company, or any on which a duty hath been or shall be paid; and from and after the first day of March next, we will not purchase or use any East-India tea whatever; nor will we, nor shall any person for or under us, purchase or use any of those goods, wares, or merchandise, we have agreed not to import, which we shall know, or have cause to suspect, were imported after the first day of December, except such as come under the rules and directions of the tenth article hereafter mentioned.

4. The earnest desire we have, not to injure our fellow-subjects in Great-Britain, Ireland, or the West-Indies, induces us to suspend a non-exportation until the tenth day of September, 1775; at which time, if the said acts and parts of acts of the British parliament herein after mentioned are not repealed, we will not, directly or indirectly, export any merchandise or commodity whatsoever to Great-Britain, Ireland, or the West-Indies, except rice to Europe.

5. Such as are merchants, and use the British and Irish trade, will give orders, as soon as possible, to their factors, agents, and correspondents, in Great-Britain and Ireland, not to ship any goods to them, on any pretence whatsoever, as they cannot be received in America; and if any merchant residing in Great-Britain or Ireland, shall directly or indirectly ship any goods, wares, or merchandise, for America, in order to break the said non-importation agreement, or in any manner contravene the same, on such unworthy conduct being well attested, it ought to be made public; and, on the same being so done, we will not, from thenceforth, have any commercial connexion with such merchant.

6. That such as are owners of vessels will give positive orders to their captains, or masters, not to receive on board their vessels any goods prohibited by the said non-importation agreement, on pain of immediate dismission from their service.

7. We will use our utmost endeavours to improve the breed of sheep, and

increase their number to the greatest extent; and to that end, we will kill them as seldom as may be, especially those of the most profitable kind; nor will we export any to the West-Indies or elsewhere; and those of us, who are or may become over-stocked with, or can conveniently spare any sheep, will dispose of them to our neighbours, especially to the poorer sort, on moderate terms.

8. We will, in our several stations, encourage frugality, economy, and in-dustry, and promote agriculture, arts, and the manufactures of this country, espe-cially that of wool; and will discountenance and discourage every species of ex-travagance and dissipation, especially all horse-racing, and all kinds of gaming, cock-fighting, exhibitions of shews, plays, and other expensive diversions and en-tertainment; and on the death of any relation or friend, none of us, or any of our families, will go into any further mourning-dress, than a black crape or ribbon on the arm or hat, for gentlemen, and a black ribbon and necklace for ladies, and we will discontinue the giving of scarves at funerals.

9. Such as are vendors of goods or merchandise will not take advantage of the scarcity of goods, that may be occasioned by this association, but will sell the same at the rates we have been respectively accustomed to do, for twelve months last past.—And if any vender of goods or merchandise shall sell any such goods on higher terms, or shall, in any manner, or by any device whatsoever violate or de-part from this agreement, no person ought, nor will any of us deal with any such person, or his or her factor or agent, at any time thereafter, for any commodity whatever.

10. In case any merchant, trader, or other person, shall import any goods or merchandise, after the first day of December, and before the first day of February next, the same ought forthwith, at the election of the owner, to be either re-shipped or delivered up to the committee of the county or town, wherein they shall be im-ported, to be stored at the risque of the importer, until the non-importation agree-ment shall cease, or be sold under the direction of the committee aforesaid; and in the last-mentioned case, the owner or owners of such goods shall be reimbursed out of the sales, the first cost and charges, the profit, if any, to be applied towards relieving and employing such poor inhabitants of the town of Boston as are im-mediate sufferers by the Boston port-bill; and a particular account of all goods so returned, stored, or sold, to be inserted in the public papers; and if any goods or merchandises shall be imported after the said first day of February, the same ought forthwith to be sent back again, without breaking any of the packages thereof.

11. That a committee be chosen in every county, city, and town, by those who are qualified to vote for representatives in the legislature, whose business it shall be attentively to observe the conduct of all persons touching this association; and when it shall be made to appear, to the satisfaction of a majority of any such committee, that any person within the limits of their appointment has violated this association, that such majority do forthwith cause the truth of the case to be pub-lished in the gazette; to the end, that all such foes to the rights of British-America may be publicly known, and universally contemned as the enemies of American liberty; and thenceforth we respectively will break off all dealings with him or her.

12. That the committee of correspondence, in the respective colonies, do frequently inspect the entries of their custom-houses, and inform each other, from time to time, of the true state thereof, and of every other material circumstance that may occur relative to this association.

13. That all manufactures of this country be sold at reasonable prices, so that no undue advantage be taken of a future scarcity of goods.

14. And we do further agree and resolve, that we will have no trade, commerce, dealings, or intercourse whatsoever, with any colony or province, in North-America, which shall not accede to, or which shall hereafter violate this association, but will hold them as unworthy of the rights of freemen, and as inimical to the liberties of their country.

And we do solemnly bind ourselves and our constituents, under the ties aforesaid, to adhere to this association, until such parts of the several acts of parliament passed since the close of the last war, as impose or continue duties on tea, wine, molasses, syrups, paneles, coffee, sugar, pimento, indigo, foreign paper, glass, and painters' colours, imported into America, and extend the powers of the Admiralty courts beyond their ancient limits, deprive the American subjects of trial by jury, authorize the judge's certificate to indemnify the prosecutor from damages, that he might otherwise be liable to from a trial by his peers, require oppressive security from a claimant of ships or goods seized, before he shall be allowed to defend his property, are repealed.—And until that part of the Act of the 12 G. 3. ch. 24, entitled "An act for the better securing his majesty's dock-yards, magazines, ships, ammunition, and stores," by which any persons charged with committing any of the offenses therein described, in America, may be tried in any shire or county within the realm, is repealed—and until the four acts passed in the last session of parliament, viz, that for stopping the port and blocking up the harbour of Boston—that for altering the charter and government of the Massachusetts-Bay—and that which is entitled "An act for the better administration of justice, &c."—and that "for extending the limits of Quebec, &c." are repealed. And we recommend it to the provincial conventions, and to the committees in the respective colonies, to establish such farther regulations as they make think proper, for carrying into execution this association.

The foregoing association being determined upon by the Congress, was ordered to be subscribed by the several members thereof; and thereupon, we have hereunto set our respective names accordingly.

In Congress, Philadelphia, October 20, 1774.

·G·

Letters and Diary Extracts of Josiah Quincy, Jr., 1774–1775

Josiah Quincy, Jr., ancestor of three mayors of Boston and a president of Harvard, was a young lawyer beginning his career during the 1760s, when the resistance to Great Britain began in Massachusetts. Quincy devoted much of this career and many of his personal energies, weakened by a lifelong disease, to the American cause. Called "Wilkes" Quincy, not only for his fiery devotion to liberty but undoubtedly for the strabismus which he shared with John Wilkes, he suffered for his views and actions through impaired health and through the refusal of the superior court in 1769 to admit him to practice before it, despite his qualifications.

When the Boston Massacre occurred in March 1770, Quincy refused to allow the accused soldiers to go to trial without proper defense and agreed to represent them. He was joined by John Adams with whom he shared the defense tasks. Quincy turned this potentially unpopular role into an opportunity for public discussion of the goals and means of resistance in the summary of the defense arguments. Reminding the jury—and thereby the town—of John Dickinson's arguments against the use of violence in the cause of liberty until absolutely necessary, Quincy called upon the citizens to keep resistance actions under their own control and not to allow the ministry to force them into thoughtless acts, which could only be to the advantage of the opponent.

In 1773, afflicted by "pulmonary" distress (tuberculosis? —the author of the memoir does not say), Quincy traveled to South Carolina in the hope that a sea voyage and change of climate would help his affliction. While in South Carolina and traveling through the colonies between there and Massachusetts, Quincy contacted many leaders of the earlier movements against the Stamp Act and Townshend Acts, including Miles Brewton, Charles Cotesworth Pinckney, and Christopher Gadsden of South Carolina, and John Dickinson and William Reed of Pennsylvania. While in the South, Quincy suggested to several of these men that they keep up a regular correspondence on politics. Unable to believe that the then-current lull in the opposition between Great Britain and its colonies would last, Quincy hoped to link many of the serious leaders of potential future resistance through correspondence.

As may be seen by some of the extracts printed here, Quincy had some success in his mission—especially with the outstanding leader of Pennsylvania, John Dickinson. Driven, as we can perceive in his letters, by a desire to do something personally about the renewed threat from Great Britain contained in the Coercive Acts of 1774, Quincy traveled to London in late September 1774. Hoping to use whatever influence his own knowledge and the strength of his arguments might have, Quincy visited many influential British politicians to argue for Parliament to repeal all the acts which oppressed America. Taking advantage of letters of introduction to Benjamin Franklin and others, Quincy lobbied extensively, seeing not only the "friends of America" but some of its opponents, including Prime Minister Lord North.

Quincy had traveled to Britain in "low health" which only worsened during his stay in London. Although in fear of his life if he again crossed the ocean, Quincy was determined to attend the Second Continental Congress at Philadelphia to lobby for firmness in opposition to England. Quincy embarked from England for America in March 1775. He did not survive the voyage.

While in England, Quincy kept a journal describing his experiences and wrote a stream of letters full of political advice for his friends in America. Most of these letters were addressed to his wife and intended to be read by the leaders of the resistance in Massachusetts—Samuel Adams, Joseph Warren, and John Adams among them. Other letters were sent to correspondents gleaned during the 1773 trip south, among them James Reed and John Dickinson, and probably others whose letters do not appear in the memoir from which these extracts were taken. Most of these extracts are from Quincy's letters, largely because these opinions and observations are the ones which would have reached his American correspondents, and a few journal extracts are also included. In these materials, we can only be impressed with Quincy's sense of the seriousness of his country's situation and his desire to impress upon his correspondents the *consequences* of their own actions. In particular, Quincy wants to teach them the lesson of the Townshend Acts resistance, which was that the merchants must be controlled by political bodies, lest they turn the commercial resistance only to their own advantage, and then drop it. Likewise, Quincy believed that the Americans *must* keep the option of military opposition open and must always act from strength, no matter what means of opposition they pursue. At first, Quincy was convinced that only a military confrontation would convince the British government and people that the Americans were in earnest. As his stay in Britain lengthened, Quincy increasingly came to believe that strongly pursued nonviolent resistance, particularly commercial resistance, could defend America against its opponents in Great Britain.

These extracts are taken from Josiah Quincy, *Memoir of the Life of Josiah Quincy, Jr.* (Boston: Cummings, Hilliard, 1825).

To John Dickinson, Esq.[1]
Boston, August 20, 1774.

Your sentiments relative to that "colony which shall advance too hastily before the rest, contrary to the maxims of discipline," &c. are no doubt just. Yet permit me, sir, to use a freedom, which your partiality seems to invite, and observe, that those maxims of discipline are not universally known in this early period of continental warfare; and are with great difficulty practised, by a people under the scourge of public oppression. When time shall have taught wisdom, and past experience have fixed boundaries to the movements of a single colony, its intemperate and over-hasty strides will be more unpardonable. But if we should unfortunately see one colony under a treble pressure of public oppression, rendered impatient by the refinements, delays, and experiments of the Philadelphians; of their less oppressed, and therefore more deliberate brethren;—I say, if a colony thus insulted, galled from without, and vexed within, should seem to advance, and "break the line of opposition," ought it to incur the heavy censure of "betraying the common cause?" Though not to be justified, may not its fault be considered venial? Believe me, dear sir, you know not all our patriotic trials in this province. Corruption (which delay gives time to operate) is the destroying angel we have most to fear. Our enemies wish for nothing so much, as our tampering with the fatal disease. I fear much that timid or lukewarm counsels will be considered by our congress as prudent and politic. Such counsels will inevitably enslave us;—we subjugated,—how rapid and certain the fall of the rest. Excuse my freedom of telling what I dread, though seeming to differ from those I honor and revere. We are at this time calm and temperate; and, partiality to my countrymen aside, I question whether any ancient or modern state can give an instance of a whole people suffering so severely, with such dignity, fortitude, and true spirit. Our very enemies are dismayed, and though they affect to sneer at our enthusiasm, yet they so far catch the noble infirmity, as to give an involuntary applause.

I see no reason to apprehend our advancing before our brethren, unless the plans they should adopt should very evidently be too languid and spiritless to give any rational hopes of safety to us in our adherence to them. *Sobrius esto* is our present motto. At the urgent solicitation of a great number of warm friends to my country and myself, I have agreed to relinquish business, and embark for London, and shall sail in eighteen days certainly. I am flattered by those who perhaps place too great confidence in me, that I may do some good the ensuing winter, at the court of Great Britain. Hence I have taken this unexpected resolution. My design is to be kept as long secret as possible,—I hope till I get to Europe. Should it transpire that I was going home, our public enemies here would be as indefatigable and persevering to my injury, as they have been to the cause in which I am engaged, heart and hand; perhaps more so, as personal pique would be added to public malevolence.

I would solicit, earnestly, intelligence from you, sir, while in London. I shall endeavour to procure the earliest information from all parts of the continent. As I propose dedicating myself wholly to the service of my country, I shall stand in need of the aid of every friend of America; and believe me, when I say, that I esteem none more capable of affording me that aid, than those who inhabit the fertile banks of the Delaware.[2]

To Mrs. Quincy
Falmouth, Great Britain, November 8, 1774

Since writing the above, I have been regaled with the profusions of Great Britain to—*those who have money*. I have read also about twenty of the late London papers. I would have sent them, but could not procure them. They contain the resolves of the congress relative to the late Suffolk proceedings. They also seem to breathe a spirit favourable to America. I am in some pain on finding that six men-of-war sailed for Boston, on the twenty-sixth of October. I have conversed with several sensible people here. I have not yet met one, but what wishes well to the Americans. And one or two expressed great veneration for *the brave Bostonians*.

We have a report that the congress have agreed upon a non-importation agreement; and also upon a non-exportation agreement, to commence the first of August next. I have also been informed that Lord North has desired leave of his Majesty to resign; to which the King replied,—"Your Lordship's policy hath made an American snarl, and your Lordship's dexterity must untie it, or it must *be cut*; and when Englishmen once begin that work, they will probably go much further."

From the Journal

November 11th. Though a very cold and stormy day, I viewed Plymouth Docks, and went on board and all over the Royal George, a first-rate, pierced for two hundred and ten, and carrying two hundred guns. The rope-walks, buildings, armory, arsenal, naval and warlike stores, exceed the power of the human mind to conceive, that doth not actually behold.

I will not attempt to describe what I could scarcely realize to be true, while I was actually viewing. My ideas of the riches and powers of this great nation are increased to a degree I should not have believed, if it had been predicted to me.

I also saw many 64, 74, 80, and 100 gun ships; and went on board a loaded Indiaman just arrived; but this, being after viewing the preceding magnificence, did not much move me. The various materials, and the several degrees of building, from the laying of the keel, to the finishing an hundred gun ship, which were very carefully viewed by me, in several instances, excited an astonishment I never before experienced.

To Mrs. Quincy
London, November 17, 1774

I am well informed that the friends of America increase here every day. In the west of England, a very considerable manufacturer told me, "If the Americans stand out, we must come to their terms." I find our friends here dread nothing so much as lest the congress should petition. Should they adopt that mode, it will be injurious to our cause. The ministry have carried their men at a late election, but the people seem to be rousing. You see I have been a short time in London. I can as yet communicate but little intelligence. A large field is opening to me. I am preparing for the course with feelings, which render me careless, whether I shall be pursuing, or pursued. Tell my political friends, I shall soon write to them, and that when I informed Dr. Franklin of the pains I had taken to establish an extensive correspondence, he rejoiced at it much. Let their intelligence be as frequent, and as minute as possible.

From the Journal.

November 18th. This morning, [Jonathan] Williams Esq, inspector of the customs in the Massachusetts Bay, waited upon me, and we had more than an hour's private conversation together. He informed me, that Governor Hutchinson had repeatedly assured the ministry that a union of the colonies was utterly impracticable; that the people were greatly divided among themselves, in every colony; and that there could be no doubt, that all America would submit, and that they must, and moreover would, soon. It is now not five minutes, since Mr. Williams left me, and these I think were his very words; he added, also, that Governor Hutchinson had not only repeatedly told the ministry so, as several Lords had informed him, but that Governor Hutchinson had more than once said the same to persons in the ministry, in his presence. Mr. Williams desired to wait on me to see Lord North and Lord Dartmouth,[3]—but as it was not at their Lordships' desire he made the request, I declined going for the present.

. . .

November 19th. Early this morning J. Williams Esq. waited upon me with the compliments of Lord North, and his request to see me this morning. I went about half past nine o'clock, and found Sir George Savil (as Mr Williams informed me) in the levee room. After a short time his lordship sent for Mr Williams and myself into his apartment. His reception was polite, and with a cheerful affability his Lordship soon inquired into the state, in which I had left American affairs. I gave him my sentiments upon them, together with what I took to be the causes of most of our political evils;—gross misrepresentation and falsehood. His lordship replied, he did not doubt there had been much, but added, that very honest men frequently gave a wrong statement of matters through mistake, prejudice, prepossessions, and biases, of one kind or other. I conceded the possibility of this, but further added, that it would be happy, if none of those who had given accounts relative to America had varied from known truth, from worse motives.

We entered largely into the propriety and policy of the Boston Port Bill. In the conversation upon this subject I received much pleasure. His lordship several times smiled, and once seemed touched. We spoke considerably upon the sentiments of Americans, of the right claimed by Parliament to tax,—of the destruction of the tea,—and the justice of payment for it. His lordship went largely and repeatedly into an exculpation of the ministry. He said they were obliged to do what they did; that it was the most lenient measure that was proposed; that if administration had not adopted it, they would have been called to an account; that the nation were highly incensed, &c.

Upon this topic I made many remarks with much freedom and explicitness, and should have said more, had not his lordship's propensity to converse been incompatible with my own loquacity. His lordship more than thrice spoke of the *power* of Great Britain, of their determination to exert it to the utmost, in order to effect the submission of the Colonies. He said repeatedly, "We must try what we can do to support the authority we have claimed over America. If we are defective in power, we must sit down contented, and make the best terms we can, and nobody then can blame us, after we have done our utmost; but till we have tried what we can do, we can never be justified in receding. We ought, and we shall be very careful not to judge a thing impossible, because it may be difficult; nay, we ought to try what we can effect, before we determine upon its impractibility." This last sentiment, and very nearly in the same words, was often repeated,—I thought I knew for what purpose.

To Mrs. Quincy
London, November 24, 1774

The minds of people are strangely altered in this island:—the many are now as prone to justify and applaud the Americans, as, but a little while ago, they were ready to condemn and punish. I have conversed with almost all ranks of people for these fifteen days past, and having been in very large circles of the sensible part of the community during that time, my opportunity for information was the more fortunate. I came among a people, I was told, that breathed nothing but punishment and destruction against Boston, and all America. I found a people, many of whom revere, love, and heartily wish well to us. Now is it strange that it should be so? For abstracted from the pleasure that a good mind takes in seeing truth and justice prevail—it is the interest, the highest *private interest* of this whole nation, to be our fast friends:—and strange as it may seem when you consider the conduct of the nation as represented in Parliament, the *people* know it. The following language has been reiterated to me in various companies, with approbation and warmth.

"We are afraid of nothing but your division, and your want of perseverance. Unite and persevere. You must prevail,—you must triumph."

This and similar language hath been held to me with a zeal that bespoke it came from the heart,—with a frequency that proved such sentiments dwelt upon the mind. . . .

Great is the anxiety here,[4] lest the congress should petition or remonstrate. In the arts of negotiation, your adversaries are infinitely your superiors. If that mode of proceedings is adopted by the congress, many, very many friends will sink,— they will desert your cause from despondency. At present (as I am assured and as I verily believe), could the voices of this nation be collected by any fair method, twenty to one would be in favour of the Americans. You wonder and say, "Then whence is it that they do not exert themselves?" One American phrase will give you the true reason. The people are "cowed" by oppression. It is amazing,—it is incredible how much this is the case. Corruption, baseness, fraud, exorbitant oppression never so abounded as in this island. And will you believe me when I say, that Englishmen,—that boasted race of freemen—are sunk in abject submission.

From Parliament, therefore, expect no favour, but what proceeds from fear,— from the people here, expect no aid. It is yourselves, it is yourselves must save you; *and you are equal to the task*. Your friends know this, and your very enemies acknowledge it. But they believe you are as corrupt and as corruptible as themselves; and as destitute of union, spirit, and perseverance, as the friends of freedom are in this country. For your country's sake, depend not upon commercial plans alone for your safety. The manufacturers begin to feel,—they know, they acknowledge, they must feel severely; and if you persevere, they must be ruined. But what are these men,—what are the body of this people? *The servants of their masters*. How easy it is for the ministry to frown or flatter them into silence. How easy to take the spoils of the nation, and, for a season, fill the mouths of the clamorous. It is true, your perseverance will occasion, in time, that hunger which will break through stone walls. But how difficult is it, how impracticable is it, for *mere commercial virtue* (if indeed it have any existence) to persevere. I repeat, therefore,—depend not upon this scheme for your deliverance. I do not say renounce it,—I say continue it; but look towards it in vast subordination to those noble, generous, and glorious exertions which *alone* can save you. Before I came among this people, the friends of liberty desponded; because they believed the Americans would give up. They saw the irretrievable ruin of the whole cause, lost in that fatal yielding. I feel no despondence myself,—I am sanguine my country must prevail. I feel the ardour of an American;—I have lighted up the countenances of many;—I am speaking conviction every day to more. In short, I am infected with an enthusiasm which I know to be contagious. Whether I have caught or spread the infection here, is no matter needful to determine.

To Mrs. Quincy
London, December 7, 1774.

This kingdom never saw a time in which the minds of all ranks were more upon the rack with expectation; and when I tell you that yesterday in the coffee-room adjoining the House of Commons, one of the ministerial members offered to lay a wager of seventy-five guineas to twenty-five, *that Boston was now in ashes,* —you will not think my own bosom free from anxiety! It is now more than two months since any advices have been received from America, of the state of things in your province. The subalterns of the ministry give out that the most peremptory orders went to General Gage last October, to proceed to extremities, with vigour; they therefore vapour with much vaunting upon the expectation of hearing, in a few days, that you are all subdued, and in deep humiliation. Should the reverse of this prove true, as God grant it may! your enemies will sink, and sink forever. Let me here tell you a great truth. The people of this country have too generally got an idea that Americans are all cowards and poltrons. This sentiment is propagated and diffused with great industry and success.

Now it is agreed on all hands, that your courage—your courage, I repeat it— will be brought to the test. Should it prove answerable to your ostentations,— worthy your ancestors, your friends will amazingly increase. Your hearty friends will be in raptures, and your very enemies will applaud you. I could easily explain to you the reason of all this, but I must leave you to consider of that yourselves. Read the paragraph again, and make your own reflections.

Prepare, prepare, I say, *for the worst.* I fear your delays have been your ruin. I know that your energies may already, or in future, bring upon you many and great calamities; but I am, from my own observation, and the judgment of very many others, most sure, that your forbearance, your delays, your indecision,—in short, what your enemies call your "arrant cowardice"—hath brought or will bring upon you many more, and greater evils.

These are important truths. Weigh, commune, consider, and act, as becomes your former professions, and your highest duty.

. . .

You must know that many of your friends here in both houses will not take a decisive part, till they see how you act in America. For should they take a determined part now, in favour of that country, and in a short time America should give back, their hopes of rise into power and office (which is the hope of all British statesmen) would be forever at an end. Therefore, till the colonists discover that union and spirit, which all parties here agree must force success, you are not to expect any great exertions in your favour. But when once there is a conviction that the Americans are in earnest,—that they are resolved to endure all hazards with a spirit worthy the prize for which they contend, then, and not till then, will you have many firm, active, persevering, and powerful friends, in both houses of Parliament. For, let me again tell you, that strange as it may seem, there is a great doubt here among many, whether you are *really in earnest,* in the full force and extent of those words.

To Mrs. Quincy
London, December 14, 1774

There is not a sensible man of either party here, but acknowledges your ability to save your country, if you have but union, courage, and perseverance. But your enemies pretend to be sanguine, that your avarice of commercial riches will dissolve your union and mutual confidence, that your boasted courage is but vapour, and that your perseverance will be as the morning cloud.

Let me tell you one very serious truth, in which we are all agreed, *your countrymen must seal their cause with their blood.* You know how often, and how long ago I said this. I see every day more and more reason to confirm my opinion. I every day find characters dignified by science, rank, and station, of the same sentiment. Lord—said to me yesterday,—"It is idle, it is idle, Mr ——; this country will never carry on a civil war against America, we cannot, but the ministry hope to carry all by a single stroke." I should be glad to name the Lord, but think it not best. Surely my countrymen will recollect the words I held to them this time twelvemonth. "It is not, Mr Moderator, the spirit that vapours within these walls that must stand us in stead. The exertions of this day will call forth events which will make a very different spirit necessary for our salvation. Look to the end. Whoever supposes that shouts and hosannas will terminate the trials of the day, entertains a childish fancy. We must be grossly ignorant of the importance and value of the prize for which we contend;—we must be equally ignorant of the powers of those who have combined against us;—we must be blind to that malice, inveteracy, and insatiable revenge, which actuate our enemies, public and private, abroad and in our bosom, to hope we shall end this controversy without the sharpest—the sharpest conflicts; to flatter ourselves that popular resolves, popular harangues, popular acclamations, and popular vapour, will vanquish our foes. Let us consider the issue. Let us look to the end. Let us weigh and consider, before we advance to those measures which must bring on the most trying and terrible struggle, this country ever saw."[5]

. . .

When you shall act agreeably to your past ostentations, when you have shown that you are, what Englishmen once were,—whether successful or not, your foes will diminish, your friends amazingly increase, and you will be happy in the peaceful enjoyment of your inheritance; or at least, your enemies will, in some measure, stay their intemperate fury from a reverence of your virtue, and a fear of reanimating your courage. But if in the trial, you prove, as your enemies say, arrant poltrons and cowards, how ineffably contemptible will you appear; how wantonly and superlatively will you be abused and insulted by your triumphing oppressors!

To Mrs. Quincy
London, December 16, 1774.

Permit me to congratulate my countrymen on the integrity and wisdom with which the congress have conducted. Their policy, spirit, and union have confounded their foes, and inspired their friends. All parties agree in giving them a tribute of honor and applause. I have this moment attended a desultory, despicable, because trifling, debate, in the House of Commons, relative to America. My Lord North apologized for, and endeavoured to explain away, his expression, "I will have America at my feet." The important questions relative to America will not be agitated till after the holidays are over. There is great talk, and much hope and fear about you, and your friends seem to intend pressing a suspension for three years, of all acts, made since 1764 relative to the colonies.[6] Your stanch friends say, "If they are unjust, repeal them: we then shall treat with you as friends. At all hazards recall your troops for we will not treat with the sword at our breast."

Be the event as it may, continue true to yourselves, and the day is your own. If they only suspend—do not, for heaven's sake, think of relaxing your agreements, while you are treating. Beware of the arts of negotiation; the ministry are adepts in them; at least they are skilled in the science of corruption.

To Joseph Reed, Esq., Philadelphia
London, December 17, 1774

Let me tell you a great truth, which ought at this, and every future day, to have much weight and influence in America. Few men are more ill-disposed towards that continent, than those who are under the greatest obligations to it. Thus the commercial world, like the political, gives us striking instances of favourites of America, who have among them the most sanguine conspirators against her public happiness. Nay, some who ought to have America inscribed on their furniture and equipages, and gratitude to that country written on their hearts, have uttered the bitterest things against it, with licensed freedom and insidious industry. It is true they now are about calling a meeting to petition Parliament in favour of the colonies; but is an ideot at a loss to discern the motive? The manufacturers also are on the move. If Americans continue firm to themselves, they will not only have the honour and reward of emancipating themselves; but even a whole kingdom, roused by their example,—brought to feel, by American economy, and fired by a thousand wrongs, may, peradventure, be brought once more to think a little of those great subjects, national justice, freedom, and happiness.

But by no means entertain an idea that commercial plans, founded on commercial principles, are to be engines of your freedom, or the security of your felicity. Far different are the weapons with which oppression is repelled; far more noble the sentiments and actions, which secure liberty and happiness to man.

The friends of America in the House of Commons are now concerting a plan for carrying a suspension of all acts made since the year 1764 relative to America, for three years, in which time, it is said, both sides may cool, and they may then think seriously of negotiation and compromise. I think it was Hannibal who said, "We treat with *arms* in our hands." Now whether the weapons of our warfare be commercial, or martial, methinks we should not suddenly lay them down, lest we not only lose the use of them, but become so broken for want of daily discipline, as that we shall not easily embody again, in so united and formidable a band. Besides, the arts of negotiation are much better understood in Europe than America, and great statesmen sometimes pretend to negotiate, when they only mean to corrupt. The economy or religion of British ministers will not restrain them from an essay upon those colony virtues, which, should they prove of easy impression, might hazard mighty blessings.

Let our countrymen therefore well consider how much a British ministry, as well as themselves, have at stake. No arms, no arts, no plots, or conspiracies will be thought unlawful weapons. Let them look all around them, and be on their guard at every point. The blessings of the wise, and the prayers of the pious, universally attend you; even throughout this nation.

My dear sir, before I close, I cannot forbear telling you that I look to my countrymen with the feelings of one, who verily believes they must yet seal their faith and constancy to their liberties, with blood. This is a distressing witness indeed! But hath not this ever been the lot of humanity? Hath not blood and treasure in all ages been the price of civil liberty? Can Americans hope a reversal of the laws of our nature, and that the best of blessings will be obtained and secured without the sharpest trials?

To Mrs. Quincy
London, December 22, 1774

Indeed if it was not for the treachery and base designs of certain merchants trading to the colonies, the manufacturers would long ago have been clamorous in your favour. I was shown two letters to two of the first manufacturing towns, written by their member now in Parliament, which I have his promise to give me a copy in a few days. As soon as I receive these copies, I shall transmit them, and they will give you great insight into the commotions now beginning to take place. Only be men of common sense, and you will do wonders. People here have no idea that any body of men can be virtuous,—but surely you have common sense, and if you have, pride will keep you from any infraction of your agreements.

. . .

[In case of suspension] Your Parliamentary friends say, "Snatch the opportunity for peace and reconciliation." Your sanguine and warm partizans say, you "are united and inspired *now*; circumstances that may never happen again." Seize the glorious, happy opportunity, for establishing the freedom and social felicity of all America! "There is a tide in the affairs of men." God direct you!

To Mrs. Quincy
Bristol, January 7, 1775.

The holy-days have been improved by me in visiting Bath, Bristol, and some manufacturing towns in the vicinity. Did Americans realize their commercial powers, spirit and obstinacy would characterize their future measures. Had the non-exportation agreement been appointed to commence on the first of March, Britain would ere this have been in popular convulsions. This is the sentiment even of adversaries.

The manufacturing towns are now in motion, and petitions to Parliament to repeal the late acts on commercial principles, will flow from all quarters. London is setting the example, which this city and other manufacturing towns are preparing to follow.

The commonalty of this kingdom are grossly ignorant; the tools of the ministry, for their reward, are incessantly retailing the same stale falsehoods, and the same weak reasonings every day. The consequences are easily conceived. The people of this country must be made to feel the importance of their American brethren. If the colonies have one spark of virtue, in less than a twelvemonth Britain must feel at every nerve. Believe me, the commonalty of America are statesmen, philosophers, and heroes, compared with the "many" of Great Britain. With the former you may reason,—the latter you must drive. I have endeavoured to study the character of both countries; this sentiment is the result of my observations.

I have lately read various letters from several inland manufacturers to their mercantile correspondents, and I find that the "address" to the people of this country, hath wrought, and is still working wonders.

. . .

The ministry, I am well satisfied, are quite undetermined as to the course they must take with regard to America. They will put off the final resolutions to the last moment. I know not, and, any further than mere humanity dictates, *I care not*, what part they take. If my own countrymen deserve to be free—*they will be free*. If born free, they are contented to be slaves, e'en let them bear their burdens.

You must know that I am a perfect infidel, in matters of mercantile virtue. It will not therefore be sufficient, when we find a commercial apostate, to mouth "perdition catch the villian." The patience, the lenity, the humanity of Americans towards public conspirators and public traitors, hath been the source of infinite mischief. From this circumstance our friends have become despondent, and our foes have taken courage. I have a thousand things to say, which I would wish to "speak without a tongue, and to be heard without ears." For this reason therefore, if the three acts relative to the Massachusetts Bay are not repealed, I intend to be in Philadelphia, in May next.

. . .

Permanent slavery, or a full deliverance from their present burdens, is the alternative now before America. No other country hath ever yet had any choice but that of the sword for their emancipation from bondage. America, favoured above the nations of antiquity, hath an alternative. If her children can withstand the blandishments of luxury, and the delusions of false pride, they may purchase liberty without its price; but if attachment to commercial leeks and onions, an idolatry equally degrading, and in the present case almost as impious as that of Egypt, have debauched the appetite and blinded all sense, they must soon make their election of the load of slavery, or the sword of blood.

To Mrs. Quincy
London, January 12, 1775

P.S. I intend to send you Burke's Speech published this day. It will be read in America with avidity and applause. I am well informed that Mr. Hayley,[7] on receiving a large parcel of letters from America without *one order* enclosed, merely said,—"I find there is not even an inclination in Boston to smuggle now."

A certain Mr ——, lately arrived from Boston, said, "A few more troops will be sufficient to enforce all the measures of the ministry."

I have neither room nor time for comment.

From the Journal

March 3d. This day being the day before my departure, I dined with Dr Franklin, and had three hour's private conversation with him. Dissuades from France or Spain. Intimate with both the Spanish and French ambassador, the latter a shrewd, great man. By no means take any step of great consequence, unless on a sudden emergency, without advice of the continental congress. Explicitly, and in so many words, said, that only New England could hold out for ages against this country and if they were firm and united, in *seven years* would conquer them.

Said he had the best intelligence that the manufacturers were bitterly feeling, and loudly complaining of the loss of the American trade. Let your adherence be to the non-importation and non-exportation agreement a year from next September, or to the next session of Parliament, and the day is won.

To Mrs. Quincy
London, January 11, 1775

The cause of the colonies every day grows more popular; that of the ministry, more desperate. The merchants are alarmed, the manufacturers are in motion, the artificers and handicraftsmen are in amaze, and the lower ranks of the community are suffering. Petitions are framing in all parts of the kingdom in favour of their own dear selves, and if America reap any advantage by this movement, be assured her tribute of gratitude is not due either to merchants or manufacturers. America might sink in bondage, and long drag the load of misery and shame, before either of these orders, as a body of men, would feel one generous sentiment, or make one feeble effort, unless their own immediate and obvious interest prompted the exertion. I say, *immediate* and *obvious,* for all know that if the distance is beyond their own nostrils, or clouded by any thing deeper than a cobweb shade, they will neither see nor understand. I speak here of the governing majoɪ ity; individuals are among them who have knowledge, sentiment, and spirit; but Heaven knows, how little, how incredibly little, these noble qualities have influence here.

There can be no doubt that the peaceful, spiritless, and self-denying warfare, in which the colonies are now engaged, would yield an ample victory; to be sure, not the most glorious or splendid of any on record, but the tinsel of splendour and the parade of glory may be dispensed with, if we can obtain the object of our wishes by attacks which are truly mock heroic, and weapons which are most certainly not spiritual.

My great doubt is, whether frugal virtue is a quality deep ingrafted in the human mind, and whether it contains a spirit sharp and active enough to cement and animate any large popular body, for any length of time.

However, if my countrymen, after deliberating, are convinced, that they can sacredly keep the pure faith of economy; that they can follow the simplicity of their fathers, and what is more, can compel and keep to the ordinances of self-denial, their whole household, I will venture to assure them, that they shall obtain a bloodless victory, and be crowned with success.

• NOTES •

1. This letter is in response to one from John Dickinson, dated "Fairhill [Pennsylvania], June 20, 1774."

2. John Dickinson had characterized himself as a farmer retired from politics in the first of his *Letters from a Farmer in Pennsylvania to the Inhabitants of the British Colonies* (1767–1768).

3. Lord Dartmouth was secretary of state for the colonies in 1774.

4. When Quincy made this kind of statement, as he frequently did, he was referring to the opinions of the British "friends of America."

5. One year before this date, Boston was near the end of a series of meetings of the "Body of the People," searching for a way to deal with three shiploads of taxed tea in their harbor. Quincy here refers to a speech he gave at one of those meetings. The meetings ended with the Boston Tea Party, 16 December 1773.

6. Quincy's "friends," British politicians and others favorably disposed to the cause of America, evidently led him to believe that suspension of these acts—all the revenue acts from the Sugar Act on, as well as the Coercive Acts—was a realistic possibility. See Chapter Eleven, "English Radicals and American Resistance to British Authority," by C. C. Bonwick.

7. George Hayley was a London commission merchant with a large American clientele, especially in Boston, who was accustomed to shipping goods worth many thousands of pounds sterling yearly to America in normal times.

The Contributors

David L. Ammerman is professor of history at Florida State University, author of *In the Common Cause: American Response to the Coercive Acts of 1774*, and co-editor of *The Chesapeake in the Seventeenth Century: Essays on Anglo-American Society and Politics*.

Colin C. Bonwick, author of *English Radicals and the American Revolution*, teaches at the University of Keele, where he is a member of the David Bruce Center for American Studies.

Ian R. Christie, professor emeritus, University College London, was elected a fellow of the British Academy in 1977. He delivered the Ford Lectures for 1984 at the University of Oxford, published as *Stress and Stability in Late Eighteenth-Century Britain: Reflections on the British Avoidance of Revolution*. Other works include *Myth and Reality in Late Eighteenth-Century British Politics* and (with Benjamin W. Labaree) *Empire or Independence, 1760–1776: A British-American Dialogue on the Coming of the American Revolution*.

Walter H. Conser, Jr., author of *Church and Confession: Conservative Theologians in Germany, England, and America, 1815–1866,* is a member of the Department of Philosophy and Religion, University of North Carolina at Wilmington. He was formerly a James A. Gray Fellow in the Department of Religion, University of North Carolina at Chapel Hill.

Paul Langford is a fellow of Lincoln College, Oxford and author of *The First Rockingham Administration, 1765–1766* and *The Excise Crisis*.

Ronald M. McCarthy, currently a visiting scholar at the Program on Nonviolent Sanctions, Harvard University Center for International Affairs, is a member of the Department of Sociology, Merrimack College.

J. H. Plumb is a professor of English modern history at the University of Cambridge and master of Christ's College, Cambridge since 1978. Among his works are *England in the Eighteenth Century, The Growth of Political Stability, The Commercialization of Leisure,* and *Georgian Delights.*

Gene Sharp is president of the Albert Einstein Institution and program director of the Program on Nonviolent Sanctions in Conflict and Defense, Center for International Affairs, Harvard University. He was formerly professor of sociology and political science at Southeastern Massachusetts University. His writings include *The Politics of Nonviolent Action, Gandhi as a Political Strategist, Social Power and Political Freedom,* and *Making Europe Unconquerable.*

Leslie J. Thomas is a professor of history at Western Washington University. His unpublished work on the Townshend Acts resistance has been cited as the most authoritative study of that campaign.

David J. Toscano has taught sociology at the University of Virginia and other institutions and is currently an attorney in private practice in Virginia.

Index

570

reaction to, 338–339

Massachusetts circular letter of 1768, 121–123, 145, 476, 478, 486, 490, 497

Massachusetts committees of correspondence, 12, 424; establishment of, 216–217, 218; Continental Association and, 248, 249, 251, 252, 257; First Continental Congress and, 246; Stamp Act circular letter from, 24, 35, 38, 40, 41, 44, 49; Tea Act resistance in, 220

Massachusetts Convention of Towns, 124, 204–205, 497

Massachusetts Council, and Massachusetts Charter Bill, 331–332, 333

Massachusetts Gazette, 279

Massachusetts General Court, 139; British concern over provincial administration and, 205–211; First Continental Congress and, 231; leadership patterns in, 497; political noncooperation and, 491; Stamp Act resistance in, 37, 44, 45–46, 49, 62, 200, 201; Townshend Acts resistance in, 139–140

Massachusetts Government Act. *See* Act for Better Government of Massachusetts Bay

Massachusetts House of Representatives, 476; Coercive Acts resistance and, 12; committees of correspondence and, 217, 218; nonimportation movement and, 157, 179–180; provincial congress and, 508; salary issues for court officials and, 216; Stamp Act resistance in, 28, 37, 63; Sugar Act resistance in, 23, 24; Townshend Acts circular letter from, 121–122, 145, 149–150, 157; Townshend Acts resistance in, 11, 140, 141

Massachusetts Indemnity Act, 475

Massachusetts Provincial Congress, 251, 256–257, 340, 431, 434–435, 440, 508, 512–513, 515

Massachusetts Superior Court: committees of correspondence and, 12; salary issues for court officials of, 215, 216–217, 493–494; Stamp Act resistance and, 63

Mauduit, Jaspar, 23

Mayhew, Jonathan, 391–392, 393, 395, 397, 399, 400, 405

Mayson, James, 445, 446

Mechanics, 497–498

Medway, Massachusetts, 513

Meetings: open resistance with, 8; spinning parties and, 500, 538; Stamp Act resistance and, 70–71

Mein, John, 125, 126, 158–159, 286, 374

Memorials, 482

Mercantilism, 362; British trade and, 363; economic conditions in empire and, 362–363

Mercer, George, 42, 56, 78

Merchants, British: alternative markets for, 288–289, 296–297; American debts in war period and, 302–305; attitudes towards colonies among, 309–318; Boston Tea Party and, 316; British monopoly of trade and, 363; changing economic conditions and, 284–285; Coercive Acts resistance and, 281–282, 317–318, 383; colonial exports and, 302–303; colonies as markets for, 363–364; commercial resistance and, 368; Continental Association weaknesses and, 375–376; debts owed, and nonimportation, 490; demands of colonies on, 312–318; dependence on colonial market of, 285; domestic demand and, 290–292; economic beliefs of, 316–317; economic effects of nonimportation movement on, 285–287, 289–295; expanded markets for, 295–296; government attitudes and, 207–209; government spending in wartime and, 297–298; increase in activity

of, 281–284; lack of gratitude from colonies to, 310–312; lobby of, 279–281; monopoly of trade with colonies of, 298–299; nonexportation and, 300–302; nonimportation movement breakdown and, 287–288; nonimportation reactions of, 199, 368; petitions and, 282–284, 312–313, 317–318, 383; political inactivity of, 305–306; reexport trade and, 383; Rockingham and, 94–95; stability of finance and, 303–304, 305; Stamp Act repeal and, 94–95, 97–100, 102, 103–106; Stamp Act resistance effects on, 74–75; 284; timing of nonimportation agreements and, 298, 299, 300; Townshend Acts resistance and, 198, 280–281, 306, 308; War of Independence and, 305

Merchants, colonial: adherence to agreements by, 373–374; Boston nonconsumption agreements and, 138–144; boycott of British products and, 72–75; commercial resistance and motivation of, 370–371; committees of inspection and, 512; Continental Association and, 245–246, 252, 500; crowd violence and, 130; economic dependence on England and, 478; economic noncooperation and, 489–490; economic resistance and leadership and, 500; exports during 1774–75 and, 302; growth of colonial institutions and, 7; indebtedness of, 304; nonconsumption movement opposition from, 136–137, 180–181; nonimportation and fears for trade of, 374, 500; nonimportation benefits and, 287, 370–371; nonimportation enforcement and, 251, 252; political noncooperation by, 490–491; Stamp Act resistance and, 58–61, 67–70, 72–75, 480–481, 490–491; Sugar Act